For an introductory text, the subject matter is refreshing and original. It is very well written and presents basic theories and more advanced concepts in an extremely clear, intuitive way. I'd recommend it to any student of macroeconomics.

Professor Paul Scanlon, Trinity College, Dublin, Ireland

This is exactly the way I teach the subject – so it is great to finally have a book which coincides with my teaching.

Professor Martin B. Schmidt, The College of William and Mary,
Williamsburg, USA

I like this text and always recommend and include it on my reading list. It is clearly written and well supported by data, graphs and nice visuals – this is one of the major strengths of the text.

Dr Catherine Pollock, Kingston University, UK

I have used Miles and Scott's book for years in my Global Economics course in the MBA program. The coverage of topics, as well as the level of difficulty, is perfect for this course. My students like what they read. I highly recommend the new edition of the book.

Professor Kevin Reffett, Arizona State University, USA

This is a very useful textbook. It combines an accessible explanation of economic theory with extensive use of examples that highlight the underlying concepts.

Professor Chris Martin, University of Bath, UK

This book brings a fresh post-crisis perspective that fully internalizes the current agenda and issues for macroeconomists. For instructors who have been scrambling for the past few years to supplement their textbook with extra readings to make the course relevant, this book will be a welcome relief.

Anil K. Kashyap, Professor of Economics and Finance at the
University of Chicago Booth School of Business, USA

Modern economic theory is often criticized for its detachment from real-world complexities. But good economics is a vital tool if we are to understand crucial challenges and policy choices – what makes countries rich or poor, what drives booms and financial crises, why there is unemployment and what we can do about it. This third edition of Miles, Scott and Breedon explains clearly the key insights of economic theory and uses a wealth of real-world data to make the relevance of the theory come alive. It is particularly valuable in its focus on the interaction between finance and the real economy, a subject inadequately addressed in much recent economics. It aims to make the reader a sophisticated consumer of economics and is excellently crafted to achieve that objective.

Adair Turner, Chairman of the Financial Services Authority, UK

MACROECONOMICS

THIRD EDITION

THIRD EDITION

MACROECONOMICS

UNDERSTANDING THE GLOBAL ECONOMY

David Miles, Andrew Scott

AND

Francis Breedon

WILEY

John Wiley & Sons, Ltd

Library of Congress Cataloging-in-Publication Data

Miles, David (David D.)
    Macroeconomics : understanding the global economy / Francis Breedon, David Miles and Andrew Scott. — Third Edition.
        pages   cm
    Revised edition of: Macroeconomics and the global business environment / David Miles, Andrew Scott. 2nd ed.
    Includes bibliographical references and index.
    ISBN 978-1-119-99572-2 (cloth) — ISBN 978-1-119-99571-5 (pbk.)
    1. Macroeconomics.   I. Scott, Andrew, 1965-   II. Breedon, F. J. (Francis J.)   III. Title.
HB172.5.M45   2012
339—dc23

                                                                                           2011045238
A catalogue record for this book is available from the British Library.

Set in 9.5/12pt Times Ten by MPS Limited, a Macmillan Company, Chennai, India
Printed in Italy by Printer Trento Srl.

Brief Contents

Contents

Pg 216
Pg 222-24

③

① Pg 269-270

②

optional
(3)

Preface

We began work on this edition with some trepidation. Much has changed in the world economy since the second edition was finalized in 2005 and many commentators claim that economics is a broken subject that needs radical change. We certainly have had much updating of statistics to do and have had to introduce new ideas and explain policies such as quantitative easing. But overall we were pleasantly surprised to find how much the underlying structure and approach of the second edition were well suited to explain the extraordinary events of the last few years. Our emphasis in previous editions on the importance of the global economy and on the critical nature of interactions between the real economy and finance, as well as our use of historical as well as contemporary data, have served us well in understanding the remarkable economic events of recent years; that and the power and flexibility of good economic theories and thinking.

Of course, the dramatic nature of events has led to some changes in the book too. We have introduced two new chapters: one on banking (which was covered in detail in the first edition but, prompted by reviewers, was dropped from the second – as with some central bankers we now regret not focusing more on banks) and one on sovereign debt and default. It would be impossible to teach macroeconomics today without such a chapter. We did not go for the 'quick fix' of apparently bringing the book up to date by adding a chapter devoted entirely to the recent crisis. Instead, we used recent events to illustrate and motivate models and concepts throughout the book. As well as drawing out the lessons of the financial crises, in this edition we have made the material more suitable to undergraduate and introductory postgraduate courses in macroeconomics as well as MBA courses.

In terms of approach, we have aimed to keep the key ingredients that we believe made the first two editions work:

- A focus on making the reader a 'sophisticated' consumer of economics. We do so by stressing the logic and intuition of economics, rather than resorting immediately to technical model building and curve shifting.
- A global outlook using historical and contemporary data from around the world.
- Introducing substantive real-world issues first to motivate students and then introducing concepts and frameworks to explain them. Rather than illustrate models with insert boxes, we integrate the facts and the analysis.
- Utilizing textbook models as well as summaries of recent and advanced research.

Given how fast the world economy is changing, we have decided to add an extra feature to the supplementary materials for this book (described in more detail below). Instead of simply reproducing charts and tables from the book in the PowerPoint™ slides, we plan to update the slides at regular intervals so that instructors using them will have up-to-date charts and tables.

TEACHING FROM THIS BOOK

Different universities and business schools tend to teach different types of macroeconomics courses and the comprehensiveness of the book easily enables this. Obviously, instructors can choose whatever sequence of topics they prefer; below we outline three different 10-topic courses that could be taught.

MACROECONOMICS: UNDERSTANDING THE GLOBAL ECONOMY

A comprehensive course covering growth, business cycles, exchange rates, stabilization policy and trade.

Lecture 1   Data and Definitions, Chapters 1 and 2
Lecture 2   Capital Accumulation and Endogenous Growth, Chapters 3, 4 and 6
Lecture 3   Technological Progress, Chapter 5
Lecture 4   Labour Markets, Chapter 7
Lecture 5   Trade, Chapters 8 and 9
Lecture 6   Fiscal Policy, Chapter 14
Lecture 7   Money and Inflation, Chapter 12
Lecture 8   Exchange Rates, Chapters 19 and 21
Lecture 9   Business Cycles, Chapter 11
Lecture 10   Stabilization Policy, Chapter 15

MACROECONOMICS: BUSINESS CYCLES AND INTERNATIONAL MACROECONOMICS

A course focusing on business cycles and the international economy, but excluding the supply-side issues of growth, labour markets and trade.

Lecture 1   Data and Definitions, Chapters 1 and 2
Lecture 2   Fiscal Policy, Chapter 14
Lecture 3   Money and Inflation, Chapter 12
Lecture 4   Consumption and Investment, Chapter 10
Lecture 5   Business Cycles, Chapter 11
Lecture 6   Stabilization Policy, Chapters 13 and 15
Lecture 7   Banking and Sovereign Debt, Chapters 17 and 18
Lecture 8   Exchange Rates: PPP, Chapter 19
Lecture 9   Exchange Rates: Exchange Rate Regimes and Crises, Chapter 21
Lecture 10   Exchange Rates: Global Capital Markets, Chapter 20

MACROECONOMICS: GLOBAL BUSINESS AND FINANCIAL MARKETS

A course focusing on the drivers of demand in world markets and the interaction between financial markets and the wider economy.

Lecture 1   Data and Definitions, Chapters 1 and 2
Lecture 2   Trade and Globalization, Chapters 8 and 9

SUPPLEMENTARY MATERIAL

WEBSITE

A robust website (**www.wiley.com/college/miles**) provides support to both students and instructors. Students are able to take practice quizzes online so as to help assess their understanding of core concepts within the text. All of the instructor's teaching aids are also provided by chapter electronically within a password-protected environment.

INSTRUCTOR'S MANUAL

This provides guidance to instructors on how best to use the textbook, through its chapter summaries, learning objectives, teaching suggestions, additional examples, answers to end-of-chapter exercises, and additional problems and solutions. This online resource also includes case studies with questions to drive classroom discussion or to help facilitate homework assignments.

TESTBANK

Offers an extensive set of multiple-choice questions relating to the concepts and topics within the text via the companion website. A customizable version is also available on the companion website.

POWERPOINT PRESENTATIONS

A set of over 1000 PowerPoint slides is available to instructors within the companion website located at www.wiley.com/college/miles.

These slides are updated at regular intervals, so that many of the charts, figures and tables will be more up to date than those in the textbook.

ACKNOWLEDGEMENTS

We remain enormously indebted to the team at Wiley. In particular, we thank Steve Hardman, who originated the project many years ago and has remained supportive ever since, and Ellie Pogson, who took the helm for this edition and steered us unerringly through a tight timetable.

Further debts have been incurred to students and fellow faculty at Queen Mary and the London Business School. In particular, we deeply thank Niki Foteinopoulou, Aurelija Polosuchina and Ozayr Safi for their able and enthusiastic assistance in producing charts, tables and other materials and to Rachel Male for helpful contributions. We would also like to thank Rosie Robertson for her persistence in the difficult but important task of securing copyright permissions. We have also benefited from extensive comments on successive drafts of all three editions from several instructors who teach macroeconomics.

REVIEWERS

Kevni Reffett, *Arizona State University*

Martin B. Schmidt, *College of William and Mary*

Chris Martin, *University of Bath*

Paul Scanlon, *Trinity College Dublin*

Michail Karoglou, *Aston University*

Catherine Pollock, *Kingston University London*

Krishna Akkina, *Kansas State University*

Samuel Andoh, *Southern Connecticut University*

Ivo Arnold, *Nijenrode University*

Charles Bean, *London School of Economics*

Raford Boddy, *San Diego University*

Phil Bowers, *University of Edinburgh*

Michael W. Brandl, *The University of Texas at Austin*

Thomas Cate, *Northern Kentucky University*

Grabriele Camera, *Purdue University*

Steven Cunningham, *University of Connecticut*

David N. DeJong, *University of Pittsburgh*

Raphael DiTella, *Harvard Business School*

Joseph Eisenhauer, *Canisius College-Buffalo*

Can Erbil, *Brandeis University*

Lynne Evans, *University of Durham*

Jean Fan, *Xavier University, Cincinnati*

Antonio Fatas, *INSEAD*

Adrien Fleiddig, *California State University-Fullerton*

Jim Fralick, *Syracuse University*

Lynn Geiger, *Eastern College*

Satyajit Ghosh, *University of Scranton*

Fred R. Glahe, *University of Colorado*

John Glen, *Cranfield School of Management*

Gregory Hess, *Oberlin College*

Beth Ingram, *University of Iowa*

Owen Irvine, *Michigan State University*

Sherry L. Jarrell, *Wake Forest University, Babcock Graduate School of Management*

Peter Jonsson, *Fayetteville State University*

Judith Jordan, *University of the West of England*

Veronica Z. Kalich, *Baldwin-Wallace College*

Tim D. Kane, *University of Texas-Tyler*

Cem Karayalcin, *Florida International University*

Yoobai Kim, *University of Kentucky*

Ben Knight, *University of Warwick*

Jim Knudsen, *Creighton University*

William E. Laird, *Florida State University*

Stefanie Lenway, *University of Minnesota, Carlson School of Management*

Thomas Lubik, *The Johns Hopkins University*

Chris Martin, *Brunel University*

Kent Matthews, *University of Wales, Cardiff*

Stuart McDougall, *University of Otago*

B. Starr McMullen, *Oregon State University*

Patrick McMurry, *Missouri Western State College*

Mico Mrkaic, *Duke University*

John Nader, *Grand Valley State University*

Akorlie Nyetepe-Coo, *University of Wisconsin-La Crosse*

Nilss Olekalns, *University of Melbourne*

Allen Parkman, *University of New Mexico*

Daniel Pavsek, *Shenandoah University*

Chung Pham, *Professor Emeritus of Economics at University of New Mexico*

Mark Pingle, *University of Nevada*

Stephen Regan, *Cranfield School of Management*

Mary S. Schranz, *University of Wisconsin-Madison*

Carole Scott, *State University of West Georgia*

Harry Singh, *Grand Valley State University*

Case Sprenkle, *University of Illinois-Champaign-Urbana*

Raymond Strangways, *Old Dominion University*

Mark Strazicich, *University of Central Florida*

Oren Sussman, *University of Oxford*

Dominic Swords, *Henley Management College*

Randolph Tan, *Nanyang Technological University*

Peter Taylor, *University of the West of England*

Paul Wachtel, *New York University, Stern School of Business*

William Weirick, *University of Louisiana*

Mike Wickens, *University of York*

Chunchi Wu, *Syracuse University*

Chi-Wa Yuen, *University of Hong Kong*

Eric Zivot, *University of Washington*

Johnson Samuel Adari, *Texas Tech University*

Francis Ahking, *University of Connecticut-Storrs*

Krishna Akkina, *Kansas State University*

Leon Battista, *City University of New York*

Edward Bierhanzl, *Florida A & M University*

Doug Bunn, *Brigham Young University-Idaho*

James Butkiewicz, *University of Delaware*

Dale DeBoer, *University of Colorado-Colorado Springs*

Erick Elder, *University of Arkansas Little Rock*

Yee-Tien Fu, *Stanford University*

Marvin Gordon, *University of Illinois at Chicago*

Satyajit Ghosh, *University of Scranton*

Brian Jacobsen, *Wisconsin Lutheran College*

Manfred Keil, *Claremont McKenna College*

Jongsung Kim, *Bryant College*

Richard Mark, *Dowling College*

Benjamin Matta, *New Mexico State University*

Ida Mirzaie, *John Carrol University*

Phil Murray, *Webber International University*

John Nader, *Grand Valley State University*

Jamal Nahavandi, *University of New Hampshire*

Luis Rivera, *Dowling College*

Malcolm Robinson, *Thomas More College*

William Seyfried, *Winthrop University*

Mohamad Shaaf, *University of Central Oklahoma*

Tayyeb Shabbir, *University of Pennsylvania*

Dorothy Siden, *Salem State College*

Robert Sonora, *University of Texas Arlington*

Jack Strauss, *Saint Louis University*

Osman Suliman, *Millersville University*

Willem Thorbecke, *George Mason University*

Charles Waldauer, *Widener University*

Chris Weber, *Seattle University*

Ky Yuhn, *Florida Atlantic University*

Finally, we thank our families – Faye, Georgia, Oscar and Harriet; Lorraine, Helena, Louis and Kit; and Jo, Lewes and Lily – for making us realize that you can still smile even when the world economy is collapsing.

The publishers would like to thank the OECD for their permission to reproduce statistical data used as examples in this book. To view OECD's full collection of economic data and analysis see **www.OECD-iLibrary.org**.

Introduction

What Is Macroeconomics?

Key Concepts

Aggregation	Long- and Short-Run Issues	Macroeconomics
Economics	in Macroeconomics	Microeconomics

Overview

In this chapter we show you what macroeconomics is about by looking at some of the big questions that macroeconomists ask: Why do some countries enjoy a standard of living many times greater than others? How does growth in productivity evolve over time? Why does the economy fluctuate between expansions and contractions? What impact do changes in interest rates or in oil prices have on the economy? Why are banks so important for the health of the economy? We draw out what is distinctive about macroeconomics and contrast it with microeconomics, illustrating this distinction by focusing on the types of risk that affect individuals and companies.

1.1 What Is Macroeconomics About?

Most books begin by defining their subject. But definitions are tricky and often are not the best way to introduce a subject. Imagine trying to interest people in tennis by defining what tennis is and how it is played. Far better to let them watch a match or try to play themselves. This approach also applies to macroeconomics. Understanding how the economy works helps us interpret the past; it makes our world more comprehensible; and it helps us think intelligently about the future. Such skills help us make better decisions. However, we think that offering a sophisticated definition of macroeconomics is a poor way to convince you of these things. To demonstrate its relevance, we prefer to illustrate the types of issues with which macroeconomics deals.

Consider the economic situation on 3 November 2010. The world's financial markets reacted favourably to US Federal Reserve Chairman Ben Bernanke's announcement that

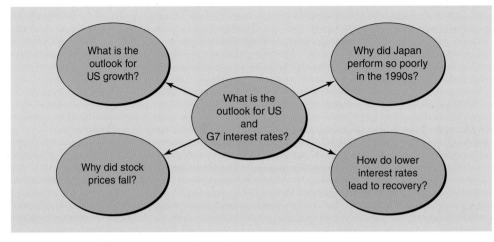

FIGURE 1.1 ● Short-run macroeconomic questions.

the Fed would spend $600 billion in a further extension of quantitative easing. This meant that the US central bank – the Federal Reserve – would be buying a huge quantity of financial assets with money that it created. (We explain what quantitative easing involves in Chapter 13.) But would this policy help the economy recover; would it simply create inflation; or would it have no effect either way? These issues raise a number of macroeconomic questions, some of which are illustrated in Figure 1.1.

These are all questions that macroeconomics tries to answer, and this textbook should give you the intellectual apparatus to understand the issues and participate in the debate. After reading it, you will be able to offer your own informed opinion about whether Bernanke did the right thing in late 2010. More important, you will be able to judge whether Bernanke's successors do the right thing in 2019.

However, macroeconomics is far more than just an intellectual toolkit for understanding current events. It is also about understanding the long-term forces that drive the economy and shape the business environment. Between 1820 and 2011, for example, the real value of the output of goods and services produced *per person* in the United States increased more than 25-fold. Over this same period, the US population increased more than 32-fold, and so the total amount of goods and services produced in the United States increased by nearly 80 000%. Not all countries have grown so much. Over the same period, output per person in the United Kingdom increased only slightly more than tenfold. Had the United Kingdom grown at the same rate as the United States over this period, it would have produced enough extra output to more than double the standard of living for *every* man, woman and child in the country. Vote-seeking politicians can only dream of that kind of largesse.

Compared to many other countries, the United Kingdom's performance was good. In 1913 the output produced per person in Bangladesh was worth roughly $737 and by 2011 this total had risen to only $1375.[1] By contrast, over this period the value of the output produced per person in China had increased from $552 to around $9987 (almost seven times Bangladeshi output), while Japan's income per person had risen to almost 16 times the Bangladeshi level (see Figure 1.2). These calculations show why a leading macroeconomist and Nobel prizewinner says: 'Once one starts to think [about questions of economic growth] it is hard to think about anything else.'[2]

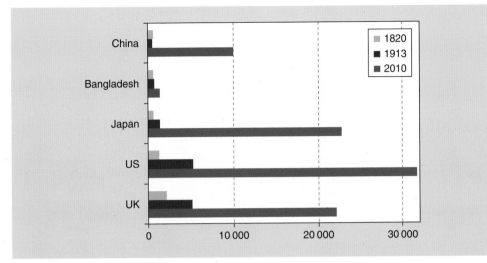

FIGURE 1.2 ● **Output differences over the long term.** The average level of output per person differs dramatically across countries. *Source:* Maddison, *Monitoring the World Economy* (OECD) and IMF *World Economic Outlook* (October 2010).

These issues raise a number of long-term macroeconomic questions, some of which are illustrated in Figure 1.3. These questions force us to examine key economic issues: the role of investment in machines and infrastructure in fostering growth; the importance of education and skills; and the critical role of technological progress, such as new inventions. These are important both for individual firms and for society. These issues are as relevant to households and businesses as are the short-term considerations about what the US Federal Reserve Board will do with monetary policy; they are probably much more important.

The above examples (the conduct of monetary policy and the sources of overall economic growth) suggest that macroeconomics is about the economy as a whole. In part this is correct: macroeconomics does focus on how the whole economy evolves over time rather than on any one sector, region or firm. Although macroeconomics often considers issues from the perspective of the firm or the individual consumer, its focus is on the overall, or *aggregate*, implications of tens of thousands of *individual* decisions that companies and households make.

(1.2) But What about That Definition?

These examples have given you some ideas about the issues that macroeconomics addresses, and they may even have aroused your interest in the subject. We hope so, because at this point we need to give you a more detailed insight into macroeconomics and its relationship with its sister discipline, microeconomics. In other words, it is time to turn to definitions.

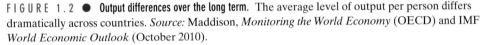

DEFINITION

Economics is the study of the allocation of scarce resources.

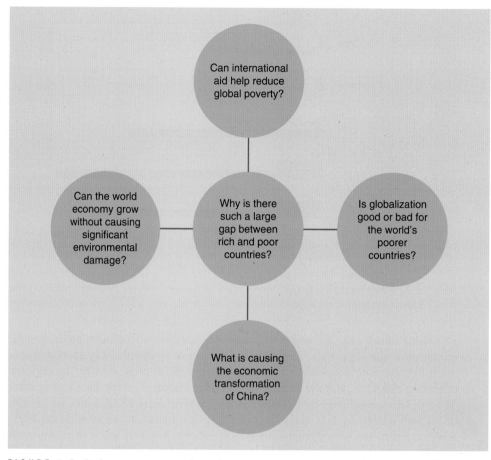

FIGURE 1.3 ● Long-run macroeconomic questions.

The basic idea is simple: each of us has an almost inexhaustible list of desires, but most of us have a finite amount of money (or, more generally, resources) with which to satisfy these desires. The British economist Adam Smith, whose book *Wealth of Nations* (published in 1776) was arguably the first treatise on economics, famously phrased this discussion in terms of whether a country should produce guns or butter. Today the choice is between more esoteric items: we all might like to buy a new top-of-the-range mobile phone *and* regularly eat steak or lobster for lunch, but household finances dictate one or the other (and you had better get used to the crummy sandwich from the snack bar if you go for the new mobile phone). Economics studies the best way to allocate the resources that are available across these competing needs. Not all these needs can be satisfied, but economics should be able to help you (and society) meet as many of them as possible.

Market economies allocate resources through prices. Prices tell producers what the demand for a particular product is: if prices are high, then producers know the good is in demand and they can profitably increase production. If prices are low, producers know that demand for the product is weak and they should cut back production. Thus the market ensures that society produces more of the goods that people want and less of those that they do not. In deciding which goods to purchase and which to avoid, consumers look at prices; by examining prices and chasing profits, producers decide which goods to provide.

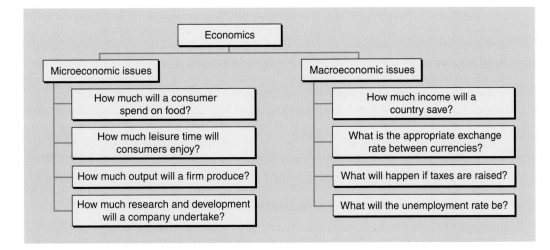

FIGURE 1.4 ● **Macroeconomic and microeconomic issues.** Macroeconomics focuses on aggregate outcome; microeconomics looks at individual markets, firms or households.

But what is *macro*economics? Broadly speaking, economics has two components: **microeconomics** and **macroeconomics**. As shown by the examples in Figure 1.4, microeconomics essentially examines how individuals, whether they be consumers or individual firms, decide how to allocate resources and whether those decisions are desirable. Macroeconomics studies the economy as a whole: it looks at the *aggregate* outcomes of all the decisions that consumers, firms and the government make in an economy. Macroeconomics is about aggregate variables such as the overall levels of output, consumption, employment and prices – and how they move over time and between countries.

In terms of prices, microeconomics focuses on, for instance, the price of a particular firm's product, whereas macroeconomics focuses on the exchange rate (the price of one country's money in terms of that of another country), the interest rate (the price of spending today rather than tomorrow) or the aggregate cost of labour (the wage rate).

1.3   The Difference between Macroeconomics and Microeconomics

These distinctions show that a grey area exists between microeconomics and macroeconomics that relates to **aggregation**: at what point do the actions of a number of firms cease to be a microeconomic issue and become a macroeconomic issue? To answer that question, let's think of another way of outlining the differences between microeconomics and macroeconomics. In microeconomics the focus is on a small group of agents, say a group of consumers or two firms battling over a particular market. In this case economists pay a great deal of attention to the behaviour of the agents on whom the model is focusing. They make assumptions about what consumers want or how much they have to spend, or about whether the two firms are competing over prices or market share, and whether one firm is playing an aggressive strategy and so on. The result is a detailed analysis of the way particular firms or consumers behave in a given situation.

However, this microeconomic analysis does *not* explain what is happening in the wider economic environment. Think about consumers' choice of what goods to consume. In addition to consumers' own income and the price of the goods they wish to purchase, their decisions depend on an enormous amount of other information. How high is unemployment? Is the government going to increase taxes? Is the exchange rate about to collapse, requiring a sharp increase in interest rates? Or consider our two firms competing over a market. If one firm is highly leveraged (i.e. it has a lot of debt), it may not be able to adopt an aggressive price stance if it fears that interest rates are about to rise sharply, because then the losses from a price war might bankrupt it. Similarly, if imported materials are important for the firm's production process, then a depreciating currency will lead to higher import costs, reducing profit margins even before the firm engages in a price war. While none of these background influences – shifts in interest rates or movements in the exchange rate – is under the control of the firm or consumer, they still influence their decisions.

KEY POINT

Macroeconomics analyses the backdrop of economic conditions against which firms and consumers make decisions.

While microeconomics is mainly concerned with studying in detail the decisions of a few agents, taking as given the basic economic backdrop, macroeconomics is about studying how the decisions of all the agents who make up the economy create this backdrop. Consider, for instance, the issue of whether a firm should adopt the latest developments in technology, which promise to increase labour productivity by, say, 20%. A microeconomic analysis of this topic would focus mainly on the costs the firm faces in adopting this technology and the likely productivity and profit gains that it would create. Macroeconomics would consider this IT innovation in the context of the whole economy. In particular, it would examine how, if *many* firms were to adopt this technology, costs in the whole economy would fall and the demand for skilled labour would rise. Combined with the resulting increase in labour productivity, this would lead to an increase in wages and the firm's payroll costs. It might also shift demand away from unskilled towards skilled workers, causing the composition of unemployment and relative wages to change.

This example reveals the differences between the two approaches. The microeconomic analysis is one where the firm *alone* is contemplating adopting a new technology, and the emphasis is on that firm's pricing and employment decisions, probably holding wages fixed. In other words, the analysis assumes that the firm's decisions do not influence the background economic environment. In contrast, the macroeconomic analysis examines the consequences when *many* firms implement the new technology and investigates how this affects economy-wide output, wages and unemployment. Both forms of analysis have a role to play, and which is more appropriate depends on the issue to be analysed and the question that needs to be answered.

1.4 A Crisis for Macroeconomics?

Many people think that the 2007–09 financial crisis was not just a crisis for the world economy, but for economists. There seem to be two strands to this argument. The first is that neither the financial crisis, nor the huge downturn that followed it, was forecast by economists. The second is that a number of standard economic models have proved inadequate as a way of explaining what happened. Economics has much to learn from this crisis and research will be clearly refocused as a result; this textbook, among many, has been substantially recast. But is it really a crisis?

The criticism over economists' forecasting failure rests on two assumptions. The first is that the crisis wasn't forecast; the second is that economics should be judged by its predictive ability. It's certainly true that only a few individuals predicted such a devastating downturn. From our experience, by early 2007 a majority of economists thought that asset markets were overvalued, that there would be a correction, and that this would cause financial pressures and a downturn. But few predicted correctly how badly the financial sector would be affected by declines in property prices or how large the impact of financial distress would be on the real economy. There seem to be two reasons for this. The first is a ubiquitous problem in forecasting. When forecasting the future, it seems natural not to take extreme positions. Put simply, if something bad is expected to happen, do you think it will be as bad as usual, not as bad as usual or the worst outcome you can think of? The reasonable perspective is to expect the average outcome. The result is that forecasters will inevitably tend to underestimate the strength and duration of what – after the event – turn out to be really sharp recessions, just as they will underestimate the strength of what turn out to be very strong booms.

The second issue is whether economics should be judged by its predictive ability. Here there appears to be a big divide between producers and consumers of economics. Among economists, forecasting is not held in high renown and is a minority occupation. However, among people who want to hear from economists, it is predictions they expect. But economists are similar to doctors in terms of their ability to predict. When you go to your doctor, you tell her your symptoms and she diagnoses an illness and recommends an intervention. If you push her, saying that you have an important meeting in three days and ask if you will be well enough to participate, you get the following response: 'I think you have X and these drugs work in three or four days. You should be okay. But if you aren't, come back and we will try something different.' You might also ask 'How should I change my lifestyle to avoid getting ill again?' and your doctor might give you a list of changes that 'should' help, but offer no guarantees that you won't get ill again. Economists are very similar. The government comes to us and says: 'Here are my symptoms.' We diagnose a recession and recommend cutting interest rates, increasing fiscal deficits and banking-sector bailouts. The government then says: 'But I have an election in 12 months; will things be better?' We reply that the measures take 12–18 months to work, that it should be okay, but, if it isn't, come back and we will try something else. Then the government might ask: 'How should we alter economic policy and regulation to avoid this happening again?' We offer a list of reforms that should help, but provide no guarantees. The medical profession isn't particularly good at prediction, but we still find it useful and helpful. That's not to say that economics is as advanced as the medical profession in terms of knowledge or the reliability of its interventions. But an inability to predict extreme and unlikely events is not grounds to dismiss a body of knowledge. Economics will never be able to predict such events reliably; nor is it alone in this failing. In fact, one of the achievements of economics is in helping us understand *why* some economic events are inherently unpredictable. More needs to be done to educate consumers of economics about how to interpret forecasts and, undoubtedly, the economics profession needs to be more modest in how it presents its forecasts.

Another widespread criticism of economics and finance is that economists have been obsessed by irrelevant theories, and bewitched by their mathematical elegance. The usual culprits mentioned here are the idea of efficient markets and the notion of rational expectations that suggest that neither markets nor individuals make obvious mistakes. The truth is, of course, that economics is a broad field with many research agendas. After all, the usual criticism of economics is that we are two-handed and can't commit to one view of the world. Those who criticize theories of efficient markets seem conveniently to ignore the significant body of economics that is concerned with the information problems and behavioural biases that can lead markets to fail. Economics is not bankrupt, nor has it ignored key themes. But there are many areas that need much more focus: imperfect information, extreme events and the interaction between finance and macroeconomics, to name but a few. In this book we give prominence to all these issues.

The dominant idea in economics is that people respond to economic incentives because they care about economic outcomes. That basic idea did not let one down in terms of understanding the crisis of 2007–10. In fact, it was the perverse incentives facing many of the players in financial markets that were the root cause of what went spectacularly wrong. All this is easier to see now than it was then. Economics proceeds by learning from big events like this. However, there is no need to doubt the usefulness of the main method of economics – which is drawing out the implications of people pursuing their own interests and responding to incentives.

SUMMARY

Economics is the study of the allocation of scarce resources. Macroeconomics studies how the economy as a whole allocates resources, for instance how the overall level of saving in an economy is determined; how the total level of investment is generated; how the level of unemployment evolves; the pattern of overall imports and exports; what determines the level of training of the workforce. Macroeconomics is therefore essentially about the backdrop of economic activity against which firms, governments and consumers make their decisions. However, this backdrop of economic activity represents nothing other than the overall effect of the thousands of decisions made by each of the millions of different consumers and firms.

Because macroeconomic factors have a huge impact on financial markets and on the demand for goods and services that companies produce, they are an important determinant of corporate performance. Businesspeople are increasingly expected to contribute to the policy debate and, because the long-run trends in the business world are driven by macroeconomic factors, a crucial part of a business education must be the study of macroeconomics.

CONCEPTUAL QUESTIONS

1. (Section 1.1) What factors do you think explain why the United States is so rich and Bangladesh is so poor? What do you think accounts for the growth that most economies have shown?

2. (Section 1.3) Consider the differing impacts of microeconomic and macroeconomic factors in the near-term prospects of:

   (a) a graduating student

   (b) a restaurant in a village

   (c) a restaurant in an airport

   (d) a manufacturer of low-price cars

   (e) a manufacturer of luxury sports cars

3. (Sections 1.1 and 1.4) Look at the last week's newspaper coverage of economic issues. How much is devoted to:

   (a) short-term macroeconomics relative to long-term macroeconomics?

   (b) economic forecasting relative to economic analysis?

   Do you think the balance is correct?

4. (Section 1.4) Knowing that some events are inherently unpredictable – such as the result of rolling fair dice – is useful. Not knowing that something is unpredictable is certainly damaging – as the history of those who were convinced that they had discovered a method to win at roulette shows. Think of ways in which negative results – such as showing that certain events cannot be predicted or that certain money-making schemes cannot work in the long run – are valuable.

ANALYTICAL QUESTIONS

1. (Section 1.1) Consider the data in Figure 1.2. What growth rate will Bangladesh have to show to catch up with the 2010 UK and US per capita income level within 10 years? 20 years? 30 years? How would population growth affect your calculations?

2. (Section 1.3) Consider an economy made up of five equal-sized firms (labelled A to E). Under one scenario the output of each firm alternates between

Firm	A	B	C	D	E
Output	1	2	3	4	5

and

Firm	A	B	C	D	E
Output	5	4	3	2	1

What is the balance between idiosyncratic and aggregate risk in this economy?

How does your answer change if each firm oscillates between

Firm	A	B	C	D	E
Output	3	3	3	3	3

and

Firm	A	B	C	D	E
Output	4	4	4	4	4

The Language of Macroeconomics: The National Income Accounts

Key Concepts

BRICs	National Accounts – Expenditure,	Real vs Nominal Variables
Chain Weighting	Income and Output Measures	Value Added
Gross Domestic Product (GDP)	of GDP	
Gross National Income (GNI)	Output and Welfare	

Overview

Macroeconomics has a strong empirical bias that is reflected in a near obsession, at least in the media, with data and statistics. But knowing how to interpret data depends on understanding what the statistics are trying to measure, and this requires a conceptual framework. In this chapter we explain key macroeconomic variables and how measures of them are constructed. Our focus is on understanding the concepts of GDP and the national income accounts.

2.1 What Do Macroeconomists Measure?

At the foundation of macroeconomics is a concern with human welfare. But human welfare is notoriously hard to measure, particularly in macroeconomics, where the relevant measure is the welfare of society as a whole. Even if we could accurately measure individual welfare, how can we compare levels of happiness across individuals and construct an aggregate measure?

Rather than try to measure welfare directly, macroeconomists take a short cut. They focus on the amount of goods and services – the 'output' – produced within an economy. The justification for this is simple: if an economy produces more output, then it can meet more of the demands of society. Using output as a measure of welfare obviously begs many questions. Does output reflect social value? What about cultural and political freedoms and problems of inequality and health? These questions suggest that output will only be an approximation to wider concepts of welfare; this is an issue that we investigate later in this chapter. But producing more output should enable a society to increase its standard of living.

2.2 How Do Macroeconomists Measure Output?

Imagine that a desert island economy produces only one good: coconuts. To measure output in this economy, you only have to count the number of coconuts that are produced. But what if the inhabitants of the island also start to catch fish? The first, and obvious, response is to count the numbers of both coconuts and fish. However, this raises difficult issues. What if one year four coconuts and two fish are produced, and the next year there are two coconuts and four fish? (Think of measuring things in terms of thousands, so four means four thousand coconuts or fish.) Has output increased, decreased or remained the same? While this example might seem trivial, the question it raises is not. Before the Second World War there was no clear answer and, rather than have a single measure of overall output in the economy, there existed a collection of disparate production numbers concerning pig iron production, railway freight tonnage and so forth. Today the most commonly used measure of the output of an economy is gross domestic product or GDP; a concept we examine in detail below.

The main problem in our example is knowing how to add coconuts and fish together. In the real economy, the problem is even more complicated: how to add together Big Macs, computers, cars, haircuts, university courses and so forth. The economist's solution to this problem is a simple one: *multiply each good by its price and then add them all together*. For instance, if coconuts sell at $1 and fish at $2, then in Year 0 we have:

Output Year 0

2 Fish @ $2 (=$4) + 4 Coconuts @ $1 (=$4) = Total Output $8

If prices are unchanged in Year 1 but production shifts from coconuts to fish we have:

Output Year 1

4 Fish @ $2 (=$8) + 2 Coconuts @ $1 (=$2) = Total Output $10

Therefore, we could say that output has increased by $2, or 25%, between Year 0 and Year 1. Because fish has a higher price it achieves a higher weight, so that the doubling of fish production more than offsets the halving of coconut output, leading to an increase in aggregate output. In order for this method to arrive at a measure of output that connects with welfare, it is critical that prices are not simply random numbers but reflect social values. At the heart of economics is the notion of markets guiding production and consumption decisions as if there were an 'invisible hand' moving resources from one use to another. The underlying idea is that prices reflect the value that society places on different goods, so that by multiplying each unit of output by its price, we can measure how society values total output.

REAL VERSUS NOMINAL OUTPUT

Crucial to measuring output is the multiplication of the quantity produced of each good by its market price (excluding any consumer or producer taxes). However, the introduction of prices adds a potential distortion – what happens if prices rise over time? For instance, assume that in Year 2 the quantity of goods provided in our coconut/fish economy does not change, but that all prices double so that a coconut now costs $2 and a fish costs $4. Using the same methodology as before, we arrive at the following measure of output:

Output Year 2

4 Fish @ $4 (=$16) + 2 Coconuts @ $2 (=$4) = Total Output $20

This suggests a problem: even though the amount of fish and coconuts produced has remained the same, our calculation suggests that aggregate output has doubled. To over-come this problem we need to distinguish between *real* and *nominal* output, or between output in *constant* and *current* prices respectively. The basic problem is that in economics we use money as a measure of value, just as scientists use grams and ounces and metres and miles. However, money does not keep a constant value over time because of inflation: after a period of 10% inflation, a $10 bill buys 10% less.

The calculations of output that we have performed so far have been for *nominal output*; that is, we multiply the output of each good by its *current* price in each year. Economists cal-culate *real output* by using for every year the same *constant prices* as weights. For instance, let us choose prices in Year 0 (coconuts cost $1 and fish $2) as our base year. Then we would calculate real output (in Year 0 $) as shown in Table 2.1. Real output increases only because the quantity of goods being produced has increased and not because prices have changed.

Nominal output changes every year because of output changes and because the weights (prices) attached to each output have altered. By using real output, we abstract from the latter and focus purely on changes in output across different industries. Because economists are ultimately interested in welfare, they want to measure the *production* of output and thus prefer to focus on real output or real GDP.

SUBSTITUTION BIAS AND CHAIN WEIGHTING

The standard method of calculating GDP described above requires the selection of a base year. The choice of a base year implies a fixing of the relative value that society places on coconuts and fish, but this may alter over time. In response to this, governments periodically change the base year and the constant prices used in calculating GDP. If relative prices alter significantly, this rebasing leads to substantial revisions in historical GDP growth figures (see Analytical Question 2 for an example). In particular, there exists a 'substitution' problem. As the price of commodities falls, consumers tend to respond by buying more of them. For instance, the price of personal computers falls by around 20% per annum, and in response purchases rise strongly (see Chapter 5). As a result, the output of goods whose relative price is falling (such as computers) tends to increase faster than average, and purchases of com-modities whose relative price is rising grow more slowly. However, in using constant prices we do not revise the weight attached to these industries: the old, comparatively high price of

TABLE 2.1 ● Calculating Real GDP.

	Coconuts	Fish	Output
Year 0	4	2	8
Year 1	2	4	10
Year 2	2	4	10

TABLE 2.2 ● Calculating Chain-Weighted GDP.

	Coconut – Output	Coconut – Price	Fish – Output	Fish – Price
Year 2	2	2	4	4
Year 3	2	3	6	3
Year 4	3	4	6	6

computers will be used as a weight for the rapidly increasing computer output, *even though relative prices have since fallen.* The use of constant prices therefore exaggerates growth after the base year because of this substitution bias. To overcome this, governments are moving away from using constant prices when calculating real GDP and instead use chain weights. Chain weights were first introduced in the United States in 1996 and are being adopted in many countries.

Using Table 2.2 we can calculate the impact of chain weighting. Let us imagine that in Year 3 of our coconut/fish economy, there is a good fish catch, making fish more abundant and cheap relative to coconuts. Using a standard base year (say, Year 2), we would calculate real GDP growth between Year 2 and Year 3 by calculating the change in the value of output using Year 2 prices. Thus output in Year 3 would be 1.4 times greater than in Year 2 (28/20 = 1.4), growth of 40%.

The key to chain weights is that rather than using constant prices, they allow prices to evolve gradually over time. Because the price weights change slowly over time, this reduces the substitution problem. Chain weights calculate the growth in GDP between Years 2 and 3 by using *both* Year 2 prices and Year 3 prices. So it proceeds in three steps:

1. Calculate output growth using Year 2 prices: 28/20 = 1.4
2. Calculate output growth using Year 3 prices: 24/18 = 1.33
3. Calculate the average of the two numbers[1] = 1.37 (i.e. 37% growth)

Notice how this method uses chain weights: Year 3 real GDP growth uses Year 3 and Year 2 prices. In this way, two successive years share some common prices, but prices are allowed to evolve over time. Comparing these results with those obtained using Year 2 prices throughout shows how chain weighting reduces average GDP growth by reducing the substitution problem (since Year 2 prices overstate the value of the extra production of cheap fish in Year 3). In 2003 when the United Kingdom introduced chain weights, the Office for National Statistics estimated that real GDP growth for 2001 was revised downwards by 0.2% through the shift from constant prices to chain weights.

INFLATION AND THE GDP DEFLATOR

Because changes in nominal GDP reflect *both* increases in output and changes in prices, while changes in real GDP only reflect output changes, we can use the gap between the two to measure price changes. In our example the nominal, or current price, level of output in Year 2 is $20. The real value of output (using Year 0 prices) is 10. So a measure of how prices, on average, have moved between Year 0 and Year 2 is determined by how much current price GDP differs from real GDP. We call the resultant index of overall prices the GDP deflator, which is defined as:

GDP Deflator = Nominal GDP/Real GDP

The percentage change in this price index from year to year is a measure of overall inflation. In our example, the price index rises from 1 to 2 – inflation is 100%.

Although the GDP deflator can be used to calculate a measure of inflation, this is not the measure to which we usually refer when discussing inflation. Normally, when we talk about inflation we are talking about changes in the price of goods and services purchased by consumers, as measured by the consumer price index (CPI), while the GDP deflator is a measure of the price of *all* output in an economy (including other elements such as invest-ment goods and government services). Another important difference between the CPI and the GDP deflator is that the CPI includes the prices of imported consumer items, while the GDP deflator includes only domestically produced goods and services. As a result, the CPI is more sensitive to external factors such as exchange rate movements.

KEY POINT

Shifts in real GDP show how production in the economy changes by using constant prices. Nominal GDP changes because of changes in production and changes in prices.

2.3   Output as Value Added

While our simple tale of coconuts and fish enabled us to focus on the critical role of relative prices in estimating output, it also simplified our story in a misleading way. When economists focus on GDP, what they want to measure is *value added*, but multiplying the quantity sold of each commodity by its price measures revenue generated. This is not the same as value added. Consider the case of a table that a retailer sells for $400. If the retailer sells 10 tables, this amounts to $4000 of output. However, before the retailer can sell the tables, other steps in the chain must occur. First, the retailer must purchase the tables from a manufacturer for, say, $200 per table. Second, the manufacturer has to purchase wood from a lumberyard at a cost, say, of $100 per table. If we were to count every stage of the produc-tion process, then output might seem to be $7000. That is:

$1000 (output from lumberyard = $100 × 10) + $2000 (manufacturing output = $200 × 10) + $4000 (output from retailing = $400 × 10) = $7000

However, this would be incorrect: the $4000 gives the value to society of the tables; that is, how much consumers are prepared to pay for them. The $7000 figure is misleading because it *double* (actually triple) *counts*. It includes the value of the wood three times: in the wood the lumberyard sells, in the table the manufacturer sells to the retailer, and then again when the retailer sells the table to the consumer. To avoid this we need *either* to ignore all the intermediate steps and the intermediate industries (the lumberyard and the manufacturer) and just focus on final sales, *or* to calculate the *value added* of each industry and then calculate output as the sum of each industry's value added.

DEFINITION

Value added is the difference between the value of the output sold and the cost of purchasing the raw materials and intermediate goods needed to produce the output.

Thus, in our example, the value added of the lumberyard industry is $1000. Value added in the manufacturing industry is also $1000 (10 tables sold at $2000 *minus* the input cost of wood of $1000). Finally, the value added of the retail outlet is $2000 (10 tables sold at $400 but purchased at $200). Combining all these, we arrive at a measure of output or valued added of $4000 – exactly equal to the final sale value of all the tables. Focusing on value added makes it clear that the contribution of each sector depends on the *additional* value it creates. In our example, the retailer adds more value than any other sector (presumably through point-of-sale information, delivery, providing warranties and so forth). However, the key point is that consumers and producers, not economists, decide the relative importance of each sector by the prices they set and are prepared to pay. If prices reflect social value, then this will produce a direct link between measures of output and welfare. Not all commentators, however, agree that such a link exists. For instance, Naomi Klein, in her bestselling book *No Logo*, comments on the 'absurdity' that a $1 white T-shirt becomes a $100 fashion item when a leading designer name is printed on it. From a value-added perspective there is no absurdity: consumers place little value on the physical manufacturing of white T-shirts, hence the $1 price tag, but consumers do place an enormous value added on marketing, advertising and design.

> **KEY POINT**
>
> GDP measures the value added produced in an economy: the difference between the value of output sold and the cost of intermediate inputs and raw materials.

(2.4) National Income Accounts

THREE MEASURES OF OUTPUT: OUTPUT, INCOME AND EXPENDITURE

Table 2.3 shows our tables example in more detail, and we can see how value added is spread across the different sectors of the economy. This is called the *output* measure of GDP: the sum of the value added created in each sector. Figure 2.1 shows a similar breakdown of value added for the US economy in 2009. The most striking feature of Figure 2.1 is how small a role the traditional sectors of the economy play: agriculture only accounts for 1% of value-added output, mining 2%, construction 4% and manufacturing 11%. In total, the industrial sector produces only 17% of GDP compared with 83% for the service sector, including government, telecoms, transport, finance and so forth. The reasons for this dominance of the service sector are twofold. First, manufacturing experiences rapid productivity growth compared to services and this tends to push down relative manufacturing prices. Second, as

TABLE 2.3 ● GDP as Value Added.

Sector	Product	Price	Profits	Salaries
Retailer	10 tables	@$400 each	750	1250
Manufacturer	10 tables	@$200 each	300	700
Lumberyard	Wood	$1000	150	850

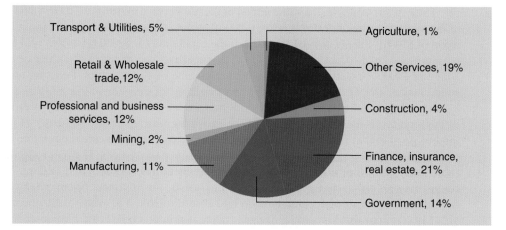

FIGURE 2.1 ● **Output measure of US GDP, 2009.** Manufacturing and agriculture account for a small proportion of modern economies. *Source:* Bureau of Economic Analysis.

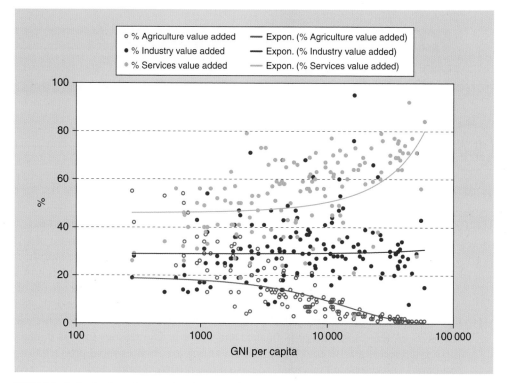

FIGURE 2.2 ● **Sectoral composition of output and GNI per capita, 2007.** As countries become richer, the share of agriculture declines and services take over. *Source:* World Bank, *World Development Indicators.*

income rises people tend to respond by demanding more services, which again pushes up the relative price of services. Both these factors tend to boost the size of the non-industrial sector in the economy. Figure 2.2 shows that as a country gets richer its share of services increases and agriculture declines. Within industrial output there is also a tendency for richer countries to move towards high-end manufacturing and away from resource exploitation. In other words, as countries get wealthier they switch more towards higher value-added outputs.

So far we have concentrated on the *output* measure of GDP. But we can show that this is identical to two more concepts: the income and expenditure measures of GDP. To create value added, factors of production – labour and capital (buildings and machines) – have to be used and of course paid. Labour will be paid wages and salaries and overtime. The owners of capital are paid in various ways: rents, dividend payments, interest payments and retained profits (if the owners of the capital are also the owners of the firm). Table 2.3 shows that *all* the value added created has to be paid out as income to either labour or capital (the sum of profits plus salaries in Table 2.3 equals the output measure of GDP). Using the income of labour and capital to calculate output is called the *income* approach to measuring GDP. We have just shown that the *income* and *output* approach both arrive at the same measure of GDP. Table 2.4 shows the income measure of US GDP in 2009 and reveals that 64% of GDP was paid out to labour and 27% in various forms to owners of capital. Figure 2.3 shows the income share of labour for a wide range of economies, which suggests that this 70–30 split of value added between labour and capital is a useful rule of thumb for most countries.

TABLE 2.4 ● **US National Income, 2009.**

Labour receives the largest proportion of GDP as income.
Figures US$bn (percentages of total in brackets).

Compensation of employees	7856	[64.2%]
Corporate profits	1263	[10%]
Rental income	222	[1.8%]
Proprietors' income[1]	1102	[8.8%]
Net interest	813	[6.5%]
Net government	1097	[8.7%]
Total national income	12396	[100%]

Source: Bureau of Economic Analysis.

[1]Income from non-corporate business activity, e.g., profits of family-run businesses.

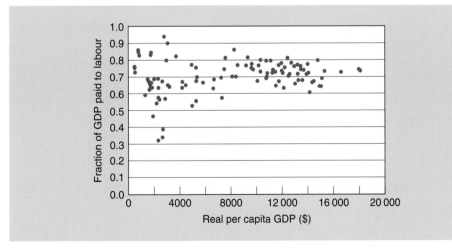

FIGURE 2.3 ● **Labour income share across countries.** Labour gets paid around 70% of GDP.
Source: Figure 5, Gollin, 'Getting Income Shares Right', *Journal of Political Economy*, April 2002, 110(2): 458–74.

There is one further way of calculating GDP: the *expenditure* method. Returning to Table 2.3, we can measure output by ignoring all the intermediate stages of production (the lumberyard and the manufacturer) and simply value the expenditure on the final good (the tables sold by the retailer). This is the expenditure measure of output and, if measured properly, this will arrive at the same answer as the income and output measure. In our example only one commodity is produced – tables – and this is bought by the consumer. But in practice, a range of commodities and services are produced and used for different purposes. The expenditure measure of output shows the breakdown across these categories.

The goods and services produced within an economy have four basic uses:

- consumption by individuals (C)
- consumption and investment by government (G)
- investment by the private sector (I)
- exports (X)

The government expenditure here is on actual purchases of goods and services (either for consumption or investment) and excludes what are called *transfer payments*, such as pensions and social security payments. Although transfer payments involve the government spending money, they do not involve the government directly purchasing the output produced by the economy and so should be excluded from our analysis here. Government consumption will include a range of activities, but a significant component will be the wages and salaries paid to civil servants in return for the services they provide. Government investment will include the building of roads, schools, tanks and so forth. In Chapter 10 we will focus in detail on investment, but note here that investment refers not to placing money in a bank account or stock market fund (these are examples of savings), but instead to firms increasing their capital stock, for instance by buying new machines, building new factories and so forth.

Demand in the economy arises from these four categories:

Aggregate Demand = Consumption + Investment
                      + Government Expenditure + Exports

or

AD = C + I + G + X

This demand must either be met from domestically produced output (Y) or from imports (M). Because expenditure on goods must equal sales of goods (demand must equal supply), we therefore have

Output + Imports = Consumption + Investment
                      + Government Expenditure + Exports

or

Y + M = C + I + G + X

From this equation we arrive at the expenditure measure of output:

Output = Consumption + Investment + Government Expenditure + Net Exports

or

Y = C + I + G + (X − M)

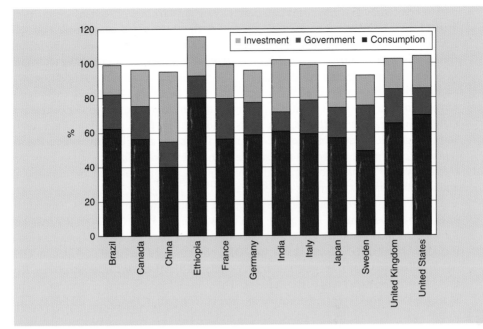

FIGURE 2.4 ● **Expenditure components as percentage of GDP, 1997–2007.** Consumption is usually the largest expenditure component of GDP, though developing countries show more variation in expenditure shares than do developed countries. *Source:* World Bank, *World Development Indicators.*

Crucial to arriving at this expenditure measure of output was the assumption that supply equals demand. To ensure this is the case, it is important to include in investment the *unsold* output that firms produce – their increase in inventories or stock building. This ensures that supply equals demand, but makes it necessary to break investment down into *gross fixed capital formation* (the new capital stock installed) and *change in inventories* (unsold output).

Figure 2.4 shows the expenditure breakdown of GDP for a number of countries between 1997 and 2007 (net exports is the missing component that makes everything add to 100%). With the exception of China (where investment and consumption are approximately equal), consumption is the single largest element of the output produced in an economy – ranging from 40% in China to 80% in Ethiopia. There is a wider range of variation in investment and government expenditure, and, as we shall see in Chapter 4, differences in investment rates are crucial to understanding differences in the standard of living across countries.

> **KEY POINT**
>
> GDP can be measured either as value of output produced, the income earned in the economy by capital and labour, or the expenditure on final products.

GDP OR GNI?

In measuring the output of an economy we need to define what we mean, for instance, by the Italian economy. Is this the output produced by all Italians (both individuals and firms) or the output produced by everyone living in Italy? In other words, how do we deal with the output created by German firms based in Italy or the earnings of Italians living abroad? In broad terms, GDP, or *gross domestic product*, is the measure of output based on Italy as a geographical concept, whereas GNI, or *gross national income*,[2] focuses on the income of a country by adding and subtracting from GDP various flows of income between countries.

To move from Italian GDP to Italian GNI we need to make several additions to GDP: all the profits Italian firms earn overseas that they *remit* (i.e. send back to Italy); all the wages and salaries earned by Italians overseas that are remitted; any other overseas investment income earned by Italian firms/households that is also remitted; and aid *received* by Italy. Several deductions also need to be made: the profits made in Italy by non-Italian firms that are repatriated; the wages and salaries earned by non-Italians based in Italy that they remit; any investment income earned by foreign investors in Italy that are remitted abroad; and any overseas aid payments made by Italy.

Thus, Italian GDP would include the output produced within Italy by Italians and anyone else, such as Germans or Albanians, who are working in Italy. However, if Albanians send some of the income they earn in Italy back to Albania, then these remittances would *not* be included in Italian GNI (only in Italian GDP), but would be included in Albanian GNI (and not in Albanian GDP). We need to draw a similar distinction for corporate profits. Consider the case of a German bank based in Rome. The value added the bank creates will be paid out in wages to its workforce and profits to its owners. The part of the profits that the bank remits to the head office of the bank in Germany will be included in German but not Italian GNI. However, these profits will be included in the measurement of Italian, not German, GDP.

For some economies the distinction between GDP and GNI is trivial, but for others (see Figure 2.5) the difference can be huge. In Ireland, GDP has been substantially in excess of GNI because so many overseas firms moved there in the 1980s and 1990s. These firms pay

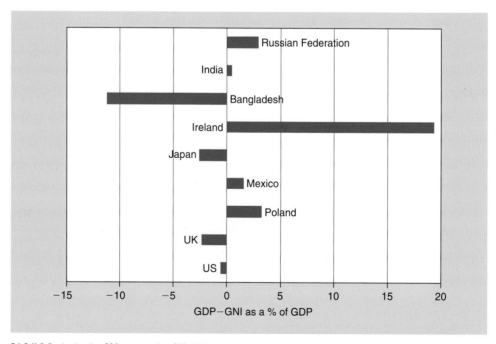

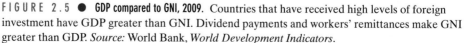

FIGURE 2.5 ● **GDP compared to GNI, 2009.** Countries that have received high levels of foreign investment have GDP greater than GNI. Dividend payments and workers' remittances make GNI greater than GDP. *Source:* World Bank, *World Development Indicators.*

wages and make profits that boost both Irish GDP and GNI. But profits repatriated out of Ireland are excluded from Irish GNI. This means that Irish GNI is 19% less than Irish GDP. A similar, but less pronounced, phenomenon occurs in Mexico and Poland, where, because of the enlargement of the North American Free Trade Agreement (NAFTA) and the European Union (EU), these countries have received much US and German foreign direct investment (FDI; for example, building of foreign-owned factories), causing GDP to grow faster than GNI. In contrast, Japan has many multinational enterprises (MNEs) that operate overseas, so that its GNI exceeds its GDP. The same holds for Bangladesh, although the explanation there is not remittances received from firms working overseas but from workers' remittances.

Is it best to use GDP or GNI as a measure of the standard of living? The answer is, it depends! Development agencies such as the World Bank like to use GNI to compare income across countries (on the basis that income that you produce in your country but that is paid to foreign entities is not really your income and vice versa for income you receive from overseas), but GDP has the significant advantage of being easier and quicker to calculate and so is far more widely reported when discussing economic growth in a country.

KEY POINT

GDP measures the value of output produced in an economy, whereas GNI shows the income earned, taking into account net worker, investor, corporate and government remittances.

(2.5) How Large Are Modern Economies?

Figure 2.6 gives some idea about the overall size of modern economies and which are the largest. It shows a snapshot of the global economy taken in 2009 in which each country's GDP is measured in US dollars (using market exchange rates). It reveals that the United States is a little smaller than the European Union (eurozone + rest of EU) and together they account for 48% of world GDP. The Chinese economy accounts for about 10% of world GDP. Given that the population of China alone is greater than those of the United States, the EU and Japan combined, world output is clearly unevenly distributed.

However, things are changing. One of the most important current macroeconomic trends is the rapid economic growth of a group of large developing economies. Often called the BRICs (Brazil, Russia, India and China), these economies have grown remarkably quickly, and look as if they may be able to sustain that growth for many years. If they do, it will not be long until these countries overtake the current rich economies of Europe and North America and become the world's largest economies. Figure 2.7 shows estimates of how long it will take this group of countries to overtake the G7 (United States, Japan, Germany, France, United Kingdom, Italy and Canada) group of large rich economies in terms of total output (though not GDP per capita) if they continue to grow rapidly.

If we are to use our estimates of GDP as a measure of the standard of living, then we should focus not on GDP but GDP per head of the population or *GDP per capita*. For instance, the economy of Poland in 2011 was worth $468 billion compared to only $55 billion for Luxembourg. However, because the population of Poland is nearly 75 times that of Luxembourg, Luxembourg has a per capita GDP over nine times larger than Poland.

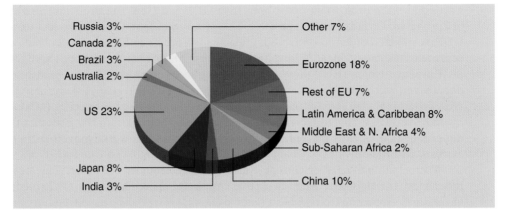

FIGURE 2.6 ● **World GDP, 2011 ($69 trillion).** The world economy is still dominated by rich advanced nations. *Source:* IMF, *World Economic Outlook* (2010).

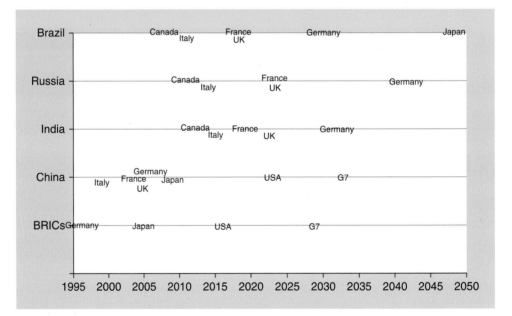

FIGURE 2.7 ● **The rise of the BRICs.** The large and fast-growing economies of Brazil, Russia, India and China are set to overtake the rich economies of the G7 by 2029 if current trends continue. Figure shows projected dates when each of the BRICs will overtake the G7 economies in terms of overall GDP. *Source:* IMF, *World Economic Outlook* (October 2010) and authors' calculations.

COMPARISONS USING MARKET AND PURCHASING POWER PARITY EXCHANGE RATES

When making international comparisons, it is necessary to convert all measures of GDP into a common currency. For instance, the output of the Japanese economy is measured in yen and the US economy in dollars. To compare them we need to convert into common units, which is often done by converting all figures into US dollars using current market exchange rates. So, in the case of Japan we can convert Japanese GDP into dollars by dividing GDP measured in yen by the current dollar–yen exchange rate. However, this method has a couple of drawbacks. First, market exchange rates can change quite quickly and dramatically, so a 10% appreciation of the yen (which can, and has, happened in less than a week) would suddenly make Japan's GDP 10% larger in dollar terms. Second, and more important, market exchange rates may not properly reflect differences in the cost of living in different countries. A dollar can buy a lot more in India when converted into rupees than it can in the United States and this should be taken into account when comparing per capita incomes.

To overcome these problems we can use purchasing power parity (PPP) exchange rates rather than market exchange rates when converting GDP into a common currency. A full analysis of PPP is provided in Chapter 19, but for now we simply note that when converting GDP per capita into another currency (usually US dollars), we use an exchange rate that reflects the cost of living in each country by calculating the exchange rate that would make the cost of a standard basket of basic goods equivalent in each country. Figure 2.8 compares GDP per capita for 177 economies with that of the United States using both market and PPP exchange rates. Although the general pattern is the same, we see that using market exchange rates we have more extreme differences. For example, using market rates we have three countries whose GDP per capita is less than 0.5% that of the United States. While using PPP we have none. This reflects the fact that poorer countries tend to have a lower cost of living, so that an American tourist would find most goods and services far cheaper in poorer countries than at home. This lower cost of living means that income per head in terms of purchasing power is actually somewhat higher in poor countries than market exchange rates would suggest.

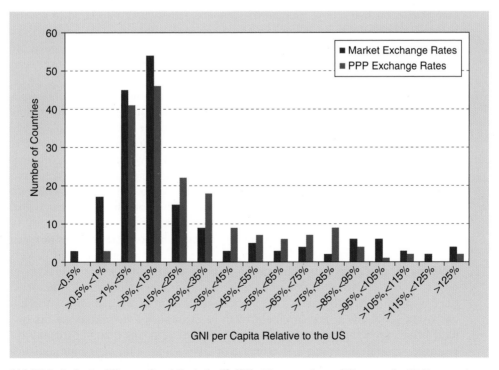

FIGURE 2.8 ● **GNI per capita relative to the US, 2009.** There are large differences in GDP per capita across countries, even on a PPP basis. *Source:* World Bank World Development Indicators and authors' calculations.

2.6   Total Output and Total Happiness

There are two interpretations of our measures of output. The most straightforward is that GDP is a measure of the scale of economic activity. But we have also referred to it as a measure of the standard of living. Is this defensible or is GDP simply too narrow a concept to be useful in measuring the standard of living? In the words of Bhutan's King Jigme Singye Wangchuk, it may be that 'Gross National Happiness is more important than Gross National Product'.

There are two separate issues lurking here. The first is a measurement one: Is GDP correctly measured and, if not, does this reduce its ability to approximate the standard of living? The second is a conceptual one: Even if it is properly measured, does GDP really capture our concepts of welfare?

MEASUREMENT PROBLEMS IN GDP

Focusing on the first issue – is GDP correctly measured – the answer is undoubtedly 'no'. One problem is that a large amount of economic activity is not declared to governments; perhaps it is illegal activity, involved with tax evasion or simply not declared to the statisticians. This underground economy is often quite substantial – Figure 2.9 shows estimates of its size relative to GDP. In some cases it amounts to close to 70%, and everywhere it is substantial.

Another problem is that GDP tends to focus on economic activity that takes place in a market transaction (whether official or underground). For instance, at any one time many families in an economy have one adult who earns an income in the marketplace, which the family uses to buy goods and services from the market, and another adult who remains outside the market but nevertheless provides goods and services: child care, cooking meals, household administration. All these activities, whether market or non-market based, produce output, and if we were to include these non-market-based activities, GDP would be substantially larger.[3] As Figure 2.10 shows, the size of this household production is substantial and for some countries takes more time than paid work.

Even for the subset of economic activity that is measured, statisticians face a number of problems estimating GDP. For example, when a new and more expensive version of a product is introduced, statisticians must decide whether the new product is similar in quality to the previous version and so the higher price is simply inflation, or whether the new product is better and so the higher price captures real economic progress. This, and other problems in measurement, such as misreported or inaccurate tax or survey data (which form the basis of the national accounts), means that statisticians are often required to admit that their first estimate of GDP – and other economic statistics – was incorrect and to revise it substantially when more information arrives. Figure 2.11 shows that these revisions are large, so that in the cases of Japan and Denmark the figure for quarterly GDP growth reported three years later is *on average* about 0.6 percentage

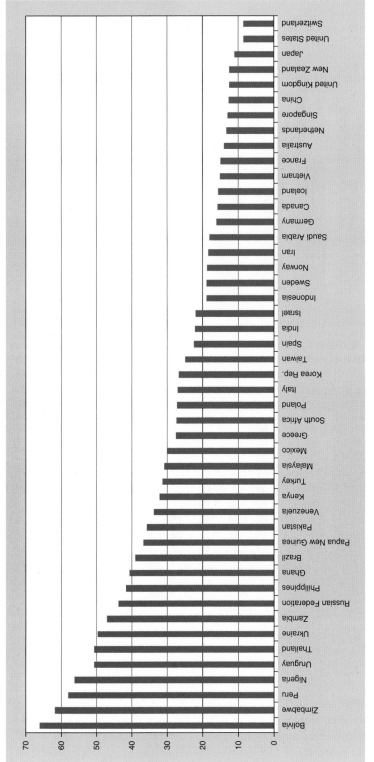

FIGURE 2.9 ● **Estimates of underground economy (% of GDP).** Some economies are characterized by large underground markets. *Source:* International Bank for Reconstruction and Development/The World Bank: Shadow Economies All Over the World. New Estimates for 162 Countries from 1999 to 2007. World Bank Policy Research Working Paper No. 5356 (June 2010). Friedrich Schneider. Andreas Buehn, Claudio E. Montenegro.

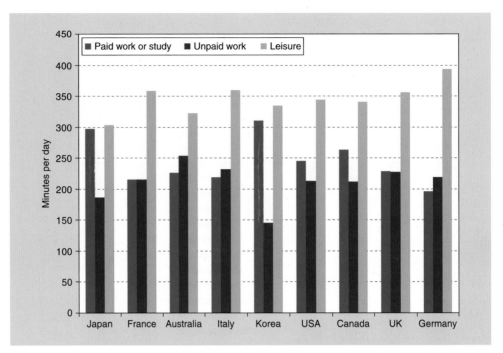

FIGURE 2.10 ● **Housework, paid work and leisure (minutes per day).** Unpaid work like cooking, cleaning and child care can take as much time as paid work for the average person. *Source:* OECD Social Indicators (2009).

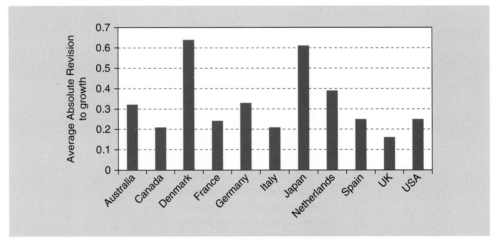

FIGURE 2.11 ● **Average absolute GDP revisions (quarter-on-quarter growth rates, 1995–2008).** Initial estimates of GDP growth are often revised substantially in subsequent years, by an average of 0.6 percentage points after three years in some countries. *Source:* OECD revisions database.

points different from the initial estimate. Given these measurement problems, the public are often rightly sceptical of official economic statistics, though the survey data for European countries in Figure 2.12 shows that public trust in UK economic statistics is particularly low despite the relatively good track record of UK GDP data shown in Figure 2.11.

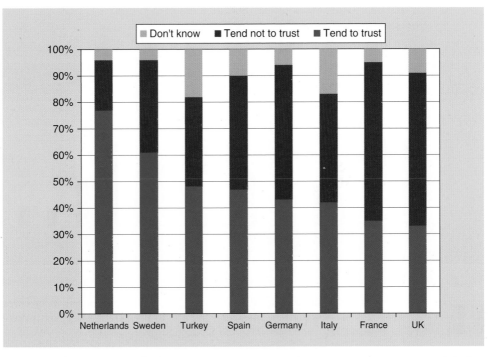

FIGURE 2.12 ● **Trust in official statistics.** Answers to the question 'Do you trust official statistics?' are generally not very positive. *Source: Eurobarometer* 67 (2007).

OUTPUT AND SUSTAINABILITY

If you borrow a huge amount of money and spend it all on a world cruise, your standard of living might improve while you are on the cruise, but you have committed yourself to many years of penury once you return and are forced to pay back the loan. It is clearly not true that your income was higher in the year you went on the cruise even though your expenditure was higher, you simply borrowed out of your future income.

A similar question occurs in the measurement of GDP. Should we measure as income activity that simply runs down future wealth? An important example of this is environmental damage and resource depletion. If our current standard of living depends on running down scarce resources or polluting the environment, then it is not likely to be sustainable and we should try to recognize this when we measure the current standard of living. Figure 2.13 shows World Bank estimates of these effects for a range of countries and for the world as a whole. Many commentators argue that these environmental effects should be subtracted from GDP to create a concept of 'green' or sustainable GDP.

OUTPUT AS WELFARE?

The second issue with GDP is whether, even if correctly measured, it reflects welfare. The nineteenth-century historian Thomas Carlyle referred to economics as 'a dreary, desolate and indeed quite abject and disturbing [subject]; what we might call . . . the dismal science'. In his opinion what is inspiring and motivating in humanity cannot be captured by

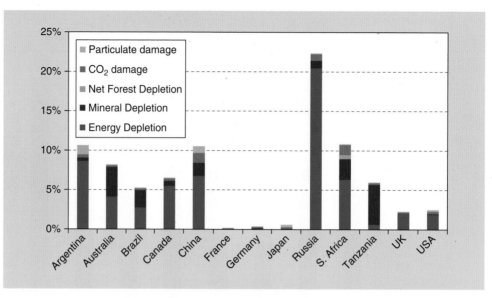

FIGURE 2.13 ● **The GNI cost of environmental depletion.** Estimates of the economic value of resource depletion and pollution help show how much economic activity depends on consuming 'natural wealth'. *Source:* World Bank Environmental Accounting (2010).

supply-and-demand diagrams. Two obvious influences on our welfare that are not measured by GDP are health and education. Being wealthy does not really compensate for poor health and low life expectancy, while greater education is generally believed to help individuals fulfil their overall potential (not just increase their future income). In an attempt to overcome these basic deficiencies of GDP as a measure of welfare, the United Nations has developed the Human Development Index (HDI), which combines data on life expectancy, years of schooling and income per capita to give a broader measure of a country's development. Figure 2.14 shows the relationship between the UN's HDI and GDP per capita. Perhaps unsurprisingly, the two measures are generally fairly similar (statistical analysis suggests that about 90% of the variation in the HDI can be explained by GDP). This is because both health and schooling are generally better in richer countries.

As well as health and education, there are many other factors that can influence people's welfare. For example, political scientists often talk about the concept of social capital, which measures the value of social networks and the extent of civic engagement. There is considerable evidence that high levels of social capital are associated with better health, less crime, better schools and so on.

Rather than try to measure all these factors, some economists have taken a different route to the measurement of welfare by asking people how happy they feel. Figure 2.15 shows how those surveys compare to standard measures of GDP per capita. Despite a few outliers (Costa Ricans claim to be the happiest people in the world despite not being rich), once again there is a relatively close link between income and happiness, with citizens of richer countries being far more likely to report themselves as happy.

There is also an interesting and important aspect of the relationship between income and happiness shown in Figure 2.15: as income gets higher, the increases in happiness that further gains in income provide get smaller and smaller. Understandably, another dollar a day given to a wealthy person will make little difference to their welfare, but it could make

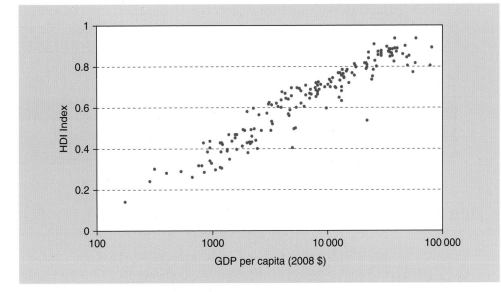

FIGURE 2.14 ● **GDP per capita and the Human Development Index.** Broader measures of welfare that include health and education are closely linked to income per capita. *Source:* United Nations Human Development Index (2010).

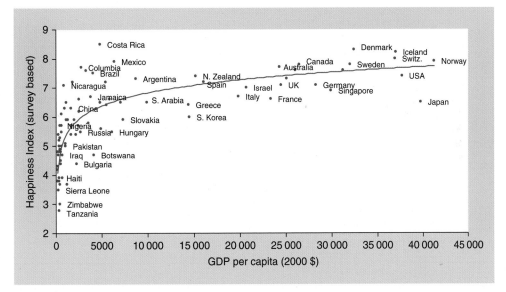

FIGURE 2.15 ● **Happiness and GDP per capita.** People from richer countries are more likely to report themselves as generally happy with life. *Source:* R. Veenhoven, States of Nations, World Database of Happiness, http://worlddatabaseofhappiness.eur.nl (2010).

a profound difference to someone living in poverty. These diminishing returns to higher income are of fundamental importance, since they suggest that transfers of income from rich to poor can, in principle, raise overall welfare and so justify a large range of government activities such as higher tax rates for richer people, welfare benefits for the poor and even international aid transfers from rich to poor countries. Diminishing returns to income also suggest that greater income inequality is – other things being equal – bad for welfare, since it results in a few rich people receiving income that they derive little benefit from while the poor remain poor. We will return to the issue of income inequality in the next chapter.

KEY POINT

GDP suffers from several measurement and conceptual limitations, but seems to correlate reasonably well with broader welfare measures.

SUMMARY

Section 2.1 suggested that central to macroeconomics is the provision of a consistent set of data on key variables. Ultimately economists are interested in welfare, but in practice they focus on output in the belief that increases in output increase a country's welfare.

In Section 2.2 we showed how macroeconomists measure output by summing the output of all the goods and services an economy produces. They distinguish between real and nominal GDP. Nominal GDP captures how both changes in prices and shifts in production affect value. By contrast, movements in real GDP reflect changes due to different levels of output and form the better measure of the health of an economy.

Section 2.3 showed how GDP is a measure of value added – the difference between the value of output sold and the cost of purchased raw materials and intermediate inputs.

Section 2.4 considered the national accounts and how the output of value added in an economy equals the income earned as well as total expenditure. Gross domestic product measures the output produced within an economy and gross national income adds and subtracts the various income flows that occur between countries. The most common measure of the standard of living in an economy is real GDP *per capita*.

Section 2.5 showed that the world economy is currently dominated by the large industrialized economies like the United States and those in the EU. However, a number of large developing economies known as the BRICs look set to catch up.

Section 2.6 looked at how GDP fails to capture a number of important influences on our overall standard of living, but, nonetheless, is still a reasonable approximation to overall welfare.

CONCEPTUAL QUESTIONS

1. (Section 2.2) '[An economist] is someone who knows the price of everything and the value of nothing' (adapted from George Bernard Shaw). Discuss.

2. (Section 2.3) Coffee beans cost only a few cents when imported, but to buy a coffee at a coffee bar costs far more. What does this tell you about value added?

3. (Sections 2.3 and 2.4) Try to explain to someone who had never thought about measuring the value of economic activity why the output, income and expenditure ways of measuring national production should give the same answer. It helps to think of a simple economy producing only two or three different things.

4. (Section 2.5) Would you expect a country where the share of wages and salaries in GDP was falling, and the share of profits and interest was rising, to be one where consumption as a percentage

of national income was also shifting? Why? Would you expect the distribution of income to become more unequal? Suppose the trends were due to demographic shifts, more specifically to a rapidly ageing population. Would this change your answers?

5. (Section 2.5) Do you think it is easier to evaluate the relative welfare of different generations of people in one country (by comparing per capita GDP over time), or to compare the relative standards of living in different countries at a point in time (by converting current per capita GDPs into a common currency)?

6. (Section 2.5) How would you treat the activities of criminals in GDP accounting? What about the activities of the police force?

7. (Section 2.6) The Beatles claimed: 'I don't care too much for money, money can't buy me love.' (Shortly after first making this claim, they joined the ranks of the richest people in the world.) Does their claim undermine the use of GDP to measure welfare?

8. Analyse the recent sectoral composition (agriculture, industry and services as a percentage of GDP) of output GDP for a selection of countries of your choice, using either national sources or the World Bank's World Development Indicators (http://data.worldbank.org/data-catalog -> WDI databank). Is the sectoral breakdown what you would expect given those countries' level of development (see Figure 2.2)?

ANALYTICAL QUESTIONS

1. (Section 2.2) The price of the four sorts of goods produced in an economy in 2010 are:

Good	A	B	C	D
Price	8	9	4	2
Quantity	1000	400	600	1000

The prices of the goods in 2011 are:

Good	A	B	C	D
Price	9	6	8	3

What is the overall rate of inflation between 2010 and 2011? Would it help to know the levels of output of goods in 2011? How might that information be used to construct an alternative measure of inflation?

2. (Section 2.2) Use Table 2.2 to calculate real GDP using constant prices for years 2, 3 and 4. How do your estimates of GDP growth compare with those achieved via chain weighting? What is the direction of the substitution bias?

3. (Section 2.3) Consider an economy with three productive sectors: mining and farming; manufacturing; and retailing. Manufacturers produce goods each year with a sale value of 500. They sell 400 to retailers and 100 direct to the private sector and to government for consumption. Retailers buy goods for 400 from manufacturers and buy 50 from the agricultural sector. Retailers sell goods for consumption for 500. Manufacturers buy goods worth 200 from mining and agricultural firms. Farmers also sell 100 direct to the private sector for consumption. Mining companies sell nothing directly to government or households for consumption.

   What is the value added in each sector and what is the total output for the economy?

4. (Section 2.4) A country has overseas assets worth 12% of GDP. Overseas assets earn a return of 7%, which is distributed back to the home country. Other countries own assets in the domestic economy worth 8% of GDP and these assets earn a return of 11%. What is the difference between GDP and GNI?

5. (Section 2.4) The national accounts of Australia for 2002 show (in A$):

Total consumption	$418 billion
Investment	$158 billion
Government spending	$125 billion
Total exports	$151 billion
Total imports	$156 billion

What is GDP? Suppose consumption increases by 10% but output only rises by 5%. Investment and government spending both increase by 3%. What happens to the gap between exports and imports?

6. (Section 2.6) Use a spreadsheet to plot the relationship between GDP per capita and the education and health components of the Human Development Index (available at http://hdr.undp.org/en/statistics/hdi/). Do these relationships make sense? Can you explain some of the outliers?

PART TWO

Economic Growth and the Supply Side

The Wealth of Nations: The Supply Side

Key Concepts

Capital Stock	Marginal Product of Capital	Pro-Poor Growth
Employment Rate	Participation Rate	Total Factor Productivity (TFP)
Growth Accounting	Production Function	Trend Growth
Labour Force	Productivity	

Overview

This chapter focuses on why GDP varies so much across countries and over long periods of time. It begins by documenting the huge increase in output that the world has experienced over the last 200 years and the benefits of this long-run growth: supporting a larger population, greater life expectancy, increasing income per head and reductions in poverty. We then analyse why GDP per capita varies so much across countries, focusing on differences in productivity and labour utilization. We argue that for sustained increases in GDP per capita, improvements in labour productivity are critical. We introduce the production function to explain how output increases over time through increases in the inputs of capital, labour and total factor productivity. We examine the magnitude of these factor inputs and how they boost output, and offer a numerical framework with which to explain observed GDP growth. We analyse the historical drivers of economic growth and establish stylized facts that we will seek to explain in later chapters.

3.1 The Importance of Economic Growth

Figure 3.1 shows growth in GDP per head across the world since 0 AD. Two facts stand out: the enormous increase in output starting in the nineteenth century and the relatively modest growth before then. Figure 3.2 shows that the rapid world growth that began around the time of the UK Industrial Revolution was not evenly spread across the world: growth in most of Europe, North America and Australasia has been significantly greater than that

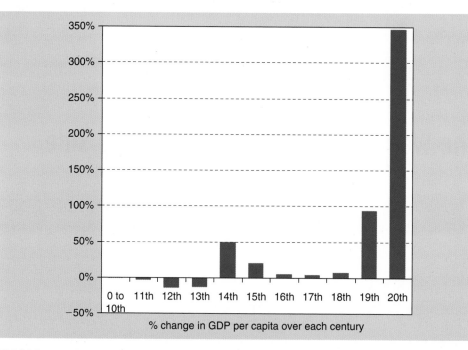

FIGURE 3.1 ● **GDP per capita, 0 AD to 2000 AD.** The twentieth century saw dramatic increases in GDP per head around the world. Despite the recent recession, average global growth so far in the twenty-first century has exceeded that of the twentieth. *Source:* Cornucopia: The Pace of Economic Growth in the Twentieth Century, NBER Working Paper 7602, March 2000. Reproduced by permission of Professor Bradford DeLong; and authors' calculations.

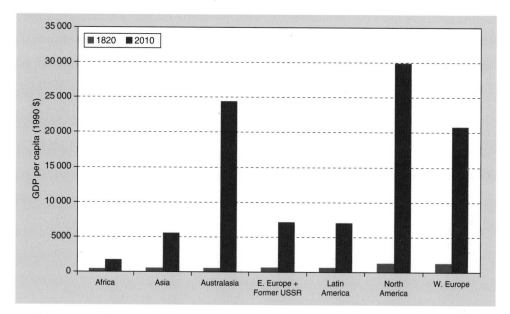

FIGURE 3.2 ● **GDP per capita by continent, 1820–2010.** The rise in GDP over the nineteenth and twentieth centuries was concentrated in North America, Western Europe and Australasia. *Source:* Maddison, *Monitoring the World Economy 1820–1998*, World Development Indicators and authors' calculations.

in Asia, South America and Africa. As a result, the gap between rich and poor countries has steadily grown over most of the last 200 years; only in the last 20 years or so have we seen some catch-up by the poorer nations (most notably the BRICs).

In this chapter we begin to develop a framework to understand this long-run growth and its cross-country variation. In this section we show how important economic growth is and how substantial the gains are from helping poorer countries grow faster. Our aim is to show that long-run growth is the most important subject in macroeconomics.

COMPOUNDING

One basic aspect of economic growth is the importance of compounding. You might think that a country that grows by 1% a year for a century would end the century with GDP 100% larger than it began with, but in fact the total increase would be about 170%. This is because as the economy grows, a 1% increase represents a larger and larger amount of output. The consequence of this is that small increases in growth have a significant impact on output if sustained for long periods. For example, 2% growth over 100 years would result in output ending up 624% higher than it began – far more than twice the increase that occurred with 1% growth. More dramatically, if China were to sustain its recent growth rates of around 8% for 100 years, the Chinese economy would end the century around 22 000% larger than it was at the beginning!

To better understand the power of compounding, consider the Rule of 70 – divide 70 by the growth rate of a country and you find out how many years it takes for a country to double its GDP. If China grows at 8% per annum, then it will take around 9 years to double GDP. If Germany grows at 2% per annum, it will take 35 years to double GDP.

LONG-RUN GROWTH AND THE BUSINESS CYCLE

Another way to see the importance of long-run growth is to consider the calculations of Nobel Laureate Robert Lucas.[1] Lucas seeks to answer two questions: How much of current consumption should an economy be prepared to give up to increase its growth rate by a specified amount? How much current consumption should an economy be prepared to give up to remove business cycle fluctuations?[2] Lucas calculates that a permanent increase in trend growth from 2% to 3% is worth 20% of current consumption for the US economy, while raising trend growth from 3% to 6% is worth 42% of current consumption, nearly $4 *trillion*. By contrast, to remove all business cycle fluctuations, the United States should give up only 0.1% of its current consumption. In other words, economic growth is a hugely important topic. While many authors have challenged the small numbers Lucas attaches to the costs of business cycles, few have attempted to challenge the relative importance he places on growth compared to business cycles.

For the intuition behind this result, consider Figure 3.3, which shows GDP for an imaginary economy growing at an underlying trend rate of 2.5% per year. The business cycle is defined (see Chapter 11) as fluctuations around a trend; in other words, the movement from A to B and then on to C and D. These business cycles contribute substantially to the volatility in GDP, but do not influence trend growth. Therefore we can link the value that people place on avoiding business cycles to how much they dislike short-run uncertainty, for example not knowing whether next year they will be at C or D. By contrast, how much they should pay to increase the growth rate depends on how they value higher output. If the

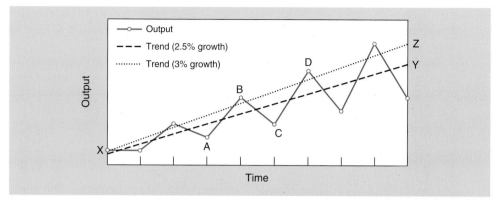

FIGURE 3.3 ● Relative importance of trend growth and business cycles. Trend growth exerts a bigger influence on welfare than business cycle fluctuations.

economy could somehow shift its long-term growth rate from 2.5% to 3%, then instead of ending up at a point like Y, it would be at Z, where output is much higher. Removing business cycles is about reducing uncertainty; boosting long-run growth is about giving people more output/income. How important business cycles are depends on how much volatility they produce and how much society dislikes uncertainty. Given the relatively small size of US business cycles (consumption growth varies between −2% and 5% at its most extreme), Lucas concluded that the main benefits flowed from higher growth – growth is much more important than short-term volatility. None of this means that business cycles are unimportant, only that the cost of business cycle uncertainty is relatively small compared to the benefits of higher long-run growth.

> **KEY POINT**
>
> The gains from boosting the long-run rate of growth in an economy are enormous and much larger than the gains from stabilizing business cycles. Even small differences in growth rates have a substantial impact over long periods of time.

3.2 The Impact of Long-Run Growth

We have already suggested how long-term increases in GDP per head lead to substantial increases in welfare. In this section we consider how these welfare gains are manifested: in increases in population and life expectancy and reductions in poverty.

GROWING POPULATION

A huge increase in world population has been both produced by, and in turn supported, economic growth. Thomas Malthus (1766–1834), an English clergyman, wrote his *Essay on the Principle of Population* in 1798 in which he prophesied that limited natural resources constrained population size.[3] With the stock of natural resources fixed, he reasoned that the

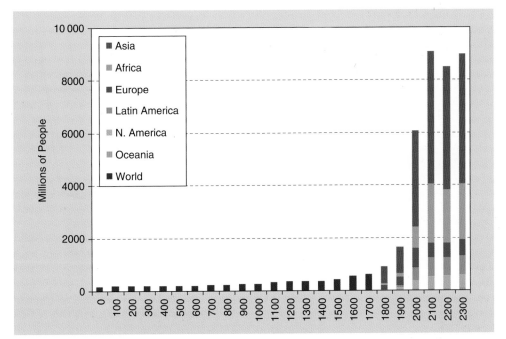

FIGURE 3.4 ● **World population (in millions) from 0 AD.** World population rose sharply in the twentieth century, but is projected to stabilize by the twenty-second century. *Source:* Kremer, *Quarterly Journal of Economics* (1993), *World Population to 2300* (2004), UN Population Division.

only way of producing more output was to use more labour. However, with a finite amount of natural resources, there was a limit to the size of the population and thus also a limit to the amount of output the population could produce. But over the last 200 years, the interaction between increases in the capital stock and increasing technological knowledge has meant that Malthusian fears of a limit on world population have not been realized. Since Malthus wrote, world population has risen more than sixfold; see Figure 3.4.

LIFE EXPECTANCY

Figure 3.5 shows how the burst in economic growth that occurred in the nineteenth and twentieth centuries has been followed by a significant increase in average life expectancy. For example, in 1662 a newborn baby in England had a 64% chance of surviving to age 6 compared to a 99% chance in modern America. Life expectancy depends on many things, not the least of which are medical knowledge and diet. Higher income helps by enabling better nutrition and financing the production of medicines and medical research.

POVERTY AND INEQUALITY

One important reason why increasing average income may not translate into a comparable increase in welfare is if the income is unevenly distributed. In one important respect, the surge in world growth in the nineteenth and twentieth centuries has been extremely unequal, since it has been concentrated in a small number of countries. Figure 3.6 shows the

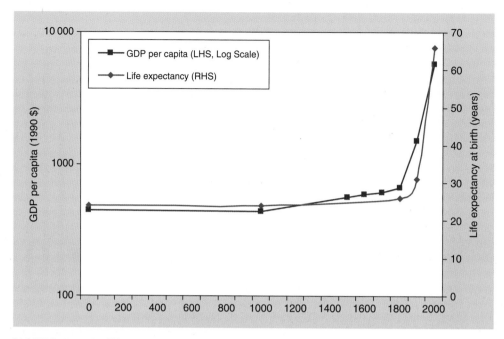

FIGURE 3.5 ● **GDP per capita and life expectancy since 0 AD.** The rise in world income per capita has resulted in increased life expectancy. *Source:* Maddison, 'The World Economy: A millennial perspective', OECD.

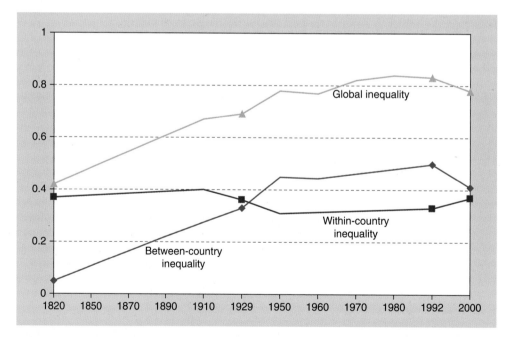

FIGURE 3.6 ● **Global income inequality since 1820.** Income inequality rose steadily until the end of the twentieth century, due to increasing inequality between countries. (Note: the measure of inequality used here is log deviation.) *Source:* Bourguignon and Morrisson, 'Inequality among World Citizens: 1820–1992', *American Economic Review* (2002), 92 (4); and authors' calculations.

impact of this uneven growth on global inequality. It demonstrates how, until recently, global income inequality was steadily rising and how that rise was almost entirely accounted for by increases in *between-country* inequality: some countries becoming rich while the rest remained poor. The rise of the BRICs at the end of the twentieth century reversed this trend and so, despite a rise in *within-country* inequality, global inequality has now begun to fall. In other words, although inequality has increased within China and India, these countries' fast growth has narrowed the gap between US and European per capita GDP on the one hand and Chinese and Indian GDP per head on the other, leading to a fall in world inequality overall.

REDUCING POVERTY

Although there are many ways to measure the level of poverty in the world, one that has gained prominence in recent years is the number of people living on less than $1 a day (using PPP exchange rates) and an alternative measure of less than $1.25 a day. By any standards, these are extremely low levels of income (not enough to provide clean water, sanitation and adequate food, let alone health and education). Yet according to the World Bank, in 1990 about 46% of the population of the developing world lived on less than $1.25 a day (about 1.8 billion people). Reducing world poverty is a major policy goal. The United Nation's Millennium Development Goals aim to reduce by half the proportion of people living on less than $1 a day from its 1990 level. As Figure 3.7 shows, progress on this aim has been impressive, with the dramatic growth of China in particular contributing to a significant reduction in poverty. By 2005, global poverty was already close to half its 1990 level despite very little progress in regions such as Sub-Saharan Africa.

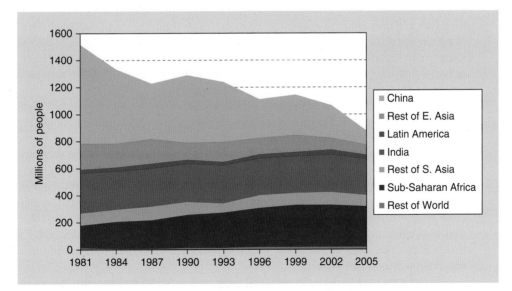

FIGURE 3.7 ● **Population with an income of less than $1 a day (millions).** Rapid growth in China has been the most important driver behind declining global poverty. *Source:* Chen and Ravallion (2008), World Bank Policy Research Working Paper 4703.

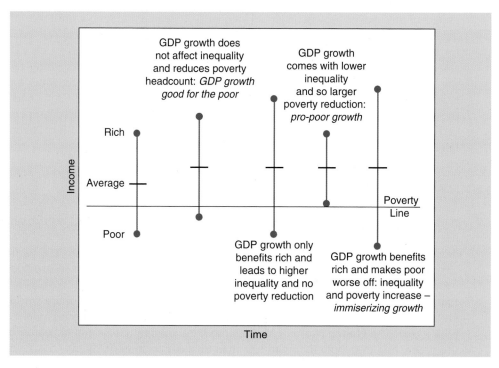

FIGURE 3.8 ● **Growth and poverty linkages.** GDP growth can theoretically have varied effects on poverty.

The number of people living in poverty depends on the level of average GDP per capita and the degree of inequality in society. Even countries with high levels of average income will have poverty if they are characterized by extreme inequality. Reducing poverty therefore requires either boosting GDP per capita or reducing inequality by redistributing resources towards the poor. In recent years the emphasis in reducing poverty has switched away from redistribution and towards GDP growth. The World Bank and IMF have begun to stress that the most effective way of reducing poverty is to boost GDP growth and, in particular, they strive to achieve 'pro-poor' GDP growth.

Whether GDP growth will automatically reduce poverty depends on its relationship with inequality; Figure 3.8 considers the various alternatives. If the benefits of GDP growth accrue only to the rich, then GDP growth will boost inequality but leave poverty unaffected. It may even be possible that GDP growth in a modern sector of the economy leads to declines in traditional sectors where the poor are mainly based. In this case, GDP growth produces widening inequality and potentially higher levels of poverty – immiserizing growth. Alternatively, if GDP growth does not affect inequality, then everyone enjoys the same proportional increase in income and poverty falls (GDP growth good for the poor). The most efficient way to reduce poverty is through pro-poor growth; that is, GDP growth that reduces inequality so that more of the benefits accrue to the poor, leading to a faster reduction in headcount poverty.

The relationship between growth and inequality is highly contentious, but a consensus is beginning to emerge. Figure 3.9 shows that there is enormous diversity in country experience, so that sometimes GDP growth leads to higher inequality, but in other cases it results in lower inequality. Among this diversity no general relationship between inequality and

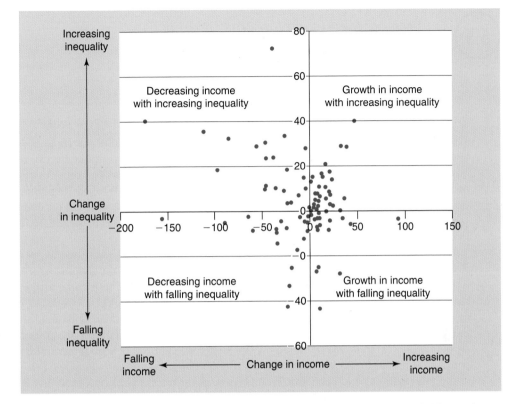

FIGURE 3.9 ● **Growth and inequality.** There is no systematic relationship between GDP growth and changes in inequality. *Source:* Adams, 'Economic Growth, Inequality and Poverty', World Bank Discussion Paper (2003).

growth can be discerned. However, if GDP growth does not on average affect inequality, then it must be the case that GDP growth reduces poverty (in Figure 3.8 this is shown as GDP growth good for the poor). Therefore, because GDP growth does not systematically affect inequality, *on average* it is good for the poor. Whether the focus is on broad geographical regions or small areas, there is a strong negative relationship between GDP growth and poverty. Not all countries benefit equally from this relationship: South Asia has seen fast GDP growth but a disappointing reduction in poverty, while the Middle East and North Africa saw very little GDP growth but a sharp fall in poverty. In other words, the Middle East experienced more pro-poor growth. It is a subject of active research as to which policies produce pro-poor growth. The strongest empirical support comes for policies such as orderly land reform, female education and financial development.

KEY POINT

GDP growth on average does not affect inequality and so helps reduce poverty. Pro-poor GDP growth increases average GDP per capita, reduces inequality and leads to the most rapid reductions in poverty.

3.3   Explaining Cross-Country Income Differences

To understand why some countries produce high levels of GDP per capita compared to others, consider the following identity:

$$\text{GDP/Population} = (\text{GDP/Hours Worked}) \times (\text{Hours Worked/Employment})$$
$$\times (\text{Employment/Labour Force}) \times (\text{Labour Force/Population})$$

This equation enables us to perform a simple decomposition of GDP per capita. The first term on the right-hand side (GDP/Hours Worked) is called hourly productivity: it records how much GDP is produced for every hour worked in an economy. The other three terms on the right-hand side reflect the labour market. The term (Hours Worked/Employment) is the average hours worked per person employed. But not everyone in society is employed: some individuals do not want to participate in the labour market, such as children, retired individuals or parents staying at home raising children, while others do want to participate but are unable to find a job. These individuals are captured in the last two terms on the right-hand side. The term (Employment/Labour Force) is called the employment rate: it is the proportion of individuals who want a job and who have one. This is equal to one minus the unemployment rate: the proportion of individuals who are willing to work but do not have a job. The final term (Labour Force/Population) is called the participation rate. It is the percentage of the population who wish to have a job and be part of the labour force. The participation rate will depend on demographic factors (number of school-age children and pensioners, and so forth), cultural factors (attitudes towards child care, female participation in the labour force) and economic factors (how generous are pensions, how easy it is for firms to hire part-time workers and so forth).

Table 3.1 shows for a sample of OECD (Organization for Economic Cooperation and Development) countries the breakdown of GDP per capita across these four components. The United States has the highest level of GDP per capita – around $47 209 per person – but it does not have the highest hourly productivity. The reason the United States scores so well on GDP per capita is that average hours worked is high and the United States performs well in achieving low unemployment and a high participation rate. It is interesting to compare Germany and the United Kingdom: both countries have roughly similar GDP per capita, even though German hourly productivity is around a quarter more than the United Kingdom's. The reason is that UK employees work around 13% longer hours on average, and experience a lower unemployment rate and a higher participation rate.

From Table 3.1 it can be seen that there are two broad sets of policies required to raise GDP per capita. The first are those that focus on boosting hourly productivity; the second are labour market policies aimed at lowering unemployment and raising the participation rate. Although both channels are important, only the first – raising hourly productivity – can produce sustained faster growth. There is a limit to how low unemployment can fall and how many people are prepared to work, but no such limits constrain hourly productivity.

> ### KEY POINT
>
> GDP per capita is the product of hourly productivity and the average number of hours worked across the population. Hours worked can be affected by labour market policies such as lowering unemployment and raising participation rates, but this cannot occur indefinitely. Boosting hourly productivity is the only means to achieve sustained long-run growth.

TABLE 3.1 ● **Decomposition of GDP per Capita, 2008, US$ PPP.**

GDP per capita varies across countries due to differences in productivity, hours worked, unemployment and population structure.

	GDP per Capita ($PPP)	Hourly Productivity ($PPP)	Average Annual Hours Worked	Employment Rate	Participation Rate
Australia	37 302	46.43	1718	0.940	0.50
Canada	38 941	44.83	1727	0.965	0.52
Denmark	38 566	49.72	1570	0.920	0.54
France	34 620	60.50	1560	0.909	0.40
Germany	36 922	57.47	1430	0.916	0.49
Greece	30 285	36.62	2116	0.933	0.42
Italy	32 695	44.55	1807	0.962	0.42
Japan	33 799	39.01	1772	0.971	0.50
Korea	26 875	25.52	2256	0.963	0.48
Mexico	15 313	20.58	1893	0.955	0.41
Netherlands	43 022	59.73	1389	0.976	0.53
Sweden	39 435	51.42	1625	0.955	0.49
UK	37 317	46.49	1652	0.946	0.51
US	47 209	56.83	1796	0.954	0.48

Source: OECD, Word Bank World Development Index and authors' calculations.

3.4 The Production Function and Factor Inputs

The productivity of each hour worked will depend on many things: the capital stock the worker has to interact with, the education and skills of the employee, the level of technology in the firm, the efficiency with which a firm combines capital and labour and incentivizes good working practices, and so forth. This suggests that we can ultimately think of GDP as being produced by three factors: capital, labour and total factor productivity (or TFP), a catch-all term that reflects any factor that influences the efficiency with which capital and labour are combined to produce output. The relationship between these three inputs and GDP is called the production function and is shown in Figure 3.10.

CAPITAL STOCK

The capital stock of a country is the collection of durable assets that help generate output of goods and services. The capital stock is normally divided into three components: residential buildings, non-residential buildings and equipment (e.g. machines). As Table 3.2 shows, physical capital, especially buildings, lasts for years. A firm invests in capital to produce more output in the future, not just today. By contrast, when a firm hires a worker or uses raw materials in the production process, the service provided is more or less instantaneous. Table 3.2

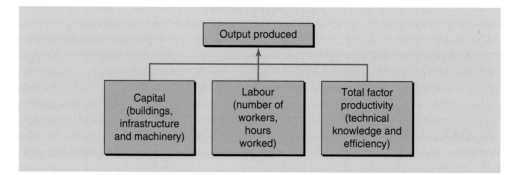

FIGURE 3.10 ● **The production function.** Output is produced by combining capital, labour and total factor productivity.

TABLE 3.2 ● **Average Length of Life of Physical Capital (in Years).**

The capital stock provides economic services over prolonged periods.

	US	UK	Germany	France	Japan
Equipment	12	13	15	11	6
Structures	40	66	57	34	42

Source: O'Mahoney, 'Measures of fixed capital stocks in the post-war period: A five country study', in van Ark and Crafts (eds), *Quantitative Aspects of Post-War European Economic Growth* (Cambridge University Press, 1996), pp. 165–214.

TABLE 3.3 ● **Capital Stock Divided by GDP, 1992.**

The capital stock is large relative to the flow of output (GDP) it produces.

	US	France	Germany	Netherlands	UK	Japan
Machinery and Equipment	0.86	0.74	0.70	0.78	0.65	1.07
Non-residential Structures	1.57	1.52	1.63	1.53	1.17	1.95
Total	2.43	2.26	2.33	2.31	1.82	3.02

Source: Table 2.1, Maddison, *Monitoring the World Economy: 1820–1992* (Paris: OECD, 1995). Copyright OECD.

indicates how long equipment and buildings last in five industrialized nations. For instance, in the United States a new machine can be expected to boost production for 12 years, while a building provides 40 years of productive services. Because capital is a stock that accumulates over time, it is much larger than the flow of GDP produced within a year. This can be seen in Table 3.3, which shows that the ratio of capital to GDP in OECD countries ranges mostly between 2 and 3.

Our interest is in the ability of the capital stock to boost output, and so we *exclude* residential structures from our measure of the capital stock. We also exclude most of the capital stock of the household sector, which consists of a vast array of consumer durables such as refrigerators, microwaves and televisions. These commodities should last (hopefully!) for years and provide a flow of services, but these are not recorded in GDP. We therefore define the capital stock as the machines and buildings used in the production of GDP. Figure 3.11 shows that for industrialized nations, buildings account for around 60% of the capital stock.

LABOUR

We have already examined in some detail the structure of the labour force. As shown in Figure 3.12, for the United States in 2011 the population consists of four categories: the employed and the unemployed (which together make up the labour force) and then those out of the labour force (those who do not want a job or cannot participate in the labour market) and those who are not of working age.

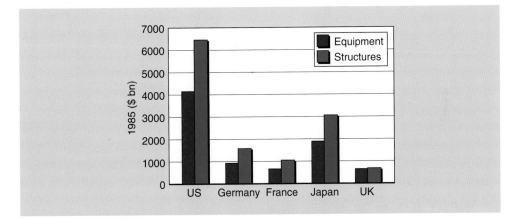

FIGURE 3.11 ● **Relative importance of structures and equipment in capital stock.** Structures are a larger part of capital stock than equipment. *Source:* O'Mahoney, 'Measures of fixed capital stocks in the post-war period: A five country study', in van Ark and Crafts (eds), *Quantiative Aspects of Post-War European Economic Growth* (Cambridge: Cambridge University Press, 1996), pp. 165–214.

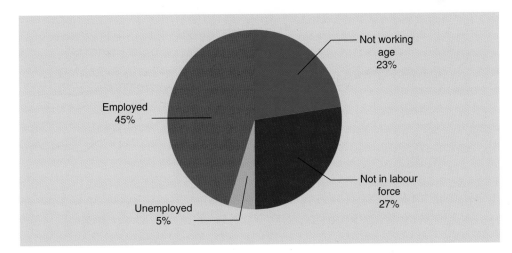

FIGURE 3.12 ● **US population by labour market status, 2011.** Around one-half of the US population participates in the labour force. *Source:* OECD.

While countries' capital stocks have increased substantially over time, statistics on labour input are more ambiguous. Figure 3.13 shows employment (in thousands) for a range of countries. In every case employment has risen,[4] but this increase has been offset by a fall in annual hours worked per person employed. Figure 3.14 shows that for these economies employees were working fewer hours in 2009 compared with the past. As a result, in many economies, especially in the more mature OECD economies, total hours worked declined during the second half of the twentieth century.

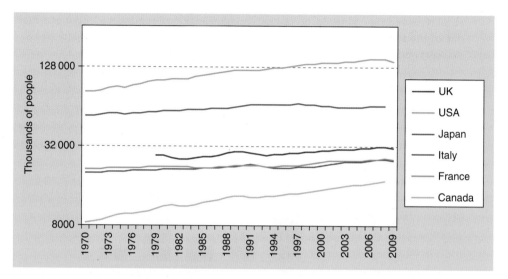

FIGURE 3.13 ● Total employment, 1970–2009. Most countries have experienced a dramatic increase in total employment due to rising populations and increasing labour market participation. *Source:* OECD.

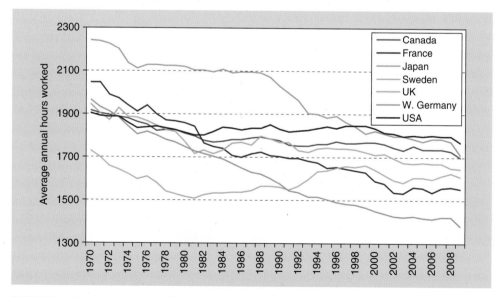

FIGURE 3.14 ● Average annual hours per worker, 1970–2009. Most countries have experienced a decline in average hours worked, due both to increased part-time working and shorter full-time working hours. *Source:* OECD.

TOTAL FACTOR PRODUCTIVITY

TFP captures the impact of *all* the factors that affect output but are not explicitly mentioned as a factor of production – it is a measure of the efficiency with which productive inputs are combined to produce output. As we have only specified the capital stock and hours worked as inputs into the production function, our version of TFP includes the effects of the level of education and skills in the workforce, technology, geography, institutions and government policies, among many other factors that we will consider in detail in Chapter 5. Figure 3.15 shows an estimate of TFP for broad geographical regions – increases in TFP have been a source of long-run growth, but also account for substantial cross-country variations in GDP.

Increases in any of these three factors – capital, labour or TFP – will boost GDP. However, given our focus in the previous section on productivity, it should be obvious that increases in output produced by working more hours are not as beneficial as increased GDP from higher hourly productivity. From the production function this suggests that we should focus on capital and TFP as the sources of long-run growth – only by providing workers with more machines and better technology is it possible to continually raise productivity.

KEY POINT

The long-run sources of growth in GDP per capita and productivity must be capital accumulation and improvements in total factor productivity.

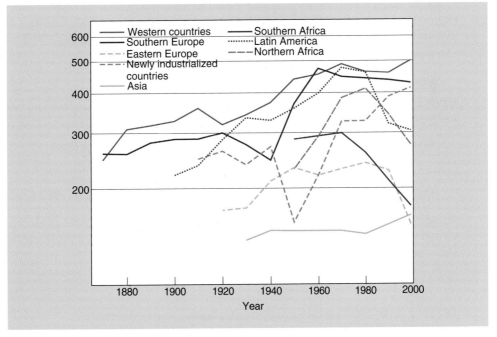

FIGURE 3.15 ● **Total factor productivity, 1870–2000.** Differences in total factor productivity are an important source of cross-country differences in GDP per capita. *Source:* Baier, Dwyer and Tamura, How Important Are Capital and Total Factor Productivity for Economic Growth?, Clemson University mimeo (2004).

(3.5)   Growth Accounting

In order to assess the relative role of capital, labour and TFP in producing GDP growth, we need to know how changes in each of the factors of production lead to changes in output. The **marginal product of capital** or the **marginal product of labour** captures this information. The marginal product of capital is the increase in output that adding one further piece of machinery generates – keeping unchanged the level of hours worked and total factor productivity. The marginal product of labour is the increase in output that results from adding one further unit of labour – keeping unchanged the capital stock and TFP. It is crucial to the definition of the marginal product that only one factor input is being changed; the idea is to isolate the role of each input.

Consider the case of a printing firm that has 20 employees and has to decide how many machines to purchase. Table 3.4 lists the output and marginal product of capital that the firm can produce using different numbers of machines when the firm has 20 employees and each machine embodies the same technology. We have assumed in this case that the marginal product of capital declines as the firm buys more machines. This is an assumption about how technology works in practice, and we will show in Chapters 4 and 6 that different assumptions about the behaviour of the marginal product of capital have enormous implications for our theories of growth.

THE COBB-DOUGLAS PRODUCTION FUNCTION

So far we have simply said that increases in capital, employment and TFP lead to increases in output. But if we can be more precise about the relationship between outputs and inputs, then we can create a much more detailed model of growth. To do this, economists often assume that a Cobb-Douglas function characterizes the production function. With a Cobb-Douglas function:[5]

$$\text{Output} = \text{TFP} \times \text{Capital Stock}^a \times \text{Hours Worked}^{1-a}$$

where a is a number between 0 and 1 so that GDP is increasing in TFP, capital and labour. It can be shown that for this production function:[6]

$$\text{Marginal Product of Capital} = a \times \text{TFP} \times (\text{Hours Worked/Capital Stock})^{1-a}$$

and

$$\text{Marginal Product of Labour} = (1-a) \times \text{TFP} \times (\text{Capital Stock/Hours Worked})^a$$

Assuming $0 < a < 1$, the Cobb-Douglas production function has a marginal product of capital and labour that are both decreasing – the more machines (workers) a firm has, the lower the marginal product of capital (labour).

TABLE 3.4 ● Output and the Marginal Product of Capital.

Number of Machines	1	2	3	4	5
Output produced	10	19	26	31	34
Marginal product of capital	10	9	7	5	3

We can use the production function and data on inputs and output to estimate the role of each factor of production in producing long-run increases in GDP – an exercise known as growth accounting. Taking logarithms of the production function gives:

$$\text{Logarithm (Output)} = \text{Logarithm (TFP)} + a \times \text{Logarithm (Capital)} + (1 - a) \times \text{Logarithm (Hours Worked)}$$

So that

$$\text{Change in Logarithm (Output)} = \text{Change in Logarithm (TFP)} + a \times \text{Change in Logarithm (Capital)} + (1 - a) \times \text{Change in Logarithm (Hours Worked)}$$

Because the change in the logarithm of a variable is approximately equal to the percentage change in a variable, this implies that

$$\%\text{Change in Output} = \%\text{Change in TFP} + [a \times \%\text{Change in Capital}] + [(1 - a) \times \%\text{Change in Hours Worked}]$$

Therefore we can calculate the amount of output growth that results from capital accumulation [$a \times \%$Change in Capital Stock] and similarly for the contribution of hours worked [$(1 - a) \times \%$Change in Hours Worked]. We attribute whatever output growth is left unexplained by changes in capital and hours worked to TFP, the unobserved factor input. In other words, TFP is calculated as a residual. All that we need to undertake growth accounting (aside from data on output, capital and employment) is therefore to find out the appropriate value of a. We can do this if we assume that capital and labour get paid their own marginal product; that is, workers' wages reflect the value of the extra output they produce, and the return earned by the owners of capital reflects the extra output that capital generates. Assuming that factors get paid what they produce, as measured by their marginal product, amounts to assuming competitive markets. If we denote the marginal product of capital by MPK and labour by MPL, then capital income is MPK $\times$ K and labour income is MPL $\times$ L. Assuming a Cobb-Douglas production function produces total output (y), capital income is $(a \times y/\text{K}) \times \text{K} = ay$ and labour income is $[(1 - a) \times y/\text{L}] \times \text{L} = (1 - a)y$. Therefore we can measure a by calculating the share of GDP paid out to capital. In most OECD economies (as we saw in Chapter 2), around 30% of GDP is paid out to owners of capital, and the remaining 70% is paid out as income to labour, so that a is approximately 0.3.

As this outline of growth accounting shows, TFP is calculated as a residual – it is the output growth that is left unexplained by recorded increases in factor inputs. As a consequence, any errors in measuring output, capital or labour will affect our estimates of the importance of TFP. Further, we have assumed a production function with only two factors of production – capital and labour – so that TFP captures all other influences. But we could extend our production function by incorporating additional variables. For instance, in Chapter 6 we will introduce human capital, a measure of the skills and education of the workforce, into the production function.

KEY POINT

Growth accounting uses the production function to calculate the importance of capital, labour and other factors of production in producing GDP growth. TFP is defined as a residual – whatever is left unexplained by other variables.

For an intuition as to exactly what growth accounting does, consider Figure 3.16. Between Year 1 and Year 2 the capital stock of the country has increased (from K_1 to K_2)

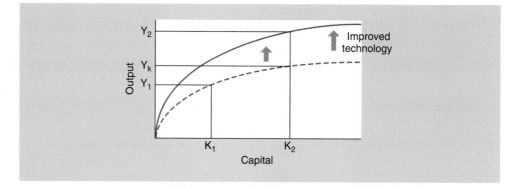

FIGURE 3.16 ● Growth accounting. Technological improvements and capital deepening drive growth.

and the technology available has improved, so the production function also shifts up as well. As a result, output increases from Y_1 to Y_2. Growth accounting calculates how much of this extra output has arisen from capital accumulation and how much from technological progress. Y_1 to Y_K gives the contribution from capital accumulation alone; that is, the output increase that comes from keeping the technology fixed but increasing just the capital stock, which means staying on the old production function. Y_K to Y_2 gives the growth that results from technological progress – this shows the extra output that technological progress produces *keeping fixed the capital stock*. Note that growth accounting distinguishes between investment in additional machines (moving along a given production function) and changes in technology (upward shifts in the production function), whereas in reality new technology comes embodied in the machines purchased this year. However, in growth accounting we are performing a *logical* analysis: How much output growth would have occurred *if* new technology were not available this year? For this logical exercise, it does not matter if capital and technology increases are always implemented simultaneously. In principle, we can disentangle the two influences.

3.6   Growth Accounting: An Application

Figure 3.17 shows the results of a growth accounting exercise for Japan, the United Kingdom, the United States and Germany for the period 1913–2008. The top part of Figure 3.17 shows the results for 1913–50. During this period in Japan, capital accumulation accounts for 1.2% annual growth in output, increased labour input for 0.3% growth per year and TFP of 0.7%. Therefore annual growth in GDP was 2.2% per year over this period (1.2 + 0.3 + 0.7). Close examination of Figure 3.17 shows:

1. 1950–73 (the so-called Golden Age) was a period of rapid output growth.
2. For Japan and Germany, labour input has detracted from recent output growth due to a reduction in total hours worked.
3. Labour input is rarely the most important contributor to growth.

Figure 3.18 shows the results of a similar growth accounting exercise for the recent performance of the BRICs. The experience of these countries varies significantly, with capital accumulation the most important element of India's growth, TFP for Brazil and labour for

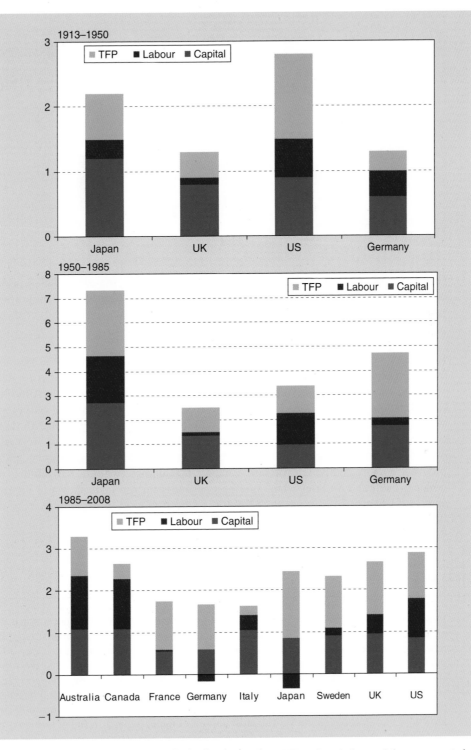

FIGURE 3.17 ● **Growth accounting for developed economies.** TFP and capital growth have accounted for the largest parts of growth in developed economies. *Sources:* Crafts, Globalization and Growth in the Twentieth Century, IMF Working Paper 11/44 (2002), OECD and authors' calculations.

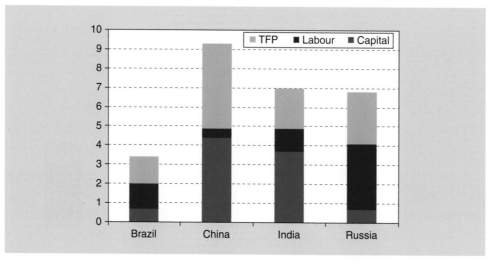

FIGURE 3.18 ● Growth accounting for the BRICs, 2000–07 (except Russia, 1998–2004). Sources of growth differ markedly between the BRICs. *Source:* OECD, 'The Growing Technological Divide in a Four-speed World' (2010) and Kvintradze, IMF Working Paper 10/89 (2010).

Russia. As we shall see in the following chapters, we should expect TFP to become ever more important over time for the BRICs.

Over the next few chapters, we will look at each of these factors of production – capital, labour and TFP – and examine more closely how they produce output growth. We will also combine all the factors of production to offer a theory of growth that helps account for the cross-country differences outlined above. In Chapter 4 we focus first on capital accumulation. Chapter 5 then incorporates into the analysis technological progress – a key component of TFP. Chapter 6 examines two different models of economic growth and assesses which one best accounts for the facts shown in Figures 3.17 and 3.18. Chapter 7 examines the role of the labour market in explaining cross-country differences in output.

SUMMARY

In Section 3.1 we showed that since the mid-nineteenth century world output has increased by an unprecedented amount. While initially focused in a small group of countries, this growth has now spread to most of the world's economies. This increase in output has vastly increased output per head, supported a rising world population, boosted life expectancy and reduced poverty. The welfare implications of economic growth are therefore enormous. If governments could raise trend growth rates, the benefits would substantially outweigh those of removing business cycle fluctuations. Even small changes in growth rates have large long-run effects. Currently, the rapid growth of the Chinese economy is the most important factor behind declining global poverty.

Section 3.2 showed that GDP per capita is driven by hourly productivity and the number of hours worked. The number of hours worked is determined by labour market variables reflecting average hours worked, the employment rate and the participation rate. In the long run continual growth in GDP per capita is driven by improvements in productivity.

Section 3.3 introduced the production function, which summarizes the relationship between factor inputs and GDP. Capital and labour are the two basic factor inputs. Total factor productivity measures the efficiency with which inputs are combined to produce output and reflects a broad range of influences. Increases in productivity depend on capital accumulation and higher TFP.

Section 3.4 used the production function to attribute growth in GDP across various factor inputs and TFP. Relying on assumptions about the marginal product of capital and labour and measuring TFP as a residual, this growth accounting offers a numerical decomposition of GDP growth.

Section 3.5 applied growth accounting to a range of countries. According to this approach, the most important variable explaining increased output across countries over the last 100 years has been capital accumulation. The next most important factor varies. For the mature industrialized nations, TFP has been important. For emerging markets, it has been increases in labour input.

CONCEPTUAL QUESTIONS

1. (Section 3.1) Examining Figure 3.2, what factors do you think explain why growth varied so much between regions?

2. (Section 3.1) Consider three economies, each of which has GDP per capita of $100. Trend growth in these economies is 2%, 2.5% and 5% respectively. Calculate GDP per capita for each economy after 5, 10, 20, 50 and 100 years.

3. (Section 3.1) If a 1% increase in GDP per head reduces poverty by 2%, then the elasticity of poverty with respect to GDP growth is 2. If population growth in this country is 2%, then in order to achieve a 2% reduction in poverty, it requires a 3% increase in GDP and a 1% increase in GDP per capita. To meet the Millennium Development targets, countries need to achieve an approximate 5% reduction in poverty per annum. Calculate the required growth in GDP for the following countries (all numbers from the African Development Bank Annual Report, 2002).

	Elasticity of Poverty with Respect to GDP	**Population Growth**
Ethiopia	0.43	2.5
Ghana	2.2	2.2
Sub-Saharan Africa	1.03	2.3
Algeria	1.87	1.9
Egypt	3.3	1.8
North Africa	2.30	2.3

4. (Section 3.2) Use Table 3.1 to calculate how much of the variation across countries in GDP per capita is due to differences in hourly productivity, average hours worked, employment and the participation rate.

5. (Section 3.3) The United States is one of the richest nations in the world and benefits from high levels of TFP. What features of US society do you think can explain this?

6. (Section 3.4) The Republic of Arden has experienced a 5% increase in output this year, a 2% rise in its capital stock and a 3% increase in hours worked. Assuming a Cobb-Douglas production function where capital income accounts for 30% of GDP, calculate how much output growth is explained by capital accumulation, labour and TFP.

ANALYTICAL QUESTIONS

1. (Section 3.4) You will need a spreadsheet for this exercise. Assume that TFP = 1 and set initial capital stock and employment to 1. Let output be given by TFP $\times$ $K^{0.3}L^{0.7}$. Calculate output, the marginal product of capital and the share of output paid to capital when labour is fixed at 1 and capital varies between 1 and 10. Repeat for the marginal product of labour when capital is set to 1 and labour varies between 1 and 10.

2. (Section 3.4) GDP in an economy is growing at 3% a year in real terms. Population is constant. The government decides to allow a significant increase in immigration so that the population (and the workforce) starts to grow by 1% a year. Output is produced in the economy according to a Cobb-Douglas production function. The share of labour income in GDP is 70%. How much higher will GDP be as a result of the new immigration policy after 20 years? How much higher will per capita GDP be?

3. (Section 3.4) Output in an economy is produced when labour hours (H) are combined with capital (K) in a way that reflects TFP to produce output (y). The relation is $y = TFP \times K^{0.27} H^{1-0.27}$. What is the share of labour income in output? What happens to the share of profits (i.e. capital's share in output) when there is a change in TFP? (Comment on your answer.)

4. (Section 3.4) Use the production function of Question 3 to calculate:

    (a) What happens to the marginal product of labour if H rises 10% with no change in other inputs?

    (b) What happens to the marginal product of capital if K increases by 15% with no change in other inputs?

    (c) What happens to the marginal product of labour and to output per person employed if labour and capital both rise by 7%?

Capital Accumulation and Economic Growth

Overview

In this chapter we examine the relationship between increases in the capital stock and economic growth. We first discuss whether an economy can keep growing if it increases only its capital stock. Under certain plausible assumptions, we show that this is not possible, and that poorer countries should therefore grow faster than wealthy ones, whose economies will depend more on technological progress than capital accumulation. We then discuss why countries with high investment rates also have high standards of living; and we consider the optimal investment rate for countries. Finally, we analyse the factors underlying the rapid growth of the Chinese economy.

4.1 Capital Accumulation and Output Growth

Figure 4.1a plots per capita real gross domestic product (GDP) and the per capita capital stock for a group of countries. Figure 4.1b focuses on the growth in GDP and capital between 1965 and 1990 for the same group of countries. Countries that have had large increases in their capital stock have also seen large increases in their GDP. For instance, Botswana during this period had a near 20-fold increase in its capital stock and, largely as a consequence, its GDP per capita more than quadrupled. This is both the largest increase in capital and the largest increase in output. Evidently capital accumulation matters greatly for both a country's standard of living and its rate of growth.

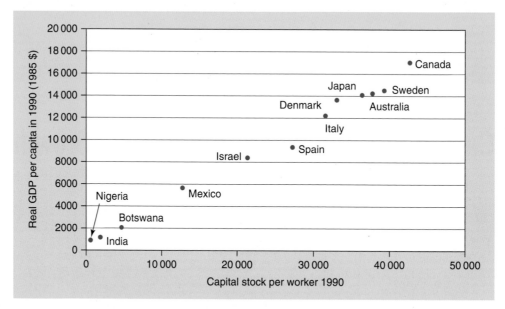

FIGURE 4.1a ● **GDP per capita versus capital stock per worker in 1990.** *Source:* Summers and Heston dataset, Penn World Tables 5.5, http://pwt.econ.upenn.edu.

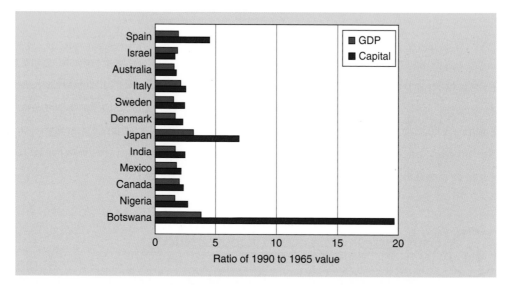

FIGURE 4.1b ● **Capital growth and GDP growth, 1965–90.** Countries that have accumulated substantial stocks of productive capital have reached higher standards of living. *Source:* Summers and Heston, Penn World Table 5.5, http://pwt.econ.upenn.edu.

HOW MUCH EXTRA OUTPUT DOES A NEW MACHINE PRODUCE?

A key question in economic growth is whether this link between more capital and higher output can be maintained indefinitely. Imagine that an economy experiences no improvement in total factor productivity (TFP, which was introduced in Chapter 3) or increase in hours worked, but only adds to its capital stock. Will this capital accumulation produce economic growth for ever or will capital accumulation eventually prove ineffective? The answer to this question depends on the behaviour of the marginal product of capital (MPK). In Chapter 3 we defined the MPK as the increase in output that occurs when the capital stock increases but TFP and labour input remain unchanged.

Consider the case of a firm that publishes textbooks and has four printing presses. The introduction of the fourth printing press enabled the firm to increase its production by 500 books per week. Will a fifth machine increase production by more than 500 books, by less than 500 books or by exactly 500 more books? If the fifth machine leads to an increase in production of more than 500 books (that is, if it causes a larger increase than the fourth machine generated), we have an *increasing marginal product of capital*; if the increased production is less than 500 books, then we have a *decreasing marginal product*; and if the increase equals 500, we have a *constant marginal product of capital*.

Why might the marginal product of capital be decreasing? Consider again the publishing company and assume that it has 10 employees, each working a fixed shift. With four machines, there are two and a half employees per machine. If we hold fixed the technology and hours worked as we increase the number of machines, we are going to encounter problems. There will be fewer and fewer operator hours to monitor the machines, so each machine will probably be less productive. Even if each new machine produces extra output, the boost in output will probably not be as high as from the previous machine. Note the importance of assuming that labour input and technology remain unchanged.

Of course, not all firms or industries will be characterized by a decreasing marginal product of capital. Consider the case of a telephone. When a country has only one telephone, the marginal product of that initial investment is zero – there is no one to call! Investment in a second telephone has a positive boost to output; there is now one channel of communication. Investment in a third telephone substantially increases communications – there are now three communication links, and so the investment increases the marginal product of capital. Adding more and more telephones increases even further the number of potential communication links. Telephones are an example of a technology that benefits from network effects, which are often characterized by an increasing marginal product of capital.

The behaviour of the MPK is a question of technology, not economics. Even so, we will show that different assumptions about the MPK have enormous implications for our models of long-run growth. If the MPK is diminishing, then it is not possible to grow for ever from capital accumulation – the output boost from investment declines with additional capital until growth does not occur. If, instead, the MPK is constant or even increasing, then capital accumulation can produce growth for ever even in the absence of labour or TFP increases.

DECREASING MARGINAL PRODUCT, OR IT DOESN'T GET ANY EASIER

In this chapter we shall assume that the marginal product of capital is decreasing for the aggregate economy and discuss what this implies for economic growth. In Chapter 6 we consider alternative assumptions and examine the empirical evidence for each case.

Figure 4.2 shows the case of diminishing marginal product of capital. At point A the country has little capital, so new investment leads to a big boost in output. At point B the capital stock is so large that each new machine generates little extra output. Figure 4.2a shows how the capital stock is related to *increases* in output (the marginal product of capital), but we can also use this relationship to draw a production function summarizing how the stock of

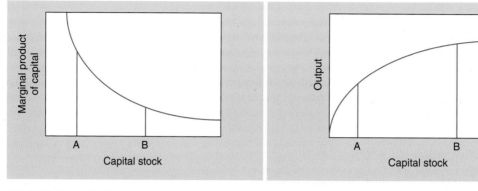

FIGURE 4.2a ● **Marginal product of capital.**

FIGURE 4.2b ● **The production function.** A concave production function implies a declining marginal product of capital.

capital is linked to the *level* of output. This is shown in Figure 4.2b. At low levels of capital, the marginal product is high, so that small increases in the capital stock lead to a big jump in output, and the production function is steeply sloped. Thus point A in Figure 4.2b corresponds to the same level of capital in Figure 4.2a. However, at high levels of capital (such as point B), each new machine generates only a small increase in output, so that the production function starts to flatten out – output changes little in this range even for large changes in the capital stock. The slope of the production function in Figure 4.2b is actually the MPK – hence at low capital the MPK is high and with high capital it is low.

> ### KEY POINT
>
> With decreasing marginal product of capital, output growth from capital accumulation eventually slows to a halt.

4.2 Savings, Investment and Interest Rates

CHOOSING THE CAPITAL STOCK

The extra revenue that a new machine contributes is the price at which output is sold (p) multiplied by the MPK. If this amount is greater than the cost of a new machine (which we denote r^0), then it is profitable for a firm to install the machinery. So if MPK $> r^0/p$, it is profitable to add to the capital stock. In Figure 4.3, the cost of an additional machine is shown by the horizontal line r^0/p. At point A, the marginal product of capital is higher than the cost of an additional machine, so the firm increases its capital stock. This continues until it reaches B, where the last machine contributes just as much to revenues as it does to costs. By contrast, at C each new machine loses money, so the capital stock should be reduced. Crucial to this analysis is the cost of capital, which will be examined in detail in Chapter 13, but for now we focus on just one element: the interest rate. We can think of the cost of

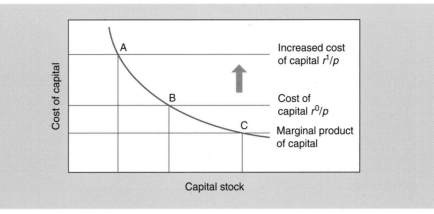

FIGURE 4.3 ● **Investment and the cost of capital.** Increases in the cost of capital reduce the optimal capital stock.

the machine as the interest rate that would need to be paid on a loan used to buy it. If we assume that it costs $1 to buy a unit of capital (so we measure everything in terms of the price of a machine), then the interest cost is just r. Therefore to be profitable, the investment project must produce at least the rate of interest. As the interest rate changes, so does the desired level of capital. If the interest rate increases, then the cost of capital shifts to r^1/p (as in Figure 4.3) and the firm desires less capital. If the interest rate falls, investment demands will be high. Therefore the relationship between investment and the interest rate is negative.

DETERMINING INTEREST RATES

When a firm wishes to increase its capital stock, it has to finance this increase at the current level of interest rates. The firm either has to use its own savings or borrow those of other economic agents. Let us assume that as interest rates increase, so does the level of savings. In other words, as banks or financial markets offer higher rates of return on savings, individuals and firms respond by spending less and saving more. Therefore the relationship between savings and the interest rate is positive (see Figure 4.4).

Consider the case where the interest rate is R_A. At this level, interest rates are so low that savers are not prepared to save much, and savings are at S_A. However, low interest rates make capital investment attractive, as the marginal product of capital is higher than the interest rate. As a result, firms are keen to borrow and desire investment, I_A. There are not enough savings to finance this desired level of investment, which frustrates firms' investment plans. Because of the gap between the marginal product of capital and the interest rate, firms are prepared to pay a higher interest rate to raise funds for investment. This puts upward pressure on interest rates, which in turn leads to increases in savings, which can be used to finance the desired investment. This process will continue – with interest rates increasing – until savings equal investment at the interest rate R_B.

We can use Figure 4.4 to analyse what happens to interest rates when there is a shift in investment or savings. Consider the case of an improvement in technology that leads to an improvement in the marginal product of capital. For a given level of interest rates this means an increase in investment, and so the investment schedule shifts to the right in Figure 4.4. If interest rates remain unchanged at R_B, then investment will be too high at I_B

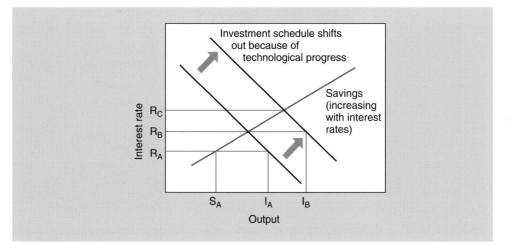

FIGURE 4.4 ● **Investment, savings and interest rates.** Technical progress increases investment and drives up rates of return/interest rates.

relative to savings. This will see firms competing for funds and bidding up interest rates. This increase in interest rates will persuade some firms not to invest and will also induce more savings, until eventually the market returns to equilibrium at R_C.

Figure 4.4 is just a supply-and-demand diagram, and interest rates are determined where the supply of loans (savings) equals the demand for loans (investment). Equilibrium in the loan market means that savings equals investment, and we will often use these terms interchangeably in this chapter. At a global level it is true that savings equals investment; in the absence of intergalactic capital markets, world investment has to be funded by world savings. At a national level, however, savings do not have to equal investment. Countries can either borrow or lend money overseas using global capital markets (see Chapter 19 for a fuller discussion). Even so, we can still expect any given country's savings and investment to be closely correlated over the long run. Countries that borrow money today (e.g. have investment greater than savings) will eventually have to repay these loans and this means that in the future savings will exceed investment. Therefore, in the *long run*, savings and investment will be similar. If there are persistent differences between savings and investment rates for a country, then this will show up in the long run as different growth in GDP and GNI.

> **KEY POINT**
>
> In the world capital markets, long-run real interest rates vary to ensure that global savings equals investment.

(4.3) Why Poor Countries Catch Up with the Rich

We return now to our discussion of decreasing marginal product of capital. Consider two economies that have similar levels of employment and TFP. This means that we can think of both economies as sharing the same marginal product curve of Figure 4.2a or, equivalently,

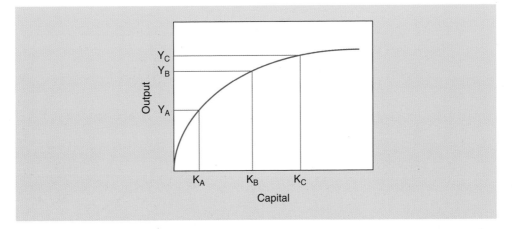

FIGURE 4.5 ● **Poor countries grow faster than wealthier countries.** A given increase in the capital stock generates more extra output for a country with relatively low capital.

the same production function as in Figure 4.2b. However, one economy has a much higher capital stock. Figure 4.5 shows these two economies as being at K_A and K_B. Diminishing marginal product implies that the economy at K_A will find it easier to grow through investment than the economy at K_B. Assume that both countries increase their capital stock by the same amount. The low-capital-stock country increases capital from K_A to K_B, while the wealthier economy moves from K_B to K_C. The result is that output in the low-capital country rises from Y_A to Y_B and in the richer economy from Y_B to Y_C. Therefore, the *same* investment will bring forth a *bigger* increase in output in the poorer economy than the richer one. In other words, because of decreasing marginal product, growth from capital accumulation becomes more and more difficult the higher the capital stock of a country becomes. This 'catch-up' result implies a process of convergence among countries and regions – for the same investment poorer countries grow faster than wealthier ones and inequalities across regions should decrease over time.

Figure 4.6, which displays the dispersion (as measured by the standard deviation) of income per head across US states, shows some evidence for this catch-up phenomenon. Since 1900 the inequalities of income across states have been dramatically reduced as poorer states, such as Maine and Arkansas, have grown faster than wealthier ones, such as Massachusetts and New York. This is consistent with the assumption of decreasing marginal product and its implication of catch-up.

Comparing income across US states is a good test of the theoretical predictions of catch-up, because our analysis depends on countries or regions sharing the same production function. This is broadly likely to be the case across US states. However, finding other examples of countries that satisfy these conditions is not easy – low-capital countries like India or Botswana also tend to have access to lower levels of technology than countries such as Japan or Australia. However, the circumstances of war and subsequent economic recovery offer some further support for assuming decreasing marginal product. Figure 4.7 shows that between 1945 and 1946, just after the Second World War, the West German capital stock and its output both fell. If there is a decreasing marginal product of capital, this suggests that after the war the ratio of output growth to capital growth (a measure of the MPK if employment and TFP don't change) should increase compared

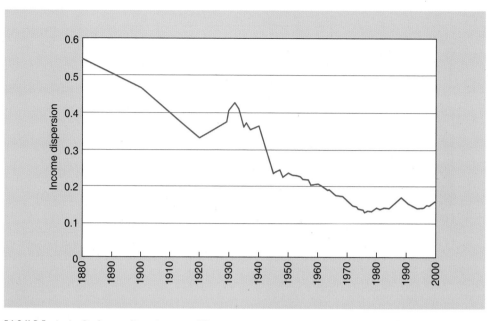

FIGURE 4.6 ● **Income dispersion across US states.** Income inequality between states in the United States has declined greatly since the end of the nineteenth century. *Source:* Barro and Sala-I-Martin, *Economic Growth* (New York: McGraw-Hill, 2003).

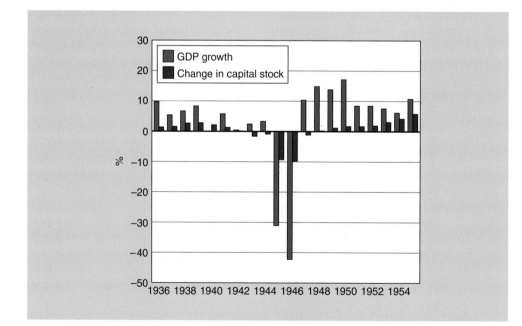

FIGURE 4.7 ● **West German GDP and capital growth, 1936–55.** West German GDP grew rapidly in the 1950s as the capital stock was rebuilt after the war. *Source:* Capital stock data from Maddison, 'Macroeconomics accounts for European Countries', in van Ark and Crafts (eds), *Quantitative Aspects of Post-War European Economic Growth* (Cambridge: Cambridge University Press, 1996).

TABLE 4.1 ● **Post-War Reconstruction in Europe.**

	Pre-War Year GDP Same as 1945	Year Reached Pre-War High
Austria	1886	1951
Belgium	1924	1948
Denmark	1936	1946
Finland	1938	1945
France	1891	1949
Germany	1908	1951
Italy	1909	1950
Netherlands	1912	1947
Norway	1937	1946

Source: Crafts and Toniolo, 'Postwar growth: An overview', in Crafts and Toniolo (eds), *Economic Growth in Europe Since 1945* (Cambridge University Press, 1996).

with the pre-war situation. Relatively small amounts of investment should produce high GDP growth after 1946, exactly what Figure 4.7 shows happened between 1947 and 1952. Table 4.1 shows a similarly sharp bounce back in output after the Second World War for other European nations. As a consequence of the war, European output and capital declined sharply to levels seen several decades earlier. However, within only a few years these countries had regained the lost output, as the depressed level of capital meant that investment benefited from a high marginal product of capital.

> **KEY POINT**
>
> Due to decreasing marginal product of capital, capital-poor countries should grow faster than capital-rich nations, and similar regions should display convergence in income levels over the long run.

4.4 The Growing Importance of Total Factor Productivity

In this section we show a further implication of a diminishing marginal product: total factor productivity (TFP) is more important for wealthier economies than for poorer ones. To see the intuition behind this result, imagine two publishing firms, each with 10 employees. One firm has three printing presses, while the other has 10. Consider the impact that one more machine will have for each firm compared to the introduction of new software that improves the productivity of all machines. For the firm with only three machines, the technological progress (the new software) will have only a limited effect – with only three machines, the software will not improve productivity a lot. However, this firm gains significantly from the introduction of a new machine, because its capital stock is so low that its marginal product of capital is high. By contrast, the other firm already has as many machines as employees, so it will benefit very little from an additional printing press. But with 10 machines to operate, the technological progress will have a more substantial impact. If we apply this example to countries, we can expect capital accumulation to be more important to growth relative to TFP for poorer nations and the opposite for capital-rich countries, as we saw in Chapter 3.

To show this argument graphically, consider the production function in Figure 4.8. In Year 0 the production function is the solid line, but because of technological progress, the production function shifts up: for a given level of capital, the improved technology increases output. Now consider two economies – A and B – both of which increase their capital stock by the same amount. For country A, the capital stock has risen from K_0^A to K_1^A. Without technological progress, the increase in output would have been Y_0^A to Y_*^A. However, because of technological developments, more output can be produced for any given level of capital, so that with a capital stock K_1^A Country A can produce Y_1^A in Year 1.

In Figure 4.8 we see that output has increased by a total of $Y_1^A - Y_0^A$, of which $(Y_*^A - Y_0^A)$ is due to the addition of extra capital and $(Y_1^A - Y_*^A)$ is due to technological progress. We can use the same argument for Country B and show that capital accumulation (without technological progress) leads to an increase in output of $(Y_*^B - Y_0^B)$, whereas at this new higher level of capital (K_1^B), the improved technology increases output by $(Y_1^B - Y_*^B)$. As the diagram shows, the proportion of growth that TFP explains is higher in Country B than in Country A: technological progress has a bigger impact for capital-rich countries. This implies that wealthier economies, such as those belonging to the OECD, will have a much greater dependence on TFP for producing economic growth than less developed nations. By contrast, emerging economies will be more reliant on capital accumulation than they will on TFP, a conjecture that Figure 4.9 supports. For the periods shown, we suggest that the OECD countries were high capital stock countries, the Asian economies low-capital-stock countries, and Latin American economies in the middle. Clearly, TFP has been much more important for growth among the more developed nations.

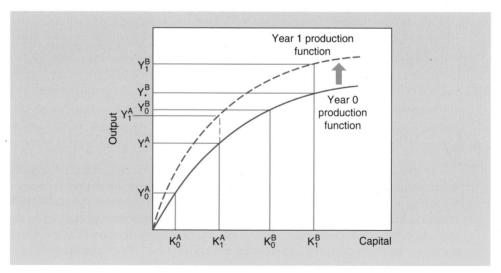

FIGURE 4.8 ● **The impact of technological progress and economic maturity.** The greater the capital stock, the more valuable is technological progress.

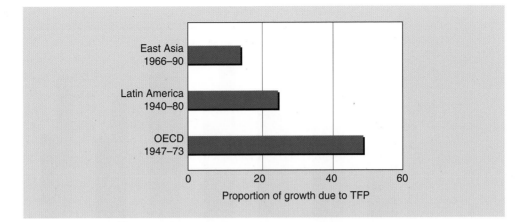

FIGURE 4.9 ● **Importance of TFP in growth.** Richer countries get more growth from TFP. *Source:* Crafts, 'Productivity growth reconsidered', *Economic Policy* (1992), 15: 388–426.

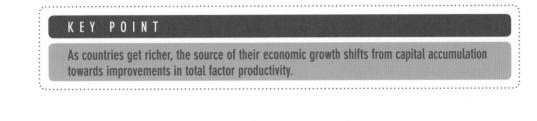

KEY POINT

As countries get richer, the source of their economic growth shifts from capital accumulation towards improvements in total factor productivity.

(4.5) The End of Growth through Capital Accumulation

THE STEADY STATE: A POINT OF REST

We have just shown that with a declining marginal product of capital, the relative importance of capital accumulation declines as the capital stock increases. In this section we go further and show how countries *always* reach a point where they cannot grow any more from capital accumulation alone. This point is called a steady state and should be considered as an equilibrium for the model with decreasing MPK.

INVESTMENT AND DEPRECIATION

Two factors cause the capital stock to change over time. The first is that firms invest in new machinery and structures, so that the capital stock is increasing. But another factor, 'depreciation', reduces the capital stock. Whenever they are used, machines are subject to wear and tear and breakdown. Economists call this process of deterioration *depreciation* – the reduction over time in the productive capabilities of capital. Note that economists use the term depreciation in a different sense than accountants do. In accounting, depreciation refers to reductions in the book value of an asset, which may bear little relation to the physical ability of a machine to produce output. Because of depreciation, we need to distinguish

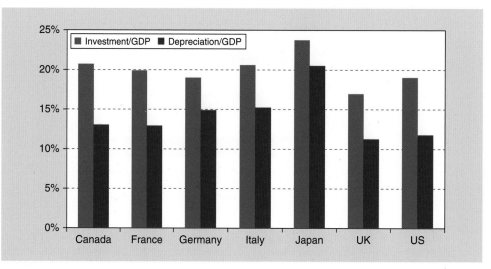

FIGURE 4.10 ● **Investment and depreciation in selected OECD countries in 1999–2008.** Gross investment exceeds net investment substantially due to depreciation on large capital stock of OECD countries. *Source:* OECD.

between different measures of investment. Gross investment is the amount of new capital being added to an economy. It includes both the repair and replacement of the existing capital stock as well as new additions. Net investment equals gross investment less depreciation, and represents the increase in the capital stock from one year to another. Figure 4.10 shows, for a sample of developed economies, gross investment and depreciation as a percentage of GDP. This figure suggests that net investment is typically about 5–10% of GDP.

Allowing for gross investment and depreciation, the capital stock evolves over time as

$$K(t) = K(t-1) + I(t) - D(t)$$

where $K(t)$ is the capital stock at time t, $I(t)$ is gross investment and $D(t)$ is depreciation: $I(t) - D(t)$ is net investment. The steady state is the point at which the capital stock does not change, so that $K(t) = K(t-1)$, which can only occur when $I(t) = D(t)$ so that gross investment equals depreciation and net investment is zero. The country purchases just enough machinery each period to make up for depreciation.

CONVERGENCE

So far our analysis has been based only on a technological assumption about the marginal product of capital. To complete our model of growth we need to make two further assumptions – one economic and one about technology. The economic assumption we make concerns gross investment, which for simplicity we assume equals a fixed proportion of output: for example $I(t) = bY(t)$, where $Y(t)$ is GDP. How much of GDP is invested varies across countries, but let us assume that 20% of output is invested; that is, $b = 0.2$. In Figure 4.11 we show the production function of the economy and the investment function that this implies. Because investment equals 20% of output, the investment line is just a scaled-down version of the production function. The other assumption we make is about technology and concerns depreciation. We assume that this occurs at 5% per annum – in other words, around

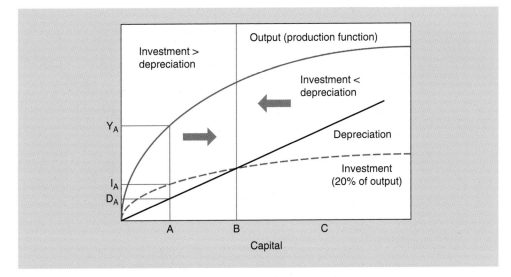

FIGURE 4.11 ● **The steady state.** If the stock of capital is below B, net investment is positive and the capital stock is growing. If the capital stock is above B, depreciation exceeds gross investment and the capital stock declines.

5% of the capital stock is retired or needs to be repaired each year. Therefore $D(t) = dK(t)$, where $d = 0.05$. Note that investment is a proportion of output and thus is related to the production function, while depreciation is linked to the capital stock. Figure 4.11 shows depreciation as a straight line – if you double the capital stock, you double depreciation.

Consider point A in Figure 4.11. At this level of capital stock, I_A (20% of the output produced) gives the amount of investment. At this level of capital, depreciation is only D_A, so that gross investment exceeds depreciation, net investment is positive and the capital stock is increasing. As the capital stock increases, the gap between investment and depreciation narrows. Decreasing marginal product implies that each new machine leads to a smaller boost in output than the previous one. Because investment is a constant proportion of output, this means that each new machine produces ever smaller amounts of new investment. However, depreciation is at a constant rate: each new machine adds 5% of its own value to the depreciation bill. At point B, the depreciation and investment lines intersect. This defines the steady-state capital stock, where gross investment equals depreciation. At this point the last machine adds just enough extra output to provide enough investment to offset the extra depreciation it brings. At this point the capital stock is neither rising nor falling but stays constant.

Imagine instead that the economy starts with a capital stock of C. At this point depreciation is above investment, net investment is negative and the capital stock is declining. The country has so much capital that the marginal product of capital is low. As a consequence, each machine cannot produce enough investment to cover its own depreciation; firms are not providing enough investment to cover maintenance and repairs, and so the capital stock moves back to the steady state at B. Therefore when the capital stock is below its steady-state level, it is increasing, and if it is above the steady-state level, capital declines. Regardless of where the economy starts from it will end up at the steady state – the steady state is the equilibrium for the model with decreasing MPK. Without diminishing MPK, the production function would not flatten out, a steady state would not exist, and capital accumulation could produce output growth for ever.

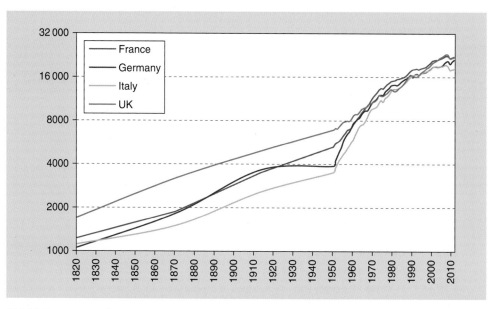

FIGURE 4.12 ● **Convergence in real GDP per capita in Europe, 1820–2010.** Levels of output in the major four European industrial countries have converged since the end of the nineteenth century. *Source:* Maddison based on data from Table D1.a, pp. 194–5, *Monitoring the World Economy 1820–1992* (Paris: OECD, 1995). Updated to 2010 by author using IMF data.

Assuming that countries share their steady state, then eventually they will all converge on approximately the same output per capita – diminishing MPK therefore predicts a process of catch-up across countries. Supporting evidence for this is offered in Figure 4.12, which shows real GDP per capita between 1820 and 2010 for four major European countries. In 1870 the United Kingdom was substantially wealthier than other European nations. However, by 2010 these large gaps in the standard of living had been substantially reduced: the gap between the richest and poorest countries was only 12%, relatively small by historical comparison.

KEY POINT

Decreasing marginal product of capital implies the existence of a steady state to which the economy eventually converges. At the steady state, the economy does not grow through capital accumulation and investment equals depreciation.

4.6 Why Bother Saving?

INVESTMENT AND THE STANDARD OF LIVING

Because the steady state is the point at which there is no growth in output through capital accumulation, growth at the steady state must be due either to increases in labour input or to improvements in TFP. Assuming that countries cannot continually reduce their

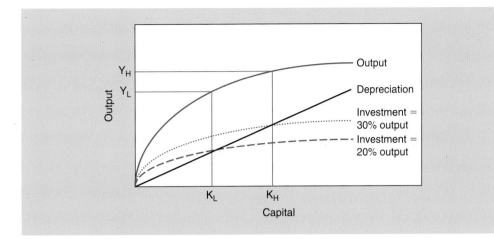

FIGURE 4.13 ● **Steady state depends on investment rate.** The higher the rate of investment, the greater the steady-state capital stock.

unemployment rate, and that all countries eventually have access to the same technology, this implies that at the steady state countries will all grow at the same rate – the rate of technological progress. Whether one country is investing more than another does not matter – *at the steady state, capital accumulation does not influence the growth rate*. Why, then, should countries encourage high levels of investment if such investment makes no difference to the long-run growth rate?

The answer to this question is simple. While the investment rate makes no difference to the trend growth of the economy, it does influence the *level* of the steady-state capital stock. The more investment a country does, the higher its steady-state standard of living.

To see this, imagine two countries, one of which invests 20% of its output and the other 30%, as in Figure 4.13. Otherwise both countries are identical: they have access to the same production function, have the same population and the same depreciation rate. For both countries their steady state occurs at the point at which investment equals depreciation – K_L for the low-investment country and K_H for the high-investment country. Therefore, the level of output in the low-investment country is Y_L, substantially below Y_H. Countries with low investment rates will therefore have a lower standard of living (measured by GDP per capita) than countries with high investment rates. Low investment rates can only fund a low level of maintenance, so the steady state occurs at a low capital stock and, via the production function, at a low output level. However, at the steady state, both countries will be growing at the same rate – the rate at which technological improvements lead to improvements in the production function. Therefore, while long-term growth rates are independent of the investment rate, the *level* of GDP per capita is definitely related to the amount of investment. As Figure 4.14 shows, the implication that high-investment countries are wealthier than low-investment countries is supported across a wide range of economies.

KEY POINT

The higher the investment rate of a country, the greater its steady-state capital stock and its output level.

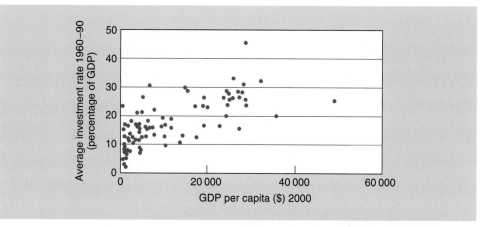

FIGURE 4.14 ● **Output and investment in the world economy.** Higher investment countries tend to have higher incomes – each point represents the income level in 2000 of a country mapped against its average investment rate from the previous 40 years. *Source:* Summers, Heston and Aten, Penn World Table 6.1, http://pwt.econ.upenn.edu.

THE LONG RUN IS A LONG TIME COMING

Decreasing marginal product of capital and the concept of a steady state suggest that in the long run a country's growth rate is independent of its investment. However, this is only a long-run result; in the short run (which may last several decades), high-investment economies can grow faster than low-investment countries.

Consider the high- and low-investment countries of Figure 4.13. At K_L, the low-investment country has no more scope for growth through capital accumulation – it is already at its steady state. However, also at K_L, the high-investment country still has gross investment in excess of depreciation, so its capital stock will continue to rise until it reaches its steady state at K_H. Therefore, while the low-investment country shows zero growth, the high-investment country shows continual growth *while it is moving towards its steady state.* If the transition from K_L to K_H takes a long time (more than 25 years), then our model can still explain why investment and growth are strongly correlated.

Examining our model and using plausible numbers for investment rates and other key economic parameters shows that the movement from K_L to K_H does indeed take a long time. For instance, after 10 years only 40% of the distance between K_L and K_H has been travelled; after 20 years just under two-thirds of the gap has been reduced. Therefore decreasing marginal product of capital can explain correlations between investment and economic growth over long periods, as economies move to their steady state. This result also implies that if a country can raise its investment rate substantially it will benefit from higher GDP growth for several decades.

> ### KEY POINT
>
> In the steady state, long-run growth is independent of the investment rate. The transition to a steady state can take several decades and, during this period, higher-investment countries will experience higher growth.

How Much Should a Country Invest?

The previous section showed that countries with high levels of investment will also have high levels of GDP per capita. Does this mean that countries should seek to maximize their investment rate?

THE GOLDEN RULE AND OPTIMAL LEVEL OF INVESTMENT

The answer to this question is 'no'. Output per head is an imperfect measure of the standard of living. The trouble with investment is that for a given level of output, the more a country invests the less it can consume. For instance, an economy with an investment rate of 100% would have an enormous level of GDP per capita, but it would only produce investment goods. However, at the opposite extreme, an economy with an investment rate of zero would have high consumption today but low consumption in the future, because depreciation would cause its capital stock to decline continually, leading to lower levels of future output. The situation is like that in the fishing industry. Overfishing reduces the stock of fish and diminishes the ability of the fish to breed, making future catches and future consumption low. However, catching no fish at all would lead to a rapid increase in fish stocks, but we would have none to eat. Ideally, we want to catch enough fish every day both to sustain a constant stock and also to provide enough for our consumption.

Economists have a similar concept in mind when they consider the ideal rate of investment. This ideal rate is called the 'Golden Rule' rate of investment. We have shown that countries with different levels of investment have different steady states and so different levels of consumption. The Golden Rule compares all of these different steady states (i.e. it examines different investment rates) and chooses the investment rate that delivers the highest consumption in the steady state.

If for simplicity we ignore the government sector and assume no trade, then from Chapter 2 we know that consumption must equal output less investment ($C = Y - I$). In the steady state, investment also equals depreciation ($I = dK$), so steady-state consumption, C^{ss}, must equal output less depreciation ($C^{ss} = Y - dK$). According to the Golden Rule, the capital stock should be increased so long as steady-state consumption also rises. Using our expression for steady-state consumption, we can see that increases in capital boost consumption as they lead to higher output. Each extra unit of capital boosts output by the marginal product, so that steady-state consumption – other things being equal – is increased by MPK. But other things are not equal, because the addition of an extra unit of capital also increases depreciation by d, which tends to lower steady-state consumption. Therefore the overall effect on steady-state consumption from an increase in capital is

Change in steady state consumption from increase in capital
    = Marginal Product of Capital – Depreciation Rate = MPK – d

For low levels of capital, MPK exceeds d and steady-state consumption increases with the capital stock and higher investment. But as the capital stock increases, the marginal product of capital declines, until eventually MPK = d. At this point, steady-state consumption cannot be raised through higher investment. Further increases in the capital stock would decrease MPK to less than d – steady-state consumption would be declining. Therefore the Golden Rule says that to maximize steady-state consumption, the marginal product of capital should equal the depreciation rate.

What level of investment does the Golden Rule suggest is optimal? To answer this question, we need to make an assumption about the production function. We shall assume, as previously, that output is related to inputs via a Cobb-Douglas production function where $Y = TFP \times K^aL^{1-a}$. In Chapter 3, we stated that this leads to:

$$MPK = aY/K$$

so that the Golden Rule implies that steady-state consumption is maximized when

$$MPK = aY/K = d$$

However, we also know that in the steady state, investment equals depreciation, or, using our earlier assumptions

$$I = bY = dK = depreciation$$

or

$$bY/K = d$$

Comparing the Golden Rule condition and this steady-state definition, we can see that they can only both be true when $a = b$; that is, when the term that influences the productivity of capital in the production function (a) equals the investment rate (b). When we discussed the Cobb-Douglas production function in Chapter 3, we showed how a was equal to the share of capital income in GDP, which empirically was around 30–35%. Therefore, the Golden Rule suggests that the optimal investment rate is approximately 30–35% of GDP – investment at this rate leads to the steady state with the highest level of consumption.

Table 4.2 shows average investment rates for a wide range of countries. Singapore, China and Japan stand out as having high investment rates, and France, Germany and Italy fare reasonably well, but the United States and the United Kingdom score poorly according to this test. The United States and the United Kingdom are underinvesting relative to the Golden Rule, and if this continues, they will eventually have a much lower future level of consumption than if they invested more (all other things being equal).

TABLE 4.2 ● Investment as a Percentage of GDP, 1980–2009.

Country	Investment Rate	Country	Investment Rate	Country	Investment Rate
Argentina	19.0	Germany	20.9	Spain	24.1
Australia	24.5	India	23.8	Sweden	18.8
Brazil	22.5	Israel	20.5	UK	17.4
Canada	20.6	Italy	21.1	US	18.5
Chile	20.8	Japan	27.1	Zambia	15.4
China	33.7	Mexico	19.9	Low Income	17.9
Congo	11.3	Russia	20.5	Middle Income	24.0
Egypt	22.0	Singapore	33.9	High Income	21.2
France	19.9	South Africa	19.0	World	21.7

Source: World Development Indicators and authors' calculations.

We should stress that at this point we are assuming that countries *only* differ in their level of investment, but in Chapter 5 we will consider many other ways in which they vary. One of these is in the quality of financial systems. Higher investment is only good for an economy if the financial system efficiently allocates investment to projects with a high rate of return.

> ### KEY POINT
>
> An investment rate of around 30–35% of GDP leads to steady states with high levels of consumption. Investment rates above or below this range lead to lower levels of steady-state consumption – either because the capital stock is too low, which leads to low output, or because capital stocks are so high that investment crowds out consumption.

INVESTMENT AND THE DEMOGRAPHIC TRANSITION

As Table 4.2 shows, most developing countries have investment rates well below the Golden Rule. The main reason for this is that incomes are so low that they are needed to support consumption, leaving little for savings and investment. An important element of these low savings and investment rates is the fact that low life expectancy encourages high birth rates (to ensure that some family members reach adulthood), so much of a household's income is used to support children. Against this background, it is possible to see how improvements in health can result in a reduced ratio of children per adult and so release resources for saving and investment.

Figure 4.15 illustrates how this demographic transition takes place.

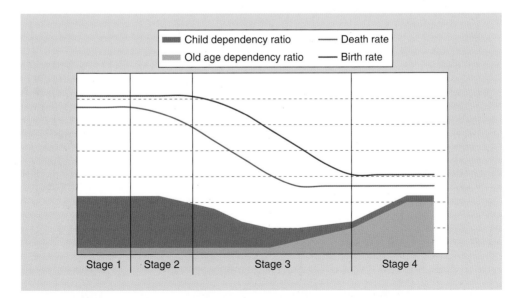

FIGURE 4.15 ● **The demographic transition.** Falling death rates and birth rates associated with improved health can lead to a temporary fall in the overall dependency ratio.

- *Stage 1:* Before the transition, the country is characterized by high death rates (deaths per 1000 people per year) and high birth rates (births per 1000 people per year). Child dependency ratios (population aged 0–14 as a share of population aged 15–64) are high and old age dependency ratios (population aged 64 and over as a share of population aged 15–64) are low.
- *Stage 2:* Improvements in health outcomes cause death rates to decline, reducing child dependency ratios as adults tend to live for longer.
- *Stage 3:* Falling death rates also encourage lower birth rates, resulting in a dramatic reduction in child dependency ratios.
- *Stage 4:* Birth and death rates eventually stabilize at lower levels and old age dependency ratios rise, offsetting the reduction in child dependency ratios.

Figure 4.15 shows how in Stage 3 of the demographic transition, total dependency ratios (the sum of child and old age dependency ratios) are temporarily very low indeed, releasing resources for investment. It is notable that most periods of rapid growth (ranging from the UK Industrial Revolution to the Asian Tigers) have coincided with a demographic transition.

4.8　China: A Big Tiger

In many ways China's economic miracle follows the textbook model of capital accumulation discussed in this chapter. In fact, in some ways the most puzzling aspect of China's economic development is that it has taken so long to occur. Figure 4.16 shows how, prior to

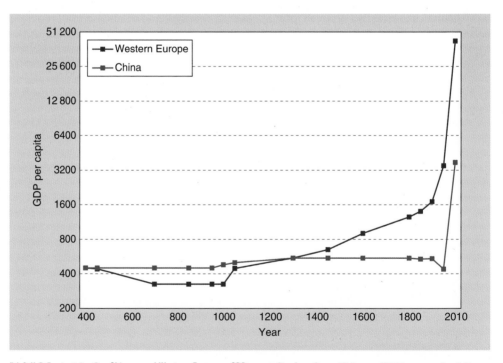

FIGURE 4.16 ● **Chinese and Western European GDP per capita since 0 AD.** Chinese GDP per capita fell behind that of Western Europe some time around the fourteenth century, but is now catching up again. *Source:* OECD, Madisson.

the twelfth century, China is estimated to have had a higher income per capita than Western Europe. Subsequent to that, Chinese GDP per capita stagnated, while that of Western Europe took off – even though many of the key inventions that help stimulate European growth (such as paper and printing) were Chinese in origin. In Chapter 5 we discuss some of the possible reasons for this puzzle.

CHINA'S DEMOGRAPHIC TRANSITION

Although numerous factors lie behind China's rapid economic development that began in 1978, an important one is the demographic transition. Figure 4.17 shows how China's total dependency ratio has fallen from around 80% in the early 1960s to 40% today. This dramatic change in dependency ratio is partly due to the adoption of a one-child policy, but also the effect of rising income in reducing fertility rates. Over the same period the savings rate has risen from around 20% to over 40%, and it is these savings that have been used to support the very high investment rates shown in Figure 4.18. The magnitude of these demographic effects are substantial – a low dependency ratio means a large working-age population and high investment – and according to some estimates they account for around 2% of Chinese GDP growth per annum over the past decades.

However, since 2010, the increased old age dependency ratio has meant that China's overall dependency ratio has started to rise again. This means that China is now entering Stage 4 of the demographic transition outlined above. Coping with this rising dependency ratio will be one of the major challenges facing the Chinese economy over the next few decades, since high savings and investment coupled with a rapidly growing labour force have underpinned much of China's economic growth in recent years. Lower growth, lower investment and the need to develop pension support for an older population will be significant challenges for the country.

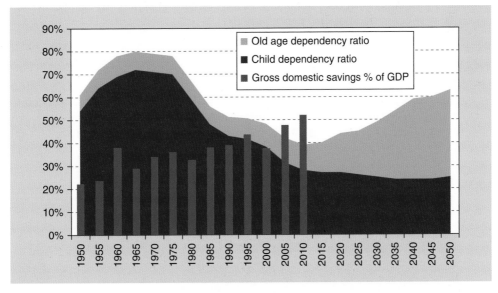

FIGURE 4.17 ● **The Chinese demographic transition.** Falling death rates and birth rates resulted in China's dependency ratio falling below 40% by 2010. This allowed savings rates to rise significantly. *Source:* UN population division and World Development Indicators.

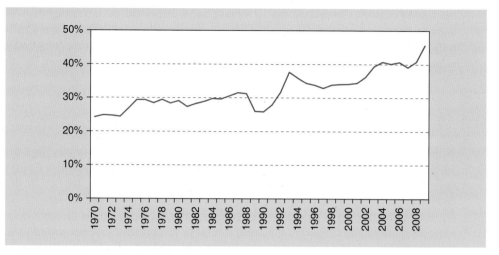

FIGURE 4.18 ● **Chinese investment rate.** High levels of domestic savings have financed high and rising investment rates. *Source:* World Development Indicators.

GROWTH ACCOUNTING FOR CHINA

Table 4.3 shows a simple growth accounting exercise for China since 1953. Unsurprisingly, it highlights the importance of capital accumulation in China's growth. However, comparing China with the other fast-growing East Asian economies, we find that China's recent growth has in fact relied less on labour and capital than most of these countries. In fact, as Figure 4.19 shows, China's balance between capital, labour and TFP since 2000 mirrors most closely that of Hong Kong, suggesting perhaps that China is reasonably well placed to continue its rapid growth even in the face of the declining growth of capital and labour inputs that may occur once its dependency ratio rises.

INCOME INEQUALITY IN CHINA

China's economic development has been unusual, in that it has been associated with an increase in income inequality (recall from Chapter 3 that, on average, there is no tendency for economic growth to result in increases in inequality). Figure 4.20 shows how the Gini

TABLE 4.3 ● **Growth Accounting for China.**

	1953–77	1978–99	2000–07
Physical capital	3.66	4.69	4.40
Labour quantity	1.05	1.36	0.50
TFP	1.75	3.65	4.40
Total GDP	6.46	9.72	9.30

Source: Wang and Yao, 'Sources of Chinese Economic Growth 1952–99', World Bank Discussion Paper (July 2001) and OECD.

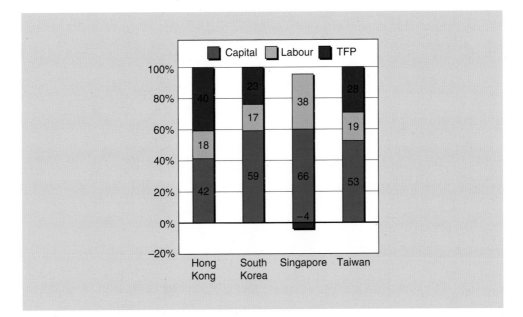

FIGURE 4.19 ● **Growth accounting for Asian Tigers, 1966–90.** Increases in inputs of labour and capital accounted for most of the growth of the Asian Tigers over the period when they increased output most rapidly. *Source:* Young, 'Tyranny of numbers: Confronting the statistical realities of the East Asian growth experience', *Quarterly Journal of Economics* (1985), 110: 641–80.

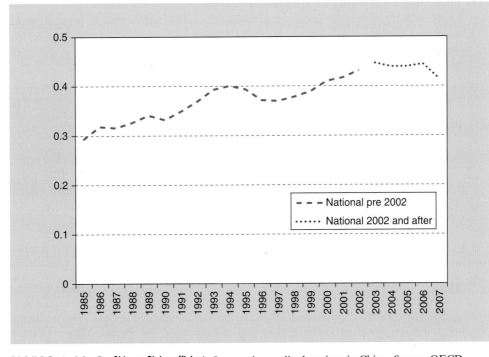

FIGURE 4.20 ● **Chinese Gini coefficient.** Income inequality has risen in China. *Source:* OECD.

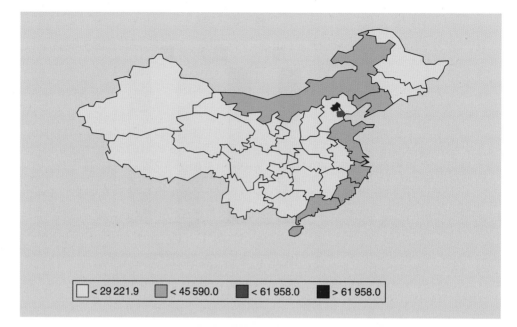

FIGURE 4.21 ● **GDP per capita by region in China, 2009.** China's income is concentrated in the eastern coastal regions. *Source:* Deutsche Bank Research.

coefficient, a standard measure of inequality, for China has risen steadily over the last 20 years. This is largely due to the uneven geographical distribution of income within China, as it is the cities of the eastern seaboard that have undergone the most rapid industrialization. Figure 4.21 shows how the coastal regions in the east have benefited disproportionally from economic growth. Recently, however, the Chinese government has become increasingly focused on the issue of inequality and, as Figure 4.20 shows, there is some evidence that the steady upward trend in inequality is coming to an end.

> **KEY POINT**
>
> Although China faces many difficult issues before its development process is complete, it would appear to be showing a magnified version of the growth seen earlier in East Asia – rapid GDP growth rates produced by high levels of investment and employment growth. But unlike many of the Asian tigers, China has also seen significant TFP growth in recent years.

SUMMARY

This chapter has examined the link between the capital stock, the standard of living and economic growth. In Section 4.1 we reviewed a concept central to our discussion: the marginal product of capital, the additional output that investment in a new machine brings. The marginal product of capital can be either increasing, constant or decreasing. We discussed the consequences of assuming a decreasing marginal product of capital, whereby each new machine leads to a smaller increase in output than the last machine.

In Section 4.2, the assumption of a decreasing marginal product of capital was used to show how interest rates keep savings and investment balanced over the long run.

In Section 4.3, we demonstrated how the assumption of a decreasing marginal product implies that capital-poor countries will grow faster than capital-rich ones, so that countries or regions will show convergence.

In Section 4.4, we saw that a decreasing marginal product also implies that wealthier countries will depend more on TFP improvements than on capital accumulation.

In Section 4.5, we explained the reasons why, under decreasing marginal product, countries will eventually arrive at a steady state where investment equals depreciation – where for a given investment rate, a country cannot grow any further through capital accumulation, and growth is due either to improvements in TFP or to increases in employment.

In Section 4.6, we saw that the steady state level of capital depends crucially on the investment rate. The higher the investment rate is, the larger the steady-state capital stock and the higher the level of output.

Section 4.7 introduced the Golden Rule of investment. Using the Golden Rule, we can show that an investment rate between 30% and 35% of GDP leads to steady states with high levels of consumption. We also saw how the demographic transition can be the underlying cause of high rates of investment and growth.

Finally, in Section 4.8 we considered China's economic growth, which appears to be repeating the same general pattern seen in many rapidly developing economies: a demographic transition leading to high investment and employment growth, but with some signs that TFP is making an increasing contribution.

CONCEPTUAL QUESTIONS

1. (Section 4.1) Consider separately the case of decreasing, constant and increasing marginal product of capital, where investors can either invest in a bank account and earn interest rate R or invest in the capital stock of a country. Using a diagramatic analysis, examine in each case where investors will place their funds and the implications for convergence.

2. (Section 4.1) What technologies might generate an increasing marginal product of capital? Do they experience increasing marginal product over all ranges?

3. (Section 4.2) Using Figure 4.4, show what happens to interest rates, investment and savings when (a) there is a downward reassessment to the productivity of capital and (b) a demographic shift whereby the proportion of 45–64 year olds increases (an age group with high savings).

4. (Section 4.3) After the Second World War, Germany experienced rapid growth in output from relatively little investment. But between 1913 and 1929, its GDP growth was on average 0.1% and showed no such sharp recovery from the First World War. What might explain these differences?

5. (Section 4.8) What can mature industrialized nations learn from the rapid growth of China?

6. (Section 4.8) In 2002 the US economy measured $10.4 trillion, Japan $4.2 trillion, Germany $1.9 trillion and China $1.22 trillion. Assuming trend growth of 2.5% in the three OECD nations, how long until China overtakes them if it grows at 5% per annum? 7%? 9%?

ANALYTICAL QUESTIONS

1. (Section 4.1) Use a spreadsheet to consider the Cobb-Douglas production function where $Y = TFP \times L^{0.7} K^a$. The marginal product of capital is given by $a \times Y/K$. Setting TFP and $L = 1$, examine the behaviour of the MPK as it varies between 0.3 and 1.

2. (Section 4.5) The steady-state level of consumption in an economy (C^{ss}) is equal to steady-state output (Y^{ss}) minus steady-state depreciation. The latter is the depreciation rate (d) times the steady-state capital stock (K^{ss}). We assume here that there is no technological progress. Thus

$$C^{ss} = Y^{ss} - dK^{ss}$$

What is the impact on steady-state consumption of a small increase in the steady-state capital stock? What level of investment maximizes the steady-state rate of consumption?

3. (Section 4.6) Use the Cobb-Douglas production function of Question 1 where $a = 0.3$ and a depreciation rate of 0.1. Examine the steady-state outcomes of an economy that invests 20% and 30% of GDP. How many periods would it take for an economy with a 20% investment rate to reach its new steady state if it increases its investment rate to 30%?

4. (Section 4.7) Consider the economy of Question 3 and compare the steady-state level of consumption as you change the investment rate. Show that the Golden Rule result of setting the investment rate equal to a in the production function optimizes consumption in the steady state.

5. (Section 4.7) The simple Golden Rule says that the optimal level of capital is one where the marginal product of capital equals the depreciation rate. If people attach less weight to the enjoyment they get from consumption in the future than consumption today, then does it make sense to abide by the Golden Rule? Is there a better rule? If such an economy ever found itself with the Golden Rule level of capital, should it preserve the capital stock by setting gross investment equal to depreciation?

CHAPTER 5

Total Factor Productivity, Human Capital and Technology

Overview

In order to account for the magnitude of cross-country differences in income and to better explain the evolution of GDP per capita over time, we extend our model of capital accumulation to include changes in total factor productivity (TFP). We focus in particular on the role of human capital and institutions in influencing the wealth of nations. We show how countries with high TFP not only produce more output from a given capital stock, but will also choose a higher level of steady-state capital. We introduce technological progress into our analysis and show how this leads to the continual evolution of the steady state so that even rich nations experience persistent growth. Technological progress and TFP growth are shown to be all the more important when we extend our model to include factors of production such as land that are in fixed supply or depletable and finite resources such as oil.

5.1 The Role of Total Factor Productivity

We have described **total factor productivity** as reflecting the influence of *any* factor that affects output other than capital accumulation or labour input. In this chapter we examine the role of TFP and explicitly identify some of its influences. Allowing for variations in TFP enables us to better explain the wide variations in GDP per capita without having to rely solely on capital accumulation.

Consider an economy that increases its efficiency in producing output from a given level of capital: in other words, it increases its TFP. This increase might arise from an improvement in education or an improvement in technology, which is the example shown in Figure 5.1.

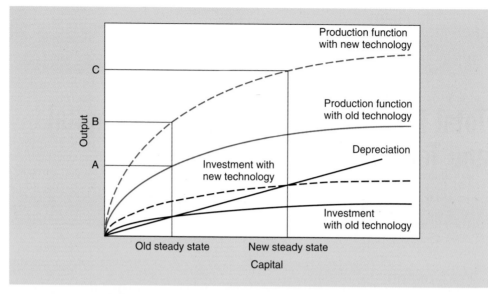

FIGURE 5.1 ● **The impact of TFP on output.** Technical progress increases output directly (A→B) and has a further effect (B→C) through its impact on the steady-state capital stock.

This leads to the production function shifting upwards: for a given level of capital, the higher level of TFP enables more output to be produced (B instead of A). So one reason GDP per capita varies so much across countries is differences in TFP. Countries that use the latest technology effectively and possess the most efficient social organizations will produce the highest level of output from a given level of capital – they will be on the TFP frontier. But only a few countries will be on this frontier – for other countries, geography may have an adverse effect on the economy, corruption may be rampant or vested interests in society may prevent the adoption of new technologies.

From Figure 5.1, we can see another implication for countries with higher TFP. The upward shift in the production function that comes from higher TFP means that even if a country does not change its investment rate, it can reach a higher steady state. Recall from Chapter 4 that the steady-state capital stock is the point where investment equals depreciation. Higher TFP means more output and so, for the same percentage investment rate, the country can provide more investment and can thus cover a larger amount of depreciation. Therefore, a higher level of TFP enables a higher steady-state level of capital to be supported. Thus countries with high TFP will have higher levels of output, not only from the upward shift in the production function but also because of the increase in the steady state of capital stock.

KEY POINT

Increases in TFP boost GDP through two channels: (1) the direct effect of the upward shift in the production function so that, for given capital, firms can produce more output; and (2) an indirect effect whereby, for the same investment rate, an increase in TFP leads to an increase in steady-state capital and output.

5.2 Human Capital

HUMAN CAPITAL AND ECONOMIC GROWTH

So far, our production function has only allowed a role for labour in terms of hours worked. There is another way in which labour can contribute, though, and that is through **human capital**. Human capital refers to the skills and knowledge that accumulate over time in individuals, the labour force and society. Many different skills make up human capital: learning acquired at school, on-the-job training, learning by doing and shared social knowledge and conventions. Like physical capital, and unlike hours worked, human capital is durable – it can provide benefits over several periods. Being durable, it can be increased by investment, such as in education or training. Sadly, human capital can also be decreased through depreciation. How much of this chapter will you remember tomorrow? Next year?

By introducing human capital into our model, we now have three factors of production: physical capital, human capital and hours worked. In addition, we still have a TFP term reflecting all other influences. This TFP term is different from that in Chapter 4, as we have now explicitly included human capital as a factor of production, leaving a diminished role for TFP. Allowing for education extends our growth model in three main ways.

1. Using Figure 5.1, we can see that the effect of boosting human capital is to shift the production function so that more output can be produced for a given level of physical capital. We should expect countries with high human capital to produce higher levels of growth (until they reach a higher steady state), which is exactly what is shown in Figure 5.2.

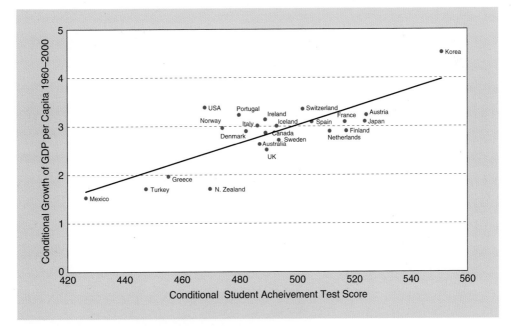

FIGURE 5.2 ● **Education and economic growth.** There is a significant relationship between educational outcomes and economic growth among OECD countries – even after controlling for other factors. *Source:* Eric A. Hanushek and Ludger Woessmann, 'How much do educational outcomes matter in OECD countries?', (2010).

2. From Figure 5.1 we can see that countries that boost their human capital will see an improvement in their steady state. This means that mature industrialized economies, such as the OECD nations, that have reached their steady state can still produce growth if they can improve their human capital and so boost the steady state. Table 5.1 shows an extended growth accounting exercise for OECD countries that allows for human capital. While the contributions to growth of capital accumulation and TFP dominate, differences in human capital (here denoted 'Labour – Skills') do play an important role in explaining growth rates.

3. Adding human capital to our model helps provide a richer story about investment flows between countries. If countries differ only in their capital stocks and have identical TFP, then diminishing marginal product of capital implies that investment should flow to predominantly poor countries. For instance, if the only difference between countries was in their capital stock, then the MPK in India would be about 50 times higher than in the United States.[1] In response to such enormous differences, we would expect huge investment flows from the United States to India. However, we do not observe flows of this nature in the data, suggesting that there are other influences on US MPK that offset the influence of diminishing returns. Examining Figure 5.3, we can see that higher human capital in the United States

TABLE 5.1 ● Contribution of Education to Annual Output Growth, 1950–90.

Human capital helps explain long-run trend growth.

	France	Germany	Japan	UK	US
Annual Growth (%)	5.04	5.92	9.27	3.03	3.65
Capital	2.40	3.19	4.33	2.40	1.62
Labour – Hours	−0.09	0.01	0.89	−0.09	0.58
Labour – Skills	0.39	0.19	0.52	0.20	0.48
Total Factor Productivity	2.34	2.53	3.53	0.52	0.97

Source: Crafts, 'Productivity growth reconsidered', *Economic Policy* (1991), 15: 387–426.

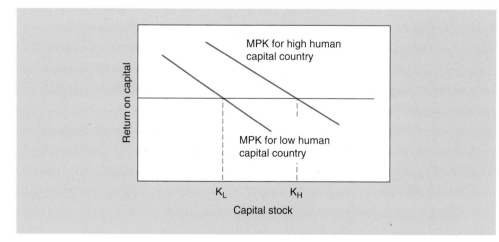

FIGURE 5.3 ● **Effect of education on the marginal product of capital.** Differences in education can explain why investment still flows to rich countries.

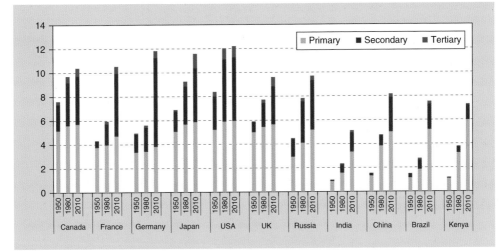

FIGURE 5.4 ● **Years of schooling by level.** Average years of formal education is rising in all countries, but richer countries have substantially higher levels of education. *Source:* Barro, R. and J.W. Lee, v.2.0, 07/11 – Educational Attainment for Total Population 1950–2010.

could explain this. Differences in the level of human capital between the United States and India (see Figure 5.4) mean that the United States is characterized by a higher MPK schedule, so that, for any given level of capital, investment earns a higher return in the United States than in India. Because of the differences in human capital, both countries face the same return on investment when India has capital stock K_L and the United States has K_H. Human capital offsets the effects of diminishing marginal product of capital and helps explain why investment doesn't flow to only low-capital-stock countries.

KEY POINT

Differences in human capital help explain output differences across countries – high human capital produces more output and increases the steady state. Continual improvements in education can help achieve long-run growth even in the capital-rich OECD nations. High levels of human capital can offset the impact of diminishing marginal product of capital and help explain why investment still flows into capital-rich countries.

INCREASING HUMAN CAPITAL

Figure 5.5 shows spending per student against educational attainment (in mathematics) for a range of OECD countries. Although there is a significant tendency for students in countries that spend more to achieve higher scores, there is also a great deal of variation not explained by the level of spending. This may suggest that how governments allocate their spending is also very important.

There are a number of problems that reduce the efficiency of educational expenditure in poorer countries. For example, in rich OECD countries, the cost of providing a year of

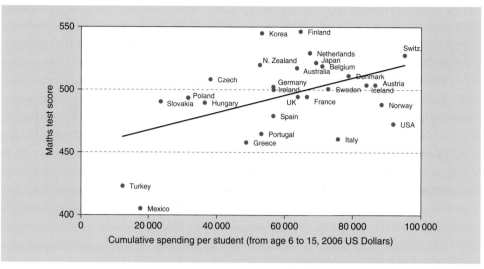

FIGURE 5.5 ● **Relationship between educational outcomes and expenditure on education.** Greater expenditure per student does tend to improve educational outcomes even after controlling for other factors. *Source:* Hanushek and Woessmann, 'How much do education outcomes matter in OECD economies?' (2010).

TABLE 5.2 ● **Determinants of Efficient Education Expenditure.**
Teacher salaries and pupil–teacher ratios do not seem to be strongly correlated with educational performance. The first column shows the number of studies considered, the second column shows the number of studies where the variable listed is important, the third column expresses this as a percentage.

Primary Schools	Number of Studies	Positive and Significant Relation	Confirmation Percentage
Teacher's salary level	11	4	36.4
School teacher–pupil ratio	26	9	34.6
Teacher's years of schooling	18	9	50.0
Teacher's experience	23	13	56.5
Class instructional time	17	15	88.2
Class frequency of homework	11	9	81.8
School library	18	16	88.9
School textbooks	26	19	73.1
Secondary Schools			
Teacher's salary level	11	2	18.2
School teacher–pupil ratio	22	2	9.1
Teacher's experience	12	1	8.3
Class instructional time	16	12	75.0
School textbooks	13	7	53.8

Source: Fuller and Clarke, 'How to Raise the Effectiveness of Secondary Schools? Universal and Locally Tailored Investment Strategies', Educational and Social Policy Discussion Paper Series No. 28 (Washington, DC: World Bank, 1994).

education for a university student is around 18 times that for a year of primary school. In poor nations the ratio is much higher – around 89. On average most countries spend 15–20% of average GDP per capita on each child at primary school, although this tends to be higher for the richest economies. The situation for tertiary education is very different, with poorer countries spending around 1000% of average GDP per capita on each college student, compared to around 100% for richer nations. From the national perspective, this suggests that poorer nations should focus more on primary education and that money spent on tertiary education may produce a lower return.

So what forms of educational expenditure are most effective at increasing human capital? This is the critical question in how government educational policies can help boost long-run growth. Table 5.2 shows a survey of several studies of developing economies. The survey examined in what percentage of research studies particular features have been shown to have improved human capital. While this is a contentious area, it is interesting to note that raising teacher salaries and reducing class sizes are not guaranteed to be effective means of improving educational performance. Instead, instructional time in class seems to be the factor that contributes most, at both the elementary and secondary levels.

5.3   Total Factor Productivity

EMPIRICAL IMPORTANCE OF TFP

Our model can now account for differences in GDP per capita through variations across countries in physical *and* human capital. However, Figure 5.6 shows that there remains a substantial role for TFP in explaining the wealth of nations. Figure 5.6 suggests that if a country has high TFP, it is highly likely that it also has high productivity and GDP *even*

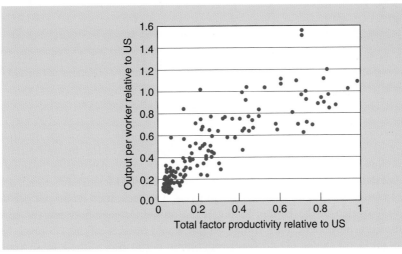

FIGURE 5.6 ● **Output and TFP across countries.** Differences in TFP account for major differences in GDP. *Source:* Hall and Jones, 'Why Do Some Countries Produce so Much More Output per Worker Than Others?' NBER Working Paper 6564, *Quarterly Journal of Economics* (1999), 114(1): 83–116. © by the President and Fellows of Harvard College and the Massachusetts Institute of Technology.

TABLE 5.3 ● Explaining Differences in Output per Head.

Variations in capital and education can account for only some of the cross-country variations in GDP per capita. Each column shows productivity in a country relative to the US if the only difference from the US was the factor input listed at the top.

	Capital	Education	TFP	Output per Worker
Canada	1.00	0.90	1.03	0.93
Italy	1.06	0.65	1.21	0.83
France	1.09	0.67	1.13	0.82
UK	0.89	0.81	1.01	0.73
Spain	1.02	0.61	1.11	0.68
Japan	1.12	0.80	0.66	0.59
Mexico	0.87	0.54	0.93	0.43
Korea	0.86	0.76	0.58	0.38
Iran	0.98	0.47	0.64	0.30
Chile	0.99	0.66	0.40	0.26
Peru	0.94	0.62	0.41	0.24
Egypt	0.45	0.58	0.72	0.19
Pakistan	0.58	0.39	0.57	0.13
India	0.71	0.45	0.27	0.09
Sudan	0.84	0.34	0.23	0.07
Lesotho	0.68	0.48	0.19	0.06
Kenya	0.75	0.46	0.17	0.06
Rwanda	0.44	0.34	0.29	0.04
Uganda	0.36	0.39	0.22	0.03

Source: Hall and Jones, 'Why do some countries produce so much more output per worker than others?' *Quarterly Journal of Economics* (1999), 114(1): 83–116. © by the President and Fellows of Harvard College and the Massachusetts Institute of Technology.

without knowing the country's physical and human capital. Table 5.3 develops this theme by examining how much of productivity differences can be accounted for through variations in physical and human capital and TFP. Table 5.3 shows that output per worker in India is 9% of the level of the United States. If India had the same level of TFP and educational achievement as the United States but differed only in its capital stock, then its output per worker would be 71% of that of the United States. If the only difference between the countries was educational achievement, then Indian output would be 45% of the US level. But the most important factor explaining differences in output per worker in the United States and India is total factor productivity. According to Table 5.3, even if India had the same capital stock and educational achievements as the United States, its output would only be 27% of the US level. Therefore, low output in India is due not only to low factor inputs but also to the relative inefficiency with which India uses these factor inputs. As Figure 5.6 shows, this finding is not restricted to India – differences in total factor productivity can account for much of the differencs in output per worker across countries.

> ### KEY POINT
>
> Even after removing human capital from TFP, differences in TFP still account for substantial variation in GDP across countries.

THE IMPORTANCE OF INSTITUTIONS

Why do some countries use factor inputs more efficiently than others? The scope of factors that might influence TFP is huge, ranging from technology, government policy and legal institutions to sociocultural norms, religious beliefs, geography, and climate. The breadth of this list reveals that explaining economic growth is not the sole province of economics.

One element of TFP that many economists, inspired by the work of Nobel Laureate Douglass North, feel is critical is **institutions**. The definition of 'institutions' is a broad one, reflecting the 'rules of the game' in society; that is, the explicit and implicit behavioural norms that provide economic incentives to society. These institutions are not limited to government organizations that sit in a building, but extend to a wide range of social behaviour and influences.

Whilt this broad definition of institutions is important for understanding the mechanisms of economic growth, it makes it extremely difficult to find a reliable way of measuring the quality of institutions. For this reason, many researchers focus on a narrower concept relating to the role of government institutions concerning:

- *Property Rights:* is there an independent legal system that upholds the rights of owners of private property?
- *Regulatory Institutions:* do governments act to curb monopoly powers and abuse of workers and consumers?
- *Macroeconomic Stabilization:* are there institutions, such as independent central banks and fiscal rules, that help achieve low and stable inflation, sustainable public finance, and low levels of unemployment?
- *Social Insurance:* does the government provide for groups disadvantaged by geography, disease, famine, or other external circumstances? Does the government help achieve equal opportunities for broad segments of the population?
- *Conflict Management:* do there exist political institutions that can legitimately arbitrate between inconsistent demands of different political or ethnic groups without producing conflict or rebellion?
- *Political Rights:* are there sufficient constraints on the actions of powerful interest groups or political parties to stop them exploiting their power in ways harmful to the economy?

Because of the importance of institutions and governance, the World Bank has developed a range of indicators to measure their quality across countries. These measures of institutions reflect six themes:

- *Voice and accountability:* a measure of civil liberties and political rights.
- *Political Stability and Lack of Violence:* a measure of the likelihood that the government will be overthrown by unconstitutional means.

- *Government Effectiveness:* a measure of the quality of public services and bureaucracy and the independence of the civil service.
- *Regulation Quality:* measured by the status of effective curbs on excessive bureaucracy, price distortion, and other market-unfriendly policies.
- *Rule of Law:* measured by perceptions of incidence of crime, the predictability of the judiciary, and enforcement of contracts.
- *Corruption:* indicated by measures of bribe-taking and other corrupt behaviour.

The economic importance of these measures of institutional quality can be readily seen in Figure 5.7. High-quality institutions, as measured by an average of these six indicators, produce higher levels of GDP per capita, faster growth rate, and less volatility in output.

While these results show the importance of institutions, they also raise two key issues relevant for emerging markets. The first is that, although institutions are widely recognized as being important, this does not mean that there is widespread agreement as to what these institutions should look like. The type of institutions that succeed in a country may depend on the culture and history of the nation and be difficult to duplicate in another society. The institutions that successfully generate GDP growth in India and China, for example, may need to be different from those of the United States and Europe. The other implication is that if economic growth depends on adopting the 'correct' institutional structure, then achieving economic success in emerging markets may be extremely difficult. It is relatively straightforward for a country to change its economic policies by, for example, increasing its education spending, privatizing its utilities, or reducing its trade barriers. Changing the underlying cultural norms that make up its institutional structure is much more difficult.

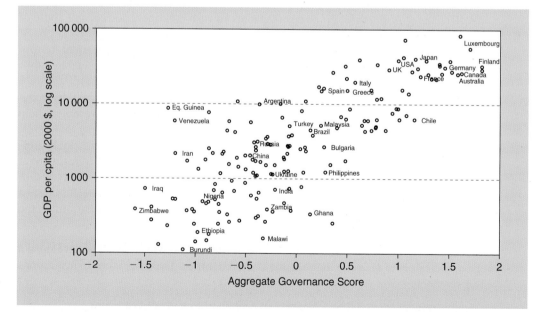

FIGURE 5.7 ● **Institutions matter.** Variations in institutions are strongly correlated with differences in GDP per capita. *Source:* World Bank Governance Database (2011).

> ### KEY POINT
>
> A key determinant of TFP is institutions. The quality of governance, related to the rule of law and the absence of corruption, is a critical component of institutions.

RENT SEEKING AND CORRUPTION

Why are institutions so important? In Chapter 2 we showed how GDP is a measure of the value added that a society produces. We also saw how total income in society is equal to the value added produced. But while society can only earn income by producing value added, the same is not true at the individual level. An individual can either earn income by adding value (what we will call being an entrepreneur) or through taking the value added that someone else has produced, in which case they are a **rent seeker**. A classic example here might be the difference between a merchant (entrepreneur) and a pirate (rent seeker).

The ultimate sources of economic growth lie in innovation and in creating output. For the good of society as a whole, as few people as possible should engage in rent-seeking activity. Rent seeking lowers growth in three ways:

- The rent-seeking sector absorbs labour that would otherwise go into entrepreneurial activities.
- By earning income from the value added that entrepreneurs create, rent seekers act as a tax and decrease the supply of entrepreneurs.
- If the rewards to rent seeking are high, the most talented people become rent seekers and the quality of entrepreneurs suffers.

The costs of rent seeking can be enormous. For instance, in 1980, rent seeking cost the Indian economy the equivalent of an estimated 30–45% of GDP and lowered Indian TFP growth by 2% per year between 1950 and 1980.[2]

As a leading social historian has commented, 'It is often assumed that an economy of private enterprise has an automatic bias towards innovation, but this is not so. It has a bias only towards profit.'[3] Institutions are needed to ensure that individuals do not engage in rent-seeking behaviour, but rather they make profits in ways that increase the value added of their societies. The role of institutions in achieving this is profound and may help explain why the Industrial Revolution happened in Western Europe in the eighteenth century rather than 400 years earlier in China. In 1400, China had a higher level of per capita output than Western Europe ($450 in 1985 prices compared to $400) and had introduced many innovations. Yet, by 1820, Chinese output was unchanged, while that of Europe had risen to $1050 and continued to rise throughout the Industrial Revolution.

One explanation for this poor performance is the allocation of talent in China and the weak social incentives to take part in entrepreneurial activity. As one author notes:

What was chiefly lacking in China for the further development of capitalism was not mechanical skill or scientific aptitude, nor a sufficient accumulation of wealth, but scope for individual enterprise. There was no individual freedom and no security for private enterprise, no legal foundation for rights other than those of the state, no alternative investment other than landed property, no guarantee against being penalized by arbitrary exactions from officials or against intervention by the state. But perhaps the supreme inhibiting factor was the overwhelming prestige of the state bureaucracy, which maimed from the start any attempt of the bourgeoisie to be different, to become aware of themselves as a class and fight for an autonomous position in society.[4]

Many economic historians believe that the Renaissance period in Western Europe – with its emphasis on rationality, individuality, and the introduction of a legal system recognizing individual property rights – provided exactly this scope for private enterprise and triggered the Industrial Revolution. The result was a social system that not only encouraged individuals to take up commercial activity to earn profit, but also encouraged higher output and greater productivity.

The above analysis assumes that it is fairly easy to identify a rent seeker and an entrepreneur, but this is not necessarily so. For instance, is a lawyer engaged in an expensive lawsuit concerning intellectual property rights a rent seeker or an entrepreneur? We shall, for fear of an expensive lawsuit, leave you to decide for yourself. Another question is whether or not rent seeking is a problem for modern industrialized economies. Researchers Murphy, Shleifer and Vishny (to widespread amusement in the economics profession) actually do identify lawyers as rent seekers. They also identify engineers as entrepreneurs, and suggest the number of students enrolled in engineering courses as a measure of how much talent a society allocates towards value-added endeavours. Using these definitions, they studied the growth performance between 1960 and 1985 of 91 countries to determine the influence of student enrolments in engineering and law on economic growth. The results suggest that every 10% increase in engineering enrolments boosts growth by 0.5% and that every 10% increase in legal enrolments *lowers* growth by 0.3%. It would probably be unfair to change educational policy on the basis of these results (and one wonders what the analysis would be if either engineers or lawyers were replaced by economists), but it does suggest that rent seeking can become a problem for modern economies. What matters for growth is not just education, but the use that society makes of that education.

Corruption is a form of rent seeking that is present in many countries. Empirical research suggests that corruption does adversely affect TFP and the level of output in an economy. Table 5.4 shows the most and least corrupt countries (as surveyed annually by Transparency International, www.transparency.org) and confirms that the least corrupt economies (10 is no corruption, 0 is complete corruption) are richer than the most corrupt. However, with international investment flows growing in importance, it should be remembered that it is not just the nationality receiving the bribe that matters but also who pays the bribe. Table 5.5 shows, for a sample of countries, which nations have companies most likely to pay a bribe (10 being companies who do not pay bribes).

A final influence on TFP that we shall consider is the level of trust. While it is important to have a good rule of law, not every transaction can be enforced through legal means. For this reason, an indispensable part of a successful economy is trust between contractual partners. This aspect of institutions is captured in the concept of **social capital** – a cultural phenomenon denoting the extent of civic-mindedness of members of a society and the degree of trust in public institutions. Societies marked by high social capital will also be marked by cooperation, and this is more likely to lead to higher value-added activities rather than to rent seeking, corruption, and crime. The role of social capital has been invoked as one reason (among several) why the former communist economies performed so poorly when they began the transition to capitalism. The transitions of these nations have often been characterized by disappointing GDP performance, even though they had high levels of physical and human

TABLE 5.4 ● Corruption Perceptions Index, 2010.

High score means less corrupt. Selected countries.

Country	Score	Country	Score
Denmark	9.3	China	3.5
New Zealand	9.3	Thailand	3.5
Singapore	9.3	Greece	3.5
Sweden	9.2	India	3.3
Canada	8.9	Mexico	3.1
Netherlands	8.8	Argentina	2.9
Australia	8.7	Indonesia	2.8
Hong Kong	8.4	Ethiopia	2.7
Germany	7.9	Vietnam	2.7
Japan	7.8	Nigeria	2.4
UK	7.6	Ukraine	2.4
Chile	7.2	Pakistan	2.3
US	7.1	Kenya	2.1
France	6.8	Russia	2.1
Spain	6.1	Venezuela	2.0
Poland	5.3	Sudan	1.6
South Africa	4.5	Iraq	1.5
Malaysia	4.4	Afghanistan	1.4
Italy	3.9	Myanmar	1.4
Brazil	3.7	Somalia	1.1

Source: Transparency International.

TABLE 5.5 ● Bribe Payers Index, 2008.

High score means less likely to pay a bribe.

Country	Score	Country	Score
Belgium	8.8	Spain	7.9
Canada	8.8	Hong Kong	7.6
Netherlands	8.7	South Africa	7.5
Switzerland	8.7	South Korea	7.5
Germany	8.6	Taiwan	7.5
UK	8.6	Italy	7.4
Japan	8.6	Brazil	7.4
Australia	8.5	India	6.8
France	8.1	Mexico	6.6
Singapore	8.1	China	6.5
US	8.1	Russia	5.9

Source: Transparency International.

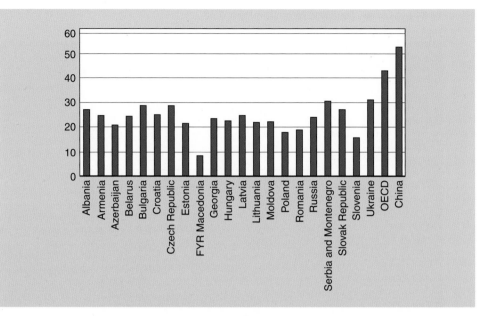

FIGURE 5.8 ● **Social capital in transition economies, 1995.** Formerly socialist economies in transition often have poor social capital. *Source:* Raiser, Haerpfer, Nowotry and Wallace, Social Capital in Transition: A First Look at the Evidence, European Bank for Reconstruction and Development Working Paper No. 61.

capital. However, they also scored poorly on institutional quality, especially corruption and financial systems. Figure 5.8 also shows that these economies were marked by relatively low rates of social capital compared to other nations – membership of civic societies and degree of trust are much lower in these nations than elsewhere.

KEY POINT

Successful economies need institutions that encourage individuals to earn their income through engaging in value-added activities rather than rent seeking.

5.4   The Importance of Technological Progress

Our focus on institutions and TFP helped to explain the variation in GDP per capita across countries. We now use TFP to account for another deficiency in our model based just on physical and human capital. For a given level of TFP, diminishing MPK means that countries eventually reach a steady state, and at this point there is no further growth in the economy. But, as we saw in Chapter 3, although growth has slowed down, the rich OECD nations continue to show positive trend growth. More than 150 years after the Industrial Revolution, it is implausible that they have not yet reached their steady state. To explain this continual growth in rich nations, we need to examine the role of **technological progress**.

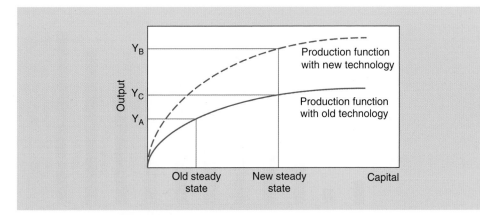

FIGURE 5.9 ● **Technological progress and growth accounting.** Technical progress increases output directly and has a further effect though its impact on the equilibrium capital stock.

An improvement in technology acts as an increase in TFP – similar to that in Figures 5.1 and 5.3 – which leads to higher output and further growth. Because technological progress occurs continuously, this suggests that the steady state of the economy is forever shifting. When technological progress occurs at a modest pace, the shift in the steady state is small and the GDP growth created is moderate. But during periods of major technological developments, the shift in the steady state might be substantial and produce fast growth for many years until the new steady state is reached.

Because technological progress increases the steady state, a growth accounting analysis will show output growth from both TFP and capital accumulation. This can be seen in Figure 5.9, where the increase in TFP and the resulting change in the steady-state capital stock leads to an increase in output of $Y_B - Y_A$. $Y_B - Y_C$ gives the direct increase in output from technical progress, but the additional capital accumulation resulting from technical progress leads to a further rise in output of $Y_C - Y_A$. Technological progress ensures that capital accumulation continues indefinitely as the steady state continuously changes. Without technological change, the economy settles down to a static steady state and shows no growth.

KEY POINT

Because of technological progress the steady state continues to evolve. This leads to higher output because: (1) capital becomes more productive, and (2) the steady-state capital stock increases.

This analysis suggests that the incentives for firms to engage in research and development increase as countries approach their steady state. We would therefore expect mature economies to focus more on R&D than emerging markets, which will focus more on capital accumulation. Figure 5.10 supports this hypothesis by showing the substantive increase in R&D expenditure experienced by South Korea. Rapid growth in South Korea was initially based around high rates of capital accumulation, but as diminishing MPK began to set in, increasing emphasis was placed on R&D. As shown in Figure 5.11, spending on R&D is highest among the richest countries, who rely on it as their driver of growth.

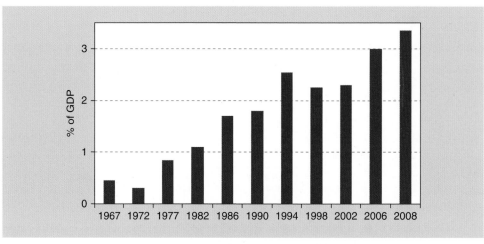

FIGURE 5.10 ● **South Korean R&D as percentage of GDP.** As countries approach their steady state, R&D becomes more important. *Source:* OECD, Main Science and Technology Indicators.

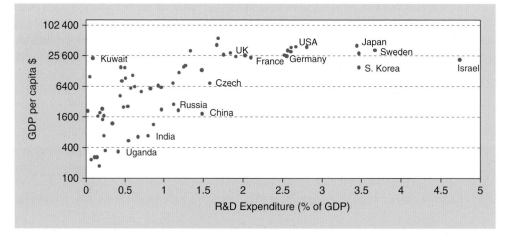

FIGURE 5.11 ● **Rich countries do more R&D.** *Source:* World Development Indicators (2007).

If technological progress is the main source of growth for the richest nations, then we can expect them to grow more slowly than countries that are not yet at their steady state and that can still grow through capital accumulation alone. Richer countries will experience slower growth due to diminishing MPK and the trials and tribulations that accompany R&D.

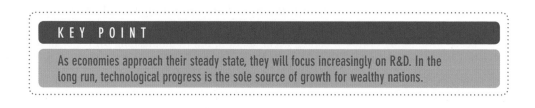

KEY POINT

As economies approach their steady state, they will focus increasingly on R&D. In the long run, technological progress is the sole source of growth for wealthy nations.

5.5 Scarce Resources and the Production Function

So far our analysis has focused on the key inputs of the production function; capital, labour (and human capital) and TFP. There are a number of other factors of production, such as energy and land, that are needed to produce output. These factors can have important implications for growth, since they are either in fixed supply (like land) or declining supply (like oil) and so can act as a brake on growth.

Take the example of land. It is a simple matter to extend the Cobb-Douglas production function that we introduced in Chapter 3 to include another factor of production:

$$\text{Output} = \text{TFP} \times \text{Capital Stock}^a \times \text{Hours Worked}^b \times \text{Land}^{1-a-b}$$

so that

$$
\begin{aligned}
\text{Change in Logarithm (Output)} = \ & \text{Change in Logarithm (TFP)} \\
& + a \times \text{Change in Logarithm (Capital)} \\
& + b \times \text{Change in Logarithm (Hours Worked)} \\
& + (1 - a - b) \times \text{Change in Logarithm (Land)}
\end{aligned}
$$

In this production function we have retained the assumption of constant returns to scale (a and b are both less than 1, so $a + b + (1 - a - b) = 1$), which means that if you double the capital stock, hours worked and supply of land you also double output (we will see what happens when you relax this assumption in Chapter 6). However, we now have the problem that the supply of available land is fixed and so it is not possible to increase output through that route. This means that even if we double both the capital stock and hours worked, output no longer doubles since the restricted supply of land limits the productivity of capital and labour. Consider the agricultural sector and its output. Continually increasing the amount of farm labour and machinery used on a farm can only result in decreasing productivity of that labour and capital, as the amount of land that can be cultivated is limited.

Including fixed factors of production like land in the production function seems to return us to the dismal predictions of Thomas Malthus that we discussed in Chapter 3. It seems that as population rises, wages and living standards will fall even if the capital stock rises in line with population growth, as land acts as a constraint. But such a prediction ignores the role of TFP. Rising TFP can lead to rising productivity and living standards even in the presence of scarce resources, though TFP must rise more to generate the same productivity gains in a world of scarce resources.

If we now think of a non-renewable resource like oil, the problem become worse since, unlike land, oil cannot be reused each period; oil consumed today permanently reduces the stock of oil available in the future. This means that growth and output based purely on that resource are ultimately unsustainable. But in the case of oil and energy resources in general it is clear that one source of energy could in principle be substituted for another or even by a new technology. So it is less clear that energy is a scarce resource in the long run. Overall, adding scarce resources to the production function once again highlights the importance of TFP for long-run growth.

KEY POINT

Adding scarce resources like land into the production function shows how limited resources makes growth more difficult to sustain.

SUMMARY

In order to account for wide variation in GDP per capita across countries, we have to introduce variations in total factor productivity to supplement the effect of capital accumulation. In section 5.1, we showed that higher levels of TFP not only enable greater output to be produced from a given capital stock, but also lead to a larger steady-state capital stock. The richest nations define the TFP frontier, although many countries will find themselves unable to reach this level.

In section 5.2, we talked about human capital. Reflecting the skills and knowledge of the workforce, human capital contributes to explaining differences in income unrelated to physical capital. Increases in human capital offset the effects of the diminishing marginal product of capital and help explain why not all investment flows to the poorest countries. For wealthy nations at their steady state, increases in human capital trigger further increases in output and investment.

In section 5.3, we saw that, even allowing for differences in human capital, there remains a substantive role for TFP in accounting for income differences. TFP reflects myriad influences, but one of the more important is the role of institutions, broadly conceived, in providing incentives for individuals to make profit in ways that are advantageous for society. Good governance, lack of corruption, an optimal allocation of talent, and high social capital are all important in boosting TFP. There is some evidence that ownership of substantial raw materials may harm GDP through adverse effects on institutional quality.

In order to explain continual growth in rich nations, we introduced technological progress in section 5.4. Technological progress increases over time, boosting output and the capital stock. With no technological progress, the capital stock reaches its steady-state level and the economy ceases to grow. Technological progress provides two additional channels for growth: it produces more output from a given level of factor inputs, and it boosts the desired level of capital. For countries at their steady state, technological progress is the long-run source of growth, so the importance of R&D to a country increases with its income.

In section 5.5, we discussed the impact of introducing scarce resources like land into the production function. We saw how the limited supply of these resources makes economic growth more difficult to sustain.

CONCEPTUAL QUESTIONS

1. (Section 5.1) Consider an economy well known to you and assess which factors of its TFP are relatively strong compared to other countries and which ones are relatively poor. What steps could be taken to improve TFP?

2. (Section 5.2) Do you think that the marginal product of human capital is decreasing or increasing? Why?

3. (Section 5.2) Should developing countries spend money on establishing universities in their own countries?

4. (Section 5.3) What steps could a government take to remove corruption?

5. (Section 5.3) Considering the importance of institutions, what advantages and disadvantages are there to joining the EU for the various ex-communist economies such as Poland and the Czech Republic?

6. (Section 5.4) In this chapter we have assumed that the level of technology can be adjusted independently of the capital stock. However, in practice, investing in new technology means investing in new machines. Use Figure 5.11 to analyse the implications of this.

7. (Section 5.4) How would a technological development that boosted output but produced a higher depreciation rate affect output and capital?

8. (Section 5.5) Is it better to develop your own technological champions or to rely on foreign direct investment?

9. (Section 5.6) Will scarcity of resources return us to the world envisaged by Thomas Malthus or will technology overcome this limitation?

ANALYTICAL QUESTIONS

1. (Section 5.1) Consider an economy in which output in period t is produced by the Cobb-Douglas production function:

$$Y_t = A_t K_t^b L_t^{1-b}$$

Y_t is output at time t; K_t is capital at time t; L_t is labour employed at time t; A_t is TFP at time t.

(You can review the Cobb-Douglas function in Chapter 3.) Saving, which equals gross investment, is 25% of output. The depreciation rate of capital is 5% in the period. Initially, TFP is constant at 1, labour input is constant at 100, and b is 0.3.

(a) Calculate the initial steady-state level of output.

(b) What happens in the short run if TFP suddenly rises from 1 to 1.2?

(c) What is the new long-run level of steady-state output, assuming TFP stays at 1.2?

(d) What is the growth in the capital stock between the old steady state and the new one?

2. (Section 5.2) Consider an economy in which output in period t is produced by the Cobb-Douglas production function:

$$Y_t = A_t HK_t^a K_t^b L_t^{1-b}$$

Y_t is output at time t; K_t is capital at time t; L_t is labour employed at time t; A_t is TFP at time t; HK_t is human capital; and a and b are both greater than 0.

(a) What happens to GDP when human capital is increased?

(b) Assuming $0 < a < 1$, what shape is the marginal product of human capital?

(c) As K is increased, what happens to the marginal product of human capital?

3. (Section 5.2) What do you think accounts for the results of Table 5.2?

4. (Section 5.3) visit http://info.worldbank.org/governance/wgi/sc_country.asp/and compare the institutional quality of two countries of your choice.

5. (Section 5.3) The quality of financial institutions is important for the level of TFP. Consider the merits and demerits of bank-based systems compared to those relying on equity markets. Should governments privatize the financial system or leave it under state control?

6. (Section 5.3) Consider Table 5.3 and assess the relative importance of investment, education, and TFP in explaining cross-country income differences.

7. (Section 5.4) What difference is there between invention and innovation? How do these affect the marginal product of capital over time?

8. (Section 5.4) What explanations can you suggest to account for Figure 5.12? Why do some countries do more R&D than others? Does this matter?

CHAPTER 6

Endogenous Growth and Convergence

Key Concepts

Colonialism	Curse of Natural Resources	Overseas Development Assistance
Conditional Convergence	Endogenous Growth	Poverty Traps
Constant and Increasing MPK	Geography	Steady State Determinants

Overview

In this chapter we develop endogenous growth models. These models drop the assumption of decreasing marginal product of capital (MPK), denying the existence of a steady state so that capital accumulation can produce growth for ever. Interactions between physical and human capital are suggested as one reason why the MPK may not be diminishing. If these interactions are pronounced, poverty traps may exist, condemning poor regions to remain poor in absolute terms.

We examine historical growth patterns and find that, across a wide sample of countries, no pattern of convergence exists; on average, poor countries do not grow faster than wealthy ones. However, when we consider similar countries, we find strong evidence in favour of convergence. We reconcile this evidence by introducing the idea of conditional convergence – among countries that share a similar steady state, poorer countries will grow faster than wealthier ones – but comparing across countries with different steady states, we should find no clear patterns of convergence. We then consider what determines a country's steady state and how policy measures might affect it. We review the poor economic growth performance of Africa, focusing on policies, geography, colonialism and institutions, and conclude by examining the historical record and principles underlying development aid.

(6.1) Endogenous Growth

The Solow neoclassical model that we have developed so far offers a rich framework for analysis, especially when we allow for differences in total factor productivity. However, it is not a very satisfactory model for explaining long-run growth. Once countries reach their long-run steady state, continual growth only occurs through changes in technological progress. However, the model is focused on capital accumulation and provides no explanation for what drives technological progress. In other words, it offers an *exogenous* theory of long-run economic growth. By contrast, **endogenous growth** theories try to outline in detail the mechanisms that cause long-run economic growth. There are many ways of explaining economic growth, and endogenous growth theory refers to a wide range of models, but in essence they are of two types. One type produces continual growth by avoiding the notion of a steady state so that capital accumulation can produce growth without limit. The other type focuses on endogenous explanations of how total factor productivity changes over time.

GROWTH WITHOUT END

To remove the steady state from our analysis, we need to drop the assumption of decreasing MPK. If instead we assume a **constant MPK**, then the production function becomes a straight line, as shown in Figure 6.1. Every new machine installed leads to an increase in output identical to the increase from the previous machine. If investment is a constant proportion of output (as we previously assumed), the investment schedule is also a straight line and no longer flattens out. In this situation, as shown in Figure 6.1, the investment and depreciation lines do not intersect, and no steady state exists. Investment always exceeds depreciation and so the capital stock is always growing and GDP growth does not slow down. With constant MPK, long-run growth becomes endogenous and is explained by investment.

The absence of a steady state rules out the convergence result we stressed in Chapter 4: poor countries need no longer grow faster than wealthier nations. This model also suggests

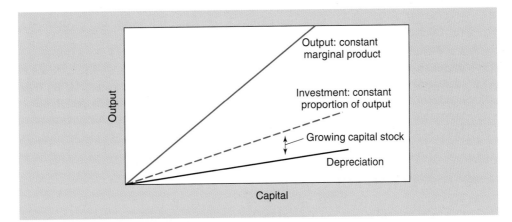

FIGURE 6.1 ● **Constant marginal product and endogenous growth.** With a constant marginal product of capital, there is no steady-state level of the capital stock.

that if government policy can boost investment, it not only increases the capital stock but *permanently* affects the growth rate. To see this, consider the following. The change in the capital stock equals investment less depreciation. If investment equals a proportion (*s*) of output, and depreciation is a proportion (d) of the capital stock, then

Change in capital stock = Investment − Depreciation = $sY − dK$

A constant MPK implies that doubling the number of machines doubles output. Therefore output is simply a multiple of the capital stock or $Y = AK$, where A reflects total factor productivity. Therefore

Change in capital stock = $sY − dK = sAK − dK$

The percentage growth in the capital stock is equal to the change in the capital stock divided by capital (K), so we have

Growth in capital stock = Change in capital stock/Capital stock
$$= sY/K − dK/K = sA − d$$

so that the increase in the capital stock depends positively on the investment rate, *s*. Therefore, if the government can change the investment rate, it leads not just to a one-time increase in the *levels* of capital and output (as in Chapter 4), but to a *permanent* increase in the *growth rates* of capital and output.

KEY POINT

Endogenous growth models explain long-run growth by avoiding the assumption of diminishing MPK and so avoid the existence of a steady state. Assuming constant MPK means that investment affects both the level of GDP and its long-run growth rate.

WHY CONSTANT MARGINAL PRODUCT?

The previous subsection has shown that dropping the assumption of declining MPK leads to very different growth implications. But is a constant MPK justifiable? Assuming a Cobb-Douglas production function where $Y = AK^aL^b$, then the MPK = $AK^{a−1}L^b$. If $a < 1$, then $a − 1$ is less than zero and an increase in the capital stock reduces the MPK (e.g. there is decreasing MPK). If instead $a = 1$, then $a − 1 = 0$ and the MPK = $AK^0L^b = AL^b$ so that increasing the capital stock has *no* effect on the MPK (there is constant MPK). Therefore, endogenous growth would seem to hinge on $a = 1$. As discussed in Chapter 4, however, we know that capital income is around 30% of GDP, so $a = 0.3$. Surely this rules out a constant MPK and endogenous growth?

A BROADER CONCEPT OF CAPITAL

One way to generate a constant MPK is to focus on positive interactions between physical and human capital. The more human capital there is in a country, the higher the marginal product of physical capital. That is, the more skilled the workforce, the higher the

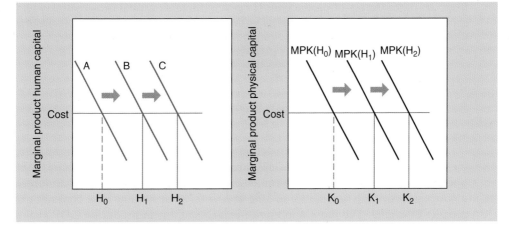

FIGURE 6.2 ● **Interaction between human and physical capital.** Increases in human capital generate more investment in physical capital and vice versa. As the productivity of human capital rises from A to B, the stock of human capital increases from H_0 to H_1 and this raises the productivity of physical schedule from MPK(H_0) to MPK(H_1). The resulting increase in physical capital ($K_0 \rightarrow K_1$) further boosts the productivity of human capital (B $\rightarrow$ C).

productivity of machines. However, the higher the level of physical capital in an economy, the greater the marginal product of human capital. That is, the more machines in an economy, the greater the return from investing in skills and education. By focusing on a broad measure of capital (both physical and human), this interaction may sustain constant MPK.

Figure 6.2 shows how these forces interact. Each panel shows the marginal product of human or physical capital, and each marginal product curve is drawn for a fixed level of the other form of capital. *Therefore, holding fixed the other form of capital, both display decreasing marginal product.* Let us assume that an increase in technological knowledge boosts the marginal product of human capital – skilled labour is now more productive. This shifts the marginal product of human capital curve out from A to B in the left panel of Figure 6.2. Assuming no change in the cost of education, this encourages the economy to increase its stock of human capital to H_1. This increase in human capital boosts the productivity of physical capital – the marginal product curve shifts out to MPK(H_1) in the right-hand panel. Given the cost of capital, this means that the economy increases its capital stock to K_1. However, this new higher level of physical capital means that the marginal product of human capital improves, and the marginal product curve for human capital shifts out to C. As a result, more human capital is accumulated to reach the level H_2. This increase in human capital in turn shifts the marginal product of physical capital out [to MPK(H_2)], and the virtuous circle continues. Therefore, although each category of capital on its own has decreasing marginal product, if we think of capital as including both human and physical capital, then we have constant marginal product of capital.

By using a Cobb-Douglas production function extended to allow for human capital, we can show this effect more easily. In this case the production function becomes

Output = A × (Human capital)^b × (Physical capital)^a × (Hours worked)^c

The marginal product of human capital is b × output/(human capital), and for physical capital it is a × output/(physical capital). Both marginal products are declining, keeping fixed the other factors of production. However, if human capital is increasing with physical capital, for example human capital = D × physical capital, then we can substitute out human capital from the production function and arrive at

Output = (A × D^b) × (Physical capital)$^{b+a}$ × (Hours worked)^c

If $b + a = 1$, then this becomes

Output = A* × (Physical capital) × (Hours worked)^c

where A* = A × D^b

This is the same AK production function (e.g. Y = AK) that we outlined when we discussed the straight-line production function in Figure 6.1. The closer $b + a$ is to 1, the more the production function becomes a straight line and the slower the MPK diminishes. Therefore, even if $a = 0.3$, as previously suggested, so long as $b = 0.7$ then we may have constant marginal product of capital. The more important human capital is in producing GDP growth, the more chance we have of endogenous growth being important.

ENDOGENOUS GROWTH AND GOVERNMENT POLICY

The key to producing a constant MPK was a spillover between human and physical capital – when education improves, benefits spill over to firms' investments. Spillovers are a form of market imperfection: left to its own devices, the market will not arrive at the best outcome, and this suggests a potentially useful role for government intervention. When each firm assesses whether to undertake investment, it compares the benefits and costs of the project. But each firm considers only the private benefits for itself; it does not factor in the additional benefits in the form of higher education and increased marginal product of human capital. As Figure 6.3 shows, the result is that the social return exceeds the private return, due to the gains of workers when firms invest. Because of the low private return, the firm underinvests and chooses the capital stock A, where the private return equals the cost, rather than capital stock B, where the social return equals the cost. The government can rectify this situation by offering a subsidy so that the cost to the firm falls. Thus, while the firm still chooses investment by equating private return to cost, it now chooses the socially optimal investment level B. Therefore, endogenous growth theory can provide a rationale for the government to boost long-run economic growth.

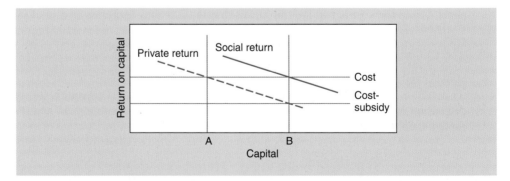

FIGURE 6.3 ● **Spillovers and subsidies.** A subsidy to bring down the cost of capital can induce firms to undertake the right level of investment (level B) even though they take account only of private returns.

> ### KEY POINT
>
> Interactions between physical and human capital can postpone diminishing MPK and even lead to an endogenous growth model with constant MPK. Because of the existence of these spillovers, government policy can be used to improve the economy.

6.2 Poverty Traps

There exists a third possibility about the MPK – the case of **increasing marginal product**. If the marginal product is increasing, this yields even richer growth implications. In particular, we can explain the existence of **poverty traps** that keep poor regions or countries poor. Figure 6.4 shows two regions in an economy, one with a low capital stock (A) and another with a high capital stock (B). For Region A, the MPK is less than the cost of investment, so it does not invest. However, because we are now assuming that the MPK is increasing with the capital stock, the capital-rich Region (B) will make the investment because its MPK exceeds the cost of investment. Depreciation and no investment will lead to Region A seeing its capital decline and becoming poorer, while continued investment and increasing marginal product will lead to high output and accelerating growth in Region B.

Increasing marginal product means that countries and regions don't show signs of catch-up, or convergence, but instead *diverge* – the rich get richer while the poor remain poor. Under this assumption, one would expect to find economic activity heavily concentrated in a few successful areas that showed continual high growth rather than spread equally across regions. Given that 54% of global GDP is produced from an area that accounts for only 10% of global land, and that the United States produces 50% of its GDP from only 2% of its land mass while the least productive 50% of US land accounts for only 2% of its GDP, there is some support for this view. Figure 6.5 shows the average growth in per capita output between 1960 and 2007 for over 100 countries. There are four groups of countries.

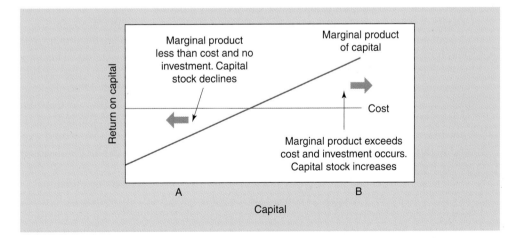

FIGURE 6.4 ● **Increasing marginal product and poverty traps.** If the marginal product of capital increases as capital employed rises, then poverty traps are possible.

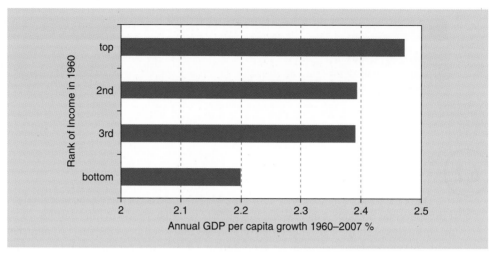

FIGURE 6.5 ● **Economic growth ranked by initial income.** The very poorest countries have not grown faster than the average – quite the reverse. *Source:* Penn World Table 6.1.

The bottom quartile was the poorest 25% of countries in 1960, the top quartile was the richest 25% of the countries, and the other quartiles reflect intermediate ranks. Overall, the gap between rich and poor countries widened between 1960 and 2007, with the poorest countries having the lowest growth.

The assumption of increasing marginal product could also help explain why, in global capital markets, investment flows mostly to wealthy nations. Between 1970 and 1994, the poorest 20% of countries received only 1% of total gross global capital flows, or the equivalent of 6 cents per person. By contrast, the richest 20% of the countries received 88% of total capital flows, or $189 per person. If the marginal product of capital is increasing, then the return to investment will be highest in the richest nations, and investors will rationally avoid portfolio investment in poor, undeveloped nations.

What justification can we give for increasing MPK? Observing many industries, professions and even neighbourhoods, we can see that individuals tend to associate with individuals of similar levels of human capital. For instance, the quality of economists within an academic department (or students within a university) tends to be similar, although quality will vary widely across different universities and business schools. This may have to do with interdependencies in the production function – it is important to avoid 'weak links in the chain'. For instance, the space shuttle *Challenger* exploded because one of its many thousands of components malfunctioned. That small imperfection destroyed a complex scientific project. Companies can fail because of bad marketing, even if the rest of the firm functions well. With such strong interdependencies (spillovers), we would expect to find highly skilled individuals working with each other, while less skilled individuals also group together.

These interdependencies typify poverty traps. In a poverty trap, the individual's incentive to avoid poverty is weak. If you are surrounded by high-quality human capital, then you have a large incentive to increase your human capital. However, if you are surrounded by low-quality human capital, your incentives are poor – with many weak links in the chain, your gains from increased education are going to be much smaller. This is why individuals and nations can get stuck in a poverty trap.

> **KEY POINT**
>
> If the MPK is increasing, then poverty traps exist whereby poor nations receive no investment and remain poor, while rich countries continue to invest and grow, leading to divergence in incomes across countries.

6.3 Convergence or Divergence?

In previous sections we have shown how different assumptions regarding the MPK produce fundamentally different implications for growth. In outlining each of these alternative assumptions on the MPK, we have shown evidence that is consistent with each theory, but which theory best explains the facts?

The key distinction between the Solow or neoclassical growth model, based on the assumption of decreasing marginal product, and the endogenous growth theories of this chapter is convergence. With decreasing marginal product, we expect to find convergence – poorer countries should grow faster than rich ones. According to endogenous growth theories, there should be no such simple negative correlation between initial income and subsequent growth. Therefore, to test the competing theories we should simply examine historical evidence. If there is a negative correlation, we have convergence, and the neoclassical model based on decreasing marginal product is the more appropriate framework.

Figure 6.6 shows the level of GDP per capita in 1960 and the average growth rate between 1960 and 2007 for a wide range of countries. Considering all countries together,

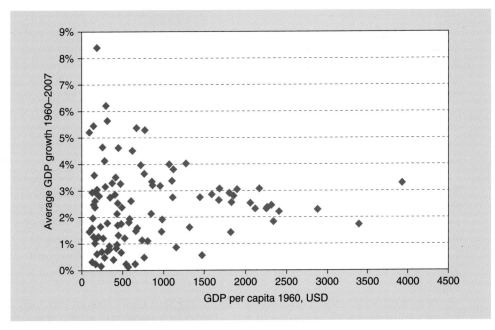

FIGURE 6.6 ● **Convergence – all countries.** There is no tendency for convergence across all countries. *Source:* Penn World Table 6.3 GDP Per Capita of 1960 Mapped Against Average GDP Growth Rates between 1960 and 2007.

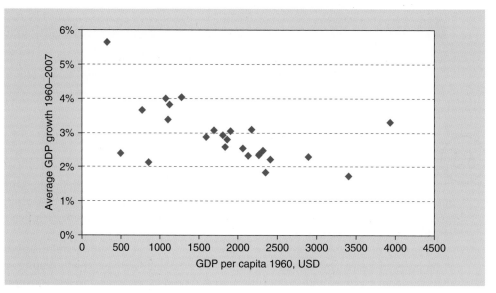

FIGURE 6.7 ● **Convergence – OECD economies.** Within OECD countries, convergence seems to exist. *Source:* Penn World Table 6.1.

there is no evidence of convergence; there is no negative correlation between initial income and subsequent growth. While some poor countries grow very fast, there is a range of growth experiences – some grow quickly, while in others, standards of living fall further.

Figure 6.6 considers a broad range of different economies including developed (OECD) countries, African countries, emerging markets in Asia and some formerly communist economies. If, however, we consider groupings of economies based on similar characteristics, then different results appear. Figure 6.7 shows the same data, but focuses on just the OECD economies – there is now substantial evidence of convergence. The fastest-growing OECD nations were those that were poorest in 1960. Spain, Portugal and Mexico, for example, have grown faster than Germany, France and the United Kingdom. Figures 6.8 and 6.9 show similarly strong evidence in favour of convergence when we examine US states and regions in Western Europe. Convergence is also found when similar charts are drawn for Canadian provinces and Japanese prefectures.

These figures show that when we consider regions or economies that display similar characteristics, we find strong evidence of convergence, so that within similar groups, relatively poor countries grow faster than the relatively rich. We can think of groups of countries as being like different species. Elephants are one species: if you find a small elephant, it is probably still growing and is on its way to becoming the size of an average elephant. But now look at squirrels. Small squirrels will grow to catch up with average squirrels, but they will not catch up to average elephants; all squirrels are small relative to elephants.

Proponents of the neoclassical model refer to the 'iron law of convergence': when they look at similar groupings of regions, they find that, on average, about 2% of the discrepancy between rich and poor regions is removed each year. This convergence occurs slowly – it takes 35 years to reduce the discrepancy by half. However, the evidence suggests that, although it may be slow, some form of convergence is occurring whereby poorer regions

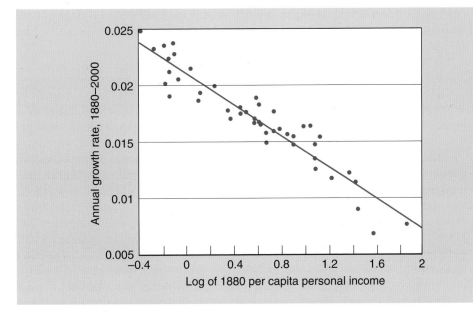

FIGURE 6.8 ● **Convergence – the US states.** Output converges within the United States.
Source: Barro and Sala-i-Martin, *Economic Growth* (New York: McGraw-Hill, 2003).

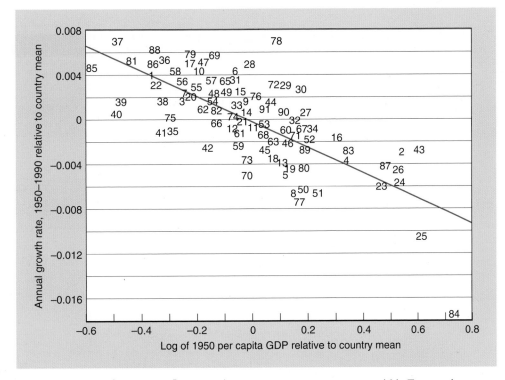

FIGURE 6.9 ● **Convergence – European regions.** Output seems to converge within Europe also.
Source: Barro and Sala-i-Martin, *Economic Growth* (New York: McGraw-Hill, 2003).

(such as the south of Italy or Maine and Arkansas in the United States) do grow faster than wealthier regions (such as the north of Italy or Massachusetts).

RECONCILING THE EVIDENCE

When we consider all countries simultaneously, we find no evidence in favour of convergence (Figure 6.6), but when we consider similar groupings of economies, we find strong evidence (Figures 6.7–6.9). How can we explain this?

The explanation is based on the idea of **conditional convergence**. The neoclassical model does *not* imply that capital-poor countries grow faster than capital-rich countries. Instead, it implies that, among countries sharing the *same* steady state, we will find convergence. To see this, consider Figure 6.10, where we show four economies (A, B, C and D) that differ only in their steady-state capital stock. Countries A and B tend towards steady state 1, while C and D tend towards steady state 2. Note that we have assumed that all four economies share the same production function (they have access to the same technology, the same human capital and so forth), so we are also assuming that their steady states differ only because of differences in investment rates. If we ignored their different steady states and examined all four countries simultaneously for convergence, we would find none. Countries B and D are near their steady state and will grow more slowly than A and C. Overall, we will find no clear negative correlation between initial income and subsequent growth. However, when we compare similar groupings that share a steady state (A and B; C and D), then we will find convergence. Conditional convergence helps explain the mixed evidence in support of convergence in Figures 6.7–6.9, but it also raises the question of why the steady state differs across countries.

> ### KEY POINT
>
> There is no evidence that income levels across all countries are converging, but when similar countries are examined, then the evidence for convergence is strong. This is consistent with the Solow model of decreasing MPK but where countries have different steady states.

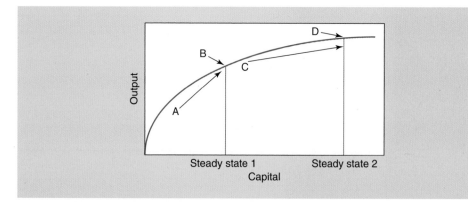

FIGURE 6.10 ● **Conditional convergence.** Countries that start out with capital stocks A and B converge on a lower steady state than countries that start out with capital at C or D.

6.4 Determinants of the Steady State

We have already discussed a wide range of factors that should influence the steady state of the economy – investment, human capital, allocation of talent, corruption and governance, to name a few. But can we use data to assess which of these factors is most important in influencing the steady state?

According to the Solow model, fast-growing economies are those that are far from their steady state. Therefore we have that

Growth in GDP per capita = b × [Steady State GDP − GDP(0)]

where GDP(0) denotes initial income and b is a positive coefficient that determines how rapidly a country converges to its steady state. But our previous reasoning tells us that steady-state GDP is influenced by numerous factors such that

Steady State GDP = (a1 × Education) + (a2 × Investment) + (a3 × X)

where X reflects the influence of any other variables that influence steady-state GDP and a1 and a2 are coefficients that reflect the impact of education and investment on steady-state GDP respectively. We can combine these two equations to get

Growth in GDP per capita = (b × a1 × Education) + (b × a2 × Investment)
+ (b × a3 × X) − (b × GDP(0))

or

Growth in GDP per capita = (c1 × Education) + (c2 × Investment)
+ (c3 × X) − (b × GDP(0))

It is possible to use econometrics, the application of statistical methods to economic data, with published data on GDP, investment, education and different choices for X (e.g. openness, corruption and so forth) and estimate this equation to answer the following questions:

1. *Do countries show convergence?* If GDP growth is *negatively* related to initial income (b > 0), then we have convergence.
2. *Which variables influence the steady state?* Any variable for which c1, c2 or c3 is statistically significant can be said to affect the steady state.
3. *What impact does a variable have on steady-state GDP?* The coefficients c1, c2 and c3 can be used to calculate the long-run impact of different variables on GDP.

Not surprisingly for such an important topic, there is much argument over the appropriate econometric techniques that should be used to estimate this equation and to identify robustly the factors that determine growth. Even so, a number of general points related to the questions above can still be made about this empirical literature.

1. The data seem to support the notion of conditional convergence (b > 0), not surprisingly given Figures 6.7–6.11. This finding in favour of convergence suggests that the marginal product of capital is decreasing and not constant or increasing as in the endogenous growth models. In Section 6.1, we argued that interactions between physical and human capital could lead to a constant MPK if b = 0.7, but estimates from these growth equations suggest that b = 0.3.[1] In other words, interactions with human capital slow down the rate at which the MPK declines, but they are not strong enough to lead to a constant MPK.

2. Most studies find a robust positive effect on the steady state from investment, health and education.

3. The effect of other variables is more controversial and often harder to robustly detect. With relatively few countries to examine and with so many variables being highly correlated (such as health, education and openness), it is difficult reliably to identify the main determinants of the steady state. Some variables, such as openness, are frequently found to be significant, but they sometimes appear to lose their importance when other variables are introduced. Table 6.1 summarizes which economic variables are found to influence the steady state robustly, which ones frequently are found to influence long-run GDP, and which variables have been found important by some researchers, but are not always prevalent.

GOOD AND BAD STEADY STATES

Table 6.2 shows for a selection of countries some of the key variables that influence the steady state. Given our steady-state analysis and the concept of conditional convergence, the table makes for sobering reading. Conditional convergence says that countries that are furthest away from their steady state grow fastest. This is hardly reassuring for the African countries listed who tend to score poorly across most of the indicators, suggesting a poor steady state and poor growth potential. By contrast, India would appear to have better

TABLE 6.1 ● **Determinants of Steady State.**

Many variables are found to have an impact on steady state, but the most robust are investment, education and health.

Always Significant	Frequently Significant	Often Significant	Sometimes Significant
Education – primary school enrolment	Regional dummies (Latin America, Sub-Saharan Africa – negative)	Real exchange rate overvaluation (negative)	Government consumption (negative)
Investment	Rule of law	Black market premiums (negative)	Financial sophistication
Health – life expectancy	Political rights	Primary products (% exports – negative)	Inflation (negative)
	Religious dummies (Confucian, Jewish, Protestant)		Ethnic diversity (negative)
	Openness Degree of capitalism		Civil liberties Revolutions, coups, wars (negative)
			Religious dummies (Buddhism, Catholic)
			Public investment

Source: Sala-i-Martin, 'I just ran four million regressions', *American Economic Review* (May 1997), 87(2): 178–83.

TABLE 6.2 ● **Determinants of Steady State for Selected Countries, 2001.**

Steady state determinants vary widely across countries. Civil Liberty is an index reflecting democratic and political freedoms (1 being highest level of freedom). Fertility is average births per female. Government consumption and investment are expressed as a percentage of GDP, and education and life expectancy are recorded in years.

Country	Civil Liberties (2011)	Fertility (Births per Female) (2009)	Government Consumption (% GDP) (2009)	Education — Average Years of Schooling (2010)	Investment (% GDP) (2009)	Life Expectancy (Years) (2009)
Egypt	5	2.9	11.4	6.4	19.3	70.3
South Africa	2	2.5	21.9	8.2	19.4	51.6
Nigeria	4	5.6	4.8	–	8.8	48.1
Sierra Leone	3	5.2	13.8	2.9	15.1	47.9
US	1	2.1	17.2	12.4	14.2	78.7
South Korea	2	1.3	16.0	11.6	25.9	80.3
Italy	2	1.4	19.7	9.3	21.9	81.3
France	1	2.0	24.6	10.4	19.0	81.1
Japan	2	1.4	19.7	11.5	20.4	82.9
Australia	1	1.9	17.0	12.0	27.5	81.5
Brazil	2	1.8	21.8	7.2	16.5	72.6
Sweden	1	1.9	27.8	11.6	16.6	81.4
Mexico	3	2.1	11.6	8.5	22.4	75.3
India	3	2.7	12.0	4.4	36.5	64.1
Turkmenistan	7	2.4	9.9	–	11.4	65.0

Source: World Bank World Development Indicators except Civil Liberties Index which is from Freedom in the World 2011 (freedomhouse.org).

fundamentals and should benefit from higher growth. These numbers show that being poor does not guarantee growth. But if these poor nations could shift their steady states (and Table 6.1 suggests that government policy can have both positive and negative influences on the steady state), then their growth prospects would improve.

> **KEY POINT**
>
> Econometric studies find that investment, health, education, initial income, and openness to trade are important determinants of a country's steady state.

6.5 Why Is Africa So Poor?

Economic growth in Africa (particularly Sub-Saharan Africa) has been continually disappointing. Figure 6.11 shows growth in real GDP per capita for a range of countries since 1820. For the entire period, Africa has been both the poorest and frequently the

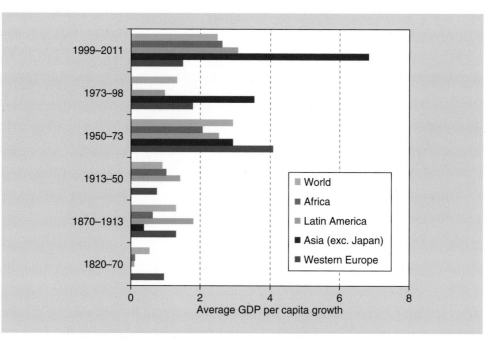

FIGURE 6.11 ● **Performance of major regions, 1820–2011 (1990 $ GDP per capita).** Africa's poor economic performance has been a persistent feature of the world economy. *Source:* Maddison, *Monitoring the World Economy 1820–1992*; OECD and IMF WEO Database.

slowest-growing region so that, as a result, 19 out of the 20 poorest nations in the world are in Africa. Although there have been some success stories, most noticeably Botswana and Mauritius, the region has remained a challenge to policymakers.

Our steady-state analysis helps to explain why Africa has seen such poor growth. Africa scores poorly on many of the key determinants of the steady state: low investment, low educational achievement and low scores on measures of social infrastructure. Moreover, Africa's strong protectionist policies have limited its ability to show convergence. But why has Africa had such low investment and consistently inappropriate government policies?

EFFECTS OF GEOGRAPHY

One widely cited explanation of Africa's poor growth focuses on its **geography** and the related issues of climate and disease. As Figure 6.12 shows, GDP is strongly related to latitude, with incomes generally lower in tropical areas near the equator (though Singapore and Hong Kong are two important exceptions). There is a tropical climate in 93% of Sub-Saharan Africa. The most successful economic areas in Africa are in the north and the south, which are the only non-tropical areas of the continent. The five North African nations have a GDP per capita (2009) of $4523, non-tropical South Africa's 2009 GDP per capita was $5786, while tropical Sub-Saharan Africa's was only $1127. In terms of climate, soil, disease and ecology, tropical regions suffer many handicaps. Agriculture is less productive in tropical areas, and agricultural (and non-agricultural) innovations tend to be designed for the temperate regions, making their adoption problematic in the tropics. These factors place a major restraint on Sub-Saharan Africa's standard of living.

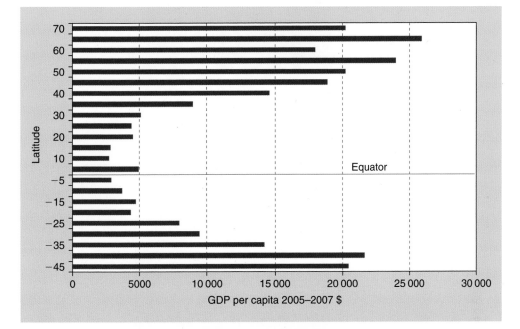

FIGURE 6.12 ● **GDP per capita by latitude.** Incomes tend to be lower closer to the Equator.
Source: Kummu, M. and Varis, O. 'The world by latitudes: A global analysis of human population, development level and environment across the north-south axis over the past half century', *Applied Geography* (2011), 31(2): 495–507. Science Direct-Elsevier.

Linked to the tropical climate are the acute problems that Africa faces from malaria. Every year an estimated 2 million Africans die from malaria (over 20% of total African deaths). Although modern medicine has dramatically reduced the threat of malaria in Southern Europe, the Caribbean and parts of North and South Africa, eradicating malaria from tropical regions remains a huge task. Historically, malarial countries have grown more slowly than others. Between 1965 and 1990, real output per capita in African countries with severe incidence of malaria grew only 0.4% per year, while in other African countries it grew by 2.3%.

Africa also faces serious problems from the spread of AIDS. By 2009, over 15 million Africans are estimated to have died as a result of AIDS. Of the 33 million people with the HIV virus, 22 million are in Sub-Saharan Africa. Because the incidence of AIDS is highest in the age group that is most economically active, this represents a heavy burden in lost output as well as lost lives.

As well as a high proportion of land in the tropics, Bloom and Sachs[2] suggest that Africa's growth is restricted because it is poorly placed to benefit from trade. As Table 6.3 shows, Africa has the highest proportion of its population living in landlocked regions. As a result, trading costs for African economies are much higher than for economies closer to ocean coasts. One way to measure transportation costs is to examine the gap between the cost of imports inclusive of freight and insurance costs, and the cost of exports measured as freight on board; in other words, the cost of a commodity before it is exported and the cost when it arrives. The gap between these prices is 3.6% in the United States, 4.9% in Western Europe, 9.8% in East Asia, 10.6% in Latin America and an extraordinary 19.5%

TABLE 6.3 ● **Geographical Characteristics of Selected Regions.**

Relative to other regions, Sub-Saharan Africa suffers from a large amount of tropical land and landlocked geography.

	GDP Per Capita ($)	Population (millions)	Land Area (mill km²)	Land in Tropics (%)	Population w/100km Coast (%)	Population w/100km Coast/River (%)	Landlocked Population (%)	Distance to Core Market (km)	Coastal Density (pers/km²)
Sub-Saharan Africa	1865	580	24	91	19	21	28	6237	40
Western Europe	19230	383	3	0	53	89	4	922	109
East Asia	10655	1819	14	30	43	60	0	3396	381
South Asia	1471	1219	4	40	23	41	2	5744	387
Transition Economies	3902	400	24	0	9	55	21	2439	32
Latin America	5163	472	20	73	42	45	3	4651	52

Source: Bloom and Sachs, Geography, Demography and Economic Growth in Africa, Brookings Papers on Economic Activity (1999).

in Sub-Saharan Africa. While part of these costs are undoubtedly due to poor transport infrastructure, they also reflect geographical location. If trade is important for growth, geography will act as a handicap for Africa.

COLONIAL INFLUENCES

If geography is a determining influence on economic performance, then Africa has a difficult future ahead because its geography cannot be altered. The existence of these natural handicaps can be used to justify special efforts on the part of rich countries to help fund R&D and treatment of diseases such as AIDS, malaria, TB and others that afflict Africa.

An alternative view argues that geography is not the main determinant of economic success. Instead, it is the quality of institutions that explains low GDP in Africa, and these are in turn explained by the interaction between geography and **colonialism**. In particular, tropical countries provided an inhospitable environment for Western colonists and this affected the institutional structures that they imposed on the countries they colonized.

This alternative argument has two stages. The first is to show that geography is not destiny. Proponents of this position do this by pointing out that Africa's geography has not always hampered its development. In 1500, there were many examples of flourishing African cities that were at least on a par with those of Western Europe (see Figure 6.13).

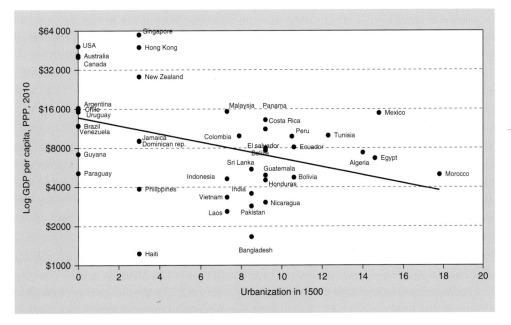

FIGURE 6.13 ● **Urbanization in 1500 versus GDP per capita in 2008.** Poorer countries today were among the most urbanized in 1500, suggesting perhaps that colonial history is more important than geography in explaining why Africa is poor. *Source:* Daron Acemoglu, Simon Johnson and James A. Robinson 'Reversal of fortune: Geography and institutions in the making of the modern world income distribution', *The Quarterly Journal of Economics* (November 2002), 117(4): 1231–94. Oxford University Press.

The second stage of the argument is to offer an alternative explanation for Africa's poor performance. Theorists reason that, where European settlers faced adverse geography (with high settler mortality rates due to tropical diseases and conflict) or a large and developed indigenous population, they did not establish large colonial populations. Instead, the colonizers developed institutions that focused on extracting rents from a country and exporting it to the colonial power – Belgium's King Leopold and his control over the Congo is a famed example. By contrast, in sparsely populated areas or those with a climate more similar to that of Europe, large colonial settlements were set up and the settlers designed institutions aimed at generating value added. After various colonies became independent nations, these institutional forms persisted. In former colonies with large settler populations, high-quality value-adding institutions were established and used, which boosted GDP growth. By contrast, in those with bad geography or large and urbanized indigenous populations, rent-seeking institutions were established. Politics became a battle for control of the state, and society became focused on rent seeking and not entrepreneurship. According to this argument, geography has no direct impact on GDP – its influence works entirely through its impact on the quality of a country's institutions and not all ex-colonies fare badly (e.g. United States and Australia), depending on the interaction of geography and institutions.

ARTIFICIAL BORDERS

Another important route through which colonial history still influences African economic development today is through the creation of artificial borders. Colonizers generally created country borders that suited their needs rather than those of the indigenous population. As a result, many African countries are composed of several large but distinct cultural groups, each with its own language and practices. Ethno-linguistically diverse nations tend to have poor government policy. Such polarized societies may be more prone to competitive rent seeking – each group tries to extract resources from other ethnic groups – and will find it more difficult to reach agreement over public goods (for instance the location of roads and transport routes). This in turn leads to bad social infrastructure, because it produces a gap between the return to individuals and that to society. Easterly and Levine[3] found that high levels of ethno-linguistic diversity are associated with the existence of substantial informal markets, lower financial development, low provision of infrastructure and low education.

Ethno-linguistic diversity may also lead to civil war. Civil wars tend to damage an economy more than conflicts between different nations. Civil wars are fought entirely on a country's own territory and so destroy much of its capital. They tend to leave a legacy of distrust that reduces social capital and hinders economic growth even after the conflicts are over. One study finds, however, that if a society is ethnically either homogenous or very diverse, then the risk of a civil war is not high. Only societies with a few large and competing ethnic groups have a high risk of civil war.[4] This is another way in which institutions can help support economic growth – by helping large but non-majority ethnic groups feel engaged in society and policy and ensuring that power and voice are spread across a population.

Table 6.4 shows two measures of artificial borders. The first is based on a fractal index that measures how straight a country's borders are. A straight border is usually an indication of colonial influence in the creation of a country, since borders that grow slowly over time tend to follow geographical or ethnic lines that tend to be more 'squiggly'. The second

TABLE 6.4 ● Artificial Borders.
Although North America has the most artificially straight borders, Africa's borders separate a far higher share of its ethnic groups.

	Europe	Asia	Africa	North America	South America
Percentage of population belonging to groups partitioned by border	19.9	20.6	48.0	7.6	15.2
Fractal Index of borders (low figure = straighter borders)	0.052	0.037	0.028	0.027	0.036

Source: Alesina, Easterly and Matuszeki, 'Artificial states', NBER Working Paper 12328 (2006).

measure shows the extent to which ethnic groups are 'cut' by a political border line and shows the percentage of a country's population that belongs to a partitioned group. It shows that North America has the lowest fractal index, indicating that it has the highest proportion of artificially straight borders (such as the one between the United States and Canada). However, in the case of North America these borders have not resulted in much separation of ethnic groups. In Africa, on the other hand, not only is the fractal index low, there is also a large proportion of the population that belongs to an ethnic group that has been separated by a border. It is these borders that have added to the institutional problems facing African countries.

Table 6.5 shows the relative standing of institutions in a sample of Southern and Eastern African countries. It shows that, as regions, they do have relatively poor-quality institutions and that, within regions, the richer nations (Botswana and South Africa) have better institutions.

TABLE 6.5 ● Institutional Quality in Africa, 2009.
Africa is characterized by poor governance and institutional quality, although there are some exceptions. Countries are ranked by percentile (0 is the worst and 100 is the best).

Country	Voice and Accountability	Political Stability	Government Effectiveness	Regulatory Quality	Rule of Law	Control of Corruption
Botswana	58.8	79.7	70.0	69.0	67.0	75.7
Democratic Republic of Congo	8.5	2.8	1.9	4.3	1.9	2.9
Kenya	37.4	12.3	31.0	47.1	15.1	11.9
Mozambique	46.9	63.7	43.8	41.9	33.5	41.4
Nigeria	24.2	4.2	8.6	25.7	10.4	14.8
South Africa	66.4	44.3	67.6	64.3	56.1	60.5
Tanzania	43.69	47.6	39.0	38.1	40.1	40.5
Uganda	33.2	15.1	33.8	46.7	40.6	21.4
Zimbabwe	6.6	9.9	2.4	1.4	0.9	1.9

Source: Aggregate Governance Indicators 2009, World Bank, http://www.worldbank.org/governance/wgi/sc_chart.asp.

6.6 The Curse of Natural Resources

Another group of countries that sometimes – though not always – have a disappointing record on growth are those that are heavily reliant on natural resources, particularly oil. Figure 6.14 shows how countries that are highly dependent on natural resource exports have tended to grow more slowly. There are a number of reasons for this poor growth performance:

- *The Dutch disease:* so called because it was first noted when the Netherlands discovered large gas deposits in the North Sea, the Dutch disease occurs because factors of production are diverted to the resource industry and away from other export industries – like manufacturing – primarily due to a stronger exchange rate (we will return to this point in Chapter 19). This has a negative impact on growth, both because the resource is limited and so cannot be the source of long-run growth and because resource industries do not generally create many spillovers of the sort described in the rest of this chapter, so diverting production from manufacturing to resource exploitation reduces the capacity for endogenous growth.

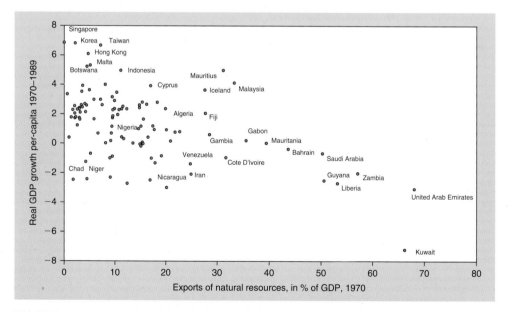

FIGURE 6.14 ● **The curse of natural resources.** Countries that depend on natural resource exports tend to grow more slowly than others. *Source:* Sachs and Warner, 'The curse of natural resources', *European Economic Review* (May 2001), 45(4–6): 827–38. Elsevier.

- *Macroeconomic volatility:* commodity prices tend to be quite volatile and so if your economy is reliant on commodity exports, price fluctuations can have a significant impact on the foreign currency earnings of your economy and can be a major source of economic volatility.
- *Conflict:* there is evidence that resource-based economies are more likely to experience civil conflict, either due to greed (rebel groups hope to profit from the resource) or grievance (local groups feel insufficiently compensated for the negative impact of resource exploitation such as land expropriation and pollution). There is evidence that these conflicts are more likely in oil-based economies or economies with 'lootable' resources such as gems.
- *Weakening institutions:* resource-based economies tend to offer more opportunities for bribery and other rent-seeking behaviour, as those in charge of the allocation of rights, to and income, from the resource will often fall prey to corruption. Additionally, resource economies tend to have a higher incidence of authoritarian governments (possibly because of the higher risk of civil conflict) and they also tend to be more unequal, as the owners of the resource benefit disproportionally from its exploitation. All of these factors tend to weaken institutions and hamper growth.

Interestingly, there is evidence that countries that start with strong institutions are less likely to experience an increase in corruption or a weakening of institutions. For example, Botswana started to exploit its mineral resources in the 1970s and has experienced extremely rapid growth and improvements of living standards since then (though it has suffered from a high level of HIV infection and high levels of inequality). The fact that Botswana had strong institutions before it began exploiting its resources and that those institutions remain strong today seems to be an important reason for its economic success.

> ### KEY POINT
>
> Evidence suggests the economies based on natural resource exports tend to perform badly. This is partly due to factors of production being diverted into the resource industry and partly because of the weakening of institutions that resources can create.

6.7 Does Aid Work?

In the Monterrey Conference of 2002, the rich economies reconfirmed their aim of donating 0.7% of GDP as overseas development assistance (development aid given by rich countries to poor nations, not including disaster relief or food aid). However, as Figure 6.15 shows, very few of the major donors are even close to that target. One reason for this is that the balance of evidence suggests that this aid has done very little to boost GDP or reduce poverty in the recipient. To some extent the failure of aid in the past reflects failures of both donors and recipients in administering its delivery, but there are also some strong arguments to suggest that even well-administered aid may not be effective.

We can use our growth models to explain the disappointing results of development aid. According to Section 6.5, Africa suffers from a number of factors that lead it to have a poor steady state, a low MPK and a low investment rate. Our analysis in Chapter 4 says that countries with high investment rates have high GDP. Based on this kind of thinking, aid policy in the 1950s and 1960s was to provide funds to boost investment. However, if a country has

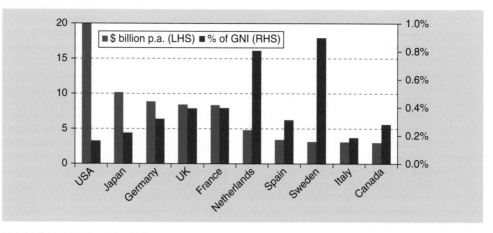

FIGURE 6.15 ● **Major aid donors.** Very few countries have achieved the target of donating 0.7% of GDP. *Source:* OECD.

a low MPK, any funds it receives will not be invested but used for other purposes due to low rates of return on investment projects. Only if aid changes investment incentives or if a country has a high MPK but is short of funds will aid boost investment.

This discussion has so far focused on the failures of aid due to the nature of recipient economies, but a further reason why aid has not always been successful in raising GDP is the motivation of donor countries in giving aid. Many countries focus on providing aid to former colonies, and during the Cold War the United States and the Soviet Union often used aid as a political rather than economic instrument. Certainly, Figure 6.16 indicates that aid is not necessarily directed to where poverty is most acute.

Table 6.6 summarizes the evidence on aid effectiveness from a recent meta-study (a study of studies). Overall, it shows that the balance of evidence across 103 studies is that

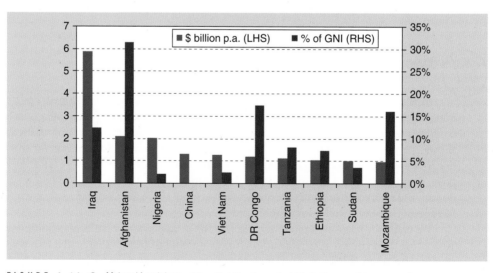

FIGURE 6.16 ● **Major aid recipients.** The distribution of aid is influenced by many factors. *Source:* OECD.

TABLE 6.6 ● **Evidence on Aid Effectiveness.**
The balance of evidence suggests that development aid has no significant effect on economic development.

Hypothesis Tested	Number of Studies Evaluated	Consensus of Results
Does aid increase saving and investment?	43	75% of aid is crowded out by lower saving
Does aid increase growth?	103	No significant effect
Is aid effective in moderation but harmful in excess?	22	No evidence
Is aid more effective when policy is good?	28	No evidence
Is aid effective when local institutions are strong?	10	Some evidence but too few studies

Sources: Doucouligos, H. and Paldam, M. 'The aid effectiveness literature. The sad results of 40 years of research', *Journal of Economic Surveys* (2009), 23: 433–61 and Doucouligos, H. and Paldam, M. 'Conditional aid effectiveness. A meta study', *Journal of International Development* (2010), 22: 391–410.

there is no significant effect of aid on growth. Studies of the direct impact of aid projects tend to find positive effects, but it seems that these positive effects are offset by negative indirect effects such as rent seeking, and the aid-related Dutch disease (where factors of production are diverted from private-sector export industries towards aid-related activities). There is also evidence that aid reduces other forms of investment so that, on average, $1 of aid spending only results in a $0.25 rise in investment.

Table 6.6 also summarizes the evidence on a number of hypotheses concerning aid. First, some have speculated that aid is less effective when granted in large amounts. In fact, the evidence suggests that small-scale aid is no more effective than large amounts. Second, many donors have been convinced by the argument that aid is effective in countries with good policies, while in fact the balance of evidence suggests that this is not the case. Finally, some writers have proposed that aid is more effective in countries with strong institutions. The evidence suggests that this might be true, but there are too few studies of this proposition to be sure of that result.

KEY POINT

The balance of evidence suggests that aid has not systematically boosted GDP growth. This may be due to deficiencies in how it has been administered or to the fundamental economic distortions that it creates.

SUMMARY

In section 6.1, we showed that assuming that the MPK is constant rather than decreasing leads to dramatically different predictions from the growth model we developed in Chapters 4 and 5. With constant marginal product, a steady-state level of output does not exist, and we should not expect to find convergence across countries. Interactions between physical and human capital may postpone diminishing MPK and even lead to a constant MPK.

In Section 6.2, we saw that, if spillovers and interactions are particularly marked, it may even be that the MPK is increasing, in which case poverty traps may exist. In a poverty trap, individuals have poor incentives to invest in either human or physical capital. As a result, wealthy nations get wealthier while the poorer nations stay poor.

In Section 6.3, we considered the evidence for different assumptions about the MPK. When we examined growth since 1950 among a wide range of countries, we found no evidence of convergence; poor countries do not grow faster than rich countries. This suggests that the assumption of diminishing MPK is inappropriate. However, when we considered similar groupings of countries, like the OECD nations, we found strong evidence of convergence. We introduced the notion of conditional convergence, which is the idea that countries grow fastest when they are furthest away from their steady state, but that different countries will have different steady states. As a result, only similar nations will show any evidence of convergence.

In Section 6.4, we examined what determines the steady state of a nation and found that investment, health, education, and an open economy are important.

In Section 6.5, we reviewed the disappointing growth performance of Africa. For over two centuries, Africa has been both the poorest and the slowest-growing region in the world economy. In part this can be attributed to Africa's poor steady state due to low levels of investment, education, the closed nature of African economies and poor social infrastructure. However, ethnic diversity, the landlocked nature of much of Africa and its tropical climate and diseases are also important. Africa also suffers negatively from poor-quality institutions, which may be a legacy of the interaction between geography and colonialism.

In Section 6.6, we assessed the evidence on the poor growth performance of many natural resource-based economies. There is evidence that natural resource exploitation diverts factors of production from other more growth-enhancing activities, as well as weakening institutions and increasing the likelihood of civil conflict. However, there is some evidence that countries with strong institutions can manage their resource wealth without these negative effects.

In Section 6.7, we considered the role of developmental aid for poor countries such as those in much of Africa. Every year rich nations spend around 0.25% of their GDP on overseas development assistance. Overall, the balance of evidence suggests that this aid has not been effective. One reason why aid has not always been effective in boosting GDP is that it has often been used by donor countries to achieve political rather than economic aims.

CONCEPTUAL QUESTIONS

1. (Section 6.1) Do models that assume decreasing MPK offer a theory of economic growth?

2. (Section 6.1) Can human knowledge and ingenuity support a constant MPK?

3. (Section 6.2) If individuals live in an area characterized by a poverty trap, will they not just move to a prosperous region? Should policymakers therefore worry about poverty traps?

4. (Section 6.3) Can conditional convergence explain *any* pattern of cross-country differences in standards of living?

5. (Section 6.4) Do empirical studies of the determinants of the steady state tell us anything more than that the richest economies are OECD economies? Are OECD economies a successful blueprint for emerging nations, and can their key factors be easily transplanted? Why?

6. (Section 6.4) What role can governments play in improving the steady state? What does this imply about the relationship between the size of government and GDP per capita?

7. (Section 6.5) What steps can a country take to change its institutions? What difficulties might it experience?

8. (Section 6.5) What incentives do pharmaceutical companies have to undertake R&D in medicines for treating AIDS? Malaria? Erectile dysfunction? What can policymakers do about this?

9. (Section 6.7) Does it matter if development aid just boosts government consumption in poor African economies? Why or why not?

10. (Section 6.7) If it is good institutions rather than good policies that matter, what implications does this have for aid agencies?

ANALYTICAL QUESTIONS

1. (Section 6.1) Assume that there are no diminishing returns to capital and that, as shown in Figure 6.1, output is simply a constant proportion (*a*) of the capital stock. Investment is also a constant fraction (*b*) of output, and depreciation is a proportion (d) of the capital stock. The change in the capital stock is total investment minus depreciation. Show how the proportionate rate of change of the capital stock depends on the relative magnitudes of *a, b* and d. What happens to the growth of capital if *b* doubles from 0.1 to 0.2?

2. (Section 6.3) Suppose that two economies share a common steady state so that there is convergence between them. The poorer country closes 2% of the income gap between them each year. What proportion of the initial gap in income between the two countries is closed after 20 years? After 40 years how much of the initial gap remains?

3. (Section 6.3) Repeat the analysis of Figure 6.10 when the high-investment-rate economy also has access to more productive technology. What does this imply about the scale of inequality we should expect to find across countries?

4. (Section 6.3) Draw the MPK schedule so that, over a certain initial range of capital, there is increasing MPK and then this is followed by diminishing MPK, until the MPK declines to a level higher than that achieved in poor countries. What pattern of cross-country growth will this produce? How does this compare with the data described in this and earlier chapters?

CHAPTER 7

Unemployment and the Labour Market

Key Concepts

Active Labour Market Spending	Employment Rate	Participation Rate
Beveridge Curve	Labour Force	Real Wage
Employment Protection Legislation (EPL)	Marginal Product of Labour	Unemployment Rate
	Natural Rate of Unemployment	Wage Bargaining

Overview

In this chapter we consider the final determinant of how much output a country can produce: the number of people employed. We begin by reviewing the key data definitions for the labour force and examine how these variables differ across countries and demographic groups. We then complete our analysis of long-run growth by examining the impact of capital accumulation and technological progress on the labour market and show how higher productivity generates higher wages but may not change the unemployment rate. This leads to the notion of a country's natural rate of unemployment – a long-run equilibrium concept that determines what fraction of the workforce is economically active. We show how this natural rate depends on the structure of product and labour markets and review its key determinants. We examine how the natural rate is related to flows into and out of unemployment and to employment protection legislation and labour market reform.

7.1 Labour Market Data

Not everyone in the population is involved in the labour market, as shown in Figure 7.1. The first important distinction is between the working-age population (normally defined as those aged between 15 and 64) and the rest of the population. But not all of the working-age population is in the labour market. Many will be taking full-time educational courses, some will be institutionalized (for instance, in jail), others sick or simply not wanting a job (for instance, those who remain at home raising children or caring for relatives). The remainder – all those of working age who are willing and able to work – make up the **labour force**.

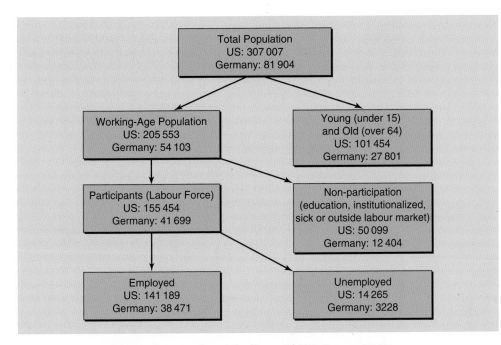

FIGURE 7.1 ● Labour market status of population (thousands) 2010. *Source:* OECD.

The proportion of the civilian non-institutional population who are in the labour force is called the **participation rate**. The labour force in turn is made up of those who have a job – the employed – and those who are willing to work but do not have a job – the unemployed. The proportion of the labour force employed defines the **employment rate** and the proportion of the labour force unemployed defines the **unemployment rate**.

One complication in measuring unemployment is who counts as being unemployed. The best measure is one based on survey data that counts respondents as being unemployed if they do not have a job but are actively seeking work. But some countries calculate unemployment numbers on the basis of whether individuals are entitled to receive unemployment benefits. Because not everyone without a job receives unemployment benefits, and because not everyone receiving benefits is looking for a job, this is not a reliable indicator of unemployment. When examining cross-country evidence on unemployment, consistent definitions based on survey data are important.

Table 7.1 shows variations across OECD countries for a range of labour market variables. For every variable there are major cross-country differences and these will make a significant difference to GDP per capita. For instance, in Italy only around 57% of the population is employed, compared to 68% in the United States. The average of hours worked is also larger in the United States.

TABLE 7.1 ● Cross-Country Variation in Labour Market Statistics, 2009.

Early retirement index is 100 – participation rate of 55–64 years; weekly hours excludes self-employed.

	% of 15–24 Year Olds in Employment	Early Retirement	% of Women Employed	% Part-time Employment	% Part-time Jobs Held by Females	Average Usual Full-time Weekly Hours	Employment Rate	Unemployment Rate
Australia	61.0	33.3	67.5	24.7	70.9	42.5	72.0	5.7
Czech Republic	26.5	40.4	57.5	3.9	68.7	41.1	65.4	6.8
France	31.1	58.6	60.3	13.3	79.8	39.3	64.1	9.1
Germany	46.6	36.2	66.1	21.9	80.4	40.0	70.4	7.8
Italy	21.7	43.3	46.8	15.8	77.6	39.8	57.5	7.9
Japan	39.9	20.2	65.0	20.3	69.9		70.0	5.3
Netherlands	67.8	38.3	71.4	36.7	75.0	37.5	75.8	3.9
New Zealand	51.6	20.5	69.6	22.5	71.9	42.8	72.9	6.3
Norway	53.2	27.2	76.0	20.4	70.8	38.0	76.5	3.2
Spain	30.8	43.3	53.9	11.1	79.3	40.3	60.6	18.1
Sweden	38.0	26.7	71.5	14.6	64.2	38.7	72.2	8.5
Switzerland	61.9	22.9	75.6	26.2	81.1	40.9	79.2	4.2
United Kingdom	52.1	33.9	67.1	23.9	75.8	42.0	70.6	7.8
United States	46.9	34.8	66.2	14.1	66.5	41.3	67.6	9.4

Source: OECD, Labour Market Statistics (2011).

(7.2) A Long-Run Model of the Labour Market

Chapters 3 to 6 focused on long-run developments in GDP per capita and on how capital accumulation and technological progress affect output. We now complete this analysis by considering how these factors affect the labour market.

LABOUR DEMAND AND THE PRODUCTION FUNCTION

The key feature of the production function for the labour market is the **marginal product of labour** (**MPL**) – the amount of extra output that one more worker can produce *keeping fixed the stock of capital and the level of technology*. The MPL is assumed to be decreasing with the level of employment – 'too many cooks spoil the broth', as shown in Figure 7.2.

When a firm considers how many workers to employ, the MPL plays a key role. Each additional worker produces extra output equal to the MPL. If the firm can sell this output for a price P, then hiring one more worker yields additional revenue of P × MPL. Every additional worker increases a firm's costs: the firm has to pay wages, employment taxes, recruitment and training costs and so forth. We summarize these costs in a wage term, W. If P × MPL exceeds W, then hiring an extra worker leads to an increase in profits, while if P × MPL is less than W, profits fall. Alternatively, we can say if MPL > W/P, the firm should hire workers, and if MPL < W/P, the firm should reduce its workforce. The term W/P is the **real wage** and reflects how much the firm has to pay its workforce relative to the price of its output. The firm is at its profit-maximizing employment level when the real wage just equals the MPL.

We can use the MPL to arrive at a labour demand curve – a relationship between the firm's real wage and the level of employment demanded by firms. As we change the level of the real wage, as in Figure 7.3, we alter the desired level of employment. Therefore the MPL traces out a negative relationship between real wages and labour demand; in other words, *the MPL curve is the labour demand curve*.

We now use this result to show what happens to labour demand when there is capital accumulation and technological progress. An increase in either the stock of capital or the level of technology means that each worker becomes more productive – for a given level

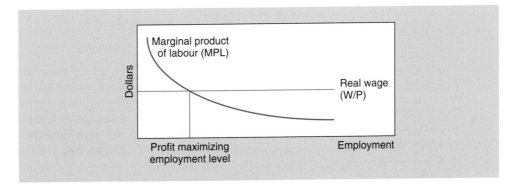

FIGURE 7.2 ● **Diminishing marginal product of labour (MPL).** As more hours are worked, with a fixed stock of machines and a given technology, the marginal product of labour falls.

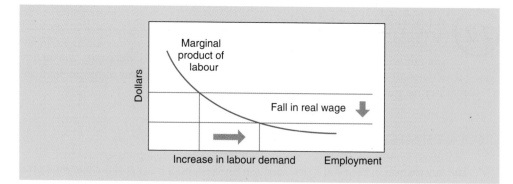

FIGURE 7.3 ● **Declining real wage leads to higher labour demand.** A fall in real wages will raise the firm's profit-maximizing level of labour demand.

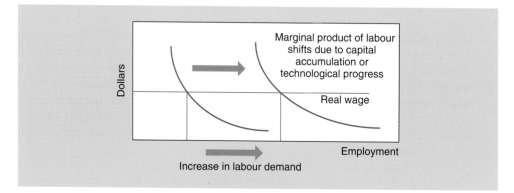

FIGURE 7.4 ● **Effect of capital accumulation and technological progress on labour demand.** More capital and better technology increase the marginal product of labour and raise the demand for labour at a given real wage.

of employment, the marginal product of labour increases, and the MPL curve shifts out, as in Figure 7.4. Because the MPL and labour demand curves are the same, investment and technological progress shifts out the labour demand curve to the right.

LABOUR SUPPLY

To complete our analysis, we must also consider labour supply. When the real wage increases, it affects the supply of labour in two ways. First, it becomes more expensive *not* to work. The cost of enjoying another hour of leisure is the wage you would have earned if, instead, you worked. An increase in real wages makes leisure more expensive and, in itself, leads to an increase in the supply of labour. This is called the *substitution effect* – as the price of a good increases (in this case leisure), people substitute something for it (in this case work).

But there is a second, offsetting effect when the real wage rises. People become wealthier and want to consume more of most goods, including leisure. This *income effect* leads people to consume more leisure and supply less labour as real wages rise. What happens to the supply of labour when wages increase depends on whether the income effect or the substitution effect dominates. In Figure 7.5a we show the case in which the substitution effect dominates and labour supply is increasing with the real wage. In Figure 7.5b, the income effect dominates. Finally, in Figure 7.5c, we show what happens if the income and substitution effect exactly offset each other.

The case shown in Figure 7.5c offers the best explanation of the long-run facts of the labour market – no trend increase in unemployment, but substantial increases in both labour productivity and real wages. To see why, consider Figure 7.6. As capital accumulation and technological progress grew between 1900 and 1950, the MPL increased, causing an outward shift of the labour demand curve. But the labour supply curve is vertical – no additional hours are supplied. As a result, firms compete among themselves for workers and bid wages up. Firms are prepared to pay these higher wages because productivity has increased. But because of the vertical supply curve, the higher wages do not lead to extra hours worked. Competition between firms continues until the real wage has been bid up to offset the productivity improvements, and firms no longer wish to hire more worker hours. At this point, labour demand is once more equal to labour supply. Further increases in labour demand bring forth additional increases in wages. The long-run impact of capital accumulation and technological progress is therefore an increase in average wages and no change in employment. Further long-run productivity improvements, whether from capital accumulation or technological progress, feed through one for one into real wages.

Figure 7.6 suggests that over time the employment rate remains approximately constant. Over the business cycle, employment/unemployment will show short-term fluctuations around this level, but eventually it will return to this *equilibrium* level. Economists refer to this equilibrium as the **natural rate of unemployment**. The natural rate is a long-run concept that characterizes the average unemployment rate over, say, a decade.

KEY POINT

Over the long run, increases in the capital stock and technological progress shift the labour demand curve but, because of a limited labour supply response, they produce equal increases in productivity and wages and no change in the employment rate.

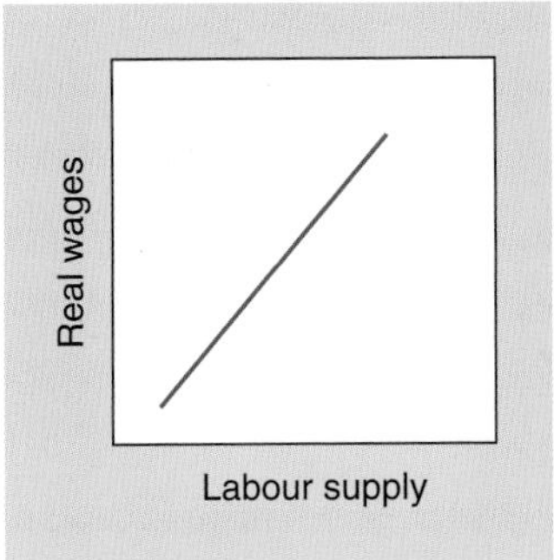

FIGURE 7.5a ● Substitution effect dominates.

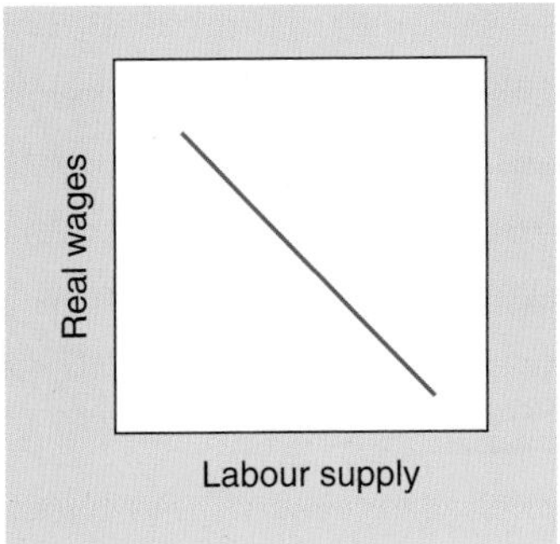

FIGURE 7.5b ● Income effect dominates.

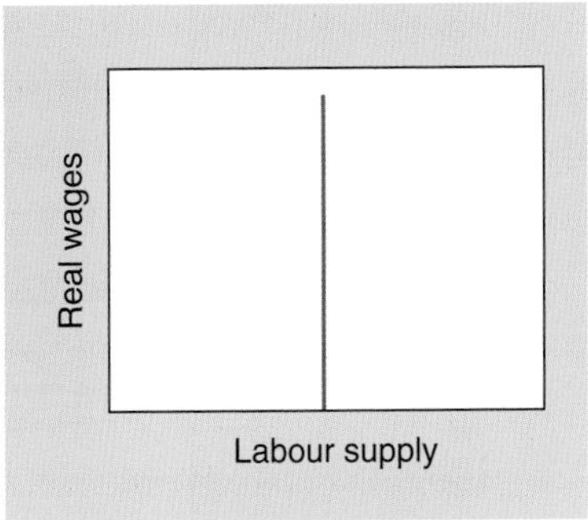

FIGURE 7.5c ● Income and substitution effect cancel out. How labour supply responds to a wage depends on the relative size of the income and substitution effects.

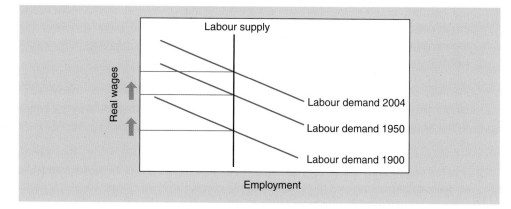

FIGURE 7.6 ● **Long-run model of labour market.** If the long-run supply curve of labour is vertical, rightward shifts in the demand for labour generate higher real wages at a constant level of employment.

7.3   The Natural Rate of Unemployment

Figure 7.7 shows OECD estimates of the natural rate of unemployment for several countries. These marked variations in the natural rate of unemployment reflect differences in the underlying structure and policies of countries, as we outline in this section.

INTUITION BEHIND THE MODEL: COMPETING MONOPOLY POWERS

In outlining our model of unemployment, we move away from the assumption that the labour and product markets are competitive. Instead, we examine a model where both firms and workers have monopoly power – they can influence the prices or wages that they charge and do not have to accept the going market rate.

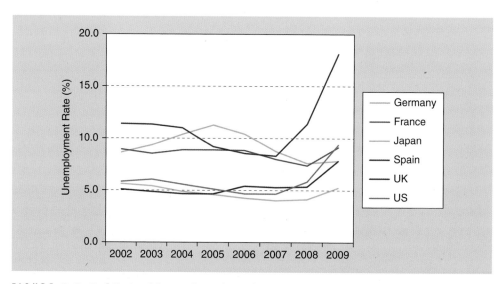

FIGURE 7.7 ● **Estimates of the natural rate of unemployment.** *Source:* OECD.

When firms have monopoly power, they set price above cost. This means that they try to set prices at a certain level above wages (an important component of costs) and thus put downward pressure on the real wage (the wage relative to prices). Monopoly power in the labour force reflects workers' ability to influence their own wage rather than have to accept the established market rate. The most obvious form of such monopoly power is trade unions, and this is how we will think of monopoly power in the model. However, you do not need to belong to a trade union to be able to influence your wage. Many workers have some form of monopoly power simply because of the hassle to the firm of hiring a replacement, including having the position vacant for a time and advertising and hiring costs. For all these reasons, the firm has an incentive to keep people in employment, which gives employees some ability to influence their wage relative to the market average. We assume that workers seek as high a real wage as possible, but the higher unemployment is, the more cautious they are in their wage demands.

This model suggests that unemployment is the mechanism that reconciles the monopoly demands of firms and workers. Market equilibrium requires that the demands of firms and workers be in agreement. This can only occur when unemployment is at a level that leads unions to seek real wages consistent with the profit margins that firms seek. The more monopoly power either firms or workers have, the higher the natural rate of unemployment will be.

KEY POINT

To explain unemployment, we need to introduce monopoly power in the product and labour markets.

7.4 A Diagrammatic Analysis

Figure 7.8 shows the model diagrammatically. The horizontal line is the firm's price-setting curve: it shows the real wage consistent with the firm's desired profit margin. For simplicity, we assume that the only costs a firm faces are its wages, that the marginal output of workers is constant and that the firm wants a profit margin of x%. The price (P) of the firm's output therefore equals $W(1 + x/100)$, where W is the wage rate (or unit labour cost). This pricing rule sets $P/W = 1 + x/100$ or alternatively $W/P = 1/(1 + x/100)$. Again for simplicity, we also assume in Figure 7.8 that the firm's desired profit margin (x) is always the same, regardless of the rate of unemployment – the price-setting curve, therefore, is a flat line.

The other part of Figure 7.8 is the wage-setting curve. This downward-sloping line shows the real wage that trade unions seek for a given unemployment rate. The higher the level of unemployment, the more restrained unions' wage demands are. The intersection of the price- and wage-setting curves is an equilibrium point where the real wage that firms are prepared to pay equals the real wage that the unions demand. This is the natural rate of unemployment. *Only at this level of unemployment are the wage demands of workers consistent with the profit margins that firms seek.*

Consider the case where unemployment is at the low rate of U_L. With unemployment so low, the real wage demands of workers are too high for firms. Unemployment will start to rise above U_L towards the natural rate as firms reduce employment. Rising unemployment leads unions to moderate their wage demands. Eventually, the increase in unemployment produces enough wage restraint that the demands of firms and workers are consistent, and unemployment stabilizes at its natural rate.

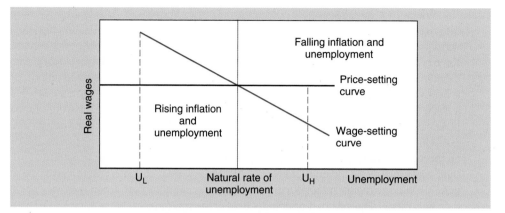

FIGURE 7.8 ● **Determinants of the natural rate of unemployment.** When unemployment is above the natural rate, the wage that firms are prepared to pay exceeds the wage that labour is able to negotiate; the opposite is true when unemployment is below the natural rate.

If, instead, the unemployment rate is above the natural rate, for instance at U_H, the process works in reverse. At this level of unemployment, union wage demands are modest, and firms can achieve a high profit margin. In response they start to hire more workers, so that unemployment falls towards the natural rate.

> ### KEY POINT
>
> Unemployment is the mechanism that reconciles the wage demands of workers with the profit margins sought by firms. The greater the monopoly power of either firms or workers, the higher the unemployment rate.

7.5 Determinants of the Natural Rate

We have characterized the behaviour of firms by the price-setting rule

$$W/P = 1 / (1 + x/100)$$

where x is the firm's desired mark-up. We can also characterize the behaviour of unions by

$$W/P = A - bu$$

where u denotes the unemployment rate, so that union wage demands are lower when unemployment is high. The constant A reflects the factors that influence the wages that trade unions demand, and the coefficient b determines the sensitivity of wage demands to unemployment.

In equilibrium, the wage demands of workers must be consistent with the price-setting decisions of firms, so that

$$1/(1 + x/100) = A - bu$$

We can rearrange this to arrive at an expression for the natural rate of unemployment (u^*):

$$u^* = (1/b) (A - 1/(1 + x/100))$$

Therefore, we can think of three separate influences on the natural rate:

1. *Product market power* (*x*). The greater is monopoly power in the product market, the higher is unemployment.
2. *The sensitivity of wage demands to unemployment* (*b*). Unemployment is the means of reconciling the competing demands of firms and workers. The less responsive wage demands are, the higher unemployment must be.
3. *The monopoly power of trade unions* (*A*). The greater the strength of the unions, the higher their wage demands will be. This leads to higher unemployment.

We now proceed to examine the institutional factors that affect each of these three influences.

PRODUCT MARKET COMPETITION AND THE NATURAL RATE

As we change the monopoly power of firms and the size of their profit margin, we shift the position of the price-setting curve and change the natural rate of unemployment. In a country with more powerful monopolies, firms set prices that are high relative to wages, which implies a low real wage. The price-setting curve shifts down, leading to a higher natural rate of unemployment. The intuition is straightforward: monopolists charge a higher price and produce less output and thus set a lower level of employment. In order for unions to accept these low real wages, unemployment has to be high. Therefore less competitive product markets lead to higher unemployment. Figure 7.9 shows that, across OECD countries, economies with less competitive product markets do have lower employment rates, as our model predicts.

THE INFLUENCE OF LABOUR MARKET STRUCTURE

Figure 7.10 shows two economies that differ only in their labour market structure. The economy in which workers have more monopoly power has a wage-setting curve further to the right and has a higher natural rate of unemployment. The labour force may be able

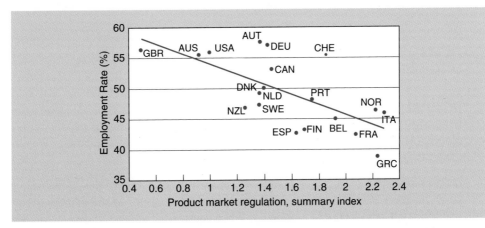

FIGURE 7.9 ● **Employment and product market competitiveness in OECD countries.** More regulated and less competitive product markets lead to lower levels of employment. *Source:* Nicolleti, Bassanini, Ernst, Jean, Santiago and Swaim, Product and Labour Markets Interactions in OECD Countries, Economic Department Working Papers 312.

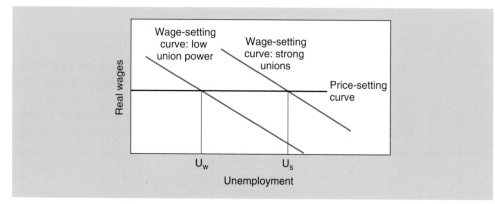

FIGURE 7.10 ● **Stronger unions lead to higher unemployment.** If labour power increases, it may cause higher unemployment with little gain in terms of higher real wages. Here, because the price-setting curve is flat, more labour union power simply increases unemployment from U_w to U_s.

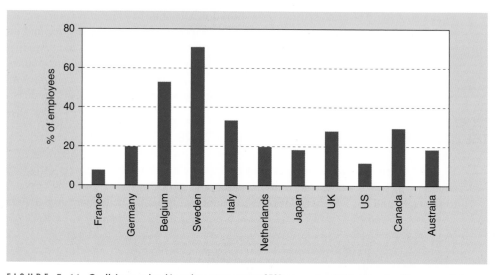

FIGURE 7.11 ● **Union membership and coverage among OECD economies, 2007.** The significance of labour unions differs substantially across countries. *Source:* OECD.

to exercise more monopoly power for five reasons: (1) strong trade union membership and union rights; (2) generous unemployment benefits; (3) large numbers of long-term unemployed; (4) regional and skill mismatch; and (5) high levels of taxes on labour. We now consider each of these factors and how they vary across countries.

UNION MEMBERSHIP The more members a union has, or the more people its negotiations cover, the more monopoly power the union can exploit. Figure 7.11 shows measures of trade union strength across OECD economies. When considering union influence, we need to distinguish between membership and coverage. Coverage (or collective bargaining) refers to the proportion of the workforce whose pay is determined by union negotiations – within a firm or industry, wage negotiations by unions are often extended to non-union members. Empirical studies suggest that coverage influences unemployment more than union membership does.

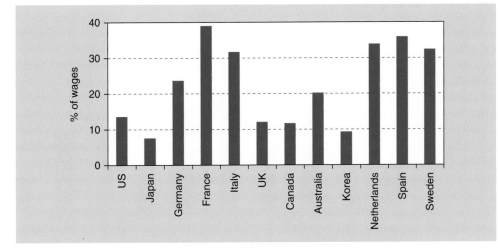

FIGURE 7.12 ● **Unemployment benefit replacement ratios, 2007.** Replacement ratio shows unemployment benefit as a share of previous earnings. *Source:* OECD.

UNEMPLOYMENT BENEFITS   If unemployment benefits are high and last for a long time, they increase the monopoly power of those employed in two ways. First, generous benefits cushion the effects of being unemployed and lessen the motivation to look for new work. This reduces competition for jobs. Second, generous unemployment benefits also reduce the cost of becoming unemployed and these make the employed more aggressive in their wage demands.

Figure 7.12 shows the **replacement rate** for a variety of OECD economies. The replacement ratio is unemployment benefits expressed as a percentage of previous earnings. Most countries have reasonably generous replacement rates for the first year, but after this benefits fall substantially. This is intended to give people protection against the initial shock of unemployment while minimizing the negative impact (the rightward shift in the wage-setting curve due to the reduced threat of unemployment). The positive effects of unemployment benefits arise from two sources: first, as an insurance policy to workers; and second, because governments are effectively subsidizing job searches. Benefits encourage the unemployed worker to spend more time searching for a job that is more suitable to them rather than having to accept a first job offer. The better the match between job and worker, the higher the productivity in a country, so subsidizing job searches has social benefits.

PROPORTION OF LONG-TERM UNEMPLOYED   The monopoly power of those in employment is lessened if the unemployed compete effectively with the employed for jobs. However, the greater the proportion of long-term unemployed, the less intense this competition is. The longer people are unemployed, the more work-relevant skills they lose, and the lower their chance of becoming employed. As a result, the greater the proportion of long-term unemployed, the more monopoly power the employed possess. This leads to a rightward shift in the wage-setting curve and upward pressure on unemployment.

Figure 7.13 shows, for a variety of economies, the proportion of unemployed who have been unemployed for six months or more and for a year or more. Those countries in the figure with high levels of unemployment (e.g. France, Germany and Italy) also have high levels of long-term unemployed. Note the low levels of long-term unemployed in the United States. As we shall see, the American labour market is particularly effective at finding jobs for the unemployed quickly.

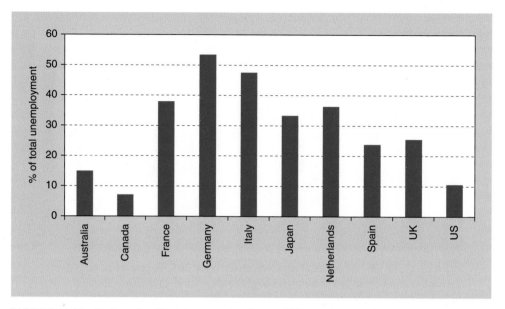

FIGURE 7.13 ● **Proportion of long-term unemployed among OECD economies, 2008.** In Europe the proportion of those unemployed who have been without work for many months is higher than in North America and Japan. *Source:* OECD.

REGIONAL AND SKILL-BASED MISMATCH   If one area of the economy is booming but is in a different part of the country from an area that is doing badly, then the employed will face weaker competition from the unemployed if there is little mobility across regions (see Figure 7.14). Similarly, if the unemployed are mostly unskilled, but the employed have high levels of skill, then unemployment will not effectively restrain the wage demands of the employed. Therefore, for a given level of unemployment, the greater the regional or skill mismatch, the higher the natural rate of unemployment.

One simple measure of labour market efficiency is the **Beveridge curve**. This shows the relationship between the vacancies rate (job openings as a percentage of the workforce) and the unemployment rate. Naturally, there is a negative relationship between the two, as rising unemployment is generally associated with fewer vacancies and vice versa. The position of the unemployment/vacancies curve is a measure of labour market mismatch. If the economy can simultaneously support significant unemployment and vacancies, then the labour market is not functioning efficiently. Figure 7.15 shows the Beveridge curve for the United States between 2000 and 2010. Over most of this period the relationship between unemployment and vacancies was remarkably stable and indicated a relatively efficient matching process. However, around 2009, the curve appeared to move out as vacancies increased without a corresponding fall in unemployment. This move could either represent a short-term timing effect, as unemployment tends to fall more slowly than vacancies rise at the end of the recession, or a longer-term shift in the whole Beveridge curve – indicating decreased efficiency of the US labour market.

LABOUR AND CONSUMPTION TAXES   Because of taxes, it is important to distinguish between the *consumer* and the *producer* real wage – a distinction we have ignored so far. The real wage is the nominal wage divided by the price, but the relevant wages and prices differ for the producer and the consumer. For consumers, the wage is what they receive after the deduction of taxes. The producer wage is the gross wage that firms pay out plus any additional employer

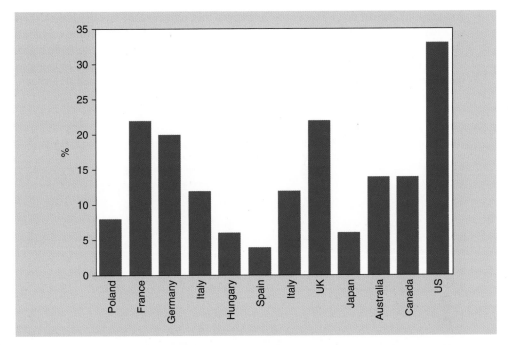

FIGURE 7.14 ● **Percentage of population who change regions per year.** Labour mobility is higher in the United States than in most other developed economies. *Source:* OECD.

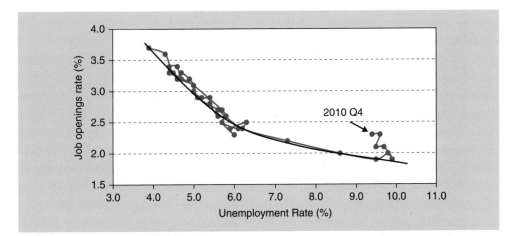

FIGURE 7.15 ● **The Beveridge curve, USA, 2000–10.** The relationship between the vacancy rate and the unemployment rate is usually quite stable. An outward shift in the Beveridge curve may indicate a less efficient labour market. *Source:* Bureau of Economic Analysis, Bureau of Labour Statistics and Congressional Budget.

taxes or social security contributions. Two tax rates influence the gap between the producer and consumer real wage: payroll taxes (taxes that either the employer or employee pay and that are normally related to social security contributions) and income taxes. Some economists also include consumption taxes such as VAT (value-added tax) and GST (goods and services tax), since these reduce consumers' purchasing power. However, since these taxes are paid whether you are employed or not, it is not clear how much they influence the labour market (the same is true to a lesser extent for income tax). These tax wedges shift the wage-setting curve further to the right and thus increase the natural rate. The wage curve shifts out because the higher taxes are, the greater the wage that unions seek to provide a given real standard of living for their members. As Table 7.2 shows, these tax wedges are large in most developed countries.

TABLE 7.2 ● Tax Wedges in OECD Countries, 2009.

Tax wedges drive a gap between the real wages workers take home and the cost of labour to employers. In many developed economies these tax wedges are very large.

Country	Income Tax	Social Security Contributions		Total Tax Wedge
		Employee	Employer	
Belgium	21.1	10.7	23.3	55.2
Hungary	15.9	12.8	24.6	53.4
Germany	17.3	17.3	16.3	50.9
France	9.9	9.6	29.7	49.2
Italy	15.0	7.2	24.3	46.5
Sweden	13.9	5.3	23.9	43.2
Finland	18.6	5.1	18.7	42.4
Czech Republic	8.3	8.2	25.4	41.9
Greece	7.1	12.5	21.9	41.5
Denmark	29.1	10.3	0.0	39.4
Spain	10.3	4.9	23.0	38.2
Netherlands	15.1	13.8	9.1	38.0
Turkey	10.5	12.9	14.2	37.5
Norway	19.1	6.9	11.3	37.4
OECD average	13.2	8.5	14.8	36.4
Poland	5.6	15.5	12.9	34.0
United Kingdom	14.6	8.3	9.6	32.5
Canada	13.9	6.5	10.3	30.8
United States	13.4	7.0	9.0	29.4
Switzerland	9.4	10.0	10.0	29.3
Japan	7.0	10.8	11.4	29.2
Australia	20.7	0.0	6.0	26.7
Korea	3.8	6.9	8.9	19.7
New Zealand	18.4	0.0	0.0	18.4
Mexico	3.5	1.2	10.5	15.3

Source: OECD.

KEY POINT

Competition between the employed and the unemployed is critical in maintaining a low natural rate of unemployment. Strong trade unions, high benefits, a large proportion of long-term unemployed, regional and skill mismatches and high taxes all reduce competition between unemployed and employed and lead to higher unemployment.

7.6 What Lowers Unemployment?

The previous section focused on factors that increase the natural rate of unemployment. Here we discuss influences that *lower* unemployment. We focus on two such beneficial factors: active labour market spending and coordinated wage bargaining. In each case, the effect is to shift the wage-setting curve leftward and to lower the natural rate of unemployment.

ACTIVE LABOUR MARKET SPENDING

Active labour market spending refers to a range of policies that governments use to boost employment and reduce unemployment (see Figure 7.16). One policy is to assist the unemployed's job search: improving information flows about job availabilities, helping individuals with application forms and interview techniques, and offering retraining. Other active labour market policies subsidize the creation of jobs for the unemployed, offer loans to individuals who want to start their own businesses, subsidize firms that hire those who have been unemployed for a long time and so on.

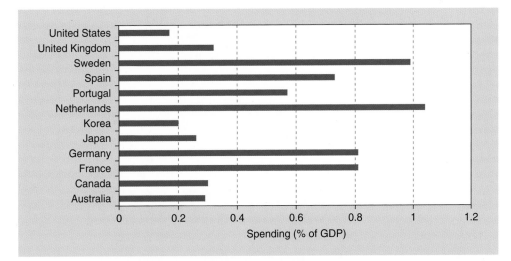

FIGURE 7.16 ● **Active labour market spending (% GDP), 2008.** In continental Europe, governments have devoted substantial resources to trying to make labour markets work better. *Source:* OECD.

COORDINATED WAGE BARGAINING

In Section 7.3, we argued that the stronger the monopoly power of unions, the higher the natural rate of unemployment. Yet some countries with the most extensive union coverage (in particular Scandinavia) also have low unemployment rates. To explain this, we need to recognize that whether or not unions are bad for unemployment depends on *both* the degree of monopoly power the workforce possesses *and* how it exercises this power. In particular, if wage bargaining occurs at a highly centralized level between unions and firms, then the adverse unemployment effects may be small.

Consider the case of numerous strong unions, each of which negotiates separately with its employers and tries to achieve as high a wage as possible compared with other unions. Of course, not all unions can do this – they cannot all outperform each other. Their uncoordinated attempts at boosting wages only generate higher unemployment to restrain their wage demands. If, instead, the unions coordinate their bargaining, they will realize that additional wage demands will only boost unemployment (especially if employer organizations are also coordinating their negotiations). As a result, their wage demands will be more modest and unemployment will reconcile the competing demands of firms and the workforce at a lower equilibrium level.

Figure 7.17 shows estimates of how centralized wage bargaining has been in different countries and compares *the level of centralization (or coordination) with unemployment rates*. This figure offers some support for the notion that both coordinated wage bargaining and decentralized labour markets produce lower unemployment.

> ### KEY POINT
>
> Unemployment is caused by the interaction of the monopoly power of firms and workers. Active labour market policies reduce the monopoly power of workers and coordinated wage bargaining restrains the use of monopoly power.

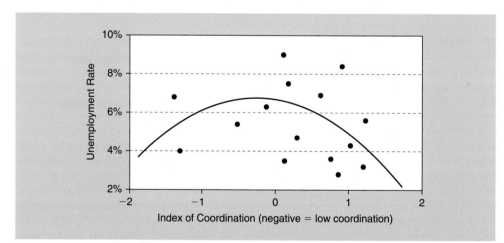

FIGURE 7.17 ● **Coordination of wage bargaining and unemployment across OECD countries.** *Source:* Autiero, 'Labour market coordinaton systems and unemployment performance in some OECD countries', *The Journal of Socio-Economics* (2008), 37(5): 1846–55. Elsevier; and authors' calculations.

(7.7) A Flow Approach to the Natural Rate of Unemployment

To enhance our understanding of the labour market, we now take a different perspective that focuses on flows into and out of unemployment. This enables us to review the effectiveness of **employment protection legislation (EPL)**, which aims to reduce unemployment by restricting the ability of firms to fire workers.

Every period, some of those who are employed lose their jobs. This may be for voluntary reasons (they did not like their job and quit) or involuntary ones (their firm is downsizing and they are fired). These inflows increase unemployment. However, in every period other people cease to be unemployed. They either withdraw from the labour force or find work. The natural rate of unemployment is an equilibrium at which there is no tendency for unemployment to change. But for unemployment not to be changing, the inflow into unemployment must equal the outflow. We can use this fact to derive an expression for the natural rate of unemployment.

The inflow *into* unemployment equals the number of people employed (L) multiplied by the probability that a person loses his or her job (p). The outflow *from* unemployment equals the number of people who are unemployed (U) multiplied by the probability of an unemployed person finding a job (s).

The natural rate of unemployment occurs when inflows and outflows equal each other, that is when

Unemployment inflows $= p\text{L} = s\text{U} =$ Unemployment outflows

We know, by definition, that employment plus unemployment equals the labour force (LF), so that LF = L + U or L = LF – U. We can therefore write our equilibrium condition as

$$p\,(\text{LF} - \text{U}) = s\text{U}$$

As the unemployment rate (u) equals the unemployed divided by the labour force (U/LF), we can write this expression as

$$p\,(\text{LF/LF} - \text{U/LF}) = s\text{U/LF}$$

or

$$p(1 - u) = su$$

where u is the unemployment rate (U/LF). Rearranging this gives us an expression for the natural rate of unemployment

$$u^* = p/(p + s)$$

In other words, the natural rate of unemployment, u^*, depends positively on p, the probability that an employed person becomes unemployed, and negatively on s, the probability an unemployed person finds a job.

THE IMPACT OF EMPLOYMENT PROTECTION LEGISLATION (EPL)

EPL is a label for a variety of measures that governments take to protect those in employment from dismissal. These include laws about formal dismissal practices, severance pay, notice periods, the number of warnings firms have to give a worker before he or she can be fired, whether government has to approve a corporate downsizing and so forth.

Table 7.3 shows considerable variation in the scale of EPL among OECD economies. For instance, according to the OECD, US employers face no meaningful administrative processes before they can dismiss workers and legally have to offer no notice or severance pay, even after 20 years of service. By contrast, in Belgium, firms have to give 9 months' notice to workers with more than 20 years of tenure. Most countries require no severance pay within the first year of employment, but Portugal and Turkey require 20 months of severance pay after 20 years of work. Such large institutional differences in EPL significantly affect the operation of labour markets. The final column of Table 7.3 shows the OECD's overall assessment of the severity of employment legislation. Southern European countries tend to have the highest level of EPL, while the English-speaking countries have the lowest levels.

EPL seeks to make it costly for firms to fire people and so tries to produce a lower value of p (probability of becoming unemployed) and a reduction in the natural rate of unemployment.

TABLE 7.3 ● Indicators of Strictness of Employment Protection, 2008.*

OECD ranking of administrative restrictions on dismissal process. Final column shows overall ranking. Scale from 0 (least restrictions) to 6 (most restrictions).

	Protection of Permanent Workers against (Individual) Dismissal	Regulation on Temporary Forms of Employment	Specific Requirements for Collective Dismissal	OECD Employment Protection Index
Australia	1.37	0.79	2.88	**1.38**
Brazil	1.49	3.96	0.00	**2.27**
Canada	1.17	0.22	2.63	**1.02**
China	3.31	2.21	3.00	**2.80**
France	2.60	3.75	2.13	**3.00**
Germany	2.85	1.96	3.75	**2.63**
India	3.65	2.67	0.00	**2.63**
Italy	1.69	2.54	4.88	**2.58**
Japan	2.05	1.50	1.50	**1.73**
Korea	2.29	2.08	1.88	**2.13**
Russian Federation	2.79	0.79	1.88	**1.80**
Spain	2.38	3.83	3.13	**3.11**
Sweden	2.72	0.71	3.75	**2.06**
Switzerland	1.19	1.50	3.88	**1.77**
Turkey	2.48	4.88	2.38	**3.46**
United Kingdom	1.17	0.29	2.88	**1.09**
United States	0.56	0.33	2.88	**0.85**

Note: *For France and Portugal, data refer to 2009.

Source: OECD, see www.oecd.org/employment/protection.

EPL also adversely affects s – the probability of the unemployed finding a job. When hiring employees, firms have to remember that at some future date they may wish to terminate the employment. The more costly it is to fire people, the more expensive it is to hire them. Therefore we can expect EPL to have offsetting effects on unemployment – it lowers job destruction rates but reduces job creation. Its overall impact on unemployment is an empirical question.

Figures 7.18a–7.18f (and associated econometric work) show that for OECD economies:

- Countries with strong EPL have low employment rates – increased hiring costs reduce the demand for labour.
- EPL is not correlated with unemployment. This suggests that the reduction in employment is matched by a similar fall in the participation rate and in the size of the labour force. A key reason for the drop in participation is that EPL makes part-time jobs less attractive for employers and the absence of such jobs reduces female participation in the labour force.
- Countries with strong EPL have lower levels of outflows *and* inflows into unemployment (both p and s decline). This explains why unemployment does not vary with EPL – the declines in inflows and outflows offset each other.
- Countries with strong EPL have greater job security and longer job tenure, but unemployment also lasts longer. EPL, therefore, benefits workers who are employed at the cost of those without jobs.

The benefits of EPL tend to accrue to those already in work, while the disadvantages hurt the unemployed. Why would a country adopt legislation that benefits the employed at the expense of the unemployed? Political considerations help answer this question. In most economies, around 90–95% of the labour force is employed. Further, in countries with strong trade unions, the demands of the employed can be easily coordinated and voiced,

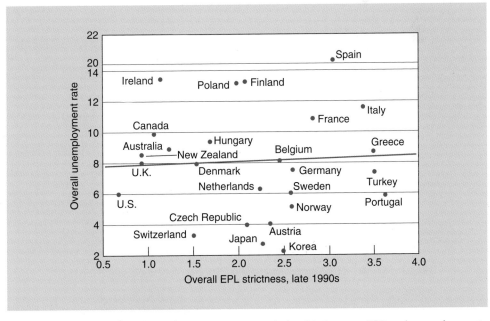

FIGURE 7.18a ● **EPL and unemployment.** No strong relationship between EPL and unemployment.

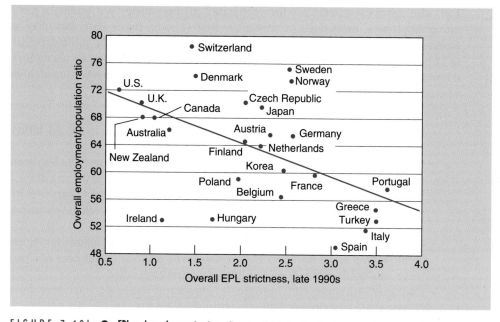

FIGURE 7.18b ● **EPL and employment rates.** Strong EPL typically means a lower employment rate.

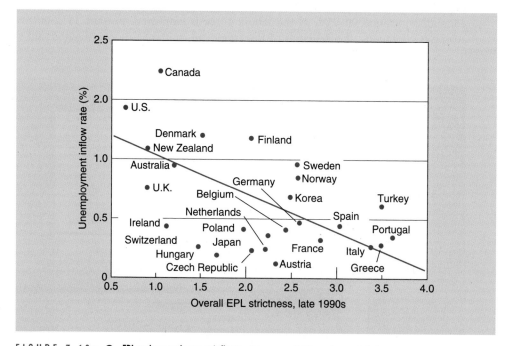

FIGURE 7.18c ● **EPL and unemployment inflows.** Stronger EPL reduces job losses.

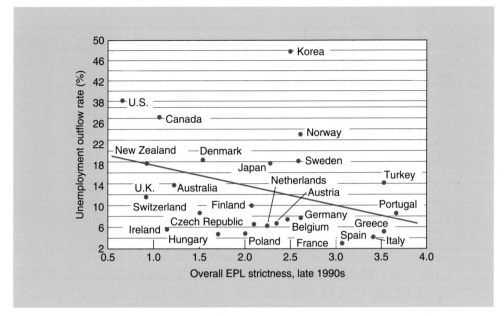

FIGURE 7.18d ● **EPL and unemployment outflows.** Strong EPL lowers job-creation rate.

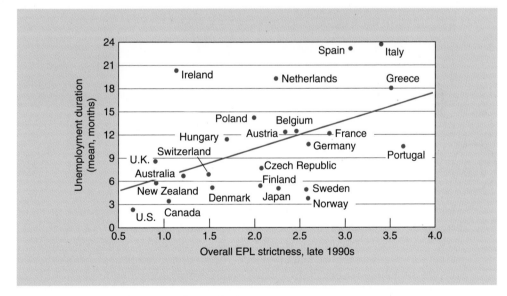

FIGURE 7.18e ● **EPL and unemployment duration.** Stronger EPL increases length of employment.

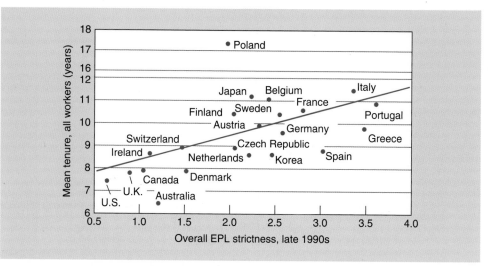

FIGURE 7.18f ● **EPL and duration of employment.** EPL improves job tenure. *Source:* All diagrams OECD, *Employment Outlook* (June 1999).

whereas the unemployed have no such organization. As a result, governments come under political pressure to adopt EPL.

> ### KEY POINT
>
> Unemployment depends on both the probability of the employed being fired and the probability of the unemployed being hired. EPL tries to lower unemployment by reducing the firing rate. It also tends to lower the hiring rate, however, so that overall it does not reduce unemployment. Instead, it increases job tenure and the length of spells of unemployment.

7.8 Labour Market Reform

There is currently growing support for continental Europe to enact labour market reform, which would remove government restrictions, reduce the power of unions and increase the role of market forces. The motivation for this is based on our theoretical framework, which suggests that lower benefits, weaker unions and less EPL will stimulate labour market turnover and reduce unemployment. Further motivation comes from the relatively low rate of unemployment in the United States, which, according to most of the statistics we have examined in this chapter, has a low level of government intervention in the labour market. Final evidence comes from countries such as Chile and the United Kingdom that enacted labour market reform and then saw unemployment decline.

There are, however, also arguments against market-orientated reform. One maintains that, while such reforms lower unemployment, they bring other concerns. Deregulated labour markets have experienced dramatic increases in income inequality, which offset the advantages of low unemployment. The other criticism is that because more flexible labour markets lower wages and produce greater inequality, they also lead to higher levels of crime. Crime is expensive for society (just think how much richer you would be if there was no need to pay insurance premiums against theft or pay taxes to finance the police force and prisons). Figure 7.19 shows the size of the prison population as a share of the total population for various countries. In the case of the United States, the prison population is currently about 1% of the total population (2% of the workforce). If this criminal population is linked to the greater flexibility of US labour markets (and this is by no means an accepted proposition), then labour market reform becomes less attractive. It can cost over $40 000 a year to keep a person in prison – considerably more than paying for continental European levels of social security. Of course, the key issue here is whether inequality, rather than other features of a society, produces the crime.

Finally, it is argued that market-orientated reform may not be the only way to reduce unemployment. It is useful here to examine why unemployment declined in the 1990s in the United Kingdom and the Netherlands. Table 7.4 shows estimates about why unemployment

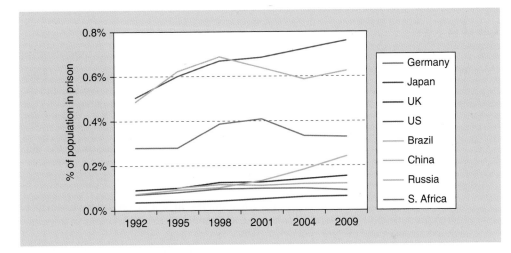

FIGURE 7.19 ● Prison populations. *Source:* OECD.

TABLE 7.4 ● Explaining Netherlands and UK Unemployment Declines.

The decline in unemployment rates in the United Kingdom and the Netherlands in the 1990s was substantial, but the factors explaining the fall in joblessness are very different.

Changes in:	Netherlands	UK
Union density	−0.83	−1.47
Union coverage	0.58	−1.25
Active labour market spending	−1.09	0.16
Union + employer coordination	−2.53	0
Benefit replacement rate	−0.41	−0.48
Tax wedge	−0.24	−0.72
Total	**−4.52**	**−3.76**

Source: Nickell and Van Ours, 'The Netherlands and the UK: A European unemployment miracle', *Economic Policy* (2000), 30: 135–80.

fell in each country. The differences are clear. The United Kingdom has focused on a market-orientated approach by weakening union strength and lowering replacement rates and tax wedges. By contrast, the Netherlands reduced unemployment though increased active labour market spending and coordination measures.

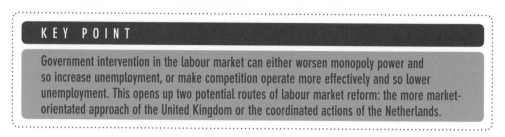

KEY POINT

Government intervention in the labour market can either worsen monopoly power and so increase unemployment, or make competition operate more effectively and so lower unemployment. This opens up two potential routes of labour market reform: the more market-orientated approach of the United Kingdom or the coordinated actions of the Netherlands.

SUMMARY

We have completed our long-run analysis of the economy by providing a model of the labour market in which capital accumulation and technological progress increase the demand for labour and produce rising productivity and real wages and a higher standard of living.

In Section 7.2, we explained the concept of a natural rate of unemployment – a long-run equilibrium to which the economy tends to return.

In Sections 7.3 and 7.4, we outlined a model of the natural rate based on the interaction between producers and the labour force, where both possess a degree of monopoly power. Unemployment reconciles the conflicting profit demands of firms with the real wage aspirations of workers.

In Section 7.5, we saw that stronger trade unions, high levels of unemployment benefits, a large proportion of long-term unemployed, substantial regional variations in unemployment, high labour taxes and greater monopoly power among firms lead to higher unemployment. We also looked at the Beveridge curve, which shows the relationship between unemployment and vacancies, which is one measure of labour market mismatch.

In Section 7.6, we also examined two factors, active labour market spending and coordinated wage bargaining, that lower unemployment.

In Section 7.7, we outlined a model of the natural unemployment rate based on inflows and outflows into unemployment. We showed that EPL varies across countries. The greater the degree of EPL, the lower are inflows into unemployment. However, this is offset by the fact that employment protection also reduces outflows from unemployment. As a result, the data suggest that employment protection does not influence the aggregate unemployment rate, but instead increases job tenure and the duration of unemployment.

In Section 7.8, we discussed the advantages of current proposals to decrease the strength of EPL in continental Europe. One of the potential disadvantages was the possibility of greater income inequality.

CONCEPTUAL QUESTIONS

1. (Section 7.1) A country has a working-age population of 70 million, a total population of 100 million, unemployment of 5 million and employment of 45 million.

   (a) What is its labour force?

   (b) What is its participation rate?

(c) What is the participation rate as a proportion of the working-age population?

(d) What is its unemployment rate?

2. (Section 7.1) In Greece, the participation rate (as percentage of working-age population) in 1998 for men aged 15–24 was 44%; aged 24–54, 94%; and aged 55–64, 57%. For the United States, these numbers were 68%, 92% and 68%. In Greece, the corresponding figures for women were 37%, 59% and 24%; and for women in the United States, 63%, 76.5% and 51%. What do you think explains these cross-country differences?

3. (Section 7.2) If the population was prepared to work substantially longer hours for higher wages, what would be the long-run impact of capital accumulation and technological progress on the labour market?

4. (Section 7.3) What influences the wage demands that you make of your current, or potential, employer?

5. (Section 7.5) How do the following affect the natural rate of unemployment?

(a) An increase in tariffs on imported goods.

(b) Making unemployment benefits taxable.

(c) More expenditure on retraining programmes for the unemployed.

(d) Increases in indirect taxes on product prices.

(e) Increases in income tax on labour income.

6. (Section 7.5) Find the latest unemployment rate and job openings rate for the US economy (www.bls.gov – job openings are on the Jolts database). Are the two numbers consistent with the Beveridge curve shown in Figure 7.15?

7. (Section 7.7) If generous welfare payments support the long-term unemployed, is employment protection legislation a good thing?

8. (Section 7.8) Is there a link between the flexibility of US labour markets and the country's large prison population?

ANALYTICAL QUESTIONS

1. (Section 7.2) A family has a target of $1500 for the income that it needs to earn each week. Both adults in the family work at flexible jobs where they have a choice over how many hours to work. They decide that the relative number of hours they should work should be equal to the ratio of their hourly wage rates. The female earns $20 an hour and the male $15. How many hours does each of them work? What happens when the female gets a 20% wage rise to $24 an hour? What happens if both adults get a 20% pay rise? What does this imply about their income and substitution effects?

2. (Section 7.2) Using a spreadsheet, consider the Cobb-Douglas production function:

$$Y_t = A_t K_t^b L_t^{1-b}$$

where Y_t is output at time t; K_t is capital; L_t is labour hours worked; A_t is total factor productivity at time t; and b is 0.3. Analyse how the marginal productivity of labour changes when:

(a) A increases by 10%.

(b) K increases by 10%.

(c) L increases by 10%.

(d) b falls from 0.4 to 0.3.

3. (Section 7.4) In an economy, firms set prices at a mark-up of 20% over costs. Costs are all in the form of wages, so that $P = (1.2)W$. Trade unions enter into bargains with firms on wages. The higher is unemployment, the less powerful are unions and the lower is the real wage they can achieve in negotiations. The real wage that gets negotiated is:

$W/P = 1 - 2u$

where u is the fraction of the workforce unemployed. What is the equilibrium fraction of the labour force unemployed?

4. (Section 7.4) Consider the economy described in Question 3. The government now decides to charge income tax on wages at a rate of 15%. Companies have to pay tax on their profits of 20%; profits per unit produced are simply price minus cost, and the cost is the wage. Assume that firms continue to want to get a net-of-tax profit margin of 20% of costs. Trade unions bargain so that real wages *after income tax* are still given by the expression $1 - 2u$. What happens to the equilibrium unemployment rate?

5. (Section 7.7) Suppose the probability of a worker losing his or her job in a year is 2%. The probability of someone unemployed finding a job within a year is 40%. What is the equilibrium unemployment rate? What happens if the government takes measures to free up the labour market that will double the chances the unemployed have of finding a job and also double the chances of those with jobs becoming unemployed?

CHAPTER 8

International Trade

Key Concepts

Comparative Advantage	Heckscher-Ohlin Model (H-O)	Stolper-Samuelson Theorem
Competitiveness	Hotelling Rule	Strategic Trade Policy
Factor Endowments	New Trade Theory	Terms of Trade
Factor Price Equalization	Opportunity Cost	Vested Interest
Gravity Model	Prebisch-Singer Hypothesis	

Overview

The global economy is becoming more interconnected. In recent decades, world trade has increased faster than world gross domestic product (GDP). We consider the advantages of free trade by outlining the theory of comparative advantage, which shows that all countries – even those that are less efficient at production – can benefit from trade. The Heckscher-Ohlin model tells us in which industries a country has a comparative advantage: those that require the intensive use in production of factors that a country possesses in abundance. We examine the evidence for this model, and consider other factors that help explain observed patterns of trade. How much a country gains from trade depends on the terms of trade – the price of exports relative to imports – and we examine how this has varied for a range of countries.

We then consider why protectionism enjoys political support. We outline the Stolper-Samuelson theorem, which states that some groups in society lose because of free trade while others gain, and we consider to what extent increasing levels of trade can explain widening income inequality. We consider the case for subsidizing key industries to boost a nation's competitiveness and argue that this confuses trade with economic growth. Finally, we consider the ideas and applicability of 'new trade theory', which maintains that, for some industries, protectionism or export subsidies can benefit an economy.

8.1 Patterns of World Trade

Figure 8.1 shows that world trade has consistently been growing faster than world output, so that the world economy is becoming increasingly interconnected. Table 8.1 shows that in 2009 total world trade was $15.1 trillion, with merchandise trade accounting for 78% of this total. The largest component of this merchandise trade is manufacturing, which makes up around 55% of *total* world trade. This implies that manufacturing is heavily exposed to fluctuations in the world economy; Chapter 2 showed that manufacturing accounts for 20–35% of most countries' GDP.

Table 8.2 shows which countries are most involved in international trade. It is striking how China is now the number 1 country in terms of merchandise exports. The EU, the United States and Japan together account for about 34% of merchandise exports. But,

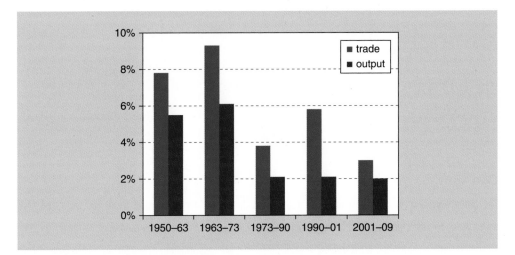

FIGURE 8.1 ● **Growth in world merchandise trade and output.** World trade grows faster than GDP as the world becomes more open. *Source:* WTO, Annual Statistical Report (2010).

TABLE 8.1 ● **Composition of World Trade, 2009 ($ bn).**

Merchandise	11 786
Agricultural	1169
Mining	2263
Manufacturing	8355
All commercial services	3350
Transportation services	700
Travel	870
Other commercial services	1780
Total	15 136

Source: WTO, International Trade Statistics (2010).

TABLE 8.2 ● Top 20 Exporters of Merchandise Goods, 2009 ($ bn and %).

Large economies account for a smaller proportion of trade than world GDP.

Rank	Exporters	Value ($ bn)	Share of World Trade
1	EU trade with rest of world	1528	16.2
2	China	1202	12.7
3	United States	1056	11.2
4	Japan	581	6.2
5	Korea, Republic of	364	3.9
6	Hong Kong, China	329	3.5
	domestic exports	17	0.2
	re-exports	313	3.3
7	Canada	317	3.4
8	Russian Federation	303	3.2
9	Singapore	270	2.9
	domestic exports	138	1.5
	re-exports	132	1.4
10	Mexico	230	2.4
11	Taipei, Chinese	204	2.2
12	Saudi Arabia	192	2.0
13	United Arab Emirates	175	1.9
14	Switzerland	173	1.8
15	India	163	1.7
16	Malaysia	157	1.7
17	Australia	154	1.6
18	Brazil	153	1.6
19	Thailand	152	1.6
20	Norway	121	1.3

Source: WTO, Annual Report (2010).

as we saw in Chapter 2, these regions combined produce around 50% of world GDP. Therefore, relative to their size, these regions are underrepresented in world trade. This is, in fact, a general rule – large economies tend to be more closed; that is, exports are a smaller proportion of their GDP than they are in smaller economies. The most obvious example of this is Hong Kong, which accounts for 3.5% of world trade even though its population is only 7.5 million – around 2% of the population of the pre-enlargement EU and 2.6% of the United States. Table 8.3 summarizes the geographical flow of world trade. The major trade flows are within Europe and within Asia. The largest cross-regional trade flows are between Europe and Asia.

TABLE 8.3 ● Regional Trade Flows, 2009 ($ bn).

Internal trade within region, Europe and Asia are largest trade blocs, followed by North America.

Origin	Destination							
	North America	Latin America	Europe	CIS	Africa	Middle East	Asia	World
World	2026	437	5105	311	391	510	3197	12 178
North America	769	128	292	9	28	49	324	1602
South and Central America	115	120	90	6	13	11	96	459
Europe	366	75	3620	147	162	154	426	5016
CIS	23	5	239	87	7	14	63	452
Africa	66	9	149	1	45	12	85	384
Middle East	60	5	76	4	34	107	357	690
Asia	627	95	641	57	102	163	1846	3575

Source: WTO, Annual Statistical Report (2010).

KEY POINT

Trade is increasing at a faster rate than output, leading to increased global interactions. Manufacturing trade accounts for around two-thirds of total trade. The gravity model of trade explains the value of trade between two countries by the product of their GDPs and their distance from one another.

8.2 Comparative Advantage: How Countries Benefit from Trade

The Nobel Prize-winning economist Paul Samuelson was once challenged by the mathematician Stanislaw Ulam to name one proposition in the social sciences that was both true and non-trivial, and in response he named the theory of comparative advantage. This theory says that *all* countries can benefit from trade, even if they are less productive in *every* industry than other nations. What matters is *not* whether a country is the most productive in the world at producing a commodity. Instead, countries gain from trade by exporting commodities in which their productivity disadvantage is least pronounced; that is, by specializing in what they are least bad at – or *comparatively* good at.

Comparative advantage says that nations should specialize in their productive activities and should focus on those activities in which their advantage is greatest or their disadvantage least. This is exactly what happens in everyday economic life. Consider the case of a highly qualified lawyer who can earn $1000 an hour. Let us assume that this lawyer has high productivity in whatever she does. For example, she can type twice as fast as her personal assistant, can make a better meal in less time than the chef in her firm's cafeteria, and can drive across New York more directly and quickly than a taxi driver. She is also, of course, more productive as a lawyer than her assistant, the chef or the taxi driver. In other words, the lawyer has an absolute advantage in all these activities. However, the optimal strategy for her is not to do everything herself. Every hour she spends typing up case notes, making meals or driving herself around town costs her $1000. Far better to use this time on legal work and then purchase the other services at a cheaper rate. The lawyer will focus on the activity that is most productive for her. A similar argument applies to the other characters. The chef would earn little as a lawyer, is a hopeless typist and cannot drive. His comparative advantage is to cook. His best strategy is to specialize as a chef and then purchase whatever legal or transport services he needs. In everyday life we all specialize in activities that we are *relatively* good at – this is the theory of comparative advantage.

To demonstrate in detail the theory of comparative advantage, we consider Terrania and Oceania, two economies that each produce two commodities: coconuts and fish.[1] Comparative advantage relies on many assumptions, but the two key ones for our purposes are that trade between countries is competitive – countries cannot exploit a monopoly position – and that, within a country, factors of production (i.e. capital and labour) are mobile, and the economy has a constant natural rate of unemployment (see Chapter 7).

We assume that Terrania's population is 10 and Oceania's is 40. The key to our analysis is productivity levels in each country. We assume that in Terrania it takes 2 people to produce a bag of coconuts and 5 to produce a bag of fish. By contrast, in Oceania it takes 8 people to produce a bag of coconuts and 10 for a bag of fish. Table 8.4 shows the state of production technology. These assumptions imply that Terrania is more efficient than Oceania in producing both commodities. Oceania therefore has an absolute advantage in neither industry. However, because of comparative advantage, both countries can gain from free trade. The key concept is **opportunity cost**.

In economics, every activity has an opportunity cost. Opportunity cost is what you could have done had you not pursued your current activity – it is the opportunity you forgo when you make a choice. For instance, the opportunity cost of us writing this textbook is the research papers we could have written instead or the consulting income we might have earned. In our example, the opportunity cost of producing more fish is producing fewer coconuts. This happens because if unemployment remains constant, Terrania can only increase fish production by moving labour from coconuts into fishing. Because every bag of fish requires 5 people to produce it, while a bag of coconuts needs 2 people, the opportunity cost of producing 1 bag of fish for Terrania is 2.5 (=5/2) bags of coconuts. However, in Oceania it takes 8 people to produce a bag of coconuts and 10 to produce a bag of fish. For Oceania the opportunity cost of producing 1 bag of fish is therefore 1.25 (=10/8). In other words, it is cheaper in an opportunity cost sense for Oceania to produce fish than it is for Terrania. *Oceania is said to have a **comparative advantage** in producing fish.*

We now show diagrammatically how both countries benefit from free trade. We assume that on world markets 2 bags of coconuts can be exchanged for 1 bag of fish. We shall show

TABLE 8.4 ● Production Technology for Terrania and Oceania.

The table shows the number of individuals in each country required to produce one bag of commodity listed in the first column.

	Terrania	Oceania
Coconuts	2	8
Fish	5	10

that, at this world price, free trade benefits both Terrania and Oceania. Note that this is *not* the only price at which trade benefits both countries, but neither is it the case that at *all* prices trade benefits both countries. So long as the market price falls between the opportunity cost of each country, then trade will benefit them both simultaneously.

The solid triangular area in Figure 8.2 shows Terrania's production possibility set: all the combinations of coconuts and fish that Terrania can produce given its workforce and technology. Terrania has a workforce of 10 people and requires 2 people to produce 1 bag of coconuts. Therefore, if everyone specializes in coconut production, the country can produce at most 5 bags of coconuts and 0 bags of fish. This gives us the top point in the production possibility set. If instead Terrania devotes all its resources to fish production (which requires 5 people per bag), it can produce 2 bags of fish and 0 bags of coconuts. This gives us the other extreme point on the production possibility frontier. However, there are also many intermediate positions where Terrania does not specialize, but allocates some labour to coconut production and some to fish. Terrania can reach any point on the line drawn between these two extreme points of specialization and the slope of the line reflects the opportunity cost – how much of one commodity is forgone by producing more of the other. All points on this line represent where Terrania is producing the maximum amount of coconuts and fish it can produce given the allocation of labour between the two industries. However, Terrania can also produce output inefficiently, so that the shaded triangular area gives the full set of production possibilities.

The production possibility set shows the consumption possibilities for Terrania if it does not trade – in this case, Terrania can only consume what it produces. However, if Terrania starts to trade, it can sell 2 bags of coconuts for 1 bag of fish, as shown by the trading line in Figure 8.2. If Terrania concentrates on coconut production, it has 5 bags of coconuts that it can swap on international markets for 2.5 bags of fish.[2] Therefore, allowing for trade, Terrania can consume 5 bags of coconuts and 0 bags of fish, or it can consume 0 bags of coconuts and 2.5 bags of fish. It can also consume any combination between these two extreme points if it decides to sell some, but not all, of its coconut production. Because the trading line lies everywhere above the production possibility set, Terrania can do better for itself through international trade than if it tries to be self-sufficient. The optimal strategy for Terrania is to specialize entirely in coconut production and then sell coconuts to acquire the

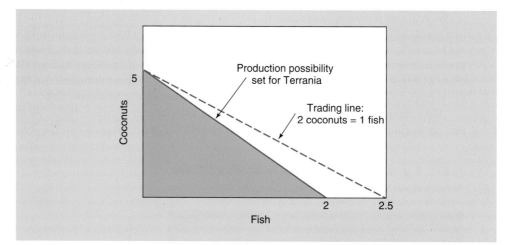

FIGURE 8.2 ● **Production and trading sets for Terrania.** Trade allows Terrania to achieve higher levels of consumption than when relying on domestic production.

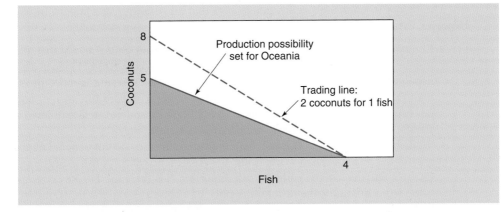

FIGURE 8.3 ● **Production and trading sets for Oceania.** Oceania, too, can enjoy the scope to consume more of both goods once it trades and specializes in producing the good in which its comparative advantage lies.

amount of fish it wants to consume. After all, even though we are producing an economics textbook, we have no desire to purchase one! This separation of production and consumption enables the economy to operate efficiently.

Table 8.4 shows us that Terrania is more efficient at producing both coconuts and fish. Therefore, it is hardly surprising that the country benefits from free trade. Can we show that Oceania, which is relatively inefficient, also benefits? Figure 8.3 shows the production and trading possibilities for Oceania. Oceania has 40 people, and it takes 8 to produce a bag of coconuts and 10 to produce a bag of fish. Therefore at most Oceania can produce 5 bags of coconuts and 0 bags of fish or 4 bags of fish and 0 bags of coconuts. Again, the shaded area shows the production possibility set. The same international prices apply to Oceania, so it can swap 2 bags of coconuts for 1 of fish. Therefore, if Oceania focuses on fish production and produces 4 bags, it can trade and obtain up to 8 bags of coconuts – compared to only 5 if it is self-sufficient. Thus *both* Terrania and Oceania can benefit from trade even though Oceania has no absolute advantage in either industry. It is comparative advantage that matters and, as a result, both countries gain.

But, as we noted earlier, not all possible prices make trade beneficial. For instance, if international prices are 2.5 bags of coconuts for 1 bag of fish, Terrania is no better off with trade – it can do just as well being self-sufficient. If Terrania does not trade, Oceania loses the benefits of free trade. Rather than do that, Oceania can suggest alternative prices (for instance, 2 bags of coconuts for 1 of fish) until both countries benefit. Therefore, unless prices are restricted – through tariffs or other forms of protectionism – they will eventually move to a range that promotes trade.

KEY POINT

Comparative advantage means that all countries can benefit from free trade even if they are characterized by low levels of productivity. Underlying this result is the concept of opportunity cost, which means that countries have a comparative advantage in industries at which they are relatively or comparatively best.

The theory of comparative advantage says that all countries can benefit from trade. However, there are some things that comparative advantage does *not* imply:

- Comparative advantage says that all countries gain from trade, but not that all countries become wealthy. As we saw in Chapters 3 to 6, the standard of living in a country depends on its *absolute* productivity. In our example, Terrania is more productive than Oceania and so has a better standard of living (compare the level of coconuts per capita in each country). However, both Terrania and Oceania will have higher standards of living under trade, *compared to* self-sufficiency.
- While both Terrania and Oceania benefit from trade, they do not benefit equally. The greater the price of fish in world trade, the greater the gains for fish exporters such as Oceania and the less the gains for fish importers like Terrania. The key concept here is the *terms of trade* – the ratio of the price of a country's exports to its imports. The higher the terms of trade, the more the country benefits from trade.
- Comparative advantage only says that a country gains from trade in the aggregate. It does not say that *every* citizen benefits. For example, the fishing industry in Terrania will not benefit from trade with Oceania. We will examine the distributional implications of free trade in detail later.

Figure 8.4, taken from a seminal study, shows empirical support for comparative advantage. The figure demonstrates, for a variety of industries, the relative productivity of the United States (compared to the United Kingdom) and the relative amount of exports from the United States in each industry. The scale shows that for every industry, productivity in the United States was greater than in the United Kingdom. In other words, the United States had an absolute productivity advantage in all industries. Yet the United Kingdom still managed to export more than the United States in several industries (where the ratio of US to UK exports is less than 1). We can see from Figure 8.4 that the United Kingdom out-exported the United States in those industries in which the US productivity advantage was least pronounced. In other words, the United States focused its export performance on those industries in which its productivity advantage was greatest compared to the United

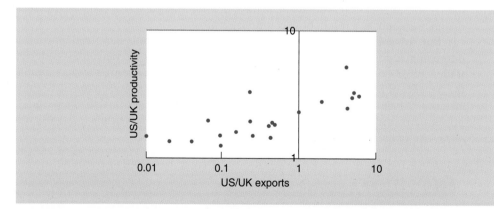

FIGURE 8.4 ● Comparative advantage in the United States and the United Kingdom, 1937. Just before the Second World War, the United States and United Kingdom appeared to specialize in production and export of goods where they had comparative advantages – although the United States had an absolute advantage in production of nearly all goods. *Source:* G.D.A. MacDougall, 'British and American Exports', *Economic Journal* (1951), 61: 703–707.

Kingdom (pig iron and motor cars). This left the United Kingdom to specialize in those industries in which its productivity deficit was *smallest* (beer and textiles) – exactly what comparative advantage implies. One implication of comparative advantage is that industries in a country are not just in competition with the same industry overseas, but also with other industries in their own country. Figure 8.4 suggests that, even if the US steel industry can match the Korean steel industry in terms of productivity, US steel producers still may not succeed internationally if they have below-average productivity in the whole economy. The reason is that while US steel producers compete with Korean steel producers in terms of output, they compete with other US firms for inputs such as management, workers and capital. If US steel firms are less productive than other US sectors, then they will struggle to compete even if they are more productive than Korean steel producers.

> ### KEY POINT
>
> Comparative advantage implies that all countries gain from trade, but not that all countries gain equally from trade or that all countries will have the same income level.

8.3 The Terms of Trade

The **terms of trade** is the ratio of the price of a country's exports to the price of its imports. The higher the terms of trade, the more benefits a nation captures from trade. Figure 8.5 shows variations in the terms of trade between 1970 and 2009 for Australia, Japan, the United Kingdom and the United States. Australia has a large proportion of commodity exports and has experienced the most volatile terms of trade, as the price of much of its exports (commodities) has varied significantly against the price of the goods it imports (mainly manufactures). Up until 2004 commodity prices had tended to fall relative to manufactures, but that was dramatically reversed following the boom in commodity prices in the late 2000s. Changes in the terms of trade affect the magnitude of the gains that countries reap from free trade. Between 1970 and 2002 the terms of trade for the United States fell by 22.5%. Over this period US imports were on average 10% of GDP (beginning at around 5% and ending at 14%). Therefore, a 22.5% increase in the price of imports relative to exports means that the US gains from trade *fell* by around 2.25% of GDP (22.5% of 10%). This does not mean that the United States did not gain from trade – comparative advantage tells us otherwise. But adverse shifts in the terms of trade meant that the United States gained *less* than it otherwise would have done.

Adverse shifts in the terms of trade have been a particular problem for countries that export mainly agricultural products, as shown in Figure 8.6. Up until 2004 the price of agricultural goods had tended to fall in real terms (i.e. relative to the price of other goods) as both production and productivity rose, but food became a smaller share of developed countries' expenditure. The prediction that commodity prices fall in value over time is known as the **Prebisch-Singer hypothesis**. This prediction was based around the idea that the elasticity of demand for food with respect to income was low. The implication of this is that rising income would not produce much extra demand for food. With productivity growth occurring due to the application of machinery and fertilizer, the result was supply growing faster than demand and so prices falling. As well as a low income elasticity, food is also thought to have a low price elasticity, so commodity prices have to fall sharply to bring supply and demand

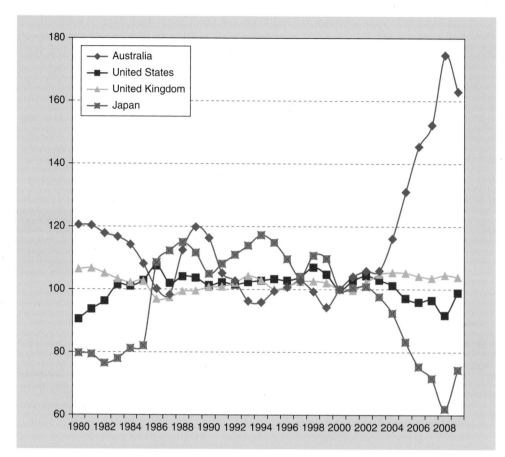

FIGURE 8.5 ● **Terms of trade for Australia, Japan, the United Kingdom and the United States.** Terms of trade display substantial variation over time. *Source:* World Bank, World Development Indicators (2011).

into balance. These assumptions predicted that agricultural commodity prices would show a long-term decline relative to other prices.

However, the Prebisch-Singer hypothesis has undergone a dramatic reversal in recent years as agricultural goods and metal prices have soared. Most suggest that the rise in price of agricultural goods (and other commodities) is due to increased demand from the BRIC nations; see Figure 8.7. Because of the relatively low starting point and the rapidity of income growth in China and India, these countries have seen sharp increases in demand for food: rice, meat and so on. The sharp increase in demand has outstripped the ability to produce more supply. In fact, climate problems and drought in countries such as Australia have led to supply problems exacerbating food price increases. Furthermore, because so much of Chinese growth comes from its manufacturing sector, its demand for metals grows strongly each year and far outstrips new discoveries, leading to a dramatic increase in metal prices.

KEY POINTS

Variations in the terms of trade influence the magnitude of a country's gains from trade. Commodity exporters have recently seen a dramatic improvement in their terms of trade.

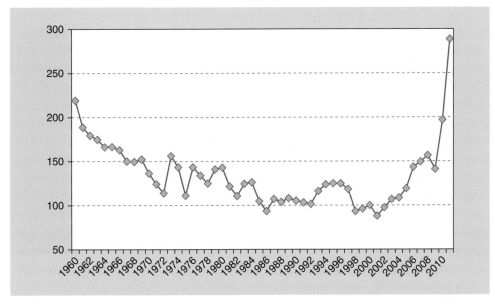

FIGURE 8.6 ● **Real agricultural raw material prices.** Basic indicators show an adverse term of trade shift for agricultural exporters until quite recently. *Source:* World Bank, GEM (2011).

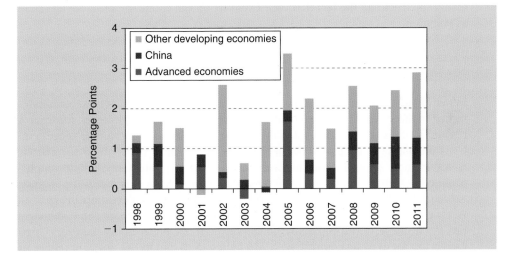

FIGURE 8.7 ● **Contribution to global demand growth for major crops.** Developing economies, particularly China, are making an increasing contribution to demand for agricultural commodities.

NATURAL RESOURCES

Rising commodity prices mean that natural resources such as minerals, fuels, fisheries and forestry represent a significant and growing share of world trade. In 2009 about 30% of merchandise trade was in these resources, though as Figure 8.8 shows, this trade was dominated by fuels (mainly oil). As well as being economically important, these resources present some unique economic problems. We saw in Chapter 6 how countries dependent on resource

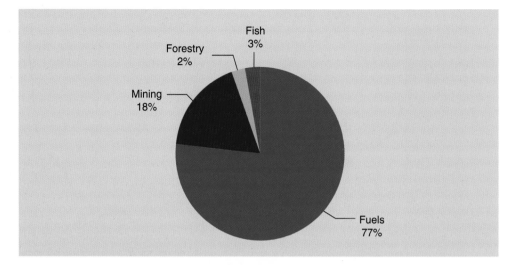

FIGURE 8.8 ● **Trade in natural resources, 2010.** Fuels, mainly oil, dominate natural resource trade. *Source:* IMF World Economic Outlook (2011).

exports may suffer from slow growth (the curse of natural resources). Furthermore, natural resources create problems associated with their exhaustibility, their uneven distribution across countries and the fact that their exploitation can create important externalities such as pollution.

PRICING DEPLETABLE RESOURCES: THE CASE OF OIL

In our discussions above regarding the recent price trends for agricultural commodities, we turned to the standard economic toolkit of supply and demand. However, for some natural resources – those that are finite and depletable – a different framework is suggested.

Commodities such as wheat can be grown from year to year, subject to environmental issues; in some sense, we can think of them as having a potentially infinite supply. Other commodities, such as gold or copper, are in finite supply; we may discover new geographical sources of these commodities, but the Earth is in effect not creating any new supplies. Among this class of commodities is a particularly interesting group: depletable commodities. For instance, oil is a depletable commodity as it is in finite supply and every barrel of oil used is lost for ever. By contrast, gold is in finite supply, but its use does not reduce its stock and so it is non-depletable.

The case of depletable and finite resources raises the issue of how quickly such resources should be exploited in practice. How much should we use today and how much should we leave to future generations? The American economist Harold Hotelling came up with a simple answer to this question, which also gives a simple prediction of how resource prices should behave in the long run.

To fully understand the Hotelling model, first think about what the optimal price would be for the very last barrel of oil. At this point with no more oil left, the optimal price would be the price at which demand for oil is zero. If this were the price, then even though there is no oil this is not a problem, as no one would want to buy oil. This price of oil is termed a 'backstop' price and is shown as Pb in Figure 8.9. This price will be determined by the use that

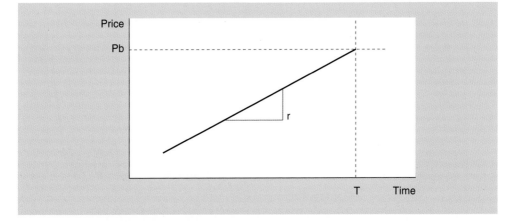

FIGURE 8.9 ● **The Hotelling rule.** The rule predicts that the price of an exhaustible natural resource rises at the rate of interest (r) to reach the backstop price (Pb) when it is economically exhausted.

is made of oil and of course what other rival sources of fuel are available that can be used instead of oil. Therefore, the optimal price of oil when oil reserves are exhausted is pinned down by this backstop price.

The next part of Hotelling's insight is to work backwards and calculate the price today. Imagine that oil is expected to run out at time T and we know that the optimal price then is Pb. Oil producers therefore have a choice. They can either earn Pb (net of extraction costs) next period or sell oil today at $P(T-1)$. Pb is money earned next period, while $P(T-1)$ is money available today, so the producer actually compares $P(T-1)(1+r)$ and $Pb-(1+r)$ is the interest that the producer can earn on its revenue between now and next period. If $P(T-1)(1+r) > Pb$, then the producer pumps oil today. This will, however, lead oil prices to fall, until eventually $P(T-1)(1+r) = Pb$. If instead $Pb > P(T-1)(1+r)$, then the oil producer waits and pumps next year. This will cause $P(T-1)$ to rise due to oil shortages, until eventually $P(T-1)(1+r) = Pb$. The same logic also holds between every period, so arbitrage by oil producers leads to oil prices rising at the rate of interest. Hotelling therefore predicts that the social optimum for depletable and finite resources is achieved when the price of the resource net of extraction costs grows at a rate equal to the rate of interest, as in Figure 8.9.

A problem for the Hotelling rule is that it seems to predict a relatively smooth path for resource prices, while in practice they have tended to be extremely volatile. Figure 8.10 shows the nominal and real price for oil over more than a century and demonstrates that although oil prices have increased over time, they have not risen at a smooth rate in the manner suggested by Figure 8.9. What could explain such volatility? First, the Hotelling rule does not necessarily predict smoothly growing resource prices, since unexpected changes to the key determinants could cause commodity prices to jump up or down. For example, an unexpected change in the path of interest or the backstop price could cause a significant change in prices today. For instance, the rapid growth of the BRICs will undoubtedly lead to a sharp increase in the backstop price for oil and so to a sharp increase in prices today. Variations in the real rate of interest in recent years will similarly cause sharp changes in current oil prices. Similarly, new discoveries of the resource could cause a significant price fall today, as they can extend the period until the resource is exhausted or discoveries of rival technologies would lead to sharp declines in prices.

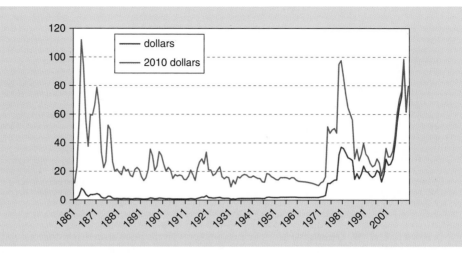

FIGURE 8.10 ● **Oil prices, 1861–2010.** Both real and nominal oil prices have been very volatile. *Source:* BP Statistical Review (2011).

8.4   In What Goods Will Countries Trade?

The theory of comparative advantage says that all countries benefit from trade and must have a comparative advantage in some industries. But what can we say about the type of industry in which a country has a comparative advantage?

The **Heckscher-Ohlin (H-O) model** answers this question. Based on certain key assumptions, the H-O model predicts that a country possesses a comparative advantage in a good whose production requires the intensive use of a factor input that the nation possesses in abundance.

> **KEY POINT**
>
> A country possesses a comparative advantage in a good whose production requires the intensive use of a factor input that the nation possesses in abundance.

China, for example, with its 1.2 billion population, should have a comparative advantage in labour-intensive commodities; Saudi Arabia has a comparative advantage in exporting oil-based products; and Canada has a comparative advantage in commodities that require the extensive use of land.

How well does H-O account for the actual pattern of trade? Table 8.5 shows the composition of trade between China and the United States and demonstrates that H-O can explain some trading patterns. In commodities that require more skilled labour, R&D and high-quality capital (chemicals and aircraft), the United States exports substantial amounts to China. However, in commodities that require more intensive use of labour and less sophisticated capital and technology (clothing and other consumer goods such as DVD players), then China exports these to the United States.

TABLE 8.5 ● **Chinese–US Merchandise Trade, 2009.**
The China–US trade pattern offers support for the Heckscher-Ohlin model.

	Export to China (% of Total)	Export to US (% of Total)
Textiles, leather and footwear	1.0	16.4
Chemicals and chemical products	13.5	3.4
Iron and steel	1.6	2.2
Transport equipment	11.0	2.2
Automotive products	3.0	1.5

Source: OECD STAN database (2010).

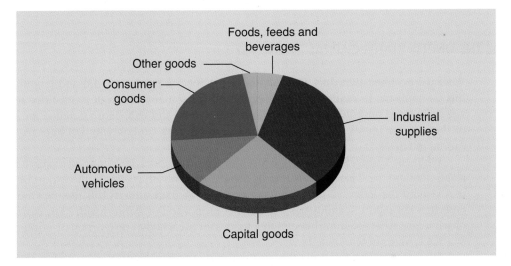

FIGURE 8.11 ● **Composition of US merchandise imports, 2009.** Even though the United States is a capital rich country, its imports tend to be capital intensive. *Source:* US Census Bureau.

However, although H-O scores some successes, many features of international trade conflict with its simple predictions. Figure 8.11 shows the composition of US merchandise imports in 2009 and reveals that the United States, despite having a high capital stock, imports mainly capital-intensive goods. How can we explain this?

DIFFERENCES IN TASTES

The H-O model assumes that all countries have the same preferences, so that trade patterns reflect only supply considerations. However, variations in demand also explain trade patterns. For instance, the US state of Virginia exports 30 tons of poultry feet to Southeast Asia every month.[3] The H-O model cannot account for this trade, because the United States does not have a comparative advantage compared to Asia in poultry production. This trade literally results from different tastes – Southeast Asian cuisine, but not American, uses chicken feet. Therefore, the United States may import capital-intensive goods because the US demand for such goods may be so overwhelming that it has to import them, even though it has a comparative advantage in producing those commodities itself.

However, differences in tastes are unlikely to explain the pattern of trade shown in Figure 8.11. First, US capital-intensive imports are surely too big to be explained by taste differences. Second, if the United States has a bias for any particular commodity, it is for luxury goods that require substantial amounts of skilled labour as input. Differences in tastes are not, therefore, enough to rectify the H-O model completely.

TRADE RESTRICTIONS

The H-O model assumes the existence of free trade. Even though trade restrictions have been reduced over time, they still distort trade patterns. As we shall see in the next chapter, there exist substantial tariffs and quotas that prevent the operation of free trade and interfere with the predictions of the H-O model.

IS THE UNITED STATES CAPITAL INTENSIVE?

We have assumed that only two factors of production exist – capital and labour – but this is simplistic. In reality, output is produced using many different inputs: raw materials, skilled and unskilled labour, land, machinery and so forth. More detailed modelling of these factor inputs, in particular human capital, may explain why US imports are so capital intensive.

While the United States has high levels of physical capital, its labour force also has high levels of schooling. This suggests that its comparative advantage lies in the export of goods that require the intensive use of human capital. The data support this theory. One study finds that US exporting industries use a higher proportion of workers with 13 or more years of schooling, whereas import-competing industries use a higher proportion of workers with 8 or fewer years of schooling.[4]

Table 8.6 breaks down the types of goods that some countries exported or imported in the mid-1960s. If a country exported a good that involves the intensive use of a factor, it is marked with an X. If it imported such a commodity, it is marked with an M. The table reveals some plausible results: the United States exports goods that require the intensive use in production of human and physical capital; Canada exports land-intensive commodities; Germany and Japan have a comparative advantage in goods that require skilled labour; Mexico imports capital-intensive goods; and the Philippines exports commodities that require unskilled labour. Thus, a more detailed breakdown of factors of production shows more support for the H-O model. However, the H-O model is still not entirely vindicated. The authors of this study examined whether the export–import patterns in Table 8.6 were consistent with independent measures of factor abundance in each country. While there were some successes, there were also many failures.

DIFFERENCES IN TECHNOLOGY

As well as assuming that countries are identical in their tastes, the H-O model also assumes that they all have access to the same technology. Therefore the only explanation for trade is supply-side differences in factor abundance. However, at any given time, countries will be using different technologies. This is another reason why trade may not agree with the predictions of H-O. British wine is to be appreciated more for the effort taken in producing

TABLE 8.6 ● Factor Intensity of Trade for Selected Countries, 1967.

M means the country imports goods that use the factor in the relevant row relatively intensively. X means that the country exports these kinds of goods.

	US	Canada	Germany	Japan	Mexico	Philippines
Capital stock	X	X	M	M	M	M
Labour force	M	M	M	X	X	M
Professional/technical workers	X	M	X	X	X	M
Management workers	M	M	X	X	X	M
Clerical workers	M	M	X	X	X	M
Sales workers	M	M	M	M	X	X
Service workers	M	M	M	M	X	X
Agricultural workers	X	X	M	M	X	X
Production workers	M	M	X	X	M	M
Arable land	X	X	M	M	X	X
Forest land	M	X	M	M	X	M
Pasture land	M	X	M	M	X	M

Source: Bowen, Leamer and Svelkauskas, 'Multicountry, multifactor tests of the factor abundance theory', *American Economic Review* (1987), 77: 791–809.

it rather than its taste – the lack of sunshine means that, regardless of cost structure, the United Kingdom will always import wine. The lack of suitable weather means that TFP for British wine making is low compared to other countries.

INTRA-INDUSTRY TRADE AND IMPERFECT COMPETITION

One particular problem for the H-O model is that, especially among OECD countries, much trade is intra-industry. An example is France selling Peugeot cars to Italy and Italy exporting Fiats to France.

Consider the following measure of intra-industry trade for a particular sector:

1 – absolute value (export – imports) / (exports + imports)

The term absolute value (exports minus imports) is the value of net exports, ignoring whether they are positive or negative. This measure ranges from 0 to 1. Imagine a country that specializes in car production and exports many cars, but imports none. In this case, our measure of intra-industry trade (given that imports of cars are 0) would be 1 – exports/exports = 1 – 1 = 0. If instead the country has no car industry, so that car exports are 0 but imports are large, the measure would be 1 – imports/imports = 1 – 1 = 0. Therefore, if trade in an industry is in only one direction (exports or imports), this measure is 0. When a country both imports and exports cars, so that net exports are 0, the measure is 1 – 0/(exports + imports) = 1. Therefore, the closer this measure is to 1, the greater the extent to which trade is intra-industry.

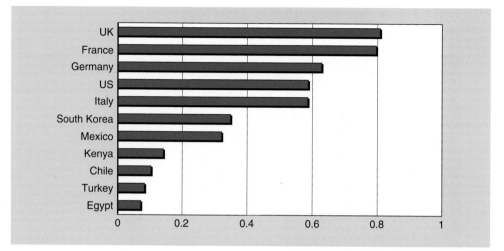

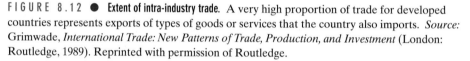

FIGURE 8.12 ● **Extent of intra-industry trade.** A very high proportion of trade for developed countries represents exports of types of goods or services that the country also imports. *Source:* Grimwade, *International Trade: New Patterns of Trade, Production, and Investment* (London: Routledge, 1989). Reprinted with permission of Routledge.

Figure 8.12 shows measures of intra-industry trade for 11 countries and reveals considerable intra-industry trade among the most developed nations. The H-O model cannot explain this – what type of factor endowment can explain why Italy produces Fiats while the French produce Peugeots? We therefore need a different model.

To develop this model, we make two assumptions. The first is that consumers like variety. On entering a car showroom, they wish to select from a range of colours, models and manufacturers rather than be faced with no choice. Because consumers value variety, the producer of each different type of car has some monopoly power – consumers do not treat Fiats and Peugeots as identical. The second assumption is that car production is characterized by increasing returns to scale: the more cars that are produced, the lower the unit cost. Therefore, if restricted to a small output, the costs – and therefore the price – of the car will be high.

Now consider what happens when the economy is closed to trade. Consumers want a wide range of models to choose from, but this means that production runs have to be inefficiently small and car prices will be high. Although consumers value product variety, there is a limit to what they are prepared to pay for it. As a result, the country will produce a limited range of products to benefit from the increasing returns to scale, for example Italian consumers would buy Fiats; the French, Citroëns; and the Germans, Volkswagens. Now consider what free trade between countries does. Because car producers can now sell to export markets, they can achieve large production runs with no increase in the level of demand in their domestic economy. Therefore, they can keep costs and prices low. Meanwhile, consumers can now choose among different car models at reasonable prices, because producers are still benefiting from increasing returns. German consumers can now choose to buy Volkswagens, Fiats or Citroëns. Trade in this case is still beneficial – production is efficient, and consumers benefit from greater product variety – but the pattern of intra-industry trade looks different from what H-O predicted. While the theory of comparative advantage focuses on trade being driven by differences in relative productivity, this approach to trade focuses on consumers' preferences for variety. It seems that this preference is so strong that substantial gains from trade are possible even if productivity is the same across countries.

> ### KEY POINT
>
> The Heckscher-Ohlin model explains trade through differences in factor endowments: a country has a comparative advantage in producing goods that require as an input a factor the country possesses in abundance. While this helps explain substantial amounts of trade, we also have to allow for differences in tastes, trade restrictions and high levels of intra-industry trade.

8.5 Distributional Impacts of Trade

The theory of comparative advantage is unambiguous – free trade is good for a country. Why, then, do countries clash so often over trade and why are trade restrictions so common? Figure 8.13 shows that, although many people in different countries do have positive attitudes towards trade, there is also substantial opposition. To try to explain these conflicts, we focus on four issues: the effect of trade on the distribution of income; concern over a nation's competitiveness; alternative theories of trade (so-called new trade theory) arguing that countries can benefit from trade restrictions; and political economy arguments that see trade barriers as the result of the interaction of different interest groups. In the next chapter, we extend this argument to consider the pros and cons of globalization, especially the role of trade liberalization for developing economies.

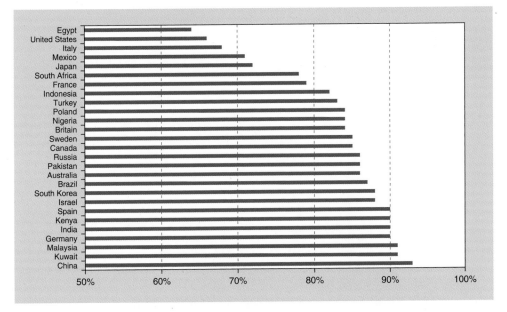

FIGURE 8.13 ● **Is trade a good thing?** Percentage who agree that trade is a good thing by country, 2007–09. *Source:* Pew Global Attitudes Project.

TRADE AND INCREASING INCOME INEQUALITY

Comparative advantage shows that a country *as a whole* can benefit from free trade; it does not show that *everyone* within a country benefits. Some groups within society are better off as a result of trade, but the standard of living of others declines. However, because the country as a whole benefits from trade, it is possible that the gainers *could* compensate the losers and still benefit from trade. Without this redistribution, though, trade will generate losers.

The **factor price equalization theorem** says that as trade occurs, relative factor prices in each country eventually converge. In other words, wages and the cost of capital adjust until they are in the same ratio across countries. Consider a country that has an abundance of capital (say, the United States) and another country whose comparative advantage lies with labour-intensive commodities (say, Mexico). H-O says that the United States will export capital-intensive commodities to Mexico and import labour-intensive goods. As a result, the demand for capital will increase in the United States but the demand for labour will fall, and the demand for labour will rise in Mexico but the demand for capital will decline. This will put downward pressure on both US wages and the Mexican rental price of capital. As a result of trade, wages should fall in the United States and rise in Mexico, and the rental price of capital should increase in the United States and fall in Mexico. In fact, we can go further and say that factor prices should be equalized across countries – Mexican and US wage costs should become the same.

Figure 8.14 shows hourly manufacturing wages for a selection of countries. There is huge variability. Given the factor price equalization theorem, it is understandable that free trade troubles many people. If US wages fall to Mexican levels, then free trade will lead to serious social problems in the United States. However, the situation is not as dramatic as Figure 8.14 suggests. Factor price equalization implies that *identical factors of production should be paid the same even if they are in different countries*. But unskilled labour in the United States is not the same as unskilled labour in Mexico. In a US factory, unskilled workers have access to much higher levels of capital and probably to higher levels of technology. Therefore, US unskilled workers will have a higher level of productivity than Mexican workers and US firms can pay a higher wage. If the productivity of US workers is twice that of Mexican workers,

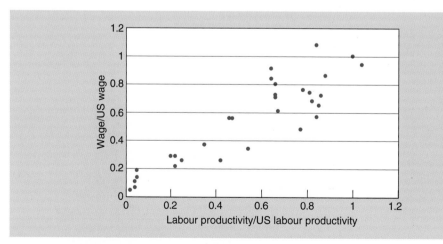

FIGURE 8.14 ● **Relative wages and productivity.** Wage differences across countries largely reflect differences in labour productivity. *Source:* Trefler, 'International factor price differences: Leontief was right!', *Journal of Political Economy* (1993), 101: 961–87.

then their wage can be twice as high. Factor price equalization refers to productivity-adjusted wages (unit labour costs), rather than to the hourly wage rate. The data in Figure 8.14 support the theory: countries with high productivity can pay high wages without violating factor price equalization. As a consequence of trade, wage differentials reflect productivity differences rather than any scarcity value. Through trade workers get paid what they are worth in terms of their productivity. High wages can only be justified by high productivity.

Nevertheless, even though US and Mexican unskilled wages do not have to be equal, the factor price equalization result still implies that unskilled wages fall in the United States as a result of trade with Mexico. The benefits of free trade in the form of lower import prices partly offset this fall. However, we have one more important trade result to outline: the **Stolper-Samuelson theorem**. This says that trade increases the real income of owners of the abundant factor of production and decreases the real income of owners of the scarce factor. In our United States–Mexico example, this means that the real income of US skilled labour increases, while that of unskilled workers declines.

It is estimated that increases in trade account for 5–20% of the increase in inequality that the United States experienced in the 1980s and 1990s. The reason for this relatively modest impact is that, although imports increased sharply during this period, they remained a minor part of the economy, and imports from low-wage economies were an even smaller component.

KEY POINT

Trade has substantial distributional implications so that, although the country as a whole benefits, some sectors gain and others lose. As a consequence of trade, wage differentials reflect productivity differences across countries.

8.6 Competitiveness

One reason governments often engage in restrictive trade policies is the issue of **competitiveness** – the ability to outperform rival nations in certain key high-value-added activities. Paul Krugman attacked this notion of competitiveness, and the following section is a summary of his critique. Krugman's main criticism is that comparative advantage says that *all* countries can benefit from trade, whereas the competitiveness argument implies that trade is a zero-sum game – if one side wins, then the other side loses.

Competitiveness makes sense in a business setting. Consider the constant battle for market share between Coca-Cola and Pepsi. Coke can only gain market share at the expense of Pepsi, so the rationale for competition here is clear. But comparative advantage says that this analogy cannot be carried over to countries. What is good advice to CEOs may not be sensible for heads of state.

IS TRADE BETWEEN COUNTRIES ADVERSARIAL?

Imagine that Pepsi introduces a new wonder drink that tastes fantastic and sells for half the price of other soft drinks. This would be unmitigated bad news for Pepsi's rivals. The marketing manager for Coca-Cola will not enthuse to its board that employment and wages in Pepsi factories are booming, increasing the potential market for Coca-Cola. Neither will the manager stress the benefits to Coke's own workforce of the availability of a cheaper and better-tasting product. Pepsi and Coca-Cola are adversaries.

But what if Korea announces a new, smaller and cheaper computer chip that increases processing speed 20-fold? Is this bad for the United States? It is almost certainly bad news for computer chip manufacturers in the United States, but not for the rest of the US economy. Two things have happened:

- First, US firms can now get access to cheaper and better products that will improve productivity in a range of industries and therefore increase the US standard of living. An example of this effect is that when the United States in 2002 increased tariffs on steel imports to help protect the US steel industry, other firms that required steel as an input formed the 49-to-1 group. The name signified that, for every employee in the steel industry, there were 49 employees in US industries that would now have to pay more for their steel. Protectionism helped the steel industry, but not the considerable number of other industries that rely on steel as an input – e.g. auto manufacturers, food processing and so on.
- Second, the Korean economy will be performing strongly on the strength of the additional profits, investment and employment that this innovation generates. This, in turn, will increase the demand for US goods in Korea.

Of course, trade restrictions could prevent the importation of the new technology or prevent US firms from exporting to Korea. Then these benefits will not materialize. But if there is free trade, the innovation will benefit the United States. This example shows clearly the difference in perspective between being the CEO of a company and the leader of a country.

Competitiveness confuses two distinct notions: economic growth and comparative advantage, or absolute and relative productivities. Advocates of competitiveness want their country to focus on high-productivity industries. Capital accumulation, education and technological progress are means of increasing productivity. Therefore, government policies that encourage the development of capital- and skill-intensive industries are to be welcomed. However, all of this is about the *absolute* level of productivity. By contrast, comparative advantage tells us that trade is about *relative* productivity. It is, of course, better for a country to have high productivity, but whether it does or not, free-trade policies improve welfare. In other words, a country should invest in education, encourage investment and try to stimulate technological progress, but these policies should not interfere with free trade between countries.

The danger with a single-minded obsession with competitiveness is that it leads one to think of success as doing better than other countries. But Chapters 3 to 6 suggested that a country should try to maximize its own productivity growth rather than outperform rivals. Consider the imaginary case in which the French and German economies are both experiencing long-run productivity growth of 2% per year, but the Germans suddenly achieve an increase of 4%. In some sense, the French have lost their competitiveness, but what does this mean? France will experience some disutility from this faster German growth rate (individual happiness does depend in part on comparisons with your neighbours, and a much larger German economy would probably affect the role of France in international politics). But, in essence, nothing has happened to the French standard of living – it is still growing at 2% per year.

Failure to recognize this distinction between absolute and relative productivities can lead to trade restrictions. Comparative advantage shows that all countries gain from trade, which therefore implies that all countries lose from trade barriers. This reasoning underpins Krugman's statement that competitiveness is a dangerous obsession.

> **KEY POINT**
>
> Comparative advantage implies that trade between countries is not a zero-sum game, so trade should not be viewed as a competition in which a country has to outperform its rivals.

8.7 Strategic Trade Theory

We have so far taken a passive view of comparative advantage: according to H-O, the resource endowments of a country determine competitive advantage. However, alternative models, known as **new trade theory**, imply that simply accepting a country's current comparative advantage is not optimal and that anti-free-trade policies can be used to transform comparative advantage. For instance, Switzerland has a comparative advantage in the production of precision-engineered luxury watches – an advantage that partly reflects historical accident. At some point in the past, Switzerland had many craftsmen who could produce high-quality watches, so the industry was established in Switzerland. A range of industries then developed nearby to supply components, and an expanding workforce acquired the skills to make watches. Thus Switzerland established a reputation for producing fine watches. The status of the Swiss watch industry reflects a comparative advantage accumulated over many years, an advantage that reputation and know-how have strengthened. This suggests that countries do not need to accept as inevitable their current comparative advantage. Perhaps government policies (such as import protection or export subsidies) can develop an industry that will eventually become the country's comparative advantage.

Consider the aircraft industry, which is characterized by extreme increasing returns to scale – because of huge development costs, average unit production costs decrease sharply as output increases. Consider the interaction between two firms: the US firm Boeing and the European conglomerate Airbus. This example combines many features. The industry is a large and important one – Boeing is the United States' largest exporter. The industry is high tech/high value added and of strategic importance to the United States and Europe. Europe and the United States have continually clashed over whether government support of Boeing and Airbus violates free-trade principles.

To develop our model, we utilize Table 8.7, which is a payoff matrix showing the profits that Boeing and Airbus earn in response to different actions by each firm. To keep the analysis simple, we focus on the case in which each firm simply decides whether to enter the market or not. The first number in each cell gives the profits that Boeing earns, and the second those that Airbus earns.

We treat Boeing and Airbus symmetrically – each gets the same profits if they find themselves in the same circumstances. Table 8.7 shows that if both Boeing and Airbus produce planes, then each loses $100 million. The reason is that if they share the market, then neither benefits from increasing returns to scale, so costs are high; competition also keeps prices low, and both lose money. However, if Boeing enters but Airbus does not, then Airbus makes zero profits, and Boeing earns $500 million. Boeing captures the whole market, with

TABLE 8.7 ● Airbus–Boeing Payoff Matrix – No Government Intervention.

The first figure in each cell represents the payoff to Boeing, the second figure is the payoff to Airbus.

		Airbus	
		Enter	Don't Enter
Boeing	Enter	–$100m, –$100m	$500m, 0
	Don't Enter	0, $500m	0, 0

benefits from increasing returns to scale and a monopoly position. If only Airbus enters the market, it makes $500 million, and Boeing earns zero. Obviously, if neither enters the market, each makes zero profit.

The best strategy for each firm depends on what it thinks the other firm will do. If Boeing knows that Airbus is going to enter the market, its best strategy is to withdraw; in this case, it makes zero profit rather than losing $100 million. If, however, it knows that Airbus has no intention of entering the market, then Boeing's best strategy is to enter. The same considerations hold for Airbus. If Boeing is already in the market and is committed to maintaining a presence, Table 8.7 says that Airbus should choose not to enter. In that case, Europe would not have an airplane manufacturing industry and would have to buy planes from an American monopoly provider.

We now show how this model provides different policy implications from those of comparative advantage. Imagine that Europe decides it needs an airplane manufacturing industry and offers a subsidy to Airbus of $200 million if it produces planes. Table 8.8 gives the new payoffs to Boeing and Airbus.

Airbus's profits remain unchanged if it does not enter – the subsidy is only paid if Airbus produces. However, if Airbus enters, profits increase by $200 million, the amount of the subsidy. Thus if Boeing enters the market, the subsidy converts the operating loss of $100 million for Airbus into a total profit of $100 million, while if Boeing withdraws from the market, Airbus's profits are now $700 million. The European subsidy – the instrument of **strategic trade policy** – changes the industry; regardless of what Boeing does, Airbus's optimal strategy is to produce planes. Therefore Boeing has to select a strategy by comparing outcomes along the top row of Table 8.8. Given that the subsidy means that Airbus is definitely going to enter the market, Boeing either loses $100 million by producing, or earns zero profits by withdrawing. The best strategy for Boeing is therefore to cease production and leave the market to Airbus. The European subsidy has worked spectacularly. In return for a subsidy of $200 million, Europe gains monopoly profits of $500 million and Europe acquires a comparative advantage in an industry perceived as being of strategic economic importance.

This example (based on imperfect competition and increasing returns) makes a focus on competitiveness seem more sensible than a search for comparative advantage. In this model, trade is a zero-sum game – what Airbus captures, Boeing loses. Furthermore, trade protection measures (subsidizing Airbus) increase welfare for Europe – contrary to what the static theory of comparative advantage implies. If this model captures important aspects of reality, then free-trade policy may not be best, and government interventions in key industries can bring benefits.

However, we should not end our account of the model here. By paying a subsidy to Airbus, Europe has captured the market, but the US government is unlikely to remain

TABLE 8.8 ● Airbus–Boeing Payoff Matrix – European Subsidy $200m.

		Airbus	
		Enter	Don't Enter
Boeing	Enter	–$100m, $100m	$500m, 0
	Don't Enter	0, $700m	0, 0

TABLE 8.9 ● Airbus–Boeing Payoff Matrix – US and EU Pay $200m Subsidy.

		Airbus	
		Enter	Don't Enter
Boeing	Enter	$100m, $100m	$700m, 0
	Don't Enter	0, $700m	0, 0

inactive while its largest exporter ceases production. Table 8.9 shows the payoffs if the United States also pays a $200 million subsidy to Boeing.

The best course of action for Boeing now is to produce no matter what Airbus does. The EU subsidy also means that Airbus's optimal strategy is to produce no matter what Boeing does. Therefore, both firms enter the market and the relevant cell is the top left corner of Table 8.9 – both firms make profits of $100 million. However, this profit includes the subsidy – each firm has an operating loss of $100 million because prices are set too low and costs are high. The US retaliatory action makes the EU intervention no longer advisable. Europe is now paying a subsidy of $200 million so that Airbus can make an operating loss of $100 million. Only air travellers in other countries gain from the subsidies. Competition between Airbus and Boeing leads to cheaper airplanes, which in turn leads to cheaper travel. European and American taxpayers overpay for this benefit, but citizens of other countries benefit without having to finance the subsidy.

Given that both firms are losing money without the subsidies, this situation is unlikely to continue. Three possible outcomes suggest themselves:

- Boeing and Airbus come together and agree to coordinate their price setting and both raise prices in order to restore profitability.
- Subsidies continue, but each firm tries to produce products that do not compete so fiercely against the other, enabling prices to rise. For instance, Boeing has been researching the development of extremely fast planes while Airbus has developed a large-capacity plane.
- The EU and the United States effectively engage in a poker game whereby they raise the subsidies they provide in the hope that the other country pulls out from the competition. This would be likely to trigger complaints by the losing country to the World Trade Organization regarding unfair subsidies.

So does new trade theory support strategic trade policy? We have shown that *under some circumstances* trade can be a zero-sum game and that suitable policy can lead a country to gain a comparative advantage in a key industry. However, the model also suggests many caveats. First, strategic trade policy works only under specific conditions: substantial increasing returns and imperfect competition. Such industries account for only a small part of the economy, and therefore the potential gains from strategic trade policy, even if successfully implemented, are small. Second, the benefits of strategic trade policy depend on how other countries react. Retaliatory responses or trade wars produce losses that outweigh any gains from import restrictions or subsidies. Therefore, new trade theory offers not general prescriptions for trade policy, but insights for specific circumstances.

> ### KEY POINT
>
> Some industries characterized by increasing returns and imperfect competition may benefit from trade restrictions or subsidies – in contradiction to the implications of comparative advantage. Such policies may, however, trigger a trade war between nations and are probably applicable to only a narrow set of industries.

8.8 Political Economy and Vested Interest

A major reason why governments implement trade restrictions stems from political lobbying. The Stolper-Samuelson theorem says that with free trade some groups in society lose, and others gain. The groups that lose may lobby the government for protection from foreign competition. Whether they succeed depends on how strategically important they are to the government, how forcefully they make their argument, and how strong are the arguments of the groups that stand to gain . Often the group that stands to lose from free trade is a readily identifiable industry that is concentrated in a particular region. Further, although the region may be small relative to the economy, each individual in it stands to lose substantial amounts, for instance their job. By contrast, those who gain may be a large but diverse group, each of whose members only benefit slightly from free trade. Such diffuse groups will also find it expensive to coordinate their efforts in lobbying for reductions in trade protectionism.

Consider US tomato producers concerned about cheaper Mexican imports. Millions of US consumers will benefit from cheaper imported tomatoes – but by only a few cents per purchase. By contrast, if millions of consumers buy Mexican tomatoes, thousands of workers on US tomato farms will become unemployed and lose their income, as will the farm owners. Comparative advantage tells us that the combined gains of consumers are greater than the tomato industry's losses. But the large number of consumers, their widespread locations and their small individual gains mean that they will not combine to lobby the government in support of cheap Mexican tomatoes. The tomato industry, however, will lobby vociferously against them. The government will therefore face pressure from an anti-trade lobby, but no corresponding support for free-trade policies. If the tomato-growing industry is concentrated in a particular region, then the political representatives for that area will be sensitive to the lobbying, as will the government, if it is worried about an election. As a result of these factors, the US tomato industry was given exemptions when the United States and Mexico ratified NAFTA. This political economy argument helps explain why governments adopt economic policies that are not economically efficient. It is often easier for a government to provide protection to a sector rather than to allow that sector to undergo a potentially painful process of relocation and restructuring.

Empirical analysis of industries that are most likely to receive protection from trade pressures in OECD countries shows that they tend to have high levels of employment, high employment/output ratios, a high proportion of unskilled workers and monopoly power. The adverse distributional implications of free trade, which lead governments to try to protect high-employment, unskilled industries, explain the first three findings. Coordination effects explain the final factor: it is much easier for an industry concentrated around a few firms to finance and coordinate a lobbying effort than for an industry that has many small firms.

SUMMARY

In Section 8.1, we reviewed evidence that world trade has been increasing at a faster rate than world GDP, so that the world is becoming increasingly interconnected. The majority of trade is in manufactured goods.

In Section 8.2, we saw that economists' support for free trade is based on the concept of comparative advantage, which says that all countries can benefit from trade if they specialize in goods in which their productive advantage is greatest or their productive inefficiencies are least. A country's gains from free trade depend on the terms of trade. In Section 8.3, we saw that, over the past few year, terms of trade have shifted to benefit commodity-exporting nations.

In Section 8.4, we examined evidence for the Heckscher-Ohlin model, which says that countries have a comparative advantage in goods whose production involves the intensive use of a factor that the country possesses in abundance. This prediction accounts for some of the observed patterns of trade, but tariffs and differences in tastes and technology lead to anomalies. The H-O model also fails to account for the substantial amount of intra-industry trade, which requires a model that combines increasing returns with consumers' desire for variety.

In Section 8.6 we saw that, even though economic theory clearly shows the advantages of free trade, trade restrictions remain popular because countries try to maintain their 'competitiveness' in certain industries. The distributional implications of free trade, discussed in Section 8.5, help explain this support for trade restrictions.

In Section 8.7, we examined new trade theories, combining increasing returns and imperfect competition, which suggest that under certain circumstances restrictive trade policies can be beneficial. However, in Section 8.8, we saw that restrictive trade practices are largely the rational response of governments to lobbying pressures, and that they usually come at the cost of economic inefficiency.

CONCEPTUAL QUESTIONS

1. (Section 8.1) Why is world trade rising faster than world output? Why is there so much trade in manufactured goods?

2. (Section 8.2) Review your transactions in the marketplace over the last week. What is your comparative advantage?

3. (Section 8.2) Very few individuals are self-sufficient and most engage in the marketplace. Why, then, do so many people not accept the theory of comparative advantage?

4. (Sections 8.2 and 8.7) The automobile manufacturer VBW is threatening to remove production from your country because productivity in its plants is too low. However, if the government pays a large enough subsidy, the firm will stay. Examine the merits and demerits of such a policy for the firm, government and consumers.

5. (Section 8.3) In some OECD countries, agriculture is heavily protected and governments provide public support, at least in part to preserve traditional lifestyles. What are the merits and demerits of using trade restrictions to achieve this aim?

6. (Section 8.4) What is the comparative advantage of your country? Can the Heckscher-Ohlin model explain it?

7. (Section 8.4) Although world coffee prices have risen recently, they remain low and volatile. Can coffee producers learn anything from the actions of oil-exporting nations in using OPEC as a cartel to raise oil prices?

8. (Section 8.5) What can governments do to ease the distributional effects of trade within a country?

9. (Section 8.5) Figure 8.10 suggests that trade makes wages reflect productivity within a country. Is this fair?

10. (Section 8.6) Imagine a reunion in 10 years' time with your classmates. Under one scenario, you find that although your income rose 50%, everyone else's income rose 100%. Under another scenario, your income fell by 25%, but everyone else's fell by 50%. Which of these scenarios do you prefer? What does this imply about competitiveness?

11. (Section 8.7) An emerging market wishes to develop a presence in a key high-technology industry. It realizes that, at the moment, it could not possibly compete with existing firms, but it believes that if it were sheltered from competition via import restrictions for several years, it could compete. (This is the *infant industry* argument for trade restrictions.) What are the likely problems with such an approach?

12. (Section 8.8) Does popular resentment against free trade simply reflect economic illiteracy or more deep-seated political issues?

ANALYTICAL QUESTIONS

1. (Section 8.2) In Country A, it is possible to produce a car with the same resources that would produce 1000 toy cars. In Country B, producing a car uses resources that could produce 3000 toy cars. Show with a diagram how both countries can be better off if the international terms of trade between cars and toy cars is 1 car to 2000 toy cars. Suppose the country that is relatively good at making toy cars is poor and feels that it cannot waste resources on consuming toy cars. Does this affect your analysis?

2. (Section 8.2) Consider again the two countries in Question 1. Country A has a per capita GDP 10 times that of Country B. The government of Country B decides that concentrating on producing toy cars is harmful because it sees few countries in the rich, developed world that use more resources on building toys than on manufacturing automobiles. It places a 50% tariff on imported automobiles (so that if the world price of an automobile is $10 000, the domestic price will be $15 000). There is no change in world prices as a result of this. What is the impact of the tariff on the structure of domestic production? Is anyone better off? Is anyone worse off?

3. (Section 8.5) A small industrialized country initially has no trading links with a large, but closed, centrally planned economy that shares a border. Wages per hour for skilled and unskilled workers are $25 and $12, respectively, in the industrialized economy. The centrally planned economy suddenly undergoes a peaceful revolution and the border with its industrial neighbour is completely opened to trade. In the formerly centrally planned economy, skilled workers get paid $5 an hour and unskilled workers $2 an hour. Productivity in the formerly centrally planned economy is one-fifth that of the industrial country in all sectors and for all workers. What would factor price equalization imply happens to wages in the industrial country?

4. (Section 8.7) How would the situation shown in Table 8.9 change if the EU increased its subsidy from $200 to $300m? If you were the CEO of Airbus, how would you use this subsidy to improve your market position? How might Boeing respond?

CHAPTER 9

Globalization

Key Concepts

Foreign Direct Investment	Import Substitution	Tariffs
Global Capital Flows	Infant Industry	Trade Liberalization
Globalization	Multinational Enterprises (MNEs)	World Trade Organization (WTO)
Immigration	Non-Trade Barriers	

Overview

In economic terms, globalization is where barriers between national markets (whether for goods and services, capital or labour) disappear and a single market with a single price is created. The first wave of globalization began in the early nineteenth century as transport costs fell; it came to an end in the early twentieth century due to the First World War and an increase in trade restrictions. After the Second World War, national governments coordinated to create international institutions such as the IMF, the World Bank and GATT. The resulting decline in trade tariffs initiated a second wave of globalization, which accelerated in the 1980s and 1990s as increasing numbers of emerging markets adopted trade-orientated policies.

Advocates of globalization argue that it brings many benefits: from world peace, the static gains of comparative advantage through to the beneficial effects on long-run growth. We review the evidence supporting these arguments and assess the benefits of trade liberalization for emerging markets. While economists tend overall to look kindly at globalization, there is also much vocal criticism. We consider these criticisms, including the loss of national sovereignty and cultural diversity, and the impact of multinational enterprises (MNEs) and the World Trade Organization (WTO).

9.1 Globalization: A Long-Term Perspective

Globalization refers to the way in which national economies are becoming increasingly interconnected with one another. This interconnection reveals itself in three main markets:

- In 1990 trade in *goods and services* (total exports) amounted to 16% of GDP for OECD economies and 21% for emerging markets. By 2008 these numbers were 29% and 37% respectively.
- There have been increased *capital* flows both between OECD nations and also between OECD and emerging markets. For example, foreign direct investment (FDI) was 1.2% of world GDP in 1995 but had reached 3% by 2008.
- While *labour* flows have not attained their nineteenth-century highs, immigration has risen sharply in recent years.

Figure 9.1 shows that this increasing interconnection is strongly related to a significant liberalization of goods and financial markets by countries around the world.

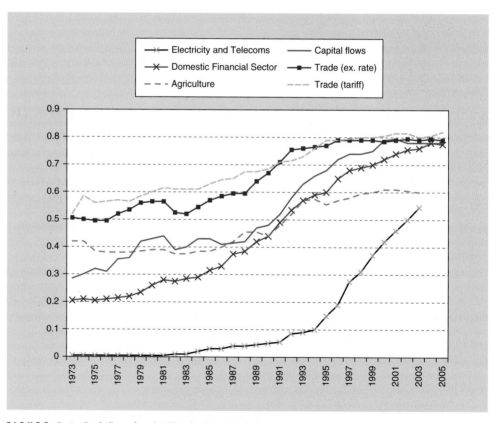

FIGURE 9.1 ● **Indices of market liberalization.** Globalization has been associated with significant deregulation of many markets by most countries. *Source:* IMF Occasional paper 268. Ostry, Jonathan, Alessandro Prati, and Antonio Spilimbergo, Structural Reforms and Economic Performance in Advanced and Developing Countries (2009).

WHEN DID GLOBALIZATION BEGIN?

World trade has been increasing for centuries as explorers have discovered trade routes and the technology of transport has improved. The great voyages of Christopher Columbus to the Americas in 1492 and Vasco da Gama to India in 1498 are dramatic examples of this long-running process of globalization. While these heroic journeys opened up new trading opportunities, the trade tended to be in high-value-added items that played a relatively small role in the economy. If trade is substantial, then prices for the same commodities should be similar in each location. Large price differentials can only persist if traders cannot buy commodities in the cheap location (which pushes up prices) and sell them in the more expensive location (which depresses prices). Trade forces prices to converge. Figure 9.2 shows evidence suggesting that a first wave of globalization started to have an impact in the early nineteenth century. The difference in price between Amsterdam and Southeast Asia for three traded goods – cloves, black pepper and coffee – began to narrow sharply.

The driving force behind this first age of globalization was dramatic declines in transportation costs. These declines were driven by the shift from sail to steam; larger, faster and more reliable ships; the introduction of refrigeration for agricultural trade; the opening of the Suez and Panama Canals; and improvements in navigation, finance and insurance. By the early twentieth century, this globalization process had led to high levels of integration, reflected in the following observation from John Maynard Keynes:

> *What an extraordinary episode in the economic progress of man that age was which came to an end in August 1914 . . . The inhabitant of London could order by telephone, sipping his morning tea in bed, the various products of the whole earth, in such quantity as he might see fit, and reasonably expect their early delivery upon his doorstep; he could at the same moment and by the same means adventure his wealth in the natural*

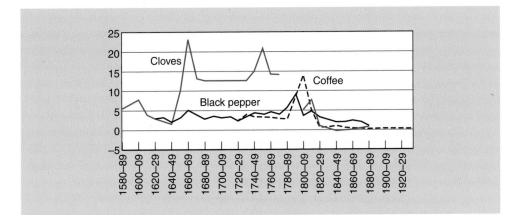

FIGURE 9.2 ● **Price differentials between Amsterdam and Southeast Asia (%).** As trade in many commodities increased sharply in the nineteenth century, international price differences fell. *Source:* Taken from material contained in *Southeast Asian Exports since the 14th Century: Cloves, Pepper, Coffee and Sugar* compiled by David Bulbeck, Anthony Reid, Lay Cheng Tan, and Yiqi Wu. Reproduced here with the kind permission of the publisher, Institute of Southeast Asian Studies Singapore, www.iseas.edu.sg/pub.html.

resources and new enterprises of any quarter of the world, and share, without exertion or trouble, in their prospective fruits and advantages. (The Economic Consequences of the Peace, *1920*)

Figure 9.3 shows the annual growth in world trade over the last 100 years (excluding the World Wars of 1914–18 and 1939–45). Before 1914 world trade grew at an average of 5% per year, although it fluctuated widely depending on the business cycle. After the end of the First World War in 1918, trade resumed but collapsed dramatically during the early 1930s. The United States and the rest of the world were in the midst of the Great Depression and, to prevent imports from capturing domestic demand, the United States enacted protectionist measures. Other countries retaliated, and trade declined.

By the end of the Second World War, most countries wanted to construct international institutions that would minimize the threat of conflict and foster international economic relations. To promote these goals, the International Monetary Fund and the World Bank were founded, and the General Agreement on Trade and Tariffs (GATT, which was later transformed into the World Trade Organization) was enacted. Through a series of negotiations, GATT achieved reductions in trade tariffs and other barriers to trade, as shown in Figure 9.4. As a result, the world witnessed a second wave of globalization, which accelerated in the 1980s and 1990s as increasing numbers of emerging markets adopted trade-orientated policies in an effort to boost their GDP growth. Figure 9.3 also shows how cyclical world trade is – the Great Recession in 2009 led to a dramatic decline in world trade in that year.

DIFFERENCES BETWEEN TWO WAVES OF GLOBALIZATION

The first wave of globalization was driven by falling transportation costs and came to an end due to war and increasingly protectionist trade policies. By contrast, the second wave of globalization has been driven by a reversal of trade policies and increasing trade liberalization. The impacts of transport costs and trade policy in driving globalization are summarized in

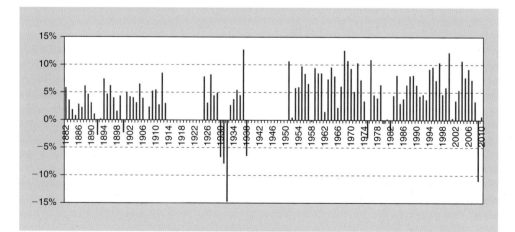

FIGURE 9.3 ● **Annual growth in world trade, 1882–2010.** Since the end of the Second World War, the volume of world trade has risen at an annual rate of over 5%. *Source:* Maddison, *Monitoring the World Economy: 1820–1992* (1995), OECD, updated using WTO data.

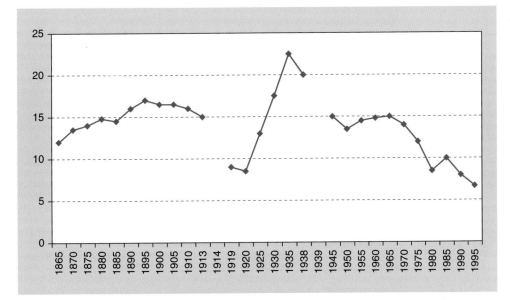

FIGURE 9.4 ● **Average tariffs since 1865.** Tariffs have steadily declined since the Depression. *Source:* Clemens and Williamson, Why Did the Tariff–Growth Correlation Reverse after 1950?, NBER working paper, WP 6181.

Table 9.1, which also documents the progress of globalization in labour and capital markets. According to the data, contemporary globalization in the goods market has passed the highs of the first wave of globalization to reach unparalleled levels. By contrast, while immigration has recently increased, it has not yet reached the levels of the end of the nineteenth century. Capital markets, on this measure, are of a similar scale, size and role to those of the first wave of globalization.

There are other differences between these two waves of globalization. In the earlier wave, trade tended to be rather simple, with raw materials and agricultural goods going in one direction and finished manufactured goods in the other. The value-added chain today is, however, far more complex and involves many more stages. To exploit the comparative advantage of different countries, firms have sliced up the production process and located different stages in different countries. As a consequence, it is estimated that around one-third of all trade is intrafirm; that is, multinational enterprises (MNEs) with production distributed across many countries shipping products at various stages of completion to different parts of the company around the world. Not only does this make the structure of trade today different from the past, but the existence of MNEs and strategic alliances among major companies creates large and powerful economic entities with which governments have to deal.

> ### KEY POINT
>
> Globalization began in earnest in the early nineteenth century, driven by falling transport costs. The First World War and increasing use of trade restrictions saw this first wave come to an end by 1914. A second wave began after the Second World War and has been mainly driven by falling trade tariffs due to international trade negotiations.

TABLE 9.1 ● **Two Waves of Globalization.**

The first wave of globalization was driven by falling transport costs and the second and most recent wave by falling tariffs.

Epoch	Intercontinental Commodity Market Integration		Migration and World Labour Markets		Integration of World Capital Markets
	Change in Price Gaps between Continents	Why They Changed	How the Migrant Shares Changed in the Receiving Countries	Why They Changed	What Happened to Integration
1820–1914	Price gaps cut by 81%	72% due to cheaper transport, 28% due to pre-1870 tariff cuts	Rise in migrant shares (e.g. from 9.6% to 14.6% in US 1850–1910)	Passenger transport cost slashed (Immigration policies remain neutral)	60% progress from complete segmentation towards market integration
1914–1950	Gaps double in width, back to 1870 Level	Due to new trade barriers only	Drop in migrant shares (e.g. from 14.6% to 6.9% policies in US)	Restrictive immigration policies	Revert to complete market segmentation
1950–2000	Price gaps cut by 76%, now lower than in 1914	74% due to policies, freeing trade, 26% due to cheaper transport	Rise in migrant shares (e.g. from 6.9% to 9.8% in US)	Transport costs drop again (no net change in immigration policies)	Again 60% progress from complete segmentation towards market integration
Overall 1820–2000	Price gaps cut by 92%	18% due to policies, 82% due to cheaper transport	No clear change in migrant shares	Policy restrictions, offsetting the transport improvements	60% progress from complete segmentation towards market integration

Source: Lindert and Williamson, Does Globalization Make the World More Unequal?, NBER Working Paper, WP 8228 (April 2001).

(9.2) The Benefits of Trade Liberalization

The removal of trade restrictions, or **trade liberalization**, has been the subject of much criticism, and we shall review in the next section arguments against globalization. For now we focus on the alleged advantages of trade liberalization.

TRADE, PEACE AND COMPARATIVE ADVANTAGE

One long-running historical claim is that trade between countries helps reduce the risk of war between them. Montesquieu in his 1748 work *The Spirit of the Laws* argues that 'commerce cures destructive prejudices', while Immanuel Kant argued that sustainable peace could be built on a combination of democracy, international organizations and economic interdependence.

In Chapter 8 we reviewed the theory of comparative advantage, which argued that all countries benefit from free trade and the removal of trade restrictions. The essence of comparative advantage is that countries gain by focusing on producing goods at which they are most efficient and purchasing other commodities more cheaply from abroad. These gains help produce an increase in the *level* of real GDP per capita. This is a *static* gain, because once resources have been fully switched to the more efficient sector, the gains from trade are complete. The logic of comparative advantage implies that all countries gain, although they do so in varying amounts. For instance, agriculture is a heavily protected sector across the world, so there are significant gains for agricultural exporting nations.

TRADE AND LONG-RUN GROWTH

A more controversial issue concerns the *dynamic* benefits of trade liberalization.

Proponents of trade liberalization suggest that emerging markets should adopt outward-looking policies based around free trade, exports, trade liberalization and encouraging inward FDI. Opponents counter that they should adopt inward-looking policies based around protective trade policies to encourage the development of domestic industries and **import substitution**, substituting imports with domestically produced goods. This prompts an important question: Does the removal of trade restrictions influence the trend growth of an economy?

During the 1950s, when many emerging markets were gaining colonial independence, inward-looking strategies dominated. The overriding policy philosophy was well summarized by the Indian premier Jawaharlal Nehru when he said: 'I believe as a practical proposition that it is better to have a second rate thing made in one's own country than a first rate thing one has to import.' The economic rationale behind this policy was a desire for countries to promote domestic high-value-added sectors, such as manufacturing, rather than relying on primary raw materials. This desire was driven by two concerns:

- The Prebisch-Singer hypothesis, outlined in Chapter 8, that the terms of trade for agricultural products fall over time so the gains from trade will diminish.
- A belief that technological progress and TFP growth occur mainly in the manufacturing sector rather than agriculture. If, due to comparative advantage, the manufacturing sector of the economy shrinks, this would lead to a fall in TFP growth and slower long-term growth.

To avoid these concerns, manufacturing was protected by trade barriers. This would give countries an opportunity to build up their proficiency in these industries until they were able to compete at a global level and trade protection could be removed. This is known as the **infant industry** justification for trade protection. A new industry in an economy cannot hope to compete with more experienced rivals in other countries, but, through experience and learning by doing, it can become competitive.

But there are powerful arguments that instead suggest that openness is good for the growth of emerging markets. These arguments point out that one problem with imposing high tariffs on importing manufactured goods is that it raises the price of capital machinery that domestic manufacturers need. A given amount of money for investment purposes will therefore buy fewer machines and lead to a smaller increase in the capital stock. The other problem with the infant industry/import substitution argument is that it ignores the fact that imports can be a source of TFP growth. By restricting imports, not only are domestic firms forced to pay higher prices for capital goods, they may have to utilize inferior domestic technology. This argument that imports can help boost TFP growth may also apply to the service sector, where it is claimed that emerging markets with weak financial systems might benefit by allowing the import of more efficient financial services from advanced nations. The same argument also applies to other service industries such as airlines and telecoms.

Most emerging markets have now abandoned import substitution policies and lowered trade tariffs sharply (see Table 9.2). Why didn't import substitution work?

- This infant industry argument needs to be applied selectively rather than across all sectors. If used selectively, it may sometimes work, as proven by our related discussion of strategic trade policy and Boeing/Airbus in Chapter 8 and by evidence in both the recent and historical experience of emerging markets. For instance, South Korea has managed to develop an extremely competitive steel industry in this way. However, if the argument is applied generally to most industries, then governments end up paying too much in subsidies. This puts a strain on fiscal finances and leads to substantial rent seeking and inefficiencies in both industry and government.
- Import substitution led to high capital goods prices and domestic firms having to use low-level technology.
- If an industry had not become competitive after several years, governments have found themselves extending the protectionism rather than removing subsidies and tariffs and seeing the industry suffer from global competition.

KEY POINT

The link between trade openness and long-run growth is ambiguous from a theoretical perspective. However, in practice many emerging markets have moved away from import substitution policies towards export openness and trade liberalization.

TRADE LIBERALIZATION AND ECONOMIC GROWTH: THE EMPIRICAL EVIDENCE

As the previous section makes clear, theory is ambiguous about how trade liberalization affects long-run growth. Although most emerging nations are now pursuing policies of openness, we must review the empirical evidence to determine the effects of either closed or open trade policies.

TABLE 9.2 ● Trends in Average Tariffs among Emerging Markets.

During the 1980s and 1990s, emerging markets moved away from import substitution and reduced trade tariffs sharply.

Country	Earliest (1960–70)	Earliest (1980–85)	Average (1986–90)	Average (1991–95)	Average (1996–2002)	Latest (2003-09)
Argentina	181	28	25	11	14	11
Bangladesh		100	93	63	26	16
Bolivia		12	18	10	9	7
Brazil		44	42	17	13	13
Burundi		38	37	7	21	14
Cameroon		28	32	19	18	18
Chile	83	35	17	11	8	4
China		50	39	40	14	9
Colombia	47	61	29	14	12	11
Costa Rica		21	19	12	7	6
Côte d'Ivoire		31	26	22	15	13
Egypt		47	40	33	30	11
Ghana		43	19	17	16	12
Guinea		76	10	11	17	14
India		74	94	54	31	14
Indonesia	58	29	26	20	7	6
Israel		8	7	8	8	3
Jordan		16	16	17	15	11
Kenya		40	40	30	20	12
Korea	40	24	18	10	9	7
Libya		13	23		20	
Malawi		22	18	20	16	12
Malaysia		11	15	14	9	7
Mexico		27	14	13	17	9
Morocco		54	23	24	34	15
Nigeria		33	32	33	25	11
Pakistan		78	67	57	24	15
Peru	73	19	41	17	14	7
Philippines		41	28	23	8	5
Sierra Leone		26	31	30	16	

(Continued)

TABLE 9.2 ● (Continued)

Country	Earliest (1960–70)	Earliest (1980–85)	Average (1986–90)	Average (1991–95)	Average (1996–2002)	Latest (2003-09)
Singapore	1	0	0	0	0	0
South Africa		29	15	9	13	8
Sri Lanka		41	28	24	16	10
Taiwan, Prov. of China		31	15	11	9	5
Thailand		32	40	32	17	11
Tunisia		24	26	28	36	20
Turkey		40	27	27	14	1
Uruguay	384	47	30	16	12	10
Average	**108**	**36**	**29**	**22**	**16**	**10**

Source: UNCTAD Trade Analysis and Information System.

Figure 9.5 shows that there exists a strong negative correlation between tariffs and GDP: countries with low tariffs tend to have high GDP. But it is well known in economics that correlation does not imply causation. In other words, Figure 9.5 does not show conclusively that trade liberalization *causes* faster GDP growth. There are two main problems: omitted variables and simultaneity.

OMITTED VARIABLES Countries that lower their tariffs may also introduce many other reforms. For example, they may improve education, reform institutions, improve their banking system and so forth. It may be these other reforms that really improve GDP, rather than trade liberalization. Countries with high tariffs may have poor economic policies in other areas. For instance, many ex-communist economies have high tariffs and many market interventions and inefficiencies, as well as having low GDP. Therefore, the strong correlation in Figure 9.5 might really reflect the influence of a third variable rather than trade liberalization itself.

To see the problems that this causes econometrically, consider the case where

GDP per capita = (a × Financial Sector Reform) + (b × Capital Stock) + (c × Openness) + u

where a, b and c are positive coefficients and u is a random variable that on average equals zero. Let us also assume that countries tend to do financial-sector reform at the same time as they reduce tariffs and increase openness, so that Financial Sector Reform and Openness are correlated:

Financial Sector Reform = d × Openness

If the econometrician mistakenly does not include Financial Sector Reform in the regression and instead estimates

GDP = (b × Capital Stock) + (f × Openness)

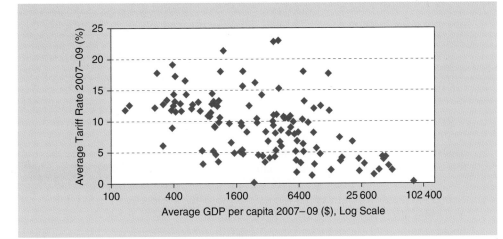

FIGURE 9.5 ● **Tariffs and GDP.** Countries with high tariffs tend to have lower GDP per capita.
Source: World Development Indicators and UNCTAD.

then the estimate of f will be c + (a × d). In other words, the econometrician will overestimate the effect of openness as c + (a × d) rather than the true value, c. If c were negative – that is, trade liberalization decreases GDP – then this bias may even be large enough to make us think that trade liberalization was beneficial when it was actually harmful.

SIMULTANEITY It may be the case that countries with high GDP have low tariffs. If this is so, then we will once again overestimate c and the impact of trade liberalization. Why might countries with high GDP have low tariffs? One reason is that poor countries tend to have weak systems for collecting taxes from labour income and so have to rely more on tariffs. Richer countries rely on tariffs less. Another reason is that, as we saw in Chapter 8, trade leads to some sectors expanding and some declining. Rich countries have more substantial welfare systems and so will be able to support the losers from free trade more easily and thus will lower tariffs more. As a result, rich countries will have lower tariffs.

Both of these problems can be overcome in our econometric estimation if we focus on a component of openness that is not affected by GDP (although it may in turn influence GDP) and is unlikely to be correlated with other policy variables. We can think of this as the *exogenous* component of openness – the portion of a country's openness that is unaffected by policy variables. Because this component is unaffected by GDP and uncorrelated with policy variables, we will be able to estimate correctly how openness affects GDP in a way not influenced by the problems of simultaneity and omitted variables.

A natural way of estimating this exogenous component of openness is to focus on the role of geography, based on the simple idea that countries nearer to one another should trade more – the so-called gravity model of trade. If we find that countries that do more trade than others for geographical reasons also have higher GDP, we can be reasonably confident that openness boosts GDP. Using this approach, for instance, we find that Japan's trade (exports plus imports) should be around 40% of GDP due to its nearness to other countries, whereas, in reality, its trade is 25% of GDP. From this we can infer that Japan has relatively closed trade policies. By contrast, Singapore's geography predicts a trade share worth 108% of GDP compared to an actual trade share (in 1985) of 318% due to highly trade-orientated policies. Using these trade shares predicted by geographical distance as our measure of openness, we find that the more open countries do have higher GDP[1] and that the result is stable and significant.

While this evidence is suggestive, it is not immune to criticism. In particular, it is vulnerable to the criticism that perhaps openness induced by policy has a different effect on GDP than geography-induced openness. In other words, this result cannot be used to argue that lowering tariffs will increase GDP growth. However, a more recent study[2] of the link between trade liberalization and growth takes a different perspective, although it finds similar results. On average, that study found that trade liberalization boosts GDP growth by around 1.5% per annum, suggesting substantial dynamic gains from trade. The interesting feature of this study is that rather than just compare across countries and see how differences in trade policy influence GDP, it also focuses on how countries respond over time to changes in their own trade policy. Figure 9.6 shows the average pattern of GDP growth after trade liberalization from a large sample of countries. This suggests that on average trade liberalization leads to improved growth performance for emerging markets. But there is considerable variation across countries in the success of trade liberalization. Trade liberalization tends to boost growth but it is not guaranteed – in the case of several countries GDP actually falls after trade liberalization.

So what lessons can we learn from this empirical evidence?

- There is little evidence that supports the idea that inward-looking, high-tariff policies boost growth. The econometric evidence tends to support the opposite – that open trade policies systematically boost GDP; a result consistent with China's rapid growth since opening up for trade.
- The finding that trade liberalization tends to boost GDP growth does not imply that countries should rapidly remove trade restrictions across all sectors. It leaves

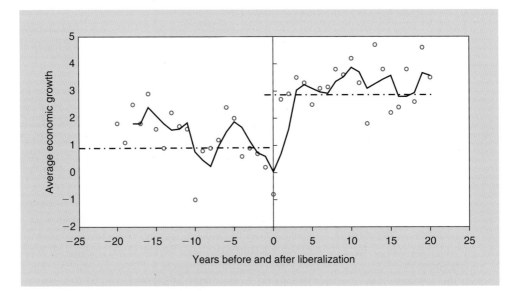

FIGURE 9.6 ● **Impact of trade liberalization on economic growth.** Trade liberalization increases GDP growth on average, but not always. *Source:* Wacziarg and Welch, Trade Liberalization and Growth: New Evidence, NBER Working Paper 10152 (2003).

open the issue of whether a gradualist or radical approach to trade liberalization is required.

- An exclusive focus on trade liberalization may be unwarranted. Although the data support trade liberalization as a means of boosting GDP growth, the same evidence can also be used to criticize governments and institutions that place an excessive faith in trade liberalization *alone* as a means of boosting GDP. Trade liberalization may work as an important component of a wide range of policy reforms.

LIBERALIZATION AND GROWTH: THE CASE OF INDIA

An important example of the impact of liberalization is India. From the 1950s to the 1970s India operated a policy of import substitution where high tariffs, licensing requirements and government monopolies reduced competition and foreign access and supported local producers. Figure 9.7 shows how, prior to 1991, average tariff rates on manufacturing were over 100% and around 90% of imports were subject to non-tariff barriers (mainly import licences restricting the amount imported). Although there were some tentative steps towards liberalization in the 1980s, significant reform did not occur until 1991 when, following an economic crisis, the government cut both tariff and non-tariff barriers significantly, allowed more foreign investment and broke up a number of state monopolies.

At first sight, the dramatic difference in India's average GDP per capita growth rate of 5% post-1991 compared with the 2.6% average achieved before then (1960–91) makes a clear case in favour of liberalization (particularly since poverty reduction has also accelerated significantly). But, as Figure 9.8 shows, there is some evidence that India's growth acceleration began in the 1980s before the liberalization (though high levels of government borrowing and spending in the late 1980s may explain this). More importantly, it is clear that a number of policies pursued before the liberalization, such as significant investment in education, were important in explaining the success of the liberalization policy.

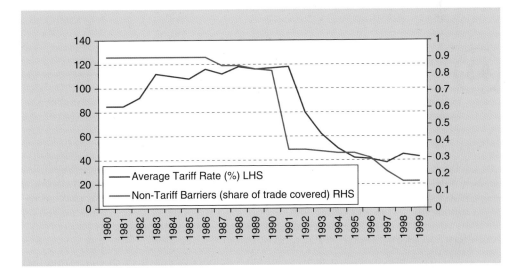

FIGURE 9.7 ● **Trade barriers in India.** India undertook a significant trade liberalization in 1991. *Source:* Kumar and Mishra, Trade Liberalization and Wage Inequality: Evidence from India, IMF Working Paper 05/20.

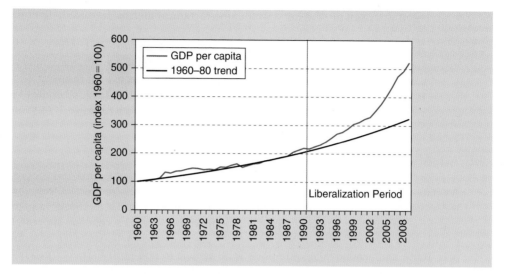

FIGURE 9.8 ● Indian GDP per capita, 1960–2009. Income growth in India has been significantly higher since trade liberalization. *Source:* Kumar and Mishra, Trade Liberalization and Wage Inequality: Evidence from India; IMF Working Paper 05/20 and authors' calculations.

KEY POINT

Econometric evidence suggests that increased openness to trade does raise the long-run rate of economic growth, although it is difficult accurately to isolate the impact that trade policy alone has on GDP. Although, on average, trade liberalization boosts growth, success is not guaranteed.

9.3 Foreign Direct Investment and Multinationals

The second area in which globalization has occurred is in international capital flows (financial capital, not the physical capital we discussed in Chapter 4). Figure 9.9 shows how cross-border capital flows increased steadily over the last 20 years or so, before collapsing in 2009 due to the global financial crisis. As Figure 9.9 shows, these flows take many forms ranging from bank loans to equity purchases; we will look at all these financial instruments in Chapters 16 and 17. In this section we focus on foreign direct investment (FDI), which is where a foreign firm takes a controlling interest in a local firm (either by purchasing a controlling interest in an existing firm or building a new factory or firm on a 'greenfield' site). By definition, it is this type of investment that is undertaken by multinational enterprises (MNEs), who have become controversial players in the globalization process.

Advocates of multinationals point out a number of benefits that come from their FDI. First, FDI by MNEs tends significantly to increase overall investment in recipient countries and MNEs tend to pay higher wages and undertake more research and development than local firms, all of which are likely to improve the living standards of citizens in recipient countries. Second, as Table 9.3 shows, there is evidence that FDI results in a transfer of technology to local firms, raising their productivity. Finally, FDI tends to be a less volatile source of foreign financing than other capital flows. This can been seen in Figures 9.9 and 9.10, where the fall in FDI in 2009 was far less dramatic than other inflows.

Critics highlight the influence that large MNEs can have on governments receiving FDI. As Table 9.3 shows, there is evidence that FDI decisions are influenced by the tax regime, so countries wishing to receive greater FDI may be persuaded to make tax (and perhaps employment and environmental) laws more favourable to MNEs. This process is called the 'race to the bottom', as governments compete with one another to offer the lowest

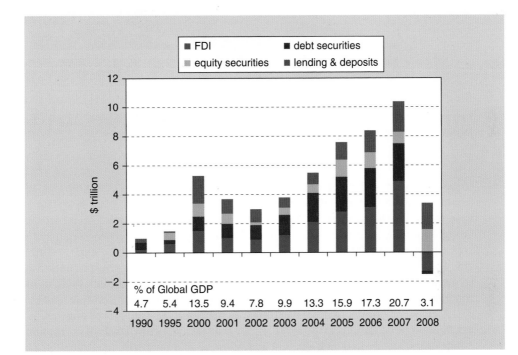

FIGURE 9.9 ● **Global capital flows, 1990–2008.** Global capital flows increased steadily until the financial crisis. *Source:* McKinsey Global Institute.

TABLE 9.3 ● **Impact of Taxes on Behaviour of Multinationals.**

Multinational firms can respond in a number of ways to changes in taxation in host nations. For example, they can restructure themselves so that profits can be shifted to lower tax locations, or they can change their level of investment in new or existing locations. The consensus of studies suggests that firms engage in all three.

Firm Behaviour	Impact of a 1 Percentage Point Increase in Tax
Change in profit due to profit shifting	−1.2%
Investment in new locations	−0.4%
Investment in existing locations	−0.65%

Source: de Mooij and Ederveen, 'Corporate tax elasticities: A reader's guide to empirical findings', *Oxford Review of Economic Policy* (2008).

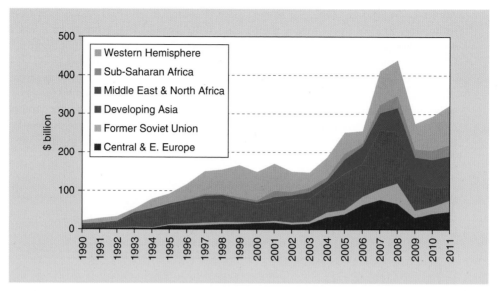

FIGURE 9.10 ● **FDI flows.** FDI tends to be more stable than other capital flows. *Source:* IMF World Economic Outlook (2010).

corporate tax rates. If governments do cut corporate tax rates, then unless they can increase labour income taxes, they will not have enough revenue to finance the welfare state and will have to reduce their generosity. Globalization may remove the ability to protect workers at the same time as it increases the need for this protection. The same argument can be applied to government regulations concerning environmental protection, working standards and minimum wages. One way to overcome this problem is for governments to agree to common standards. For instance, the EU has rules restricting the subsidies that its member countries are allowed to pay to firms in order to prevent a race to the bottom, and efforts to create global environmental standards such as the Kyoto agreement are ongoing. It is also worth noting that there is evidence that FDI is attracted by low levels of corruption, good public infrastructure and high levels of education, so that the desire to attract FDI need not create negative incentives for policymakers.

9.4 Immigration

The third route through which globalization has increased connections between countries is through immigration. Figure 9.11 shows that immigration into a number of OECD economies has risen in recent years and is increasingly becoming a policy issue. A common fear about immigration is that it will lead to an increase in unemployment for native workers. Table 9.4 shows that this fear is largely unfounded – the balance of evidence suggests that immigration has a small and probably temporary effect on the unemployment of native-born workers. Another concern is that immigrants receive more in public spending than they pay in taxes. Again, Table 9.4 suggests that this concern is not borne out in practice: unemployment among immigrants is indeed higher than for native-born workers (and the unemployed do indeed receive benefits without paying tax), but the age profile

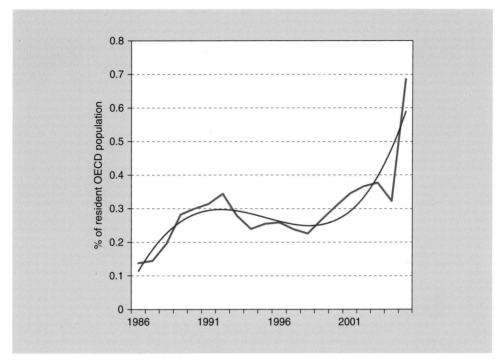

FIGURE 9.11 ● Net migration in OECD countries. Immigration has increased significantly recently.
Source: OECD.

TABLE 9.4 ● The Economic Impact of Immigration.

Studies suggest that increased immigration has a small impact on wages and a minimal impact on unemployment of native-born workers. They also suggest that immigrants on average pay as much in tax as they receive in government spending and transfers.

Hypothesis Tested	Number of Studies	Consensus of Results
Does increased immigration reduce the wages of native-born workers?	18	1 percentage point increase lowers wages by 0.12%
Does increased immigration increase unemployment of native workers?	9	Very small impact. 1 percentage point increase raises unemployment by 0.024 percentage points – probably temporary
Net fiscal impact of immigrants	15	Neutral/positive

Sources: Longhi, S., Nijkamp, P. and Poot, J., The Fallacy of 'Job Robbing': A Meta-Analysis of Estimates of the Effect of Immigration on Employment, Tinbergen Institute Discussion Papers 06-050/3, Tinbergen Institute (2006); Longhi, S., Nijkamp, P. and Poot, J., A Meta-Analytic Assessment of the Effect of Immigration on Wages, Tinbergen Institute Discussion Papers 04-134/3, Tinbergen Institute (2004); Weber, R. and Straubhaar, T., 'Immigration and the public transfer system: Some empirical evidence for Switzerland', *Review of World Economics (Weltwirtschaftliches Archiv)*, (1996), 132(2): 330–55.

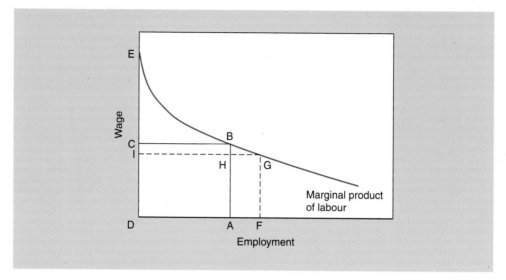

FIGURE 9.12 ● **Effect of Immigration on Labour and Capital.** Income.

of immigrants (who are generally younger than the average of the native population) renders them more likely to make a positive contribution to the public finances.

One concern that has some justification is that immigration reduces the wages of native-born workers. Table 9.4 suggests that for every 10% increase in foreign workers, the wages of native workers falls by around 1.2%.

We can use the marginal product of labour to understand the impact of immigration on the economy. Figure 9.12 shows that, before immigration occurs and at the prevailing wage, employment is A and wages are C. Total labour income is given by the rectangle ABCD and the remaining output (BCE) is paid out as capital income, so that total output equals capital plus labour income – as in Chapter 2. With an influx of immigration, employment rises by AF, which, as discussed above, lowers wages to the new level, I. Labour income is now given by FGID, with AFGH being the earnings of immigrant workers and AHID the earnings of native workers. The fall in wages has reduced the earnings of native workers by HBCI – the bigger the fall in wages caused by immigration, the bigger this negative impact on native workers. While native workers lose (depending on the magnitude of the wage fall), the owners of capital gain – capital income is now GEI. The increase in capital income is made up of HBCI (the gain from native workers) and the area GBH. The area GBH is known as the migration surplus – it is the gain to society from the increase in labour supply that immigration brings about. The extra output that immigrants produce is not all paid out as wages, and hence society gains by the excess – GBH. While this is the net gain from immigration (ignoring any fiscal calculations), there is also the distribution effect that reallocates HBCI from native workers to owners of capital.

KEY POINT

Immigration does not seem to have a large or long-run impact on unemployment for native workers, but instead causes wages to fall. Not all the extra output that immigrants produce is paid out in wages, so that overall the receiving country gains — even though native workers lose while owners of capital gain.

(**9.5**) Problems of Globalization

Although we have seen that the balance of evidence suggests that globalization has helped raise incomes. particualrly for developing economies, there are a number of other concerns that have caused many commentators to argue that globalization is detrimental.

GLOBALIZATION AND INEQUALITY

The evidence we have seen so far in this chapter and in Chapter 3 suggests that globalization may have been important in reducing *global* poverty and inequality by contributing to rapid growth in countries like China and India. However, there is some evidence that globalization has increased inequality in developed countries. As Figure 9.13 shows, most OECD economies have experienced an increase in inequality over the last 30 years. As we saw in the case of immigration, it is possible that globalization is responsible for this, as increases in the supply of labour to firms in developed countries have lowered wages and raised the rate of return of owners of capital. In essence, prior to globalization developed countries experienced a relative shortage of unskilled and semi-skilled labour and a relative excess of capital. After globalization the potential supply of labour has increased dramatically and so capital is now scarcer and more valuable. This has lowered wages relative to the return on capital and so increased inequality.

ENVIRONMENTAL DAMAGE

Critics of globalization fear that it leads to environmental damage in two ways. First, due to the power of MNEs, governments abandon efforts to protect the environment through legislation. Second, increased levels of trade lead to greater use of fuel and more environmental

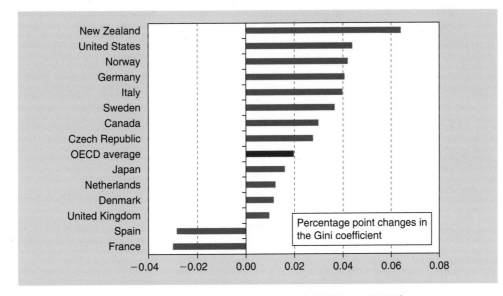

FIGURE 9.13 ● **Change in income inequality in OECD countries (mid-1980s to mid-2000s).** Most OECD countries have experienced an increase in income inequality. *Source:* OECD.

damage. Further, much of this trade seems 'pointless'; the United Kingdom, for instance, exports almost exactly the same number of pigs as it imports.

The need for governments to agree to global environmental standards to stop countries competing with one another along this dimension is connected to our next topic: the race to the bottom. The evidence regarding whether FDI worsens pollution is inconclusive, depending on which environmental indicator is considered. For instance, urban air pollution seems uncorrelated with FDI. Furthermore, there is a strong correlation between GDP and environmental regulation, so that if FDI does raise GDP, it may also lead indirectly to improvements in the environment. There is also evidence that trade protectionism can damage the environment.

What about fuel? That global trade leads to an increase in fuel use is undeniable. One cause of this is that airline fuel is frequently tax exempt, so that the full cost of environmental damage is not paid by exporters and, as a result, trade is too extensive. The other issue is whether or not the trade is 'pointless'. For instance, on average, every month Sweden imports 1305 metric tons of bottled water and exports 791 metric tons. Can this be justified? The main cost of this trade pattern is the additional transport costs – it would be cheaper for Sweden to consume its own water rather than ship it overseas and import other water. However, this cost can be offset by three factors. The first is that competition is increased through imports. This will lead to lower prices. Existing consumers of bottled water pay less. Because prices fall, more bottles are sold as consumption rises. The second benefit is that the variety of products available increases. If consumers value variety, this will also boost welfare. If the competition and variety effects are large enough, they can offset the higher transport costs. Third, increased trade in environmental goods such as solar panels may offset the negative impact of transport

THE ROLE OF THE IMF AND THE WORLD BANK

Following the end of the Second World War a number of international financial institutions (IFIs) were created that aimed to avoid the economic mistakes that had led to the Great Depression and the rise of Nazism. The most important of these are the International Monetary Fund (IMF) and the World Bank. Since both these institutions were created to manage international capital flows and economic development, their profile has risen as the world has become more globalized.

Although both institutions are financed in the same way (contributions by their 'shareholders', who are the member countries) they have distinct roles. The World Bank's focus is on long-run growth and economic development and so it makes long-term, low-interest-rate loans for development projects as well as administering a large number of aid programmes and technical assistance in developing economies. The IMF, on the other hand, has a shorter-term focus and is charged with achieving stability in the international monetary and financial system. It does this through three functions:

- *Surveillance*: monitoring government policies to see if countries are in danger of experiencing a balance of payments crisis.
- *Technical assistance*: the IMF helps governments implement economic reforms.
- *Lending assistance*: when countries experience a balance of payments crisis, the IMF lends funds.

The emphasis in IMF lending has always been on repayment; the IMF will not loan funds unless a country accepts certain conditions on its future economic and financial policies (this is referred to as *IMF conditionality*).

The IMF in particular receives plenty of criticism for the way in which it operates. One major criticism of both institutions is that they tend to support a particular set of policies, such as lowering public spending and liberalizing markets. These policies are sometimes referred to as the 'Washington Consensus' (since both institutions are based in Washington, DC). Nobel prize winner Joseph Stiglitz (a former chief economist at the World Bank) argues in his book *Globalization and Its Discontents* that the IMF's role in forcing governments to cut back expenditure in order to receive loans worsens the economic crisis in a country. Furthermore, he argues that the IMF in particular focuses on pure market-based policies, such as deregulation and privatization, which not only may adversely affect social order and poverty, but are also more extreme than richer nations are prepared to implement themselves.

The IMF is also criticized for acting in the interests of the international financial community rather than the countries to which it lends. For instance, critics of the IMF argue that by its insistence on repayment, it ensures that although the international financial companies are repaid their loans, poor countries are saddled with higher debts.

The IMF also receives criticism from another perspective: that it interferes too much with markets and creates instability. A common version of this criticism is that through offering loans to countries experiencing a balance of payments crisis, the IMF encourages countries to pursue unsustainable policies and persuades international banks to lend money knowing that eventually the IMF will bail out both the country and investors. As a result, the international financial system displays more volatility than if the IMF did not intervene.

CULTURAL AND POLITICAL CONCERNS

We have focused above on the economic implications of globalization, but many of the criticisms are more politically focused. Globalization produces a greater role for markets, so naturally globalization is seen critically by those with anti-capitalist views. Globalization also means that more resources are being allocated by market mechanisms and this may lack political legitimacy. For instance, consider the case of a country that has banned child labour but now, because of globalization, finds itself importing textiles made using child labour. No democratic decision has been made in the importing country, yet market forces have brought about this change. This is also an example of where countries begin to lose their national sovereignty – domestic rules cease to have jurisdiction. Other examples of this loss of sovereignty are connected to the power of MNEs and IFIs that lead domestic governments to alter their policies. A loss of cultural sovereignty is also a common criticism of globalization. Globalization has led to a proliferation of global brands and an alleged homogenization of cultures: 'Americanization' or 'Europeanization'.

This is a wide and varied list of criticisms of globalization. We have covered cultural change, environmental problems, inequality and poverty, the monopoly power of MNEs, instability and insecurity. What is interesting is that these were precisely the criticisms made of industrialization in the nineteenth century as *domestic* markets began to grow and restructure the economy. Governments then realized that in order to bring out the best features of markets, they would have to intervene to restrict industrial pollution, introduce town planning and health regulation, implement schemes to help the poor, create government organizations to restrict monopoly abuse by firms and provide regulation and insurance to preserve stability in the banking system. In other words, in response to the growth of markets we saw the development of national governments, institutions and regulations to reduce the disadvantages of markets and support the advantages. What this argument suggests is that with the development of global markets, we require national governments to agree to international standards and help construct global institutions in order to optimize the contribution that global markets make to welfare. In the next section we will review the global institutions that currently exist to support global markets.

> **KEY POINT**
>
> Global markets are raising many concerns relating to inequality, instability, the power of MNEs and IFIs, environmental damage and the ability of governments to protect and offer social support to their citizens.

9.6 The WTO and the Future of Trade Liberalization

An important driver of trade liberalization since the Second World War has been the WTO (World Trade Organization) and its predecessor the GATT (General Agreement on Tariffs and Trade). Its key role has been to organize a series of multilateral negotiations and agreements to reduce tariff and non-tariff barriers (the WTO also has a role in settling trade disputes). As Table 9.5 shows, these agreements, called trade rounds, have until recently been very successful both in terms of reducing tariffs (and non-tariff barriers) and increasing the number of countries participating in negotiations.

The WTO is currently engaged in the ninth round of trade negotiations, the Doha Development round, which was instigated in November 2001. Compared to previous trade rounds, the agenda for the Doha round is very broad and ambitious: to continue to reduce tariffs in manufacturing, to extend reductions into services and agriculture, to limit and reduce the role of non-tariff barriers, to focus on intellectual property rights and environmental regulation, to improve transparency in government procurement and develop internationally minded competition policy, and a focus on a range of policies to try to make the benefits of trade negotiations more available to developing nations.

Progress with the Doha round to date has been limited, however. Not all countries accept the need for such a broad agenda and the United States, European Union and Japan show limited enthusiasm for removing agricultural protectionism, while many emerging markets are reluctant to liberalize their service sectors. As a consequence, the round, which was scheduled to be completed in 2005, is, at the time of writing, still not complete and is at risk of failing altogether. Figure 9.14 shows estimates of the economic benefit of completing the Doha round and suggests that it could raise world GDP by around $50 billion.

> **KEY POINT**
>
> The WTO is responsible for leading global trade negotiations and enforcing existing agreements. Despite an impressive track record of successful trade agreements, the latest WTO-led trade negotiations, called the Doha round, have run into difficulties.

TABLE 9.5 ● Impact of GATT/WTO Negotiations on Tariffs.

Through a series of trade negotiation rounds, GATT achieved substantial declines in tariffs.

	Average Cut in All Duties (%)	Remaining Duties (% 1930 Level)	Number of Participants
Pre-GATT (1935–47)	33.2	66.8	23
First round 1947	21.1	52.7	23
Second round 1949	1.9	51.7	13
Third round 1950–51	3	50.1	38
Fourth round 1955–56	3.5	48.9	26
Dillon round 1961–62	2.4	47.7	26
Kennedy round 1964–67	36	30.5	62
Tokyo round 1974–79	29.6	21.2	99
Uruguay round 1987–94	38	13.1	125

Source: Yarbrough and Yarbrough, *The World Economy* (Fort Worth, TX: Dryden Press, 1997).

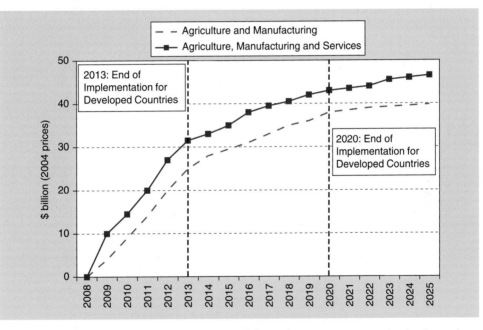

FIGURE 9.14 ● **Estimated gains from completing the Doha round.** Estimates suggest that implementing the 2008 proposals of the Doha round would increase global GDP by almost $50 billion. *Source:* Bouet and Laborde, The Potential Cost of a Failed Doha Round, IFPRI (2009).

SUMMARY

Section 9.1 argued that globalization could be defined as the emergence of a single market in goods and services, capital and labour. A first wave of globalization began in the early nineteenth century, due to falling transportation costs, and came to an end in the early 1900s due to the First World War and growing trade restrictions. A second wave of globalization began after the Second World War due to a continual process of lowering trade tariffs among

OECD nations. This process accelerated in the 1980s and 1990s as increasing numbers of emerging markets embarked on trade liberalization.

Section 9.2 reviewed the economic benefits of trade liberalization. Increased economic interdependence is believed to reduce the chances of war and international conflict. Increased trade also enables a more efficient use of resources and achieves the static gains of comparative advantage. Economic theory is ambiguous as to whether openness to trade increases the long-term growth of an economy, but, given the failure of import substitution policies, a number of countries have reduced trade barriers, a policy that econometric evidence suggests should boost growth.

In Section 9.3 we saw that foreign direct investment and multinational enterprises are increasing in importance and encourage convergence between countries through an increase in the capital stock and technology transfer to the recipient country. However, there is a concern that some policies aimed at attracting FDI may have adverse effects.

Section 9.4 showed how immigration is increasingly becoming a policy issue in OECD economies. Our analysis suggests that overall a country benefits from immigration; although the wages of native workers fall, this is offset by rising capital income.

Section 9.5 focused on the numerous criticisms that are made of globalization. These include fears of growing inequality and poverty; environmental damage; the loss of governments' ability to protect their citizens; and the lack of legitimacy of global markets, global firms and international institutions. Many of these global problems have been addressed at a national level by national governments and regulations. Some problems require an increased role for global institutions if they are to be overcome.

In Section 9.6 we considered the role of the WTO, which tries to help achieve negotiated reductions in trade barriers and ensure fair trade.

CONCEPTUAL QUESTIONS

1. (Section 9.1) What do you think the term 'globalization' means? Is it just an economic phenomenon?

2. (Section 9.2) Trade liberalization shows that it is a mistake for policymakers to think that 'exports are good and imports are bad'. Discuss.

3. (Section 9.2) Imagine that

$$GDP = (0.2 \times \text{Financial Sector Reform}) + (0.4 \times \text{Capital Stock}) - (0.05 \times \text{Openness})$$

But that

$$\text{Financial Sector Reform} = 2 \times \text{Openness}$$

If an econometrician ran a regression of GDP on the capital stock and openness, what effect would he or she find from openness? Explain your answer.

4. (Section 9.3) What are the limits and constraints to establishing global institutions and regulations? What does this imply about the process of globalization?

5. (Section 9.3) To what extent does the focus by economists on the economic gains from globalization fail to recognize the concerns of non-economists?

6. (Section 9.3) On what policies would governments need to focus to make sure that trade liberalization did not adversely affect poverty?

7. (Section 9.3) As an alternative to globalization, many critics are advocating a 'buy local' campaign. Assess the merits and disadvantages of this policy.

8. (Section 9.4) Does the world economy need stronger or fewer international financial institutions? Why?

PART THREE

Business Cycles and Economic Policy

Consumption and Investment

Key Concepts

Average Propensity to Consume (apc)	Keynesian Cross	Precautionary Savings
Borrowing Constraints	Marginal Propensity to Consume (mpc)	Procyclical
Cost of Capital	Multiplier	Q Theory of Investment
Intertemporal Budget Constraint	Optimal Capital Stock	Substitution and Income Effects
IS-LM Model	Permanent Income	

Overview

This chapter examines the determinants of consumption and investment. Consumption is the largest component of demand in the economy and plays an important role in business cycle fluctuations. Saving is that part of income not spent on consumption and so can be channelled into investment. First we consider the influence of current and future income on consumption and how interest rates, borrowing restrictions and financial deregulation influence savings. We then go on to see how investment is influenced by similar factors but is far more volatile than consumption.

10.1 The Importance of Consumption

Economists pay enormous attention to consumers' expenditure because they are interested in welfare, which, to a significant extent, comes from the utility people get from consuming goods and services. Consumption represents the largest part of overall spending and is a key determinant of gross domestic product (GDP). Table 10.1 shows the proportion of GDP accounted for by consumption in a sample of countries. The size of consumption varies across economies. For the majority, it is around 50–70% of GDP. For the developed economies, consumption averages around 65% of GDP. There is a greater range for the non-OECD economies, from 94% in the Central African Republic to 25% in Equatorial Guinea.

TABLE 10.1 ● Consumption as a Proportion of GDP, 2008.

Argentina	59
Bangladesh	79
Botswana	48
Brazil	60
Central African Republic	94
Czech Republic	50
Denmark	48
Equatorial Guinea	25
Norway	40
Philippines	77
Sweden	47
Thailand	56
UK	64
US	71

Source: World Bank, World Development Indicators.

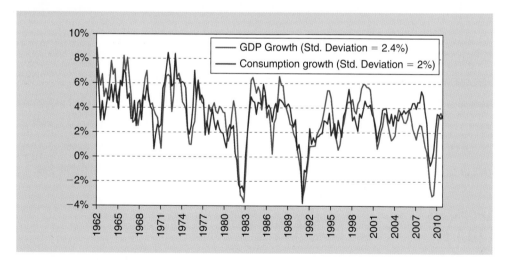

FIGURE 10.1 ● Consumption and GDP growth in Canada, 1962–2011. *Source:* OECD.

The importance of understanding the role of consumption in business cycle fluctuations is illustrated in Figure 10.1, where we see that the cyclical fluctuations in Canadian GDP are closely mimicked by fluctuations in consumption. This figure also illustrates another fact: *while consumption closely follows GDP fluctuations, it is not quite so volatile.* Consumption tends to be a bit smoother than income. Understanding why consumption changes are smoother than output changes will be a major focus of this chapter.

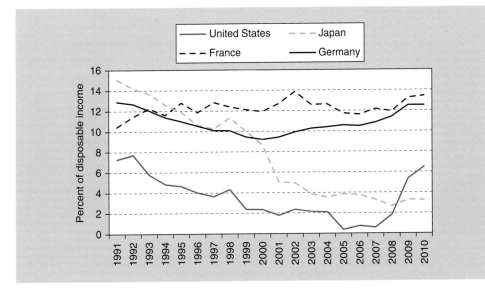

FIGURE 10.2 ● **Savings rates in United States, Japan, France and Germany.** There are substantial variations in savings rate over time and across countries. *Source:* OECD.

In analysing the determinants of consumption, we are also analysing saving decisions. What people do not spend out of their disposable income (that is, total income, including wages, interest payments and dividends, and social security payments, less tax payments), they must save. And, as we saw in Chapter 4, the level of savings in a country is a crucial determinant of its long-run steady state and helps determine the rate of investment. Investment can be financed by domestic or foreign saving, but in practice domestic saving is the key source of funds. Figure 10.2 shows that savings rates vary significantly both across countries and over time.

> **KEY POINT**
>
> Consumption is the largest part of GDP in nearly all countries. Saving – the difference between income and consumption – is the source of investment.

10.2 The Basic Keynesian Model of Consumption

The economist John Maynard Keynes said:

> *The fundamental psychological law, upon which we are entitled to depend with great confidence both a priori from our knowledge of human nature and from the detailed facts of experience, is that men are disposed, as a rule and on the average, to increase their consumption as their income increases, but not by as much as the increase in their income.*[1]

In other words, we should expect to see a very close relationship between current consumption and current income – both for an individual and for an economy. Evidence in support of this can be seen in Figure 10.3, which shows that in the United States consumption rises closely in line with disposable income.

In Keynes's work an important concept is the **marginal propensity to consume**, or mpc. The marginal propensity to consume is the extra amount an individual will spend if you give him or her an extra $1. If the mpc is 80%, or 0.8, then from every extra dollar of income, the individual spends 80 cents. A key task of this chapter is to examine the determinants of the mpc. The mpc may not be constant – it may vary with income. But, for the moment, we will assume that people spend a constant fraction of every dollar they receive.

The mpc only tells us how much *additional* income an individual spends. What about someone who receives no income? This individual will still need to consume goods and services, whether financed by begging, borrowing or stealing. Therefore, even at zero income, an individual will have positive levels of consumption. In Figure 10.4 we show how individual consumption is linked to income according to this simple Keynesian model.

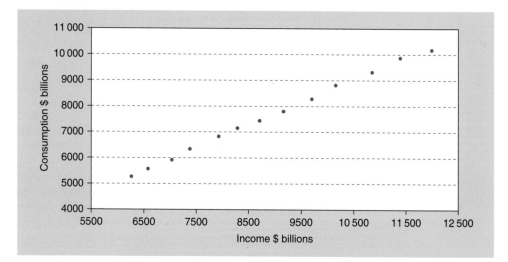

FIGURE 10.3 ● **Consumption and disposable income in the United States, 1996–2009.** Consumption tracks current income very closely. *Source:* World Bank, World Development Indicators.

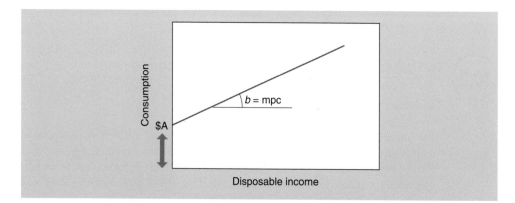

FIGURE 10.4 ● **The Keynesian consumption function.** The Keynesian consumption function has consumption rising with current income but by less than 1:1. The mpc (*b*) is less than 1.

At zero income the individual spends $A; A could be any amount, such as 100 or 1000. For every extra dollar, he or she spends b dollars, where b is the mpc. If he or she spends 80 cents out of every dollar, then $b = 0.8$. Therefore consumption is given by

Consumption = A + ($b \times$ Disposable Income)

or

$$C = A + (b \times Y)$$

The mpc is given by b, but we can also define the **average propensity to consume** – how much of an individual's total income he or she spends (recall that the mpc is about how much of your *additional* income you spend). The average propensity to consume (apc) is just consumption divided by income, or C/Y. Given our expression for consumption, this is

$$C/Y = A/Y + b$$

As income gets larger, the term A/Y goes towards zero, so that eventually the apc is the same as the mpc. Because consumption plus savings equals income (C + S = Y), the apc equals 1 minus the savings rate (S/Y).

Why have we spent so much time outlining the concept of the mpc? For Keynes, the level of demand in the economy is key to understanding business cycle fluctuations and, in turn, the mpc is the key concept in influencing demand. To see why, consider again the national accounts identity from Chapter 2:

Output = Consumption + Government Expenditure + Investment

or

$$Y = C + G + I$$

where we have for ease of analysis ignored net exports (X – M). We showed in Chapter 2 how the income and output measures of GDP were equivalent, so using this fact and our expression for consumption we can rewrite this as

$$Y = A + bY + G + I$$

which can be rearranged as

$$Y - bY = A + G + I$$

or

$$Y = [1/(1 - b)] \times [A + G + I]$$

In other words, GDP equals the sum of A plus government expenditure and investment, all divided by $(1 - b)$. If the government can increase G by $100 million, then according to this expression, GDP will increase *by more than $100 million*. If G increases by $100 million, then Y rises by $100 million/$(1 - b)$. If $b = 0.8$, then GDP increases by $500 million, while if the mpc (b) equals 0.9, GDP increases by $1000 million. The expression $[1/(1 - b)]$ is called the **multiplier** and it represents the total impact on the economy of an initial increase in demand. The larger the mpc, the bigger the multiplier.

Why does this multiplier exist? When the government spends $100 million, it purchases goods with this money, which increases the incomes of the firms and workers that produce these goods. Because of the mpc this extra income is spent on other goods and services, further increasing income and consumption elsewhere in the economy. But this additional income is also spent, so that the initial increase in government expenditure sets in motion a sequence of rising incomes and consumption throughout the economy, which serves to magnify the initial demand boost. The higher the mpc, the greater the impact on consumption at every stage of the process and so the greater the ultimate increase in demand.

KEY POINT

Keynes' concept of the mpc is important in understanding demand in an economy because it contributes to a multiplier effect upon an initial increase in demand.

10.3 The Permanent Income Model

Whereas current consumption undoubtedly does depend on current income, the model we have outlined is rather simplistic because it assumes that nothing else matters. According to this model, an individual looks at his or her monthly salary cheque and spends a constant proportion of it. But consider whether this insight holds true for the following characters:

- A senior in college has a current income of $3000 from various part-time jobs, but Goldman Sachs offers her a job when she graduates with a starting salary of $80 000.
- A bond trader at Morgan Stanley is currently earning $500 000 a year, but rumours of redundancies are rife.
- The tax authorities refund $25 000 to someone in a steady job who has mistakenly overpaid taxes in recent years.

If we are thinking about how consumption is linked to current income – that is, the marginal propensity to consume – then in each of these three cases we would arrive at different answers. Although the student's current income is low, she will probably wish to spend substantially more than she is currently earning because of her high future income (assuming that the bank will loan her the money). The Morgan Stanley trader has a very high current income, but uncertainty about the future will lead him to accumulate savings in order to prevent consumption from crashing if he loses his job. The third case involves a one-time windfall receipt of income that will not be repeated. The consumer therefore has to choose between spending it all today or spreading it out over several years.

All of these examples suggest, as does common sense, that when deciding how much to consume, households think about their income over the future as well as what they currently earn. These ideas lead us to a broader theory of consumption, called the *permanent income theory*,[2] which provides a much richer model of the determinants of the mpc. To understand this theory, we outline a simple and stylized model of income over a person's life.

THE INTERTEMPORAL BUDGET CONSTRAINT

Any model of consumption must contain two ingredients: the constraints consumers face and also their preferences. We focus first on their constraints.

Consider a person whose life consists of two periods (if it cheers you up, let the periods last for many years). Denote labour income in the first period by $Y(1)$ and in the second period by $Y(2)$. For instance, if the individual is a student in the first period, $Y(1) = 0$, but $Y(2)$ will be positive – her salary. If instead the individual is currently working but will retire next period, then $Y(1)$ is positive and $Y(2)$ zero. We shall denote consumption in the first period by $C(1)$ and in the second by $C(2)$. For ease of analysis, we also assume that the individual has no wealth at the beginning of the first period. This means that at the end of the first period the individual's bank balance is $Y(1) - C(1)$. If the individual has saved money, $Y(1) > C(1)$, the bank balance is positive. If instead she borrowed money to finance high consumption $[Y(1) < C(1)]$, then she owes the bank money. Assuming that the bank pays out interest r (or charges an interest rate on loans of r), then at the beginning of the second period the bank account has funds worth

$$(1 + r) \times [Y(1) - C(1)]$$

Therefore, the maximum amount of money the individual has to spend in the second period is given by

$$Y(2) + (1 + r)[Y(1) - C(1)]$$

Assuming that the individual does not wish to leave any inheritance, she will spend this entire amount on second-period consumption so that

$$C(2) = Y(2) + (1 + r)[Y(1) - C(1)]$$

In order to arrive at the intertemporal budget constraint, we need to do a little rearranging. First, we collect on one side all the consumption terms and on the other all the income terms. This gives

$$(1 + r)C(1) + C(2) = (1 + r)Y(1) + Y(2)$$

If we finally divide through by $(1 + r)$ we have the **intertemporal budget constraint**

$$C(1) + C(2)/(1 + r) = Y(1) + Y(2)/(1 + r)$$

When we divide a number by $1 + r$ we *discount* the number. Discounting is a way of valuing future amounts of income or spending in terms of today's money. Imagine that I have $100 and the interest rate is 10%; that is, $r = 0.1$. Therefore I can turn $100 of cash today into $110 in a year's time. This also means that if I were to calculate today the value of $110 received in a year's time, I would put it no higher than $100; that is, 110/1.1.

> ### KEY POINT
>
> The intertemporal budget constraint says that current consumption plus discounted future consumption must equal the sum of current income and future discounted income.

The key constraint that the individual faces is a *lifetime* budget constraint. While in any one particular year an individual can save or borrow, over his or her lifetime total discounted expenditure must equal total discounted income. The intertemporal budget constraint reveals immediately the importance of the future. How much consumers can spend today, $C(1)$, depends on their expectations of future income, $Y(2)$, as well as future consumption, $C(2)$, and current income, $Y(1)$.

In the case of two periods, we can show the intertemporal budget constraint diagrammatically. Figure 10.5 shows the different combinations of first- and second-period consumption that the individual can afford on the assumption that today's income is $Y(1)$ and tomorrow's is $Y(2)$. Assuming that an individual can borrow against future income, she could choose to

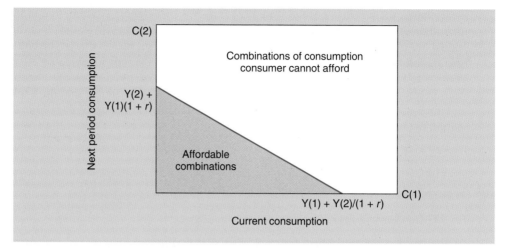

FIGURE 10.5 ● **The intertemporal budget constraint.** The intertemporal budget constraint shows combinations of first- and second-period consumption that an individual can afford given lifetime income.

consume the whole of today's income [$Y(1)$] plus an amount equal to the maximum she could borrow against tomorrow's income: $Y(2)/(1 + r)$. Therefore the *maximum* first-period consumption is given by the point on the horizontal axis at which $C(1) = Y(1) + Y(2)/(1 + r)$ and $C(2) = 0$. At the other extreme, if an individual were to save all her current income – that is, $C(1) = 0$ – she would start the final period of her life with accumulated wealth of $Y(1)(1 + r)$, to which she would add final-period income $Y(2)$ to enjoy a maximum final-period consumption of $Y(2) + Y(1)(1 + r)$. These two extreme points involve setting consumption to zero in one period, but the consumer can, of course, reallocate consumption between time periods. Every \$1 of reduced first-period consumption translates into an extra \$$(1 + r)$ in the second period, so the slope of the line linking these two extreme points is simply given by one plus the interest rate. Any point on the straight line joining these two extremes or any point within the shaded triangle represents bundles, or combinations, of consumption that the consumer can afford, given lifetime income.

CONSUMER PREFERENCES

The intertemporal budget constraint shows what the consumer can afford; it does not say what he or she prefers. To find this out we need to know about consumer preferences. Economists draw *indifference curves* to characterize preferences between commodities (and we can think of consumption today and consumption tomorrow as two distinct commodities). Indifference curves show combinations of consumption of the two commodities between which an individual is indifferent. Consider the points A and F in Figure 10.6. Point A involves high first-period consumption but very little in the second period. By contrast, F involves a lot of second-period consumption but not much in the first period. Both points are on the same indifference curve, which means that the consumer is equally happy with either bundle. The additional second-period consumption that F implies just compensates for the loss of first-period consumption compared to A.

The slope of the indifference curve tells us how willing a consumer is to substitute between first- and second-period consumption. Consider points A and B. At point A, the

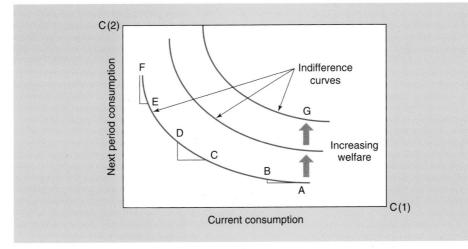

FIGURE 10.6 ● **Consumer indifference curves.** Indifference curves indicate consumption bundles that yield equal pleasure.

consumer has very little second-period consumption but lots of first-period consumption and we have drawn a very flat indifference curve. This means that the consumer is prepared to give up quite a lot of first-period consumption in return for only a small amount of extra second-period consumption. We are in effect assuming that when a consumer has a lot of one commodity but very little of another, he places a higher value on the scarce commodity. The same logic explains why the indifference curve is so steep between points E and F. In this case, the consumer has an abundance of second-period consumption and so is prepared to forgo quite a lot of this in return for a small increase in initial consumption. Finally, between points C and D the consumer is willing to trade roughly equal amounts of first- and second-period consumption – when he has similar amounts of both commodities, they are valued roughly equally.

The previous discussion was about different combinations of first- and second-period consumption that yield the same welfare. However, comparing points A and G we see that they both have the same amount of first-period consumption, but G involves more second-period consumption. Therefore the consumer prefers bundle G to bundle A and these different combinations are on different indifference curves. The higher the indifference curve, the more the consumer prefers the consumption bundles.

THE CONSUMER'S CHOICE

If we put together the intertemporal budget constraint and the indifference curves, we have a complete analysis of the consumer's consumption decisions. Assuming that consumers want to maximize their welfare, they will want to choose the combination of first- and second-period consumption that puts them on the highest indifference curve that their intertemporal budget constraint makes feasible. This is shown in Figure 10.7 as point A – where the budget constraint just touches the highest achievable indifference curve. We have drawn Figure 10.7 to produce roughly equal amounts of first- and second-period consumption. This result is achieved by an indifference curve with the curvature shown. As explained above, these indifference curves imply that consumers dislike volatile consumption – they prefer

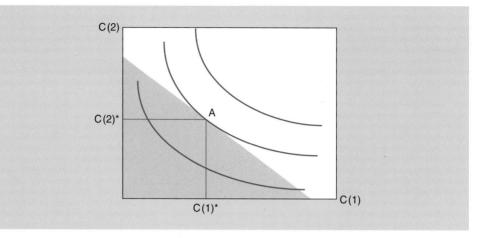

FIGURE 10.7 ● **Consumer's optimal choice.** Consumers choose the affordable consumption bundle that gives the highest welfare.

roughly equal amounts of consumption in each year. This is why they are prepared to give up a lot of second-period consumption at F (see Figure 10.6) for only a small gain in terms of first-period consumption.

RESPONSE TO AN INCREASE IN CURRENT INCOME

Figure 10.8 shows how we can use our model to analyse the effect of a temporary one-time increase in current income. It considers the case in which current income is higher by $100 000 but no change is expected in the second period. If all income is used to finance current consumption, then instead of consuming $Y(1) + Y(2)/(1 + r)$ the consumer can now spend $Y(1) + 100\,000 + Y(2)/(1 + r)$. Similarly, if the consumer saves everything, then maximum second-period consumption rises from $Y(1) (1 + r) + Y(2)$ to $(Y(1) + 100\,000) (1 + r) + Y(2)$. The effect in Figure 10.8 is for the whole intertemporal budget constraint to shift outwards to the right. The increase in lifetime income means that consumption increases, but the increase in current income leads to a roughly equal increase in *both* first- and second-period consumption. This is because of our assumption about indifference curves: that the consumer prefers to divide consumption fairly equally between both periods rather than experience substantial swings. This implies that, in response to a temporary increase in income, the mpc in this two-period model will be approximately 50% – half the income is spent now and half later. The person who received the one-time tax refund would spend half the refund money now and the other half in a later period. Arguing analogously, we also note that if there are 10 more periods, then the mpc would be about 10%.[3]

KEY POINT

A one-time rise in income is likely to cause consumption to rise by less than it would with a permanent income increase, and the mpc will be low.

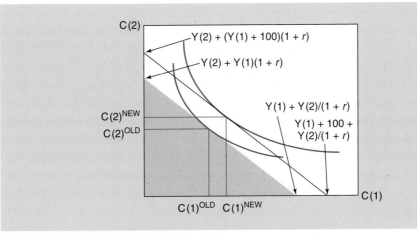

FIGURE 10.8 ● **Impact on consumption of increase in current income.** Both current and future consumption increase when current income rises in the forward-looking model.

RESPONSE TO INCREASES IN FUTURE INCOME

Now consider the case in which first-period income remains unchanged but tomorrow's income is expected to be $100 000 higher. The maximum amount of first-period consumption that can be financed (by borrowing on the basis of all future income) is $Y(1) + (Y(2) + 100\,000)/(1 + r)$ and the maximum second-period consumption is $Y(1)\,(1 + r) + Y(2) + 100\,000$ (see Figure 10.9).

As in the previous case, the consumer's lifetime income has risen, and she responds by spreading the increase equally between both periods. The result is that current consumption rises even though current income has not changed. This would suggest that our graduating student will respond to her employment letter from Goldman Sachs by going out and spending, even though her current income has not changed.

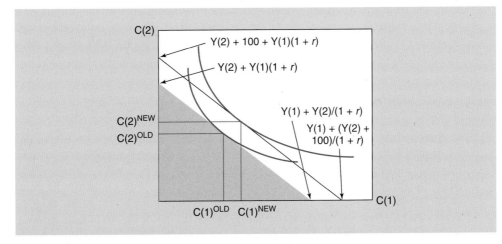

FIGURE 10.9 ● **Impact on consumption of increase in future income.** Because of borrowing, both current and future consumption increase when agent expects higher future income.

PERMANENT INCOME

Our previous two examples show that current consumption rises by a similar amount in response to an increase in current income and an increase in future income.[4] This is very different from the simple Keynesian model in which current income is all that matters. In the forward-looking model, the consumer sets consumption considering lifetime rather than current income and, given our assumptions on indifference curves, does so in a way that tries to avoid large changes in consumption. Consider the extreme case in which the consumer wishes to set first- and second-period consumption to be the same. (For simplicity, assume that interest rates are zero.) Under these assumptions the intertemporal budget constraint is

$$C(1) + C(2) = Y(1) + Y(2)$$

If the consumer sets consumption to be the same in each period, then $C(1) = C(2) = C$ so we have

$$2C = Y(1) + Y(2) \text{ or } C = (1/2)[Y(1) + Y(2)]$$

that is, consumption is set equal to average lifetime income or what is called **permanent income**. Any change in permanent income is immediately reflected in current consumption. When first-period (or second-period) income increases by $100 000, then permanent income (and consumption) increases by only (1/2) ($100 000) = $50 000 and the mpc is 50%.

Therefore, the forward-looking model has as its main relationship the link between consumption and permanent, rather than current, income, and the mpc is determined by the influence that current income has on permanent income. This permanent income model helps explain one of the key facts of Figure 10.1: in a recession, consumption does not fall as much as GDP does, nor does it rise as much in a boom. In a recession, GDP and income are temporarily low and so the fall in current income is greater than the fall in permanent income. As a consequence, the mpc is low and consumption falls by less than income. Exactly similar reasoning holds during a boom so that, over the whole, business cycle consumption fluctuates by less than income.

The assumption of zero interest rates in our example means that permanent income only depends on labour income. However, with positive interest rates, consumers earn interest on their wealth and this has to be factored into our concept of permanent income. Once again, the principle of consumption smoothing dominates, so that the consumer spends from this wealth equally over time. In the extreme (and, sadly, unrealistic) case in which the consumer lives for ever, this implies that the consumer spends only the interest payments in order to maintain a constant level of wealth.

TEMPORARY AND PERMANENT INCOME CHANGES

We can combine our previous analysis of how current consumption responds to increases in current and future income to show how the mpc out of permanent income shocks differs from that of temporary shocks. In response to a $100 000 increase in current income, we found the consumer would spend around 50% today and the rest tomorrow. In response to a $100 000 increase in *future* income, we suggested that around 50% would be spent now and the rest tomorrow. A *permanent* increase in income of $100 000 is extra income today *and* next period; combining these two results, we conclude that the consumer has an mpc out of additional permanent income of around 100% in the current period as well as the next period.

> ### KEY POINT
>
> The mpc out of shocks to permanent income is much greater than that out of temporary shocks. In the case of permanent shocks to income, the implications of the forward-looking model and the Keynesian consumption function are very similar: consumers will spend most of any increase in current income.

SAVING FOR A RAINY DAY

The permanent income model has important implications for savings. Consider the case in which savings are negative; that is, consumption is greater than current income. This, in turn, implies that average lifetime income is greater than current income, such as when the individual feels that his or her income will rise in the future. By contrast, consider the case in which savings are positive, so that current income exceeds consumption and average lifetime income. In these circumstances, the individual thinks that his or her income will fall in the future. Therefore, according to the permanent income model, saving is for a 'rainy day' – people only accumulate assets if they believe that their income is going to fall. For instance, if the individual is retiring from work in the next period, his income will fall to zero and he should be saving now in order to finance his retirement. Conversely, as we saw, the student who is waiting to begin employment with Goldman Sachs should be borrowing heavily and then using her high future income to repay her bank loan.

(10.4) The Importance of Current Income Revisited

The forward-looking model of consumption is not consistent with the central assumption of the Keynesian consumption function that there is a simple and stable relationship between current consumption and current income. Instead, it emphasizes the importance of future income in influencing current consumption decisions. In this section, however, we add two different features to the forward-looking model, each of which reinstates the importance of the link between current income and consumption. The first factor we add is consumer uncertainty about future income; we then examine the implications of constraints on how much individuals can borrow.

THE IMPORTANCE OF UNCERTAINTY

So far we have been assuming that people have knowledge of current and future incomes. In practice, however, future earnings are highly uncertain. This is likely to affect savings and consumption decisions through influencing the mpc. One study[5] suggests that as much as 46% of personal-sector wealth is the result of higher savings aimed at insuring against future income uncertainty.

Let's consider two different people. Mr Grey has taken a safe job with the IRS that pays a steady income for ever. He is a reliable and boring type – a James Stewart character from a Frank Capra film. Then there is Ms Purple, who has piled all her savings into setting up a software company that has generated her a first-year income of $90 000, but whether she will even have a company in two or three years is anyone's guess – she is more a Sharon Stone type in a late 1980s thriller. Let's assume that Mr Grey also earns $90 000 doing his repetitive tasks. Mr Grey should not worry about volatility in his future income and as a result will be inclined to spend more; in other words, he will have a high mpc. By contrast, the entrepreneur must remember that her income could fall to zero any day. Since dramatic swings in consumption are unpleasant for consumers, Ms Purple is likely to save in order to accumulate assets for precautionary reasons. Note that these savings are for precautionary reasons and are different from the rainy-day savings we mentioned above. You save for a rainy day because your best guess is that your income will fall. In contrast, **precautionary savings** provide individuals with insurance against their income turning out worse than they forecast. The more uncertainty there is about income and the more risk averse consumers are, the greater are precautionary savings.[6]

> **KEY POINT**
>
> Introducing precautionary savings makes current income more important than future income.

Future income is uncertain: I may fall ill and be unable to earn, my boss may be replaced by my arch-rival who forces me out of the firm and so forth. Given news about a $100 000 increase in both current and likely future income, the mpc will be a lot higher out of the former. There is no need to do any precautionary saving in respect to current income.

BORROWING CONSTRAINTS

There is another way of reinstating the close link between current consumption and current income that characterizes the basic Keynesian model. For the forward-looking model to be relevant, individuals must not be affected by **borrowing constraints**. Consider again the student with a job offer from Goldman Sachs. The only way she can spend more than her current income is if a bank is persuaded to loan her funds. If banks refuse, then it does not matter what the student's permanent income is – she can only finance consumption equal to current income. This situation is shown in Figure 10.10. If the consumer could borrow from the bank, her budget constraint is given by the line ABC. However, if the bank does not grant her credit, then first-period consumption cannot exceed first-period income and the budget constraint becomes ABD. With this budget constraint, the consumer chooses first-period consumption C*(1) and consumption during the next period of C*(2). Therefore, she consumes too little in the first period and then too much in the second period. The inability to borrow reduces her welfare because she is on a lower indifference curve.

We can use Figure 10.10 to examine the impact of credit liberalization on an economy. During the 1980s a number of European economies instituted a process of financial deregulation. The result was a much greater degree of competition between financial institutions and the introduction of overseas banks eager to grab market share. The consequence was a surge in bank lending, as banks competed among themselves for new customers. In order to attract market share, banks became willing to lend on anticipation of future incomes and large loans were offered for house purchases. The budget constraint thus shifted from ABD to ABC and current consumption rose strongly. Furthermore, if consumers expect rising future income, then according to our 'rainy-day' story, savings will go negative as consumers avail themselves of the opportunity to smooth their consumption over time. Figure 10.11 shows that this

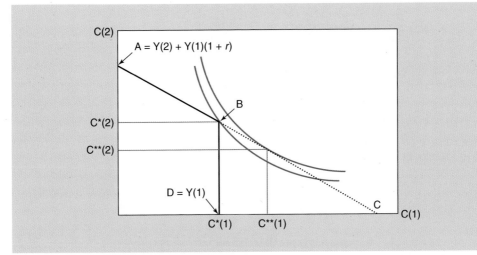

FIGURE 10.10 ● **Borrowing constraints make consumption equal to current income.** If consumers are unable to borrow, then current consumption depends on current rather than permanent income. If there were no borrowing constraints, consumption in period one would be C**(1), which is greater than Y(1).

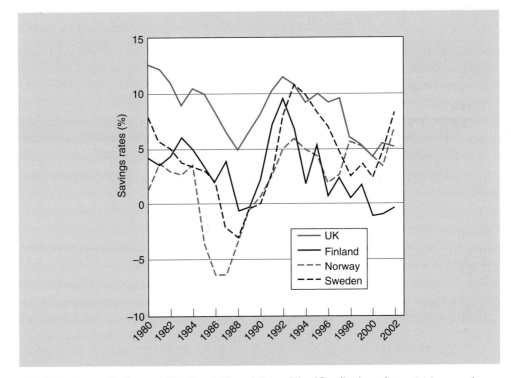

FIGURE 10.11 ● **Impact of 1980s financial deregulation on UK and Scandinavian savings.** The increased ability of banks to lend in the 1980s led to dramatic falls in the savings rate in the UK and Scandinavian economies. *Source:* OECD, *Economic Outlook* (2003).

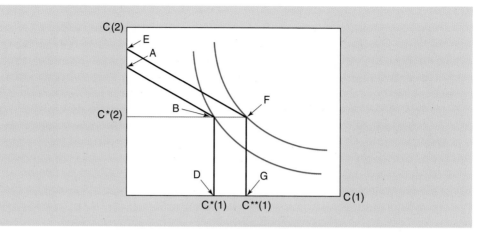

FIGURE 10.12 ● **Increases in income create high mpc under borrowing constraints.** With borrowing constraints, increases in current income feed through into current consumption only.

is exactly what happened in Sweden, Norway, Finland and the United Kingdom – countries where rapid financial deregulation took place in the 1980s.

In the case of borrowing constraints, the mpc is very high – individuals have too low first-period consumption and too high second-period consumption. They would like to reallocate this consumption, but cannot because they cannot borrow. Therefore, when they receive more current income they will spend most of it – there is no point in saving money when consumption next period will already be too high. This situation is shown in Figure 10.12, where the increase in current income shifts the budget constraint from ABD to EFG. In this case, the increased income leads entirely to higher extra first-period consumption and has no effect on second-period consumption.

KEY POINT

If borrowing constraints are important, it is current income rather than future income that matters.

(10.5) The Influence of Interest Rates

Because of the importance of consumption as a component of GDP, the influence of interest rates on consumption is an important aspect of monetary policy. In the basic Keynesian model, all that matters for consumption is current income, so that interest rates have only an indirect effect. For savers, a higher interest rate means greater income because of higher interest payments. However, for debtors the higher interest rates reduce their income available for discretionary consumer spending. The extra income gained by creditors should equal the income loss to debtors, so overall aggregate income has not changed. However, there may still be an influence on consumption. Creditors tend to have low mpc – they do a lot of saving – whereas debtors have a high mpc, which helps explain why they are debtors. The interest rate increase therefore leads to a redistribution of income from those with a propensity to spend towards those with a tendency to save. The result will be a fall in consumption. This fall in consumption, via the multiplier effect outlined at the beginning of the chapter, will lead to a fall in GDP and rising unemployment, potentially generating a further fall in consumption.

In the forward-looking model, the effect of interest rates is more direct but also more ambiguous, as shown in Figure 10.13. An increase in interest rates leads the budget constraint to tilt from AB to CD. Higher interest rates mean that, for the same second-period repayment, the consumer can afford a smaller loan in the current period – more money has to be spent on interest payments. Therefore, on the horizontal axis, the budget line shifts inwards. However, if the consumer saves his or her first-period income, then the higher interest rates lead to greater second-period interest income and lead the budget line to shift *up* on the vertical axis. Because the budget line tilts, interest rates have two conflicting effects on consumption. One impact, called the *substitution effect*, causes a fall in first-period consumption and is best reflected in the inward shift on the horizontal axis from B to D. The interest rate is an intertemporal price for the consumer – every \$1 of current consumption means \$$(1 + r)$ less future consumption. If the interest rate increases, this makes first-period consumption more expensive and so the consumer substitutes away towards second-period consumption by saving more. The other influence is the *income effect*. When interest rates increase, savers receive higher interest payments and can afford to spend more; this is the reason the intercept on the vertical axis shifts up from A to C. This higher income means that the consumer can spend more over his or her lifetime and, because of consumption smoothing, this will lead to an increase in first- and second-period income.

For savers, the income effect leads to higher current consumption. However, for debtors, the higher interest rates mean higher debt interest payments and so *lower* lifetime income and lower current consumption. Therefore, for debtors, the income effect of higher interest

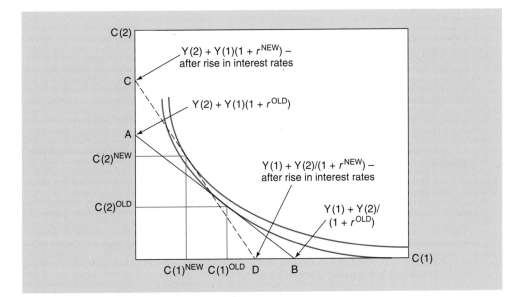

FIGURE 10.13 ● **Impact of interest rates on consumption.** Increases in interest rates lead to lower consumption as a result of income and substitution effects.

rates leads to lower current consumption. For borrowers, the effect of higher interest rates is unambiguous: current consumption falls. For savers, however, consumption can either rise or fall depending on the relative strength of income and substitution effects. In Figure 10.13 we have shown the substitution effect dominating so that consumption falls; this outcome is also supported in the aggregate consumption data. However, the impact of interest rates on consumption is relatively small, partly due to offsetting income and substitution effects.

> ### KEY POINT
>
> Under both Keynesian and forward-looking models, interest rates affect debtors and savers differently. In forward-looking models, the effects on savers are complicated by substitution and income effects.

(10.6) The Role of Wealth and Capital Gains

We have so far focused only on income and interest rates as influences on consumption, but another important influence is wealth. The household sector does not hold all its money in a bank account but also owns stocks, bonds and real estate. Changes in the value of these other assets will affect consumer wealth and also consumer spending.

What is the marginal propensity to consume out of wealth? The analysis closely parallels that for the mpc out of income. Assuming that consumers are forward looking, they will not consume all their wealth today but only a small proportion of it – the rest they will leave for later years. We can expect the mpc of wealth to be much lower than that for income. Income is a *flow*, something that is received every year, whereas wealth is a *stock* and needs to be maintained if it is to last for many periods. The result is that consumers spend a much higher proportion of their annual income than of their current wealth.

The existence of capital gains raises issues about how to measure the savings rate. The savings rate is defined as unspent income divided by income and, as measured by the national accounts, income *excludes* capital gains but *includes* interest payments and dividends. As we saw in Figure 10.2, in the late 1990s the US savings rate fell dramatically, as measured by the national accounts, but at the same time the US stock market boomed. Between 1989 and 1999 the Dow Jones index of US stock prices increased fivefold. Consumers borrowed from banks using these capital gains as collateral in order to finance consumption, and the result was a sharp fall in savings. But does this give a misleading impression of household finances?

National accounts measures of savings ignore the financial resources available to the consumer through capital gains. Including capital gains dramatically changes the performance of the US savings rate. Figure 10.14 shows the national accounts (NIPA) measure of savings along with an alternative measure that includes realized capital gains (i.e. capital gains that have been banked via selling stock) in its concept of income. This adjusted series suggests that US consumers save a much higher proportion of their income and that this proportion has changed very little. Figure 10.14 also shows the savings rate for US consumers including unrealized gains in the measure of disposable income. Far from showing a dramatic decline in US savings in the 1990s, the chart suggests that, until the bear market that started in 2001, *savings* had actually increased, so that US consumers were being cautious in the rate at which they were spending these capital gains. Given the very sharp falls in stock prices in 2001 and 2002, such caution was amply justified by subsequent events.

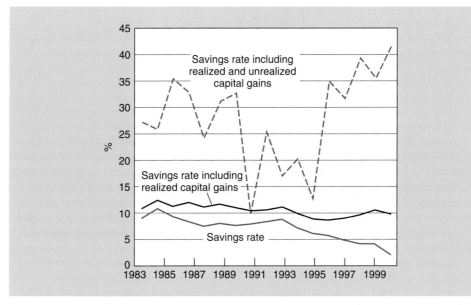

FIGURE 10.14 ● **US savings rate and importance of capital gains.** The US savings rate in the 1980s and 1990s would have been much higher if capital gains were factored into the concept of disposable income. *Source:* Peach and Steindal, 'A nation of spendthrifts?', *Current Issues in Economic and Finance* (September 2000), 6(10): 1–30.

It is now clear that many of the apparent gains in wealth that seemed to have been generated by stock price rises in the late 1990s evaporated in the bear market of 2001 and 2002. Those households that borrowed on the basis of apparent stock market wealth in 1998 and 1999 may well have regretted their decisions by 2002, when stock prices were around 50% lower. Because of this sort of stock price volatility, how much of a rise in stock prices to treat as real income is very hard to gauge. The same issue is true of gains in wealth for owners of real estate. In fact, there is an added factor here. Even if a big rise in property prices is permanent and not reversed in future years, it is unclear how much of a real gain this generates for a home owner. If there is a general rise in prices of properties in areas where I want to live, then I may be no better off. I would certainly be overestimating my wealth if I counted all the rise in the value of my current house as a gain without taking account of the fact that, if I buy a new house, I will have to pay an inflated price for my new property. And if I never plan to move, in what sense am I really better off if my property is worth more? Problems in measuring wealth and the issue of how changes in the market value of tangible assets might affect consumption are hard to figure out.

KEY POINT

The dependence of the mpc on consumers' expectations of future income, whether they perceive income increases to be temporary or permanent, the importance of uncertainty and the variable impact of capital gains, combined with the issue of whether they have access to credit – all of these make the mpc a difficult number to pin down. This suggests that governments have limited ability to influence consumption reliably by shifting taxes or moving interest rates.

(10.7) Demographic Influences in the Life-Cycle Model

We have omitted much of the richness of individual lives in the simple two-period models that we looked at earlier in this chapter. However, this richness affects both consumption and savings. The profile of income over individual lives is likely to be uneven and, as a consequence, we can expect people's savings behaviour to be different at different points in their *life cycle*. Most people earn low amounts in their teens and often into their twenties as they get a formal education. They then (usually) start work, and their income tends to rise as they become better at what they do and get promoted. At some point, productivity declines and earnings fall. The profile of earnings over working life depends on the work people do. Professional football players' productivity declines sharply in their thirties, but a professor of English literature might not peak until her late fifties (at which point she can understand *Finnegan's Wake*). The Rolling Stones's earnings seem to rise as they move into their seventies. But usually income tails off sharply as people move near or into retirement.

Consumption is also likely to vary dramatically over the life cycle. Most people are single in their early adult life, during which period consumption is relatively low. However, as they become older they may have a family, with consumption increasing as a result. Eventually children grow up, leave home and (hopefully) stop relying on parental income, at which point household consumption falls. During retirement, consumption tends to continue to fall (perhaps the desire for extravagant skiing holidays in Aspen declines as the ability to get out of bed in the morning diminishes).

Support for these demographic shifts in consumption and income is shown in Figure 10.15 and Table 10.2. These show how consumption and income vary across a large sample of

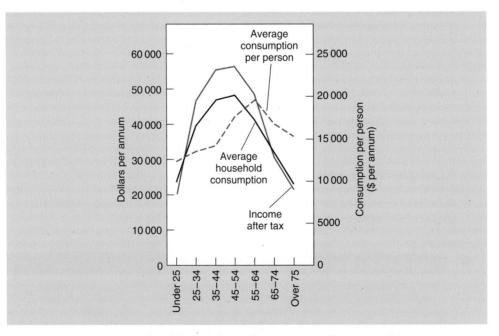

FIGURE 10.15 ● **Consumption and income over the life cycle – average US consumer, 2001.** Consumption and income vary with age, peaking in middle age and then declining. *Source:* Bureau of Labor Statistics, *Consumer Expenditure Survey* (2003).

TABLE 10.2 ● Savings Rates by Age, 2001.

Under 25	25–34	35–44	45–54	55–64	65–74	Over 75
−13.3	20.2	20.4	21.6	20.2	1.1	−3.4

Source: Bureau of Labor Statistics, *Consumer Expenditure Survey* (1991).

107 000 US households as the age of the reference adult in the household varies. The income profile is exactly what we outlined, except that income remains significant at the end for people older than 75 because measured income in this survey includes interest earnings and pension payments.[7]

With income and consumption following such different paths, the household has to use savings to offset the differences. Table 10.2 shows the savings that accompany Figure 10.15: early in adult life consumers borrow and then repay their loans and accumulate funds, which they then run down slightly during retirement.

Although the life-cycle model achieves many empirical successes, it does have some problems. In particular, older generations tend not to spend their savings at a very rapid rate, if at all. Two possibilities are frequently stressed to account for the reluctance of older generations to reduce their savings dramatically: uncertainty and bequests. First, uncertainty is critical. People don't know exactly when they are going to die. So the simple life-cycle theory that says that people should decumulate wealth in retirement and have negative savings rates does not translate easily to a model in which people are uncertain about how long they will live. You may be afraid that you will live too long and run out of money, so you try to avoid exhausting your stock of wealth during retirement. And, of course, many people want to hand over substantial bequests to their heirs. The relative importance of uncertainty over longevity and the desire to leave a bequest are controversial as explanations for the surprisingly high savings rates of retired individuals, with some studies suggesting that these motives account for more of US wealth than life-cycle savings.

> **KEY POINT**
>
> Because savings are likely to vary substantially over people's lives, changes in the overall demographic structure of a country are likely to have a significant impact on its aggregate rate of saving.

(10.8) Investment and the Capital Stock

Understanding what drives investment is critical not only for understanding capital accumulation and movements in countries' standard of living, but also for understanding the volatility of activity from year to year. Movements in investment expenditure tend to be sharper than shifts in other components of expenditure. Figure 10.16 shows a time series of the percentage change in real GDP and private-sector investment for the United States.

Table 10.3 summarizes investment and GDP information for a range of developed economies. Here we define investment broadly to include spending on new plant and machines, buildings (including residential home building) and inventory. The long-run

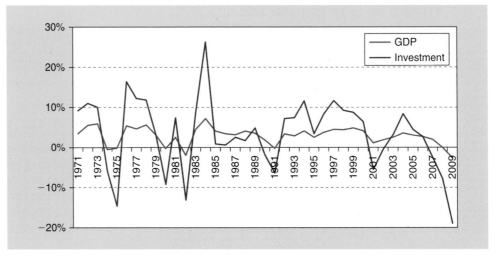

FIGURE 10.16 ● **Percentage change in US GDP and private-sector investment.** Investment is procyclical and much more volatile than GDP. *Source:* World Bank, World Development Indicators.

TABLE 10.3 ● **The Volatility of Investment.**

Investment is more than twice as volatile as GDP.

1970–2009	% Change in GDP (Standard Deviation)	% Change in Investment (Standard Deviation)
Germany	1.97	6.00
Japan	2.79	6.08
UK	2.22	8.50
US	2.19	8.95

Source: World Bank, World Development Indicators.

trend in investment expenditure and in GDP is similar in all of these economies. But investment is much more volatile than GDP. In the big economies, changes in investment are more than twice as volatile as changes in GDP.

Changes in investment and GDP are highly correlated; investment is **procyclical**. That is, when output in the economy as a whole is rising rapidly, investment expenditure tends to increase sharply; when output growth falls, investment expenditure tends to decline markedly. Movements in investment expenditure may be disproportionately important in driving the business cycle.

When we talk about investment, we should be precise about what we mean. In Figure 10.16 and in Table 10.3, investment means the accumulation of physical capital. We are not talking about expenditure on the education system or on research and development. What we mean is investment in machines, buildings and so on – tangible assets used in the production process. Expenditure on these kinds of capital assets is extremely important. As we saw in Chapter 4, investment expenditure is a substantial proportion of overall spending in developed economies – accounting for around one-quarter of GDP, while in some developing nations the ratio is even higher. For example, China's investment-to-GDP ratio is close to 40%.

As well as physical investment and capital, developed economies are increasingly dependent on intangible assets such as copyrights and brands. Calculations by Robert Hall suggest that perhaps 40% of the value of corporate assets in the United States reflects the worth of intangibles.[8] It is possible that, once we account for intangible assets, the difference in overall investment rates between the United States and some other countries is not so great.

As we noted in Chapter 4, there is a distinction between total (or gross) investment and net investment, which is net of depreciation of existing capital.

KEY POINT

Investment is an important element of GDP and tends to be more volatile than GDP.

(10.9) The Optimal Stock of Capital

It makes sense for a company to expand its stock of capital if the cost of the additional investment turns out to be lower than the value of the extra profit that the new machines generate. But it makes no sense to continue investing if the extra revenues from the new machine do not at least cover its cost. So we can think of the **optimal capital stock** as being that level beyond which extra returns are lower than cost, and below which extra returns exceed cost. Figure 10.17 shows a simple illustration of the determination of the desired capital stock. On the horizontal axis, we measure the total value of the machines that are already in place (that is, the capital stock), and on the vertical axis, we measure costs and marginal rates of return. It is important to be clear about the units in which we are measuring costs and returns here. When we think about costs, we are measuring the *extra* resources that are used over a particular period as a result of installing one extra unit of capital. Let us think of that period as one year. We can then measure the cost of capital as the resources

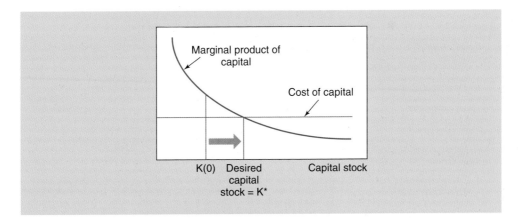

F I G U R E   1 0 . 1 7   ●   **What determines investment?** The optimal level of the capital stock is where the cost of capital just equals the marginal productivity of capital.

that a company has to come up with to enjoy the use of a particular lump of capital for 12 months. And we measure the marginal product of capital as the *extra* profit that the company derives from having that capital in place over that period.

Of course, it is arbitrary to think of the period over which we measure extra profits, and the cost, as precisely 12 months. We should really think about how long the capital is in place and the stream of extra profit that it can generate over that period. You can hire, or rent, some pieces of capital for a day. If I hire a van to help me move furniture into my new house, then the relevant cost of capital is the one-day rental cost, and the gain is whatever monetary value I can put on the benefits of using a van for 24 hours. If we can buy a machine today and sell it again in a few months, then the relevant period to calculate profits against cost is a few months. Many machines remain in place for longer periods, perhaps 10 or 20 years. When we think about the extra profit that such a machine can earn and about its cost, then we may need to form expectations of those benefits and costs over many years. So, although we have simplified the time period to one year for our example, in practice the type of capital we are talking about greatly affects the time period for measuring costs and benefits.

Let us, for the moment, return to the somewhat abstract world depicted in Figure 10.17 and focus on how we actually measure the cost of capital. We need to think about the extra resources that using a piece of capital for 'a period' consumes. This cost reflects several things. First, there is the cost of the funds tied up in the machine. Suppose that you bought a piece of capital machinery on 1 January and borrowed the money to finance the purchase. A major element of the cost of capital would then be the interest rate on the borrowed funds. If you sold the machine again at the end of the year, a second element of cost would be the change in its value, which itself reflects both depreciation (or wear and tear) and the change in the market price of that sort of capital.

So two of the major elements in the **cost of capital** are changes in the value of the machine and the cost of using funds. That second element – the cost of funds – is more subtle than simply the rate of interest. Most corporations, in fact, do not finance their investment expenditure by borrowing from banks, so we need to think about more than just a bank interest rate. Companies finance investment from many sources: they issue shares, retain profit, issue bonds and sometimes rely on credit from suppliers of capital goods. The cost of capital should reflect the cost of each type of finance and its relative importance. Table 10.4 shows that, in the last quarter of the twentieth century, companies in Germany, Japan, the

TABLE 10.4 ● The Financing of Investment: Flow of Funds Estimated (%).

	Germany	Japan	UK	US
Internal finance	78.4	69.9	95.6	94.0
Bank finance	12.0	30.1	15.0	12.8
Bond finance	−1.0	3.4	3.8	15.3
New equity	20.02	3.4	−5.3	−6.1
Other	10.6	−6.8	−9.1	−16.0
Data sample	1970–94	1970–94	1970–94	1970–94

Note: Internal finance comprises retained earnings and depreciation. The 'Other' category includes trade credit and capital transfers. The figures represent weighted averages where the weights for each country are the level of real fixed investment in each year in that country.

Source: Corbett and Jenkinson, 'How is investment financed?', *Manchester School* (1996), LXV: 69–94.

United States and the United Kingdom, in aggregate, relied on internal funds for a far higher proportion of their investment than borrowing from banks or issuing new debt or equity.[9] Naturally, internal finance is not free!

When a company uses some of its profits to finance investment, there are opportunity costs involved. The company is using money that it could otherwise pay out to shareholders as dividends. And once the dividends are distributed to shareholders, they could earn a rate of return that reflects the investment opportunities open to investors. So we should think of the cost of internal finance as reflecting the rates of return that investors might earn on the funds if they were available to them. Those funds could be invested in the stock or bond markets or put in banks, so the overall cost to a firm of using internal finance should reflect the varying rates of return that could be earned on a whole range of financial assets.

And then, of course, there is risk. The shareholders in a company may perceive investments in that company as more risky than putting money in the government bond market or buying a diversified portfolio of equities. In this case, the cost of capital to the individual firm will reflect not just the rates of return that could be earned on other assets, but also a risk premium to reflect greater uncertainty over returns.

In figuring out the cost of capital, as well as the required rates of return that investors might expect on different assets, we must also consider the impact of the tax system. Interest on debt is usually tax deductible to corporations, so this helps determine both the relative attractiveness of debt and equity to companies and the overall level of the cost of capital. Tax also plays a key role in calculating the marginal product of capital. Companies pay tax on profits that they earn, and these taxes are a deduction from the available profits. In fact, the tax system is much more complicated than this. Depreciation of capital is often tax deductible, and companies may enjoy tax incentives to undertake investment.[10] We shall see below that the impact of taxes on investment differs in important ways across countries.

KEY POINT

The optimal amount of capital is that level above which additions to the stock increase costs more than they increase revenues. At this point, the marginal product of capital equals the marginal cost of capital; the latter is often called the marginal user cost of capital.

(10.10) Declining Marginal Product of Capital

Figure 10.17 depicts a situation where the marginal product of capital falls with the value of the capital stock. This is probably plausible for an individual company. The greater the capital stock, the larger the level of output and, beyond a certain point, price probably has to fall to sell more of a product, so marginal profitability declines. If the cost of capital is either flat or increasing, and the marginal product of capital schedule, at least beyond some point, begins to decline, then there will be a unique desired capital stock. In Figure 10.17, initial capital is at level $K(0)$ and desired capital is at level $K(*)$. If there are costs in adjusting the capital stock quickly, then investment will be undertaken to close the gap between $K(0)$ and $K(*)$ over some period; but we will not jump straight to the new level. The amount of time taken to close the gap between current capital and optimal capital reflects the size of the gap and the costs of installation of capital.

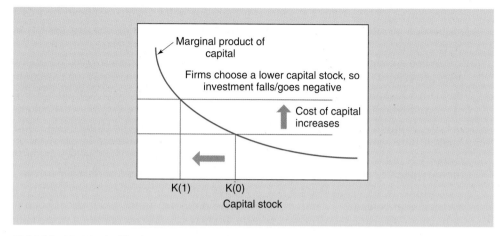

FIGURE 10.18 ● **What happens when interest rates increase?** A rise in the cost of capital, other things remaining equal, reduces the optimal capital stock.

We can use this framework to analyse the impact of changes in some of the main determinants of the capital stock. Figure 10.18 shows what happens when the cost of capital increases. If firms were initially at their optimal capital stock, so that K(0) coincided with K(*), then anything that causes the cost of capital to increase will take the new optimal level of capital *beneath* the current level (to K(1)). Many things could increase the cost of capital. Investors may suddenly come to see the risks of investing in corporations as having increased, in which case the risk premiums on corporate capital will rise, meaning that the required rates of return on new investment need to be higher. Or, the monetary authorities (central bank) may increase interest rates, which may cause bond prices to fall, thereby increasing companies' nominal cost of borrowing. (The lower bond prices are, the greater is the cost for firms in selling bonds to finance investment; we explore the link between bond prices and the required rates of return of investors in Chapter 16.) Unless there is an offsetting increase in expectations of inflation, then the *real* cost of borrowing has risen, and the cost of the capital schedule will move up. The negative impact of a rise in interest rates on investment is one of the important factors that lies behind the IS curve that we will outline in Section 10.13. We might, in fact, expect investment to be more sensitive to a change in interest rates than is consumption expenditure. In addition, because the user cost of capital depends on much else besides interest rates, other factors will also drive investment. Changes in the tax system (for example, reductions in the generosity of deductions of interest charges against taxable profit) could have the same impact as a movement in interest rates.

If the cost of capital increases, for whatever reason, then the optimal stock of capital will be lower. However, companies may not be able to reduce their capital stock instantly to a lower level. The transition from K(0) to K(1) following a rise in the cost of capital could, in fact, take years. If a firm finds that its optimal capital stock is substantially beneath its current level of capital, then it may decide to undertake zero *gross* investment for some years and allow depreciation gradually to reduce its capital.

Note that all this tends to make investment expenditure volatile. Small movements in the cost of capital could take the equilibrium level K* from being slightly in excess of K(0) to well beneath it. If a company found that K* was in excess of K(0), it would want to undertake positive net investment, which, given depreciation, could imply substantial levels of *gross* investment. But if K* then dipped beneath K(0), the firm might find it optimal to reduce gross investment to *zero*, as we have noted. This is one reason why investment expenditure might be more volatile than consumption expenditure. It would be unusual for an individual to decide to cut consumption to *zero* in response to news about interest rates or future incomes, but it is not unusual for firms to move from substantial *net* investment to zero *gross* investment from one year to the next.

KEY POINT

Like consumption, the cost of borrowing is an important determinant of investment.

One of the main driving forces behind investment expenditure is technological advances. Many companies spend a lot of money on computer systems, because computer hardware and software technology has advanced so dramatically in the last 20 years that one generation of machines is virtually obsolete within a few years. Again, we can use the simple framework we have developed to analyse the impact of technological breakthroughs. If a new invention dramatically increases the productivity of capital, then the marginal product of capital schedule will shift significantly outwards. Figure 10.19 illustrates this. After a technological breakthrough, you might expect dramatic investment for substantial periods. You might also expect existing machines that have become obsolete to be scrapped. Technological progress can simultaneously increase both gross investment and the scrapping of existing machines. So its overall impact on the value of the net capital stock may not be dramatically positive, but its impact on productivity may, nonetheless, be profound. We see here another reason why investment expenditure is likely to be more volatile than consumption expenditure. Technological breakthroughs often profoundly affect the structure of the capital stock and can be sudden and hard to predict.

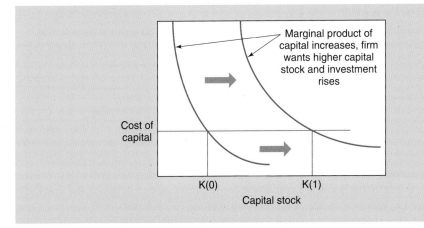

FIGURE 10.19 ● **What happens with a technological breakthrough?** An increase in productivity raises the optimal stock of capital.

(10.11) Investment and the Stock Market

We noted above that in the largest developed economies, corporations finance most of their investment expenditure from internal resources; ultimately this is shareholders' capital. The stock market valuation of companies' existing capital reflects the return that shareholders might earn on funds. So we should expect to see a link between levels of investment that companies undertake and the stock market. In fact, the link was elegantly and formally set out many years ago by James Tobin, who developed the so-called **q theory** of investment. Tobin noted that if the value of a company on the stock market was substantially more than the replacement cost of the assets that the firm employs (most of which we will assume are some form of capital equipment), then in principle that company has a major incentive to increase investment. When we think about the replacement value of capital here, we mean the current cost of buying the sorts of machines that the company uses. If the ratio between the value of its shares and the replacement cost of that firm's capital stock is greater than 1, then the stock market is valuing the firm at more than it would cost to replace all its capital by buying new machines. If that were the case, a company would have an incentive to replicate itself by expanding its capital stock, and its stock market valuation would rise by more than the cost of the investment. The company could finance the purchase of the new machines from its existing shareholders, who would enjoy immediate gains as the firm's stock market value increased by more than the cost of the new machines. The ratio between the value of a firm's shares (or its stock market valuation) and the replacement cost of its capital stock is Tobin's 'q'.

Consider the example of a small company that produces specialized pistons for high-performance car engines. Suppose that the stock market valuation of this company is $200 million. The assets of the company are really of two sorts: (1) the physical plant, machinery and buildings with which it produces pistons; and (2) its less tangible assets, like the experience of its workforce and the value of the techniques that the firm has developed. Suppose that the firm can hire more workers with the same skills and at the same cost as the current workforce, and that it can sell more pistons on the same terms as existing output. This means that doubling the productive capacity – buying new machines, getting new buildings, hiring more workers and so on – should double the value of the firm. Suppose that the existing machines, buildings and such like have a replacement cost of $150 million. Because the existing company is valued at $200 million, and it costs $150 million to double productive capacity, the company could increase its market value by $200 million by spending $150 million; obviously this is a good deal.

In this example, Tobin's q is well in excess of 1 (it is $200/150 = 1.333$), so there is a clear incentive to invest. Note that we specified that the firm could expand production by taking on extra workers who were no more costly and no less productive than the existing ones. We also assumed that the firm could sell the extra pistons at no lower a price and, further, that the techniques it had developed (whose worth the market value of the existing firm reflected) could be applied as productively to the operation of the new machines as the old ones. These assumptions ensured that the value of existing assets was a guide to the increase in value that expanding capacity would bring. (Put more technically, we needed to ensure that the average q on the existing assets was equal to the marginal q on new investments.)

The q theory has a simple prediction for the relationship between the level of investment and the value of the stock market, and Figure 10.20 depicts it. If the q of a company exceeds 1, that company should find that the cost of buying machines is below the value that the stock market will then place on those machines. This is an incentive for a firm to expand and start investing, which will be in the interest of its shareholders. By the same token, if Tobin's q is less than 1, then the stock market is valuing the capital of a company at less than

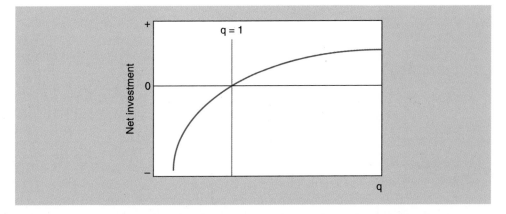

FIGURE 10.20 ● The q theory of investment. When q is above 1 there is an incentive to undertake net investment because the rate of return on capital is larger than the cost of capital.

its replacement cost. This means that, were a company to undertake investment, it would find that the cost of buying the machines was greater than the value the market placed on those machines. Firms would have no incentive to invest under such circumstances. In fact, they should start selling their capital, because they would get more for it on the secondhand market than the value shareholders placed on it.

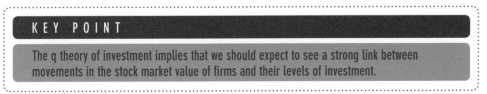

KEY POINT

The q theory of investment implies that we should expect to see a strong link between movements in the stock market value of firms and their levels of investment.

The q theory is closely linked to the idea that firms should invest if the rate of return on new capital exceeds the cost of capital. To see this, assume that a firm can get a return on new investment that is close to the return on its existing capital. Then a good way to measure the marginal rate of return is to take the ratio between the profits earned on the existing capital and the replacement cost of that capital. (For simplicity, we assume here that it is an all-equity-financed firm, but this is not essential to the logic of the argument.) This ratio tells you the average rate of return given the actual purchase price of machines, and this is the relevant number when considering buying a new machine. So our measure of the rate of return is

Profits / Replacement cost of capital

What about the cost of capital? If a firm is generating just enough profits to satisfy its shareholders, we would expect that the ratio of profits to stock market value is equal to the shareholders' required rate of return. So a measure of the cost of capital is

Profits / Stock market value of firm

The ratio of our measure of the rate of return to the cost of capital is therefore

[Profit / Replacement cost of capital] / [Profit / Stock market value of firm]
= Stock market value of firm / Replacement cost of capital = q

Thus q is the ratio of the rate of return to the cost of capital. As noted above, if q > 1, the rate of return exceeds the cost of capital, and the capital stock should be expanded. If q < 1, the rate of return falls short of the cost of capital, and the capital stock should not be expanded.

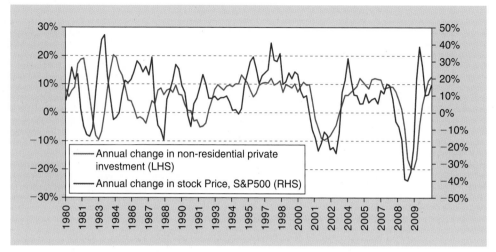

FIGURE 10.21 ● US stock prices and investment. There is at best only a weak link between movements in stock prices and changes in investment. *Source:* OECD.

The q theory of investment implies that there should be a positive link between stock market valuations (relative to the purchase cost of plant, machines, buildings and so forth) and the level of investment. But empirical evidence suggests that there is not such a clear link. Figure 10.21 plots changes in the level of investment expenditure in the United States charted against the change in stock prices. While the two move roughly in line, the correlation between them is not very high. Similar pictures could be drawn for all the major economies.

What are we to make of the relatively weak link between stock prices and levels of investment? The most natural interpretation may be that corporations do not find sudden shifts in stock market valuations informative when it comes to predicting rates of return that they can earn on new investment. Given the volatility in stock prices, often apparently unrelated to shifts in fundamental factors that might influence profitability, they may be right. If stock prices have a tendency to become unconnected with fundamental economic forces – supply and demand for goods – then firms would not be helping their shareholders by undertaking massive bouts of investment every time the stock market moved up sharply, only to slam on the brakes when stock prices plummet. Another practical problem with measuring q is that intangible assets are important and not included in the replacement cost of capital and so q may be mismeasured.

(10.12) Cash Flows and Investment

Relatively heavy reliance on internal resources to finance investment suggests that shifts in current profits may have more influence on levels of investment expenditure than do movements in stock prices, or even shifts in expectations of future profits. Of course, this isn't how we analysed investment expenditure in the abstract models outlined above. There, what really mattered was the relative magnitude of the cost of capital and the marginal rate of return on new investment. Current cash flow or the amount of internal revenue that the company generated played no role. Investment depended completely on the *potential* returns and costs of new investment rather than on the revenue generated by existing capital. If current profits were, in fact, a key determinant of investment expenditure, it would not only be in marked contrast to the simple model, it would also suggest that resources could become significantly misallocated. If existing cash flow, rather than potential profitability, determines investment, then in periods of buoyant profits, companies might tend to overinvest and they might under-invest when current profits were low. Investment could also destabilize the macroeconomy. Corporate profits and revenues would tend to be high during booms, and if investment also tended to be high, it would exacerbate the economic cycle; similarly, corporate revenues would tend to fall in recessions, and investment expenditure might also decline.

Because of the influence on business cycles, it is important to find out whether or not the cash flow story of investment is correct. This is a controversial area, and the evidence is not straightforward. The problem is that movements in current profits not only generate shifts in available resources (i.e. in cash flow), they also, plausibly, should influence expectations of the *future* profitability of investment expenditure. Even a high correlation between current profits and levels of investment would not prove that available cash flow is the key variable that drives investment. It could simply reflect a strong correlation between expectations of high future profitability on capital and high current profitability. Indeed, it would be bizarre if such a correlation did not exist.

So an apparent link between current cash flows and investment expenditure does not indicate that something has gone wrong with how corporations make investment decisions. There are, nonetheless, worrying signs. Surveys in the United States[11] and in the United Kingdom[12] in the 1990s revealed that companies seemed to apply unusual criteria in deciding whether to undertake investment projects. Specifically, they appeared to require rates of return on investment expenditure that are often dramatically higher than the rates of return that investors typically receive on funds. It looks, at face value, as if firms are requiring hurdle rates of return[13] on potential new investment projects that are much larger than the rates of return with which you might expect investors to be content. Could this affect the relatively low levels of investment expenditure in the United Kingdom and the United States? Again, the evidence is far from conclusive. Managers of corporations, who are used to inflated forecasts of profits about projects from those in the company who have the most to gain from expansion, may tend to correct for this excess optimism by applying a higher discount factor. Of course, this isn't the right way to handle excess optimism; a better strategy would be to scale back the inflated expectations of profits that come from the planning department. But, as a rough-and-ready response to institutionalized excess optimism, it is at least understandable.

(10.13) The IS Curve

We can use the simple framework for thinking about consumption that we introduced at the beginning of this chapter to start to build up one side of the famous **IS-LM model**, designed to show how changes in elements of spending and in monetary conditions interact to drive the overall level of income in an economy.[14] We shall be developing the component parts of the overall IS-LM model over several chapters; we start here by considering further the implications of the dependence of consumption on income.

At this early stage of developing the IS-LM model, we are assuming that only consumption varies with income and that all the other factors of demand (planned investment, government expenditure and net exports) are exogenous, or given, amounts. Note that we refer to *planned* investment rather than just investment. From our analysis of GDP in Chapter 2, it will be remembered that investment equals investment in physical capital plus any increase in inventories, or unsold output. The latter will be important whenever overall spending in the economy differs from planned levels.

Assuming a closed economy and using our simple Keynesian consumption function, total planned expenditure (PE = C + G + I) in the economy equals

$$PE = A + b(Y) + G + I$$

So planned aggregate spending depends on actual income. Actual income has to be the sum of consumption, investment and government spending. If actual income equals planned expenditure then PE = Y, which implies that

$$PE = Y = A + b(Y) + G + I$$

which, as before, implies that

$$Y = [A + I + G]/(1 - b)$$

So when planned aggregate expenditure equals actual income, the level of income is a multiple of the components of demand that are independent of income, the expression in square brackets. Shifts in those components have a multiplied impact on demand and income. As noted previously, the multiplier is $1/(1 - b)$, which depends positively on the marginal propensity to consume.

What happens when planned expenditure and actual spending do not coincide? Consider Figure 10.22. On the horizontal axis we measure actual income, which, given GDP accounting, is equivalent to output. On the vertical axis we measure planned aggregate spending. A 45-degree line is drawn on the figure and when actual and planned spending are equal – which is something we will require for an equilibrium – we need to be on this line. The line PE–PE shows how planned spending varies with actual income. Because the propensity to consume is b, a number we plausibly take to be less than one but positive, the slope of the PE–PE line is less than 45 degrees. Its slope reflects how much planned spending rises as actual income goes up one dollar. Since we assume that the only component of demand that depends on current income is consumption and that the marginal propensity to spend is b, then this slope is b – demand increases directly through increases in consumption of $\$b$ for every $\$1$ increase in output.

Suppose that firms assess that the level of output they should produce to satisfy planned spending is at level Y_1. This is in excess of the level of output consistent with output being equal to planned spending, which is level Y^*. If firms produce Y_1, they will find that, so long as the

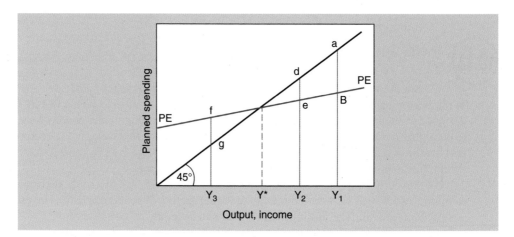

FIGURE 10.22 ● **The Keynesian cross.** Planned spending and actual spending only coincide at Y*.

government spends G, then the overall level of demand, given firms' own planned investment, will fall short of Y_1. The vertical distance aB shows the difference between actual output and planned spending at a production level of Y_1. That distance is equal to unplanned inventory accumulation. Since we count inventory accumulation as a part of investment, then we can interpret the vertical distance aB as the difference between actual investment and planned investment.

Unplanned inventory accumulation is likely to encourage firms to reduce their output. Wise and far-sighted firms who could work out where they went wrong in the first period, when they expected planned spending to be at Y_1, might decide to produce Y^* in the second period. If so, we would then go straight to the equilibrium, where plans and outcomes for spending are consistent. But maybe firms only scale back their plans partly and aim to produce Y_2 in the next round of production. In this case they would still accumulate unwanted inventories, but at the lower rate of de; eventually firms would converge on Y^*.

A similar story would unfold if firms had been too pessimistic about equilibrium output. Had firms anticipated that only at output level Y_3 would production match planned spending, they would have found that demand exceeded their expectations and that inventories would be drained by the amount fg. Only when they increased output up to level Y^* would unanticipated reductions in inventories cease.

In Figure 10.22, the point at which the 45-degree line and the planned expenditure line intersect is the point at which actual and planned spending coincide; this crossover point of the two lines is what gives the **Keynesian cross** its name. At this point the economy can be considered to be in equilibrium – planned output equals actual output. To demonstrate graphically how the multiplier works, we can return to our simple Keynesian cross model and show how important are shifts in investment, government spending and the exogenous (to income) element of consumer spending (A) to the determination of income. Figure 10.23 shows that a given rise in G, I or A has a long-run effect on output that is much greater than the original stimulus – greater in fact precisely by the magnitude $1/(1 - b)$.

Figure 10.24 shows that if we look at two economies with different propensities to consume, the impact of extra investment or government spending will be greater in the

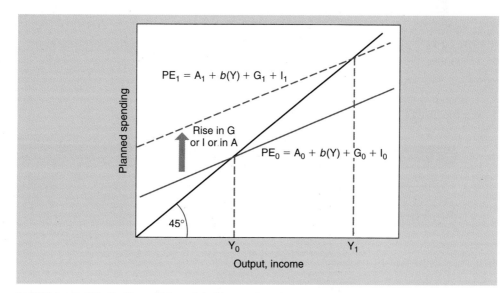

FIGURE 10.23 ● **The multiplier and the IS curve.** The rise in spending exceeds the initial rise in demand.

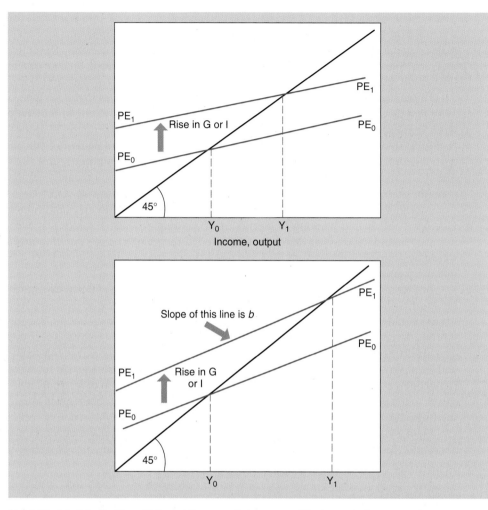

FIGURE 10.24 ● **The multiplier and the propensity to consume.** The larger is the propensity to consume, the steeper is the line PE and the greater is the multiplier.

economy with the larger propensity to consume. The economy with the larger marginal propensity to consume has a larger multiplier.

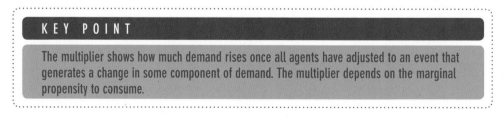

KEY POINT

The multiplier shows how much demand rises once all agents have adjusted to an event that generates a change in some component of demand. The multiplier depends on the marginal propensity to consume.

BUILDING UP THE IS CURVE

In the Keynesian cross diagram shown in Figure 10.22, we focused on shifts in consumption induced by changes in disposable income. Let us assume that, in aggregate, consumption and investment are negatively affected by a rise in the interest rate; an assumption that is consistent with empirical evidence from developed countries. It is the influence of interest rates on the components of aggregate demand that leads us to the IS curve we mentioned earlier in this chapter.

We would certainly expect that overall planned spending would decline with higher interest rates. Figure 10.25 shows that in the Keynesian cross diagram, the implication of this is that the higher interest rates are then, other things being equal, the lower will be the equilibrium level of output. When interest rates increase from r_0 to r_1, the aggregate spending schedule shifts down from PEr_0 to PEr_1 – in part because consumption is likely to be lower. As a result, the equilibrium level of output falls from Y_0^* to Y_1^*. If we vary the interest rate and calculate the equilibrium level of output for each rate, we would trace out a negative relation, shown in Figure 10.26. Figure 10.26 is the IS curve – it is built up by using Figure 10.25 to draw a PE schedule at various interest rates and calculating the

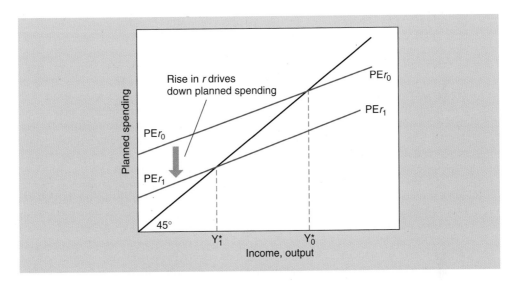

FIGURE 10.25 ● **Aggregate demand and a rise in interest rates.** A rise in interest rates reduces some components of spending and causes equilibrium income and output to fall.

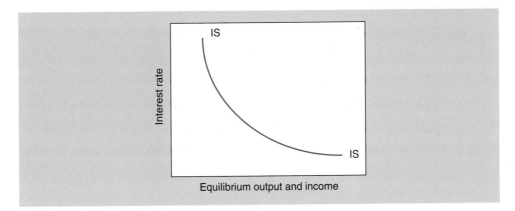

FIGURE 10.26 ● **The IS curve.** The IS curve shows combinations of interest rates and income consistent with equilibrium in the demand for goods and services.

equilibrium level of income consistent with actual and planned expenditure being equal for each interest rate. The IS curve gives policymakers an indication of the effects of interest rates on economic output.

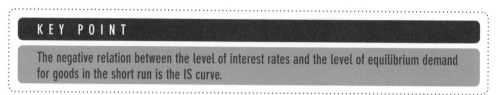

KEY POINT

The negative relation between the level of interest rates and the level of equilibrium demand for goods in the short run is the IS curve.

SUMMARY

In Section 10.1, we discussed the importance of consumption. Consumption accounts for around 60% of GDP and is closely tied to GDP growth over the business cycle. Consumption decisions also determine savings, which is a key determinant of the long-run standard of living.

In Section 10.2 we saw that, traditionally, Keynesian economics has given a key role to consumption in influencing the impact of fiscal policy on the economy. The key concept is the *marginal propensity to consume* – how much of an extra dollar of income is spent by an individual. In Section 10.3, we introduced the permanent income model, which offers a richer framework and has consumers smoothing their lifetime income by setting consumption equal to permanent income. The mpc then depends on whether changes in income are perceived as temporary or permanent. In Section 10.4, we saw that it also explains savings as dependent on future income expectations: if income is expected to grow, then savings are negative.

In Section 10.5, we examined how the forward-looking model can produce a close relationship between current consumption and income, like the Keynesian model, but for different reasons. One reason is that individuals are sometimes unable to borrow; the other, that individuals are unsure of future income expectations and so base their current expenditure decisions on current income. In the forward-looking model, the impact of interest rates is ambiguous depending on the relative strength of income and substitution effects. For borrowers, the effect is for current consumption to fall, but for savers, the net effect is indeterminate.

In Section 10.6, we examined the additional role of wealth in consumption choices and noted the difficulties for policymakers in predicting mpc that are introduced by capital gains and consumers' expectations and uncertainty levels. In Section 10.7, we noted that, as well as depending on future income expectations, the pattern of consumption is also influenced by demographic considerations – in particular, the number of children in a household. Profiles of both income and consumption vary systematically with age, meaning that savings rates are also age dependent.

In Section 10.8, we discussed two reasons why investment expenditure is important: it is the means whereby the capital stock grows (or at least is preserved) and it is a significant, volatile and procyclical element of overall spending. In Section 10.9, we suggested that investment depends on expectations of the profitability of new capital relative to its cost. The cost depends on interest rates, the tax system, depreciation and movements in the price of capital goods. Section 10.10 showed how declining marginal product of capital gives a simple relationship that can relate the cost of capital to the optimal capital stock.

In Section 10.11, we explored Tobin's q theory. According to this theory, there should be a link between the stock market value of firms and their incentives to invest – summarized in deviations in Tobin's q from unity. But, in Section 10.12, we saw that financing constraints are one reason why that theory may not really be very satisfactory.

Tracing through the impact of shifts in incomes and in interest rates on consumption and investment allows us to build up a simple model of the demand side of the economy. In Section 10.13, we examined the role of the mpc and planned expenditure in creating a multiplier effect on output in an economy and looked at the Keynesian cross diagram, which relates planned expenditure and output. We saw that the Keynesian cross and the IS curve are useful building blocks in this analysis.

CONCEPTUAL QUESTIONS

1. (Section 10.1) Is there a useful distinction to be made between consumers' expenditure and consumption for (a) services, (b) non-durable goods, (c) durable goods? Might spending on these different components react very differently to changes in income and to interest rates?

2. (Section 10.3) Draw indifference curves for a patient consumer compared to an individual with a need for instant gratification.

3. (Section 10.3) What would the budget constraint look like if it were only possible to borrow at an interest rate higher than the deposit rate?

4. (Section 10.3) When inflation increased sharply in the 1970s, the savings rate increased. Evaluate the role of interest rates and current and future income in explaining this phenomenon.

5. (Section 10.3) The permanent income model assumes that you treat your current financial wealth and the present value of your discounted future income in the same way. Discuss the plausibility of this result.

6. (Section 10.4) What would be the impact on savings if the government introduced an unemployment insurance scheme?

7. (Section 10.7) In the two-period model the consumer aimed to die with zero assets. What would be the planning horizon of parents who wished their children to enjoy the same standard of living that they experienced? What is the planning horizon if every generation feels this way?

8. (Section 10.7) How would an increase in the popularity of annuities affect levels of inheritances in a country? (Annuities are contracts where in exchange for handing over a lump sum of money today, a person receives a certain [known] amount of money each year until death.)

9. (Section 10.8) Can a country invest too much? How might you assess what is too much?

10. (Section 10.9) Suppose that firms extrapolate from recent growth in demand to future growth in demand. They invest when capital is insufficient to meet projected demand. If current capital exceeds what is required to meet expected demand, investment is cut to zero. How could an economy that worked like this generate investment-led business cycles?

11. (Section 10.9) Suppose that interest rates rise sharply but are expected to fall again in a year or so. How do you think this would affect the level of investment in machines with short lives and those with very long useful lives?

12. (Section 10.10) Suppose that an invention renders much of existing production techniques in a sector of the economy obsolete. What would happen to the stock prices of firms and to investment in the sector? What does this tell you about q theory?

13. (Section 10.13) Use the Keynesian cross diagram to show how a fall in government spending can affect consumption.

ANALYTICAL QUESTIONS

1. (Section 10.2) A consumer expects to earn the following sequence of income over the next five decades:

   4   7   10   19   0

(a) Using the forward-looking consumption smoothing model, calculate consumption, savings and wealth for the consumer in each decade (assuming that interest rates are zero).

(b) The government introduces a tax system to pay benefits to all those earning less than 8. As a result, the net-of-tax income that the individual earns (including benefits) changes to:

8   8   10   14   8

Recalculate consumption, savings and assets for each decade. What impact does the benefit system have on consumption?

2. (Section 10.2) Consider an individual who is planning his consumption over five periods during which he expects his income to be 4, 10, 16, 12 and 8.

(a) What is his permanent income?

(b) What is his marginal propensity to consume out of a temporary increase that boosts first-period income to 6?

(c) What is the mpc if the income increase of 2 is expected to continue into the second period?

(d) What is the mpc if the income increase of 2 is expected to continue for every period of the consumer's life?

3. (Section 10.13) Suppose that $C = 100 + 0.7\,Y$, $G = 50$, $I = 120$

In a closed economy $Y = C + I + G$

(a) What is the equilibrium level of Y?

(b) What happens if the level of consumption becomes $C = 130 + 0.7\,Y$?

(c) What happens if the level of consumption becomes $C = 120 + 0.85\,Y$?

Illustrate your answers using the Keynesian cross diagram.

4. (Section 10.5) Consider the same consumer as in Question 1, but now the consumer is unable to borrow – wealth always has to be positive.

(a) How does your answer to Question 1a change?

(b) How does your answer to Question 1b change?

(c) What difference is there in the way fiscal policy influences the economy in these two situations? Why?

5. (Section 10.5) Consider a consumer who expects to receive income in five periods of 4, 12, 23, 16 and 0. In response to 5% interest rates, the consumer defers savings and aims for her consumption to grow by 1 every period. If interest rates are 10%, then she wishes her consumption to increase by 2 every period.

(a) Calculate consumption and savings in each period when interest rates are 5%.

(b) Repeat these calculations for interest rates at 10%. Comment on the relative income and substitution effects.

6. (Section 10.6) Using the same simple model of the economy as in Question 3, now allow for the impact of interest rates on consumption. The consumption function is:

$$Y = 120 + 0.7Y - 10r$$

where r is the level of interest rates.

Calculate the equilibrium level of income when interest rates are 1, 2, 3, 4, 5, 6, 7, 8, 9 and 10%. Draw the resulting IS curve.

7. (Section 10.9) A delivery company can buy a new truck for $50 000. It can finance the purchase with a bank loan. The annual interest rate is 12%. Interest payments are tax deductible and the corporate tax rate is 30%. The company estimates that it will be able to sell the truck a year later for $30 000. Any capital loss is tax deductible. What is the annual user cost of the truck?

8. (Section 10.9) Consider again the delivery company in Question 7. The company estimates how much extra pre-tax income a given number of new trucks will bring in. Here is the schedule:

Extra trucks	Extra Income (Pre-Tax $)
10	300 000
20	570 000
30	840 000
40	1 000 000
50	1 150 000

How many trucks should the firm buy?

9. (Section 10.10) An all-equity company (which has no debt) has a stock market value of $540 million. Its tangible assets comprise land, buildings and machines. The land is worth $100 million. The buildings are worth $120 million. The replacement value of the machines is $300 million. What is Tobin's q? Why might q differ from unity? The intangible assets of the company include the value of its reputation. Does the fact that these assets might have value imply that the company should expand?

CHAPTER 11

Business Cycles

Key Concepts

Business Cycle	New Keynesian Models	Real Business Cycle Theory
Demand Shocks	Okun's Law	Recession
Depression	Output Gap	Supply Shocks
Frisch-Slutsky Paradigm	Propagation Mechanism	

Overview

Business cycles are medium-term fluctuations in the economy; that is, fluctuations that are normally completely contained within a decade or less. The business cycle involves oscillations between periods of high and low activity, or expansions and contractions. In this chapter we outline the main statistical facts that characterize business cycles and how the business cycle affects different industries and different individuals. We consider whether business-cycle fluctuations are bad for the economy or whether they may have beneficial effects. Understanding the business cycle requires identifying the shocks that trigger fluctuations and the various economic mechanisms that propagate these shocks over time. We view a range of different business-cycle theories, outlining the shocks and propagation mechanisms they assume and reviewing the evidence in support of each. We also describe a simple supply-and-demand model with which to analyse the effects of these shocks and propagation mechanisms.

11.1 What Is a Business Cycle?

One way of defining the business cycle is that it is the fluctuations in output around its trend. The production function tells us that, for a given level of capital, labour and technology, a certain amount of output can be produced. This is what we have referred to as the trend level of output. However, at any point in time, output does not have to equal its trend value. Firms can always produce less output if they do not work at full capacity or if they do not work their labour force at full efficiency during its working shift. Therefore, output can always be below this trend level. But output can also exceed the trend level predicted by the production function. For instance, workers can be persuaded to work overtime for short periods and machines can be utilized at more than full capacity during intense periods of production. Firms cannot maintain these high levels of activity indefinitely: eventually the workforce needs a rest, and if machines are used too intensively they will break down and there will be stoppages. But, for short periods, this intensive use of factors of production enables output to be above its trend. These fluctuations of output above and below the trend level provide one definition of the **business cycle**. Figure 11.1 shows an estimate by the OECD of the trend (or potential) level of output for Italy, as well as its gross domestic product (GDP). Figure 11.2 shows the gap between Italian GDP and potential output, which is one measure of the business cycle. When output is above trend, the economy is in the boom phase of the cycle, and when it is significantly below trend, the economy is in **recession**.

The measure shown in Figure 11.2 is sometimes referred to as the 'output gap', the distance between potential output and current GDP. The output gap is a popular concept used to explain how monetary policy operates. When the output gap is large and negative, GDP is far below its potential level and factors of production are not being used intensively. By contrast, when the output gap is positive and large, GDP exceeds potential output by a large margin. This can only be the case if factors of production are being used intensively, so that overtime is high and machines are operating a full shift. In these circumstances, inflation is likely to be rising. If firms are already at full capacity when they receive additional orders, these orders cannot easily be met, so the firm will start to increase prices to choke off demand. In addition, overtime costs more than normal working hours, so costs will increase, which also puts upward pressure on prices. Therefore, a large positive output gap is associated with either high or rising inflation, while a large negative gap leads to subdued inflation.

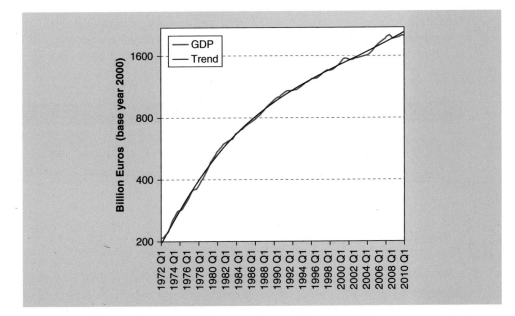

FIGURE 11.1 ● Italian GDP and trend GDP. GDP isn't always equal to its trend level but fluctuates around it – these are business-cycle fluctuations. *Source:* OECD, Economic Outlook Database.

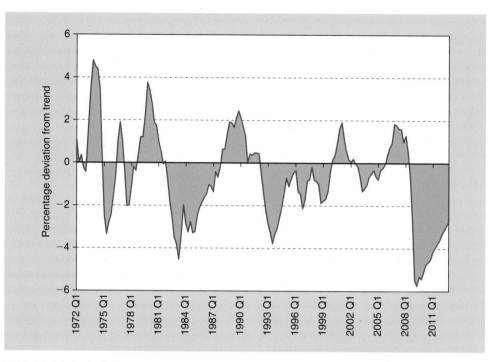

FIGURE 11.2 ● Italian output gap, 1970–2011. The output gap is a measure of the business cycle. *Source:* OECD, Economic Outlook Database.

As Figures 11.1 and 11.2 make clear, business cycles are only temporary – whether in an expansion or a recession, output is eventually expected to return to its trend level. But the economy can remain either above or below its trend level for several successive years. In other words, expansions last for several years and then are replaced by recessions, which are also persistent. In this chapter we will try to explain why the economy experiences these oscillations and also to document how persistent each stage of the business cycle is.

> **KEY POINT**
>
> The business cycle is the continual process whereby the economy enjoys an expansion, endures a recession and then again experiences an expansion. Business-cycle fluctuations occur over the medium term and are usually complete within a decade.

(11.2) Measuring the Business Cycle

We do not actually observe the business cycle – we only observe GDP. To measure the business cycle, we have to make assumptions about trend output. To further complicate matters, economists use a variety of terms when discussing business cycles: booms, recessions, expansions, contractions, depressions, growth recessions and other expressions. What do these terms mean?

One often cited definition of a recession, particularly in the United States, is when an economy has experienced two successive quarters of negative growth. Therefore, if an economy grows by –0.3% and –0.5% in two quarters, it is in recession. Unfortunately, this definition is somewhat restrictive. Imagine that over the last three quarters output growth had been –15%, 0.01% and –35%. This economy is clearly in recession, but does not conform to our two consecutive quarter ruling. We need a more flexible way of defining recessions. The authoritative National Bureau of Economic Research in the United States provides one such definition. A business-cycle committee, which examines recent trends in output and other variables as well as different sectors of the economy, decides whether the economy is in recession. It declares a recession if economic activity contracts across a wide range of variables and a broad range of sectors. Table 11.1 shows the NBER estimates of the phases of US business cycles over the past 150 years.

In many economies, recessions – that is, genuine falls in output – are quite rare. However, growth recessions are more common. A growth recession occurs when, although the economy is still expanding, the growth is less than the economy's long-run trend rate. The output gap is falling during a growth recession, as output growth is below trend. For instance, growth may slow down to 1% even though over the last three years the economy has been expanding at 5% per year. Such a slowdown is a growth recession, but not a recession itself – the economy is still expanding, but not as fast as previously.

Another term used when the economy is performing weakly is **depression**. As with much business-cycle terminology, depression does not have a precise definition.[1] Loosely speaking, it signifies a bad recession: one that is both long-lasting and in which output declines substantially. This does not specify how bad or long-lasting a recession has to be to be called a depression. Probably the key difference between a recession and a depression is that, as Figure 11.2 demonstrates, recessions tend to be short-lived and output soon returns to its trend value. The economy shows momentum between good and bad periods. However, in a depression the economy seems to have lost all momentum – the downturn lasts so long that the economy seems unable to recover on its own without a dramatic policy intervention.

The most famous example of an economic depression is the one that affected many countries between 1929 and 1932. Table 11.2 shows the percentage decline in output between 1929 and 1932 of the countries that were most affected by the Great Depression. Throughout this three-year period, output in these countries fell sharply. Both the extent of these declines and the duration of the contraction make this period a depression rather than a recession.

MEASURING THE OUTPUT GAP

The concept of an output gap is widely used by economists and policymakers as a measure of the cycle. Estimating the output gap is not easy, since the concept of potential or trend output on which it relies is hard to pin down. In practice, three main methods are used to estimate the output gap:

- Estimate trend output using statistical trend fitting and then define the output gap as the difference between actual output and the trend.
- Estimate a production function like the one we looked at in Chapter 3 and use that to generate estimates of potential output.
- Use a range of current data like business surveys of capacity utilization to estimate the output gap directly. So, for example, if businesses are reporting that they operating below normal capacity, then that indicates a negative output gap.

TABLE 11.1 ● Dating of US Business Cycles.

US business cycles vary in their duration: on average, contractions are shorter than recessions.

Reference Dates		Duration (in months) of		
Trough	Peak	Contraction	Expansion	Cycle
12/1854				
12/1858	06/1857	18	30	
06/1861	10/1860	8	22	40
12/1867	04/1865	32	46	54
12/1870	06/1869	18	18	50
03/1879	10/1873	65	34	52
05/1885	03/1882	38	36	101
04/1888	03/1887	13	22	60
05/1891	07/1890	10	27	40
06/1894	01/1893	17	20	30
06/1897	12/1895	18	18	35
12/1900	06/1899	18	24	42
08/1904	09/1902	23	21	39
06/1908	05/1907	13	33	56
01/1912	01/1910	24	19	32
12/1914	01/1913	23	12	36
03/1919	08/1918	7	44	67
07/1921	01/1920	18	10	17
07/1924	05/1923	14	22	40
11/1927	10/1926	13	27	41
03/1933	08/1929	43	21	34
06/1938	05/1937	13	50	93
10/1945	02/1945	8	80	93
10/1949	11/1948	11	37	45
05/1954	07/1953	10	45	56
04/1958	08/1957	8	39	49
02/1961	04/1960	10	24	32
11/1970	12/1969	11	106	116
03/1975	11/1973	16	36	47
07/1980	01/1980	6	58	74
11/1982	07/1981	16	12	18
03/1991	07/1990	8	92	108
11/2001	03/2001	8	120	128
06/2009	12/2007	18	73	81

Source: NBER (www.nber.org).

TABLE 11.2 ● **Percentage Output Declines during the Great Depression.**

Depressions are characterized by dramatic and long-lasting falls in output.

Argentina	−13.72
Australia	−5.78
Austria	−19.79
Belgium	−7.09
Canada	−24.08
Chile	−30.02
France	−14.66
Germany	−23.50
Mexico	−17.66
New Zealand	−14.64
UK	−5.09
US	−26.99
Venezuela	−21.20

Source: Maddison, *Monitoring the World Economy 1820–1992* (Paris: OECD, 1995).

Of course, these three measures rarely agree, particularly during large recessions like that of the late 2000s when it is possible that the downturn was so severe that it has actually reduced potential output (for example, through capital scrapping, when bankrupt firms end up allowing capital to be destroyed rather than selling it to other firms buyers are hard to find). If the trend and business cycle are not independent, then estimating the output gap becomes very difficult.

11.3 Characterizing Business Cycles

Business cycles are not just a feature of modern OECD economies – even the Bible describes seven years of feast followed by seven years of famine. Figure 11.3 shows annual growth in real GDP since 1971 in Germany and Peru. It reveals a pattern of oscillation between periods of high and low growth.

The nature of business-cycle fluctuations differs across countries – for instance, Peruvian growth varies much more than that of the postwar United States – but they all show the general pattern of expansions followed by contractions. Why do such different economies experience business-cycle fluctuations? Later we will provide a model to explain these fluctuations, but for now we shall use a simile. The economy is like a reservoir. With no wind or disturbance, the water will be still. However, as soon as something is thrown into the water, it sets in motion a wave-like pattern on the surface. If a pebble is thrown in, the waves will be small and will not extend far. If an automobile is thrown in, the waves will be bigger and more pronounced. In other words, different disturbances evoke different

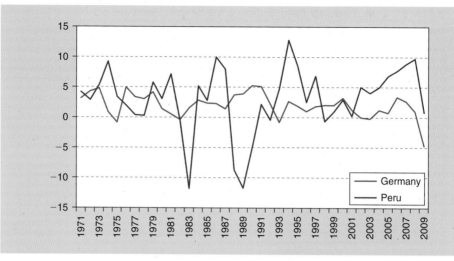

FIGURE 11.3 ● **Annual GDP growth in Germany and Peru, 1971–2009.** Although their frequency and amplitude change, all countries in all historical periods have experienced business-cycle fluctuations. *Source:* IMF, *International Financial Statistics.*

fluctuations in the water, but all disturbances evoke a wave-like motion. Economists think in a similar way about the economy. Its structure is such that any disturbance, such as an increase in the price of oil or in interest rates, sets in place a long-lasting reaction in which output fluctuates between high and low periods of activity.

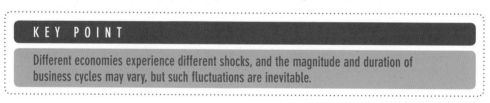

KEY POINT

Different economies experience different shocks, and the magnitude and duration of business cycles may vary, but such fluctuations are inevitable.

WHAT DO BUSINESS CYCLES LOOK LIKE?

We have said that a business cycle consists of two stages: an expansion and a contraction. There are many differences between these two stages of the business cycle. The first is that expansions tend to last longer than recessions. Table 11.3a shows estimates of the patterns of recessions and expansions for countries between 1980 and 2010. Overall, the duration of business cycles is very similar for poor and rich countries. For all income groups expansions tend to last about three years on average, while contractions last just over a year. The amplitude of the cycle varied significantly across income groups. High-income countries have a relatively shallow cycle, with expansions of about 14% and downturns of less than 7% on average. All other income groups experience much larger expansions and contractions, so poorer countries tend to have more pronounced business cycles overall. Table 11.3b shows business cycles by region and highlights how Eastern European countries and those in Sub-Saharan Africa have experienced the most severe downturns over the period, both with an average GDP contraction of over 15%. Over the same period, Asian countries have tended to experienced long and large expansions, which accounts for their far greater average GDP growth.

TABLE 11.3 ● Average Duration and Amplitude of Business Cycles by Income Level and by Region, 1980–2010.

11.3a ● Average Duration and Amplitude of Business Cycles by Country Income Level

Income	Average Duration (In Quarters)			Average Amplitude (%)		Average GDP Growth Rate (%)
	Expansion	Contraction	Cycle	Expansion	Contraction	
High Income	13.3	4.8	19.1	14.0	−6.6	2.8
Upper Middle Income	11.1	4.5	16.3	17.2	−10.8	2.9
Lower Middle Income	10.4	4.9	15.4	20.8	−14.5	2.4
Low Income	12.9	4.4	19.5	24.8	−12.6	3.2

11.3b ● Average Duration and Amplitude of Business Cycles by region

Region	Average Duration (In Quarters)			Average Amplitude (%)		Average GDP Growth Rate (%)
	Expansion	Contraction	Cycle	Expansion	Contraction	
G7	13.4	5.1	19.7	11.2	−6.8	2.1
Africa	7.6	6.2	13.9	18.3	−15.0	2.6
North Africa	9.7	3.8	13.8	14.7	−4.8	4.4
Latin America	8.6	4.8	13.5	16.2	−13.0	2.6
Asia	19.0	3.4	25.2	30.8	−11.6	5.0
Eastern Europe	12.5	4.6	17.8	25.0	−15.9	1.5

Source: Authors' calculations.

11.4 Business Cycles as Aggregate Fluctuations

CO-MOVEMENT ACROSS VARIABLES AND ACROSS SECTORS

The business cycle is a prime example of a macroeconomic phenomenon – an event that has an impact on the majority of people. Admittedly in a recession some firms or individuals will be doing well: in a recession, bankruptcy advisers' workload will soar, and firms can still get lucky by introducing a new product that consumers really want. However, most firms in most industries will be performing below average in a recession.

Figure 11.4 shows this common aggregate experience by examining the four main productive sectors of the UK economy: manufacturing, services, construction and the public sector. The output of all four sectors tends to move together, although the magnitude of the fluctuations differs greatly between them.

The sector most exposed to the business cycle is construction – output growth in this industry has hit peaks of 16% and declines of 13% in a year. The manufacturing sector is also volatile – over the same time period, growth and declines reached as much as +8% and −14% respectively. By contrast, the service and public sectors show muted business-cycle

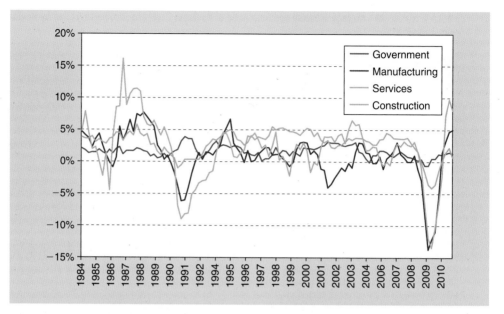

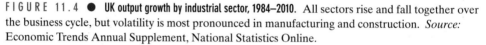

FIGURE 11.4 ● **UK output growth by industrial sector, 1984–2010.** All sectors rise and fall together over the business cycle, but volatility is most pronounced in manufacturing and construction. *Source: Economic Trends Annual Supplement, National Statistics Online.*

fluctuations. Output growth in the public sector has varied between 4% and 0, although for most of the time it lies in the range of 0 to 2%. The service sector shows more variability, with fluctuations between 6% and –4%, but this is still less volatile than either manufacturing or construction output. Therefore, while most sectors show a business-cycle pattern, some are more exposed than others.

Like business sectors, most aggregate economic variables display a strong cyclical pattern, although some do not. For example, wage growth displays little volatility over the business cycle and a much lower correlation with GDP than other economic variables. Trying to explain why wages show such a weak cyclical pattern when unemployment and employment are so strongly cyclical is a key challenge to business-cycle theorists and an issue we will examine in Section 11.7.

GDP AND UNEMPLOYMENT: OKUN'S LAW

A key business-cycle relationship is between GDP and unemployment. When GDP growth is strong, unemployment falls; when the economy moves into recession, unemployment starts to rise (and employment falls). This relationship is not immediate but normally involves a lag of around six months between changes in GDP and subsequent changes in unemployment. The stability of this relationship leads to a simple rule of thumb first proposed by Arthur Okun in 1962, now called Okun's Law. The 'Law' states that for every 2% output falls below trend, the unemployment rate rises by 1%. Figure 11.5 shows the Okun relationship for the US between 1949 and 2010 and confirms that it is generally pretty reliable. Note that the largest deviation from Okun's Law comes at the end of our sample, where unemployment seems much higher than can be explained by the output gap.

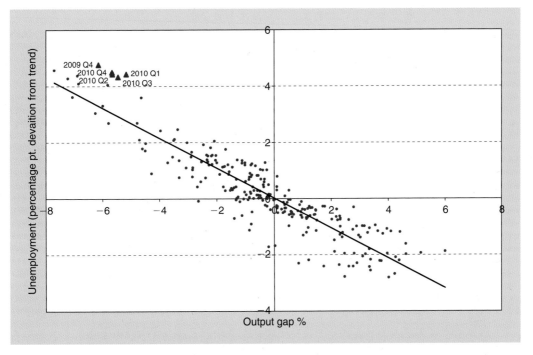

FIGURE 11.5 ● Okun's Law for the US, 1949–2011. There is a relatively stable relationship between the output gap and deviations of unemployment from the natural rate, called Okun's Law. *Source:* Bureau of Economic Analysis, Bureau of Labour Statistics and Congressional Budget Office.

CO-MOVEMENTS ACROSS REGIONS

Regions within a country are strongly connected, so we would expect to find positive co-movement between them. Table 11.4 shows the correlation of output across US states between 1986 and 2009. If the correlation is positive, then output growth tends to be high in each state when overall US output growth is high. The closer the correlation is to 1, the stronger the co-movement. If the correlation is negative, then output in the state tends to be low when the rest of the economy is doing well. If the correlation is zero, then there is no consistent pattern between how output at the state level varies with the national business cycle. Table 11.4 shows that the majority of regions face similar business-cycle experiences: over half the states have a correlation coefficient greater than 0.6 and many have a correlation coefficient above 0.8. Only South Dakota has a negative correlation coefficient.

CO-MOVEMENT ACROSS COUNTRIES

It is understandable why sectors within an economy tend to share a common business cycle. If the manufacturing sector is doing well, it will generate demand for new buildings that will encourage the construction industry and will also generate increased demand for the serv-ice sector (increased estate agency services, mortgage demands, insurance policies and so forth.). National economies are also linked together: when the US economy is growing fast,

TABLE 11.4 ● Output Correlations across US States, 1986–2009.

Alabama	0.77	Kentucky	0.68	North Dakota	0.04
Alaska	0.37	Louisiana	0.55	Ohio	0.75
Arizona	0.91	Maine	0.60	Oklahoma	0.32
Arkansas	0.66	Maryland	0.71	Oregon	0.74
California	0.90	Massachusetts	0.60	Pennsylvania	0.85
Colorado	0.69	Michigan	0.53	Rhode Island	0.47
Connecticut	0.84	Minnesota	0.84	South Carolina	0.88
Delaware	0.63	Mississippi	0.48	South Dakota	−0.22
DC	0.28	Missouri	0.71	Tennessee	0.78
Florida	0.86	Montana	0.60	Texas	0.83
Georgia	0.85	Nebraska	0.54	Utah	0.72
Hawaii	0.44	Nevada	0.91	Vermont	0.53
Idaho	0.69	New Hampshire	0.65	Virginia	0.77
Illinois	0.94	New Jersey	0.80	Washington	0.61
Indiana	0.80	New Mexico	0.43	West Virginia	0.31
Iowa	0.58	New York	0.90	Wisconsin	0.87
Kansas	0.75	North Carolina	0.86	Wyoming	0.34

Source: Authors' calculations from data from Bureau of Economic Analysis, www.bea.doc.gov.

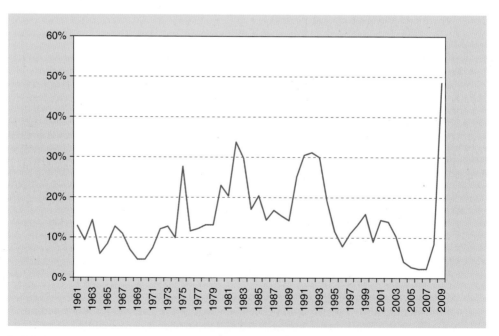

FIGURE 11.6 ● **Share of countries with falling output.** Business-cycle conditions tend to be similar in different economies. *Source:* World Bank, World Development Indicators and authors' calculations.

it generates demand for non-US goods and that helps output grow faster in other countries. As a result, we should expect to see signs of a common business cycle across countries.

Figure 11.6 shows how synchronous recessions were across the world economy between 1961 and 2009. The major recessions of the mid-1970s, early 1980s and early 1990s are clearly shown, but they are dwarfed by the most recent recession of the late 2000s, where almost half the world's countries experienced falling output simultaneously.

> ### KEY POINT
>
> The key feature of business cycles is that they are an aggregate phenomenon. Business cycles are characterized by co-movement; that is, many economic variables from different sectors and regions of the economy, and also from different countries, display similar behaviour at roughly the same time.

(11.5) Have Business Cycles Changed?

While business cycles have been a feature of economies for most of recorded history, their nature is not constant. Figure 11.7 shows how GDP volatility (for the United States) has tended to fall over time, culminating in the 'Great Moderation' of 1984 to 2007, when output volatility in the United States and other major economies fell to very low levels. Stock and Watson estimated that between 20% and 30% of the reduction in volatility was due to

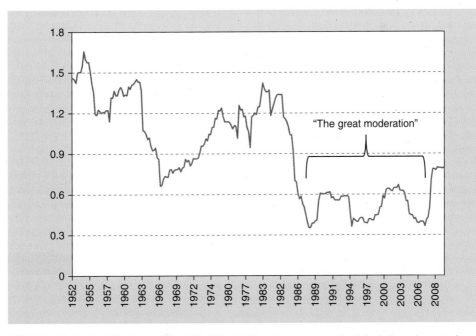

FIGURE 11.7 ● **US output volatility, 1952–2010.** Rolling five-year standard deviation of quarterly output growth. *Source:* OECD and authors' calculations.

improved monetary and fiscal policy.[2] A further 20% to 30% was due to identifiable good luck in the form of an absence of large productivity and commodity price shocks. The rest (40% to 60%) was unexplained. Unfortunately, some people – particularly in the financial sector – felt that the Great Moderation was a permanent feature of the economy and with reduced volatility they were prepared to take larger risks. As a result, it seems in retrospect that the low volatility of the Great Moderation was a contributing factor to the scale of the financial crisis as it encouraged a false sense of security. This led to greater risk taking, which in particular took the form of higher levels of debt and borrowing. The Great Moderation of 1984–2007 came to an end with the Great Recession of 2009–10 and a renewed awareness of aggregate risk. The rise in perceived aggregate risk has caused substantial revaluations to real estate and equity prices and undermined the stability of the banking sector and government debt; issues we will examine in considerable detail in the following chapters.

KEY POINT

Business cycles may have grown less volatile since the middle of the twentieth century, though the extremely low volatility of the 'Great Moderation' was exceptional.

11.6 Are Business Cycles Bad?

In Chapter 3 we outlined an argument of Nobel Prize winner Robert Lucas that said that the benefits to boosting the long-run rate of economic growth were enormous and that the gains from eliminating business-cycle fluctuations were fairly small. In this section we reexamine this argument. Lucas is correct in saying that the benefits from boosting long-run growth are large *relative* to the gains from removing business cycles. However, are the gains from eliminating business cycles so small?

In essence, Lucas's argument is that consumption does not vary much over the business cycle and that, according to some measures, investors do not need to be compensated much for bearing risk (although our analysis of equity markets in Chapter 16 suggests that this is not uncontroversial). Lucas's conclusions are based on fluctuations in *aggregate* consumption. However, business-cycle volatility affects some sectors more than others. For some individuals, consumption volatility will be much greater than Lucas's calculations suggest. Figures 11.8 and 11.9 show this. These are taken from a study of UK households that examined the impact of the 1990–91 recession on the consumption of different individuals and households. Recessions hit the young and the unskilled much more than they affect prime working-age professionals. Therefore, focusing on aggregate consumption underestimates the volatility that some consumers face.

KEY POINT

Although the long-run impact of business-cycle volatility on aggregate economic performance may not be dramatic, the short-run effect on the welfare of households may be significant, because the impacts of recessions are not shared equally. They hit certain households disproportionately hard.

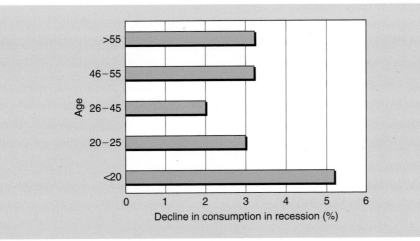

FIGURE 11.8 ● **Impact of recession on consumption by age.** The impact of recession is felt the most by the young and the least by those of prime working age. *Source:* Clark, Leslie and Symons, 'The cost of recessions', *Economic Journal* (1994), 104: 10–37. Reprinted with permission of Blackwell Publishers.

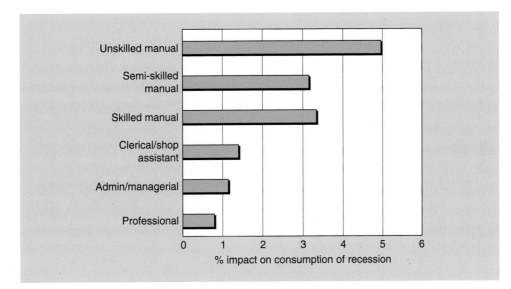

FIGURE 11.9 ● **Impact of recession on consumption by occupation.** Recessions are particularly costly for those with fewer skills. *Source:* Clark, Leslie and Symons, 'The cost of recessions', *Economic Journal* (1994), 104: 10–37. Reprinted with permission of Blackwell Publishers.

Table 11.5 shows how the consumption costs of recession are distributed across the population. Most of the population (57.7%) experiences small declines in consumption as a result of recession – between 0 and 2%. In all, nearly three-quarters of the people suffer, at most, a 4% decline in their consumption. For this group, Lucas's calculations would seem to apply: business cycles involve relatively small variations in consumption. However, a small group suffers disproportionately. For 1% of the population (and, if the sample is

TABLE 11.5 ● Distribution of Consumption Costs of Recession.

The majority of individuals suffer very little from recessions, but a sizeable minority is badly hit.

0–2%	2–4%	4–6%	6–8%	8–10%	10–12%	12–14%	14%
57.7	16.5	13.4	5.4	3.4	0.3	0.3	0.3

Source: Clark, Leslie and Symons, 'The cost of recessions', *Economic Journal* (1994), 104: 10–37.

representative of the UK population, that is 600 000 people), consumption declines more than 10%; and for 15% of the population, it falls more than 6%. Figure 11.9 also suggests that those who suffer the most tend to be the poorest in society, unskilled workers rather than professionals, which suggests that these declines in consumption will substantially affect their standard of living.

Research by Justin Wolfers, based on survey evidence of what makes people happy and depressed, also suggests that business-cycle volatility might be more costly than the Lucas calculations imply.[3] Wolfers finds evidence that people are much more averse to spells of unemployment than to inflation. He finds that the levels of volatility in developed countries in recent years reduced well-being by the equivalent of raising unemployment by a quarter of a percentage point.

Business cycles may also be costly because their volatility may influence long-run growth in the economy. Business cycles create volatility not just in output but also in other variables, such as corporate profits and firm cash flow. This volatility may restrain investment. Firms will be reluctant to commit cash or borrow funds to finance investment if there is a substantial risk of a serious downturn in the economy. Therefore, the greater the magnitude and duration of recessions in an economy, the lower the investment rate and, potentially, the lower the long-run growth rate. Business-cycle volatility may also hinder growth through other channels. During recessions, unemployment increases. If learning by doing is important, then those who become unemployed will lose certain skills, and their productivity will decline. This will hinder their efforts to regain employment when recovery occurs and may permanently diminish output.

Nonetheless, it is not obvious that business-cycle volatility is bad for growth. Indeed, recessions may even be good for the average growth rate. In an expansionary phase, when the economy is growing strongly, it is costly for firms to stop production and add new machinery or rearrange the production process to boost efficiency. However, during a recession machines are idle and workers have spare time; this is a good time for firms to restructure and try to boost productivity. Intense competition during recessions also gives firms the incentives to reorganize. In other words, recessions may act like a pit stop for the economy during which efficiency and productivity improve, so that growth can accelerate when the economy recovers.

Theory therefore is ambiguous about whether business cycles are good or bad for long-run growth, so we now turn to some empirical evidence. Figure 11.10 shows the volatility of output growth between 1961 and 2009 for almost 200 countries, plotted against the average growth rate for each country over this time period. Overall the data suggest a weak, but negative, relationship – in other words, volatile business cycles are probably bad for growth – although clearly other things also affect growth. One study finds that every 1% increase in business-cycle volatility leads to a 0.2% reduction in growth.[4] This implies that if Portugal could reduce its business-cycle volatility to the US level, its trend growth rate would be 0.4% higher; or if the United States could reduce its business-cycle volatility to that of Sweden, US trend growth would be higher by 0.15%.

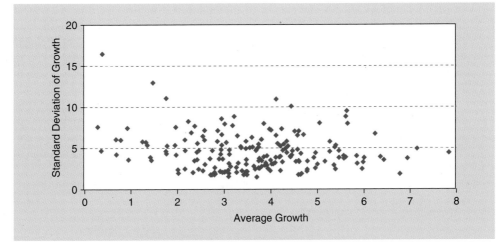

FIGURE 11.10 ● **Trend growth rates and business-cycle volatility, 1961–2009.** There is some evidence that volatile business cycles lead to low growth, but it is very weak. *Source:* World Bank, World Development Index and authors' calculations.

11.7 The Frisch-Slutsky Paradigm

We have already implicitly discussed the main ideas behind the **Frisch-Slutsky paradigm** when we drew an analogy between business cycles and reservoirs.[5] The Frisch-Slutsky paradigm identifies three components in business cycle fluctuations, as shown in Figure 11.11.

The first component is an impulse or a shock that triggers business-cycle fluctuations. In terms of our metaphor, the impulse is the pebble or automobile that is thrown into the reservoir. However, as in our metaphor, the fluctuations that are produced may have a different pattern from the impulse that started them. This is because the impulse acts through a **propagation mechanism** that converts one-time shocks into persistent business-cycle fluctuations – the pebble interacts with the structure of water to produce a wave.

Most economists agree about what business cycles, the third part of the model, look like. Therefore, debate focuses on the first two components of the Frisch-Slutsky paradigm: which shocks are most important and what economic factor converts these shocks into the business cycles that we observe. Although economists disagree over which of them is most important in explaining observed output fluctuations, there is broad agreement over which shocks are candidates for causing business cycles. These include monetary and fiscal policy shocks, shifts in desired consumption and investment, terms of trade shocks (including oil

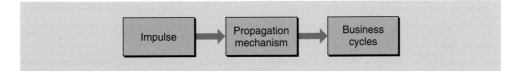

FIGURE 11.11 ● **Frisch-Slutsky business cycle paradigm: A theoretical characterization of business cycles.**

prices), technology shocks and shocks to the financial structure. But the most substantial debate is over what mechanism propagates business cycles. This is because the nature of the propagation mechanism determines how policymakers should respond. Policymakers can do little to reduce the likelihood of technology or terms of trade shocks. The issue is, instead, whether policymakers can, or should even try to, offset the business-cycle fluctuations that these shocks cause.

In the rest of this section, we outline two different views of business cycles. One says that business cycles are the efficient response of markets to shocks that have affected the economy; in other words, business cycles are a sign that the market is working correctly. The other viewpoint, which we shall call Keynesian, is that business cycles are a sign that the market is failing to operate.

REAL BUSINESS CYCLE THEORY

The last 20 years have seen substantial debate in academic journals about business cycles. **Real business cycle theory** has generated much of this debate.[6] Real business cycle theory created several controversies, but here we focus on only two:

- The first is its claim that technology (or more generally total factor productivity, TFP) shocks cause business cycles. Traditionally economists believed that variations in demand caused business cycles and that changes in TFP drove long-run growth but not business cycles. Real business cycle theory's rejection of demand shocks and its use of the same model to explain growth *and* business cycles is therefore radical.
- The other controversy concerns the propagation mechanism. Real business cycle theory says that the profit-maximizing decisions of consumers and firms convert technology shocks into business-cycle fluctuations. When technology improves, firms want to hire more workers and capital. The capital stock cannot be increased instantaneously but, once in place, it leads to high demand for labour and rising wages. This, in turn, leads to higher personal income and thus higher consumption. The effect of the positive technological development is thus spread over several periods.

This view that the propagation mechanism is the efficient operation of the market is particularly controversial. In essence, real business cycle theory says that booms are a time of high productivity and good technology shocks. As a result, firms want to produce high levels of output, to employ many workers and to invest in new machinery. Because productivity is high, firms will pay high wages. So economic expansions happen because it is a good time to be economically active. By contrast, recessions happen because productivity/technology is poor. It is a bad time to produce, and firms will not wish to pay high wages, invest or hire workers. With wages low, workers will not be eager to work. Recessions are simply bad times to be economically active. Note that in this theory, individuals make the decision not to engage in high levels of economic activity based on the market prices in the recession, the 'invisible hand'. This result tells us that the market is efficient. Of course, this doesn't mean that recessions are good – everyone would prefer to be in a boom than a recession. It does, however, mean that because the economy is experiencing low productivity, it is optimal for the economy to be in recession; in other words, governments should not try to kickstart the economy.

As an analogy, consider agricultural production and employment, which vary substantially over the year, reaching a peak at harvest time and a trough during the winter. Governments do not respond to the dramatic decline in output, investment (sowing) or employment during these winter months by aggressively cutting interest rates or trying to boost government expenditure. They recognize that winter is a bad time for farmers and employees to work, so output is low. Real business cycle theorists make essentially the same argument regarding business-cycle fluctuations. Although recessions may be bad in the sense that we would rather not have them, given the circumstances (bad weather, adverse technology shock), the economy is inevitably in recession, and the government should not try to alter output or employment.

This claim that recessions are optimal market responses to bad economic events is understandably controversial. As our seasonal analogy suggests, it also raises interesting issues. Governments do not express concern over seasonal downturns, and economists rarely use anything other than seasonally adjusted data. This suggests that volatile output is not necessarily bad – the key issues are what produces this volatility and how the economy responds to it.

Are real business cycle theorists correct in their claims that recessions are an optimal response by the market to bad technology shocks? To answer this question we need to look more closely at real business cycle theory by focusing on its model of the labour market. As we noted earlier in this chapter, wages fluctuate relatively little, but employment fluctuates a lot. Over the business cycle, we see volatility in output, employment and investment, but much less volatility in interest rates, inflation and wages. In other words, quantity variables are more volatile than price variables. To explain this, we have two main camps. One camp, which includes the Keynesian models that we will soon discuss, says that markets sometimes do not work well and that prices are sluggish. As a result, the economy can only respond to adverse shocks through big changes in output or employment. The other camp, to which the real business cycle model belongs, says that markets work well and that individuals are very responsive to changes in prices.

How does real business cycle theory explain this? When the economy experiences a positive technology shock, then the marginal product of labour is high. At a given wage, firms now want to hire more workers, so the labour demand curve shifts to the right. How this increase in labour demand affects wages and employment depends on the slope of the supply curve. Figure 11.12 shows two different possibilities. In Figure 11.12a the labour supply curve is steep – even with higher wages, firms are not able to employ more people. In this case, fluctuations in labour demand lead to large changes in wages, but no change in employment. However, this is inconsistent with the business-cycle facts that we documented earlier. But if we assume a flat labour supply curve, so that in response to small changes in wages individuals are prepared to change their hours worked dramatically, then this model can explain the high employment variability and low wage movement that we see over the business cycle. To explain business-cycle fluctuations, therefore, the real business cycle model needs to assume that labour supply is very responsive to changes in wages, as in Figure 11.12b. Are real business cycle models justified in assuming such a flat labour supply curve as in Figure 11.12b? As we have seen, according to real business cycle theory, recessions are periods of low total factor productivity, which means a low marginal product of labour, so firms are not prepared to pay high wages. The theory suggests that people respond to these low wages by choosing not to work many hours, which leads to a fall in employment and a rise in unemployment.

However, studies suggest that people are not very responsive to changes in wages. In fact, studies of the responsiveness of prime working-age males reveal that their labour supply hardly varies with changes in wages – Figure 11.12a would capture their behaviour much better. Other demographic groups show more responsiveness, but probably not enough to justify the flat labour supply curve in Figure 11.12b. We see some support for Figure 11.12b

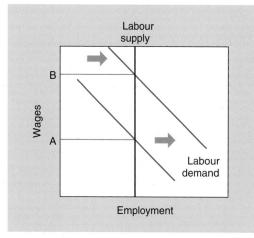

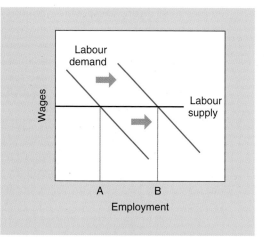

FIGURE 11.12a ● Business cycles with inelastic labour supply.

FIGURE 11.12b ● Business cycles with elastic labour supply. To explain the observed business-cycle pattern of employment and wages requires an elastic labour supply curve.

when we consider those who change their employment status over the business cycle rather than just vary the hours they work. For instance, some people may not find it worth while to seek employment when wages are low because they have to pay for, say, child care. However, when wages rise above a certain level, these people do find it profitable to work a full shift. As a result, their employment is very responsive to changes in wages.

Nevertheless, even this variation of employment does not empirically account for the business-cycle facts – most people's labour supply decisions are just not responsive enough to changes in market prices. As a result, real business cycle theory has had to develop and extend the model of Figure 11.12b by introducing other impulses, such as changes in tax rates, that in addition to technology shocks lead to shifts in the labour supply curve. However, these extensions still struggle to capture the full flavour of observed business cycles. As a result, these models have developed three additional features to improve their empirical realism. The first is that they introduce money and monetary policy – something that we will also do in subsequent chapters. Second, as well as allowing for supply shocks they introduce demand shocks: shifts in consumption, government expenditure or monetary policy. Finally, and critically, they introduce sticky prices into their analysis. These extended models are known as New Keynesian models and have served as the workhorse model in central banks over the last decade. Introducing sticky prices is a different way of explaining why we see such little price variability and such large fluctuations in output and employment. It assumes not that people are very responsive to prices, but that prices do not change much because they are fixed or sticky.

KEY POINT

Real business cycle theory attributes volatility in the aggregate economy to the impact of total factor productivity (TFP) shocks, such as technology and other supply factors. According to this framework, shocks to the level of aggregate demand do not play a significant role and business-cycle fluctuations may represent the optimal and efficient response of firms to bad shocks.

THE KEYNESIAN VIEWPOINT

In 1936 John Maynard Keynes (1883–1946) published *The General Theory of Employment, Interest and Money*. This was a defining moment for macroeconomics. Keynes wrote his masterpiece in the wake of the Great Depression of 1929–32. His basic message was that in certain circumstances the market mechanism may not work. For various reasons, he argued that prices, wages and interest rates might be unable to change enough to prevent the economy getting caught in a period of low output and high unemployment. If the market works well, then prices and wages should fall until demand and employment increase. Keynes argued that prices may not be able to fall and, even if they did, it may exacerbate matters. Keynes was essentially arguing that microeconomics – the study of the marketplace and how prices and individuals interact – may not be relevant for studying the aggregate economy. In other words, macroeconomics needed different models and tools.

The General Theory was innovative not just in its analysis of the Great Depression but also in its suggested remedy. If markets could not restore prosperity on their own, then governments had to. If prices could not be relied on to create demand, then governments needed to pump demand into the economy by raising government expenditure, cutting taxes or lowering interest rates. The differences between this approach to business cycles and that of real business cycle theory are many. This Keynesian perspective says that recessions are caused not by adverse supply shocks, but by too low a level of demand. Furthermore, recessions are not occasions when individuals optimally choose to produce low output, but periods when the market does not work properly, leading to suboptimally low output. In other words, recessions are bad, and the government should and can improve things.

Essentially, Keynesian economics is about malfunctioning markets. Of course, a market can fail in many ways, and there are many different markets to fail. As a result, Keynesianism has many different strands. Some Keynesians think that it is the labour market that does not function well and that wages do not change, so that unemployment can become too high. Others argue that product-market monopolies keep prices too high and output too low, so that unemployment is too high. Another camp argues that flaws in the credit markets and banking sector produce fluctuations and recessions. Of course, all three markets could operate poorly, and the interactions among them could produce large fluctuations and inefficient business cycles.

Keynesian models are therefore many and varied, linked by the common theme of market failure. In many of these models, the market failure is of a particular form – what economists call a 'strategic complementarity' – a situation in which whether a person acts in a particular way depends on whether someone else is also acting in that way. Consider whether you want to go to a party this evening. You are probably more likely to go if you think that your friends will be there. Just knowing the cost of attending the party – for instance, cab fares, gifts and so forth – does not provide enough information to make a decision. This is an example of a strategic complementarity, in which you are more likely to do an action if others are as well.

Keynesian models invariably involve strategic complementarity. Consider the example of an economy dominated by two large industries. Each industry is contemplating a major investment programme that will substantially increase productivity and output, but will be extremely costly. The investment will only prove profitable if the economy has enough demand to purchase the extra output. If each industry makes the investment, productivity and wages will be so high that the economy will have enough demand to make the investment profitable. If only one industry undertakes the investment, demand will not be high enough, and the expanding industry will make a loss. In this situation, each industry will only undertake the investment if it thinks that the other industry will, too. This raises the possibility of a coordination failure: what if each industry wants to make the investment but thinks that the other industry will not? Then neither industry will invest and the economy remains at a low level of output. If each industry could be persuaded that the other will invest, then the economy would be at a high level of output.

This example introduces another common feature of Keynesian models: multiple equilibria. This example has two outcomes: either both industries invest and the economy booms, or neither does and the economy remains at low output. This offers a different perspective on business cycles: expansions are periods when everyone is confident and the economy performs well, but recessions are periods of coordination failure when pessimism takes hold and the economy is at a low activity level. In this case recessions are clearly bad – it is better to be at the high output level. What should the government do? In our example the solution is simple. The government has to promise that it will always provide enough demand in the economy to purchase the production of firms. Then each industry knows that if it makes the investment, it can sell its output and make profit, no matter what other industries do. As a result, all industries make the investment and the government never actually needs to buy anything – because all firms expand, there is enough demand from the private sector.

A popular strand of Keynesian thought is that prices and wages are sticky: that they do not adjust in response to changes in output or employment. As a result, over the business cycle, we get large fluctuations in output and employment, but little fluctuation in prices and wages. One explanation for this price stickiness is that firms are monopolists and set too high a price – as a result, their output is lower and they need fewer employees, so unemployment will be higher.

To see how this fits in with our discussion of strategic complementarities, consider that the demand for a firm's product depends essentially on two factors: the price of the product relative to other commodities and the total amount that people want to spend. The latter factor depends on the stock of money in the economy. However, what this money can buy depends on the price level. The higher the price level, the fewer commodities this money can buy. When a firm sets its price, it tends to think only of how its price affects its attractiveness relative to other commodities. This gives it an incentive to lower its price, but it ignores an additional channel. If a firm lowers its price, then it increases the amount that individuals are prepared to spend on all commodities – the amount of money that they hold can now buy more. However, this effect is small if only one firm lowers its price, and it boosts demand for all products (this is the strategic complementarity), not just those of the firm itself. Therefore, the firm ignores this additional benefit from cutting prices when it selects its own price and as a result sets prices too high. But the same reasoning leads all firms to set prices too high, so that output and employment are too low.

If somehow all firms could be persuaded to lower their prices, then the economy would have more demand and output and employment would be higher. The existence of this strategic complementarity – specifically in this case an aggregate demand externality – means that prices are too sticky and do not adjust to clear the market. This problem can only be overcome if government tries to boost the demand for all commodities. In this simple model, if firms will not lower prices, then the government should increase the money supply.

KEY POINT

In Keynesian models, markets do not function well, individuals may act in an uncoordinated way and arrive at a bad equilibrium; in these circumstances, the government can and should improve things.

11.8 Aggregate Demand and Aggregate Supply

Broadly speaking, two categories of impulses might trigger business-cycle fluctuations: aggregate demand shocks and aggregate supply shocks. In this section we use fluctuations in the aggregate supply-and-demand curve to construct a simple way of thinking about business-cycle fluctuations.

AGGREGATE DEMAND

Aggregate demand measures the claims made on output produced. We saw in Chapter 2 that we can categorize the use made of output produced into four components: consumption, investment, government expenditure and net exports. As Table 11.6 shows, consumption is the largest component of demand, and investment the most volatile domestic component.

To construct our model of business cycles, we need to use the concept of an aggregate demand curve. Figure 11.13 shows this negative relationship between demand and prices. When prices are high, demand is low: output is too expensive. (One reason is that the amount of goods that financial wealth can purchase falls if output prices are higher.) We are interested in shifts in the demand curve; that is, changes in the amount of demand in the economy even without a change in prices. Figure 11.13 shows the example of an increase in aggregate demand that shifts the demand curve to the right. This means that at the price P, demand in the economy is now Y(1) and not Y(0). Note that this shift has nothing to do with changes in prices – at unchanged prices, individuals wish to buy more.

What might cause such a shift? Aggregate demand consists of consumption, government expenditure, investment and net exports. We are looking for shocks to aggregate demand – unexpected increases in any of these components. For instance, consumers may decide that they would rather save less out of their income than they have previously, perhaps because the population is getting younger on average, or social forces glamorize conspicuous consumption, or the population just feels more optimistic about the future. Any of these events would lead to an increase in aggregate demand through a shift in consumption. Similarly, an increase in the optimism of firms regarding investment prospects, a change of government to a party that favours increased government expenditure or a sudden shift in world demand towards the products a country produces will all lead to shifts in aggregate demand and affect business-cycle fluctuations.

TABLE 11.6 ● **Volatility of GDP Components.**

Volatility (standard deviation) of annual change of GDP components, 1970 to 2009.

	Germany		Japan		UK		US	
	% of GDP	Volatility	% of GDP	Volatility	% of GDP	Volatility	% of GDP	Volatility
Consumption	58%	1.75	54%	2.38	62%	2.50	66%	1.88
Government Consumption	20%	2.02	15%	2.27	20%	1.49	16%	1.70
Investment	22%	6.00	29%	6.08	18%	8.50	19%	8.95
Exports	27%	5.67	12%	8.06	26%	4.49	9%	5.97
Imports	26%	4.55	11%	8.03	27%	5.34	11%	7.42

Source: World Bank, World Development Indicators.

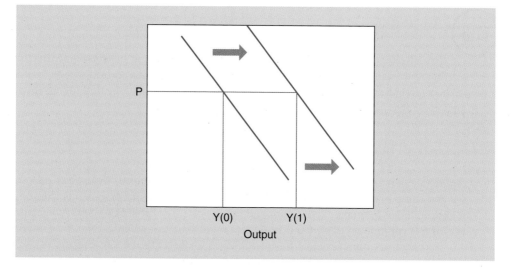

FIGURE 11.13 ● **Shifts in aggregate demand curve.** The aggregate demand curve shifts right when, at a given price, the level of demand increases.

However, a complete model of business cycles needs to contain both supply and demand features. Chapters 3 to 7 outlined in detail the development of the supply side of the economy. There we listed the determinants of supply as the capital stock, employment and total factor productivity (TFP). However, our analysis omitted prices: if all prices are doubled (including wages and the rental cost of capital), then this should make no difference to the capital stock, employment or TFP, and so no difference to output. In other words, Chapters 3 to 7 suggest that the supply curve should be vertical. We illustrate this in Figure 11.14. There is a fixed level of output that can be provided, which the capital stock, employment and TFP determine, regardless of the price level.

Figure 11.14 shows that, with this model of the supply side, we cannot account for the business-cycle properties that we observe through shocks to aggregate demand. When the demand curve shifts out, this means that at a given price the economy has more demand. However, firms cannot provide any more output to meet this extra demand – they can only produce their full-capacity output and no more, and capital, labour and TFP pin down this level of output. The extra demand only pushes up prices, from P(0) to P(1). As prices rise, they choke off demand until demand equals the output that firms can produce. This model implies that when demand varies output does not change, only prices fluctuate; clearly, this is no good as a model of business cycle fluctuations. However, if the supply curve is not vertical but upward sloping, then changes in demand generate both changes in output and changes in prices, as in Figure 11.15. The flatter the supply curve, the more output varies and the less prices change – similar to what we observe over the business cycle.

Figure 11.15 implies that when firms start to receive increased orders, they meet this extra demand by some combination of raising prices and increasing output. Therefore, Figure 11.15 can account for business cycles, but its plausibility depends on the answers to two questions: Are firms prepared to meet increases in demand by expanding output rather than just raising prices? And why would firms not just raise prices when demand increases?

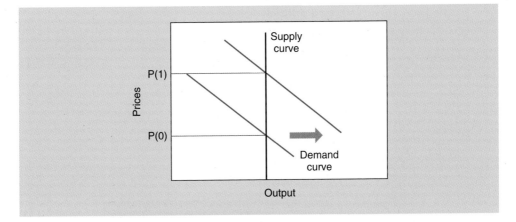

FIGURE 11.14 ● **Business cycles with vertical supply curve.** With a vertical long-run supply curve, an increase in demand only raises prices and leaves output unaffected.

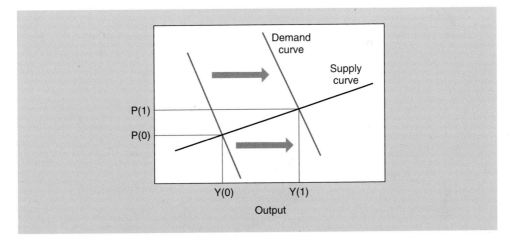

FIGURE 11.15 ● **Business cycles with short-run supply curve.** With an upward-sloping short-run supply curve, firms respond to increases in demand by raising output.

Figure 11.16 shows the results of a Bank of England survey that asked firms how they respond to increases in demand. The huge percentage of respondents who would increase output even if this means working more overtime, hiring more workers or increasing capacity is striking. Only 12% of firms gave increasing prices as one of their main responses. Figure 11.16 gives very strong practical justification for the flat supply curve in Figure 11.15.

There are two reasons why firms seem willing to increase output rather than raise prices when demand increases. The first is that firms only periodically review prices, so that for significant periods prices are fixed. For instance, mail-order firms and restaurants print catalogues and menus in advance and cannot alter prices between printings. This makes prices sticky and costly to change, an example of what economists call 'nominal rigidities'. Figure 11.17 shows that firms from the same Bank of England survey only occasionally review their prices – the rest of the time prices are fixed, and either output or delivery lags vary when demand changes. While 22% of firms review their prices daily, over a quarter review them

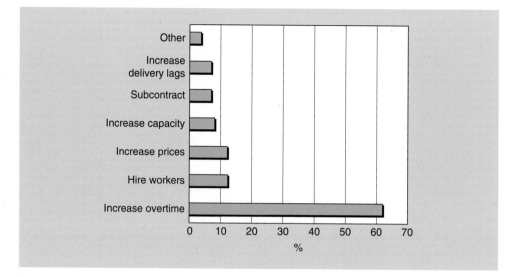

FIGURE 11.16 ● **How firms respond to increased demand.** Survey evidence suggests that most firms respond to higher demand more by raising output than by increasing prices. *Source:* Hall, Walsh and Yates, How Do U.K. Companies Set Prices?, Bank of England Working Paper 67 (1997). Reprinted with the permission of the Bank of England.

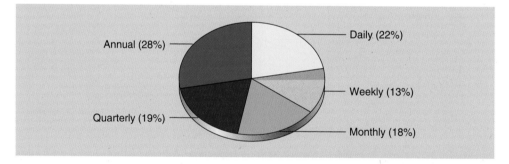

FIGURE 11.17 ● **Frequency of price reviews.** The majority of firms review their prices once a month or less. *Source:* Hall, Walsh and Yates, How Do U.K. Companies Set Prices?, Bank of England Working Paper 67 (1997). Reprinted with the permission of the Bank of England.

once a month, and another 19% only once a quarter. Therefore, firms may not change prices in response to every change in demand – prices are sticky.

Prices are also sticky because firms choose not to change them. Figure 11.18, also from the Bank of England survey, shows the number of price changes that firms made in a year. Even though 22% of firms review their prices daily, only 6% change their prices more than 12 times a year. In total, almost 70% of firms change their prices only every six months or more; firms do not adjust prices frequently in the short run.

However, if we assume that firms are maximizing profits, why don't they increase prices by more when they have the opportunity to increase them? Firms don't raise prices for many reasons. The first is that, when they do raise prices, they lose customers and thus revenue.

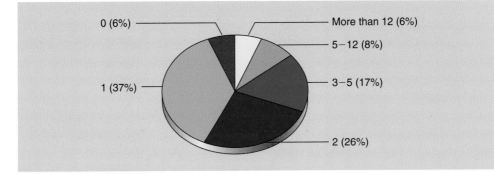

FIGURE 11.18 ● **Frequency of price changes over one year.** The majority of firms change prices twice a year or less. *Source:* Hall, Walsh and Yates, How Do U.K. Companies Set Prices?, Bank of England Working Paper 67 (1997). Reprinted with the permission of the Bank of England.

If the firm has many competitors, none of which has raised its prices, then the firm will be wary of doing so itself for fear of losing revenue and profit. The second reason is costs. A standard result in microeconomics is that firms maximize their profits when they set price equal to a mark-up over their marginal cost, where the mark-up depends on how much monopoly power the firm has. According to this formula, firms should only change prices when either the mark-up they demand changes, or their costs do. Therefore, the behaviour of marginal costs is crucial in determining the slope of the supply curve. If marginal costs do not alter much when the firm increases output, then it should increase output, not change its prices. It can thus be profit maximizing for firms not to increase prices even if they have the opportunity – this is what economists call 'real rigidities'. Similarly even if marginal costs increase with output, firms may not change prices if they are prepared to take a lower mark-up. Therefore, a combination of nominal rigidities (that is, firms cannot change prices because of fixed contracts, existing advertising or price stickers) and real rigidities (that is, firms not wanting to raise prices even when they make a price review) means that in the short run the supply curve is not vertical and variations in demand lead to changes in output and prices, as in Figure 11.19.

> **KEY POINT**
>
> Price stickiness means that short-run aggregate supply curves are unlikely to be vertical.

RELATIONSHIP BETWEEN SHORT-RUN AND LONG-RUN SUPPLY CURVES

Doesn't this contradict our supply-side model outlined in Chapters 3 to 7? The answer is no, because the analysis in those chapters focused on long-run developments in the economy, how the level of output varied from decade to decade. When we analyse business cycles, we are considering fluctuations that complete themselves within a decade. We can therefore think of the vertical supply curve of Figure 11.14 as being a long-run supply curve and the flat curve of Figure 11.15 as a short-run supply curve.

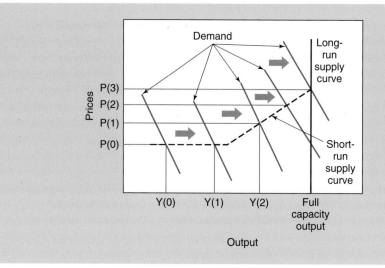

FIGURE 11.19 ● Supply-and-demand model of the business cycle.

The long-run supply curve shows the level of output that an economy can produce when machines and labour are working at full capacity for a given level of TFP. As Figure 11.19 shows, demand increases at this full-capacity level produce price increases because firms cannot produce any more output: the marginal cost of output soars as firms find it increasingly difficult to produce any more, so prices rise.[7] However, firms are not always at this full-capacity output. Machines may be lying idle, and employees may not have enough work to keep them fully occupied. In these circumstances, when a firm receives new orders, it has the spare resources to boost output without increasing costs – the machines and workers are already there and are not being used. As a result, the supply curve will be flat, and as Figure 11.19 shows, any increases in demand boost output rather than prices. However, as output increases, fewer machines are idle and all potential employee hours are being used. Under these circumstances, firms will have to use overtime, hire more workers or invest in new machinery to meet rising orders. As a result, marginal costs begin to increase, and the firm responds to extra demand by a combination of raising output and raising prices. The supply curve is no longer flat but increasingly slopes upwards.

Figure 11.19 suggests the following pattern for prices and output over the business cycle. Consider an economy in recession with output Y(0) – the economy has a large negative output gap because GDP is far below its capacity level. As demand increases, the economy grows to Y(1) but experiences little inflation – firms meet the increase in orders by boosting output, not prices. At Y(1) the output gap has shrunk, so that when demand continues to increase, firms still increase production but also start to pass along price increases to customers. Output rises to Y(2) and prices to P(1), and the economy grows until it reaches full-capacity output, and prices are at P(3). At this point the economy is on the long-run supply curve and firms cannot boost output – any additional increase in demand feeds straight through into inflation. Therefore, in the latter stages of an expansion, output growth slows and inflation increases. Policymakers will try to allow growth during the recovery stage but prevent demand from increasing when the economy is at full capacity. Figure 11.19 shows why central bankers analyse information about the output gap so closely: it indicates potential inflation.

WHEN DOES THE SHORT RUN BECOME THE LONG RUN?

How do we link the short- and long-run supply curves? The long-run supply curve moves over time as the capital stock and the level of technology change, so that the full-capacity level of output increases. However, the capital stock and technology change slowly and only increase substantially over decades. Within a business cycle, which tends to last less than a decade, they change little, so that the full-capacity output level is roughly fixed; in other words, over the business cycle, the long-run supply curve does not move. This is consistent with the definition of business cycles as medium-term fluctuations around the trend level of output.

DO SUPPLY SHOCKS CAUSE BUSINESS CYCLES?

Figure 11.19 shows fluctuations in demand causing business cycles while the supply curve remains fixed. However, supply shocks can also affect business-cycle fluctuations. When we discussed real business cycle theory, we mentioned one source of supply shock: technological innovations. There are, however, many other sources of supply shock. The most obvious example is an increase in the price of commodities such as oil, which, as we saw in Figure 8.10, has shown considerable volatility over time.

Oil is an important input into the production process of many commodities. If the price at which firms sell their product does not change, but their input costs have risen, then the profit margin will decline and the firm will start to scale back production. For the same price, firms will now want to supply less output, and the supply curve shifts in, as in Figure 11.20. As a result of this adverse supply shock, output falls and the economy goes into recession. However, while a demand shock moves the economy into recession but lowers prices, a negative supply shock leads to a fall in output and increases in prices. In other words, with oil price increases, producers cut back on production but also try to recapture their profit margins by raising prices.

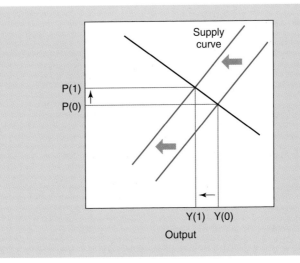

FIGURE 11.20 ● Adverse supply shock causes recession.

There are wider sources of supply shocks than oil price increases: anything that alters the output firms provide at a given price shifts the supply curve. For instance, increases in indirect taxes will act as negative supply shocks because for the same retail price, firms now receive a lower profit margin. Increases in the power of workers, stemming, for instance, from new industrial relations legislation, that lead to a rise in wages would also be a negative supply shock. Credit crunches that lead to disruptions in the supply of credit are a negative supply shock, as well as being a negative demand shock.

11.9 So What Causes Business Cycles?

In outlining the Frisch-Slutsky approach to business cycles, we commented that although there was broad agreement over the list of candidate shocks for explaining the business cycle, there was no consensus over which of these many shocks is most important. The problem is partly that we have to infer from the data which shocks are hitting the economy, and different assumptions lead to different conclusions about the importance of shocks. Table 11.7 shows the results of one study that attempted to discover the ultimate source of business cycles among the G7 nations. It distinguishes among three distinct causes of business-cycle fluctuations: nominal demand shocks (due to variations in the money supply), real demand shocks (shifts in consumption, investment or fiscal policy not related to monetary policy) and supply shocks. The results vary from country to country, but essentially show that demand shocks tend to cause most business-cycle volatility.

> **KEY POINT**
>
> While economists accept a role for supply-side shocks in the business cycle, they see fluctuations in demand as the major source of business-cycle volatility.

TABLE 11.7 ● Causes of G7 Business Cycles, 1973–95.

Demand shocks explain the majority of business-cycle fluctuations.

	Percentage of Nominal Demand Shocks	Output Volatility Real Demand Shocks	Explained by Supply Shocks
US	37	52	11
Germany	98	2	
UK	57	43	
France	3	67	30
Italy	35		65
Canada	45		55

Source: Canova and Nicolo, On the Sources of Business Cycles in the G7, Universitat Pompeu Fabra mimeo.

SUMMARY

In Section 11.1, we described business cycles as medium-term fluctuations in the economy around its long-run trend rate of growth. Business-cycle fluctuations are normally, although not always, finished within a decade. In Section 11.2, we saw the difficulty of developing definitions for recessions and expansions. In Section 11.3, we discussed measuring business cycles and reviewed evidence that expansions tend to last longer than recessions, although the economy changes more dramatically each period in a recession.

In Section 11.4, we noted that the key feature of the business cycle is co-movement: economic variables tend to move up and down together, as do different sectors and regions of the economy. To a lesser extent, countries also tend to show similar cyclical movements, although this is not always the case. In Section 11.5, we saw that there is some evidence that output has tended to become less volatile, but that the Great Moderation of 1984–2007 was exceptional.

In Section 11.6, we discussed the benefits from eliminating business-cycle fluctuations. These are not trivial, and they arise from the beneficial impact on growth through encouraging investment by reducing uncertainty. Because the impact of recessions tends to fall disproportionately on the poorer members of society, reducing business-cycle fluctuations also reduces inequality.

In Section 11.7, we examined two major theories about the origins and meanings of business cycles. For Keynesians, the business cycle reflects a market failure, and recessions are a time of suboptimally low output. The market failure can be caused by numerous factors and often relates to coordination failures in either the product, labour or asset market. In contrast, real business cycle theory says that recessions are the result of bad technology shocks that make it optimal for firms to produce little and workers not to work many hours. However, to account for the observed high variation in output and employment but low volatility in prices and wages, the real business cycle model has to rely on an implausibly high sensitivity of individuals' labour supply to changes in market prices.

In Section 11.8, we showed how a simple supply-and-demand model can be used to account for business-cycle fluctuations, although to account for the low variability in prices but high volatility in output, we have to utilize a short-run supply curve. The short-run supply curve describes the fact that in response to new orders, firms may not just increase price but will also boost production. We argued that there are real and nominal rigidities, such that firms decide only infrequently whether to change prices and often decide not to. Finally, in Section 11.9, we saw that research suggests that the most important sources of business-cycle fluctuations are changes in demand, with variations in supply playing only a supporting role. The standard workhorse model of the business cycle in policy institutions is a New Keynesian model. While allowing for supply shocks, the main source of business-cycle volatility are demand shocks and the main propagation mechanism is through sticky prices and/or wages.

CONCEPTUAL QUESTIONS

1. (Sections 11.3 and 11.5) Why are recessions shorter than expansions?

2. (Section 11.6) Are recessions a good time for reorganizing and improving the efficiency of firms?

3. (Section 11.6) If the economy goes into recession, how will it affect you? Consider not just your income but the prices of any assets you might own or commodities you purchase. How can you minimize this impact?

4. (Sections 11.6 and 11.7) In a recession, share prices tend to be low and companies can be bought at low prices and workers hired for low wages. Given that recessions are only temporary, what stops you from buying loads of stocks in a recession and then selling them during an expansion?

5. (Section 11.7) If rising inflation after an oil price increase leads the central bank to increase interest rates dramatically, what is the impulse behind this business cycle and what is the propagation mechanism?

6. (Section 11.7) How much of your weekly shopping is on commodities with 'sticky' prices, prices that firms cannot immediately change? Are these sticky prices relevant or can they be negotiated? How do you think the introduction of barcoding and computer pricing have influenced price behaviour?

7. (Section 11.7) Travel on a train between Paris and Madrid and the view from the window changes, fluctuating between green land and a heavy concentration of economic activity. What explains this bunching of activity over space? Could similar factors explain the bunching of activity over time (the business cycle)? If so, how should governments respond to the business cycle?

8. (Section 11.7) What role do you think consumer and firm psychology has in driving the business cycle through fluctuations in demand?

9. (Section 11.7) What are the impulses and propagation mechanisms of real business cycle theory and Keynesian models?

10. (Section 11.8) Real business cycle theory implies that negative total factor productivity shocks cause recessions. What do you think such shocks might be?

ANALYTICAL QUESTIONS

1. (Section 11.1) Output in an economy is given by the following numbers:

Year	1	2	3	4	5	6	7	8	9	10
Output	1	1.2	2.8	4.3	5.2	6.1	6.7	7.4	8.9	10

(a) Assume that a simple straight line between Year 1 and Year 10 is a good estimate of trend GDP. Calculate the output gap.

(b) In Year 11 output is measured at 10.5. How does this change your estimate of trend output? What about your estimated output gap in Year 10?

(c) In Year 11 output is instead measured as 12. What happens now to your estimate of trend output and the output gap? Discuss the problems that this suggests in using the output gap to measure the current state of the business cycle.

2. (Sections 11.1 and 11.7) You will find a spreadsheet useful in answering this question. Let the output gap in Year 0 and Year 1 be 0. Furthermore, let the output gap today equal 0.9 of yesterday's output gap less 0.9 of the output gap two periods ago, e.g. $Y(t) = 0.9Y(t-1) - 0.9Y(t-2)$.

(a) Calculate the output gap for Years 1 to 20.

(b) An unexpected shock in Year 2 increases the output gap to 11. What happens to the output gap now until Year 20?

(c) What happens to the amplitude and duration of business cycles when the shock is 12 instead?

(d) What happens to the amplitude and duration of business cycles when the output gap follows the rule $Y(t) = 0.5Y(t-1) - 0.5(Y(t-2)$?

When it is $Y(t) = 0.1Y(t-1) - 0.1Y(t-2)$?

What about $Y(t) = Y(t-1) - Y(t-2)$?

(e) Consider again the case where $Y(t) = 0.1Y(t-1) - 0.1Y(t-2)$. What happens to fluctuations when $Y(2)$, $Y(3)$ and $Y(4)$ are increased by 1, $Y(5)$, $Y(6)$ and $Y(7)$ are lowered by 1 and the same three-period oscillatory pattern is imposed for the remaining years? What does this tell you about the relative role of propagation and shocks in explaining persistent business-cycle fluctuations?

3. (Section 11.7) Consider the real business cycle model of Figure 11.11a. How does the labour supply curve need to shift for the model to explain business-cycle fluctuations? What might cause such a shift?

4. (Section 11.7) An economy is dominated by two industries, both of which are considering whether to initiate a major investment project. If both industries invest, then employment and productivity are high and each industry makes profits of $5 billion. However, if neither industry invests, the economy is weaker and each industry makes $1 billion profit. If only one industry invests, then the industry that doesn't invest makes $2 billion profit, but the additional costs of the investing industry mean that it loses $1 billion.

   (a) If each industry assumes that the other one will not invest, what is their optimal course of action?

   (b) What if they assume that the other industry will invest?

   (c) What is the role of changing business optimism in this economy?

   (d) How do your answers change when government offers an investment subsidy worth $3 billion to each industry? Is society better off?

5. (Section 11.8) Use a supply-and-demand model to analyse the impact of an oil price shock on the economy. After an increase in oil prices, what is likely to happen to profits, unemployment, income and consumer confidence? How will this further affect your analysis? How useful is the distinction between supply and demand shocks?

CHAPTER 12

Money and Prices

Overview

This chapter focuses on the nominal side of the economy: money and prices. We examine the historical behaviour of prices and the surge in inflation that occurred in the twentieth century. We consider how to measure the price level and the rate of inflation and compare their different meanings. We discuss why policymakers want to control inflation and the costs of inflation.

Money is intimately linked to prices — after all, we quote prices of goods and services in terms of money. We review the historical development of money — from commodity money to paper money — and examine how governments and the banking sector create money and credit.

We then consider the interaction between money and inflation. We first discuss hyperinflations — inflations of more than 50% per month — and show that they really always originate in fiscal policy, when governments print money to finance their activities. We review the concepts of seignorage and the inflation tax and compare them across countries. We then discuss a more general link between money and inflation and outline the quantity theory, which forms the basis of monetarism: the idea that inflation can be controlled by controlling the money supply.

12.1 Rising Prices

THE HISTORICAL RECORD

Although historical evidence regarding the scale of economic activity is often obscure, we have much more evidence about the price of different items. The various receipts, invoices and advertising leaflets that accumulate in pockets and wastepaper baskets amount to a substantial historical legacy. From these we can construct price indexes that reflect the costs of buying a representative collection of consumer goods over time. For example, we could go to a supermarket on 1 January 2012 and buy a typical household's weekly groceries for $120. When purchased on 1 January 2013, the same groceries might cost $125. With this information we can construct a *price index* that has a value of 120 in 2012 and 125 in 2013. This implies an **inflation** rate (the annual percentage change in prices) of 4.2% [100 × (125 – 120)/120]. Price indexes often are set at a value of 100 in a particular year – usually the year used to construct the average basket of goods. In our example, the index would have been 100 in 2012 and 104.2 in 2013.

Figure 12.1 shows the behaviour of UK prices between 1264 and 2008.[1] (A detailed examination and a cross-reference with UK history reveals many interesting events,[2] but we want to see the broad characteristics of price behaviour.) Between 1264 and around 1930 prices showed no persistent trend, though there was a significant increase in prices around the sixteenth century (primarily associated with the influx of gold and silver from the Americas). Prices sometimes rose sharply (e.g. during the Napoleonic Wars, 1790s to 1815 and the First World War, 1914–18), but then fell sharply. But after 1930 things changed and prices continued to increase – by 46-fold between 1930 and 2009. As Figure 12.2 shows, after 1945 annual inflation was always positive. Before 1945 the United Kingdom had experienced extreme inflation, large deflations (falls in prices) and frequent small deflations, which overall kept the price level reasonably constant over long periods.

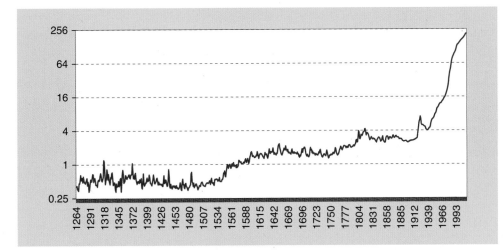

FIGURE 12.1 ● **UK prices, 1264–2010.** Until the twentieth century, prices showed no upward trend, experiencing both increases and decreases. In the twentieth century prices increased sharply. *Source:* Lawrence H. Officer, What Were the UK Earnings and Prices Then?, MeasuringWorth (2009), http://www.measuringworth.com/ukearncpi/.

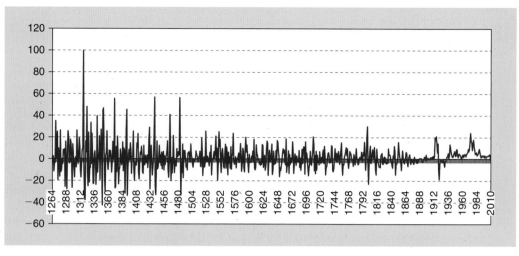

FIGURE 12.2 ● **UK inflation, 1264–2010.** Since 1945, inflation has been consistently positive. *Source:* Authors' calculations from Figure 12.1.

Although not all countries experienced the United Kingdom's overall price stability prior to 1930, most countries did see prices surge during the second half of the twentieth century. Figure 12.3 shows the same pattern for the United States.

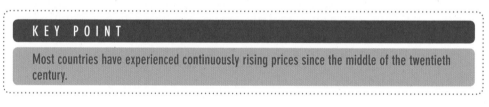

KEY POINT

Most countries have experienced continuously rising prices since the middle of the twentieth century.

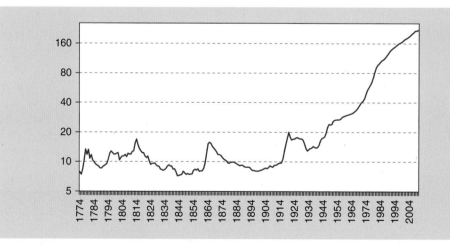

FIGURE 12.3 ● **US prices, 1774–2010.** US inflation shows a familiar pattern: while prices rose and fell during the 1800s, inflation has been consistently positive since 1950. *Source:* Lawrence H. Officer, The Annual Consumer Price Index for the United States, 1774–2010, MeasuringWorth (2010), http://www.measuringworth.com/uscpi/

THE RECENT EXPERIENCE

Figure 12.4 shows the inflation experience among the seven leading industrialized nations over the past four decades. We can note five distinct periods. The first covers 1973–76, when inflation increased in all countries. Economists refer to this period as OPEC I. In October 1973 Arab nations, through a cartel of oil producers known as the Organization of Petroleum Exporting Countries (OPEC), embargoed oil sales at the time of the Yom Kippur War with Israel. As a result, oil prices increased from $3 a barrel to $11.65 (see Figure 12.5 for the history of oil prices over this period). Industrialized nations were heavy importers of oil and had low oil stocks in the early 1970s, so the increase in oil prices led to a rapid increase in inflation.

By 1977 most countries had stabilized their inflation in response to OPEC I, but in 1979 OPEC again raised oil prices (OPEC II), which peaked at over $36 a barrel in 1980. Inflation surged again, although, as Figure 12.4 shows, the increase was more restrained. The increase in oil prices and the associated rise in interest rates led to a global recession. This slowdown in the economy and a sharp fall in oil prices produced the third stage in Figure 12.4: lower inflation among the industrialized nations in the 1980s. Inflation fell and economic growth increased significantly in the industrialized world in the 1980s. The strength of this boom and the strong growth in all countries led to another increase in inflation by the end of the decade, so that governments again raised interest rates and economic growth slowed. In the 1990s inflation continued to fall until, by 2000, it was at its lowest level since the 1970s. Since then inflation has remained low despite a significant rise in oil (and other commodity) prices recently.

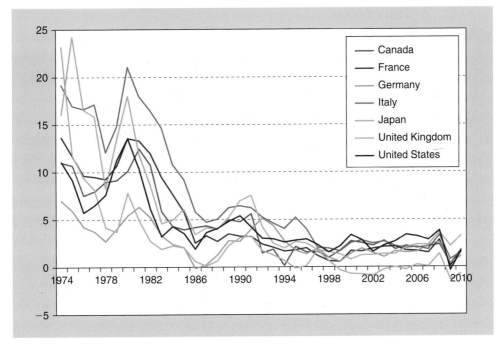

FIGURE 12.4 ● **G7 inflation, 1974–2010.** Inflation surged after increases in oil prices in 1973 and 1979 and after high global growth in the late 1980s, but it was subdued by the end-of-the-century inflation. *Source:* OECD.

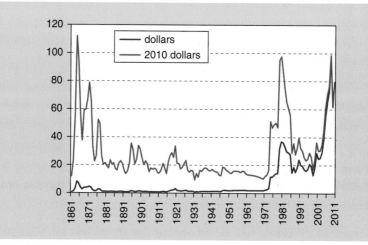

FIGURE 12.5 ● Oil prices, 1861–2011. In recent decades high-inflation periods have followed big rises in oil prices. *Source:* BP Statistical Review (2011).

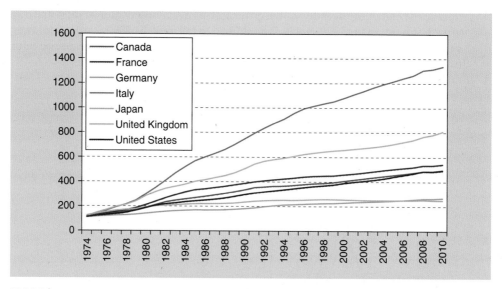

FIGURE 12.6 ● G7 price levels, 1974–2010. Persistent differences in average inflation rates have led to big differences cross-country in how the level of prices has changed over time. *Source:* OECD.

We have stressed the co-movements in inflation across countries, but differences are also significant. High inflation means something different to an Italian than to a German. These differences in annual inflation rates lead to big differences in price changes over long periods. Figure 12.6 shows how prices have changed across countries. Prices are set equal to 100 in each country in 1974, so that an index of 500 in 2004 means that prices have risen fivefold over that 30-year period. Japan has had the lowest inflation over this time period, so goods that used to cost ¥100 now cost the equivalent of around ¥250. By comparison, Italy has seen large increases in prices: a commodity that used to cost 100 lira now typically costs the equivalent of around 1300 lira (though prices are now quoted in euros).

> **KEY POINT**
>
> Global events, particularly changing prices of oil, have caused developed nations to experience similar patterns of inflation. But small differences in inflation rates can cause dramatic price differences between countries over time.

(12.2) Measuring Inflation

Price indices measure the cost of purchasing a bundle of commodities. However, different agents buy different bundles of commodities, and each bundle defines a different price index. The most important indexes are consumer price indexes (CPIs, which are sometimes called retail prices indexes, RPIs), which measure the cost to the consumer of purchasing a representative basket of commodities. This basket includes both goods and services; commodities purchased in shops, through mail order or the Internet, and commodities produced either domestically or abroad. Individual prices are weighted together based on how much the average consumer spends on each item. Like with GDP, most countries allow the basket of goods used to measure inflation to change every year and then use chain weighting to link the results together. Consumer prices also include any consumption taxes (e.g. general sales tax or goods and services tax, GST, or value added tax, VAT). The CPI is the most important inflation measure because central banks often use it as a policy target.

HOUSING COSTS IN THE CPI

Although the concept of a consumer price index is relatively straightforward, various countries and economies have different ways of measuring the overall index of consumer prices, which can make inflation measures hard to compare. One area that has proved particularly troublesome is how to include the cost of owner-occupied housing in the CPI. At first sight, the answer seems simple: just include the cost of buying houses in the index. Although a house purchase is a significant one-off expenditure, it occurs only rarely, so the average consumer in the average month will spend only a fraction of their income on housing. However, there are two main problems with this approach. First, the purchase of a house is not like buying bread, in the sense that the benefit to the consumer (eating the bread) occurs very soon after the purchase. With housing, the benefit of living in the house is spread over many years and so its impact on the CPI should perhaps also be spread. (The same issue also arises with other durable goods like cars and washing machines.) Second, and more important, houses are not consumed in the conventional way since they can be sold again after many years of occupancy, quite possibly for a higher price than when they were purchased. This makes them like a financial asset as well as a consumer good. The cost to a consumer of housing should be net of (i.e. exclude) the prospective financial gain, though this is of course not known at the purchase date. To get round this problem countries have adopted different approaches. In the case of the United Kingdom Retail Price Index (RPI), mortgage payments are used to proxy for the cost of owner-occupied housing. Most countries, however, adopt the concept of imputed rent, so that the cost of owner-occupied housing is the rent you would have to pay to live in the property if you did not own it (which is inferred using data from the private rental market). While this approach is probably the most sensible, many countries do not have a developed rental market to use as a comparator and so many countries choose not to include housing costs in their consumer price indices at all.

OTHER PRICE INDICES

We can also construct price indexes for producers' input and output prices. Producer *input* prices measure the cost of the inputs that producers require for production. Industrialized nations import many of these raw materials, so that fluctuations in exchange rates will affect changes in producer input prices.[3] Producer *output* prices, or 'factory gate prices', reflect the price at which producers sell their output to distributors or retailers. Factory gate prices exclude consumer taxes and reflect both producer input prices and wages and labour productivity.

Governments and central banks pay attention to producer prices because they can help predict future changes in consumer prices. Consider an increase in oil prices that increases producer input price inflation. Because the prices of commodities, such as oil, are volatile, the firm may not immediately change its factory gate prices – customers dislike frequent changes of prices. Instead, firms will monitor oil prices, and if they remain high for several months, eventually output prices will increase. This may not immediately result in higher consumer price inflation. Instead, retailers may decide to absorb cost rises and accept a period of low profit margins – they may think that the increase in output prices is only temporary or intense retail competition may mean that they are unable to raise their own prices. However, if output prices continue to increase, eventually retail prices will follow.

The gross domestic product (GDP) deflator is another common measure of prices and inflation. In Chapter 2 we discussed how this is constructed and noted that because it is based on GDP, this measure of inflation only includes domestically produced output and does not reflect import prices. Furthermore, because GDP is based on the concept of value added, it does not include the impact of taxes on inflation.

Each of these different inflation measures reflects different commodities, so on a year-to-year basis, they can behave differently from each other. However, the various prices tend to move in a similar manner over long periods, as Figure 12.7 shows.

KEY POINT

The choice of index and method of calculation used to measure inflation can create significant differences in the measured rate of inflation, although most commonly used methods reveal similar trends.

All measures of inflation mismeasure actual inflation to some extent. Every year the quality of existing products improves, and firms introduce new products. If a toothpaste manufacturer increases its price when introducing a new tube that is easier to squeeze, how should our price index reflect this? The toothpaste costs more, but in part this reflects the improved quality of the overall product. Some of the increased cost of purchasing the representative basket of goods reflects improvements in product quality rather than the increased cost of buying *exactly the same* commodity.

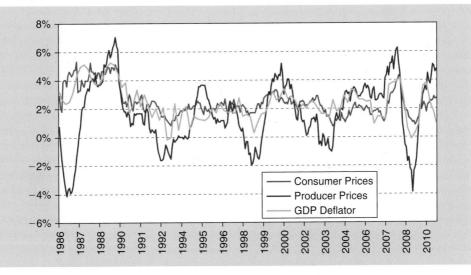

FIGURE 12.7 ● **Different measures of Danish inflation, 1986–2011.** Although inflation measures differ from one another each year, over time they show similar trends. *Source:* OECD.

Improvements in computers and medical services illustrate this problem dramatically. Virtually no households had computers 40 years ago. Twenty years ago some households did have machines, but their capabilities were massively inferior to even the cheapest desktops available today. No PC today has as little computing power as a state-of-the-art machine had in the early 1970s. Medical services pose even deeper measurement problems. Some operations that are now relatively routine – cataract removals or hip replacements – were not feasible a few decades ago. Many drugs that exist today were not available even five years ago; how do we work out the impact of Viagra on average prices?[4] People might have paid fortunes for Viagra or hip replacements in the past, but the technology and know-how did not exist. In a fascinating article, Matthew Shapiro and David Wilcox show how issues around pricing medical services over time suggest that price indices in the United States probably overstate inflation by around 1% a year.[5]

(12.3) The Costs of Inflation and the Dangers of Deflation

As a result of the high levels of inflation in the latter part of the twentieth century, the control of inflation now dominates economic policy. Public opinion seems to support the notion that inflation damages an economy. Figure 12.8 shows evidence from a survey asking people in the United States, Germany and Brazil whether they would prefer low inflation at the cost of high unemployment or low unemployment at the cost of high inflation. Except for Brazil, a high-inflation economy, most people prefer low inflation even if it entails higher unemployment.

IS MONEY NEUTRAL?

While public opinion seems firmly against inflation, economists find it more difficult to explain why people feel this way. Economists use money and prices as *nominal* measures of economic activity. This is analogous to using miles or kilometres to measure distance.

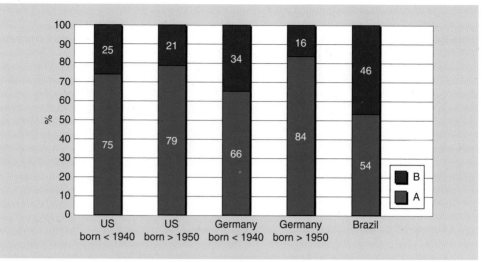

FIGURE 12.8 ● **Public attitudes to inflation.** Defeating inflation is seen as hugely important for the general population. A is the proportion of people who prefer 10 years of 2% inflation and 9% unemployment, and B is the proportion of those who prefer 10 years of 3% unemployment and 10% inflation. *Source:* Shiller, 'Why do people dislike inflation?', in Romer and Romer (eds), *Reducing Inflation: Motivation and Strategy* (Chicago: University of Chicago Press, 1997).

Inflation means that something that cost $10 last year now costs $11; the commodity itself has not changed – only its price is different. To continue our analogy, it is as if the distance we use to define a mile has changed, so that one year (2004) we measured the distance between London and Boston as 3250 miles (using '2004 miles'), but in the next year we say that it is 3500 miles (using '2005 miles'). Of course, the true distance has not changed at all; all that has changed is the units we use to measure distance – a '2005 mile' is a bit shorter than a '2004 mile'. The same is true for inflation: after 10% inflation, a dollar buys 10% less.

Economists refer to money as a 'veil' – it is merely a system used to price things and should not influence the real economy. It does not matter whether I measure the distance between London and Boston in miles or kilometres, the actual distance that needs to be travelled does not change. Similarly, it does not matter if we use 2004 prices or 1960 prices in the economy; the real side of the economy remains unaltered. This belief that, in the long run, money is neutral helps explain the different results shown in Table 12.1; 84% of ordinary citizens agree that preventing high inflation is as important as preventing drug abuse and deteriorating school standards. By contrast, economists are almost equally divided over the same question.

To understand why changes in prices should be neutral for the economy, consider the following example. Suppose that while you are reading this chapter, the government introduces a new law that doubles all prices and wages immediately. In other words, what used to cost $5 now costs $10, and if you previously earned $40 000, you will now earn $80 000. All bank accounts, loans and asset prices will likewise be doubled. The exchange rate will depreciate by half, so that the price of imports or exports remains unchanged in real terms for their purchasers. A new currency will be introduced and all old currency will be worth twice its face value. So all prices double,[6] but aside from causing confusion (which we will discuss later), how is it costly to society?

TABLE 12.1 ● How Important Is Preventing Inflation?

Shows response to the question: 'Do you agree that preventing high inflation is an important national priority, as important as preventing drug abuse or preventing deterioration in quality of our schools?' While the general population believes that defeating inflation is hugely important, there is less consensus among economists.

	1	2	3	4	5
	Fully Agree		Undecided		Fully Disagree
All US Citizens	52	32	4	8	4
Economists	18	28	11	26	18

Source: Shiller, 'Why do people dislike inflation?', in Romer and Romer (eds), *Reducing Inflation: Motivation and Strategy* (Chicago: University of Chicago Press, 1997).

KEY POINT

Economists consider money to be a neutral, nominal measure of economic activity, rather than a measure of real changes.

COSTS OF INFLATION

However, this hypothetical example is unrealistic. One problem is that most tax systems are specified in nominal, not real amounts. For instance, most countries do not tax income below a certain threshold. But as inflation increases, so do wages and income, and more people earn above the threshold and have to pay tax. Wages are only increasing in line with inflation; real incomes are not changing. But the increase in nominal income means that more people are paying tax, which makes them worse off.

The taxation of interest rates causes a similar problem. Tax is usually levied on the nominal interest rate, for example if interest rates are 10% and the tax rate is 50%, the net-of-tax interest rate is 5% [10% × (1 – 0.5)]. However, two components make up the nominal interest rate: one term reflects expected inflation, the other reflects the real interest rate. The term reflecting inflation compensates the saver for rising prices. If inflation is 5%, then a good that costs $100 at the beginning of the year costs $105 by the end of the year. Therefore, investors need to earn at least 5% if they are not to lose by investing their money. The reward to saving is the difference between the nominal interest rate and expected inflation. This is called the *real* interest rate. With an interest rate of 10% and an inflation rate of 5%, the real interest rate is 5%. After a year, the saver's $100 becomes $110, and after allowing for inflation (what used to cost $100 now costs $105), the real return is $5 or 5%. However, taxation usually applies to the whole nominal interest rate – even the part that compensates for inflation. For instance, with 50% tax rates, 5% interest rates and 0% inflation, the pre-tax real interest rate is 5% and *net of tax* is 2.5% [5 × (1 – 0.5) – 0 = 2.5]. If inflation and interest rates both increase by 5%, the pre-tax real interest rate remains unchanged, but the net-of-tax real interest rate falls to 0% (0.5 × 10 – 5 = 0). If interest rates and inflation reach 15% and 10% respectively, the pre-tax real rate remains 5%, but the net real rate is now –2.5%; that is, 0.5 × 15 – 10.

Inflation also exerts a cost by reducing the value of cash. Unlike bank deposits, notes and coins do not earn interest, so there is no compensation for inflation. As a result, the value of notes and coins falls as inflation increases (this is called the **inflation tax**, to which we will return later). As inflation increases, firms and individuals will hold less cash at any one time, so they will need to make more trips to the bank to withdraw cash and spend more time keeping their cash balances at low levels. We call these costs 'shoe-leather costs'. Taken literally, this phrase refers to the wear and tear that repeated trips to the bank to withdraw funds exact on people's shoes! But it also captures a more general tendency to spend time managing finances (when inflation is 20% per month, unpaid invoices become urgent) rather than engaging in productive activity. Despite the trivial-sounding name, these costs can be substantial: it has been estimated that shoe-leather costs can exceed 0.3% of GDP when inflation is 5%.[7]

Another cost of inflation is *menu costs*. Changing prices is costly for firms. One obvious cost is physically changing prices: printing new menus or catalogues, replacing price labels and advertisements in stores and the media. The higher inflation is, the more often these prices have to change and the greater the cost to firms. Moreover, marketing departments and managers have to meet regularly to review prices, which is also costly. The lower inflation is, the less often these meetings need to be held.

Another unrealistic feature of our example of a costless increase in prices was that all prices simultaneously increased by exactly the same amount. As a result, there were no relative price changes (for instance, CD players did not become relatively more expensive than concerts), there was only a general increase in prices. In practice, although all prices might eventually increase by the same amount, they will not increase at the same time, which reduces the overall efficiency of the price system. For the market to work well, firms and consumers must respond appropriately to relative price changes. If the demand for a firm's product increases, the price of the product will rise. This will encourage firms to produce more of that commodity and less of others. Prices therefore signal what consumers want. But inflation interferes with this signal. Producers may not know whether a price increase reflects increased demand for their product or just reflects a general increase in prices. Furthermore, some prices respond more quickly than others, which redistributes income among individuals. For instance, if wages respond slowly to rising commodity prices, inflation will hurt consumers because their real income will fall. Table 12.2 suggests that this may help explain public resentment of inflation.

The volatility of inflation is also a problem because it often leads to uncertainty: with very volatile inflation, firms and consumers may not know whether inflation next year will be 1% or 10%. If inflation is predictable, contracts can be written to minimize its costs. But if inflation is different from what was expected when contracts were written, the parties to the contracts will not get the return they were expecting. These are redistribution effects – some

TABLE 12.2 ● **Does Income Lag Inflation?**

Response to: 'How long will it be before your income catches up with inflation?' One reason individuals dislike inflation is a belief that their wages rise slower than inflation.

	Up to a Month	Next Negotiation	Several Years	Never	Don't Know
US	0	7	39	42	11
Germany	0	8	40	40	12
Brazil	2	19	17	28	14

Source: Shiller, 'Why do people dislike inflation?', in Romer and Romer (eds), *Reducing Inflation: Motivation and Strategy* (Chicago: University of Chicago Press, 1997).

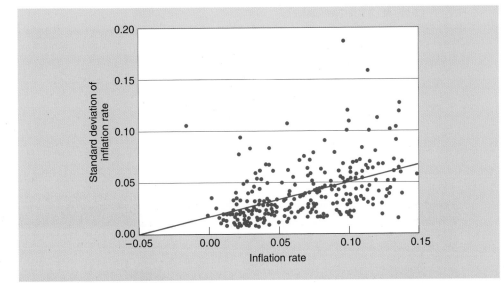

FIGURE 12.9 ● **Inflation and inflation volatility.** Countries with high inflation also have more volatile inflation. *Source:* Barro, Inflation and Economic Growth, NBER Discussion Paper 5326 (1995).

parties gain, others lose – but they can still have an overall impact on society. For instance, unexpectedly high inflation is particularly hard on retired people whose savings are invested in banks. Interest rates may only compensate for expected inflation, so unpredictable inflation will tend to impoverish the elderly. No one knows whether inflation will be less than or greater than what they expected it to be. Volatile inflation makes writing contracts riskier, so fewer contracts will be written and less money will be saved. All of this will hurt the economy. While these costs come from volatility in inflation, they are also indirectly related to the level of inflation. As Figure 12.9 shows, countries with high inflation tend also to have volatile inflation.

Inflation also harms long-run growth. Evidence suggests that an increase in inflation of 10% leads to a decline in growth per year of between 0.2 and 0.3% and a fall in investment/GDP ratio of 0.4–0.6%.[8] However, we can only identify these costs if we look at countries whose inflation rates exceed 15%. At lower rates, inflation does not seem to adversely affect long-run growth.

Inflation may also seem costly for another reason: it complicates economic life. Imagine that every year the distance that we called a mile got smaller by a variable amount. This is analogous to how inflation every year reduces the value of what money can buy. Dealing with these changes would be a computational burden. What year was the atlas printed that tells you how far apart two cities are? In what year was the speed control in your car installed or the speed limit signs on the highway erected? The scope for confusion and mistakes would be considerable. Not only do these annual changes in value lead to costly calculations, people may not respond rationally to price changes. Table 12.3 shows that when people's salary rises by the same amount as inflation, so that their real income remains unchanged, nearly half of respondents would feel better off. Table 12.3 shows evidence of what economists call *nominal illusion*: people mistake nominal changes for changes in a real variable. If prevalent, this behaviour will be another source of inflation costs.

TABLE 12.3 ● **It's Just an Illusion?**

Responses to: 'I think that if my pay went up I would feel more satisfied in my job, more sense of fulfilment even if prices went up just as much.' Individuals seem to react inappropriately to purely nominal variables.

	1 Fully Agree	2	3 Undecided	4	5 Fully Disagree
All US Citizens	28	21	11	14	27
Economists	0	8	3	13	77

Source: Shiller, 'Why do people dislike inflation?', in Romer and Romer (eds), *Reducing Inflation: Motivation and Strategy* (Chicago: University of Chicago Press, 1997).

KEY POINT

The costs of inflation include readily measurable penalties from taxes on wages or interest and the inflation tax, as well as costs that are more difficult to measure, including complications, possible effects on long-run growth, uncertainty, menu costs and lags in price or wage changes.

THE COSTS OF DEFLATION

It is not just rapid increases in the general level of prices that can cause economic damage. General declines in prices – deflation – can also pose problems. Indeed, the dangers of deflation became more of a concern in some developed countries in the early 2000s than the risks of inflation. In the United States, consumer price inflation fell to around 1% in 2003; with price indices probably overstating the effective inflation rate, it is possible that the general level of prices actually fell near that time, at least in some quarters. In Japan the general level of prices fell steadily from around the middle of 1999. And as prices fell, consumers became convinced that prices would continue falling.

Why should falling prices cause problems? There are three main reasons. First, what matters for real economic decisions is the real interest rate: the return on saving (or cost of borrowing) after accounting for inflation. When real interest rates are high, the cost of borrowing and the return to saving are substantial, so there is an incentive for people to save more. This may mean weaker consumption spending and weaker investment by companies. Sometimes this is appropriate: in an economy that is overheating and where inflation pressures may be high and rising, slowing the pace of spending is helpful. But when prices are already falling, cutting demand is not likely to be helpful. Yet falling prices will mean a high real rate of interest unless nominal rates of interest can be taken to very low levels. Nevertheless, the level of nominal interest rates cannot fall below zero (or at least much below zero). If it did, people would just hold their savings in cash (which pays zero interest) rather than hold it in a bank, where with negative interest rates the money value of saving would actually fall. So there is a potential for a vicious circle to develop, with falling prices driving up real rates of interest in a way that cannot be offset (beyond some point) by lowering nominal interest rates. In Chapter 13 we will discuss quantitative easing, a monetary policy tool that can be used when nominal interest rates approach zero, the effectiveness of which has not yet been reliably measured.

A second, related problem with deflation is that the real burden of debt – most of which is fixed in nominal terms – rises when prices fall. This makes those who have borrowed to finance spending less well off if prices and the nominal level of incomes fall. If the real burden of debt rises enough, bankruptcies will follow. Of course, there is another side of this: those who have lent money are – other things equal – better off when prices fall. But it is plausible that the cut in spending from those who lose out is greater than the rise in spending from those who gain. After all, the savers are those who have a tendency to save their resources while the borrowers have a tendency to spend what they can.

Finally, as we discussed above, there is some evidence that people suffer from money illusion, in the sense that they are less concerned if their real wages fall due to inflation than if their nominal wages are cut (i.e. they would prefer a 2% wage rise when inflation is 4% to a 2% wage cut when inflation is zero, even though both involve a *real* wage cut of 2%). Figure 12.10 shows the importance of this effect in practice, by demonstrating how wage settlements tend to cluster around zero and as a result negative wage settlements are less likely. This effect, known as downward nominal wage rigidity, means that industries in which significant real wage cuts are required in order to maintain jobs are more likely to achieve that end when inflation is relatively high.

The experience of Japan at the end of the 1990s and into the 2000s – where inflation became negative and nominal interest rates fell to zero – seems to confirm the costs of deflation. Japan has been trapped in a period of high unemployment (for Japan) and the level of consumer and investment spending has stagnated.

KEY POINT

Falling prices discourage spending, drive up real interest rates and increase the real burden of debt.

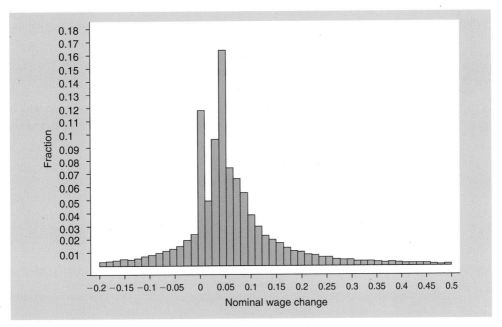

FIGURE 12.10 ● **Distribution of UK wage settlements in 1993.** Wage settlements of no change are more common than might be expected and so very small wage increases and wage cuts are less common than might be expected. *Source:* Nickell, S. and Quintini, G. 'Nominal wage rigidity and the rate of inflation', *The Economic Journal* (John Wiley & Sons Ltd, 2003).

(12.4) The Nature of Money

In everyday conversation, when people talk about someone having lots of money, they really mean that she is rich: she has wealth. In calculating a person's wealth, we convert the components of that wealth – cars, stocks and shares, houses, gold, pension rights, yachts, works of art – into money values. But just because we can put a dollar value on your car or the current assets in your pension fund does not make them money, in the sense that an economist uses the word. A car or a house is not money, because money by definition can be used to make a transaction, which implies that it is an acceptable means of payment. Try paying for a pair of Nike sneakers with a few bricks from the side wall of your house!

What counts as money is a matter of convention and convenience. For instance, in North Carolina in 1715, 17 commodities were declared to be legal tender, including wheat and maize. Money is whatever people will accept in return for handing over goods. What is acceptable as money to *me today* depends crucially on what I expect its acceptability will be for *others tomorrow*. Acceptability limits what items can serve as money. Historically, the need for acceptability led societies to use precious or rare commodities as money, but over time we have switched to money that has value only because government legislation says it has value, what we call *fiat money*.

Money makes an economy much more efficient. Suppose that money did not exist and that people had to rely on barter – swapping goods directly rather than accepting money as payment for them. To get through the week in a barter economy, you would need to have some goods that the producers of petrol, milk, electricity, bread, movies, newspapers and so forth wanted to swap with you. As economists, we make money by giving lectures, writing books and thinking profound thoughts on, for example, the role of money. But how could we find someone willing to swap 10 gallons of petrol on a wet night at 2.30 A.M. for some economics advice? And how does the person who sells petrol buy this book (assuming that we don't frequent the petrol station)? She needs to find a bookseller who wants to trade a few cans of petrol in exchange for this fine text. Tricky, to put it mildly.

Barter relies on a double coincidence of wants: you need to find someone who has the commodity you want and who also wants the good that you are willing to trade. This is costly in three ways:

- Transaction costs are high; you have to find out what commodities people are willing to exchange and then you have to decide on a price.
- When you go shopping, you have to carry around with you many different commodities in the hope that you can barter some of them.
- You cannot consume this sample of commodities because you need them to make transactions.

KEY POINT

Any commodity may be acceptable as money, if people are confident that they can use it to get something else they value. Using a common currency boosts this confidence and is an improvement over bartering.

THE ROLE OF MONEY

Money avoids these costs because everyone accepts it in exchange for commodities. The publisher sells this book for money and can then use money to buy petrol. Note that the publisher values not the money itself, but only what it can purchase. Similarly, the owner of the petrol station accepts money for petrol only because she can then use it to buy what she wants.

Money offers substantial efficiency gains over barter because it fulfils three key roles: it acts as a medium of exchange, a unit of account and a store of value. We have already discussed the importance of money as a medium of exchange. But also important is its role as a unit of account: the language in which prices are quoted. We could measure the prices of commodities in terms of almost anything, for example a loaf of bread. But it is bizarre to quote prices in terms of a commodity when transactions do not actually involve the exchange of that commodity. Why would we quote the price of boots, paper towels, computers and motorbikes in terms of numbers of loaves of bread when nobody would pay for those things at a store with a truck full of loaves? It makes sense to quote prices in terms of what we will hand over when we purchase goods.

The final role for money is as a store of value – money needs to be a durable commodity that can transfer purchasing power from one period to another. Even in the simplest pre-industrial societies, there was a gap between the times when people wanted to sell what they produced and the times when they wanted to buy what they consumed. As the local baker, I may want to sell all my loaves by 10 A.M. each day. Due to the drudgery of my life, I tend to want to spend much of the proceeds of my bread sales on alcohol, which I generally consume after 6 P.M. So I need a means of holding the revenue from my bread sales until the bars open at 6 P.M. Holding my bread revenues in the form of money lets me do this.

A BRIEF HISTORY OF MONEY[9]

- *3000 BC and before: Units of account.* Commodities such as barley or cattle are widely used as a unit of account (in Mesopotamia, for example, a shekel of barley was a standard weight), but money as a storable and transportable commodity is not yet developed.
- *Around 1000 BC: Early money.* Some civilizations move to precious objects as a standard. Cowrie shells (especially the species *Monetaria Moneta*) are widely used throughout Asia and Africa. (They were still used in parts of Africa until the nineteenth century.) Precious metals are also used, but smelting technology is not sufficiently advanced to create a reliable quality of gold or silver.
- *Around 550 BC: The first gold and silver coins.* The Kingdom of Lydia under King Croesus develops an improved smelting technique to create pure gold and silver. Lydia also produces standard weights of gold stamped with the king's symbol to signify their weight and quality. Thus the first pure gold coins are created.
- *960 AD: Paper money* is widely introduced into China by the Song Dynasty. Initially, the notes give the owner a claim to some other object of value, but eventually the money is printed without any backing in order to help fund government spending. By 1455 excess money printing had led to high rates of inflation and paper money is abandoned by the Ming Dynasty.

- *1542: Gresham's Law.* Henry VIII, struggling to finance his profligate spending, follows the example of many rulers before him (e.g. Roman Emperor Nero) and mints coins debased by non-precious metals, thus allowing him to create more coins and so finance more spending. The eminent financier Thomas Gresham observes that only the debased coins are used for transactions as people hang on to the more valuable pure coins. This supposedly leads him to formulate Gresham's Law: *bad money drives out good.*
- *Around 1550: Spanish silver.* The vast silver mines of Potosi in Bolivia and Zacatecas in Mexico allow the Spanish Empire to mint a huge number of *real de a ocho* (also known as pieces of eight, Spanish dollars, pesos, dollars, yiyals, yuan and yen). These coins are used throughout the known world and come close to becoming a universal currency.
- *1668: The first central bank.* Sweden's Riksbank is established, but is not initially allowed to issue bank notes. It is not until 1897 that it is given the *exclusive* right to issue bank notes. It is this monopoly over note issuance that characterizes the modern central bank and gives it control of short-term interest rates.
- *1871–1914: The pure gold standard.* Most countries found themselves moving away from a bimetallist standard (with both gold and silver coins circulating) to a pure gold standard. This often occurred when the bullion price of silver rose relative to gold and so people found it profitable to melt down the silver coins they owned and sell them for gold. For example, when Isaac Newton in his role as the head of the English Royal Mint set the conversion rate of silver shillings to gold guineas at 21 to 1, it soon became profitable to melt down the shillings and sell them as bullion; another example of Gresham's Law in action.
- *1896: The bimetallist debate in the US.* A limited supply of gold left the US economy experiencing deflation and recession. The Democratic presidential nominee William Jennings Bryan proposed that this could be alleviated by reintroducing silver currency alongside gold and so increase the money supply. He lost the election and so the pure gold standard was maintained. Many argue that Frank L. Baum (a disappointed supporter of Bryan) wrote *The Wonderful Wizard of Oz* as an allegory of the bimetallist debate with Dorothy, flanked by the industrial and agricultural workers (and Bryan himself in the form of the Cowardly Lion), being forced to follow the yellow brick road by the financial interests of the east and west coasts. But the answer to their problems lie in the silver slippers worn by Dorothy (these were changed to ruby in the film as they looked better in Technicolor).
- *1914–73: The decline of the gold standard.* After the Second World War the major economies were keen to avoid the economic mistakes of the inter-war period that had led to the great depression and, arguably, the rise of Nazism. One problem was the gold standard itself, since most countries had suspended the link between their currencies and gold during the First World War and in the Depression, and were unwilling to return to it in its original form. (Winston Churchill as Minister of Finance had returned to the standard in 1925 after the link with gold was suspended in the First World War and had plunged the UK economy into recession, forcing it to leave the gold standard again in 1931.) But a number of countries that had broken the link with gold had ended up with a hyperinflation. The solution they came up with at the Bretton Woods Conference of 1944 was for the United States to stay on the gold standard and for all the other major economies to use US dollars to back their currencies rather than gold. Although this worked for a while, many countries (most notably France) complained that they were effectively being forced to lend

money to the United States (since they needed to hold dollar assets to back their currencies). Eventually they broke their link with the dollar and in 1973 the United States finally broke its link with gold.

- *1973: Pure fiat money.* Most countries now use fiat money, which is paper currency not backed by a valuable commodity (fiat from the Latin for 'let it be done', indicating that it is backed by government decree alone). If you go to the European Central Bank or the US Federal Reserve Board with a euro or a dollar, you will not be given gold or silver. The one modern exception is countries that operate a currency board (see Chapter 21), such as Hong Kong, which is committed to swapping the national currency for dollars at a fixed rate. In this case, US dollars fulfil the role of a precious commodity.

KEY POINT

Fiat money solves the key problems of using commodities as money, and most countries today use it, even though it can result in excess money printing and high inflation.

12.5 The Money Supply

Typically, part of a person's wealth is in some form of money, but most of it is not. While people own bills (or bank notes) and coins, they may also hold part of their wealth in various types of bank deposits. In addition, they may hold stocks and shares, either directly or through pension plans. Many people also own their homes, though often they also have a large liability in the form of a mortgage. People can use some of the forms in which they hold wealth to buy other commodities quickly and easily. I can easily use money in my bank account to buy goods and services. But other financial assets are harder to exchange for goods and services. I cannot easily get my hands on the assets in my pension fund until I retire. And if I own stocks and shares, I have to sell them and transfer the proceeds into a bank account before I can write a cheque (or use a debit card) on that account to buy goods.

Financial assets therefore have a spectrum of spendability, or *liquidity*. Some financial assets are readily available to use to buy goods and services – bills and coins, for example – and we will certainly want to call them *money*. Others (stocks and shares, life insurance policies or pension fund assets) are less liquid and should not count as money. Somewhere in between bills and coins and stocks and shares held in pension funds, are assets whose availability to buy commodities is less clear. I cannot use a 90-day deposit with a bank to finance a last-minute weekend at a ski resort unless I can switch the deposit into a current account. However, the 90-day deposit is clearly closer to being 'money' than are the stocks and shares in my pension fund. So when we think about measuring the money supply, we should be aware that in modern economies the answer to the question 'What is the money supply?' has no simple answer. It depends on what measure of money you want to use.

We can start with the narrowest definitions of money (bills and coins) and then add increasingly less liquid assets. Bills and coins are readily acceptable in exchange for goods and services almost anywhere. In fact, it is stated on most paper currency that people *have to* accept them, by law, in exchange for goods and services. But often people are less willing to accept a cheque. So current accounts are *somewhat* less liquid than dollar bills. Other types of bank accounts that do not have chequing facilities are even less liquid, because we would usually need to transfer the money from them to a current account, or else cash in those deposits in (i.e. turn them into bills and coins), before we could use them to complete a transaction.

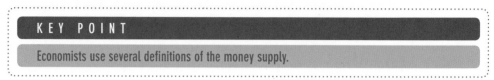

KEY POINT

Economists use several definitions of the money supply.

Table 12.4 shows increasingly wider definitions of the US money supply and illustrates what the stock of different types of money was in 2010. The narrowest definition in the table is the monetary base, which is made up of currency and commercial bank reserve deposits at the central bank. The important feature of this type of money is that it can only be created by the central bank (the Federal Reserve in the United States) and so this gives the central bank a fundamental role in the monetary system. The monetary base is also called fiat money, high-powered money and M0 (though in some countries M0 is just notes and coins). The next definition is M1, which is made up of currency plus demand deposits (that is, money available at short notice from commercial banks) and other deposits against which cheques can be written (including traveller's cheques). M1 represents funds that can readily be used to make transactions. Adding savings deposits to M1 gives us M2. (M2 includes other liquid forms of savings, including money market mutual funds and short-maturity eurodollar deposits.)

DEFINITIONS

Monetary base = notes and coins and reserve deposits at the Federal Reserve
M1 = notes and coins + traveller's cheques + demand deposits + other chequable deposits
M2 = M1 + retail money market mutual funds + savings and small time deposits + overnight repurchase agreements

Table 12.5 shows the levels of M1, M2 and M3 in the European Monetary Union in 2010. The definition of the various money stocks is close to, but not identical with, those used in the United States. Most notably, in the Eurozone the M3 measure is considered the most important, while it no longer exists as a measure in the United States.

DEFINITIONS

M1 = currency + overnight deposits
M2 = M1 + deposits with agreed maturity up to 2 years + deposits redeemable at notice up to 3 months
M3 = M2 + repurchase agreements + money market mutual funds + debt securities up to 2 years' maturity

TABLE 12.4 ● US Money Supply ($ bn), 2010.

The US money supply consists mostly of credit rather than currency.

Currency in Circulation	Monetary Base	M1	M2
888	2032	1744	8629

Source: St. Louis Federal Reserve Monetary Trends.

TABLE 12.5 ● European Monetary Union Money Supply (€ bn), 2010.

As in the United States, the European money supply is mainly made up of credit money.

Currency	Monetary Base	M1	M2	M3
790	1073	4705	8400	9524

Source: European Central Bank, www.ecb.int.

(12.6) How Banks Make Money: The Money Multiplier

As Tables 12.4 and 12.5 show, the stock of currency (that is, bills and coins) is a small part of the wider definition of the money supply in both the United States and Europe. Bills and coins are about 10% of M2 in the US and 7% and 3.5% respectively of M3 in the European Monetary Union and the UK. In this section we will show how, from a relatively small amount of currency, the commercial banking sector can create many more large bank deposits through a mechanism called the **money multiplier**. The money multiplier means that only a relatively small part of the money supply is under the *direct* control of the monetary authorities. In Chapter 15 we shall explain how central banks try to control the money supply and set interest rates. Here, however, we focus on how commercial banks make money, or create the gap between M3 and currency.

RESERVE REQUIREMENTS

A critical variable for commercial banks is their reserves, which are either cash held in the banks' vaults or money the banks hold on deposit with the central bank. How much a bank can lend depends on its level of reserves. If a bank extends too much credit, it risks exhausting its reserves. If a high proportion of its customers simultaneously write cheques or make payments from their accounts, the bank will not have the cash to honour its commitments to the other banks that have received these payments. Banks and the monetary authorities thus closely monitor the level of reserves. Most countries set a *reserve requirement*: a floor below which the ratio of reserves to chequable deposits must not fall. For instance, if the reserve ratio is 5%, a bank that has deposits worth $100 billion must have reserves of at least $5 billion. The value of the reserve requirement varies across countries. Some countries set a low ratio, and banks themselves often choose to use a higher one. Historically, many countries used the reserve requirement as a key part of monetary policy and to control the money supply. More recently, countries have used the reserve requirement to ensure a stable and prudent financial system more than a way of implementing monetary policy.

Although the reserve requirement limits the ratio of reserves and deposits, in effect it also constrains banks' ability to issue loans, because every time a bank issues a loan, *it also creates a deposit*. When you get a loan, the bank either sends you a cheque for you to deposit in another bank or credits your own account with the funds. This is how commercial banks create money: they essentially swap a loan note, which doesn't count as money, for a bank deposit, which does count as money. Therefore, a $10 000 loan creates a $10 000 deposit and, with a 5% reserve requirement, requires an additional $500 of reserves. If the bank already has a reserve-to-deposit ratio of 5% and cannot obtain new reserves, it cannot grant this additional $10 000 loan.

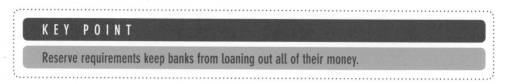

THE MONEY MULTIPLIER

To see how the money multiplier works, consider the case of Loans 'R' Us which has reserves of $5 million and deposits of $100 million, so that it satisfies the minimum reserve requirement of 5%. The central bank purchases from Loans 'R' Us $1 million worth of government bonds by placing $1 million in the Loans 'R' Us bank account at the central bank. Loans 'R' Us reserves are now $6 million against deposits of $100 million – it now exceeds the minimum 5% requirement, so it can lend $1 million to Greedyforfinance.com. It credits the latter's account with $1 million. Loans 'R' Us now has reserves of $6 million and deposits of $101 million. It has lent the full $1 million of extra reserves out, but the reserve requirement ratio is still close to 6%. Loans 'R' Us can lend *another* $19 million until its deposits reach $120 million, and the reserve requirement reaches 5%. At this point Loans 'R' Us can lend no more. Therefore, an extra $1 million of cash or reserves enables (though certainly does not force) the commercial banking sector to create $20 million of additional deposits. In this example, the money multiplier is 20: $1 million of reserves is turned into $20 million of M3. The magnitude of the money multiplier can depend on the reserve requirement. In fact, when banks want to lend the maximum amount consistent with a given level of reserves we have

Money multiplier = 1 / Reserve requirement

so that a reserve requirement of 10% (0.1) would lead to a money multiplier of 10 (1/0.1).

The principle at work with the money multiplier is similar to our discussion of how the government issues paper currency backed up by its holdings of precious commodities. Because people only take a certain amount of paper currency a day to the central bank and demand to swap it for a precious metal, the central bank can issue more paper money than it has precious metal. For instance, if on average 5% of people want to swap paper for metal, then if the central bank has $5 million of gold, it can issue $100 million of paper money. This is exactly what commercial banks can do. If, on average, only 5% of their customers want to come and withdraw their account in cash, the commercial bank can issue $100 million of loans backed by its own reserves of $5 million.[10]

Table 12.6 shows this process. Ms A deposits $100 in cash with Loans 'R' Us which increases its reserves by $100. But Loans 'R' Us has to pay interest on this deposit and thus wants to lend money out to earn interest. However, Loans 'R' Us cannot lend all $100 out, because tomorrow Ms A may wish to withdraw her cash. Based on its experience, Loans 'R' Us calculates that, on average, its customers withdraw 5% of their deposits a day in cash, and therefore it decides that it can only lend out $95, which it does to Mr B, whose deposit increases by $95. However, on average, Mr B will only want to withdraw 5% of these funds tomorrow (0.05 × 95 = $4.75), so Loans 'R' Us can lend the remainder ($95 – $4.75 = $90.25) to Mrs C, whose account is credited with this amount. But like the other customers, Mrs C will only withdraw on average 5% of her deposit (= $4.51), so that Loans 'R' Us can lend another $85.74 to Dr D. We could carry on this way for many pages (which would be very boring), but eventually we would find that from the original $100 deposit, the bank increases the money supply by $2000.

TABLE 12.6 ● **The Money Multiplier.**

Using a reserve requirement, banks can make loans and dramatically increase the money supply.

	Deposit	Reserves	Loan
Ms A	$100	$5	$95
Mr B	$95	$4.75	$90.25
Mrs C	$90.25	$4.51	$85.75
Dr D	$85.74	$4.29	$81.45
⋮	⋮	⋮	⋮
Total	$2000	$100	$1900

> **KEY POINT**
>
> The money multiplier calculates the amount of money banks can create by loaning money that they are not required to keep on reserve.

12.7 Seignorage and the Inflation Tax: How Governments Make Money from Money

Issuing paper money is a high-profit-margin activity: the face value of currency normally far exceeds its production costs. The profit made from printing money is called **seignorage** and equals the amount of new currency that the monetary authority issues. Along with raising taxes and issuing debt, printing money is one of the three ways in which a government can finance its activities.[11] Historically, seignorage was important for monarchs, whose one reliable source of revenue was the profit from minting coins.[12] However, in the modern economy, taxation revenues are much more substantial, and with highly developed government debt markets, seignorage for most countries is a relatively small source of finance. As Figure 12.11 shows, for most OECD nations seignorage accounts for less than 1% of GDP, although it is more important for emerging markets in which tax and bond market infrastructure is less developed.

Closely related to seignorage is the **inflation tax**. Seignorage looks like a good way to raise revenue, because it means that governments have to collect less revenue through taxes. However, this ignores a crucial link between issuing money and creating inflation: the subject of the rest of this chapter. Notes and coins do not earn interest; bank deposits do. Therefore inflation reduces the value of the cash holdings of individuals – after 10% inflation, a $10 bill is worth only $9 in real terms; it is as if the government has taken a dollar from your wallet. However, $10 in a bank account earning 12% interest (2% real interest and 10% for anticipated inflation) does not lose its value. Therefore

Inflation tax = Inflation × Currency[13]

How is seignorage linked to the inflation tax? By definition

Seignorage = Change in currency

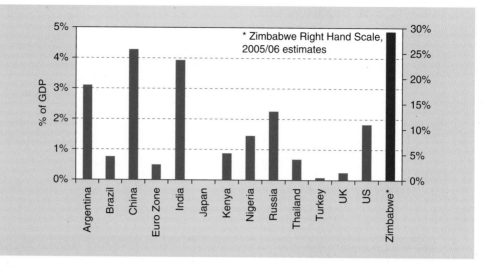

FIGURE 12.11 ● **Seignorage, 2008 (% GDP).** For most countries seignorage is an unimportant source of revenue, but for some countries it is substantial. *Source:* IMF, *International Financial Statistics.* Calculated as change in monetary base divided by nominal GDP.

Expressing everything relative to the size of the stock of currency, we have

Inflation tax/Currency = Inflation rate

Seignorage/currency = Change in currency/Currency

Therefore, if the inflation rate equals the growth in the money supply, then seignorage and the inflation tax are equivalent. In a later section, we outline a theory that makes exactly this claim: in the long run, changes in the money supply are proportional to inflation. If that is right, then in the long run the inflation tax is also proportional to seignorage.

This equivalence between seignorage and the inflation tax throws additional light on Figure 12.11. The amount of seignorage collected depends on the rate of inflation and on how much cash is circulating in an economy. China and Pakistan have a less-developed credit industry, so cash is much more important in these societies than in the United States or the United Kingdom, and so, as a result, is seignorage.

SEIGNORAGE AND CENTRAL BANKING

In many ways, the standard definition of seignorage is out of date given how modern central banks operate. Implicit in the measurement of seignorage is the idea that governments print money and then spend that money directly. But in almost all countries it is the central bank that is responsible for printing money and it will use any new money it prints (not including that printed to replace worn-out notes) to purchase financial assets – usually government debt. This means that the revenue it derives from issuing money is in fact the interest earned on those financial assets. Effectively the central bank ends up with a balance sheet made up of interest-bearing assets (mainly government debt) and non-interest-bearing liabilities (currency). So we can define central bank revenue as the interest it earns from its assets:

Central Bank Revenue = Interest rate × Currency

Of course, most, if not all, of this revenue ends up being remitted to the government, who is usually the central bank's sole shareholder.

> ### KEY POINT
>
> In developed countries, seignorage is not a major source of government revenue and is often linked to inflation.

(12.8) Hyperinflation

In the rest of this chapter, we focus on the link between money and prices and, in particular, on whether inflation is always a result of increases in the money supply. Before doing so, we discuss **hyperinflations.** Technically, hyperinflation occurs when inflation is running at more than 50% per month, which translates to an annual rate of about 12 875% due to compounding $(12\,875=((1+(50/100)^{12})-1)\times100)$. Hyperinflations have their origins in fiscal policy (the government's decisions about spending and taxation) rather than monetary policy (the government's policies for investing and loaning money). While many countries have experienced hyperinflations, it has been a particular scourge recently in two regions: Latin America and the formerly socialist economies. Of the 28 recorded hyperinflations of the twentieth century, 17 occurred in Eastern Europe and Central Asia, 5 in Latin America, 4 in Western Europe and 2 each in Africa and Southeast Asia. Table 12.7 shows the six highest recorded monthly inflation rates, though measuring inflation during a hyperinflation is not easy and some (like that of Zimbabwe) have been estimated from a range of sources. In all these cases the cause of high inflation was the same: a large fiscal deficit that, without tax increases or the ability to issue bonds, led governments to finance their activities through the inflation tax by printing money. Unless a government reforms its fiscal position, it will have to print money and create inflation. Furthermore, inflation will increase continuously while the authorities pursue this policy.

TABLE 12.7 ● **Highest Monthly Inflation Rates.**

Country	Month with Highest Inflation Rate	Highest Monthly Inflation Rate	Equivalent Daily Inflation Rate	Time Required for Prices to Double
Hungary	Jul. 1946	$4.19 \times 10^{16}\%$	207%	15.0 hours
Zimbabwe	Nov. 2008	79 600 000 000%	98%	24.7 hours
Yugoslavia	Jan. 1994	313 000 000%	64.6%	1.4 days
Germany	Oct. 1923	29 500%	20.9%	3.7 days
Greece	Nov. 1944	13 800%	17.9%	4.3 days
China	May 1949	2178%	11%	6.7 days

Source: Table 2 from Steve H. Hanke and Alex K. F. Kwok, 'On the measurement of Zimbabwe's hyperinflation', *Cato Journal* (Spring/Summer 2009), 29(2).

To see why inflation increases when the government resorts to seignorage, consider again the definition of the inflation tax as inflation multiplied by non-interest-bearing money. We can think of the inflation rate as the tax rate and the stock of non-interest-bearing money as the tax base; that is, the thing that is getting taxed. As tax rates increase, all other things being equal, the tax base shrinks as individuals shift to commodities with lower or zero taxes. Therefore, as inflation increases, people try to get rid of their cash holdings by spending them – in other words, the demand for money falls. When the demand for a good falls, its price also declines, which for money means that it buys less as inflation increases the price of other goods. In other words, the real money supply falls. However, the government has to raise all its revenue from the inflation tax so, as the real money supply falls, the inflation rate has to rise. But, of course, this only causes the demand for money to fall further and the inflation tax to rise. Lags in the collection of taxes exacerbate the situation. If inflation is running at 5000% per month, then tax revenues collected with a lag of a few months are effectively worthless, which increases the fiscal deficit. This is an example of the Laffer curve that we will discuss in more detail in Chapter 14 – which shows how a higher tax rate does not necessarily bring forth greater tax revenue.

Therefore, hyperinflations create a vicious circle of inadequate tax revenue, leading to a reliance on the inflation tax, which in turns leads to a decline in the demand for money and rising inflation. Rising inflation further reduces the real values of tax revenue collected and encourages the demand for money to fall further, leading to ever-rising inflation. The only way to end a hyperinflation is to solve the underlying fiscal problem.

These hyperinflations show all the signs that we documented above: large fiscal deficits, excessive reliance on monetary financing, and large reductions in the real money stock as people sought to avoid the inflation tax, which required even larger increases in inflation. For instance, in Germany between 1923 and 1924, the government issued currency to finance 88% of expenditure, but between the beginning and end of hyperinflation, the real money stock fell by 99.9%. Most of these hyperinflations ended the same way: with a new currency, fiscal reform, a return to a fiscal surplus that removed the need to print money, and the establishment of an independent central bank with the constitutional ability to ignore the demands of the fiscal authority.[14] Some, like that of Zimbabwe, resulted in the abandonment of their own currency and adoption of other countries' currencies (the South African rand, Botswanan pula and US dollar were adopted for all transactions soon after the introduction of the Z$100 trillion note).

KEY POINT

Hyperinflation can result when governments have large fiscal deficits and try to resolve the problem by printing money rather than raising taxes or issuing bonds.

12.9 Monetarism and the Quantity Theory of Money

We have throughout this chapter been discussing the nominal side of the economy and referred often to the link between money and prices. We now focus on this in more detail by considering the claims of **monetarism**, the idea that money supply growth causes inflation. One of the famous concepts in economics – the **quantity theory of money** – underpins this belief.

Nobel Laureate Milton Friedman is one of the most famous exponents of monetarism. In a seminal work, he and his co-author Anna Schwartz studied the relationships between money, output and inflation.[15] Friedman concluded that 'Inflation is always and everywhere a monetary phenomenon'. Some critics of monetarism argue that this statement is vacuous. Inflation is essentially a change in the price of money: a $10 bill buys less because of inflation. Therefore, to claim that inflation is always and everywhere a monetary phenomenon is as true, but as empty, as saying that, in the words of Frank Hahn, 'The price of peanuts is always and everywhere a peanut phenomenon'.

We start with a relationship that, by definition, has to hold: the *quantity equation*. Let M denote the stock of money, P the price level in the economy and T the volume of transactions. In a monetary economy, money has to back transactions, but the money supply can be less than the value of all transactions if the same bills are used repeatedly. For instance, if I pay the baker $5, the baker pays the butcher $5 and the butcher pays the petrol attendant $5, a single $5 bill can finance $15 worth of trade because it is used three times. Economists call the number of times that money is used for transactions in a period the velocity of circulation (V). By definition

$$M \times V = P \times T$$

Rather than focus on transactions, it will be easier to focus on the overall value added in the economy; in other words, the level of total output (GDP or Y). Value added is a different concept from the number of transactions, but the two are likely to be closely linked. We can therefore rewrite the quantity equation as

$$M \times V = P \times Y$$

which implies that

%change in money supply + %change in velocity

≈ %change in prices(inflation) + %change in output

So far we have only developed an identity – a relationship that has to hold true by definition. To convert this into a theory of inflation, we need to make two more assumptions.

STABLE DEMAND FOR MONEY

The first is that the velocity of circulation does not change – the percentage change in velocity = 0. For the moment, assume that M measures a narrow monetary aggregate, such as M1, and that an individual wishes to keep two months of her annual expenditure in a current account or in cash. Her annual expenditure is simply $P \times Y$, so money demand (M^d) = $(2/12) \times P \times Y$. But the quantity equation tells us that $M \times V = P \times Y$, so this assumption about money demand means that V = 6, which is, of course, a constant. Therefore, the percentage change in velocity = 0, and the quantity equation becomes

%change in money = %change in prices + %change in output

The same conclusion holds for any alternative assumption about how many months of expenditure the individual wants to hold in her bank account.[16]

LONG-RUN NEUTRALITY: OUTPUT INDEPENDENT OF MONEY

Assuming that the velocity of money is constant means that increases in the money supply feed through into increases either in prices or in output. Our second assumption is that changes in output are independent of changes in the money supply; in other words, **money is neutral**. In discussing the costs of inflation earlier in this chapter, we outlined the logic behind this argument. Money is a nominal variable that we use to measure economic value. Just as whether we use miles or kilometres does not influence the distance between Tokyo and New York, neither should it matter if things cost $10 or $20, as long as all prices double. Our analysis holds irrespective of whether things are priced in euros, dollars, Disney dollars, or whether things are priced as they were in 1950 or 2015.

Consider again our analysis in Chapters 3–7 of what determines a country's level of output. We discussed how, via the production function, capital, labour and total factor productivity influenced output. These were links between *real* variables. We discussed many factors behind long-run growth, but did not mention the average level of prices or the money supply. Over the long term, the level of real output (Y) should be independent of shifts in the money supply and prices. Instead, real factors like the efficiency with which machines are used, the numbers of new and useful inventions, the willingness of people to work and so on determine a real magnitude like total output. We would not expect shifts in the price level or in the stock of money to affect these factors substantially. Instead, output grows at a rate (g) that is independent of the money supply but dependent on technology and other factors. This implies that the percentage change in output = g, so we can rewrite our quantity equation as

%change in money supply = %change in prices + g

or

%change in money supply − g = inflation

In other words, inflation should be strictly related to changes in the money supply. If the long-run growth rate does not change over time, every 1% increase in the money supply will increase prices by 1%. Therefore, by assuming that the velocity of money is constant and that money as a nominal variable cannot influence real output, we arrive at a version of monetarism – changes in the money supply directly affect inflation.

KEY POINT

Monetarism suggests that inflation is the result of changes in the money supply.

Figures 12.12a and 12.12b support this monetarist view. Figure 12.12a shows the relationship between average excess M1 growth (money supply growth in excess of output growth g) and average inflation over the period 1980–2008 for a large range of countries, while Figure 12.12b shows the same for M2. Both figures support the conclusion of our monetarist argument: inflation is a monetary phenomenon, high money supply growth means high inflation. However, although Figures 12.12a and 12.12b support our quantity theory, they focus purely on long-run data. If we focus on the shorter term, the evidence is much less impressive. Figures 12.13a and 12.13b show the same countries, but focus on excess money supply growth and inflation between 2007 and 2008. The evidence is less

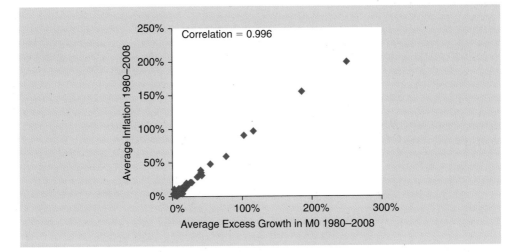

FIGURE 12.12a ● Excess money growth (M0) and inflation, 1980–2008.

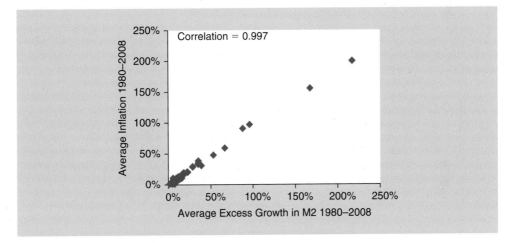

FIGURE 12.12b ● Excess money growth (M2) and inflation, 1980–2008. There is a very strong relationship between excess money growth (money growth minus real GDP growth) and inflation over the long run.

supportive: in the short run, money is a not such a strong indicator of inflation trends. Finally, Figures 12.14a and 12.14b look at the long-run relationship between excess money growth and inflation, but focus purely on countries whose average inflation was less than 5% over this period. Once again, we see a weaker relationship between money and inflation, since at low rates of inflation, changes in velocity become a more significant determinant of money growth.

Figures 12.12–12.14 tell us that the assumptions underlying our quantity theory – stable velocity of money and output being independent of inflation – are only true in the long run. Furthermore, the theory may only be a good approximation to reality when there is significant inflation.

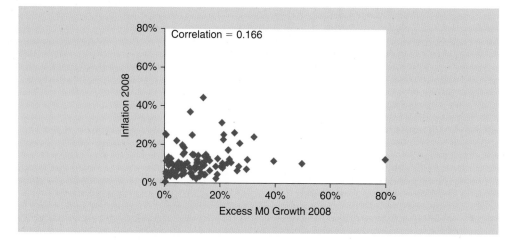

FIGURE 12.13a ● Excess money growth (M0) and inflation, 2008.

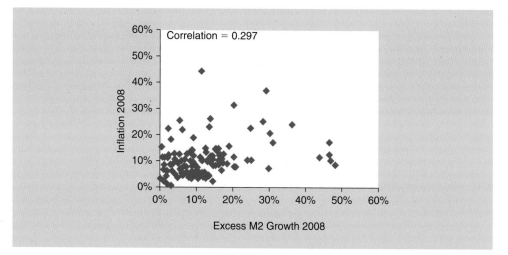

FIGURE 12.13b ● Excess money growth (M2) and inflation, 2008. In the short run the relationship is much weaker.

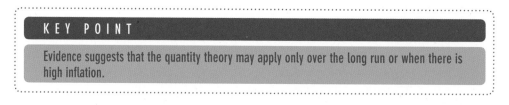

KEY POINT

Evidence suggests that the quantity theory may apply only over the long run or when there is high inflation.

In Chapter 14 we will examine why the quantity theory does not explain short-run inflation trends and show that, as a result, most governments have now moved away from the idea that they can control inflation by controlling the money supply. However, the lesson from this section is clear: as a long-run theory, the quantity equation goes a long way to explain inflation. In that sense sustained, significant inflation is always a monetary phenomenon.

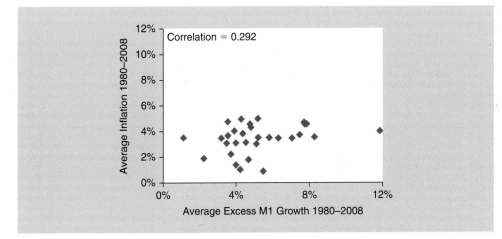

FIGURE 12.14a ● Excess money growth (M1) and inflation for low-inflation countries, 1980–2008.

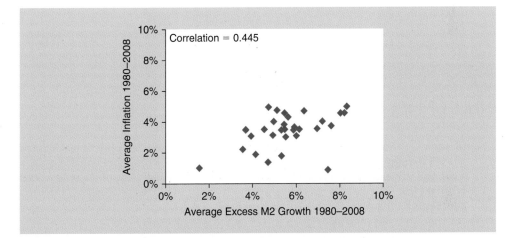

FIGURE 12.14b ● Excess money growth (M2) and inflation for low-inflation countries, 1980–2008. The relationship is also weaker for low-inflation countries. *Source:* All diagrams World Bank, World Development Indicators.

SUMMARY

In Section 12.1 we introduced the concept of inflation, which is defined as a sustained increase in prices. The twentieth century witnessed dramatic inflation compared to previous periods, but inflation at the turn of the millennium was once more very low.

In Section 12.2 we noted that there are many different measures of inflation, reflecting both consumer and producer prices. Quality improvements and technological change make measuring inflation difficult, and it is widely believed that official statistics overestimate inflation.

In Section 12.3 we discussed some reasons why the defeat of inflation is currently a main aim of macroeconomic policy, and one that receives widespread public support. Past experience of high inflation rates has convinced many people that it brings significant costs, including readily measurable penalties from taxes on wages and interest and the inflation tax, as well as costs that are more difficult to measure, such as possible effects on long-run growth, uncertainty, menu costs and lags in price or wage changes. Falling prices – deflation – can also bring problems.

In Section 12.4 we explored the nature and history of money. Money is an asset used for transactions. Originally money was a form of precious commodity, but over time the link with commodities has disappeared. Paper money now has value and is accepted in exchange as a result of government legislation and social convention.

In Section 12.5, we considered the challenges of defining exactly what is, and is not, money. Economists have created several definitions of the money supply. In addition to paper currency issued by the government, the money supply also consists of credit created via the banking system, and different definitions of the money supply include increasingly less liquid forms of money.

We showed, in Section 12.6, exactly how banks can add to the money supply by making loans of money that they are not required to hold in reserve. The money multiplier varies in inverse proportion to a bank's reserves.

In Section 12.7, we showed that the ability to issue paper currency provides governments with a source of revenue, called seignorage. Seignorage is equivalent to the inflation tax.

Section 12.8 described how hyperinflations are caused by governments resorting to seignorage as their main source of financing.

Finally, in Section 12.9, we discussed monetarism. Monetarism derives from the quantity theory of money and states that sustained inflation is caused by increases in the money supply. Assuming that the velocity of money is constant and that output is not influenced by the money supply, increases in the money supply feed through into inflation. The long-run evidence behind monetarism is strong, but the short-run support is poor.

CONCEPTUAL QUESTIONS

1. (Section 12.2) Suppose that a new drug can cure cancer. It costs a few cents to make the pill, and one pill can stop a malignant growth with zero side effects. The drug goes on sale for a few cents a pill, and although the manufacturer makes millions, the money value of the production is tiny. Is it right that GDP has not really changed much? What would the price index, both before and after the invention and sale of the drug, look like?

2. (Sections 12.3 and 12.9) Most economists – and nearly all central bankers – seem to think that inflation is costly. But the quantity theory asserts that there is no long-run link between money and output, nor between inflation and output. Can inflation be costly if the quantity theory is true?

3. (Section 12.4) Which of these is money: a credit card; luncheon vouchers; a portfolio of blue-chip equities; a $100 000 revolving credit line; a $100 dollar bill in Moscow; one million Russian roubles in New York; one million Russian roubles in Des Moines, Iowa?

4. (Section 12.4) Suppose that people could walk around with electronic charge cards that they could use to buy anything; they never need to carry currency. People would have accounts that were invested in bonds, equities and other financial assets into which their salaries, dividends and interest were paid. The portfolio manager would automatically sell assets whenever the card was used. In such a world, would money exist? Would it matter?

5. (Section 12.7) Rich people tend to hold more money than poor people; so is the inflation tax fair?

6. (Section 12.9) Suppose that thieves hijack a truckload of old paper currency on the way to the incinerator. The old currency is worth $1 billion. Who, if anyone, loses if the thieves get away with the cash?

ANALYTICAL QUESTIONS

1. (Section 12.2) The UK price index in Figure 12.1 has the value 109 in 1661, 83 in 1691, 81 in 1891, 231 in 1919, 208 in 1946, 1103 in 1975 and 5350 in 2000. Imagine a one pound note that is accidentally left in the attic of a stately home when it is built in 1661. Calculate the real value of this bank note for each of the years listed above.

2. (Section 12.3) In the United States of Albion, expected inflation is 5% and the real interest rate is 2%.

   (a) What is the nominal interest rate?

   (b) If inflation turns out to be 10% instead, what is the *ex post* real interest rate? Who gains and who loses from this error in forecasting inflation?

   (c) Recalculate your answers for (a) and (b) for net interest rates when the tax rate is 50%.

3. (Section 12.6) Main Street Bank sets its loans on the basis of a 5% reserve requirement and has $100 million cash in its vaults.

   (a) What is the maximum amount of loans the bank can make?

   (b) If the bank has made loans of $50 million to real-estate firms and is required to keep a 50% reserve requirement against such loans, how does this change your answer?

4. (Section 12.7) Let the demand for money in the economy be given by $150\,000 - [\text{Inflation}\,(\%)]^3$. Calculate the amount of revenue raised through the inflation tax for inflation rates up to 50% (a spreadsheet would help!). What inflation rate maximizes revenue?

5. (Section 12.9) The Central Bank of Arcadia has an inflation target of 2%, and forecasts real GDP growth of 2.5% with no change in the velocity of money.

   (a) What money supply growth should it target?

   (b) If the Central Bank revises its velocity forecast to 3% growth, what does this do to its money supply target?

   (c) Assume a forecast of no change in velocity. Interest rates are currently 4%, but inflation is 3% and the money supply is growing at 5.5%. Every 1% increase in interest rates leads to a 1% fall in money supply growth, a 0.5% reduction in output growth and a 0.25% increase in velocity. What level do interest rates have to be to achieve the 2% inflation target?

CHAPTER 13

Monetary Policy

Key Concepts

Credit Channel	LM Curve	Taylor Rules
Inflation Targeting	Open Market Operations	Transmission Mechanism
Intermediate Target	Quantitative Easing	

Overview

By the beginning of the twenty-first century, monetary policy was, almost always and almost everywhere, undertaken by a central bank, implemented by changing short-term interest rates and aimed at controlling inflationary pressures. How this situation came to exist and how emergency measures such as quantitative easing came to be part of monetary policy are important questions that we address in this chapter. We also consider how governments operate monetary policy, what they try to target, how they seek to achieve this and how monetary policy affects the economy. We consider what problems are created in an environment where inflation is low, and may become negative. Finally, we consider how monetary policy may be affected by developments in the banking sector.

13.1 The Influence of Central Banks

The number and power of central banks have never been greater than they are today. Before the twentieth century, the United States did not even have a central bank. Now most countries have a central bank that implements a form of monetary policy. Many more of these central banks are now independent of government than was the case even 15 or 20 years ago.[1] The Federal Reserve System in the United States had considerable independence over monetary policy for decades. But until recently, that was the exception rather than the rule. Within the last 20 years, several major central banks – the Bank of England, the Reserve Banks of Australia and New Zealand, the European Central Bank (responsible for setting monetary policy in the Eurozone) – have gained substantial autonomy to set monetary policy. Furthermore, most of these central banks set policy explicitly to control inflation.

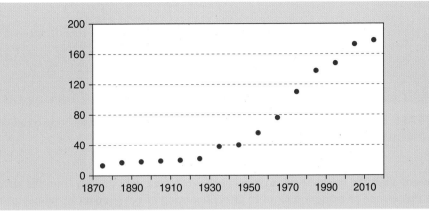

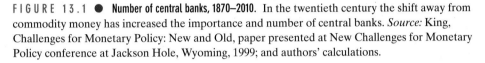

FIGURE 13.1 ● **Number of central banks, 1870–2010.** In the twentieth century the shift away from commodity money has increased the importance and number of central banks. *Source:* King, Challenges for Monetary Policy: New and Old, paper presented at New Challenges for Monetary Policy conference at Jackson Hole, Wyoming, 1999; and authors' calculations.

Why have central banks become influential in setting monetary policy and why has monetary policy become so focused on controlling inflation? As we saw in Chapter 12, until the breakdown of the gold standard, the operation of monetary policy was of limited significance, because in most countries money had always been commodity money and the central banks that then existed had little discretion and few policy choices open to them. (This, of course, was why so few central banks existed, as Figure 13.1 shows.) The breakdown of the gold standard marked the end of the long centuries of commodity moneys. For the first time, central banks, usually under the control and instruction of governments, could influence monetary conditions and faced real choices.

A STYLIZED CENTRAL BANK BALANCE SHEET

Figure 13.2 shows the balance sheet for a stylized central bank. Its key liability is the monetary base, which is composed of currency and reserve money (reserve money is usually deposits that commercial banks are required to hold at the central bank). Notes and coins are of course non-interest bearing, so the cash that you and I hold is effectively the receipt for an interest-free loan by us to the central bank. Reserves can be interest bearing (as is the case for the US, Eurozone and UK) or non-interest bearing (most other countries). The overall level of monetary base is determined by the amount of cash demanded in the economy (as we saw in Chapter 12) and the legally required level of reserves held by commercial banks. The required level of reserves (reserve money plus cash held in banks) is usually set as a percentage of total deposits held by commercial banks and can vary significantly by country, from 0% in countries like Australia and Canada to around 20% in China. A central bank can have other liabilities such as debt and equity, but these are less important in practice.

The asset side of a central bank's balance sheet is usually dominated by holdings of government debt. As we shall see later, the standard procedure through which a central bank increases the amount of monetary base in the economy is to purchase government debt from commercial banks in exchange for newly created monetary base. Most countries

Assets	Liabilities
Government Debt	Currency ⎤
Other Domestic Assets	Reserves ⎦ Monetary Base
Foreign Exchange Reserves	Other Debt and Equity

FIGURE 13.2 ● A stylized central bank balance sheet. It is a central bank's ability to create currency and reserves that makes it unique.

do not allow the central bank to purchase government debt directly from the government, as this is seen as being too close to direct financing of government by money printing. So the debt held by central banks is generally purchased from commercial banks. Another important asset that most central banks hold (though in most cases it is actually owned by the Ministry of Finance) is foreign exchange reserves. We discuss these in more detail in Chapter 21.

What makes central banks special is that they are the only institution that can create monetary base, a product held both by individuals for convenience (cash) and by banks for liquidity management and statutory reasons (reserves). As we shall see later in this chapter, although it is a central bank's control of the overall quantity of base money that is the source of its control of monetary policy, in practice it chooses to exercise that power by deciding on the level of short-term interest rates and allowing the monetary base to move to a level consistent with that. As well as their control of monetary policy, central banks also tend to act as banker to the government, agent for foreign exchange intervention and, as we shall see later in this chapter, lender of last resort to distressed banks.

MONETARY POLICY INSTRUMENTS AND TARGETS

To understand monetary policy we have to distinguish among three different elements, as shown in Figure 13.3.

- The first is the **ultimate policy target**, whether that target be inflation, output growth or employment. In practice, the ultimate target is usually inflation. However, monetary policy does not affect the economy immediately, but with a lag.

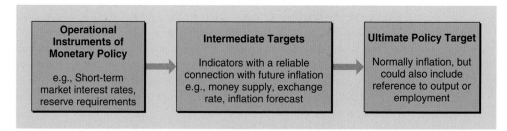

FIGURE 13.3 ● The three aspects of monetary policy. The central bank uses instruments of monetary policy to achieve an outcome for an intermediate target and in that way to control its ultimate target, usually inflation.

- In order to achieve their ultimate target, therefore, central banks try to achieve an **intermediate target**, a variable that, if it can be controlled by the central bank, will enable it to achieve its ultimate target. Central banks have used numerous intermediate targets. Money supply growth and exchange rates have often been intermediate targets. If the ultimate target of the central bank is to control inflation, then we can think of these intermediate targets as a nominal anchor – if the bank successfully meets its intermediate target, then it will keep the price level under control.
- Finally, there are the **operational instruments of monetary policy**, what the central bank uses to implement monetary policy. For most countries this is the level of short-term interest rates.

In the next section we develop a simple framework for thinking about how monetary policy can affect the level of demand in the economy, introducing the concept of the LM curve and using the IS curve, first introduced in Chapter 10, to show how shifts in monetary policy can affect the wider economy. We then focus on how monetary policy is actually implemented.

KEY POINT

Central banks are the sole supplier of base money and it is this that allows them to set monetary policy. Generally, monetary policy is set to achieve a desired rate of inflation, but since monetary policy only influences inflation with a lag, most central banks have an intermediate target as well.

13.2   Monetary Policy and the LM Curve

The IS curve shows combinations of interest rates and levels of output (or income) such that the spending plans of households and firms are fulfilled (*I*nvestment is consistent with *S*avings). However, when interest rates change, they affect not just plans on spending, but also the desirability of holding different types of financial assets. The cost of holding non-interest-bearing money (notes or bills, coins and highly liquid bank deposits that pay close to zero interest) rises with the level of interest rates; the opportunity cost of money goes up – the higher the level of interest rates, the more costly is it to hold cash that yields no interest. Furthermore, the use of money for transaction purposes suggests that as GDP rises, so too will the demand for highly liquid assets, such as cash.

To see this, consider the case of an individual choosing between holding her wealth in the form of a non-interest-bearing current account or in bonds that yield a return (in Chapter 16 we analyse the bond markets in detail). Imagine that GDP rises. So does the income of the investor, which will boost her consumption and so increase her demand for liquid assets. This will cause her to move some of her wealth from bonds and into cash. But by selling bonds, she will affect bond prices, and bond yields are interest rates. Therefore, we cannot just focus on combinations of interest rates and income levels (which is what we are looking at when we consider points on the IS curve) in isolation from conditions in the financial markets. To see how monetary policy affects demand, we need to introduce the **LM curve**, which focuses on equilibrium in the money market. In particular, it focuses on the demand and supply of money provided by the central bank. For the moment, we will assume that the central bank can control the supply of money; later in this chapter, we describe what this means and explain how open market operations work in practice.

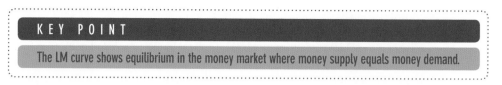

KEY POINT

The LM curve shows equilibrium in the money market where money supply equals money demand.

Let us return to the quantity equation that we introduced in Chapter 12. This says that

$$MV = PY$$

Consider the case where M denotes non-interest-bearing forms of money. We know that in equilibrium money supply equals money demand, so that $M = M^s = M^d$. With a little rearrangement, we therefore have

$$M^d/P = (1/V)Y$$

so that the demand for real money balances depends inversely on the velocity of circulation (V) and positively on the level of GDP, or income (Y). As explained in Chapter 12, the velocity of circulation is a measure of how frequently money is used for transactions. The velocity is likely to depend on the level of interest rates: when interest rates are high, then holding cash is expensive (due to the forgone interest). Individuals will economize on their cash balances and the velocity of circulation will rise, so that at a given level of income, M^d/P will fall. Therefore we can expect increases in interest rates to *lower* the demand for money and increases in income to *increase* the demand for money.

In considering the supply of money, we shall first consider the case where the central bank sets a fixed level for the money supply. Combining this with our demand for money, we have the situation shown in Figure 13.4, with equilibrium at A. We can use this to derive the LM curve, which is a curve illustrating the relationship between interest rates and income. When income increases, for a given level of interest rates, this will increase the demand for money. But if the central bank does not alter the supply of money, then the market is not in equilibrium. The only way equilibrium can be restored is if interest rates rise so that a new equilibrium is restored at B. Therefore, money market equilibrium involves a *positive* relationship between interest rates and GDP; this is the LM curve shown in Figure 13.5.

The LM curve helps show how monetary policy affects the economy. As shown in Figure 13.6, when the central bank increases the money supply from M_0 to M_1, this leads to

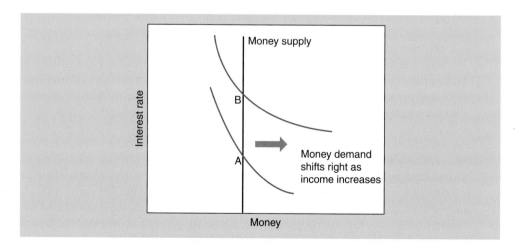

FIGURE 13.4 ● A shift in the demand for money.

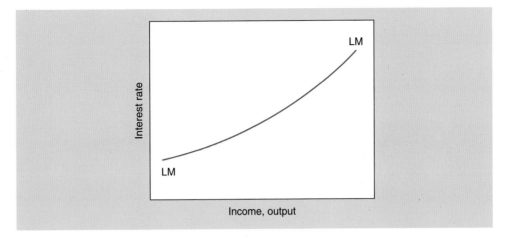

FIGURE 13.5 ● The LM curve.

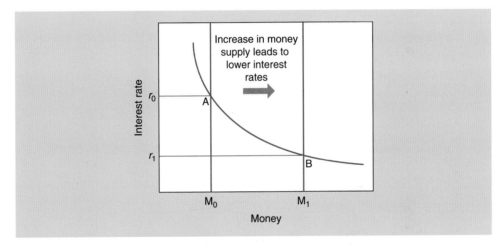

FIGURE 13.6 ● A rise in the money supply.

a fall in interest rates – assuming that income remains unchanged; the only way for money demand to equal the new, higher level of money supply is if interest rates fall to encourage higher demand. In other words, an increase in the money supply is equivalent to a rightward shift in the LM curve, as shown in Figure 13.7. In contrast, a reduction in the money supply involves the LM curve shifting leftwards.

Having developed both the IS and LM curves, we can finally complete our analysis by bringing them together, as shown in Figure 13.8. In this figure the only combinations of interest rate and output consistent with simultaneous equilibrium in the goods market (the IS curve) and the money market (the LM curve) are r^* and Y^*.

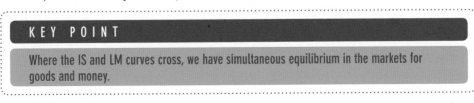

KEY POINT

Where the IS and LM curves cross, we have simultaneous equilibrium in the markets for goods and money.

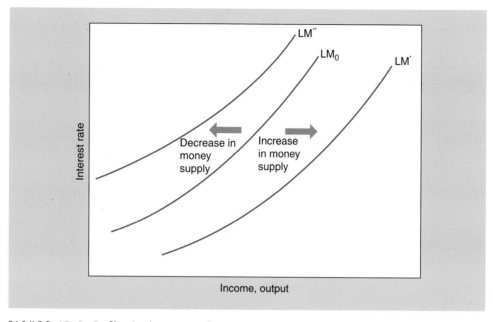

FIGURE 13.7 ● Changing the money supply.

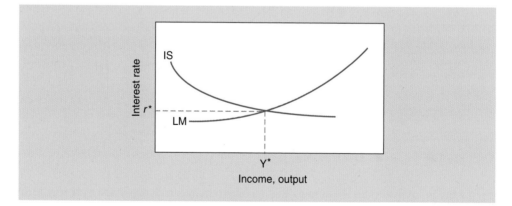

FIGURE 13.8 ● Equilibrium in the goods and money market.

Suppose, however, that the central bank does not have a target for the supply of money, but instead allows the supply of money to move so as to preserve a given level of the interest rate. Interest rate setting is now much more common among central banks than fixing the money supply. For instance, in the United States, the Federal Reserve uses purchases and sales of treasury bills – open market operations – to achieve its Federal Funds *target rate*. How does that affect the shape of the LM curve? The upward slope of the LM curve when supply is fixed reflects the fact that interest rates (r) need to go up or down as income rises or falls, so as to keep money demand (M) constant as Y fluctuates. But if M fluctuates so as to preserve a given level of r, then there will be no relation between Y and r – the LM curve will be flat at the targeted level of interest rates. So we can always think of the LM curve as showing consistent combinations of r and Y for equilibrium in the money market.

Figure 13.9 illustrates the impact of a relaxation in monetary policy. In the top panel we show a situation where there is a money supply target and the target is raised (that is, the central bank allows a larger money supply). This shifts the upward-sloping LM curve to the right. Output is higher, interest rates are lower and demand and output expand as interest-sensitive components of demand – investment, exports and consumption – react to a lower cost of funds. Looser monetary policy operates here by inducing a move down the IS curve; in contrast, easier fiscal policy operates by shifting the IS curve. The lower panel of Figure 13.9 shows a situation where the central bank operates a target for the interest rate and reduces the target level (from r_0 to r_1). In effect, the impact on the economy is the same: interest rates fall, output rises and we move down the IS curve. The distinction between the two panels of Figure 13.9 is, in some sense, not very significant. As noted above, in a world where there is no uncertainty about the demand for money schedule (and therefore no uncertainty about the position of the LM curve), the same effect can be achieved by moving the target for the supply of money by a given amount or shifting the price of money in a way that leads people to want to hold that amount more money.

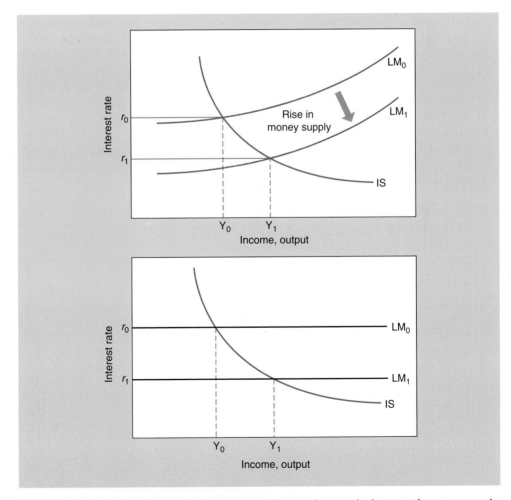

FIGURE 13.9 ● **Increasing targets.** The top panel shows an increase in the target for money supply. The bottom panel shows a cut in the target for interest rates.

(13.3) What Does Monetary Policy Target?

In the twenty-first century the most popular type of target adopted by central banks is not for some measure of the money supply nor for a given level of interest rates. Rather, it is an explicit inflation target. The Reserve Bank of New Zealand, for example, in 2000 had an inflation target range of 0% to 3%. The Bank of England's inflation target was then 2.5% per year, which was changed in 2004 to a target of 2%. The European Central Bank sought to limit inflation to no more than 2%, and to try to keep the rate of inflation close to the 2% level.

As these examples show, many governments ask their central banks currently to target inflation of around 2% per annum. Inflation is costly, as we saw in Chapter 12, so achieving a low level of inflation is desirable. But why do many governments aim at 2% inflation – if inflation is costly, why not aim for price stability and inflation of 0%?

As we discussed in Chapter 12, there are three main reasons why a zero inflation target might not be appropriate. First, official price indices do not adequately abstract from quality improvements, so measured inflation might be overstated by as much as 2%. Second, individuals are very reluctant to accept wage cuts, although they will sometimes accept a wage freeze. Allowing for a modest amount of inflation, the central bank can achieve some variation in real wages even if nominal wages are sticky downwards. Third, as a zero inflation target raises the probability that the economy may enter deflation, a rising real burden of debt and the problem of operating monetary policy when nominal interest rates reach zero are more likely to occur.

How serious is the risk of deflation in practice? Table 13.1 shows that the problem was a serious one both in the era of the gold standard (when variations in the supply of gold relative to GDP caused significant price variability, even though average inflation was very low) and in the inter-war period, which includes the Depression. But it has been less common since then, except in Japan.

TABLE 13.1 ● **Frequency of Effective Deflation, since 1870.**
Proportion of years in which CPI fell, year average basis.

	1870–1914	Inter-War	Post-War
Australia	45.5%	36.4%	1.8%
Canada	31.8%	40.9%	1.8%
UK	38.6%	36.4%	0.0%
US	25.0%	50.0%	3.5%
France	59.1%	40.9%	3.5%
Germany	38.6%	22.7%	5.3%
Italy	45.5%	31.8%	1.8%
Japan	31.4%	36.4%	12.3%
Sweden	43.2%	50.0%	1.8%
Switzerland	31.8%	50.0%	8.8%

Source: Inflation, Deflation and All That. Glenn Stevens, Deputy Governor, Australian Business Economists 2002 Forecasting Conference. Reserve Bank of Australia.

> **KEY POINT**
>
> Because inflation is costly, central banks wish to achieve a low inflation rate. However, for measurement reasons and in order to provide them with some flexibility in how they use monetary policy, central banks do not target a zero inflation rate but somewhere between 2% and 3%.

What Intermediate Target Should Central Banks Use?

In trying to achieve a given inflation target, the central bank has to use an *intermediate target*. An intermediate target is a variable that reliably tracks future inflation and that the central bank can control. The need for the intermediate target to track *future* inflation is because of the lags involved between changing monetary policy and its effect on inflation. If the central bank only responds when it sees actual inflation increasing, then by the time the policy response has an effect, inflation may be even further out of control. However, if an intermediate target – for instance, the money supply – increases, this means that future inflation will probably be high. By tightening monetary policy preemptively today in response, the central bank can then avoid the higher future inflation.

There are three main forms of intermediate targets currently in use – money supply targets, an exchange rate target and an inflation forecast relative to a target level – and we explain each in detail below. Central banks can consider using these intermediate targets individually or in combination. Figure 13.10 shows the type of intermediate targets in use over the 2000s. Over the whole decade, an increasing number of banks adopted some form of inflation target, but exchange rate targets remained the most common policy rule

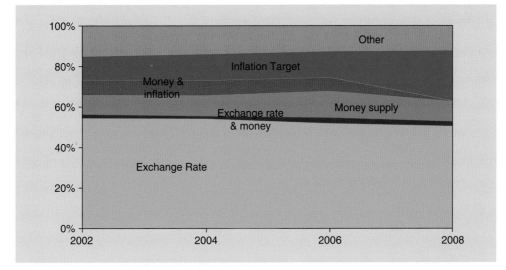

FIGURE 13.10 ● **Monetary policy targets for IMF countries.** The use of explicit monetary targets has increased over time, with inflation and exchange rate targets becoming more popular and money supply targets less so. *Source:* IMF.

overall. The European Central Bank (ECB) uses both an inflation target and a money supply target; the Federal Reserve in the United States is one of the few central banks with no explicit target; the Bank of England, the central banks of Sweden and Switzerland and the Reserve Banks of Australia, Canada and New Zealand have purely an inflation target; and Argentina and Hong Kong have an exchange rate target.

(13.5) Money Supply Targeting

Chapter 12 outlined in detail the quantity theory of money, which states that by definition:

Percentage change in the money supply + Percentage change in velocity of circulation
= Inflation + Percentage change in real output

If we add the assumption that the velocity of money is constant (or at least predictable) and that the growth of output is given by the real factors considered in Chapters 3 to 8, then we have a simple relationship between money supply growth and inflation. If velocity is constant and real output grows at a trend rate of 2.5%, then money supply growth of 4.5% will be consistent with inflation of 2%. Therefore, using a money supply growth rate of 4.5% as an intermediate target should mean that we hit a target of 2% inflation.

In the 1980s such monetarist policies were implemented in many advanced economies. While inflation did decline, the reliance solely on monetary targets was not seen as successful. In Chapter 12, we showed how the quantity theory was excellent at explaining long-run inflation, but not very successful in explaining short-run inflation. Purely relying on money supply targets to control short-run inflation proved difficult for five reasons, outlined below.

WHICH MONEY SUPPLY?

As described in Chapter 12, there are several different monetary aggregates, or money supplies. If all monetary aggregates behave similarly, then it does not matter which monetary aggregate the central bank targets. But in practice, different monetary aggregates behave in different ways. Figure 13.11 shows the behaviour of US M1 and M2 growth. Frequently while one aggregate is showing rapid growth, the other is slowing down. In 1992, should the Federal Reserve have been relaxed about inflation because M2 growth was falling to zero or deeply alarmed that M1 growth was close to 15%? Heated debate occurred during these years as to the relative merits of each monetary aggregate, and often central banks would switch from one intermediate target to another. However, in the end, none of them proved reliable and *Goodhart's Law* was established. This states that any observed regularity between a monetary aggregate and inflation will break down when central bankers try to exploit it for policy purposes.

THE VELOCITY OF MONEY IS NOT PREDICTABLE

One reason why the monetary aggregates behaved differently was because of large changes in the velocity of circulation. Figure 13.12 shows the velocity for a narrow and a broad measure of money for the United Kingdom between 1982 and 2010. Over much of the period, the introduction of ATMs (automatic teller machines) led to an increase in velocity for narrow

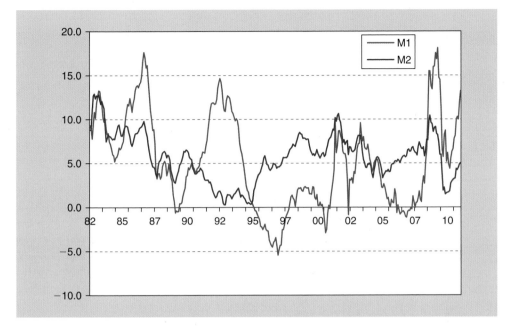

FIGURE 13.11 ● **US money supply growth, 1982–2011.** Different money supply measures show very different behaviour. *Source:* Federal Reserve Board, http://www.federalreserve.gov/releases/H6.

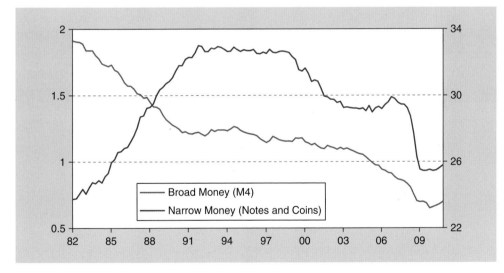

FIGURE 13.12 ● **UK velocity of money, 1982–2011.** Velocity of money has shown large and hard-to-predict changes. *Source:* Economic Trends, UK Office for National Statistics, http://www.statistics.gov.uk.

money. Because it was easier to get hold of cash, people reduced the amount they withdrew from their bank on each trip and held less cash in their wallet. But this trend was reversed in the late 1990s, partly because low inflation reduced the cost of holding cash. Over most of this period, however, the velocity of broad money fell. Changes in legislation meant that more financial institutions could make loans and the result was intense competition and an increase in credit and broad money, which lowered the velocity of broad money. If these trends were predictable, then allowance could be made for them when setting the money supply target; but they were not predicted. No one knew when these changes would come to an end nor what would happen in the year ahead. The result was to weaken considerably the link between the money supply and inflation.

CAN THE CENTRAL BANK CONTROL THE MONEY SUPPLY?

In Chapter 12 we described the money multiplier, which helps understand why the great majority of broad money is the creation of commercial banks through their credit policies, rather than something that is under the direct control of the central bank. As we shall see later, a central bank can use interest rates only to influence the cost at which a commercial bank can borrow. The central bank cannot be certain whether this cost increase is passed on to a bank's loan customers or whether its increase in lending rates will affect demand for loans. Without a predictable link between changes in interest rates and changes in the money supply, it is problematic to use monetary aggregates as a reliable intermediate target.

IS THE SUPPLY CURVE VERTICAL?

Our example of a 4.5% money supply target producing a 2% inflation rate was based on stable output growth of 2.5% per annum. In Chapter 12 we explained the idea of a vertical long-run supply curve that shifts out over time because of technological progress and capital accumulation. With a vertical supply curve, any increase in the money supply will raise aggregate demand, but lead only to higher prices and no extra output, as shown in Figure 13.13. However, firms do not usually immediately increase prices in response to an increase in demand. Either

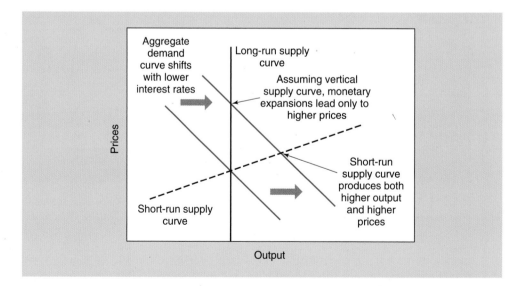

FIGURE 13.13 ● **Effects of monetary expansion on prices and output.** Assuming a long-run vertical supply curve, monetary expansions produce only inflation. With a short-run supply curve, output and prices both increase.

because of real or nominal rigidities (as described in Chapter 12), firms choose to keep prices fixed initially and increase output. While this policy is not sustainable, in the short run, while it lasts, the supply curve will not be vertical but have a flatter slope. The result is, as shown in Figure 13.13, that increases in the money supply lead to higher output and inflationary pressure in the short run. Therefore, any attempt at controlling inflation via money supply targeting must make an assumption about the current slope of the supply curve and how long it will take for the inflationary pressures to emerge. To achieve a 2% inflation target will take different money supply growth rates, depending on whether output is growing at 1% or 4% this year.

SUPPLY SHOCKS

Even if the velocity of money is constant and the money supply is under control, this does not mean that inflation will be on target. Figure 13.14 shows the case of an adverse supply shock, such as an oil price increase. Even if the money supply is controlled so that the demand curve remains fixed, the oil price increase will produce higher inflation and lower output. If these effects are only temporary, then it is less important. But if the supply shocks occur over a long period (for instance, because of a sustained improvement in technology), then the effects on inflation will be long-lasting and must be taken into account.

While the long-run performance of the quantity theory in explaining inflation is impressive, each of these five factors meant that simple reliance on monetary aggregates was insufficient to control inflation in the short run. As a former governor of the Bank of Canada said, 'We didn't abandon the monetary aggregates, they abandoned us.' As a consequence, very few countries still maintain such a pure version of money supply targeting. This does not mean that the money supply numbers are uninformative for inflation. It simply means that central banks have to monitor other variables and use additional or alternative intermediate targets.

One country that did profess faith in money supply targeting was Germany. The German enthusiasm for monetary targeting was important in establishing the 'twin pillar' approach of the ECB to monetary policy – to use both inflation targeting and monetary indicators in setting interest rates. Even in Germany, however, the use of money supply

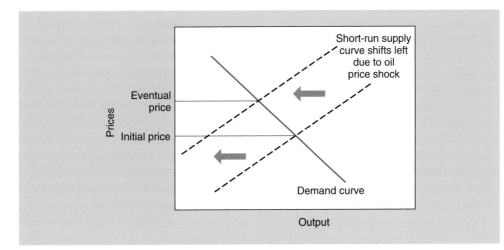

FIGURE 13.14 ● **Inflation and supply shocks.** Adverse supply shocks will also cause inflation to rise even if the money supply is under control.

targeting was not as simple as the approach outlined above. The Bundesbank would only set its money supply target after it had considered in detail the likely behaviour of velocity and gross domestic product (GDP) growth over the next year. Changes in these forecasts would lead the Bundesbank to revise its money supply targets. This focus on a wide range of variables rather than just the money supply is more characteristic of inflation targeting than straightforward monetarism.

KEY POINT

Money supply targeting is now much less common than it was in the 1980s and 1990s. This is largely a reflection of the instability in the relation between measures of the money supply and inflation.

13.6 Exchange Rate Targets

An alternative nominal anchor to money supply targets is to set monetary policy in order to achieve a target exchange rate. By dedicating monetary policy to fixing the exchange rate, the hope is to achieve inflation control. In Chapters 19 to 21 we examine in detail the behaviour of exchange rates, the links between inflation and interest rates and the relative merits of fixed exchange rates. For now, we take a more informal approach and note that if the central bank achieves a fixed exchange rate, then it is likely that over the medium term it will achieve the same inflation rate as the country with which it has a fixed rate of exchange (see the detailed discussion of *purchasing power parity* in Chapter 19).[2] In order to achieve its exchange rate target, a central bank can raise interest rates if it wants the currency to appreciate or lower them if it wishes the currency to fall (see the discussion of *uncovered interest parity* in Chapter 20).

As Figure 13.10 shows, many countries use exchange rates as a guide to operating monetary policy. However, exchange rate targets can also be costly. The main cost is that if monetary policy is used to fix the exchange rate, it cannot also be used to influence the domestic economy. This lack of an independent monetary policy was at the heart of the United Kingdom and Italy's exit from the European Exchange Rate Mechanism in 1992. The Bundesbank was raising interest rates to control German inflation at this time, and other countries in the group had to follow in order to maintain a fixed exchange rate. However, with other countries in recession, this increase in interest rates was unwelcome, and as a result of these tensions the pound sterling and the lira were forced to leave the fixed exchange rate system. For small open economies whose economy is closely tied to that of the country whose exchange rate they are targeting, fixed exchange rates seem to work well. For larger economies they are more problematic.

13.7 Inflation Targeting

The problem that many central banks encountered with pure money supply or exchange rate targets is their inflexibility – policymakers only focus on one statistic, be it the money supply or the exchange rate, in order to control inflation. No other information can be used to override the rule. Consider again the case of the United Kingdom and the Exchange Rate Mechanism. While Germany was expanding rapidly and seeing inflation increase, the United Kingdom was in recession and faced little inflationary pressure. If the Bank of England could give weight to a wide range of evidence, then it might conclude that even if sterling depreciated against the Deutschmark this would not threaten higher UK inflation. As a result, it might be able to leave interest rates unchanged. By contrast, under a fixed exchange rate the central bank does not have this discretion – regardless of what the data for output or inflation say, the central bank would have to respond to a depreciation in sterling by increasing interest rates to maintain the exchange rate target.

This example suggests the desirability of adopting a monetary policy rule that utilizes a wide range of information and that is flexible enough for policymakers to respond differently to different circumstances. However, no rule could be written down that describes how policy would be set in all possible outcomes. This leaves two alternatives. First, choose a simple rule – such as a money supply or exchange rate target – and face the occasional risk of having to abandon the rule in certain circumstances, leading to some loss of credibility. Alternatively, develop a framework that offers the central bank some discretion in how it responds to the data, but also provides a clear objective to which policy is directed and against which the performance of monetary policy can be assessed. This latter option is referred to as 'constrained discretion'.

Inflation targeting is an attempt to achieve this constrained discretion. Inflation targeting involves the central bank stating explicit quantitative targets (or ranges) for inflation for a specific time horizon. The central bank also dedicates monetary policy to achieving a low inflation rate and no other purpose. The intermediate target in this framework becomes the central bank's own inflation forecast. If the forecast is for inflation to consistently exceed its target, the central bank raises interest rates. By using the forecast rate of inflation as an intermediate target variable, the central bank can take into consideration a huge range of information. Any variable that influences inflation should be considered, including the exchange rate and the money supply. No one variable is dominant and the net effect of all of them is considered.

This obviously provides the central bank with a large amount of discretion. In order to preserve credibility, inflation targeting is characterized by vigorous efforts at communicating with the public. Through publications and speeches, the central bank reveals the logic behind its deliberations and actions, and publishes its forecasts and its analysis of how it thinks the economy and monetary policy operate. After decades of acting with the utmost secrecy, the adoption of inflation targeting has brought about a dramatic change in the behaviour of central bankers.

The belief is that by explaining in a consistent and logical manner the reasons behind monetary policy decisions, the public will appreciate that inflation targeting is desirable, should be supported and will be consistently followed. Furthermore, if this is understood, the public will not fear the central bank using its discretion to risk high inflation, but will instead expect it to use discretion to set monetary policy in a flexible manner. Advocates of inflation targeting argue that it should increase credibility. Simple, inflexible rules will inevitably be abandoned in certain circumstances, but not flexible approaches like inflation targeting.

KEY POINT

Inflation targeting is a framework for monetary policy, not a rule – it occupies a midpoint on the rules versus discretion spectrum. It provides a forward-looking discipline that should enhance credibility, but allows flexible responses to events (such as shocks to the demand for money). Inflation targeting does not provide mechanical instructions to the central bank, but allows it to use its discretion in the short run.

Inflation targeting has been enthusiastically adopted by central banks. Starting with New Zealand in 1990 and subsequently Canada, the United Kingdom, Finland, Sweden, Australia, Israel, Chile, Mexico and Brazil, inflation targeting has become a common *modus operandi*. The European Central Bank now also operates a form of inflation targeting, although it continues to place a special emphasis on the money supply figures.

In adopting inflation targeting, numerous operational issues have to be determined. What measure of inflation should be used? Which inflation rate should be the target? Should a range be targeted or a specific value? On what horizon should the central bank focus? Most countries focus on increases in consumer prices (sometimes extracting volatile components) and have a target of around 2%. Some countries specify that inflation should be below a certain limit (the ECB sets a target of 2% or less), while others allow deviations from the target rate within a narrow band (from 2004 the Bank of England targets 2.0% inflation; New Zealand, a range of 0–3%).

(13.8) The Operational Instruments of Monetary Policy

As well as the ultimate and intermediate targets, the other key component of monetary policy is the instruments that the central bank has at its disposal. Currently the key tool of monetary policy is the short-term interest rate.

How can central banks, with limited resources, control almost exactly the level of short-term interest rates? The answer is that, at least in the current state of monetary arrangements and transaction technologies, base money remains essential.

The monetary system in most developed economies is, ultimately, similar. At its centre stand commercial banks, which take deposits from the private sector, make loans and, crucially, help facilitate transactions by honouring cheques and other payment instructions from their customers. If the customers of a bank write more cheques in a working day than the bank receives in payment, that bank may have to make a net transfer of funds to another bank. For example, suppose that the customers of Deutschebank write cheques that the receivers deposit into Dresdnerbank and that compensating flows in the other direction do not match them. At the end of the day, Deutschebank needs to transfer, say, 50 million euros to Dresdnerbank. Both banks will typically have accounts with the central bank; the central bank will hold accounts for the major commercial banks that allow them to settle transactions with each other. Central banks severely limit the ability of private banks to overdraw these accounts or take their reserves below a critical threshold (the reserve requirement). This means that if, towards the end of a working day, Deutschebank has insufficient funds to transfer the necessary amount to the Dresdnerbank account, Deutschebank will need to do something.

The interbank market allows Deutschebank to borrow money from another commercial bank overnight, so that it does not go into deficit at the central bank. But suppose that most major banks are going to be overdrawn at the end of the day and that the system does not have enough funds to allow individual banks to borrow from others that had a surplus at the central bank. Suppose, for example, that a large corporation pays its tax bill on a particular day. When it pays its tax bill, it transfers a large quantity of funds from its account at a commercial bank to a government account. Government accounts are normally held with the central bank, so that clearing the cheque will result in a net drain of funds from the pool of base money available to private banks. If the central bank did nothing to alleviate this shortage, private banks would be bidding for funds on the interbank market and would begin to drive interest rates up.

In this system, central banks operate by providing reserves, mainly through so- called **open market operations** or through lending at the discount window. During a working day, a central bank may realize that the money market will run short of funds unless it acts. The central bank will then signal that the system is likely to run short of funds that day and that it will buy short-term securities[3] in exchange for cash at a specified interest rate. Every time the central bank buys a security from a private bank, that bank's reserves with the central bank are credited with the sale proceeds. So by buying securities (that is, engaging in open market operations), the central bank can help regulate the quantity of reserves in the system.

Central banks can also control reserves by supplying or absorbing them directly from individual banks. Direct lending of base money to banks (in return for securities) is generally undertaken at the discount rate. This rate is generally a little higher than the official interest rate set in open market operations in order to discourage banks from using this means. In practice, the most important use of discount rate lending is for **lender of last resort** operations. When a commercial bank is perceived to be in financial difficulty, it is quite possible that other banks will refuse to lend to it for fear that it will become insolvent before the loan is repaid. As we shall see in Chapter 17, it is quite possible that this refusal to lend could force the bank into insolvency even if its true financial position was okay. In these situations the central bank may decide to lend to the troubled bank directly at the discount rate, taking whatever assets the bank can offer in return for base money.

Finally, some central banks (most notably the European Central Bank) offer a **Lombard or deposit rate of interest** to individual banks that find themselves with excess reserves after open market operations have been completed. The deposit rate that the central bank pays to the bank that deposits excess reserves is lower than the official interest rate set in open market operations in order to discourage its use.

Figure 13.15 shows the full range of rates offered by the European Central Bank. The key monetary policy rate is the so-called repo rate, which is the rate at which standard

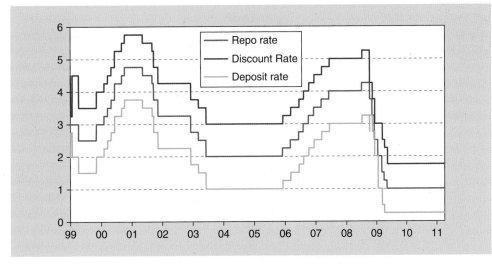

FIGURE 13.15 ● **ECB policy rates.** Although the repo rate is the ECB's key policy interest rate, it operates with a discount and deposit rate that form a corridor around the repo rate. *Source:* ECB.

open market operations are undertaken. The discount and Lombard rates form a corridor in which the repo rate can fluctuate and so limit its movements in the event of surprise changes in the demand for base money.

The key aspect to remember about all this is that the central bank has rules about how much funds the private-sector banks have to hold with it. The private-sector banks will, in certain circumstances, find that there is a shortage (or sometimes a glut) of reserves. If the central bank were to do nothing, the level of money market interest rates would move. The central bank can prevent significant movement in these money market rates by supplying or absorbing base money in return for securities. The central bank has enormous influence over the level of money market interest rates, because it can supply almost unlimited quantities of funds to the market or, by selling securities, it can drain enormous quantities of reserves from the market.

> ### KEY POINT
>
> Central banks decide the terms at which they will purchase or sell securities in their open market operations. They may also undertake emergency operations with individual banks at the discount rate and, less commonly, the deposit or Lombard rate.

Note that if commercial banks were not required to hold reserves at the central banks, the central banks would not have the power to alter interest rates. The precise nature of the reserve requirements that the central bank requires differs from system to system. In the United States, commercial banks that hold accounts at the Federal Reserve for settlement of flows are required not to be in deficit, on average, over a two-week period. Other systems require that individual banks not be overdrawn on a daily basis. Regardless of the specific detail, the key point is that failure to meet these reserve requirements is penalized by the central bank and only the central bank can supply reserves to the banking system. This is the reason behind the central bank's influence over short-term interest rates.

13.9 Controlling the Money Supply or Interest Rates?

Earlier in this chapter, we reviewed how central banks have tended to move away from trying to control the money supply to a framework of inflation targeting. We also introduced the concept of the LM curve. In doing so, we began with a simple assumption that the central bank controls the money supply. But, as Figure 13.9 showed, we can just as well use the IS-LM apparatus to illustrate the much more relevant case where the central bank sets an interest rate and allows the money supply to adapt to its new target rate of interest. Here we return to this important issue.

Figure 13.16 illustrates a situation in which the central bank has a target for some measure of the money supply. As before, we assume a negative relation between the level of the short-term nominal interest rate and the stock of money. The higher the interest rate, the more expensive it is to hold cash, the more narrow money demand falls; and the more expensive it is to borrow, the more credit and broad money decline. M^* is the target level, and MD_0 illustrates the expected position of the money demand curve. If demand for money turns out to be what the central bank anticipated, then interest rates will be R_0. But if the demand for money is either higher or lower than the central bank anticipated, interest rates

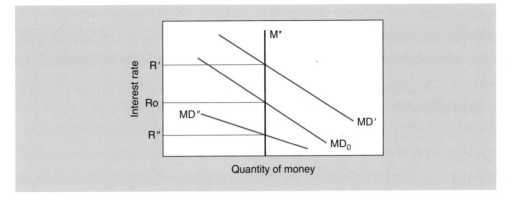

FIGURE 13.16 ● **Monetary policy when targeting the money supply.** Money supply targets imply volatile interest rates if money demand is unstable.

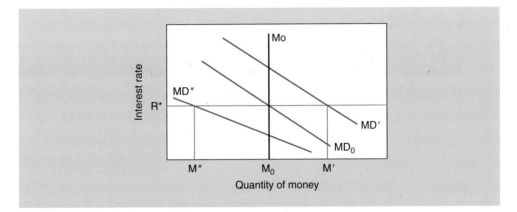

FIGURE 13.17 ● **Monetary policy when the central bank sets interest rates.** When the central bank sets interest rates, volatility occurs in the money supply.

will deviate from R_0. If demand is at level MD′ and the target does not change, monetary conditions will be tighter, and interest rates will rise to R′ to reflect the scarcity of funds. But if demand for money is lower than the central bank anticipated, at MD″ interest rates will fall to R″. With higher demand for money, the central bank will be offsetting expansion in banks' balance sheets by selling securities (that is, entering into contractionary open market operations). This will drain reserves from the banking system and cause interbank interest rates to be bid up as the commercial banks vie to attract funds. In this case, in which the central bank is targeting the money supply, fluctuations in money demand produce considerable volatility in interest rates.

Under inflation targeting, the central bank sets interest rates to achieve a particular inflation target. This case is shown in Figure 13.17. Again, MD_0 denotes the level of demand for money that the central bank anticipates. If the central bank aims to keep interest rates at R* *and* if demand turns out to be MD_0, the money supply will be at M_0. But if demand deviates from MD_0 and interest rates are kept at level R*, the supply of money will deviate from M_0. So, for example, if the money demand schedule is to the right of MD_0, the quantity of money will exceed M_0. And if the demand for money balances is substantially lower than MD_0, then so will be the stock of money.

If the demand for money schedule is predictable, there is no substantive difference between interest rate targeting and money supply targeting. The central bank could choose to specify a money supply target or a particular level of interest rate, and the two would be equivalent because each interest rate corresponds to a particular (known) level of money demand. As we discussed earlier, it was unpredictable shifts in money demand, due to technological developments and financial innovation, that contributed to central banks looking for alternatives to targeting the money supply.

(13.10) How Monetary Policy Affects the Economy: The Transmission Mechanism

We have outlined the aims of a central bank and how it adjusts the instruments of monetary policy to achieve them, but we have not yet outlined in any detail how changes in interest rates affect inflation and output. This is called the **transmission mechanism** of monetary policy – the link among changes in interest rates, changes in components of demand within the economy, and how such changes in demand can affect inflation pressures.

> ### KEY POINT
>
> It is the nature of the transmission mechanism that determines the slope of the IS curve.

Figure 13.18 outlines the main links through which the transmission mechanism works. When the central bank increases official interest rates, this will begin to have an effect on interest rates of all maturities and will influence asset prices. Assuming inflation in the short term is relatively unchanged, short-term *real* interest rates will be higher. If the markets believe that the higher interest rates are not purely transitory, this will also increase longer-term bond yields. These increases in interest rates will have a direct effect in lowering demand. As we saw in Chapter 10, increases in interest rates lead to reductions in

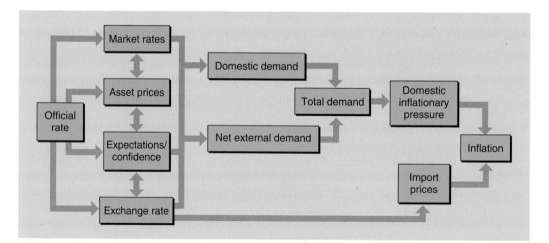

FIGURE 13.18 ● **The transmission mechanism of monetary policy.** Interest rates affect output and inflation through numerous channels. *Source:* Monetary Policy Committee, Bank of England, *The Transmission Mechanism of Monetary Policy* (1999). Reprinted with permission from the Bank of England.

consumption. In addition, higher interest rates will affect the cost of borrowing and the real rate of return that needs to be earned on investment projects, leading to a fall in investment spending. The higher interest rates will also lead to a fall in asset prices (see Chapter 16) and further reductions in consumption and investment through wealth effects and the q theory of investment (see Chapter 10). If higher interest rates are expected to lead to a future slow-down in the economy, consumer and producer confidence will also fall, which in turn will lead to retrenchment of consumption and investment plans.

The increase in interest rates will also affect external demand in the economy. As we noted earlier, higher interest rates lead to an increase in the exchange rate. The higher exchange rate makes imports cheaper, which may place downward pressure on domestic inflation. Further, the higher exchange rate makes exports more expensive and so reduces demand in the economy. The overall impact of the increase in interest rates is therefore to reduce demand in the economy.

Figure 13.18 focuses on how increases in the price of money, the interest rate, affect the economy. However, in some cases monetary policy operates less as a result of changes in the *price* of money and more through the *quantity* of lending that banks undertake. This is known as the **credit channel** of monetary policy. Increases in interest rates can produce declines in real-estate and equity prices, which reduce the collateral that firms can offer banks. As a con-sequence, banks reduce their loans to the corporate sector, which has a direct effect on con-sumption and investment. It has been argued that the credit channel, rather than inappropriate levels of interest rates, was responsible for the severity of the Great Depression. The credit channel occurred through the failure of the Federal Reserve to offset the dramatic decline in the stock of money by providing banks with cash that they could lend.[4] The Federal Reserve could have done this by buying securities (or other assets) from the banking sector and pro-viding it with loanable funds. We will return to the credit channel when we discuss the credit crunch in Chapter 17.

Figure 13.18 only outlines the channels through which interest rates affect output and inflation, not the magnitude of the effects nor how long the impact takes. Table 13.2 shows empirical estimates of the magnitude and timing of output and price effects for developed economies taken from a meta-analysis (a study of studies) of 44 individual studies compris-ing up to 120 estimates. There are a number of interesting features of Table 13.2. First, the authors find that the impact of monetary policy on the economy does not differ significantly between countries despite their differing economic structures. They do find, however, that the level of inflation has a significant effect on the impact of monetary policy on output, with higher inflation generally reducing its impact on output. This is consistent with the Phillips curve that we outline in Chapter 15. They also find that countries operating a fixed exchange

TABLE 13.2 ● Estimated Impact of a 1% Increase in Interest Rates in a Developed Economy: A Meta-Analysis.

These estimates summarize the results of 44 different studies. The base case is for a medium-sized economy with 2% inflation and a floating exchange rate, using data starting in the 1970s.

	Output Level Effect		Price Level Effect	
	Short term (1 year)	Long Term (5 years)	Short term (1 year)	Long Term (5 years)
Base case	−0.6%	−0.7%	0.1%	−1.7%
Higher (10%) inflation	−0.3%	−0.4%	−0.1%	−1.6%
Fixed exchange rate	−0.6%	−0.5%	0.2%	−1.1%

Source: De Grauwe and Costa Storti, The effects of Monetary Policy: A Meta-Analysis, CESifo Working Paper 1224 (2004).

rate regime also tend to find that monetary policy is less effective. This is unsurprising, as Figure 13.18 shows that the impact of interest rates on the exchange rate is one of the channels of through which monetary policy works.

Looking in detail at the base case of Table 13.2 (the impact of a 1% increase in interest rates in a economy with 2% inflation and a floating exchange rate), we can trace through the impact of monetary policy. Possibly the most surprising aspect of Table 13.2 is that the estimated short-run (1-year) impact of higher interest rates is actually an increase in prices. This result is called the **price puzzle** and is probably not a true feature of monetary policy but a problem in estimating its impact. Since interest rates are often increased when inflation is about to rise, if the interest rate rise is too small or too late, it is possible to see inflation rise after a rate rise and so estimates of the impact of interest rates may incorrectly attribute the increase in inflation to the rise in interest rates. Even allowing for this effect, the impact of monetary policy on prices is slow and seems to take longer to feed through than does its impact on output.

(13.11) Monetary Policy in Practice

Let us assume, as is the case in most developed countries, that the central bank sets monetary policy. In general terms, how central banks set policy is uncontroversial. The central bank will first analyse the economy and then consider how best to set the policy instruments that it has, usually short-term money market interest rates. Central banks act in light of the current economic situation and base their assessments on such crucial factors as how the policy instrument will affect the overall level of demand in the economy and how demand is linked to the ultimate policy target. A stylized description of this process is shown in Figure 13.19.

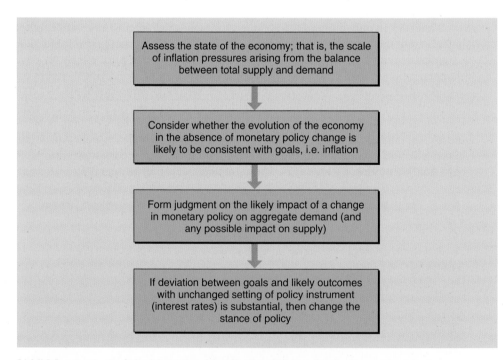

FIGURE 13.19 ● **Stylized description of the behaviour of the central bank.** Central bankers have to process a wide range of information and form views of future inflation when setting interest rates.

As this discussion and our earlier one regarding inflation targeting reveal, setting interest rates to control inflation is a complex activity. A useful way of summarizing the way interest rates are set lies in **Taylor rules**.[5] Taylor rules specify a link between the level of the short-term interest rate and output and inflation. Some proponents of Taylor rules advocate them for use in setting interest rates in practice. However, our discussion of inflation targeting outlined some problems with using fixed rules. Here, we simply propose Taylor rules as a way of approximating what central bankers try to do when setting rates. A number of studies have found that such rules provide a reasonably good explanation of actual central bank behaviour.

The following equation gives the typical structure for a Taylor rule:

$$\text{Nominal interest rate} = \text{Equilibrium nominal interest rate} + (\lambda \times \text{Output gap}) + [\alpha \times (\text{Inflation} - \text{Inflation target})]$$

where the equilibrium nominal interest rate is the real interest rate plus the inflation target and λ and α are positive numbers. The Taylor rule says that if the output gap is positive (GDP is above its trend value), then the central bank should raise interest rates. Similarly, if inflation is above its target, then interest rates also should be increased. A variety of versions of the Taylor rule exist. Some use the gap between expected future inflation and the inflation target, rather than current inflation. Also, interest rates from the last period are often included in order to smooth the changes in interest rates, something that central banks appear to do.

The positive coefficients λ and α reflect an assessment of the sensitivity of inflation and output to shifts in monetary policy *and* to the chosen trade-off between inflation volatility and output volatility. If inflation is very sensitive to changes in interest rates, then other things being equal, α will be small, similarly for λ. If the central bank will not tolerate much volatility in inflation, then α will be large, similarly for λ and output volatility. For the United States, the values of λ and α that best account for the behaviour of interest rates are about 0.5 and 1.5, respectively. This says that in response to a 1% increase in the output gap, the Federal Reserve tends to raise interest rates by 0.5%. In response to inflation being 1% above its target, the Federal Reserve raises interest rates by 1.5%. It cuts them by 1.5% when inflation is 1% below target. Broadly similar values are obtained for other countries, although differences in attitudes towards inflation mean that there are some variations.

If α equals 1, then nominal interest rates would only rise in line with inflation and the real interest rate would not alter. When α exceeds 1, then the central bank responds to higher inflation by increasing the real interest rate – it is the increase in real interest rates that makes the policy contractionary. The Taylor rule, and its ability to track actual changes in interest rates, suggests that central bankers translate the various messages conveyed by a wide range of macroeconomic variables into movements in the output gap and inflation relative to the target. Then, having formed these views, they adjust interest rates accordingly.

Figure 13.20 compares simple Taylor rule projections for some major economies (using λ and α of 0.5 and 1.5 respectively in all cases) with official interest rates. It is remarkable how closely these simple projections match actual policy. The Taylor rule projected higher interest rates than existed in all major economies between 2004 and 2008; some commentators have argued that this contributed to the subsequent financial crisis.

KEY POINT

Taylor rules specify a link between the level of the short-term interest rate and output and inflation. In practice, central bankers take account of a much richer set of data in setting monetary policy.

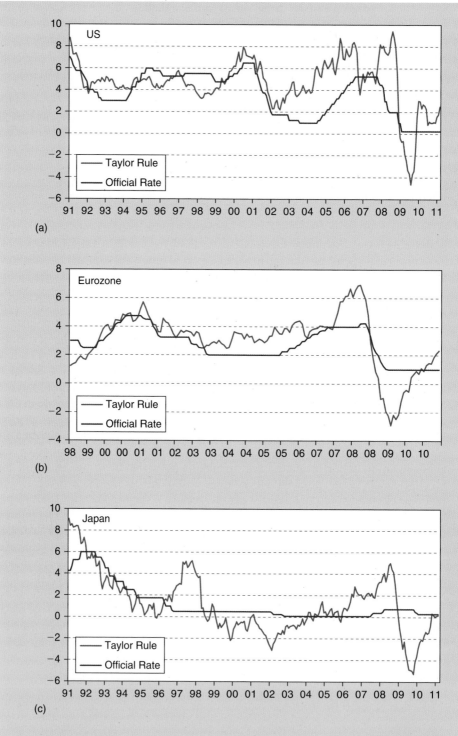

(continued)

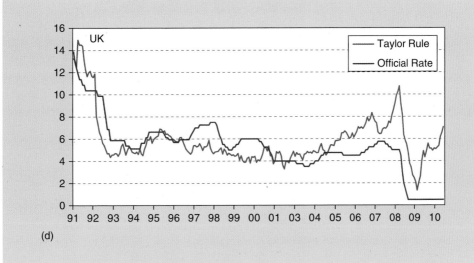

(d)

FIGURE 13.20 ● Taylor Rule projections and official interest rates for the major economies. The simple Taylor rule predicts interest rates that are close to those that were actually implemented. *Source:* OECD and authors' calculations.

(13.12) Quantitative Easing

As Figures 13.20a–13.20d indicate, there have been a number of periods in recent history when the Taylor rule suggests that due to extremely low inflation and a large negative output gap, interest rates for a number of countries should have been negative. The key episodes are Japan in 2001–04 and the United States, Japan, and Eurozone in 2009. In practice a negative interest rate cannot be implemented, since banks and individuals would prefer to hold cash (that pays a zero interest rate) than put their money in bank deposits that have a negative interest rate. So what options are left for a central bank that wishes to relax monetary policy further once nominal interest rates are at or very near zero?

In all these cases the central bank opted for some form of quantitative easing. The key idea behind quantitative easing is that when interest rates are at or near zero, the central bank can dramatically increase the supply of base money without changing interest rates. This is because when interest rates are very low, the private sector is happy to hold large amounts of non-interest-bearing base money, since it is safe and has a return similar to a financial asset. So, as Figure 13.21 shows, while a money supply of M is consistent with near-zero interest rates, so is M^{QE}. Loosely speaking, the distance between M and M^{QE} can be thought of as the scale of quantitative easing, since it is base money that the central bank creates in excess of the minimum required to keep interest rates at their target level of zero or near-zero levels. Figure 13.22 shows the substantial increases in base money created by the central banks of the United States and United Kingdom in 2008 and 2009 in their quantitative easing programmes. The main reason for understating this quantitative easing was to bring down a range of other interest rates (besides the ones controlled directly by the central bank).

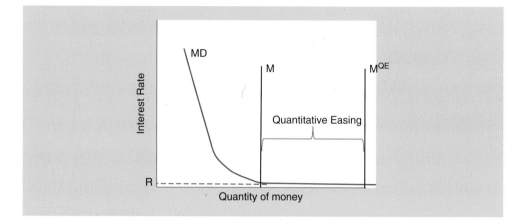

FIGURE 13.21 ● **Quantitative easing.** At very low interest rates, the central bank can dramatically increase the quantity of money without changing interest rates.

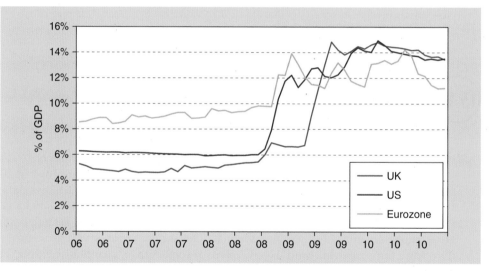

FIGURE 13.22 ● **Supply of base money.** The US and UK significantly increased the supply of base money in 2008 and 2009 as part of their quantitative easing programmes. *Source:* Various.

DOES QUANTITATIVE EASING WORK?

Although the sums of money involved are huge, it is not obvious that quantitative easing (QE) has any significant economic effects, since it has no effect on the short-term interest rates central banks usually control. But at least three channels have been identified through which QE could have an effect on the wider economy:

- *Expectations channel.* Merely by announcing such a large-scale programme, the central bank might hope to convince the private sector that the economy was more likely to recover and inflation was more likely to rise. Such expectations could cause a reduction in precautionary saving and so create growth in spending. This was considered an important factor behind the Bank of Japan's QE programme of 2001; while it is difficult to judge, it is unclear that the hoped-for boost to expectations actually occurred in that case.

- *Excess monetary base channel.* There are various formulations of this idea, but the key is that when the central bank injects excess amounts of base money into the economy, the private sector in general and banks in particular are more willing to invest in non-monetary assets like loans. Once again, this is difficult to assess, but most evidence suggests that commercial banks seem happy to absorb large amounts of base money without increasing their lending.

- *Purchases of financial assets channel.* Contrary to much popular comment, QE does not consist of throwing money out of helicopters or passing it out in the street; base money is injected into the economy through large-scale open market operations. This means that the money is used to buy financial assets – usually government debt. By buying large amounts of government debt, the central bank may make that debt more expensive and so encourage investors to sell that type of debt and go into more risky investments, such as lending to corporations. In this case there is some evidence that QE programmes that have focused on government debt (like those of the UK and Japan) have increased the price of government debt. This is likely to have encouraged investors to move into riskier investments, though the evidence is far from conclusive. The Federal Reserve and ECB have taken a more direct approach and purchased risky assets such as corporate debt directly; some have termed this policy *qualitative* easing. Its key feature has been to take risky assets out of the financial system and put them on the balance sheet of the central bank. In fact, the ECB has focused on this policy rather than quantitative easing in its standard form.

SUMMARY

In Section 13.1, we saw that the twentieth century witnessed a large increase in the number of central banks as the move away from commodity-based money gave governments more discretion over monetary policy. Monetary policy consists of three main components: an intermediate target that the central bank tries to control in order to meet its ultimate target; the instruments of policy that the central bank has at its disposal; and the ultimate policy target that the central bank wishes to achieve.

In Section 13.2, we described how the IS-LM apparatus can be used to depict how changes in monetary policy affect the level of demand in the economy. Although it is common to think of shifts in monetary policy in the context of the IS-LM apparatus as stemming from changes in the money supply, in practice central banks actually control the level of the short-term interest rate. However, this is not inconsistent with the IS-LM framework.

We saw in Section 13.3 that a belief in a vertical long-run supply curve, pessimism over the ability to fine-tune the economy and a belief that following rules will improve credibility and achieve lower inflation have all combined to persuade many central banks to target inflation, which most try to keep at around 2%.

In Sections 13.4–13.7, we noted that countries have experimented with a range of intermediate targets; money supply, fixed exchange rates and inflation targeting are the most common. In the 1980s a number of countries attempted to control inflation via controlling the money supply. However, this proved unsatisfactory in practice, so that now setting targets for inflation or for the exchange rate are the most common policies. Inflation targeting is attractive to central banks because it provides discretion as to how to respond to economic events, while still providing a rules-based framework to help promote credibility.

In Section 13.8, we saw that central banks invariably use short-term market interest rates to implement monetary policy. The central bank has control over these because it is the only supplier of reserves to the banking system. Section 13.9 showed the equivalence, under some conditions, between targeting the money supply and an interest rate. In Section 13.10, we described a model of the transmission mechanism by which monetary policy affects demand directly by changing interest rates, asset prices and exchange rates, and affecting consumption, investment and exports. Additional effects work through changes in producer and consumer confidence. Furthermore, a credit channel is believed sometimes to affect the economy. This operates through changes in the supply and demand for credit that are not directly related to interest rates. Empirical estimates suggest that the effect of changing interest rates accumulates over time and takes years to have its peak impact.

In setting interest rates, central bankers monitor a wide range of statistics. In Section 13.11, we introduced Taylor rules as a useful way of conceptualizing this process. Interest rates increase when the output gap is large and when inflation exceeds its target. Section 13.12 described the concept of quantitative easing, a policy that central banks adopt when interest rates are close to zero.

CONCEPTUAL QUESTIONS

1. (Section 13.1) Should something that has such a large impact on the economy as monetary policy be handed over to a central bank rather than being decided by elected politicians?

2. (Section 13.1) Central banks control short-term interest rates because they control the supply of base money, which is the ultimate, final form of settlement for transactions. Are central banks abusing this power by using it to determine interest rates?

3. (Sections 13.4–13.7) Why not specify a goal for the monetary authorities that includes both a price level and an unemployment target?

4. (Sections 13.7 and 13.11) Should measures of inflation include asset prices (e.g. stock prices and house prices) so that inflation targeting would require the monetary authorities to act when asset prices rise dramatically?

5. (Section 13.11) At Christmas and Easter members of the public withdraw large amounts of cash from their accounts. What should central banks do during these periods to stabilize interest rates?

6. (Section 13.11) Should central banks use Taylor rules to set monetary policy?

7. (Section 13.12) Has quantitative easing been effective?

ANALYTICAL QUESTIONS

1. (Section 13.2) Use the IS-LM apparatus to show how the change in the level of interest rates needed to bring about a given change in demand is greater, the less responsive investment and consumption are to the cost of borrowing.

2. (Section 13.2) Use the IS-LM framework to show that the level of interest rates needed to preserve demand at some given level might require negative interest rates.

3. (Section 13.11) The Federal Reserve Bank of Albion operates a Taylor rule of

$$\text{Interest rate} = \text{Inflation target} + \text{Equilibrium real interest rate} + (0.5 \times \text{Output gap}) \\ + [1.5 \times (\text{Inflation} - \text{Inflation target})]$$

It has an inflation target of 2% and believes the equilibrium real rate to be 3%. Currently the output gap is zero and trend output growth is 2% per annum.

(a) If output growth is predicted to be 4% this year and inflation 3%, to what level should interest rates move?

(b) How does your answer change if the central bank changes its inflation target to 3%?

(c) Consider again the economy in (a). What should the central bank do if it thinks that trend output growth may have increased to 3.5%? What would happen if it were wrong?

4. (Section 13.11) The Community of Pacific States (CPS) operates a Taylor rule of

Interest rates = 5% + (A × Output gap) + [B × (Inflation – Inflation target)]

Inflation is determined by a Phillips curve so that

Inflation = Inflation target + (0.5 × Output gap last year)

And interest rates have an impact on the output gap so that

Output gap = −0.5 × (Interest rates last period − 5%)

The output gap is currently 2% and inflation is 3% with a target of 2%. The central bank of the CPS is considering two alternative policy rules. One sets A = 0.75 and B = 1, whereas the other sets A = 0.25 and B = 2.

(a) Compare the behaviour of interest rates, inflation and output over the next five years for both rules.

(b) How does the volatility of inflation and output vary in each case?

(c) Examine how your answers change when the slope of the Phillips curve and the sensitivity of interest rates change.

(d) How would your answers change if inflation = last year's inflation + 0.5 × output gap last year?

5. (Section 13.11) The League of Big States (LBS) has inflation expectations of 5% and an estimated natural rate of unemployment of 5%. A 2% rise (fall) in unemployment leads to a 1% fall (increase) in inflation.

(a) What is inflation when unemployment equals 5%?

(b) What is inflation when unemployment falls to 3%?

(c) If unemployment falls to 3% but the Central Bank of LBS thinks that the natural rate has also fallen to 3%, what will happen to inflation?

(d) How will the behaviour of interest rates differ in your answers to (b) and (c) if the Central Bank uses higher interest rates to keep inflation at 5%?

(e) The Central Bank is not sure whether or not the natural rate of unemployment has changed. How will its behaviour vary depending on whether its goal is (1) to achieve inflation of 5% or less, (2) to try to maintain stable inflation and unemployment, or (3) to keep inflation in the range of 4.5–5.5%?

(f) Let inflation expectations be equal to last period's inflation. Unemployment is currently 5%, the natural rate is 5% and last year inflation was 5%. The Central Bank wants to lower inflation from 5% to 2%. Compare how unemployment and inflation vary over the next four years when (1) the government wants to achieve 2% inflation next year, (2) the government wants to achieve 2% inflation by lowering inflation by 1% each year.

CHAPTER 14

Fiscal Policy and the Role of Government

Overview

In this chapter we consider the role of government and ask why the spending of governments varies across countries. We analyse the rationale behind government intervention and the public provision of services, and consider empirical evidence on government activities in different countries. We then discuss the implications of the size of government on taxation and how it can distort resource allocation. The structure of the tax system and how it can be designed to minimize distortions is analysed. We consider the implications of governments running fiscal deficits; that is, not covering their current expenditure out of tax revenue. We discuss how deficits and the stock of debt have evolved over the last century. Finally, we consider the empirical evidence for the link between the size of the public sector and long-run economic growth.

14.1 Government Spending

Figure 14.1 shows that the size of the public sector varies considerably across countries. For instance, in France over recent decades, government spending has accounted for around 45% of GDP, while in the United States it has been around 20%. Some things that governments do are both essential and could not be done by the private sector – it is hard to see how any entity but the government could be responsible for the legal system, the police force and national defence. Some things that governments do in many countries are essential, but the private sector could do them. For example, in many countries, public-sector health and education services comprise much of total spending, but the private sector could provide these

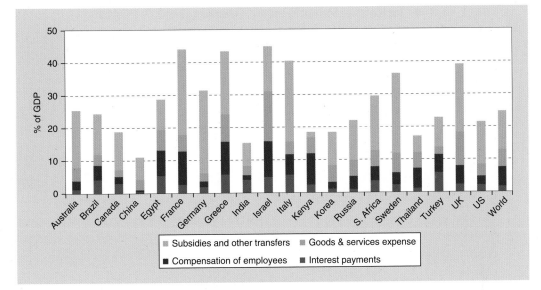

FIGURE 14.1 ● **General government spending (% GDP, 1998–2008 average).** The size of government varies across countries, but in all developed economies the state plays a major role in economic life. (Note: these figures are based on the IMF definition of government expenses that differs slightly from that used elsewhere in this chapter.) *Source:* World Bank, World Development Indicators.

services. And some government activities need not be done and, until relatively recently, were not done. For example, in most developed countries, governments provide various kinds of social security (unemployment and sickness benefits, old-age pensions). This kind of social welfare provision, or social insurance, is a relatively recent phenomenon, but one that accounts for much of the rise in the role of government in market economies.

The public sector expanded in most countries during the twentieth century. Table 14.1 shows the share of government spending in GDP for 14 industrialized nations since the second half of the nineteenth century. In 1870, government spending as a percentage of GDP averaged about 8% across these economies. Just after the end of the First World War, expenditure had, on average, almost doubled to over 15% of GDP. By 1960, the average proportion of total spending that government accounted for had risen to almost 30% of GDP. Since then, expenditure has steadily increased in most countries, so that on average the public sector now accounts for over 40% of GDP in developed countries.

Much of the rise in government spending reflects growing government consumption; that is, government spending on wages (of civil servants, soldiers, police and so forth) and on materials and supplies that public-sector workers use (e.g. office supplies, arms, fuel and electricity). This part of government spending absorbs or *directly* uses economic resources, but it excludes investment (e.g. road building). From the nineteenth century to the Second World War, the growth in overall government spending roughly mirrored the rise in government consumption. But since 1939, spending has outpaced direct government consumption. Now, on average, less than half of government spending in developed countries is consumption. The majority of government spending in developed countries now involves transfers; that is, various cash benefits, pensions, unemployment benefits, disability payments and so forth. Unlike government consumption or investment, transfer payments involve the government spending money, but without receiving any economic goods or services in exchange.

TABLE 14.1 ● The Increasing Share of Government Expenditure, 1870–2002 (% of GDP).

	Late Nineteenth Century (about 1870)[1]	Pre-First World War (about 1913)[1]	Post-First World War (about 1920)[1]	Pre-Second World War (about 1937)[1]	Post-Second World War (about 1950)	1980	1990	2002
Austria	–	–	14.7	15.2	35.7	48.1	48.6	51.1
Belgium	–	–	–	21.8	30.3	58.6	54.8	50.2
Canada	–	–	13.3	18.6	28.6	38.8	46.0	40.4
France	12.6	17.0	27.6	29.0	34.6	46.1	49.8	54.2
Germany	10.0	14.8	25.0	42.4	32.4	47.9	45.1	48.1
Italy	11.9	11.1	22.5	24.5	30.1	41.9	53.2	47.7
Japan	8.8	8.3	14.8	25.4	17.5	32.0	31.7	38.3
Netherlands	9.1	9.0	13.5	19.0	33.7	55.2	54.0	47.2
Norway	3.7	8.3	13.7	–	29.9	37.5	53.8	46.4
Spain	–	8.3	9.3	18.4	18.8	32.2	42.0	39.4
Sweden	5.7	6.3	8.1	10.4	31.0	60.1	59.1	58.0
Switzerland	–	2.7	4.6	6.1	17.3	32.8	33.5	37.6[2]
UK	9.4	12.7	26.2	30.0	32.2	43.0	39.9	40.1
US	3.9	1.8	7.0	8.6	27.0	31.8	33.3	35.0
Average	8.3	9.1	15.4	18.3[3]	28.5	43.3	46.1	45.1

Source: Data are from Tanzi and Schuknecht, The Growth of Government and the Reform of the State in Industrial Countries, IMF Working Paper, 1995; updated with data from OECD.

Notes

[1] Or nearest available year after 1870, before 1913, after 1920 and before 1937.

[2] 1992.

[3] Average; computed without Germany, Japan and Spain (all at war or preparing for war at this time).

Since the eve of the Second World War, this kind of transfer has been responsible for most of the growth of the government sector in developed countries. Across the seven developed countries for which reliable data are available, transfer payments relative to GDP averaged just under 4% in 1937. That figure had grown to over 15% by the end of the 1990s. Figure 14.1 also shows the breakdown of government spending by type and illustrates how the level of transfers differs enormously between rich and poor economies (though some rich countries like Korea and the United States have a relatively small level of transfers).

Table 14.2 shows a more detailed breakdown of general government (including central, state and local government) spending for some OECD economies in 2006. It shows that there are significant variations in spending patterns. For example, defence makes up over 11% of US central government spending, but just over 2% of Germany's. In contrast, social protection (largely transfers) is less than 20% of US spending but over 46% of Germany's.

We have not distinguished in the figures between investment expenditure and current consumption. Although most governments do give some breakdown into capital and current

TABLE 14.2 ● Breakdown of General Government Spending, 2006 (% of total).

	General Public Services	Defence	Public Order and Safety	Economic Affairs	Environmental Protection	Housing and Community Amenities	Health	Recreation, Culture and Religion	Education	Social Protection
Canada	18.6%	2.6%	4.0%	8.6%	1.4%	2.3%	18.7%	2.3%	18.3%	23.3%
France	13.2%	3.5%	2.4%	5.5%	1.6%	3.6%	13.7%	2.8%	11.3%	42.3%
Germany	13.3%	2.3%	3.5%	7.2%	1.1%	2.1%	13.6%	1.3%	8.9%	46.7%
Greece	19.2%	5.4%	2.6%	10.5%	1.4%	0.9%	11.2%	0.8%	5.5%	42.4%
Italy	17.5%	2.7%	3.8%	11.7%	1.6%	1.5%	14.1%	1.7%	9.0%	36.4%
Japan	14.0%	2.6%	3.9%	9.9%	3.4%	1.8%	19.6%	0.4%	10.6%	33.9%
Korea	13.2%	9.2%	4.7%	21.3%	3.2%	3.9%	13.5%	2.9%	15.7%	12.4%
Poland	13.4%	2.6%	4.2%	10.0%	1.4%	2.8%	10.7%	2.6%	13.8%	38.6%
Spain	11.8%	2.9%	4.8%	13.0%	2.3%	2.3%	14.6%	3.8%	11.2%	33.3%
Sweden	14.2%	3.1%	2.5%	8.8%	0.7%	1.4%	12.5%	2.0%	13.0%	41.8%
UK	11.0%	5.7%	5.8%	6.3%	2.3%	2.1%	16.0%	2.0%	13.0%	35.8%
US	13.2%	11.6%	5.8%	10.1%	0.0%	1.7%	21.0%	0.8%	16.9%	19.0%

Source: OECD, Government at a Glance.

expenditure, this does not correspond to the economic distinction between investment and consumption. This classification issue is acute for the public sector, because governments call much of what they spend on goods and services 'current expenditure' (which is often interpreted as consumption) when it is more like investment. Education expenditure helps enhance, or at least preserve, the national stock of human capital. The largest element of this expenditure is wages, but governments generally count them as current expenditure. We could make the same point about health expenditure. Firms count their expenditure to cover the depreciation of physical investment as investment; government health spending is, by analogy, a form of investment to cover depreciation of the national stock of human capital.[1]

These figures show that governments in all developed economies play a major role in the economy and that the range of government programmes is wide. Why is this? In the next section, we discuss the rationale behind government spending on goods and services and, in particular, why transfer payments have grown.

KEY POINT

The size of the public sector varies greatly across countries, but has tended to rise over time.

(14.2) The Rationale for Government's Role and the Failure of the Invisible Hand

The political economist Adam Smith had a truly profound insight. The free operation of forces in decentralized markets would lead not to chaos but to order: resources would tend to be allocated to produce goods that society valued most. He likened the operation of these forces to the workings of an invisible hand. Smith argued that market mechanisms coordinate the actions of companies and households – all serving their own self-interest – to produce things that people want in the right quantities. It was as if some giant benevolent, but invisible, hand were guiding and coordinating the millions of economic decisions made each day. But market outcomes would only be efficient under certain circumstances: when agents understand the nature of the goods that are being offered for sale; when those agents behave rationally; when goods are produced under competitive conditions (i.e. no monopolies); and when all commodities that have value are offered for sale (i.e. when markets are 'complete'). Efficiency here has a special, and unusual, meaning. The allocation of resources is efficient if a reallocation of resources (perhaps as a result of government intervention) is unable to make anyone better off without making someone worse off. We call such a situation **Pareto efficient**, named after the Italian economist Vilfredo Pareto (1848–1923).

The idea that market forces encourage the efficient use of resources is immensely powerful. There is also a simple intuition behind it: free markets tend to be efficient in this sense, because if they were not, then profitable opportunities would not be exploited. But the conditions required to operate this invisible hand efficiently are demanding. And even if those conditions exist, the resulting allocation of resources could be hugely unequal, and unsustainable in a society in which citizens vote and governments respond to majority opinion.

Smith himself was aware that the conditions needed for *laissez-faire* (or totally unregulated) capitalism to work well might not hold. He believed that government intervention when ideal free market conditions were not present *could* generate more desirable outcomes. Free markets might not produce certain goods that are desirable because it would be difficult to make people pay for them – some of these are so-called public goods; others are goods for which there are missing markets. For example, there may be no market in which I can insure myself against the risks of a permanent fall in my earning power. People might not fully take account of the consequences of producing and consuming certain goods; irrationality can make free market outcomes suboptimal and justify a paternalistic role for government. Finally, free market outcomes may generate an undesirable distribution of income. We will now consider the significance of these phenomena – we might call them market imperfections – and what they imply about the role of government.

KEY POINT

The 'invisible hand' of the free market would lead to economic efficiency under ideal conditions. Governments play a role when ideal conditions do not exist.

PUBLIC GOODS

Even at the height of laissez-faire capitalism in the mid-nineteenth century, people recognized that the state had to take responsibility for providing some things. These so-called night-watchman duties of the state were largely concerned with ensuring law and order: the legal system (crucial to the functioning of any market economy based on exchange and property rights), policing and national defence. A secure system of national defence and a well-functioning legal system are goods in much the same way that a telephone is a good. But these goods are *non-excludable* – it is hard to exclude any citizen from enjoying their benefits. If I live in a country in which crime is low, the legal system fair and the borders secure, then I benefit even if I make no contribution to paying for the police force, the army and the law courts. My consumption of these benefits, which are safe streets and peace of mind about the threat of invasion or arbitrary imprisonment, does not affect the cost of providing these services. We call goods that have this characteristic **public goods**.

The problem with public goods is that you cannot easily sell access to them: how can you get *individuals* to pay voluntarily for an army? People who live in the country benefit from the army whether they pay or not. So rational and non-altruistic people would not pay for the service and, instead, hope to get a free ride from the contributions of others. If everyone did this, the market would not provide an army.

It is the difficulty of preventing people from enjoying the benefits of these goods that makes providing them in a market problematic. When the cost of providing commodities or services to another person is close to zero at the margin and the benefits of providing them cannot easily be blocked, it is hard for commercial enterprises to produce them.

Moreover, markets for most standard (non-public) goods would not operate well unless some of these public goods were provided. Consider the importance of a police and legal system that is administered fairly and without corruption. This system is essential to the efficient running of an economy (see Chapter 4). We can see this most vividly by looking at cases in which respect for the law has broken down; such situations make the rewards of trying to expropriate the goods of others high and the benefits of actually producing goods (which are likely to be stolen) low. It is worth considering the costs of such situations and how they can trap standards of living at low levels. To do so, we introduce the notion of a Nash equilibrium.

PUBLIC GOODS AND NASTY NASH EQUILIBRIA

Most people who have read Joseph Heller's *Catch-22* remember the catch: if you were crazy, you could be declared unfit to fly dangerous bombing raids, but claiming insanity to avoid flying is the act of a sane man. In one of the scenes in the novel, a character is discovered committing a selfish act that could endanger others and is asked: 'What if everyone did that?' After some thought, he answers: 'Then I'd be a fool not to.' Economists will instantly recognize a *Nash equilibrium* here (named after the mathematical economist and Nobel prizewinner John Nash). A Nash equilibrium is a situation in which, given everyone else's behaviour, each person is acting in a way that is individually rational. The example from *Catch-22* suggests that such equilibria may not be pleasant places within which to get trapped.

In a nasty equilibrium, cheating, breaking conventions and stepping outside the law are individually advantageous, though collectively costly. Laws and social conventions can prevent societies from being trapped in bad equilibria in which standards of living are low. It is useful that a convention forbids standing on your seat at a football game to get a better view – though doing so would be rational if people around you did it, even though it would be collectively self-defeating.

The football example is trivial, but the strength of social institutions (laws, conventions, how rules are enforced and changed) in preventing inefficient equilibria may help explain the massive differences in wealth and income across countries. As we saw in Chapter 3, the differences in output across countries are far more pronounced than the differences in capital stocks employed. Total factor productivity, in which social institutions and culture play key roles, is hugely important in explaining income differences.

So one of the primary roles of government is to try, in part through the legal and police systems, to reduce corruption, theft and disrespect for the law. The World Bank also tries to reduce corruption, particularly in developing countries, because it sees how corruption can damage economic growth and standards of living.

PATERNALISM AND THE DISTRIBUTION OF INCOME: THE RATIONALE FOR THE WELFARE STATE

Many public goods (e.g. law and order, absence of corruption) are essential and the operation of markets cannot supply them. Until the middle of the nineteenth century, governments' almost exclusive role in the economy was to provide public goods. But Table 14.2 shows that today only a small part of government spending represents the provision of public goods. In most of the developed countries, the emerging economies and in the formerly centrally planned economy of Russia, spending on defence, public order, safety and general public services does not exceed 25% of all government spending and is often lower. Starting in Bismarck's Germany, in the 1880s, governments in many countries began to provide social insurance, which almost always involved redistributing income among agents. In 1870 across the industrialized market economies, average spending on transfers was less than 1% of GDP. By the start of the twenty-first century, it was almost 20% of GDP.

Governments have come to play a bigger role here for many reasons. The first is a *paternalistic* one, reflecting the belief that, left to themselves, many people will not act in their own longer-term economic interests. For example, people may not perceive how education can benefit their future incomes and, if left to themselves, they would 'underconsume' education. So governments subsidize education in most countries and force people to consume it by requiring that they stay in school until a certain age. People might also consume too much today and save too little for their old age – a decision that they might later bitterly regret. To protect people, governments in many countries force them to contribute to pension systems. And people might also fail to see the full benefits of health care, both for themselves and others, so governments subsidize health services.

These paternalistic arguments for the public sector providing some goods, and for the compulsory consumption of others, are partly behind the growth of the welfare state in many countries. Concern about the distribution of income is another reason for government involvement in the economy. The distribution of income that might arise from free market outcomes may be undesirable for many reasons. One may be that a majority of the population simply finds it ethically unacceptable that many of their fellow citizens should live in poverty. Another reason may be that risk-averse individuals, fearing the consequences of bad luck, bad genes or bad schools, may want the state to offer them insurance against misfortune in their later lives. This can be a powerful, if not altruistic, force.

A third factor may also be important. You may not care that other people live in poverty or fear the risks of becoming poor yourself, but you may not like how other people's poverty affects you. Crime, delinquency and disease are likely to be worse if a large economic underclass has poor economic prospects, bad schooling and inadequate health care. The worse these problems are, the lower the quality of life for people in general – not just for those in poverty. Governments may take on social welfare roles with the aim of improving the quality of life for all their citizens. Some writers question, however, just how much of a role is appropriate for the government to take. So how big should the government be? This is the issue we now turn to.

> ### KEY POINT
>
> There are many reasons why governments need to play a major role in the economy if markets are to work well.

(14.3) Taxation and Distortions

We cannot answer questions about the appropriate size of government simply by focusing on the merits of different spending programmes or the relative efficiency with which the private and public sectors provide services. It is also relevant to consider how public spending is financed. If government chooses to finance its spending mainly out of taxation, then we must take the economic costs of raising revenue into account when considering the optimal size of government.

TAXATION

Comparing Figures 14.1 and 14.2 shows that there is a very high correlation between spending and the overall amount of tax revenue raised in both industrialized and developing

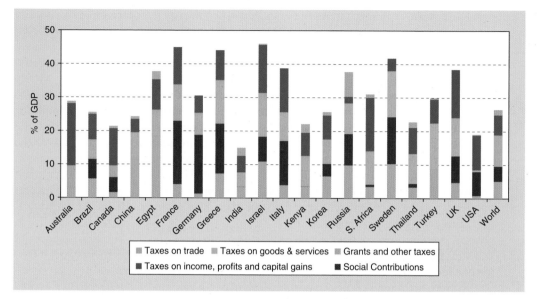

FIGURE 14.2 ● **General government revenues (% GDP, 1998–2008).** Tax receipts as a proportion of GDP, and therefore average tax rates, broadly reflect the scale of government spending. *Source:* World Bank, World Development Indicators.

countries. This is why we need to look at the costs of raising tax revenue when analysing what is the right level of government spending. It is important to note that raising revenue is not the only reason that governments tax. Taxes can be used to discourage the consumption and production of goods that have bad side effects for which consumers and producers may not pay all the costs. Taxes on tobacco, alcohol, petrol and the production of pollutants (carbon taxes) are examples of ways in which the government uses its tax powers to make market prices reflect some of the wider costs of certain activities.

But most taxes – and certainly all income taxes – are imposed to generate revenue to pay for government spending. Figure 14.2 shows how a range of governments raised revenue over the period from 1998 to 2008. Taxes levied directly on individuals (on income, property or goods and services consumed) have consistently been far more important than taxes raised from corporations. In those countries in which state pensions are generous and account for a big slice of government spending – Sweden, Germany, France and Italy – social security contributions are an important source of revenue.

There are economic costs associated with various methods of raising revenue. We do *not* mean simply how much revenue the government actually raises. There is no efficiency loss, per se, from raising the $500 million needed to build a new road by taxing people as opposed to charging fees for using the road. The costs of using one strategy or the other have to do with how particular revenue-raising schemes distort behaviour. According to Smith's invisible hand, when markets are complete and competitive, the allocation of resources is efficient: prices signal to firms and workers the value that is placed on the goods and services that they provide. Taxes drive a wedge – or create a gap – between what sellers receive for supplying goods and services and the prices that buyers pay. This can mean that highly valued activities will be underprovided if suppliers only receive a fraction of the value created. If labour income is taxed at 50%, workers only receive half of the price that buyers of labour pay; this is likely to affect labour supply. The higher taxes are, the more they will affect demand and supply decisions. This applies to direct taxes on labour incomes and profits, and to indirect taxes on the sale of goods.

So the real cost of raising revenue through taxation is that it can distort patterns of spending and labour supply, savings behaviour or other aspects of economic activity. Virtually any form of tax alters economic behaviour. Taxes on labour income are likely to influence people's choice of jobs, the number of hours they work, how hard they try to earn a bonus or how much costly training and education they undertake. Taxes on corporate profits are likely to affect the investment that companies undertake. Social security contributions, levied either on workers or on firms, will affect the cost of labour and the benefits of work and thus will tend to affect levels of employment, as seen in Chapter 7. Taxes on wealth and property influence people's incentives to save and allocate that saving. Taxes on consumption (indirect taxes) affect both the distribution of spending across commodities (because governments may tax commodities in different ways) and the supply of labour, because indirect taxes reduce the real spending power of wages.

DISTORTIONS

We can measure the costs of the *distortions* arising from taxes by thinking about how taxes affect the demand and supply for the taxed good. For taxes on earned income, the relevant good is labour. In Figure 14.3, the demand curve shows how many hours of work are demanded at different wages. Labour should be demanded up to the point at which the value of the extra output produced – which is the marginal productivity of labour (MPL) – equals the wage (see Chapter 7 for a full analysis). We can assume that the more hours worked – with a given amount of machines, computers, land and so forth – the lower, eventually, marginal productivity will be. So, in Figure 14.3 we show a downward-sloping demand for labour. Because productivity declines with hours, the wage must fall if employers are going to buy more hours of labour.

The supply of labour schedule reflects the value that people place on the time they give up when they work one more hour. We can assume that, beyond some point, people place increasingly high values on the leisure they have to give up in order to work. The money value of the leisure given up will equal the wage that a worker has to be paid to induce him or her to do the extra work. So we expect to see an upward-sloping supply of labour schedule.

We also illustrate in Figure 14.3 the effect of taxing labour income. The vertical distance t is the tax on wages. This drives a wedge between the wage that the employer has to pay and the net wage that the worker receives. If we have the kind of demand and supply schedules that economists consider normal (downward-sloping demand and upward-sloping supply), the number of hours worked will fall at the same gross wage if the tax rate rises. The supply curve will move up by the amount of the tax, since workers' supply is based on their net, or after-tax, wages, and in the figure we measure on the vertical axis gross wages, including taxes (which is what matters to firms).

The grey triangle in Figure 14.3, therefore, measures the cost of the distortion. It reflects the fall in the number of hours worked *and* the gap between the demand curve (the productivity schedule) and the supply curve (the value of leisure schedule) over that range of hours. This is a good measure of the distortions introduced by taxation because it measures the lost benefit of work: the difference between what workers actually produced (marginal productivity) and the value of what they gave up (leisure).

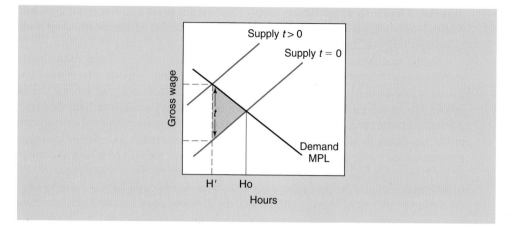

FIGURE 14.3 ● **Labour supply, labour demand and taxes.** Taxation (on wages) is distorting because it alters economic decisions relative to the invisible hand outcome. Hours worked fall from Ho to H' when tax rate *t* is levied. When a person reduces hours worked, MPL measures the loss of output; and the height of a person's supply curve measures the value of the extra leisure gained from working less. Thus the value of the distortion generated by a tax *t* is the grey triangle.

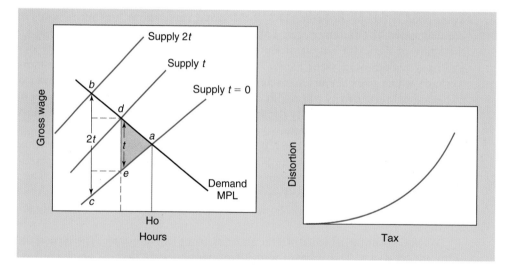

FIGURE 14.4 ● **Measuring the cost of labour taxes.** When taxes rise from *t* to 2*t* the cost of distortions more than doubles. The area *abc* is 4 times the area *ade*. Thus the cost of taxes is proportional to the square of *t*. If tax *t* is doubled, the distortion will quadruple.

This diagram implies that the cost of the tax rises with the tax rate. Not only does the cost rise but, in fact, it will tend to rise more than proportionally because we are multiplying a reduction in hours worked (which depends on the tax rate) by a *widening* gap between productivity and the value of leisure – the distance between the demand and supply curves. In fact, as Figure 14.4 shows, the cost of the tax rises with the square of the tax rate.

A key insight into the economics of taxation is that the distortions to economic behaviour that a given rise in tax creates are likely to be greater the higher the tax is (Figure 14.5).

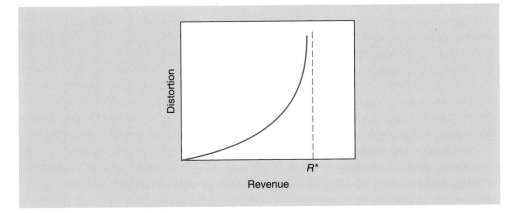

FIGURE 14.5 ● **Taxation theory.** Two important conclusions may be drawn from this figure: there is a limit to how much revenue government can raise; and the marginal cost of taxation, in terms of distortions, increases with revenue. The cost approaches infinity close to R*, the maximum revenue.

This implies that the damage that a rise in the tax inflicts is greater the higher the level of that tax to start with. A simple example may help to illustrate this. A rise in the tax rate of 10 cents on the dollar of labour income may have relatively little impact on incentives to work if it takes the overall tax rate from 5% to 15%. Workers still get to keep 85% of the wages that employers pay them. But suppose that the tax rate was already at the high rate of 80% on marginal (or extra) income. If employers do not change the amount of wages they pay, then the extra 10 cents on the dollar tax cuts the after-tax earnings of a worker in half – from 20% of the gross wage to just 10% of the wage. This example may seem far-fetched but, in fact, marginal tax rates on labour income in several European countries have, at times, been in excess of 70%.

The revenue that the government raises from income taxes increases as the tax is increased from zero, but it will ultimately fall as taxes deter ever more workers from supplying hours. The curve describing this relation between tax revenue and the tax rate is shown in Figure 14.6. This hump-shaped curve is called the **Laffer curve.**

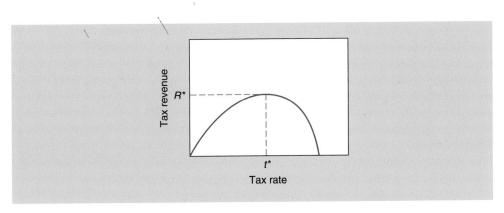

FIGURE 14.6 ● **The Laffer curve.** Beyond some point the rise in tax rates so discourages work that the overall tax revenue generated – the product of the tax rate, wages and hours worked – falls. That gives rise to the Laffer curve. The maximum tax revenue here is *R** with tax at rate *t**.

Notice in Figure 14.6 that there may be two different tax rates that generate the same level of overall revenue. The higher rate that generates a given level of revenue is one where the level of economic activity is relatively low and economic activity is taxed relatively heavily; the same level of revenue can be generated with a lower tax rate if, as a result of relatively light taxation, the amount of economic activity is higher. In Figure 14.6, the only level of tax revenue that can be generated by a single tax rate is the maximum amount of revenue, R^*. The tax rate that generates this level of revenue is denoted t^*.

Figure 14.6 suggests that it might be possible to cut the tax rate while boosting tax revenue – any cut in taxes from an original level in excess of t^* that takes the tax rate towards t^* will increase revenue and tend to boost economic activity. This argument for cutting taxes is often made by so-called supply-siders, who focus on the revenue advantages that lower taxes might generate as a result of workers' greater incentives to work and consume. The supply-side argument was the intellectual underpinning of the Reagan tax cuts in the United States during the 1980s and, to some extent, of the Bush income tax cuts in the 2000s. Figure 14.6 shows that its validity depends on taxes being beyond the level t^*. Whether that was the case in the United States in the 1980s or at the start of the 2000s is very far from clear.

What also remains unclear, even after decades of intensive research, is the scale of the damage done to economies by government intervention. The average level of taxation that governments levy varies widely across the developed countries. If higher taxes had dramatic negative impacts on incentives, we would expect income levels, growth of productivity and perhaps also levels of investment to be lower in countries with high levels of spending than in countries in which the government plays a smaller role. But if government expenditure helps boost education and health, then countries with higher taxes may have high growth. Figure 14.7 shows the relationship between government spending (as a percentage of GDP) and the growth of GDP per capita between 1990 and 2009. The relationship between these variables is not strong. Nor have more sophisticated statistical techniques established a clear link between the size of the public sector and the rate of economic growth.[2] The absence of

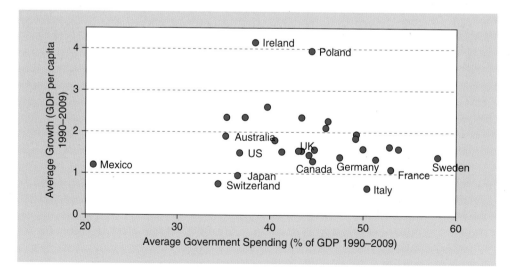

FIGURE 14.7 ● Government spending and growth: Is there a relationship? OECD countries, 1990–2009. There is no obvious, strong link between growth and the share of output accounted for by government. *Source:* OECD.

a clear link should not surprise us. What affects efficiency is how effectively the public sector provides goods and services and makes transfers. *Bad* government, not necessarily *big* government, damages a country. Furthermore, the distortions that taxes generate depend on the structure of *marginal* tax rates, not on the average tax take out of GDP. A government can raise little revenue and yet impose damaging taxes. An example would be a situation in which revenue generated was small, even though the marginal tax rates on income were 90% or more and incentives were badly damaged. The structure of the tax system probably matters more than the overall level of revenue that needs to be generated.

KEY POINT

The cost of taxes arises from the distortions to the allocation of resources that they almost invariably bring.

14.4 Deficits and Taxes

We have seen that there is a tendency for countries where the share of government spending in GDP is high to have high average tax rates. But taxes and spending do not typically match each other from year to year. Governments, like households and companies, can run deficits and incur debt. In fact, governments have a far greater ability to spend more than they raise in tax revenue than individual households have to borrow to finance their current consumption. Governments can raise revenue in the future through the tax system and, unlike households and companies, they do not have to sell commodities at market prices to raise revenue. This means that governments can usually borrow more, and at lower cost, than companies or individuals can.

Figure 14.8 shows the difference between annual US government spending and the revenue that the government raised over 200 years from the 1790s to 2010 (the total deficit). The size of the deficit is shown relative to gross national product (GNP). The three major peaks in deficits reflect wars: the Civil War of the 1860s, the First World War and the Second World War. For much of its history, except for during these wars, the US government typically ran (close to) balanced budgets; indeed, after the Civil War and the First World War, the government ran surpluses for several years and reduced the stock of debt. But for much of the period since the early 1970s, the US government has run a deficit – the first sustained period in peacetime when the government did not balance expenditure against revenue. For most of the period from the mid-1970s to the end of the 1990s, the US government ran deficits close to 4% of GNP. Only at the end of the 1990s did the US government move back into surplus, but that proved to be a temporary phenomenon. In the aftermath of the financial crisis of 2007 and 2008 the US fiscal deficit increased enormously, to a level that is unprecedented outside of major wars.

The experience of the United States since the Second World War is not unusual. Many governments in developed countries have run deficits on a scale previously only seen in wartime. In 1960, levels of government expenditure across the industrialized world were, on average, under 30% of GDP; by the end of the 1990s, expenditure was, on average, around 50% of GDP. Deficits have been generated consistently over the intervening period because the tax take out of GDP has not risen fast enough to offset increasing spending.

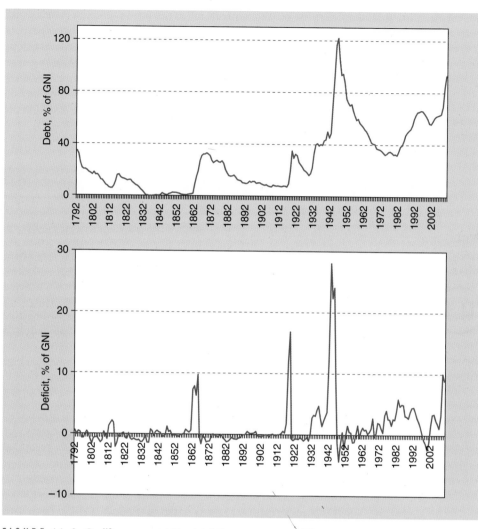

FIGURE 14.8 ● **US government debt and deficit as a percentage of GNI, 1791–2010.** The US government's stock of outstanding debt has fluctuated greatly over time, while the deficit has shown even greater variability from year to year. *Source:* Elmendorf and Mankiw, 'Government debt', in *The Handbook of Macroeconomics*, vol. 1c (Amsterdam: North Holland, 2000).

Figure 14.9 shows the fiscal deficits of some of the largest economies from 1970 to 2011. Through several business cycles, the major economies, in aggregate, have consistently run deficits; over the whole period, deficits have averaged close to 3% of GDP, and in 2011 nearly all of the large developed economies were running a large fiscal deficit in the aftermath of the financial crisis.

When a government is running a deficit, it is borrowing to finance the gap between expenditure and taxation. As a result, the stock of outstanding debt increases. Figure 14.8 showed how the stock of US government debt relative to GNP has evolved. Major wars generated a sharp rise in the stock of debt relative to GNP and the stock of debt tended to fall in post-war periods until the mid-twentieth century. Since the 1970s, however, the stock of debt has increased steadily relative to GNP, at least until the end of the 1990s. Figure 14.10

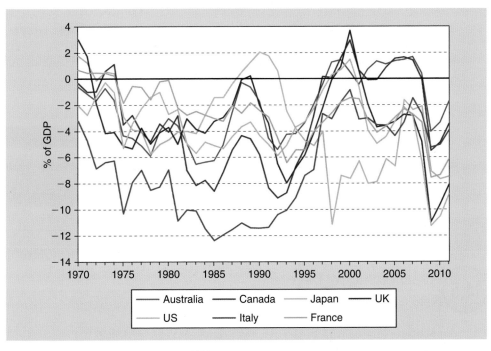

FIGURE 14.9 ● **Fiscal surplus as % of GDP, 1980–2011.** Budget deficits across the world's largest economies have fluctuated with the economic cycle: in the downturns in the early 1990s deficits rose sharply; in the upturns in the later part of the 1990s deficits fell. But with the financial crisis, deficits have ballooned in many countries. *Source:* OECD, *Economic Outlook*.

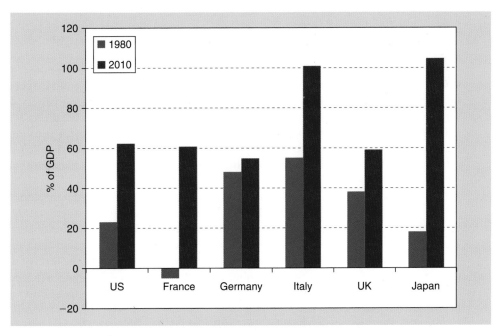

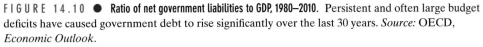

FIGURE 14.10 ● **Ratio of net government liabilities to GDP, 1980–2010.** Persistent and often large budget deficits have caused government debt to rise significantly over the last 30 years. *Source:* OECD, *Economic Outlook*.

examines recent decades in more detail. The figure shows that the stock of net government debt relative to GDP has risen in each of the biggest economies between 1980 and 2011, often sharply. Whether governments can continue to run deficits while preventing the stock of debt from rising continuously as a percentage of GDP is an important question, and we analyse it in detail in Chapter 18.

KEY POINT

In recent decades, governments across the developed world have run deficits more often than they have enjoyed fiscal surpluses. As a result, the stock of debt has risen in most countries.

(14.5) Optimal Budget Deficits

Budget deficits can be a problem or a blessing. There are powerful justifications for governments running deficits. First, governments may be running deficits to finance investment. If debt is incurred to finance investment that will boost future GDP and enhance future tax revenues, it will be self-financing. Running deficits to pay for lavish presidential palaces – which are unlikely to boost future GDP and future tax revenues – is quite a different matter from government spending to improve the transport system. So we should always ask what governments are spending their money on. If net government investments in productive assets more than match a deficit, then such deficits need not be a problem. Certainly, they need not be unsustainable, because the level of spending is likely to improve future government revenues and GDP growth itself.

Deficit financing can also be desirable when the economy suffers a temporary shock. Consider a major war, one of the biggest shocks that can hit any country. Increasing taxation to balance a budget during wartime could be undesirable, for a variety of reasons. In terms of equity, the generation that is paying for the war – in the direct sense of fighting it – should not also have higher taxes reduce its net resources for consumption. So on a pure *equity* argument, there are grounds for running a sustained deficit during wartime. But there is also a **tax-smoothing** argument – an *efficiency* argument – about distortions.

Taxes distort individual behaviour: they force people to do things differently, for example work less hard, spend less and so forth. These distortions discourage activities that are taxed heavily, even though using resources in those areas may be economically beneficial. Taxes move resources towards activities that are taxed less heavily, rather than towards those that are of greatest value. Moreover, as we showed in Section 14.4, the level of the distortion typically rises more than proportionately with the tax rate. This implies that governments should keep taxes at a smooth average level, rather than change them every period in order to balance a budget.

To illustrate the point, consider the results of two tax policies. One would keep tax rates constant at 20% through booms and recessions. The other would raise tax rates to 30% in recessions (when tax revenue would otherwise tend to fall and unemployment benefit expenditure might be high) to avoid deficits and lower tax rates to 10% in boom

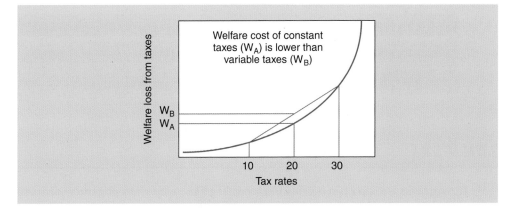

FIGURE 14.11 ● **Distortionary cost of taxes rises faster than tax rates.** Keeping taxes stable generates fewer distortions than having taxes sometimes well above, and sometimes well below, average.

times to stop a surplus from being generated. Under both policies the average tax rate over the cycle is the same, but because of tax distortions and inefficiencies, the constant 20% rule is better. Figure 14.11 shows why. Here the welfare loss from distortions due to taxation rises more than proportionately with the tax rate. Keeping tax rates constant at 20% would generate average welfare losses of level W_A. In contrast, setting tax rates sometimes at 10% and sometimes at 30% will generate an average welfare loss from taxation of level W_B – exactly halfway between the loss from a 30% tax and that from a 10% tax – which is greater than W_A.

If there are sharply rising distortion costs of taxes, then to minimize the harm of taxation, governments should *not* try to balance the budget every period with different tax rates. Instead, they should try to keep tax rates steady over the business cycle and thereby ensure an average budget balance. If the economic cycle lasts for a long time, tax smoothing can justify prolonged periods of deficit; provided, of course, that the government expects offsetting surpluses in the future.

This tax-smoothing idea has strong implications for how to deal with unexpected expensive events, such as wars (or German unification). Governments should only increase tax rates by a small amount when faced with an expensive, one-time event, but keep them at this higher level for a long time. This will spread the burden across many periods. Governments have followed this policy during wartime. We noted earlier in this chapter that government deficits in the United States have risen dramatically during wartime, but that the stock of debt had tended to fall again after the war.

Tax smoothing also has implications for long-term policy in the absence of unexpected events. *Governments should avoid changing taxes frequently.* Taxes should be set to ensure the long-run solvency of the government and not a balanced budget from year to year. Governments should expect to switch from surpluses during booms to deficits during recessions. Shifting tax rates over the economic cycle to ensure balanced budgets at all times would override automatic fiscal stabilizers and generate too much volatility in economic activity over the cycle. Raising tax rates at times of slow output growth (or falling output) and rising unemployment is likely to be destabilizing; it would aggravate recessions. Cutting taxes when demand in the economy is rising fast is likely to have a similar destabilizing effect, artificially stoking demand in booms.

> ### KEY POINT
>
> Budget deficits are not something to avoid. Matching spending to revenue in each period will generate too many sudden changes in spending and in tax rates. But deficits need to be either temporary or balanced by investment that generates higher future taxes.

SUMMARY

Governments are important because their spending represents a high proportion of overall total expenditure – on average around 40% in the developed economies. In Section 14.1, we saw that the range of activities undertaken by governments varies greatly across countries but that, overall, government spending has been expanding in recent years.

If markets worked perfectly, and if the distribution of incomes created by the 'invisible hand' of the free market were considered acceptable, there would be no role for government. But in Section 14.2, we argued that if there are market imperfections, this invisible hand result no longer holds, and government can make the economy work more effectively. Governments provide public goods, play a paternalistic role and attempt to correct undesirable distributions of income.

Financing government spending through taxes creates distortions: labour supply is affected by income taxes, and investment by companies and households is influenced by corporate taxes and taxes on saving. In Section 14.3, we concluded that the optimal scale of government is one that perfectly trades off the benefits from the government rectifying forms of market failure against the costs of raising the funds to finance spending.

Governments rarely match spending to tax revenue – fiscal deficits or surpluses are the norm. In Section 14.4, we showed that in the period since the Second World War, deficits have been much more common than surpluses.

Keeping tax rates smooth avoids excessive distortions in economic behaviour. In Section 14.5, we argued that governments should avoid rapid tax changes, aiming to balance deficits and surpluses over an entire economic cycle, rather than in each budgetary period.

CONCEPTUAL QUESTIONS

1. (Section 14.1) Figure 14.2 shows that the level of social benefits (e.g. unemployment benefits, retirement benefits and income support) varies hugely across countries. Why might this be so? Consider whether differences in the degree of inequality of pre-tax incomes might be a factor.

2. (Section 14.1) Some of the things on which governments spend money are luxury goods (goods for which the proportion of people's – or governments' – income that is spent on them is likely to rise as income grows). Health care and education may be such goods. If most goods that a government provides are of this type, the pressure for the share of government spending in total GDP to rise over time will grow. Should such pressures be resisted?

3. (Section 14.2) Should governments force people to be in school? Why or why not?

4. (Section 14.3) Resource allocation will be less distorted if taxes are levied on goods and services (including types of labour) that are in inelastic supply; that is, where changes in the price that sellers receive do not change supply much. But would this generate a fair system of taxes? What conflicts might arise between the design of a tax system that generates small distortions and one that is equitable?

5. (Section 14.5) Should there be limits on the size of budget deficit that a country can run?

ANALYTICAL QUESTIONS

1. (Section 14.2) Suppose that the average value that a person in a certain city places on having 1000 extra police officers out on the streets for a year is $10. Some people have a higher value and some a lower value. The population is 7 million. The city government decides to ask people how much they value an extra 1000 police to see if it is worth spending the $50 million a year needed. Two questionnaires are proposed. The first version of the questionnaire asks people to assess the value to them of the extra police and explains that people will pay whatever amount they answer – on the condition that the total of answers is at least $75 million. The second version of the questionnaire also asks people to reveal how much they value the extra police, but it says that everyone will pay the same amount if the police are hired, provided that the sum of the personal valuations exceeds $75 million.

   (a) What would be the results of the different surveys?

   (b) Which is better?

   (c) Does either survey give people the incentive to tell the truth?

   (d) Can you devise a survey that does make people reveal the truth?

2. (Section 14.2) Suppose that income is distributed within a country so that one-third of the population earns exactly one-third the average wage, one-third earns exactly two-thirds of the average wage and the richest one-third earns exactly twice the average wage. Initially there are no taxes and no benefits. The government then introduces a system of redistributive taxes and benefits. Those earning more than the average wage are taxed at 25% on total earnings and each of those earning less than the average wage receives the same flat-rate benefit. Total taxes received and benefits paid are equal. Assuming no change in pre-tax wages, what is the new distribution of income? Now assume that half of those with above-average incomes leave the country in response to the tax. What does the distribution of income look like then?

3. (Section 14.3) Suppose that you had information on the impact of spending on public education on the productivity of the labour force. You also have information on how education spending reduces crime. Finally, you have estimates of how raising extra taxes creates distortions to labour supply. Explain precisely how you would use this sort of information to help determine optimal spending on public education. What extra information would be valuable?

4. (Section 14.4) A government is running a balanced budget. An election is approaching and the government decides on a one-time, temporary, massive tax cut that will cut tax revenue by $50 billion in one year; after the year is over, tax rates and tax revenue return to normal. The government decides to issue perpetual bonds of $50 billion to cover the cost of the tax cut. The interest rate on these bonds is constant at 6%. The tax to pay the interest in the future will be levied on the private sector. Suppose that half of the population plans ahead and wants to leave enough in bequests to the next generation so that they are not harmed by future higher taxes. The other half of the population spends all they can now.

   (a) What is the impact of the tax cut on domestic saving?

   (b) What happens to consumption?

   (c) Who buys the $50 billion of debt?

CHAPTER 15

Stabilization Policy

Key Concepts

Phillips Curve	Ricardian Equivalence	Sacrifice Ratio
Policy Credibility	Rules and Discretion	Time Inconsistency

Overview

In this chapter we ask a big question: Can governments use fiscal and monetary policy to stabilize the economy? We saw in Chapter 11 that economies do not grow smoothly. Most advanced industrialized countries go through periods when economic growth is above the long-run average, unemployment falls and inflation is high. In other periods, output is far more sluggish, unemployment rises and inflation falls. In this chapter we consider whether fiscal policy and monetary policy can be used to make the path of output, unemployment and inflation smoother than it otherwise would be. We analyse whether trade-offs between inflation and output exist. We consider whether governments and central banks operate macroeconomic policy better when they have maximum flexibility (or discretion), or whether binding rules exist that generate better long-run outcomes although they reduce discretion in the short run.

15.1 Output Fluctuations and the Tools of Macroeconomic Policy

In Chapter 11, we introduced the concept of the output gap – the difference between gross domestic product (GDP) and its trend level. The volatility of an economy's output gap is one measure of the strength of its business-cycle fluctuations. These business-cycle fluctuations can be large, as Figure 15.1 shows. What can the government do to reduce these fluctuations? Can the government stabilize the economy by using fiscal and monetary policy?

We can use the aggregate demand-and-supply analysis of Chapter 11 to show what might be feasible. Consider Figure 15.2, which shows the case of an economy that has experienced a positive aggregate demand shock (e.g. an investment boom, a consumption surge

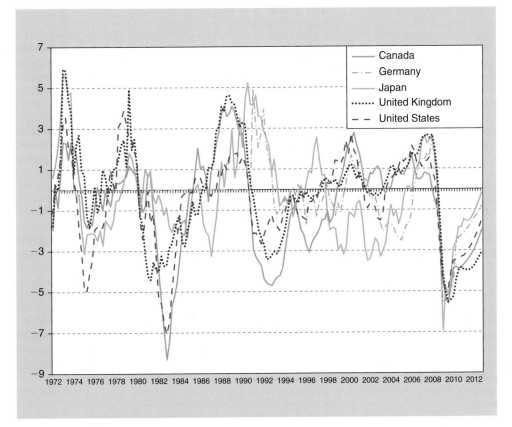

FIGURE 15.1 ● **Estimated output gaps in industrialized nations, 1980–2011.** Output shows substantial volatility over the business cycle. *Source:* OECD, World Economic Outlook Database.

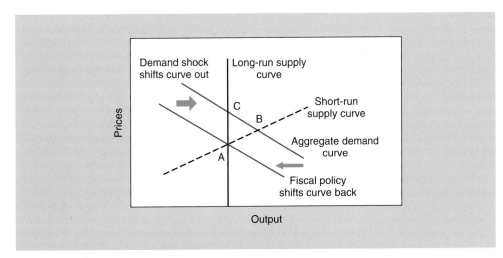

FIGURE 15.2 ● **Stabilization policy with demand shocks.** By changing monetary and fiscal policy, government may be able to adjust demand to stabilize prices and output in the face of aggregate demand shocks.

or an increase in government expenditure). In the short run, the economy moves from A to B – prices rise and output increases. However, at B the economy is producing above its trend level – the output gap is positive – so prices are rising. As prices increase, demand and output fall until the economy reaches C. The result is an increase in prices but no long-run increase in output. While moving from A to C, output and prices show considerable volatility. If the government could control the demand curve, it could reduce demand – for instance, by raising taxes, reducing government expenditure or increasing interest rates – and shift the demand curve back again. Prices would remain at A and output would not change. A similar logic holds for negative demand shocks. In this case, by boosting demand (through inter-est rate and tax cuts, or increases in expenditure) the government could avoid recession. Figure 15.2 suggests that governments might be able to stabilize output and prices by using fiscal and monetary policy to change demand.

Figure 15.3 illustrates how monetary policy operated by the central bank setting the inter-est rate can play this role using the IS-LM framework. Here the target for income is Y^*. Initially, planned spending generates an IS curve at IS_0. A surge in optimism in the private sec-tor boosts household and corporate spending plans, so the IS curve moves to IS_1. A tightening of monetary policy is required to offset the expansionary impact of this wave of optimism. The LM curve moves up from LM_0 to LM_1 as the central bank responds to the strength of demand by raising interest rates from r_0 to r_1 – exactly what is required to keep income constant.

Figure 15.4 illustrates another example of counter-cyclical monetary policy. Here, monetary policy is loosened to offset a decline in planned private-sector spending that has pushed the IS curve to the left (from IS_0 to IS_1). The LM curve shifts from LM_0 to LM_1 as interest rates fall from r_0 to r_1 – exactly enough to boost interest-sensitive spending so as to offset the fall in other components of demand.

Figure 15.5 shows the role of stabilization policy after an adverse supply shock, for instance an increase in oil prices. The increase in oil prices causes the supply curve to shift leftwards, which produces an increase in prices and a fall in output as the economy moves from A to B. B is below the trend level of output and so is not a long-run equilibrium. For the economy to return to equilibrium, either prices have to fall and the economy moves

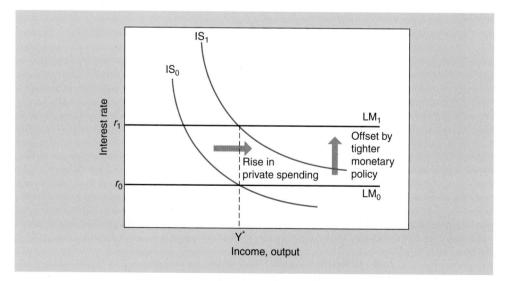

FIGURE 15.3 ● Using monetary policy to offset higher spending.

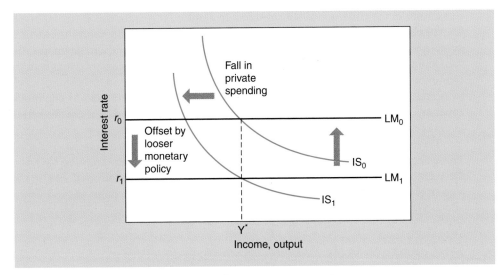

FIGURE 15.4 ● Using monetary policy to compensate for a fall in spending.

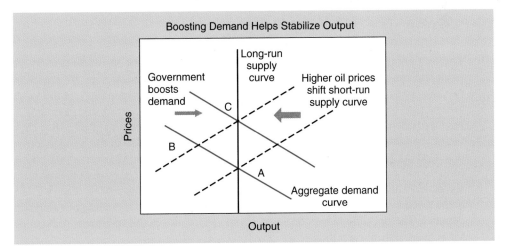

FIGURE 15.5 ● Stabilization policy and supply shocks. Using fiscal and monetary policy to boost demand helps stabilize output and avoids the need for prices to fall.

from B to A (which, given price stickiness, could take a long while), or the government boosts demand and shifts the economy from B to C. If the government does the latter, it will be stabilizing output but destabilizing prices.

KEY POINT

The idea that governments could manipulate demand and, in doing so, stabilize the business cycle was the essence of Keynesian economics in the 1950s and 1960s. There was considerable optimism that the adoption of such demand-management policies would eradicate events such as the Great Depression. The main issues concerned how best to boost demand – whether changes in interest rates, tax cuts or increases in expenditure were most effective.

Events in the 1970s and 1980s substantially reduced this optimism. Later in this chapter we will outline a powerful argument that says governments should *not* try to use fiscal and monetary policy in such a discretionary way apart from in extreme circumstances. Instead, they should generally follow fixed rules and avoid the temptation to try to stabilize the economy. We shall show that, in certain cases, we reach the counter-intuitive result that by doing so the government achieves a better outcome than if it tried to manipulate the economy. This is a positive argument for not using stabilization policy: there are better ways of doing things.

There are also negative arguments that stabilization policy will not work if it is tried. These negative arguments apply to both monetary and fiscal policy. They are based both on the fact that policymakers have only limited information at their disposal and on the time lags involved between the economy experiencing a problem and a policy response having its effect. We explore these arguments further in the next section.

(15.2) General Arguments against Stabilization Policy

AUTOMATIC STABILIZERS

The first point against an active stabilization policy is that to a significant extent government spending and revenue respond *automatically* to the business cycle. In a recession, tax revenue tends to fall due to falling incomes and private-sector spending. At the same time, government spending may automatically rise as expenditure on transfer payments such as unemployment benefit increases. As a result, even if the government does not change its tax or spending policies, a recession is likely to cause an increase in the government budget deficit as tax revenues fall and government spending rises (and vice versa in a boom). The processes underlying this natural change in the stance of fiscal policy over the business cycle are called automatic stabilizers; an increase in government borrowing during a recession helps stabilize the economy as lower taxation and greater government spending stimulate demand. The opposite occurs during a boom. These automatic stabilizers reduce the need for *active* stabilization policy.

UNCERTAINTY

In Figures 15.2 and 15.5, we assumed that the government knew by exactly how much the demand or supply curve had shifted and also what the trend level of output was. However, one of the key problems of stabilization policy is figuring out what is happening in the economy. Figure 15.6 shows a variation on Figure 15.2. In this case, the long-run supply curve has shifted out, perhaps because of some technological development, at the same time as the positive demand shock has happened. The government needs to decide how much of the increase in output has been caused by demand factors and how much by permanent supply changes. If it mistakenly assumes that the cause is nearly all demand shocks, then fiscal and monetary policy will be tightened too much and the economy will experience a sharp recession. Therefore, the government runs the risk of being the source of volatility if it uses stabilization policy when it is uncertain of the structure of the economy.

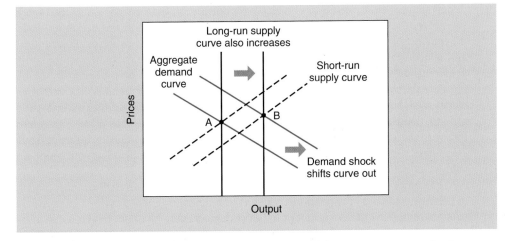

FIGURE 15.6 ● **Business-cycle expansion due to demand and supply boost.** Stabilization policy is complicated by the need to work out whether fluctuations are caused by temporary demand shocks or permanent supply improvements.

POLICY-MAKING LAGS

Monetary and fiscal policy are also subject to long lags. Stabilization policy faces three types: informational lags, decision lags and implementation lags. Informational lags arise because economic data are published only with a delay and even then are normally revised after publication. For example, in December we usually only have provisional estimates of what GDP was in June. Therefore, governments will only have statistical evidence of a boom or a recession several months after the fact. Decision lags arise because, even when it has obtained the data, the government has to decide how to respond. For monetary policy, when all that has to be decided is the interest rate, this can be done relatively quickly. However, fiscal policy involves many different tax rates, tax thresholds and thousands of government procurement decisions; fiscal policy cannot be adjusted so rapidly.

Finally, even when a government has identified an economic problem and adjusted its policy accordingly, it will take some time before the change has its full impact on the economy. This is the implementation lag. First, the policy actually has to be changed. In the case of interest rates this can be done swiftly, but for tax and expenditure plans, the process is more cumbersome and may even require legislation. Second, once policy has been changed, it has to have an effect on the economy. Empirical estimates suggest that it takes around two years before the peak impact of changing fiscal and monetary policy is achieved. Long, uncertain lags mean that stabilization policy may actually be destabilizing. By the time a government has boosted demand in response to a recession, the economy may well have recovered, thus the policy is simply adding demand to an already strong recovery.

PROBLEMS WITH FISCAL POLICY

Fiscal policy is not a very flexible tool. Changes in taxes are administratively difficult and take time. Government expenditure cannot be turned on and off like water from a tap. Government departments have to plan in advance. No one could run a government department of transportation in which expenditure on road maintenance fluctuated massively from year to year as the government tried to fine-tune the economy with sharp movements in the overall level of spending. The same is obviously true of defence, health and education spending. There is a tension, then, between sensible long-run planning for providing public-sector services and using the overall level of government spending to regulate demand in the economy. An additional problem for fiscal policy is that governments wish to achieve many objectives through tax and expenditure policies: long-run growth, redistribution, environmental concerns and political ends. These aims may conflict with the role of fiscal policy in stabilizing business cycles. This is different from monetary policy, in which the sole instrument is interest rates and the government seeks to achieve only limited aims.

The other complication in using fiscal policy is uncertainty over the impact that changes in taxes or increases in expenditure will have on demand. There are three channels through which attempts by the government to boost demand may be offset by the behaviour of the private sector: Ricardian equivalence, consumer expectations and crowding out.

RICARDIAN EQUIVALENCE

The eighteenth-century English economist David Ricardo (1772–1823) argued that whether a government financed spending by raising taxes or by issuing debt, it would have little impact on demand if people were forward-looking. The idea was that if debt was issued, people would see that this was just storing up more tax for the future. The **Ricardian equivalence principle** says that the impact of government expenditure on the economy does not depend on whether higher taxes or government debt is used to finance it. In other words, government deficits have no effect on the economy.

To illustrate the Ricardian result, consider a two-period model of the economy. The government can finance its spending (G) out of tax revenue (T) or by running a deficit and issuing debt (D). Let us suppose that the interest rate on government debt is r, and that this is the same interest rate at which households can borrow or lend. Any debt that the government issues in the first period needs to be repaid, along with interest, out of tax revenue in the second period. Finally, let us assume that households decide on consumption in the light of the value of after-tax incomes in both periods – and that, as in the analysis of Chapter 10, they need to keep the present value of consumption (C) equal to the present value of after-tax incomes (Y − T). This means that any saving in the first period (Y1 − T1 > C1) means that consumption can exceed income tomorrow (Y2 − T2 < C2), while any borrowing today (Y1 − T1 < C1) means that consumption must be less than after-tax income in the second period (Y2 − T2 > C2)

So the government budget constraint is:

$$D1 = G1 - T1 \tag{1}$$

$$T2 - G2 = D1(1 + r) = (G1 - T1)(1+r) \tag{2}$$

The household budget constraint is:

$$C2 = Y2 - T2 + (1+r)(Y1 - T1 - C1) \tag{3}$$

Equation (3) implies:

$$C2/(1+r) + C1 = Y2/(1+r) + Y1 - T2/(1+r) - T1 \tag{4}$$

This says that the present value of consumption (the left-hand side) equals the present value of pre-tax incomes (the first two terms on the right-hand side) minus the present value of taxes (the last two terms).

Equations (1) and (2) also imply:

$$T1 + T2/(1+r) = G1 + G2/(1+r) \tag{5}$$

This says that the present value of tax revenue (the left-hand side) equals the present value of government spending (the right-hand side). So finally, using (5) in equation (4) we have:

$$C2/(1+r) + C1 = Y2/(1+r) + Y1 - G2/(1+r) - G1 \tag{6}$$

This final equation says that the present value of consumption for households is the present value of pre-tax incomes (the first two terms on the right-hand side) minus the present value of government spending (the last two terms on the right-hand side). The key thing here is that this budget constraint for households makes no mention of the fiscal deficit. D1 does not feature in equation (6) – it is the present value of overall government spending that matters and not whether that spending is largely financed out of taxes raised in the first period or in the second period. The timing of taxes – which generates a fiscal deficit or a surplus – does not matter, simply the overall present value of taxes that need to be raised, which equals the spent value of spending. This is Ricardian equivalence.

Ricardian equivalence is a special result that relies on several strong assumptions. Ricardian equivalence is unlikely to hold exactly. However, it is the case that sometimes increases in the fiscal deficit have little effect on demand because of increases in private-sector saving. Unless the multiplier effects of fiscal deficits are predictable, using fiscal policy to stabilize the economy can be destabilizing.

CONSUMER EXPECTATIONS

As we saw in Chapter 10, how consumers respond to tax cuts depends on whether they perceive them as transitory or not. If consumers believe that tax cuts will be reversed as soon as the economy recovers from recession, consumption will respond only weakly, if at all. Only if the tax cuts are perceived as being permanent will consumption respond strongly. As tax cuts made to stabilize the economy are only temporary, this not only suggests that they will have only a small effect on the economy, it also adds an additional element of uncertainty as to how fiscal policy will work.

CROWDING OUT

There are a variety of different ways in which 'crowding out' works, but all have the same essential mechanism: increases in the fiscal deficit lead to higher interest rates and lower private-sector demand. If the government is trying to stimulate demand with spending that enlarges the deficit, the drop in demand due to higher interest rates 'crowds out' the government's efforts. If private-sector demand is highly sensitive to interest rates, these crowding-out effects can be substantial.

The classic way in which crowding out operates is through a larger fiscal deficit reducing the amount of funds available to other borrowers, including the corporate sector. This leads to higher interest rates, which leads to lower investment and consumption. The expenditure plans of the private sector have to be reduced in order to provide the financing for the fiscal deficit. For this channel to work, the fiscal deficit must be large relative to the amount of funds available in the loan market. In the 1950s and 1960s, when global capital flows were very small, deficits had to be financed largely through the domestic loan markets and so this channel would have been important. Given the size of global capital markets today, however, very few economies are likely to have a large enough fiscal deficit for crowding out to work through this channel. This argument is probably only relevant for the case of an extremely large US fiscal deficit. But this is a relevant case, since the US deficit in the early 1990s and the early 2000s – and particularly ten years or so later, after the financial crisis – was large and growing.

There are, however, alternative ways in which crowding out can happen. Monetary policy is set mostly by independent central banks, which may be persuaded to raise interest rates in order to reduce inflationary pressures if governments run large fiscal deficits. A non-accommodating monetary policy designed to keep the level of output steady in the wake of a rise in spending triggered by a laxer fiscal policy will generate a rise in rates. The higher rates can crowd out extra demand by curtailing interest-rate-sensitive spending. Figure 15.3 illustrated just such a case. These higher interest rates would lower consumption and investment and, through a higher exchange rate, lead to lower exports.

MONETARY POLICY

In many ways, monetary policy is a more useful tool for stabilization. Central banks can change interest rates at very short notice. The US Federal Reserve, the European Central Bank and central banks in Japan, Australia, New Zealand and the United Kingdom have regular meetings to discuss monetary policy, after which, literally within minutes, the decisions on interest rates that have been made are implemented. The lag between a decision and the implementation of monetary policy is virtually zero.

Nonetheless, many of the problems with fiscal policy are common to monetary policy. Private-sector expectations about the aims of policy are critical. Time lags between the implementation of policy (a change in interest rates) and its impact on expenditure decisions are long and variable. Much of the effects of interest rates on output and inflation may only come through after two or even three years.

Finally, although the ability to move official interest rates and other short-term interest rates is substantial, central banks do not control *real* interest rates of any maturity. So when they set monetary policy, central banks have a very indirect impact on the prices that really matter for many private-sector spending decisions. One would expect that investment decisions, precisely because they have long-term implications, would be most sensitive to shifts in long-term, real interest rates. But central banks only set short-term, nominal interest rates. This means that unless movements in interest rates set by the central bank can influence expectations of inflation and of future interest rates, they are unlikely to have a substantial impact on spending.

KEY POINT

Using stabilization policy is problematic and assumes a great deal of knowledge and proficiency among economic policymakers. Fiscal policy is not flexible enough and its impact too uncertain to be extensively used for stabilization purposes. Although monetary policy also has drawbacks, it is more suitable as a short-term demand-management tool.

FISCAL POLICY IN A LIQUIDITY TRAP

We have seen a number of theoretical and practical reasons why using fiscal policy to stabilize the economy is not generally a good idea. However, there is one set of circumstances where most economists would argue that stabilization through fiscal policy might be helpful: in a liquidity trap. The most common way to think about a liquidity trap is a situation where interest rates are at or near zero, but the economy is still in a severe recession, for example the economic situation in Japan in the 1990s and a number of major economies in the wake of the financial crisis of 2007–08. In these circumstances, a number of objections to fiscal stimulus fall away. First, the recession is so severe that the recognition and implementation lags of fiscal policy are much less likely to be a problem. Second, since interest rates are at zero and unlikely to be increased for some time, there is little or no crowding-out effect. As a result, most governments implemented stimulative fiscal policy during the financial crisis of 2008 and 2009. But, as we will see in Chapter 18, this can cause problems later when it comes to managing the extra government borrowing generated by such policies. Some argue that even in a recession and when interest rates are close to zero, the perception that fiscal deficits will have to be repaid at some point still means that the positive impact of running a fiscal deficit is offset by the negative impact of expectations of higher future taxes and so the fiscal multiplier is small. The debate about the size of the fiscal multiplier in the recession that followed the financial crisis of 2008 became intense – particularly in the United States, where influential economists like Robert Barro and Paul Krugman took dramatically different positions. Krugman argued the multiplier was significantly positive and that expansionary fiscal policy was called for; Barro – who had done much to revive interest in the concept of Ricardian equivalence – argued that it was very small and that fiscal expansion would not be effective.

15.3 The Inflation Output Trade-off

We shall now examine whether, using monetary policy, governments should seek to stabilize output. The answer to that question depends, in part, on whether there is a trade-off between inflation and unemployment.

Historically, there has been a correlation in most developed economies between the rate of unemployment and the rate of inflation. Bill Phillips, who spent most of his life as a professional economist at the London School of Economics, first noted this link.[1] Phillips observed an empirical regularity between unemployment and inflation. Specifically, he documented a negative correlation between the level of unemployment and the rate of increase in prices and wages. The lower unemployment, the higher inflation tended to be. The data he considered and the curve that explains this data are shown in Figure 15.7.

To understand this correlation, let's suppose that at some point in time people expect that inflation will be 3%. We will assume that the labour market is in equilibrium (at the existing level of real wages, all those who want to work can, and firms are employing precisely the number of people that maximizes their profits). In this case, if unemployment remains constant, wages should be increasing at the rate of expected inflation, so that real wages are expected to be steady (for the moment we ignore technological progress, which would allow wages to grow by inflation plus the rate of productivity growth). Suppose that instead of wages and prices both increasing at 3%, as people had anticipated, demand for the output of firms turned out to be higher than producers had anticipated and, in response,

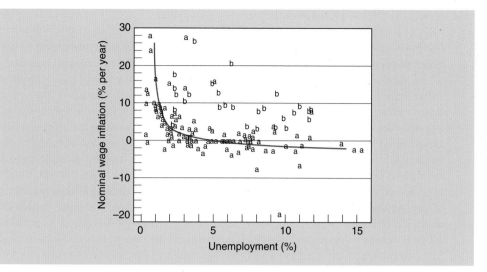

FIGURE 15.7 ● **Wage inflation and unemployment, UK, 1856–1997.** Phillips used UK historical data and found a negative relationship between (wage) inflation and unemployment. *Source:* Reprinted from Haldane and Quah, *Journal of Monetary Economics* (1999), 44: 259–78. Copyright 1999. Reprinted with permission from Elsevier Science.

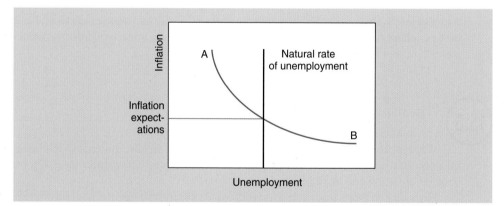

FIGURE 15.8 ● **The Phillips curve.** The Phillips curve shows a negative relationship between inflation and unemployment. Unemployment equals the natural rate when inflation equals inflation expectations.

companies increased their prices by more than 3%. If wages are fixed in nominal terms in the short run, then real wages will have fallen (nominal wages will have risen at 3% while the prices of goods will have increased by more than 3%, so real wages – the ratio of nominal wages to the price level – will have fallen). Because labour is now cheaper, firms will hire more workers to supply more output, particularly when demand is high. The end result is a negative correlation between inflation and unemployment, as illustrated in Figure 15.8.

Figure 15.8 depicts the **Phillips curve** for a given level of inflation expectations; that is, the relation between unemployment (horizontal axis) and inflation (vertical axis) holding anticipated inflation constant. We can represent the Phillips curve in a simple formula

Inflation = Inflation expectations + [A × (Natural rate of unemployment
            − Actual unemployment)]

where A is a positive number. This version of the Phillips curve states that actual inflation will equal expected inflation if output and unemployment remain at their equilibrium levels (see Chapter 7 for a full analysis of the natural rate of unemployment). This means that the point at which the Phillips curve crosses the line depicting the natural rate of unemployment gives an inflation rate equal to inflation expectations. If the level of inflation expectations changes, then the Phillips curve will shift to a new position.

Suppose that A = 0.5 and the natural rate of unemployment is 6%. Suppose, too, that everyone thinks inflation is going to be 5%, and unemployment is 6%. The Phillips curve says that in these circumstances, inflation will turn out to be 5%. But if unemployment were 2%, inflation would need to be 7%; that is, the 5% expected inflation plus an extra $0.5 \times (6 - 2)$.

In explaining why there is a negative relationship between inflation and unemployment, we made the assumption that wages could not adjust as rapidly as prices. It was because of this that the real wage changes, which in turn affects labour demand and unemployment. However, as soon as wages do adjust, the real wage returns to a value consistent with unemployment being at its natural rate. That is, the negative relationship between inflation and unemployment is only a short-run phenomenon: it is only while wages are sticky relative to prices that this trade-off between inflation and unemployment exists. When wages and prices have both fully adjusted, unemployment will be at its natural rate. Therefore, only in the short run can governments use demand management to affect unemployment.

Unemployment is a real variable that ultimately must be explained by real factors, not nominal forces. As Chapter 7 showed, the natural rate of unemployment depends on real factors such as the tax and benefits system, the power of trade unions, employment protection legislation and monopoly power in firms. The original Phillips curve contained no reference to inflation expectations or the natural rate; it simply envisaged a negative relationship between inflation and unemployment. It was through the work of Edmund Phelps and Milton Friedman that these additional aspects of the Phillips curve were introduced. As we shall see, the introduction of expectations and the natural rate profoundly changes the government's policy options.

There is one further addition to the Phillips curve that we have to make. We saw in Chapter 11 that supply shocks also contributed to inflation through adverse shifts in the supply curve. Furthermore, these negative supply shocks cause output and employment to fall. We need therefore to amend our Phillips curve to

Inflation = Inflation expectations + [A × (Natural rate of unemployment
     − Actual unemployment)] + Supply shocks

Supply shocks introduce another reason why the Phillips curve can shift. The negative trade-off between inflation and unemployment only exists for changes in demand: adverse supply shocks cause inflation and unemployment to rise together. *Therefore the Phillips curve exists as a short-run trade-off that the government faces when it uses demand management; it is not necessarily a strongly observed relationship in the data.* Figure 15.9 shows inflation and unemployment for the United States, Japan, Germany and the United Kingdom between 1980 and 2009. For Japan, and to some extent Germany, a negative relationship exists, but certainly not for the United States or the United Kingdom during this period. However, this does not mean that the Phillips curve does not exist. Any changes in inflation expectations, the natural rate of unemployment or supply shocks will shift the Phillips curve but, at any moment in time, the government still faces the Phillips curve trade-off in operating demand-management policies.

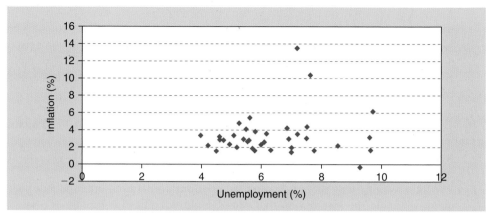

FIGURE 15.9a ● Inflation and unemployment, US, 1980–2009.

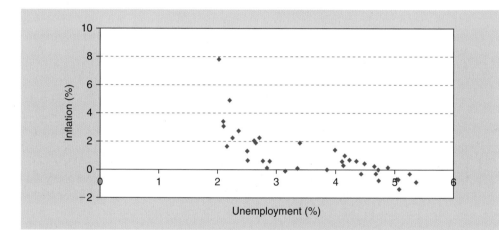

FIGURE 15.9b ● Inflation and unemployment, Japan, 1980–2009.

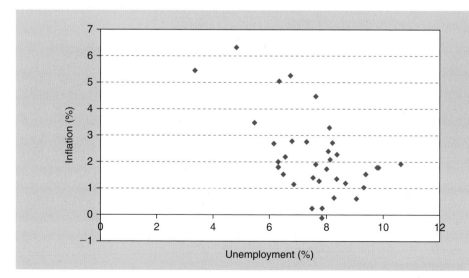

FIGURE 15.9c ● Inflation and unemployment, Germany, 1980–2009.

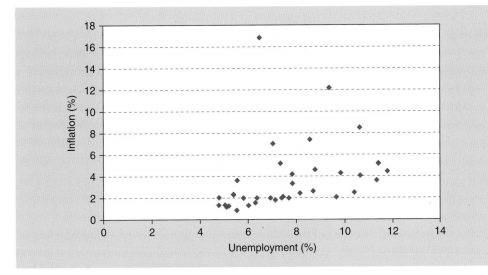

FIGURE 15.9d ● **Inflation and unemployment, UK, 1980–2009.** The Phillips curve is not always seen clearly in the data, as changes in the natural rate, supply shocks and changing expectations shift the curve around. *Source:* OECD, World Economic Outlook Database.

If there is a known, stable and predictable Phillips curve, governments have a tool to help operate stabilization policy. Using Keynesian demand management, it seems that the government could usefully increase or reduce demand depending on events in the economy. Therefore, it appears possible to achieve a preferred level of unemployment. The role of the Phillips curve is to tell policymakers the costs of a particular unemployment rate in terms of the inflation it will generate. If governments want to reduce unemployment and are prepared to pay the price of higher inflation, they simply need to increase demand within the economy, which will bid up prices and generate more inflation. To the extent that this inflation is unexpected, unemployment will be lower as we move along the Phillips curve from a point like B to one like A in Figure 15.8. Alternatively, a government may decide that inflation is too high, and the Phillips curve will tell policymakers how much unemployment they have to accept to reduce inflation. If governments believe that the inflation and unemployment combination of point A in Figure 15.8 is suboptimal and inflation too high, then the level of unemployment at B might be a price that they would pay to reduce inflation.

KEY POINT

The Phillips curve appears to provide a menu of choices for policymakers. It seems to imply that we can have 1% less inflation, but only at the expense of (1/A)% more unemployment. But, crucially, the addition of the natural rate into the Phillips curve limits this trade-off to the short run — while wages do not adjust. However, as we saw in Chapter 11, Keynesian macroeconomics tends to view price and wage adjustment as lengthy processes, if they occur at all. If this is the case, then the trade-off may exist for a substantial period of time.

(15.4) The Phillips Curve and Shifting Expectations

During the 1950s and 1960s, the Phillips curve was crucial to understanding how governments ran fiscal and monetary policy in an effort to stabilize the economy. However, Milton Friedman warned that the Phillips curve could not be used for this purpose and, if it were, the result would be ever higher inflation rates.[2] Key to Friedman's analysis is the fact that a different Phillips curve exists for each level of inflation expectations. If inflation expectations increase, then the Phillips curve shifts upwards, while a decrease in expectations leads to a downward shift. Figure 15.10, which shows UK wage inflation and unemployment, indicates that such shifts do occur. Between 1856 and 1957 (points labelled a), inflation was low and so were inflation expectations. However, between 1957 and 1997 (points labelled b), UK inflation increased substantially and so did expectations. The result was the Phillips curve shifting upwards.

Figure 15.11 illustrates Friedman's powerful argument. Suppose initially that inflation expectations are 2% and unemployment equals its natural (equilibrium) rate. The government, however, wishes to achieve lower unemployment and so increases demand by raising government spending. This leads to higher prices and inflation moves above 2%. Because of wage sluggishness, the real wage falls. This lower real wage leads to a fall in unemployment. The economy moves along a short-run Phillips curve to a point such as B – with lower unemployment and inflation above 2% (we have assumed it at 4%).

At point B one of three things will happen. First, wages may never adjust; the real wage remains permanently lower and unemployment stays at this low level. However,

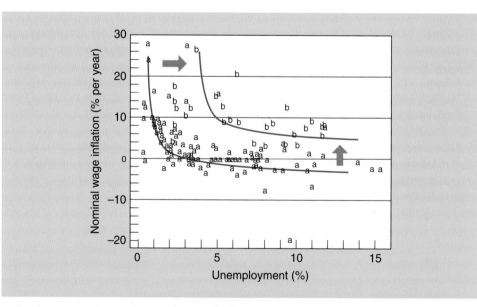

FIGURE 15.10 ● **UK Phillips curve and shifting expectations.** Increases in inflation led UK inflation expectations to rise and the Phillips curve to shift outwards. Point a denotes observations in period 1856–1956; point b in period 1957–97. *Source:* Reprinted from Haldane and Quah, The U.K. Phillips curve and monetary policy, *Journal of Monetary Economics* (1999), 44: 259–78. Copyright (1999). Reprinted with permission from Elsevier Science.

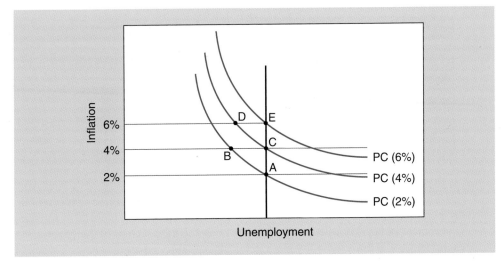

FIGURE 15.11 ● **The long-run Phillips curve.** Because inflation expectations adjust to higher-inflation outcomes, the government does not face a usable trade-off between inflation and unemployment.

for this to happen we have to discard our analysis of the natural rate as an equilibrium concept and assume that unemployment, a real variable, is determined by nominal demand rather than real supply-side factors. Second, nominal wages could adjust to the higher inflation level: the real wage returns to its equilibrium level and the economy returns to A. However, for this to happen, individuals have to display slightly strange behaviour. At B, inflation is at 4% and the economy can only be at A if individuals expect inflation of 2%. In deciding what level of wages to bargain for, workers have to form an expectation of inflation. In doing so, surely they will consider the current level of inflation. The government has already revealed that it prefers B to A, so if workers negotiate wages on the basis of 2% inflation expectations, inflation is once again likely to be 4%. The third possibility, therefore, is that workers revise upwards their inflation expectations to 4% and the Phillips curve shifts upwards to the line that we have marked PC 4%. If that happens, then if inflation remains at 4%, unemployment will move back to its natural rate (point C).

If the government wants to keep unemployment beneath its natural rate, it must increase demand again. But now, it has to generate inflation *above* 4% in order to lower the real wage. So we could move to point D with unemployment beneath its natural rate, but the inflation rate now has to be higher again, at 6%. But if the economy remains at point D, we would have to assume that workers begin to anticipate 6% inflation; inflation remaining at 6% would then imply that unemployment would move back to its natural rate at point E.

Therefore, if individuals adapt their inflation expectations in response to changes in observed inflation, attempts by governments to exploit the Phillips curve produce only higher inflation and no long-run benefits in terms of unemployment. There is a *vertical* long-run Phillips curve positioned at the natural rate. Friedman's crucial insight is that there is no usable long-run trade-off between inflation and output. The key assumption is that the natural rate of unemployment is itself independent of nominal variables and is determined by fundamental supply-side factors.

> **KEY POINT**
>
> Friedman's analysis of the Phillips curve is a forceful argument against using demand management to achieve 'full' employment. If full employment is incompatible with the natural rate of unemployment, then attempts at demand management will just result in higher inflation. However, Friedman's argument does not necessarily imply that stabilization policy must fail. After all, stabilization policy is designed to stabilize output and unemployment around some long-run trend, rather than to try to drive the level of output (or unemployment) permanently above (or below) that long-run trend.

The Friedman argument showed how important the private sector's expectations are in determining the short- and long-run responses to shifts in demand induced by movements in government policy. We will develop this theme in the next section of the chapter, when we examine the role that credibility plays in setting monetary policy. Friedman's argument also illustrated the enormous importance of the difference between shocks that might affect the natural rate of unemployment (and certainly would then affect the long-run sustainable rate of output or unemployment) and shocks that affected short-run demand. This distinction is critical to stabilization policy. Governments should not try to offset supply-side shocks that affect the natural rate of unemployment. If shocks occur that mean that unemployment can now safely be 2% rather than 4% without inflation accelerating, governments should not try to tighten policy and reduce the level of demand in the economy when unemployment falls beneath 4%. But if a temporary demand shock (for example, stock prices are bid up irrationally or consumers start spending in a wave of optimism) drives unemployment beneath its natural rate of 4%, governments might want to head off incipient inflation by reducing demand.

(15.5) Policy Credibility: The Good News about Shifting Expectations

Friedman's analysis suggests that governments should not try to exploit the Phillips curve in a regular manner, and it implies that demand-side policies cannot affect the level of unemployment. The reason for this pessimism is the fact that inflation expectations change with observed inflation. However, the importance of shifting inflation expectations also brings good news for monetary policymakers. Shifting expectations may lead to the ability to lower inflation without large increases in unemployment.

From the Phillips curve, we have that every 1% increase in unemployment produces an A% decline in inflation. Therefore, to reduce inflation by 1% we need to increase unemployment by (1/A)% – this is called the **sacrifice ratio**, how much unemployment needs to be generated to lower inflation by 1%. If, however, the government can persuade the private sector that inflation will be reduced, then inflation expectations will fall and so will inflation *without any need for higher unemployment*. Therefore, the more that inflation expectations change, the less disinflationary work unemployment has to perform.

To see how this argument works, consider Figure 15.12. Suppose that the private sector – either through inertia and myopia, or through scepticism about what government policy can actually achieve – believes that the current inflation rate is likely to stay the same. Suppose also that inflation is higher than the government wants it to be. To be specific, suppose that

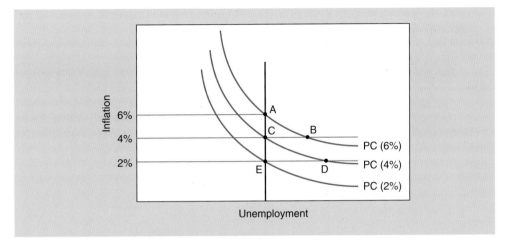

FIGURE 15.12 ● **Disinflation when expectations are slow to change.** The central bank can lower inflation either by moving along a Phillips curve by achieving higher than expected inflation (i.e. A to C) or by lowering inflation expectations (A to C) and shifting the Phillips curve down.

the inflation rate is 6% and everyone thinks that it will stay there. Suppose now that the government tries to reduce inflation. We can use the Phillips curve to work out how the economy might evolve. We start at point A in Figure 15.12. The government now tightens policy – by having the central bank increase interest rates, by cutting government spending or by increasing taxes – and by doing so lowers inflation to, say, 4%. But because people still expect that inflation will stay at 6%, they do *not* respond to this tougher policy by lowering their anticipation of future price rises, and wage settlements continue to run at a level that reflects expectations of a 6% rise in general prices. This means that wages are set too high relative to inflation, the real wage is high, unemployment increases and we move to point B.

If the economy remains at B for long enough, then eventually the private sector will adjust its inflation expectations. It will realize that the government is serious about producing low inflation and is even prepared to accept high unemployment in order to do so. If people now believe that inflation will stay at 4%, the Phillips curve shifts down and we move towards point C. But suppose that the government really wants to cut inflation to 2%. With actual inflation now at 4%, it has again to announce a tough policy of relatively high interest rates and/or relatively tight fiscal policy. If people continue to believe that inflation will stay at its current rate (4%), we have to endure the pain of higher unemployment again to drive the inflation rate down. Given expectations of 4% inflation, unemployment must rise to point D for actual inflation to be 2%. Only after another spell of unemployment do we eventually drive expectations of inflation down to 2%. Then we can return to the original level of unemployment, but with inflation at 2% rather than 6%. The government has achieved its planned disinflation, but only at the cost of a prolonged period with unemployment above its natural rate. The longer that inflation expectations take to fall, the more prolonged is this period.

But now suppose that the private sector was rational, forward-looking *and*, crucially, believes that the government will ultimately bring the inflation rate down to 2%. Then, as soon as the government announces its intentions, expectations of inflation move down from 6% to 2%. The unemployment rate does not have to increase at all. Instead, wage bargains immediately reflect expectations of 2%, rather than 6%, inflation. We move directly from point A to point E in Figure 15.12. The credibility of the government's policy, and the forward-looking nature of price setting in labour and goods markets, means that the sacrifice ratio is zero!

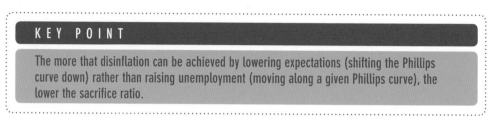

> **KEY POINT**
>
> The more that disinflation can be achieved by lowering expectations (shifting the Phillips curve down) rather than raising unemployment (moving along a given Phillips curve), the lower the sacrifice ratio.

Whether inflation expectations shift downwards depends on the credibility of the government's announced disinflation plan. Governments cannot just announce a policy of being tough on inflation and expect that inflation will immediately fall at zero cost. The private sector may have good reason *not* to believe the government. If this is the same government that started out with low inflation, but through its misguided attempts to lower unemployment raised inflation to 6%, the private sector will be extremely sceptical if the government announces a plan to reduce inflation to 2%. That was, after all, where inflation started out! In order to gain credibility, governments have to earn it – either by making tough decisions, for instance demonstrating the need to accept high unemployment in order to lower inflation, or by having a track record of always achieving low inflation. As we saw in Chapter 12, the Bundesbank achieved low inflation by international standards between 1960 and 1999 (at which point the European Central Bank took over interest rate setting) and as a result enjoyed substantial credibility. The Bank of Italy and the Bank of England have less impressive inflation records and their attempts at lowering inflation were hampered by credibility problems in the 1970s and 1980s.

Figure 15.13 shows estimates of the sacrifice ratio for OECD countries over the period 1980 to 2010. Over this period, inflation was brought down in nearly every country. But

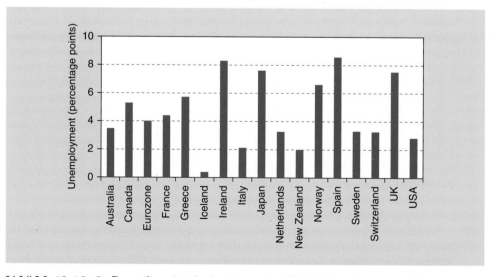

FIGURE 15.13 ● **The sacrifice ratio in developed economies, 1980–2010 (unemployment cost of lowering inflation by 1 percentage point).** The cost of bringing down inflation in the 1980s and 1990s differed substantially across countries because the credibility of policy varied. *Source:* Authors' calculations.

the cost of doing so varied greatly. In part, this was because the degree of credibility over policy at the start of this period varied significantly across countries. There is also evidence that those countries that reduced inflation the fastest (what is known as the 'cold turkey' approach to disinflation) achieved the lowest sacrifice ratios; that is, the smallest increases in unemployment.[3] When countries implement a sharp tightening of monetary policy, unemployment will rise substantially. However, this signals to the private sector the determination of the government to lower inflation regardless of the unemployment cost. As a result, inflation expectations adjust swiftly, the Phillips curve moves down and inflation falls. By contrast, if disinflation occurs slowly, expectations do not adjust quickly and the government comes under prolonged political pressure in the wake of a slow and long-lasting increase in unemployment.

(15.6) Time Inconsistency

A feature of our analysis in this chapter is the importance of expectations in determining the success of policy. In particular, we have found that the success of government actions *today* depends on the private sector's beliefs about what the government will do *tomorrow*. For instance, the success of an anti-inflation policy depends on whether the private sector believes that inflation will be low in the future. This dependence of the current situation on expectations of the future raises the problem of **time inconsistency**; that is, when the future arrives, it may no longer be optimal to carry out your plan. If people are aware of this problem, then they have no reason to believe your predictions.

The problem of time inconsistency arises in many settings: monetary policy, threatening punishments to children if they don't carry out chores or, more seriously, governments dealing with terrorists. Every government would like every potential hostage taker to think that it will never negotiate. If that really were credible, terrorists would never hijack airplanes because they would know, in advance, that governments would not give way. But after the hijack, when the plane is stuck at the airport with bombs on board and 80 million people watching on television, the government has a strong incentive to negotiate. This is an example of time inconsistency.

> ### KEY POINT
>
> A time-inconsistent policy is one in which a rule that seemed optimal at one time (e.g. we do not negotiate with terrorists) subsequently becomes undesirable. When the government announces its non-negotiating stance, it genuinely believes that it will follow this strategy. However, talk is cheap and, unless other actions are taken to make this a credible strategy, the stance will be ignored.

Time inconsistency is a major problem for governments when they wish to achieve low inflation. Consider again Figure 15.12 and a government that finds itself at A, with 6% inflation. If it successfully persuades the private sector that inflation will be 2%, then the economy will shift to E. However, if inflation expectations have fallen to 2%, why not generate inflation of 4%? This will produce a fall in inflation (from 6% to 4%) as well as a fall in unemployment, as real wages are pushed down by unanticipated inflation. If the private sector realizes that if it expects that inflation will be 2%, inflation will actually be 4%, then it won't adjust its expectations and inflation will not fall. If the government cannot credibly commit to producing low inflation, inflation will remain high.

MONETARY POLICY AS A GAME

We can show this more formally in the context of a very simple game between the private sector and the government. Consider the case in which the government can produce either low or high inflation. Table 15.1 shows the various possibilities for unemployment in this game, depending on whether inflation is greater than, less than or equal to inflation expectations.

Before we can analyse what choices the government and private sector will make, we have to know their preferences. We assume that the government likes low unemployment and low inflation, but has a stronger preference for low unemployment. Its most preferred outcome is scenario C (inflation higher than expectations and unemployment below the natural rate). Its next best outcome is A (low inflation and unemployment at the natural rate), followed by D (high inflation and natural-rate unemployment), and its least preferred is B (low inflation, high expectations and unemployment above the natural rate). In Table 15.2 we show these preferences and we attach numerical values to each outcome, reflecting the value that government places on each. The first number in each cell is the payoff to the government, and the second is that to the private sector. We assume that the private sector dislikes having its expectations turn out to be wrong; in other words, it finds only unexpected levels of inflation costly. Therefore, it is indifferent between low or high inflation so long as expectations are in line with outcomes. (This could be modified to have a preference for low inflation without altering our conclusions.) The private sector does not value

TABLE 15.1 ● Possible Outcomes in Monetary Policy Game.

The level of unemployment depends on whether inflation expectations hold or not.

Scenario	Inflation	Inflation Expectations	Unemployment
A	Low	Low	Natural Rate
B	Low	High	Above Natural Rate
C	High	Low	Below Natural Rate
D	High	High	Natural Rate

TABLE 15.2 ● Payoffs to Government and Private Sector.

The first number in each cell is the return to the government; the second is the return to the private sector. Governments will always choose high inflation, regardless of the inflation expectations of the private sector.

		Private-Sector Inflation Expectations	
		High	Low
Government's Inflation Choice	High	−3, 0	3, −3
	Low	−5, −3	0, 0

unemployment below the natural rate, because this is only achieved by real wages being low as a result of false expectations.

We can now examine the equilibrium of this game between the private sector and the government. The structure of the game is as follows: first the private sector negotiates wages on the basis of its inflation expectations, and then the government decides the level of inflation. It is crucial that the private sector makes its decision first – time inconsistency only arises because agents' expectations of the future influence the success of events today.

Consider first the actions of the government. If the private sector has high inflation expectations, then the best course of action for the government is to produce high inflation. With this outcome, unemployment equals the natural rate. If instead the government produces low inflation, then real wages will be too high (because they have been set assuming high inflation) and unemployment will be above the natural rate. Because the government places a higher weight on unemployment, the low inflation in this scenario does not compensate for the higher unemployment. Therefore, if the private sector has high inflation expectations, in this model the government will deliver high inflation. If instead, inflation expectations are low, the government will still find it optimal to produce high inflation. With low inflation expectations, high inflation leads to a low real wage and lower unemployment below the natural level. The government preference for low unemployment means that this outweighs the high inflation. The other alternative would be to have low inflation, but this would lead unemployment to be equal to its natural rate, which is not optimal for the government. *Therefore, regardless of the private sector's inflation expectations, the government will choose high inflation.* Knowing this, the private sector sets its expectations for high inflation.

The situation is illustrated in Figure 15.14. Notice that the outcome of the game is inefficient: society prefers the low-inflation, natural-rate unemployment outcome (A in Table 15.1) to the high-inflation, natural-rate unemployment outcome (D). However, it is not possible to be at A, because even if the government claims that it will produce low inflation, as soon as the private sector lowers its expectations, the government has an incentive to cheat, produce high inflation and lower unemployment. Sticking to a low-inflation policy is a time-inconsistent promise by the government and so the economy stays at a high-inflation

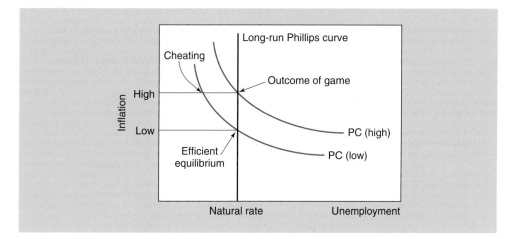

FIGURE 15.14 ● **Inflation bias.** Because the government has a preference for low unemployment, it cannot achieve a low-inflation equilibrium; inflation is too high.

outcome. The mere fact that a Phillips curve exists and may be exploited by governments creates an inflationary bias in the economy.

> ### KEY POINT
>
> If governments could remove the option to use discretionary policy and abandon the opportunity to exploit the Phillips curve, this inflationary bias would disappear. But so long as governments have a preference for lower unemployment, they will be tempted to use this option. Notice that this preference for low unemployment is futile: in equilibrium unemployment is at its natural rate, so the government never benefits from low unemployment. In other words, it might as well just focus on low inflation.

CENTRAL BANK INDEPENDENCE

How can governments overcome this problem of time inconsistency? As our analysis suggests, the answer is to give up the option of discretion and instead follow certain rules. One way in which this can be achieved is to hand control of inflation policy over to an independent central bank and give it the goal of controlling inflation *with no reference to unemployment*. By setting up incentives that penalize the central bank when inflation exceeds its target and by not making its prestige depend on unemployment, the government effectively changes the preferences of the policymaker. We saw in the previous chapter that many central banks have now become independent and that many of these have adopted some form of inflation target. Table 15.3 shows how we can incorporate this change into our theoretical game analysis. Assume that the central banker has no preference regarding unemployment, but simply prefers low to high inflation. The central bank is then indifferent between scenarios A and B (low inflation; natural-rate unemployment and low inflation; unemployment above the natural rate, respectively), but prefers these to C and D (high inflation, below-natural-rate unemployment; high inflation; natural-rate unemployment, respectively). Repeating our earlier analysis, we find that with these preferences, *the central banker will always choose low inflation, regardless of the private sector's expectations*. Given this, the private sector will set their expectations for low inflation. As a result, the inflationary bias disappears and the economy will be in a low-inflation equilibrium.

This result is obviously a paradox – by setting monetary policy without worrying about unemployment, the outcome is better than if you are allowed discretion. However, there are

TABLE 15.3 ● **Payoffs to Independent Central Bank and Private Sector.**
The first number in each cell is the return to the central bank; the second is the return to the private sector. By appointing an independent central bank to control only inflation, the preferences of the policy authority change and now can achieve the low-inflation outcome.

		Private-Sector Inflation Expectations	
		High	Low
Central Bank's Inflation Choice	High	–3, 0	–3, –3
	Low	0, –3	0, 0

many examples in which denying yourself certain options in the future actually generates better outcomes. The classical reference here is to Homer's *The Odyssey*. Odysseus knew that if he allowed himself to hear the Sirens' songs while he was still in command of his ship, the sound and sight of the Sirens would lure him towards them, where he would meet a horrible death. So he had his crew stop up their ears with wax and tie him to the mast, so that he could neither persuade the crew to change direction nor steer the ship himself. As a result, he could hear the beautiful singing of the Sirens without losing his ship or his life. This classic example illustrates the advantages of 'tying one's hands' – by denying yourself short-term flexibility, a better outcome is achieved.

The ability of independent central banks to overcome the inflationary bias of monetary policy is given substantial support in Figure 15.13. Countries with strong, independent central banks achieve substantially lower inflation. Some economists argue that all that Figure 15.13 shows is that countries that have a strong dislike of inflation achieve low inflation and have independent central banks. It is the dislike of inflation that matters rather than whether the central bank is independent. These economists argue that if society does not strongly dislike inflation, then an unelected central bank that pursues severe anti-inflationary policies will not exist for long. However, the logic of the time-inconsistency argument and the evidence of Figure 15.13 have been extremely influential over the last decade, with many governments granting substantial independence to central banks.

> ### KEY POINT
>
> It may seem strange for governments to hand such an important policy instrument over to an unelected group of officials and to ask them to target only inflation. However, our analysis shows that the fact the central bankers are unelected and do not have a policy goal of achieving low unemployment is crucial in achieving a better outcome for society.

(15.7) Rules versus Discretion

We have outlined three broad sets of arguments that suggest that in operating monetary and fiscal policy, governments may find it preferable to follow fixed rules rather than discretionary policies.

- Pragmatic concerns regarding whether the authorities have enough up-to-date and reliable information about the state of the economy and whether inevitable lags in the system will make stabilization policy actually destabilizing.
- Concerns over whether the government really has the ability to control the level of demand. The impact of fiscal deficits will, at least in part, be offset by the actions of the private sector, as we saw with crowding out and Ricardian equivalence. Furthermore, the central bank can only set the short-term nominal interest rate. The important long-term real interest rate is not under its control.
- Time-inconsistency arguments suggest that by denying themselves discretion and following fixed rules, governments can achieve better outcomes.

In combination, these three arguments have been so persuasive that most governments no longer try to use fiscal and monetary policy to fine-tune the economy. As we saw in

Chapter 13, monetary policy is now based on achieving announced targets for inflation and is operated mostly by independent central banks whose overriding aim is the control of inflation. Similarly, fiscal policy is rarely used in a conscious way to influence the business cycle.

But things were different in the slump that hit many of the rich countries after the financial crisis of 2008. Then some governments used emergency fiscal measures – including tax cuts – to boost demand. This was in a situation when interest rates had already fallen to close to zero. In more normal times, when interest rates are well above zero, governments now rarely adjust tax rates and expenditure in an effort to control the business cycle. Monetary policy is the main tool to smooth out cyclical fluctuations that otherwise might create volatility in inflation. Fiscal policy nonetheless operates to support this, because automatic fiscal stabilizers inject demand when the economy is weak and remove it when growth is strong.

Whereas the rules for operating monetary policy are now well established, this is not the case for fiscal policy and we expect this to be an area of considerable research over the next decade. Just like monetary policy, fiscal policy suffers from problems of time inconsistency. In Chapter 14 we saw that tax smoothing was an optimal policy. Tax smoothing implies that governments only need to worry about balancing their budget over a long run. Therefore, fiscal deficits are allowable today, so long as they are followed by future surpluses. Governments can thus justify not raising taxes today because of expected higher revenues in the future. But when the future occurs, the government may decide that it would rather spend these additional revenues, or even reduce taxes, rather than run a surplus. The result is that deficits are not matched by surpluses and government debt increases continually.

The perception that governments may face incentives to spend more than they raise in taxes lies behind the various balanced-budget amendments to constitutions that have been advocated in some countries (most notably the United States). The logic behind these amendments is similar to the arguments for central bank independence: governments (or politicians), if left to themselves, face too many temptations to cut interest rates or taxes, or to boost expenditure, in order to gain electoral popularity.

There are a variety of ways in which the discretion of governments in setting fiscal policy could be reduced. A particularly draconian form would be a requirement that government expenditure (or planned expenditure) could never exceed taxation in any year. In practice, to avoid the penalties of breaching this requirement, governments would generate surpluses almost every period so as to avoid even the smallest chance of not covering spending out of current taxation. A more modest balanced-budget requirement would have the government balance its budget over a longer planning horizon (maybe five or seven years, or some period reflecting the average duration of the economic cycle). Alternatively, restrictions could be placed on the size of fiscal deficit that a country can run. This was supposed to be the approach of countries in the European Monetary Union with the Growth and Stability Pact. But when France and Germany ran large deficits in 2003, they effectively ignored the rules of the pact. This illustrates the problem of time inconsistency.

Although there are analogies between balanced-budget amendments and governments handing over control of monetary policies to central banks, we should not take these too far. As we saw in Chapter 13, granting control over monetary policy to even the most independent central bank does *not* mean that monetary policy should be set to preclude stabilization. In fact, any central bank that was pursuing a target for inflation would almost certainly be loosening policy when unemployment was rising above, and output falling beneath, its equilibrium level and tightening monetary policy when the opposite was happening. The same would *not* be true, however, with a tightly specified balanced-budget amendment.

SUMMARY

In Section 15.1, we discussed how output and inflation fluctuate substantially over the business cycle. If this volatility is undesirable, governments can try to manage the level of demand in the economy using fiscal and monetary policy. This is stabilization policy.

However, we saw in Section 15.2 that achieving successful stabilization policy is fraught with problems. Knowledge about the economy and how it operates is imperfect, and macroeconomic data is only available with a delay of several months. Furthermore, the instruments of stabilization policy operate with long and uncertain lags. There exists uncertainty over the impact of these policy instruments on the economy, as the efforts of the government can be offset by the actions of the private sector. The delays and uncertainty over impact are particularly problematic for fiscal policy.

In Sections 15.3–15.5, we explored the implications of the Phillips curve. The Phillips curve is a negative relationship between inflation and unemployment. In the 1950s and 1960s, it was believed that this offered governments a trade-off between inflation and unemployment. However, recognizing the importance of inflation expectations and how they change over time led to a belief that the long-run Phillips curve was vertical. This also raised awareness of the importance of inflation expectations in achieving low-inflation outcomes.

In Section 15.6, we showed that, because expectations of the future influence events today, monetary policy suffers from a problem of time inconsistency. Governments may not find it optimal to deliver the low inflation that they promise. We showed how this leads to an inflation bias in the economy that can be removed if the government follows rules rather than a discretionary approach to policy. Handing control of monetary policy to an independent central bank is a way of overcoming this bias and has been widely adopted.

In Section 15.7, we saw that the preference for rules rather than discretion is now firmly based among macroeconomic policymakers. Whereas the rules and operating procedures are well developed for monetary policy, governments are only just beginning to investigate the fiscal rules that they should follow.

CONCEPTUAL QUESTIONS

1. (Section 15.1) How might a big hike in oil prices affect the natural rate of unemployment in a country that relies heavily on imported fuel and where oil is an essential input to the production of many goods? How might things be different for an oil-producing country?

2. (Sections 15.1 and 15.2) The natural rate of employment depends on the stock of capital, which in turn obviously depends on investment expenditure. The natural rate also depends on technical progress, which is also likely to depend on levels of investment and research and development spending. Suppose that governments can affect investment in the short term by

demand-management policies. Does it follow that demand management must have long-term impacts on the level of employment?

3. (Section 15.2) Think of how lower prices (or lower inflation) may generate greater overall demand within the economy. Could these mechanisms be more powerful than forces that reduce overall demand when prices (or inflation) rise?

4. (Section 15.2) Fiscal and monetary policy in small, open economies with fixed exchange rates are not likely significantly to influence the level of demand for the output of domestic producers. Why are things different in a country like the United States, which is not very open and has a floating exchange rate?

5. (Section 15.2) In the 1990s, as output fell and unemployment rose in Japan, the level of interest rates was cut to zero and the government ran large deficits; output remained depressed. Does this show that stabilization policy is ineffective?

ANALYTICAL QUESTIONS

1. (Section 15.2) The economy responds to changes in interest rates with a lag. Suppose that aggregate demand for goods is given by the equation

$$Y_t = A + bY_{t-1} - cr_{t-2} + e_t$$

where Y_t is demand in year t; r_{t-2} is the interest rate in year $t - 2$; and e_t is a shock to demand in period t. A = 200; b = 0.7; and c = 10.

(a) Suppose that the economy goes through many years in which interest rates are steady at 6% and there are no shocks. What is the equilibrium level of demand?

(b) Now there is a sudden, one-time shock to demand in period t of –30 (e_t = –30). Show what happens to demand over the next five years if there is no monetary policy response. (Assume that e returns to zero after the first year.)

(c) Now assume that the government immediately reduces interest rates from 6% to 3% to offset the shock. Show how the economy responds over the five years after the shock when interest rates stay at 3%.

(d) Can you devise a better response to the shock than cutting interest rates to 3% and leaving them there?

2. (Section 15.3) Imagine that the Phillips curve is

Inflation = Inflation expectations + [0.5 × (Natural rate of unemployment
            − Unemployment)]

Over the next 10 years the data are as follows:

Year	1	2	3	4	5	6	7	8	9	10
Inflation Expectations	3	3	4	4	4	4	3	3	3	3
Natural Rate	5	5	5	5	5	6	6	6	7	7
Unemployment	5	3	4	5	5.2	5.7	6.1	6.4	6.8	7.2

(a) Calculate inflation in each year.

(b) Draw a chart showing inflation and unemployment over these periods. What evidence do you have for a Phillips curve?

(c) Can you explain your answer to (b)? Can you rescue the Phillips curve?

3. (Section 15.3) Consider the following two specifications for the Phillips curve:

   Inflation = $5 - [0.3 \times (\text{natural logarithm of Unemployment rate})]$

   and

   Inflation = $5 - [0.3 \times (\text{Unemployment rate})]$

   (a) Graph each of these Phillips curves over the range of unemployment from 1 to 10.
   (b) What is the difference between the two curves? Which do you think is more plausible?
   (c) How does the sacrifice ratio differ in each case?

4. (Section 15.6) Consider the monetary policy game between the government and the private sector described in Section 15.6, but this time assume that the private sector dislikes high inflation, even if it is expected, and also values low unemployment. The payoff matrix is now

		Private-Sector Inflation Expectations	
		High	Low
Government's	High	−3, −1	3, −2
Inflation Choice	Low	−5, −3	0, 1

   (a) How does this alter your analysis?
   (b) How would you construct the payoff matrix for the case in which the government, rather than making the central bank independent, appoints a central bank chairperson with a pathological hatred of inflation?
   (c) What about if the government appoints a trade union leader as chairperson?

PART FOUR

Asset Markets and the Financial Sector

CHAPTER 16

Financial Markets: Equities and Bonds

Key Concepts		
Asset Market Bubbles	Dividend Discount Model	Fundamental Value
Capital Gain	Equities	Maturity
Coefficient of Relative Risk Aversion (CRRA)	Equity Risk Premium	Momentum
	Fixed-Income Securities	Yield Curve

Overview

The financial sector plays an important role in channelling savings into investment and borrowing to finance other sorts of spending. In this chapter we focus on the two key financial markets through which this occurs, namely the equity (or share) market and the bond market. We first contrast these two markets, showing how one gives you an ownership interest (equity) while the other gives you a fixed stream of payments and the right to force the borrower into bankruptcy if those payments are not delivered. We then look at how each of these financial instruments is valued and find that similar principles apply in each case, with the key difference being that equity gives the owner the right to future dividend payments that are not yet known, while bonds give fixed and pre-announced future payments. We also look at non-fundamental factors that seem to influence financial markets, including speculative bubbles, irrational herd-like behaviour by investors and myopia in forecasting the future.

16.1 The Financial Sector: An Overview

In the remaining chapters of this book we turn our attention to how the financial sector interacts with and influences the economy. This and the following chapter introduce the key elements of the domestic financial system: financial markets and the banking sector. Chapter 18 analyses financial distress and debt problems. Chapters 19 to 21 focus on international finance and the exchange rate.

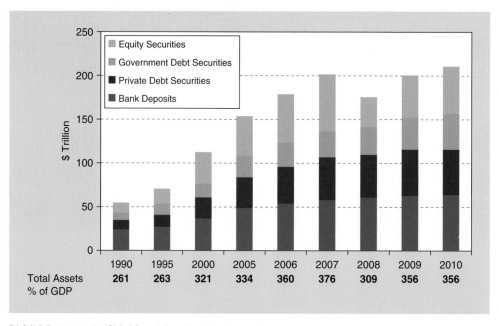

FIGURE 16.1 ● **Global financial assets.** Total financial assets were about 3.5 times more than global GDP in 2010 despite the fall in asset values. *Source:* McKinsey Global Institute.

Before looking in detail at each element of the financial system, we shall start with an overview of the sector as a whole, though here and throughout this book we largely ignore the more exotic markets such as financial derivatives that are better left to a finance text-book. Figure 16.1 shows that in 2010 the total stock of financial assets amounted to around 350% of global GDP (remember that GDP is a flow – the amount of goods and services produced in a year – so the stock of assets can easily exceed it). The major element of those financial assets is loans of different forms, made either through the banking system (as bank deposits that the banks then lend) or directly through private and government debt markets. Equities, which had been growing steadily since 2002, fell back dramatically in 2008 as the value of stock markets around the world dropped significantly.

Figure 16.2 focuses on the breakdown of those assets and liabilities by sector for Australia. Australia is typical in the sense that both the non-financial corporate sector and the government have more liabilities than assets and so are net borrowers. Those net lia-bilities are then largely matched by the net assets held by the household sector and the overseas sector. Once again, the fact that households are net holders of assets is typical of most countries. Despite the fact that many households have mortgages and other types of debt, that is more than offset by financial assets held in various forms such as pensions and insurance policies as well as standard bank deposits and direct share holdings. Australia's position as a net borrower from overseas is less typical; in fact, since the world as a whole cannot be a net debtor or creditor, Australia's position as a net debtor must be offset by net creditor positions of other countries such as China, Japan and Switzerland. We will look at these international net asset positions in more detail in Chapter 20. Finally, as is the case in most countries, Australian financial corporations have large assets and liabilities, but a net position of near balance reflecting their role of managing assets that are ultimately owned by households.

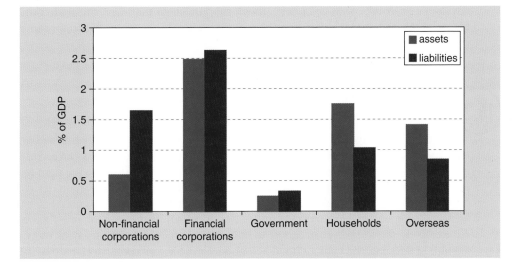

FIGURE 16.2 ● **Financial balance sheets by sector for Australia, 2008.** *Source:* OECD, *Financial Balance Sheets: Non-Consolidated Stocks* (2010); OECD, *National Accounts Statistics.*

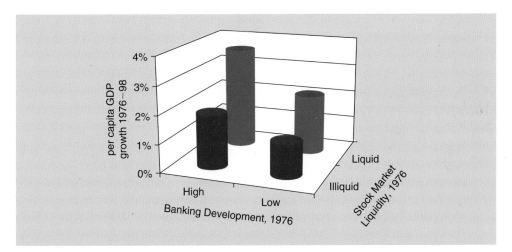

FIGURE 16.3 ● **Financial development and economic growth.** Evidence suggests that developing countries with more liquid stock markets and more developed banking sectors tend to grow faster. *Source:* R. Levine, *Finance and Development*, IMF, March 1996.

Perhaps the more fundamental question regarding the financial sector is its underlying contribution to the economy. In principle, its key role is to ensure that savings are allocated efficiently; that is, channelled to the most productive investment projects. In fact, as we saw in Chapter 5, empirical evidence suggests that the financial sector is an important driver of economic growth in developing countries. Figure 16.3 shows a summary of the evidence concerning financial development and growth in developing countries, from a study by Ross Levine. It suggests that both a large banking sector and a liquid stock market can be important for generating economic growth. In particular, by comparing measures of financial development in 1976 with economic growth subsequent to that date, the study avoids the potential criticism that it is economic growth that causes a large financial sector rather than vice versa.

(16.2) Debt and Equity

When a company is seeking to raise funds for investment, it has two broad types of finance to choose from, equity or debt. In the case of equity, the company can sell shares to investors that give them a share of the ownership of the company (and so the right to a vote on important corporate matters like the board of directors) and some portion of the future profits in the form of a dividend. The size of that dividend is not fixed and may well be nothing if the company makes no profits or decides to plough its profits back into the business. Alternatively, the company can choose to borrow the money either from a bank or by selling a bond. In this case, the bank or bond holder does not have an ownership share of the company, but is entitled to a pre-specified set of repayments in the future that pay back the debt with interest. If for any reason that company fails to make one of those payments, then the creditor is entitled to take the company to court and, potentially, force it into bankruptcy. A final, but important, difference between debt and equity is that dividends are paid after the company has paid corporation tax on its profits, while interest payments on debt are seen as a business expense and so are not subject to corporation tax. This distinction gives debt a tax advantage over equity. Figure 16.4 summarizes the differences between debt and equity.

(16.3) International Comparisons of Equity Markets

As Figure 16.5 shows, the importance of equity markets varies greatly across countries. For instance, in continental Europe stock markets have played a smaller role in funding companies than in the United States or the United Kingdom and the aggregate value of equities has constituted a smaller part of the total stock of financial assets. Where companies rely heavily on banks and bond issues to finance investment, and less on new equity issues and retained profits, the value of the equity market relative to GDP will tend to be smaller. And where private firms that are not quoted on a stock market account for a substantial part of economic activity, the importance of publicly traded stock is correspondingly lower.

Debt	Equity
Not an ownership interest	Ownership
No voting rights	Voting rights
Interest payment tax exempt	Dividends paid after corporation tax
Creditors have legal recourse if payments not made	Shareholders have no legal recourse if dividends not paid
Excess debt can lead to bankruptcy	An all-equity financed firm cannot go bankrupt

FIGURE 16.4 ● **Debt versus equity.** Debt and equity have different characteristics, though both are a form of finance.

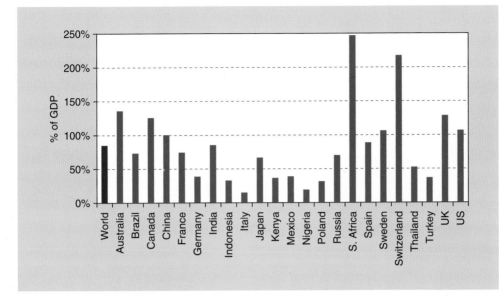

FIGURE 16.5 ● **Stock market capitalization around the world, 2010 data.** Market capitalization is the total value of shares listed on each country's stock market. *Source:* World Bank, World Development Indicators.

Another reason why the size of stock markets varies across countries is the presence of multinationals. For example, South Africa has a very large stock market in comparison to the size of its economy, largely due to the presence of multinational firms that operate across Africa and the rest of the world.

Figure 16.6 shows the nominal returns on US stocks, bonds (long-term debt), bills (short-term debt), gold and cash since 1871. The figure shows how assets would have risen in value before we adjust for inflation. However, adjusting for inflation is important. A dollar bill held since 1871 would have been worth about 7 cents, in real terms, by 2010; inflation has eroded more than 90% of its value. Gold, which is often thought to be a safe long-term investment, would have done better and been worth about $3.50 by the end of the period – still a miserable return over 140 years. Bonds would have done better still: $1 invested in the bond market in 1871 would have been worth about $32, in real terms, 140 years later. But equities do very much better. Despite big falls in 1929, in the early 1970s and in 2008 and 2009, the equity line consistently rises faster than any of the others. Note how even big shocks – like the 1987 stock market crash – have been washed away by the overwhelming tendency over the longer term for stock prices to rise faster than the prices of bonds, bills and gold. That same $1 invested in 1871 would have been worth over $6000 in real terms by the end of the period if put into US stocks. Furthermore, in almost none of the 20-year intervals from 1800 do cash (dollar bills), gold or US bonds or bills outperform US stocks.[1]

KEY POINT

Over the long term, equities have generated higher returns than nearly all other assets.

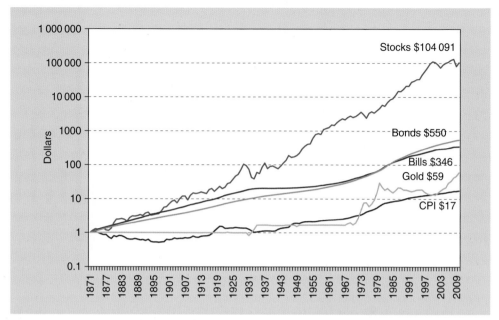

FIGURE 16.6 ● The value of $1 invested in 1871. Equities have massively outperformed other investments in the United States over the past 150 years or so. *Source:* R. Shiller, *Market Volatility*, online data, www.econ.yale.edu/~shiller/data.htm; and Reuters Ecowin.

EQUITY MARKETS

Once a company issues shares, investors are then free to sell those shares on to other investors at the going market price. It is the so-called **secondary market** for existing shares that dominates in terms of trading activity. If the company is doing well and looks set to pay larger future dividends, then the price of its shares may rise above the price the company issued them at and so the investor can make a tidy return by selling his or her shares to someone else. Share prices themselves fluctuate widely. Even if we look at averages of the share prices of many companies, which smooths out a lot of volatility, variability is substantial. Figure 16.7 shows the history of two stock price indexes for the United Kingdom and United States, demonstrating that while share prices generally go up, there can be extreme volatility – particularly recently.

The pattern of stock prices revealed in the figures and the data on the overall value of the stock markets across different countries raise several questions: Why do share prices move? Are the substantial fluctuations we observe in the stock market related to economic fundamentals or the whims of speculators? How important are equities in the portfolios of the private sectors across different countries? Why have equities in the past tended to yield greater returns than those earned on most other assets? Can we expect this excess return on equities to continue into the future? Economists have thought a lot about these questions. Equity markets fascinate them, partly because these markets seem to meet many of the strong assumptions that standard economic theory often makes: they are markets with many participants, none of whom has much monopoly power, all of whom have access to a lot of information, and most of whom want to make money. Does such a market really function well – do prices reflect a sensible judgement on the future earnings power of the

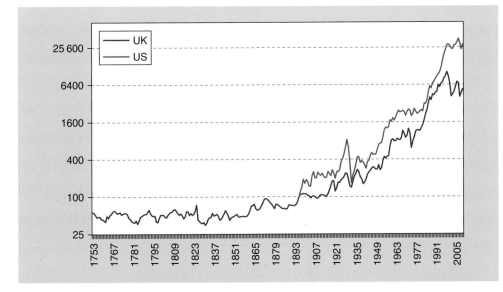

FIGURE 16.7 ● **UK and US stock indices.** UK's FT30 index and the US Dow Jones Industrial Index. *Source:* Thomson Financial Datastream.

underlying assets of corporations? Because stock markets are so important, this is not just an academic question.

We saw in Chapter 10 that investment expenditure should depend on stock prices. And we have also seen that in many of the major economies, total stock market values are large relative to the size of the economy. For both these reasons, how equity markets work has great economic significance. As well as trying to answer some of these fundamental questions about how equity markets work, we also hope to help you make sense of the massive amount of commentary on stock markets in the media. This commentary often addresses another set of issues, usually why the market went down or up yesterday. For example, a recent report we read on the day's trading in the US stock market said, 'On a wave of buying, US stocks rallied 220 points in early trading on Wall Street today.' However, because every transaction involves a seller as well as a buyer, this statement makes about as much sense as, 'On a wave of selling, US stocks rallied 220 points.'

The following section will provide a more formal analysis to help you understand how equity markets operate. This is worth doing, because how these markets work is important. It matters greatly whether stock price movements are the result of rational and reasoned responses by investors to information on the long-term economic prospects of firms or whether they are the result of a whim or of herd-like behaviour that is triggered by sports results, the weather or blind panic.

KEY POINT

The investment decisions of firms are likely to depend to some extent on movements in financial asset prices, so it would be worrisome if those financial market valuations were dissociated from fundamental determinants of corporate profitability. When markets work well, they reward those who are most efficient at producing what society wants and punish those who are not.

(16.4) The Determination of Stock Prices

Our analysis of what determines share prices starts with a model in which fundamentals pin down equity prices; that is, expectations of the future profitability of the companies whose stocks are being valued. Later we will consider additional factors, including market psychology.

Although voting rights can have economic value to shareholders, the fundamental driver of share prices is the future profitability of the firm and, in particular, the future stream of dividends that the firm will pay its shareholders out of those profits. To be more precise, theory suggests that the current share price of a company should be the *discounted sum of future dividends*. That is to say that in principle, an investor will value a share by trying to work out the future dividends she will receive from that share, but will value dividends in the distant future far less than those due imminently. More formally, theory suggests that the current share price $P(0)$ should be determined by the following equation:

$$P(0) = \frac{Div(1)}{(1 + r)} + \frac{Div(2)}{(1 + r)^2} + \frac{Div(3)}{(1 + r)^3} + \frac{Div(4)}{(1 + r)^4} + \cdots \cdots + \frac{Div(\infty)}{(1 + r)^\infty}$$

where $Div(1)$, $Div(2)$, $Div(3)$ etc. are expected future dividends 1, 2, 3 etc. periods ahead and r is the investor's required rate of return. The required rate of return can be thought of as the return an investor expects from an investment of this type expressed as a decimal, so if investors require (and in an equilibrium expect) an 8% return from their equity investments, r would be 0.08.

At first sight this equation seems daunting, as it implies that investors need to form expectations of dividends out into the infinite future. However, future dividends are discounted at an increasingly high rate, so for example since $(1 + r)^4$ is a bigger number than $(1 + r)$, the contribution of $1 earned four periods in the future is significantly less than that of a dollar earned next period. If the required return is 8% ($r = 0.08$), the value of dividends paid 10 years ahead is less than half the value of dividends paid now. So dividends far in the future may make little contribution to the current share price. Of course, in practice investors rarely hold on to their shares waiting for a long stream of future dividends; they generally hope to make much of their returns through capital gains – an increase in the share price over the period they hold it.

Overall, the expected rate of return from holding a share for a given period is equal to the expected capital gain plus the dividend yield (dividend payments expressed as a percentage of the share price). Given that investors' required return is r, in an equilibrium we need the expected return (capital gain plus dividend) to be equal to r each period, so

Expected capital gains + Dividend yield = Required rate of return

$[P(1) - P(0)] / P(0) + Div(1)/P(0) = r$

$P(1)$ is the price expected one period ahead
$P(0)$ is the price now
$Div(1)$ are expected dividends to be paid 1 period ahead.

How does this relationship fit with the previous one we looked at, showing that the share price was equal to the discounted sum of future dividends? To start with, think of the simple case where all expected future dividends are the same. In this case $P(1)$ should be the same as $P(0)$, since r and all the dividends are unchanged. As a result, there is no expected capital gain from this stock and so the dividend yield $Div(1)/P(0)$ must equal r. Of course, this is a rather unrealistic example, since the combination of economic growth and inflation should mean that the average firm is expected to pay larger and larger dividends over time. Imagine now that expected future dividends are expected to grow at a steady rate of g, so $Div(2) = Div(1)*(1 + g)$, $Div(3) = Div(2)*(1 + g)$ etc. In this case $P(1)$ will be expected to be higher than $P(0)$, since the first and all subsequent dividends for $P(1)$ will be $(1 + g)$ times larger than they were for $P(0)$ (since in period 1 the dividend that was $Div(2)$ for $P(0)$ becomes $Div(1)$ etc.). In fact, in turns out that $P(1) = P(0)*(1 + g)$, since all the dividends are $(1 + g)$ larger.

If dividends grow at steady rate g and the required return is r, then today's share price can be written:

$$P(0) = \frac{1}{(1 + r)}\left[D(1) + \frac{D(1)(1 + g)}{(1 + r)} + \frac{D(1)(1 + g)^2}{(1 + r)^2}\right.$$

$$\left. + \frac{D(1)(1 + g)^3}{(1 + r)^3} + \cdots\cdots \frac{D(1)(1 + g)^\infty}{(1 + r)^\infty}\right]$$

A bit of algebra[2] then gives us the following result:

$$P(0) = D(1)/(r - g)$$

If we rearrange this equation we get:

$$D(1)/P(0) = r - g$$

This equation says that the ratio of the next expected dividend paid to the current stock price, which is called the (prospective) **dividend yield**, is the difference between the required rate of return (r) and the long-run growth of dividends (g). Because we can accurately measure the dividend yield on a stock, or on an index of the stocks of many companies, we now have a way of judging what the gap is between the required rate of return and the anticipated growth of dividends. We just take the latest stock price and dividends and, by forming the dividend yield, we can measure the implied expected excess return over and above the anticipated growth of dividends. This simple and useful relation says that if the dividend yield is low, either the required rate of return on equities is itself low or the anticipated growth of dividends is high. It even shows how firms that currently pay no dividends can have a healthy share price so long as their expected future dividends are high.

KEY POINT

One interpretation of a low dividend yield is that people are optimistic about long-run growth in dividends. Another explanation, which is not inconsistent with the first, is that people come to see equities as less risky, so their required rate of return falls.

Either of these forces could account for a decline in the dividend yield during the early 2000s, shown in Figure 16.8. We will consider the risk premium issues in more detail shortly. But another explanation is that stock prices were just far ahead of their fundamental value by the end of the 1990s – for some reason, share prices had become higher than would be predicted by companies' earnings. In the light of the large falls in stock prices in 2008–09, this now looks more likely.

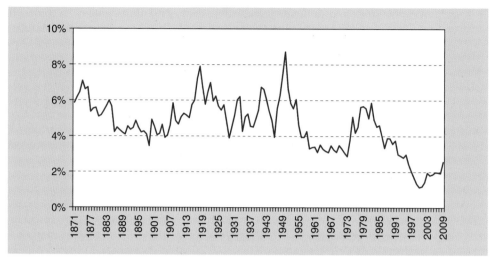

FIGURE 16.8 ● US dividend yield since 1871. Low dividend yield may indicate higher expected growth, a lower required return or simply mispricing. *Source:* R. Shiller, *Market Volatility*, online data, www.econ.yale.edu/~shiller/data.htm.

16.5   On the Unpredictability of Share Prices

We have offered a theory of what determines share prices based on fundamentals: the anticipated value of future corporate dividends. But can we use this theory to make money? That depends on how predictable stock price movements might be, which, in turn, depends on what drives share values. Our examples so far have focused on changes in stock prices that are driven by news about economic fundamentals. But rational expectations of current and future economic conditions are not the only determinants of stock prices.[3] Expectations do not have to be formed in a scientific, logical, coherent, consistent way. Indeed, many puzzles about stock market prices and movements in returns on equities are hard to square with the view that prices are the discounted value of expected future earnings *and* that people form rational and coherent expectations. We will look at some of that evidence shortly.

But even our theory of rational investors evaluating the fundamentals before purchasing a stock is consistent with volatile and unpredictable movements in share prices. Indeed, we shall now show that if the world is peopled by rational, calculating individuals, movements in stock prices over short periods should appear to be random and unforecastable. If that is so, even smart people won't be able to make money by predicting movements in stock market prices.

Assume that stock prices are equal to the discounted values of the sum of future expected dividends. We could then think of the *change* in the price of an equity over a short period as simply being equal to the *change* in the expectation of the (discounted) stream of future dividend payments – assuming that the required rate of return does not change. If this is the case, then rational behaviour makes those changes unforecastable. In other words, share prices should be unpredictable.

We should dwell on this point for a moment and illustrate it with an example. Suppose that I asked you now what your best guess is for the temperature at noon in New York City on Christmas Day, 2050. Let's say that your answer is 30 degrees Fahrenheit. Now suppose that I ask you a different question: 'What do you expect your answer will be if I ask this same question again a year from now?' Any answer other than 30 degrees Fahrenheit would be illogical. It would make no sense to say that your best guess now about the temperature in New York City at Christmas 2050 is 30 degrees, but that you also expected that your best guess about the answer to the *same* question a year from now would be different. That is not to say that when I ask you *in a year's time* that you must still answer 30 degrees. In the meantime, you may have all kinds of news about global warming and how it will affect New York and, if so, you would be perfectly reasonable to change your answer. But the key point is that you cannot *now* expect your best guess to be different in the future. Any change in expectations must be unforecastable if you are using information sensibly. In other words, while you are quite likely to change your forecast of the temperature in New York at Christmas 2050 over the coming years, you cannot predict how you will revise your forecast. That is, you should not be able to forecast changes in your own forecast.

The same logic applies to your best guess about future dividends. We have shown that the current stock price depends on your current forecast of all future dividends. Similarly, the stock price in a year will reflect your forecast in a year of all future dividends. Therefore, the difference in the share price today and next period will reflect how your forecasts of future dividends have altered. If you revise your forecasts of future dividends upwards, the share price will rise; if you revise your forecast downwards, the share price will fall. However, *you cannot today forecast how you will change your forecast* – just as with the New York temperature example, this would be irrational. Therefore, your current best guess of the next period's stock price must be today's price (plus any expected growth in dividends). Changes in future stock prices should be unpredictable (other than the 'drift' element associated with expected dividend growth). Technically this means that stock prices should follow what is called a 'random walk' (with a drift of *g*): whatever the past path of the price, the next move in expected future dividends is as likely to be up as down.

> ### KEY POINT
>
> Random fluctuations in stock prices, rather than necessarily being the result of chaos, irrational behaviour, indecision, inconsistency, bubbles or other hiccups in the market, are more or less an implication of rational and efficient behaviour.

This combination of rationality and the forward-looking nature of stock prices also explains other features of stock prices that might appear puzzling. When the central bank cuts interest rates or a firm announces an increase in dividends, the share price often falls. How can this be? We have just shown at great length that lower interest rates or higher dividends should *boost* the current stock price. However, the market expectation of future events affects share prices.

Imagine that the market expects the central bank to cut interest rates by 0.5% or expects a firm to announce a 10% increase in dividends. The market will therefore price stocks based on these assumptions. If the central bank only cuts interest rates by 0.25%, or the firm announces only a 5% rise in dividends, the market will have to change its forecast. The market now sees that interest rates will not be as low as it thought or that dividends will be lower than forecast, so the price of shares will fall. Similarly, if the central bank cut rates by 1%, or the firm announced dividend growth of 20%, the stock price would rise. Finally, if the interest rate cut was 0.5% or dividend growth was 10%, nothing would happen – the market had already forecast this, so these announcements contain no information and the market has no reason to change its forecast. As a result, the stock price does not alter.

16.6 Risk, Equity Prices and Excess Return

We noted above that, at least in the United States, the rate of return on equities over the last 100 years had, on average, substantially exceeded the rate of return available on government bonds. This makes perfect sense as long as the risk on equities substantially exceeds the risk of those other investments. But what do we mean by risk here, and how might we measure it? The answer to these questions matters a lot, because movements in the risk premium can dramatically affect stock prices. If people come to think of equities as much more risky, they might require that, on average, they offer a return of 10% more than government bonds, rather than, say, 5% more. Discounting future dividends at a rate that is higher by 5% could easily generate 40% or 50% falls in the price of equities. Anything that causes the required rate of return to increase will decrease share prices unless there are compensating shifts in future dividends. Therefore, increases in risk premiums will lead to sharp falls in share prices *even if investor forecasts of future dividends do not change.*

The simple dividend discount model for stock prices, combined with an assumption of anticipated steady dividend growth, generates a link between stock prices, the latest dividend payment and the relative magnitudes of the overall required return and the expected growth in dividends:

$$P = D/(r - g)$$

The required return on equities, r, is the sum of a safe rate and the risk premium. Let us consider some plausible magnitudes for a developed economy. The safe (real) rate might be around 3%. With a risk premium of 4%, $r = 7$%. If dividends grow in line with GDP, 2% a year might be plausible, giving a value for $(r - g)$ of 5%, so that the price-to-dividend ratio is 20. Suppose that the risk premium falls to 2%; $(r - g)$ is now 3% and the price to dividend ratio rises to 33 – an increase in stock prices of 65%!

As long as investors perceive that equities are riskier than other assets, they will have to yield a higher rate of return. Can we therefore use this perspective to explain Figure 16.6, which shows by just how much equities have outperformed rates of return than other conventional assets? The first issue to consider here is whether equities really are riskier than most other investment categories.

It may seem obvious that equities are riskier than bank deposits or government bonds, since they are far more volatile. But that is a hasty conclusion. What matters are *real* rates of returns; that is, the proportionate increase in the money value of the asset less the rise in the general cost of living. Most government bonds guarantee a nominal rate of return and, even then, that return is only guaranteed if you hold the debt until maturity and if the government has a zero probability of default. Holders of US, Italian and UK government bonds found that those assets generated substantial negative real returns through much of the 1970s because inflation was higher than expected. Holders of Russian government bonds had a much nastier shock in 1998: their market value fell by about 80% during the year. Nor do bank deposits generate predictable real rates of return; inflation is unpredictable even over a five-month horizon, let alone over five or ten years. These facts should make us think harder about the relative riskiness of equities and other assets.

TABLE 16.1 ● **The Equity Premium in the United States.**

Time Periods	Return on 'Riskless' Asset (Commercial Paper Rate)	Return on S&P Stocks	Risk Premium
1900–2000	4.10%	10.10%	5.80%

Source: Dimson, Marsh and Staunton, *Triumph of the Optimists: 101 Years of Global Investment* (Princeton, NJ: Princeton University Press, 2002).

To gauge whether the extra return over bonds or bank deposits that investors in US or UK equities have received over the last century is a fair compensation for risk, we need to use a more formal apparatus. In 1985, Raj Mehra and Ed Prescott published an influential paper on the 'equity premium'; that is, the extra return that equities yield over risk-free assets.[4] Using past data, Mehra and Prescott estimated that the US risk premium was about 6%. Another team of researchers, Dimson, Marsh and Staunton, examined excess return on equities over the past 100 years. As summarized in Table 16.1, they also found an average excess return on equities of nearly 6%.[5]

Mehra and Prescott's paper suggests that the equity premium has been too high. In other words, investors have been overcompensated for the higher risk that equities involve. Mehra and Prescott call this the 'equity premium puzzle' – the puzzle is, why do equities yield such a high rate of return?

Of course, whether this is a puzzle depends on how investors – ultimately you and me – feel about taking risks.[6] The measure of risk aversion that economists most frequently use is called the **coefficient of relative risk aversion (CRRA)**. Mehra and Prescott argued that unless for the typical investor this measure is massively above 2 (and probably above 10), standard economic theory cannot account for the observed magnitude of the equity premium.

But what does a CRRA of 2 or 10 mean, and are people this averse to uncertainty? Suppose that you have been offered a job that is potentially lucrative but risky. If the job goes well, you will get an average annual income over the next 20 years (in present value terms) of $80 000. The value of your human capital (the present value of future labour income) would then be $1.6 million (20 × $80 000). We will assume that this is your only source of wealth. But there is a 50% chance that the risky job will go badly – there are spells of unemployment and you have to change firms. These factors will have a negative impact on your reputation and your resumé. If the job goes badly, your average income over the next 20 years would be only $20 000 (in present value), so that the overall value of human capital would be $400 000 (20 × $20 000).

We can work out how risk averse you are by knowing what certain level of income in a completely safe job gives you the same utility, or happiness, level as accepting this risky job. If you would consider a safe job earning an average salary of $50 000 a year as giving you the same welfare as the risky job, you have no aversion to risk; your CRRA is 0. This is because the expected value of the average annual salary in the risky job is $50 000 – halfway between the good outcome ($80 000) and the bad outcome ($20 000) – which is exactly the same as the guaranteed income in the safe job. A CRRA of 0 therefore indicates that individuals are indifferent between certain outcomes and risky outcomes with the same average value.

However, if an investor has a CRRA of greater than 0, she would rather take the certain salary than a risky one that is only on average the same. This also implies that she would prefer a slightly lower salary if it was guaranteed rather than a higher but riskier salary. The degree of risk aversion determines exactly how much lower the guaranteed salary can be for the person to be indifferent. For instance, if you think a job that guarantees you an annual salary of $48 000 gives you the same utility as the risky job in our example, your level of CRRA is 0.21; this is close to being indifferent to risk, certainly not very risk averse. As we increase the level of risk aversion, the guaranteed income the person requires falls: for instance, with a CRRA of 0.4, the fixed income falls to $46 000. By the time the CRRA rises to 4, it implies a safe salary of only $25 000.

Remember that Mehra and Prescott concluded that unless CRRA was substantially greater than 4, standard economic theory could not account for the observed historical equity premium. As our example shows, this implies that investors would need to be incredibly risk averse. As a result, Mehra and Precott conclude that US equities have yielded far too much for the excess returns just to reflect a risk premium.

If Mehra and Prescott are right, the market has mispriced equities in the largest stock market in the world for over 100 years and by a huge magnitude. The scale of that mispricing is staggering. Suppose that equities, on average, should not yield any more than 'safe' government debt – perhaps around 2% per year in real terms. In that case, $1000 invested in 1870 in the stock market should have generated a value by 2000 of about $(1.02)^{130}$, which is about $13 122. In fact, the rate of return was more like 7% a year, so that the real value of $1000 invested in equity was by the end of the period about $6 605 000. This is about 500 times its assumed fair value, which by any criterion would imply colossal market error and overcompensation for risk bearing.

There are a variety of explanations for the equity premium; perhaps one of the most interesting is the concept of survivorship bias. When we look at stock markets today, it is natural to focus on the US market since it is by far the largest, but what about in 1870? At that date the Russian market might have seemed a good bet, but in fact your investment would have been entirely wiped out in 1917. So by focusing on the largest market today we are inadvertently picking a winner and excluding markets that either performed very badly or did not survive at all. So when we find that the US market performed better than might be expected by the average stock market, that is because we have actually picked a market with a better than average track record.

(16.7) Are Stock Prices Forecastable?

Belief in efficient (or rational) stock market pricing has taken big blows over the last 20 years. Robert Shiller led the intellectual assault on belief in stock market efficiency in a series of papers written more than 30 years ago.[7] In 1981 Shiller argued that stock prices in the United States over the 100-year period starting in 1870 were far too volatile to be consistent with a rational evaluation of the fundamental value of the corporate sector.[8]

Shiller wanted to compare the volatility of stock prices observed in practice with the volatility of share prices if they are based on rational forecasts of future dividends. However, we cannot recreate *now* what rational forecasts of future dividends were in 1870. Therefore, Shiller focused instead on the volatility of share prices, assuming that the investor had perfect foresight about future dividends. If you had known in 1870 what dividends US companies would pay over the next 100 years, then, using the logic of Figure 16.8, you could work out what the price of equities should have been over this period on the basis of this perfect foresight. (Of course, this depends on choosing a discount factor r.) Shiller argued that the actual path of dividends that companies paid over that 100-year period should have been *more* volatile than the path that it was rational to expect in 1870. In other words, if actual share prices are more volatile than Shiller's perfect foresight share price, then they must also be more volatile than share prices based on forecasts of fundamentals.

Crucial to Shiller's argument was the claim that the share price based on perfect foresight should be more volatile than the share price based on rational forecasts. The argument was subtle, some would say intellectually dangerous. An analogy might be helpful in understanding it.

Suppose that I asked you what you expected to be the average outcome of tossing an unbiased coin 100 times. You would probably say that you would expect 50 heads and 50 tails. Suppose that now I actually tossed a coin 100 times. The outcome is unlikely to be exactly 50 heads and 50 tails. I could repeat the same question to you over and over again, and toss a coin 100 times after each answer. We would find significant variability from one occasion to the next in the actual outcome of tossing a coin 100 times, but no variability in your expectation of what the result would be (you would keep saying 50 heads and 50 tails). Shiller argued analogously that the expectation of future dividends should be less variable than actual future dividends. This implied that the price calculated by discounting the actual future course of dividends (the perfect foresight price) should be more volatile than the share price that would result from people forming rational expectations of the present value of future dividends. This meant that Shiller expected the perfect foresight share price to be more volatile than the actual history of share prices. Figure 16.9 shows what he saw.

The P line is actual share prices, and the line marked 'PDV of dividends' is the perfect foresight path. Remember, the perfect foresight line should be *more* volatile than the actual prices. Clearly it is not! Shiller concluded that sensible reactions to news about future economic fundamentals were not driving variability in stock prices; if they were, we could expect the perfect foresight path to be much more variable relative to the actual path for prices.

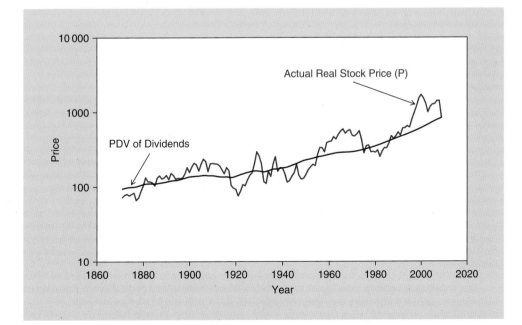

FIGURE 16.9 ● Share prices are more volatile compared to those constructed using actual dividends paid.
Source: R. Shiller, *Market Volatility*, online data, www.econ.yale.edu/~shiller/data.htm.

If Shiller is right, things are rather worrying. Big swings in prices either up or down might have much more to do with irrational sentiment than with changing expectations of future profits. But is he right? The jury is still out on this question. The statistical issues are subtle and still not resolved. Furthermore, sample selection bias, which we argued was relevant to the equity premium puzzle, is also relevant to the Shiller story. In a sense, the 100-year period between 1870 and 1970 that Shiller used for his original work was not a large sample of observations. It was one run of history for one country. And one observation is a small sample on which to base a devastating hypothesis.

In defence of Shiller, you could argue that dramatic volatility in stock prices is not confined to the United States. Huge swings in prices occur in stock markets in most countries: in the United Kingdom, share prices dropped by 35% in 1973 and by 55% in 1974. In Russia, the stock market index fell by over 80% between January and September 1998. Between 1990 and 1992, the Japanese stock market fell by 50%.

However, stock price volatility, and more specifically big drops in prices in short periods, are not inconsistent with an efficient market. If news arrives that causes a substantial change in expected future profits (on which dividends are based), prices should move a lot. Smart economists can construct stories around the events in Russia, Japan and the United Kingdom at the time of big market falls that are consistent with efficient markets. Despite this, the work of Robert Shiller began to undermine faith in efficient markets.

KEY POINT

An important insight of Shiller's was to note that although efficient markets might imply near-random behaviour in asset prices (under certain circumstances), such randomness did not imply efficiency; it was a necessary but not sufficient condition for efficiency.

(16.8) Speculation or Fundamentals?

As well as Shiller's results, there are other characteristics of equity prices that do not seem to square with the efficient market view that movements in stock prices are unpredictable. Possibly the most pervasive of these is the evidence of momentum in share prices. Go onto any financial trading floor and you are likely to find some traders avidly studying a chart of the past performance of a share price. According to our theory such effort is wasted, since only expected future events are important for predicted future share prices, not their own past history. However, as Figure 16.10 shows, empirical evidence strongly suggests that shares that have performed well in the recent past are more likely to perform well in the near future. It shows the relative performance of shares that demonstrated a strong upward trend in the previous six months against those that demonstrated a strong downward trend. The upward-trend shares tend to outperform by about 11% 12 months after they were picked – a significant difference. Figure 16.10 also shows that in the longer term **mean reversion** sets in, so that shares that have outperformed for a number of periods eventually fall back to earth (mean reversion is a statistical concept that implies that a variable tends to return to some long-term value or trend). Thus traders use a variety of tools such as technical analysis to try to find shares that will do well in the near future due to momentum, but are not about to go into reverse due to mean reversion. Why

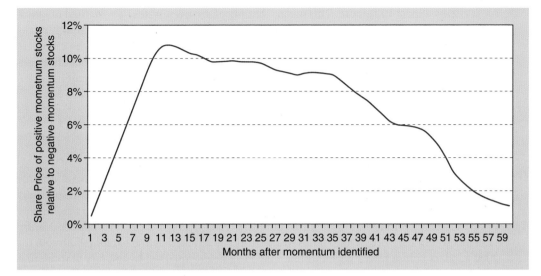

FIGURE 16.10 ● **Evidence of momentum in share prices.** The subsequent performance of shares on an upward trend relative to those on a downward trend suggests that trends tend to persist for a year or so. *Source:* Narasimhan Jegadeesh and Sheridan Titman, 'Profitability of momentum strategies: An evaluation of alternative explanations', *Journal of Finance (*2001): 699–720. John Wiley & Sons Ltd.

these simple predictable patterns exist at all is the subject of much research and controversy. Defenders of efficient markets suggest that maybe the changes in the risk premium explain momentum, while proponents of **behavioural finance** suggest that it comes from psychological biases. Evidence from psychological experiments shows strong tendencies for groups to influence each other and make common mistakes (peer group errors) or display *herding behaviour*.

16.9 Bubbles

Many commentators argue that a more extreme version of herding behaviour is behind **asset market bubbles**. A bubble occurs when an asset price deviates substantially from its fundamentals, and this difference does not disappear even if investors know that the price is above its fundamental value.[9]

With bubbles, if the deviation in the asset price is to be sustainable, the deviation from fundamentals must become ever more pronounced. We can demonstrate this with an example. Suppose that prices start out 20% above 'fundamentals', with a 1 in 10 chance of dropping back to their equilibrium level. To generate an annual average return of, say, 15%, the following equation must hold:

$$15\% = x\%(0.9) - 20\%(0.1)$$

where x is the proportionate rate of price increase *if* the bubble does not burst – which is 90% probable. There is a 1 in 10 chance that the price will fall back to its fundamental value, which is 20% lower, hence the final term in the equation. The solution to this equation is $x = 18.9\%$. Therefore, even though the price starts off 20% overvalued in a bubble, we can expect to see it rise by almost 19% more. This means that prices are even further above fundamentals if the bubble persists; and next period's value of x needs to be even higher, because if prices crash, they fall further. A key element of a bubble is that even smart investors who know it is a bubble may be tempted to join in so that they benefit from the upswing and, hopefully, get out before the bubble bursts. As George Soros, a famously successful investor, put it:

> *When I see a bubble first I do is I buy because if I am right and the bubble is going to develop, I am going to make money, and if I see a bubble and I see a flaw in the bubble then I am really happy, because then I will know that I have to sell, most bubbles you do not know that they are bubbles. (*Wall Street Journal *interview, October 2009)*

In fact, even after the event it is not always clear that a true bubble has occurred. In provocative research, Peter Garber has argued that when you look at events that researchers have universally accepted as asset price bubbles, a bubble may not really have existed.[10] For example, he argues that the events surrounding the Tulip Mania of early seventeenth-century Holland, where the price of tulip bulbs rose astronomically so that a single tulip bulb sold for 2000 guilders before prices began to fall, may have been explained by the fact that the first bulb of a new variety was far more valuable than plants derived from it. Similarly, he suggests that the South Sea Bubble in the UK in 1720, where investors clamoured to buy shares in the South Sea Company, made sense for as long as investors thought that the company opened up commercial possibilities and was supported and guaranteed by the British government. However, explaining the success of related 'bubble companies' that received huge investments with little prospect of return is more difficult. One such advertised itself as 'a company for carrying out an undertaking of great advantage, but nobody to know what it is'. The founder of this company disappeared with the funds he had raised and was never seen again. Even the Dot-Com Bubble of the late 1990s, when Internet-based companies with no profits rose to very high valuations, has been explained as a bet on uncertain future growth.[11]

16.10   What is a Bond?

A bond is basically an 'I owe you' (IOU). When a company or a government issues a bond, it promises to repay certain amounts of money at specific dates in the future. Most bonds specify the precise cash values of the repayments, and their timing, in advance.[12] These IOUs often have long lives: many governments want to borrow money for 20 or 30 years, and debt issued today may not finally be repaid until 2030 or 2040. Indeed, the first consolidated bond (consol) issued by the UK government in 1751 had an indefinite life and so is still paying interest today. Like equities, bonds are traded in a secondary market: holders of bonds can sell their claims to third parties and liquidate their holding without recourse to the issuer. For this reason, a 30-year bond – one that the issuer will not finally repay for three decades – can nonetheless be a highly liquid asset that can be bought or sold at any time.

Bonds are traded in securities markets (the bond market). This distinguishes bonds from bank debt: claims held by banks cannot, in general, be sold to a third party. And the debts that banks issue directly to the public – that is, deposits – are also not traded in a secondary market. When you want the cash you have lent to a bank, you get it from the bank rather than by selling your deposit to someone else. In this sense, bonds have more in common with equities than with bank debt, because both bonds and equities are traded securities that you can cash in by selling to other investors; the original issuer is not involved. If I own bonds issued by a company, I can sell their claims to you and liquidate my holdings without involving the company.

Bond prices are set, on a minute-by-minute basis, by market makers who typically work for large financial institutions like Morgan Stanley, UBS or Goldman Sachs. They quote prices at which they will buy and sell bonds. These prices reflect the flow of buy and sell orders that they receive. As always, the forces underlying demand and supply generate prices. Expectations about whether bondholders will really receive the money that bond issuers have promised them are crucial, as are the ways in which people value money that will only be paid 5, 10 or 20 years ahead. As people's views on these factors change, demand-and-supply curves shift, which generates changes in prices. The prices reflect the cost of borrowing money for various time periods and are a major factor behind corporate investment decisions.

The big distinction between bonds and equities is that the repayment schedule for bonds is specified in great detail, whereas equities merely represent a claim on some unspecified fraction of whatever corporate profits (after tax and interest payments) happen to exist in the future. As a result, bonds have different risk characteristics.

Bond markets are certainly big news. Figure 16.11 indicates the size of the global market, and shows both domestic bonds (those that are mainly denominated in the local currency and aimed at domestic investors) and international bonds (denominated in a foreign currency and aimed at foreign investors).

In some countries, like Japan, the government dominates the bond market. The importance of government debt reflects two factors. First, governments often need to borrow on a large scale because they cannot cover their expenditure out of tax revenue – sometimes by choice and sometimes of necessity. This is particularly true during wartime. The stock of government debt outstanding has often increased massively because of long and expensive

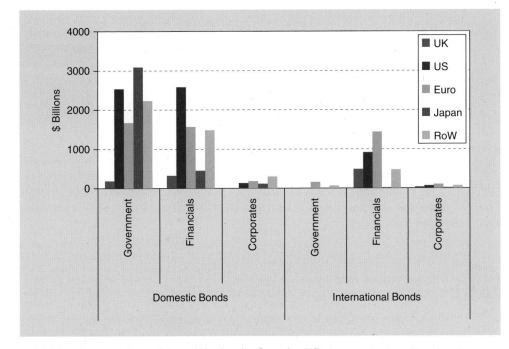

FIGURE 16.11 ● **Shares of the world bond market, September 2010.** The total value of bonds outstanding with more than 1 year to maturity, by country, issuer and type. *Source: BIS Quarterly Review*, http://www.bis.org/statistics.

conflicts. But in many countries it also increased massively in the aftermath of the financial crisis of 2008 and 2009.

Second, governments issue bonds because they cannot issue equities. Corporations have a wide choice of financing techniques; governments do not. If you think about the difference between bonds and equities, this makes sense. The returns that shareholders get from holding equities depend on the profits that companies earn, and these, in turn, reflect a company's efficiency and skill in producing things that people want. Governments, in contrast, do not aim to make profits. If they did, life would be strange. After all, governments can (in most developed countries at least) raise taxes further and thus can (within limits) generate a surplus of revenue over spending. If governments really decided to maximize the excess of their revenues over their expenditure, they could generate huge 'profits'. If governments considered it their duty to maximize profits to generate returns to shareholders, taxpayers would suffer. Furthermore, shareholders might only be willing to buy equity in governments if, in exchange, they had a say in how government was run. This is hard to square with 'one person, one vote' democracy!

So when governments want to borrow, they typically look to the bond market. Figure 16.11 shows that among the developed countries, the government issues far more bonds than non-financial corporations. But corporations are also big players in the bond market; this has long been true in the United States, and in the 1990s European companies also became significant issuers of bonds. When companies issue bonds, they are, like governments, issuing IOUs that give the holder of the bond the right to some portion of future corporate revenues.

The prices at which companies and governments can issue bonds are crucial, because they reflect the rate of return that investors demand to hand over cash now in exchange for the promise of repayment in the future. This is a key determinant of the level of corporate investment. The price at which governments can issue bonds determines the cost of the national debt. The cost of debt to companies and governments is, of course, the mirror image of the return that savers earn.

> ### KEY POINT
>
> Bond prices reflect the balance of supply and demand for debt. The flow of new bonds coming onto the market depends on the level of investment that companies wish to undertake and the needs of government to borrow.

The demand for new bonds reflects the desired level of saving of households and companies. Both demand and supply in the bond market depend on returns on other financial assets, for example equities and bank deposits. To understand how these factors affect bond prices and the volumes of debt issued, we need to understand the link between returns, or yields, and bond prices.

16.11 Prices, Yields and Interest Rates

If you buy a bond, you hold a piece of paper that gives you the right to receive cash flows at specified dates in the future. The expectation of receiving those cash flows gives your piece of paper some value today. Because there are alternatives to holding bonds – for example, putting the money in a bank where it will earn a particular rate of interest – bonds have to generate a positive expected return to make them worth holding. We can think of the price of a bond as simply reflecting the value today of all the streams of cash that it will generate in the future. Because we value the cash paid to us tomorrow less than the cash that is in our pocket today, we will discount those future receipts of cash to which a bond entitles us. So the *price* of a bond is the appropriately discounted value of all the repayments on the bond until it is finally redeemed. Those repayments come in two forms: regular **coupon** payments, plus a final payment in the last period of the bond's life (its **face value**) at the **redemption** date (when the bond matures). The *yield* on a bond is simply the rate of return that, when used to discount future cash receipts, makes their total value equal to the current market price of the bond.

We need to be more precise about these relations. If we denote the yield on a bond by y and its price by P, then the relationship between the price and the yield on a bond with n periods to maturity is given by:

$$P = \frac{C}{1+y} + \frac{C}{(1+y)^2} + \cdots \cdots + \frac{C}{(1+y)^n} + \frac{F}{(1+y)^n}$$

where C is the regular annual coupon payment on the bond, and F is the face value. Here we assume that coupon payments come at 12-month intervals, and the first coupon is paid exactly a year from today. (In practice, some bonds pay coupons more than once a year, while others only make a final repayment.) The bond **matures** (or is redeemed) n years from now. Such a bond has a residual maturity of n years; obviously as time passes, n falls. So a bond issued in 1995 with an original maturity of 30 years, and a face value of $100, will guarantee to its holder in 2025 a final payment of $100. By 2015 the bond's residual maturity is 10 years. This formula may look a little familiar, since it is based on the idea that the price of the bond should equal the discounted sum of future expected coupons and final repayment, just as the price of equity should be the discounted sum of future expected dividends.

You can see from the relation in the equation above that the prices of bonds and their yields have an inverse relationship. The higher is the yield to maturity y, the lower is the price. Figure 16.12 shows that relationship.

> **KEY POINT**
>
> The yield to maturity is a measure of the average rate of return that a buyer will earn on a bond if the buyer holds it to maturity.

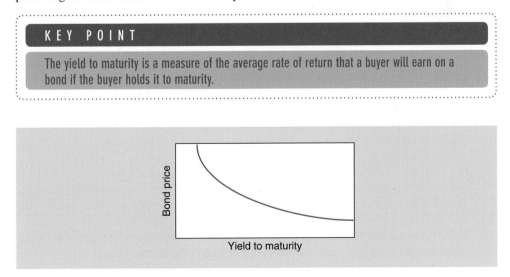

FIGURE 16.12 ● **Bond price/yield to maturity relationship.** There is a negative, non-linear relationship between the yield on a bond and its price.

If you buy a bond at a low price, then given that the issuer will make regular payments each year of $C and the bond also will generate a final payout of $F when it matures in n periods' time, the bond will generate a high return over its entire life. The higher the price you have to pay for the bond today, the less, *on average*, you will earn on it, year by year, over its life. The key point is that, unlike equities, the amount of money you get back from holding the bond is fixed in advance. This is why bonds are sometimes described as **fixed-income securities**.[13] By paying more now to get the right to those fixed future amounts, you are getting a worse deal; that is, a lower yield.

Let's take a concrete example of bond pricing: a bond with a face value of $100, a maturity of four years and a coupon rate of 8%. The issuer promises to pay $8 (the coupon rate times the face value) each year and to make a final (or redemption) payment of the full face value ($100). Suppose the next coupon payment is due a year from now, and the final coupon payment is made at the time of redemption exactly four years from now. Finally, suppose that the required yield on the bond is 6%. This means that the rate of return needed over a four-year horizon, expressed as an annual rate, is 6%.

The value of the bond will be the sum of the present values of each of the cash flows using a 6% discount rate to calculate those present values.

The first coupon is worth today: $8/(1.06)
The subsequent coupons are worth: $8/(1.06)^2$; $8/(1.06)^3$; $8/(1.06)^4$
The final repayment of the face value is worth today: $100/(1.06)^4$
Evaluating each of these terms and summing them give us the bond price today:

$$P = \$7.55 + \$7.12 + \$6.72 + \$6.34 + \$79.21 = \$106.94$$

Note here that because the yield on the bond (6%) is less than the coupon rate (8%), the price exceeds the face value. If you paid the face value of $100 (this is sometimes called the **par value**), you would be earning 8% a year because that is what the coupon rate is. But the required return is only 6%. So you are willing to pay more than $100 to buy the bond. The price will be driven up from a face value of $100 to $106.94 to generate a return of 6%. If the yield (or required return) were to coincide with the coupon rate, the annual coupons would generate a return equal to the yield as long as the price stayed at $100. If the yield were in excess of the coupon, the price would be below the face value. When governments and companies issue bonds, they typically set the coupon rate at close to what they expect the yield on the bond to be, so that bond prices are usually around face values near to the issue date; such bonds are said to be trading at par.

Figure 16.12 reveals an important fact about bonds: not only is the relationship between price and yield *inverse*, it is also non-linear. An increase in yields of a given amount has a smaller negative impact on price at high yields than at low yields. We will see below that a given shift in yields also has different impacts on the prices of bonds of different maturities.

So far we have just defined what we mean by the yield on the bond: it is simply the average return that you will earn from holding the bond *until the time at which the debt is finally repaid*. This is why we sometimes call yields 'yields to maturity' or 'redemption yields'. We do not really know yet what will determine those yields and tie down bond prices. This is a crucial and difficult question, but expectations of future short-term interest rates, which central banks largely control, should be a key part of the story.

To see the link more clearly, suppose that you wanted to invest some money for 10 years. You could buy a 10-year bond. For simplicity, let us assume that this bond will make no payments until the end of the 10 years when the issuer – a government or a company – will send you a cheque for $100 for every bond that you own. (In other words, the coupon rate is zero; such bonds are called zero-coupon bonds or sometimes 'zeros'.) Buying and holding such a bond would clearly be one way to invest money for 10 years. You could also put the money in a bank savings account in which interest was reset every month in line with money market interest rates. Those money market interest rates will be closely linked to the rates of interest that the central bank will fix (see Chapter 13).

As shown in Figure 16.13, we now have two options:

1. Buy now, at its current market price, a government bond that has 10 years still to run until maturity.
2. Put your money in a bank and leave it there for 10 years, accruing interest each month at a rate that will be reset at the beginning of each month in line with whatever short-term interest rates then rule.

Suppose that we do not care too much about the uncertainty of future short-term interest rates. Then in order to be indifferent between these two investment strategies, the yield on the 10-year government bond, a number that we know for sure today, should be nearly the same as the average interest rate that we think we are going to earn on those bank deposits if we hold them for a decade. If that was not true, then one or other of the two strategies would clearly be dominant, and if enough people agreed that one of these strategies was better than the other, there would be either massive movements of funds out of bank deposits and into bonds or huge selling of government bonds and a massive inflow of funds into banks. Such large movements would generate price changes that would eventually make the two investments similar again. Suppose that 10-year bond yields were substantially higher – given current bond prices – than people's expectations of what the average interest rate would be on bank deposits over the next 10 years. People would have an incentive to buy bonds and write cheques on their banks to pay for them. The massive increase in demand for bonds would boost their price which, as we saw

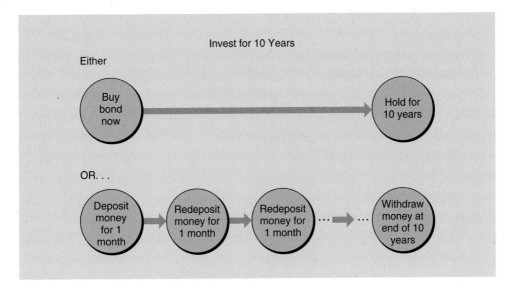

FIGURE 16.13 ● Alternative strategies for an investor with a 10-year horizon.

in the equation above, would reduce their yields. Meanwhile, the big outflows of money from banks would encourage banks to increase their deposit rates. This process would continue until the 10-year bond yield was close to the average expected interest rate on bank deposits over the next 10 years.

Let us take a concrete example. Suppose that the US Federal Reserve funds rate was 3%, and the rate on Treasury bills with one month to maturity was at the same level – reflecting an expectation that over a one-month horizon at least, the Federal Reserve was likely to hold rates steady. Now 3%, while it is above the level to which the Fed cut interest rates after the financial crisis of 2008, is nonetheless an unusually low rate for the United States. If the Federal Reserve had engineered short rates down to that level, then unless the circumstances were exceptional (as they were between 2008 and 2011), investors would not expect it to keep them there for long. Let us assume that investors thought that rates on one-month Treasury bills would have moved up to 4% by 12 months ahead because the Federal Reserve was set to increase rates. Suppose further that the Federal Reserve was expected to raise rates gradually to 5% by two years ahead and to 6% by three years ahead. After that, the consensus view was that the Federal Reserve would leave rates at 6%. Figure 16.14 shows the path along which the one-month Treasury bill rate is expected to evolve. Now consider what the yield on a bond with one year to maturity should be. If one-month Treasury bill rates are now 3% and are expected to gradually move up to 4% by a year from now, then the average of one-month rates over the next 12 months is 3.5%. This is approximately where the yield on one-year bonds should be. If you kept investing in one-month Treasury bills and as each bill matured you bought another, the average interest rate you would earn, over the year, is 3.5%. The one-year bond yield is, by definition, the return you get from holding a one-year bond to maturity, so this should be close to the 3.5% you expect to earn from buying a series of one-month bills.

What about two-year bonds? The average Treasury bill rate over the first year is expected to be 3.5%, and the average over the second year is expected to be 4.5% [(4 + 5)/2)]. The simple average of short rates over the whole two years is expected to be 4%, which is about where two-year bond yields should be. A similar argument

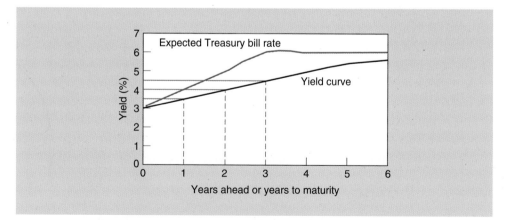

FIGURE 16.14 ● **Expected Treasury bill rate against yield curve.** The anticipation of rising short-term interest rates generates an upward-sloping yield curve.

shows that the average of one-month rates over the next three years is expected to be 4.5%. As we consider bonds with longer and longer maturities, the average of expected one-month Treasury bill rates over the time to their redemption gets closer and closer to 6% (though it always remains below 6%). The yield curve, which shows the relation between yields to maturity and time to maturity, would be upward sloping towards 6%, as Figure 16.14 shows.

> ### KEY POINT
>
> The yield curve shows the average return that is expected to be earned holding bonds of different maturities.

> ### KEY POINT
>
> Prices and yields of bonds are inversely related and are influenced by expectations of future short-term interest rates.

(16.12) Inflation and the Bond Market

By now, you should understand why people who hold conventional (fixed-rate) bonds are hit hard when inflation rises unexpectedly. An inflationary environment erodes the real value of fixed-income securities, and persistent and unanticipated inflation can inflict enormous damage to returns on bonds. The inflation rate in the 10 years from January 1970 to January 1980 was, in almost every developed country, higher than the 10-year bond yield at the start of the decade. Investors in government bonds who bought in the early 1970s invariably earned negative real returns. But the losses on bonds that the developed countries issued in the 1970s pale alongside the much greater losses on the debt of emerging countries that occurred in the 1980s and 1990s. Russia is a case in point. Yields on rouble bonds moved up sharply during the 1990s as inflation in Russia reached hundreds of per cent a year. Faced with hyperinflation, the government pushed up rouble short-term interest rates sharply, generating massive increases in bond yields and causing huge falls in bond prices that all but wiped out the value of investments.

> ### KEY POINT
>
> The inverse relationship between yields and prices makes inflation, which nearly always brings higher short-term interest rates, the enemy of the bond holder.

That inverse relationship also explains what might otherwise appear puzzling. You often hear descriptions of activity in the bond market that sound something like this: 'Yesterday was a good day for the US bond market as yields on long-dated Treasuries fell 20 basis points on expectations of further Fed easing.' Bonds are debt, and people who hold bonds own IOUs. So why are bond holders laughing when interest rates come down, which is normally thought to be bad for people who hold debt? The reason is that bonds, as we noted above, are typically *fixed-income securities*. In other words, the amount of cash that you are going to get in the future from holding a bond does not change when interest rates and yields move, *but the present value of that cash does*. Bond prices rise, leading to capital gains for bond holders.

All of this is in marked contrast to the situation in which holders of bank debt (or bank deposits) find themselves. Depositors with banks are, other things equal, better off when central banks push up interest rates, because most bank deposits are earning interest at rates that typically move closely in line with shifts in central bank rates. Note the contrast here with conventional bonds, which are fixed-income securities and the coupon payments on which are usually fixed in nominal terms in advance. The fixity of the nominal repayment schedule on bonds means that bond prices have to move when required rates of return shift. With bank deposits, the interest stream (analogous to coupons on bonds) is generally not fixed, and as the general level of interest rates moves, the stream of interest income that the deposit generates also moves, so that the value of the underlying deposit does not change. The absence of sharp changes in capital values distinguishes bonds from bank deposits and makes the return on fixed-income assets more volatile. It also means that the link between changes in monetary policy, both actual and anticipated, and the price of bonds is important. We discuss this link next.

(16.13) Government Policy and the Yield Curve

We argued above that yields on long-dated bonds are likely to reflect expectations of future short-term interest rates. This is the essence of the so-called expectations theory of the yield curve. In this section we discuss in more detail the link between what governments and central banks do, particularly in setting short-term interest rates through monetary policy decisions, and the longer-term interest rates that are likely to be important for private-sector saving and investment decisions.

Suppose, for example, that short-term (say, three-month) interest rates were currently high but were expected to fall gradually over the next 5 to 10 years. If you expect short-term interest rates to decline gradually, then the average of the interest rates over the next year will be greater than the average of the interest rates over the next three years, which, in turn, will be greater than the average of short-term interest rates over the next five years. Because the yield on one-year bonds should be linked to average short-term interest rates over a year, and the yield on five-year bonds should be linked to the average of short-term interest rates over five years, one would expect that five-year bond yields would be substantially lower than one-year bond yields. In other words, the yield curve would be sloping downwards. Clearly, if you expected short-term interest rates to rise over the next five years, then five-year bonds would tend to have much higher yields than one-year bonds. In that case, the yield curve would slope up.

Is this expectations theory consistent with the evidence? If it is, and assuming that expectations of future short-term interest rates and inflation are rational, the shape of the yield curve should help predict changes in inflation and short-term interest rates. The evidence supports this view. Figure 16.15 estimates what you would have predicted the change in interest rates to be, given the slope of the yield curve (predicted change), and what subsequently happened to average short-term (three-month) interest rates over the next five years (actual change). There is some correlation between these lines for the four countries.

The yield curve also seems to have some ability to predict future inflation. When five-year bond yields are above (below) short-term rates, evidence shows that average

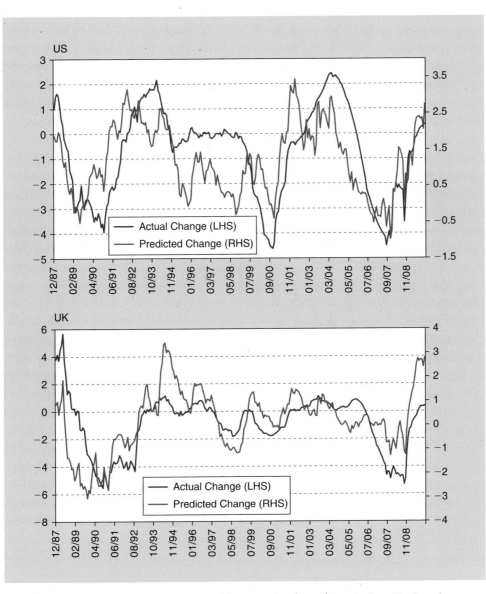

FIGURE 16.15 ● **Some evidence in support of the expectations theory of term structure.** The broad pattern of movements in short-term interest rates is explained moderately well by looking at the slope of the yield curve. *Source:* Authors' calculations.

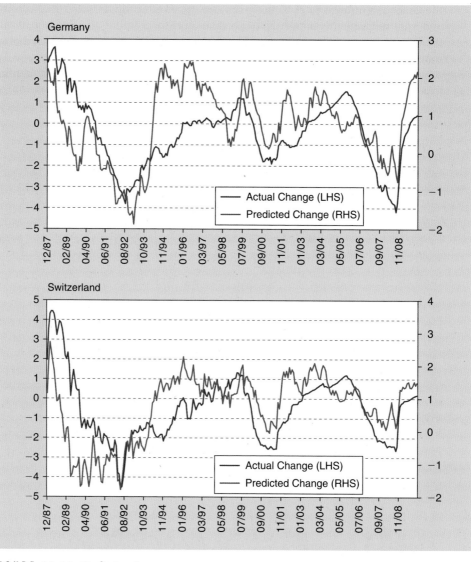

FIGURE 16.15 ● Continued.

inflation is higher (lower) over the next five years. Figure 16.16 shows the actual change in inflation against the predicted change, based on the slope of the yield curve. Clearly, the two are noticeably correlated.

The close correlation means that the slope of the yield curve tends to change over the business cycle. When an economy emerges from a recession, short-term nominal interest rates are generally low; but central banks should be expected to increase rates gradually as growth picks up and the economy moves back to full capacity. With low current interest rates and the expectation of higher rates to come, the yield curve will tend to slope upwards. During a boom, in contrast, the central bank may have raised short-term interest rates to levels substantially above the long-term average. If tightening monetary policy is effective, the market will anticipate slower growth and falling inflation, which would allow the central bank to reduce interest rates in the future. In this environment, longer-dated bonds will tend to have yields *below* short-term interest rates, and the yield curve will slope down. Inversions of the yield curve – that is, downward-sloping curves – are not common, as, over the long run, yields on long-maturity bonds tend to be higher than yields on short-dated bonds and Treasury bills. However, when inversions occur they

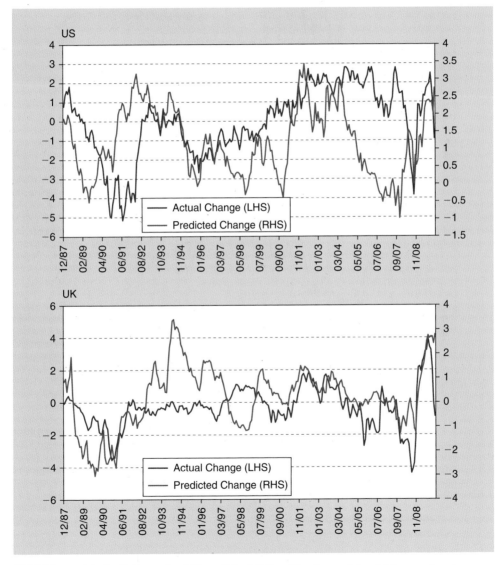

FIGURE 16.16 ● **Yield spread useful in predicting inflation.** The shape of the yield curve also gives some information about changes in future inflation: when the yield curve slopes up more than usual, inflation tends to be on the increase. *Source:* Authors' calculations.

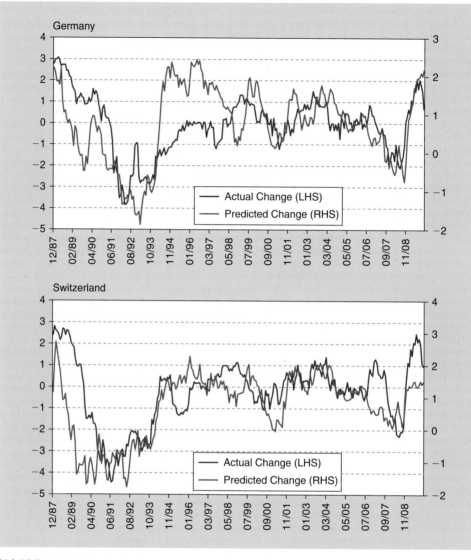

FIGURE 16.16 ● Continued.

often suggest that a recession is on its way. Figure 16.17 shows the slope of the US yield curve (10-year yields minus three-month rates) and US GDP growth. It is remarkable that each time there is a yield curve inversion (yield curve slope negative) a recession has occurred about one year later.

Because yields on bonds reflect expectations about future monetary policy, they give us useful information about the future of the economy. This information has at least three elements:

● First, we might focus on the *absolute levels* of government bond yields of different maturities. This tells us something about the level of short-term interest rates that we can expect in the future, and those levels are likely to reflect demand pressures in

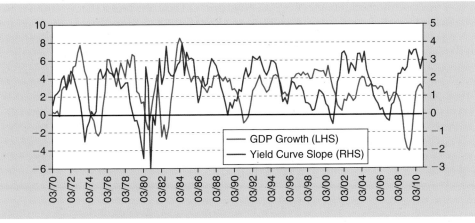

FIGURE 16.17 ● **Yield curve a good predictor of recessions.** When the US yield curve inverts (10-year yields less the three-month rates), a recession is likely to occur about a year later. *Source:* Authors' calculations.

the economy, the strength of output growth and inflation pressures. So, for example, if 10-year bond yields are at 15%, this is likely to reflect a strong belief that inflation is going to be so consistently high that the central bank will need to set short-term nominal rates at double-digit levels.

* Second, as noted above, the *slope* of the yield curve is likely to reveal something about how monetary policy will be *changing*, and that, in turn, should reflect whether the economy is slowing down or accelerating.
* Third, we can learn something about shifts in perceptions of bankruptcy risk from movements in the average *spreads* between government and corporate bonds. After the major sell-off in emerging-market bonds (particularly in Russian government bonds) in mid-1998, spreads between corporate and government bond yields in the United States widened as fears about default risks for highly indebted companies increased (we will look at this point in detail in Chapter 18).

KEY POINT

The sensitivity of bond prices to expectations of what the central bank will do in the future gives monetary policy real teeth. Even in countries in which individuals and companies do not borrow money at short-term variable rates of interest, the central bank can still significantly affect the cost of borrowing.

Remember, central banks only have *direct* influence over short-term interest rates. If individuals borrow at long-term fixed rates of interest (e.g. by taking out mortgages), or if companies issue long-dated bonds to finance investment, governments and central banks might not seem to have much influence on the relevant cost of borrowing. Not so! Long-dated bond yields depend on expectations of short-term interest rates into the future. So by influencing expectations about their *future* actions when setting short-term interest rates, central banks can *today* influence the cost of borrowing money for long periods ahead.

They can also generate big swings in bond prices. The expectation that a central bank might have to increase short-term interest rates sharply in the future can cause bond prices to decline. Given the value of the total stock of debt outstanding, big percentage changes in bond prices can significantly change the total wealth of the private sector, which, in turn, can cause major changes in consumption. Therefore, an important element in the transmission mechanism of monetary policy is the induced impact on bond yields and bond prices of central bank actions.

SUMMARY

Section 16.1 gave an overview of the financial sector, its size, how finance flows across sectors and how it is important for growth (in developing countries). In Section 16.2 we contrasted the features of debt and equity as a source of finance. Section 16.3 explored the nature of equities and compared their importance in various nations. Stock prices are important because they give an indication of the value of firms and help guide investment decisions. Fluctuations in prices also generate big movements in the wealth of the private sector and are likely to cause movements in spending.

In Section 16.4, we suggested that the value of a company's equity should reflect the expected value of the dividends that it will generate into the future or the earnings out of which dividends can be paid.

If this is how stock prices are determined, we explained in Section 16.5 why we should not be surprised by the fact that changes in stock market values appear random. Shifts in expectations and movements in required returns will drive shifts in stock prices.

In Section 16.6, we noted that stock returns in the United States have exceeded returns on bonds and most other assets by a large margin over the last 200 years. This creates another puzzle: the excess return puzzle. In part this may reflect a systematic sample selection problem – history records the deeds of the winners. If that is so, the past returns in the world's most successful large capitalist country give an exaggerated estimate of the likely returns on equities in the future.

In Section 16.7, we saw that, while volatility of stock prices per se is not inconsistent with the efficient functioning of the market, the degree to which prices fluctuate may be. In Section 16.8, we explored further the idea that stock price gyrations often appear hard to reconcile with the notion that cool-headed investors make rational assessments of future earnings of companies and discount those earnings appropriately. Some analysts suggest that herding behaviour and extrapolations from recent price movements may play a role. Asset market bubbles are another interesting market phenomenon, which we explored in Section 16.9. Finally, we analysed how bonds are priced and the link between the yields on longer-dated bonds and movements in short-term interest rates set by central banks.

CONCEPTUAL QUESTIONS

1. (Section 16.3) Firms tend to use retained earnings rather than issue new shares to finance a higher proportion of new investment. Does this mean that the stock market is largely irrelevant for companies?

2. (Section 16.4) Suppose that a company cuts its dividend today to finance more investment from retained current profit. Under what circumstances would this increase, decrease and leave unchanged the share price?

3. (Section 16.5) 'Share price changes are volatile and unpredictable, therefore the stock market is unrelated to what happens in the rest of the economy; it's just a casino.'

'Share price changes are volatile and unpredictable; therefore the stock market is efficient and helps allocate resources effectively.'

What is wrong with each of these propositions?

4. (Section 16.6) How would you judge what the equity risk premium is today? How would you assess whether it was adequate?

5. (Section 16.11) What do you expect to happen to short-term interest rates when the yield curve is unusually steep? Would you expect an inverted yield curve, where longer rates are below shorter rates, to be sustainable?

6. (Section 16.11) Suppose that yields on one-year bonds are at 6%, on two-year bonds are at 7% and on three-year bonds are at 6.5%. What does this imply about future short-term interest rates if the expectations theory of the yield curve is valid?

7. (Section 16.12) How would you expect a rise in inflation to affect the yields and prices of nominal, fixed-rate bonds? Distinguish between an anticipated and unanticipated shock to inflation and between one that was expected to persist and one that was temporary.

ANALYTICAL QUESTIONS

1. (Section 16.5) Suppose that the price of a share always either goes up by 20% or falls by 30% over the next year, whatever its current level. The chances of an upward move are 0.75 and the chances of a downward move are 0.25. The stock pays no dividends. Suppose that you know nothing about the recent performance of the stock. What is the expected rate of return on the stock? Suppose further that you now discover that over the past five years the returns on the stock have been +20%, +20%, +30%, –30%, –30%. What do you now think the expected return for the next year is?

2. (Section 16.6) In an economy, aggregate dividends paid by companies are expected to grow in line with GDP. The trend rate of growth of GDP is 2.5% per annum. The required rate of return on equities equals a safe rate plus a risk premium. The safe (real) rate is 3%, and the risk premium is 5%. What would you expect the dividend price ratio (or the dividend yield) to be? By how much would stock market prices change if the risk premium increased to 6%?

3. (Section 16.6) Suppose that you are risk neutral, so that your coefficient of risk aversion is 0. You are on a game show where you have already won $500 000. You can quit now with the $500 000 or take a chance by answering a question of which you are not sure. If you guess right, your winnings go to $1 000 000 and you walk away a millionaire. If you guess wrong, you get to keep a miserable $50 000. You assess that there is a 50:50 chance of guessing right. Should you gamble? What would the odds need to be on a correct guess to make you indifferent between gambling and quitting? Suppose that the fall-back prize if you guess wrong is $250 000. How does this change your answers to the first two questions?

4. (Section 16.7) Suppose that your weight fluctuates randomly from month to month; it is as likely to go up as down. Your current weight is 161 pounds. Looking back at records of your weight over the past year the pattern is:

Jan	Feb	Mar	Apr	May	Jun	Jul	Aug	Sep	Oct	Nov	Dec
150	145	148	153	157	155	158	160	161	159	159	161

What is your best guess on the profile of monthly weights over the next 12 months? How volatile is the path of actual monthly weights over the next year likely to be relative to your estimated profile?

5. (Section 16.11) Using a spreadsheet, calculate the price of the following bonds on the assumption that yields to maturity are 7% for all maturity dates:

(a) A bond with exactly 10 years to maturity that pays no coupon and has a face value of $100.

(b) A bond that pays an annual coupon worth 5% of face value and will pay a coupon every year for 10 years and then be redeemed for $100.

(c) A bond that pays an annual coupon worth 7% of face value and will pay a coupon every year for 10 years and then be redeemed for $100.

(d) A bond that pays an annual coupon worth 9% of face value and will pay a coupon every year for 10 years and then be redeemed for $100.

What is the percentage change in the price of each bond if yields move up from 7% to 7.5%?

6. (Section 16.11) Consider each of the bonds that you priced in Question 5. Calculate the percentage change in the price of each bond between the start of one year and the start of the following year. Assume that yields to maturity remain at a constant level of 7% throughout. Now add the coupon yield (the ratio of coupon to price) to the percentage change in price. What do the one-year returns on each bond look like? (The one-year returns are the percentage change in price plus the coupon yield.)

7. (Section 16.12) The central bank in a country has set the short-term interest rate at 6%. It is widely expected that the short-term rate will stay at this level for a year and then rise to 7% for a year before moving back to an equilibrium level of 6.5%, where it is expected to remain from two years ahead indefinitely. Assuming that the expectations theory is true, what would you expect the yield to be on government bonds of maturities from 1 year up to 10 years?

CHAPTER 17

The Banking Sector

Key Concepts

Bank Runs

Capital Adequacy

Commercial Banks

Contagion

Credit Crunch

Deposit Insurance

Investment Banks

Moral Hazard

Overview

Banks play a critical role in the economy. Retail bank liabilities are largely made up of deposits, which represent much of the financial wealth of the household sector and most of the money supply. Bank assets — loans of various sorts — represent much of the debt finance of companies, especially for small and medium-sized firms, as well as most of the credit extended to households. When banks work well, they intermediate between savers and borrowers and provide a number of services that financial markets cannot. But both their source of funds and the type of lending they undertake make them vulnerable to failure. Given the size and importance of this sector, bank failures can have major macroeconomic significance.

In this chapter we discuss the role of banks in the economy, why banks are vulnerable to failure and what happens when they do fail. We also look at how government regulation aims to mitigate the macroeconomic risks associated with banks.

17.1 The Role of Banks

Banks are financial intermediaries. They intermediate (or channel) funds from savers to those who need to borrow to finance investment or consumption. Banks fall into two main categories: **commercial banks**[1] that receive savings in the form of deposits and then lend out those funds, perhaps as mortgages or loans to firms; and **investment banks** that operate as intermediaries in financial markets. In practice, many banks operate as both retail and investment banks. Investment banks play a variety of roles. They can facilitate financial trading between other financial institutions and advise issuers (generally non-financial

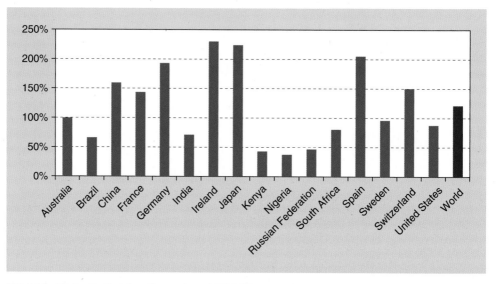

FIGURE 17.1 ● **Bank deposits as a share of GDP, 2009.** Bank deposits are large in relation to GDP, especially in highly banked economies like Japan. *Source:* World Bank, World Development Indicators.

companies) on how best to raise funds in financial markets. They can also trade in markets on their own behalf (which is called proprietary trading). In this chapter we focus mainly on commercial banking, though the link between commercial and investment banking has become an important regulatory issue in its own right.

The scale of banking intermediation both within and between countries is great. Figure 17.1 shows that across a range of countries, total bank deposits vary between about 50% and 200% of annual GDP. Although, banking is generally smaller relative to GDP for developing countries, Figure 17.2 shows that claims on banks are often a large share of total financial

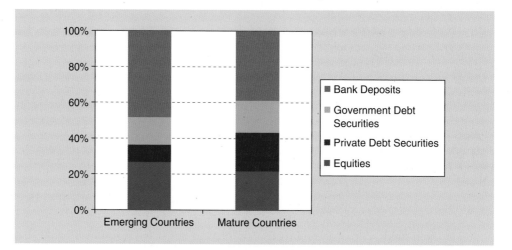

FIGURE 17.2 ● **Bank deposits as a share of financial assets, 2007.** Although the banking sector is usually smaller in developing countries than in developed, it makes up a large share of the financial sector. *Source:* McKinsey Global Institute.

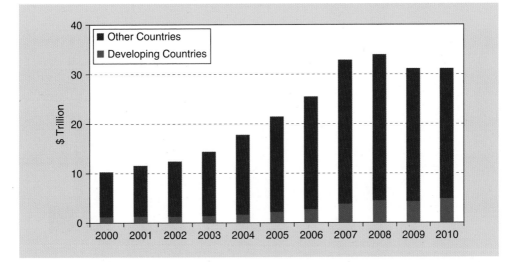

FIGURE 17.3 ● **Cross-border loans by banks.** Despite falling back in 2008, international loans by banks still total over $30 trillion. *Source: BIS Quarterly Review.*

assets. Banks are also important international lenders. Figure 17.3 shows outstanding international loans by banks, which, despite the financial crisis of 2008, have remained at over $30 trillion.

Why are banks so important in helping to finance expenditure, both within a country and between countries? After all, you could imagine a situation in which companies and individuals wanting to borrow money did so directly by approaching savers themselves, rather than go through the intermediate step of borrowing from banks. Why have banks become the middlemen? The answer to this profound question tells us a lot about the benefits, but also the potential problems, that banks create.

FUNCTIONS OF BANKS

EFFICIENT PAYMENTS SYSTEMS   For most people, the key reason they hold a bank account is to access the payments systems that the banks operate. Their salary can be paid directly into the account and then various technologies such as cheques and payments cards can be used to spend that money. For most transactions banking transfers are far more convenient than cash. Figure 17.4 gives an indication of the scale of this payments infrastructure for the United States and for the world as a whole. First, we see that in the United States there are far more bank accounts than adults, while even for the world as a whole there is an average of one bank account for every two adults. Those bank accounts are supported by a bank branch network (though the number of bank branches per adult has been falling recently), automated teller machines (ATMs) and, increasingly, point-of-sale terminals, all of which allow customers to access and spend their money. As well as payments systems for individuals, banks supply important payments systems to companies, financial markets and even to governments (though recall that the central bank is usually the official banker of the government).

ECONOMIES OF SCALE   When I take $5000 to the bank, the money, effectively, is used to finance loans to a large and diverse pool of borrowers. The bank may lend some of that

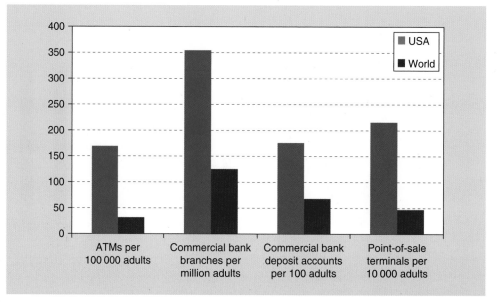

FIGURE 17.4 ● **Banking services in the US and the world, 2009.** Banking services such ATMs, bank branches and point-of-sale terminals are an important benefit of a developed banking system. *Source:* World Bank, World Development Indicators.

money to individuals who live near me who have borrowed on mortgages. Some of it may be channelled to companies at the other end of the country that are investing in high-tech ventures. Some of it may be channelled to an emerging market to help finance an office block. I acquire a diversified portfolio of loans by simply depositing my money in a bank. And this diminishes risk. It would be prohibitively costly for me to allocate part of that $5000 to a loan to help finance a house purchase by one of my neighbours, a loan to a high-tech company 1000 miles away and part of a construction company in Asia. The bank, by accumulating small deposits from many individuals, can spread the cost of allocating those funds across thousands of people, thereby reducing the transactions costs of channelling funds.

EFFECTIVE MONITORING   When considering the diversification benefits of banks, it is relatively easy to think of alternative investments that might give the same benefit. For example, putting $5000 into a mutual fund would results in my investment being spread across a huge range of companies and investments through the equity market. However, a widely noted weakness of equity markets is the lack of effective monitoring by investors. Even though holding equity in a company gives you part ownership in a firm, you are unlikely to take a day-to-day interest in the running of that firm (unless your equity holding is very large indeed). Even a professional investor is more likely to sell the shares of a company that she thinks is badly run rather than turn up at the annual general meeting and vote for change. When share ownership is widely dispersed, no one investor has a strong incentive to control the management of that firm or even spend much time understanding the details of how the firm operates. Banks can devote more time to monitoring the performance of the loans they make (if the loan is large enough to be worth monitoring). In particular, banks specialize in lending to small and medium-sized enterprises (SMEs), where understanding the details of the business is crucial. Figure 17.5 shows how SMEs in the European Union

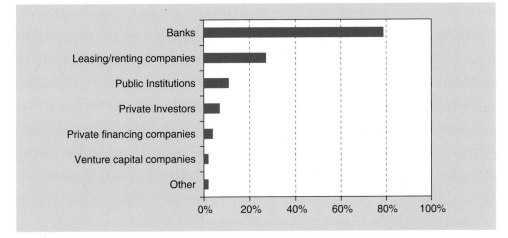

FIGURE 17.5 ● **Sources of finance for small and medium-sized businesses in the European Union.** Smaller firms rely heavily on banks as a source of finance. *Source:* EOS Gallup Europe, SME Access to Finance (2005).

are particularly dependent on banks for financing; the same is true of SMEs elsewhere in the world. Although venture capital firms specialize in equity investment in small firms and undertake a great deal of monitoring, the costs to the firm itself are significantly higher than for bank lending. Cochrane estimates that the average venture capital investment in the United States between 1987 and 2000 earned a return of about 50% (even after allowing for firms that failed),[2] at a time when banks would lend to small businesses at an interest rate only a couple of percentage points above the official rate.

MATURITY TRANSFORMATION   When I put my $5000 in the bank, I am probably not sure when I will need it again, but I know I can access it when I need it. I benefit from getting instant access to it at short notice. In contrast, the person who borrows the money from a bank usually needs it for a long time. If I am borrowing money to buy a house, I may not be able to repay most of it for 10 or even 20 years. And it may take 10 or 15 years for the flow of rents to pay off the money used to finance the construction of an office building.

KEY POINT

People who borrow typically want the money for much longer than the people who deposit the money are prepared to give up access to their funds.

This would be a major problem if all the money lent to someone who was buying a house came from one or two depositors, because at some point one or both of those lenders would probably want their money back at short notice. But suppose that the money that helps finance my house purchase comes from not one or two savers, but from a million savers. While it may be hard to predict whether an individual saver will want his money back this month or next month, the proportion of the deposits that one million savers want back at short notice is much more predictable. Banks can use the law of large numbers to get round the maturity mismatch problem. Additionally, banks can borrow or lend money to

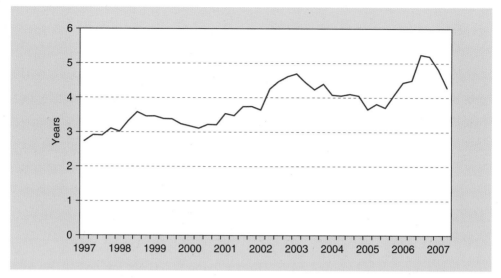

FIGURE 17.6 ● **Maturity mismatch for US banks: Average maturity of assets minus maturity of liabilities.** The average interest rate maturity of US bank assets is around three to four years longer than their liabilities.[3] *Source:* W.B. English, S.J. Van den Heuvel and E. Zakrajsek, Interest Rate Risk and Bank Profitability, Federal Reserve Board mimeo (2011).

other banks in the interbank market, should they find a mismatch of depositors and borrowers in their own bank. Therefore, they can be confident, at least in normal times, that the amount of cash being withdrawn by savers is relatively predictable and that any mismatch can be balanced by using the interbank market. As a result, almost all banks operate with a maturity mismatch, whereby they offer depositors near-instant access to their money but offer borrowers long-term loans that need not be repaid for many years.

While the maturity of loans made by banks may be very long, not all of these loans will be made at a fixed rate of interest. For example, a mortgage scheduled to be paid over 20 years may have repayments based on short-term interest rates and so the payments can change each month. Despite this, banks still face significant interest rate risk, as their average depositor receives interest payments based on short-term interest rates that change quite frequently, whilst a significant proportion of their borrowers pay a fixed interest rate. As a consequence, a sudden increase in interest rates by the central bank may require banks to pay more interest to their depositors, while still receiving the same interest from most of their borrowers. This interest rate risk is one of the many risks faced by banks and requires them to manage their financing very carefully. Figure 17.6 shows an estimate of the scale of this mismatch for the average US bank. It demonstrates that the gap between the average maturity of interest rates paid by banks' sources of funds (depositors, interbank borrowing etc.) and the maturity of the interest rates they receive on their assets (mainly loans) is about four years.

(17.2) Problems in Banking Markets

As well as providing valuable payments systems, banks help overcome two problems that would exist if savings were to be channelled directly to lenders. The first is the maturity mismatch issue – I want to have access to my savings at fairly short notice, while the person who wants to build a factory needs the money for 10 years or more. The second problem is that

I do not really want to spend my life checking to see that the 30 people I have lent money to really are using it for what they said they would. Banks help overcome these problems. But in so doing they face other severe problems. First, if I, as a depositor, have delegated to the bank the responsibility for monitoring loans made with my savings, then inevitably I will not know a lot about the real value of those loans. Most of the time, this does not matter much, because I can probably be confident that at least most of the loans that the bank makes are good and so I am going to get my money back and the bank will not become insolvent. And, most of the time, it also does not matter very much that my deposit is highly liquid (that is, I can go in and get my money back at short notice), whereas the assets backing my deposit are loans that have a long payback period, which implies that the bank cannot get its hands on the cash at short notice.

But suppose that many people start to worry about the solvency, or health, of the bank where I have deposits. Anyone worried about the health of his or her bank would want to get their money out quickly. Sometimes you have to pay a small penalty for accessing your money at short notice, although with most current accounts you can get your money back with no penalty. Suppose that my worry turns out to be pointless and the bank is perfectly solvent. The only cost I will have incurred by taking my money out and putting it back in again a few weeks later is the (probably very small) amount of interest I will have lost in the interim. In contrast, if I do not pull my money out and the bank does become insolvent, I may only get back 50 cents on every dollar that I deposited. Given the two possibilities – the bank is insolvent, the bank is solvent – I only need to attach a small probability to the insolvency outcome to make it rational for me to take my money out now.

You can see the problem here. If enough people start to worry and go to the bank to withdraw their funds, the bank is going to be in trouble. It may find that it has to try to pull in loans at short notice to pay off depositors. But trying to pull in loans at short notice itself causes problems. If companies have borrowed from the bank on overdraft, fully expecting to be able to roll the overdraft forward and not repay the money at short notice, they can get into trouble if the bank suddenly stops the line of credit. The company, in turn, may need to try to pull money in from its trade creditors (customers with unpaid invoices), who will themselves be squeezed. You can imagine a situation in which the very fact that banks try to pull in loans at short notice undermines the economic health of the people they have lent money to and thereby reduces the real value of those loans. Figure 17.7 shows how a vicious circle of

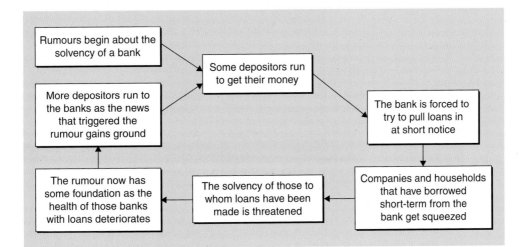

FIGURE 17.7 ● Self-fulfilling bank panic.

TABLE 17.1 ● **Payoff Matrix.**

		All Others	
		Don't Run	Run
Me	Don't Run	1, 100	0, 70
	Run	1, 100	0.777, 70

rapid withdrawal of deposits and immediate liquidation of loans can actually make a formerly solvent bank become insolvent and have serious repercussions for the rest of the economy.

A numerical example can help make the point about bank runs. Suppose that a bank has loans (its assets) that, so long as the great majority are allowed time to be paid off, will be worth 100. Should those loans need to be called in immediately – because most depositors want their money back – they will be worth only 70. Suppose that all depositors can ask for their money back at any time, but that if they have confidence that they can get all their money back they will leave their funds at the bank. Finally, suppose that deposits are worth 90, which means that as long as the bank is able to have its loans repaid over time (so that the assets are worth 100), there will be a profit of 10 for the owners of the bank.

Now consider whether an individual depositor should run to the bank and get her money back or not. The payoffs from the strategy of running or not running depend on whether other people run for their money or not. Let's assume that there are 90 depositors in all, so that each has a deposit that is worth 1.

We show the payoffs in Table 17.1. There are four possibilities: I run when others run or when they do not run; and I do not run when others also do not run or when they do. For each case we show two payoff figures: the value of my payoff as a depositor, and the value of the bank's assets.

If others don't run, the assets are worth 100 and there is plenty to pay me the 1 that is due. That is true whether I leave my deposit with the bank or whether I, in isolation, go for my money now. That is why the payoffs to me and to the bank are 1, 100 in both entries in the first column. But if I don't run while others do, all the money that is available when the other 89 run (which is the value of the loans that are called in early of 70) is gone by the time I go to the bank. That explains the bad payoff of 0, 70 in the top right entry. If I run along with everyone else, then assuming that we all arrive together, we on average get a payout of 70/90, which is 0.777. That is a bad outcome since I was due 1 – but it is better than getting nothing.

So the bottom line is that I might as well run if I think that there is any chance at all that others will. Either I will get the 1 due to me (if others do not run) or I will at least get 0.777 if others do run, which is better than the nothing I would get if I don't run. So a bank run is a Nash equilibrium – if I think others will run I should certainly run too.

> ### KEY POINT
> Banking panics can become self-fulfilling.

The film *Mary Poppins* gives a nice example of how a self-fulfilling bank panic can occur. In the film the young son of a senior banker in Fidelity Fiduciary Bank visits his father at

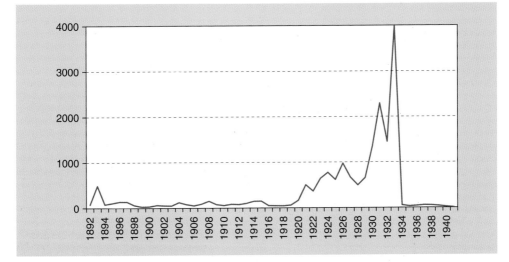

FIGURE 17.8 ● **US bank failures in the Great Depression.** Contagion meant that many banks collapsed at the same time in the Great Depression. *Source:* FDIC reports.

the bank. The owner of the bank tries to persuade the boy to deposit his two pence into the bank, but he refuses, as he wants to buy a bag of seeds to feed the birds. Customers of the bank overhear parts of this exchange and immediately wonder why the son of a senior employee refuses to put money in the bank. They guess that there is something wrong with the bank and all rush to withdraw their deposits. We do not get to see the consequences of this panic, but it is entirely possible that it could cause the failure of the bank. Such an outcome may explain why we see the senior management of the bank flying kites in the park at the end of the film.

Banking panics are unfortunately not confined to children's stories: as we will see later in the chapter, they are surprisingly common. Possibly the most famous and most economically costly banking panic occurred in the United States in the Great Depression of the 1930s. Figure 17.8 shows the number of banks that failed over this period and highlights another feature of banking panics, called **contagion**. If one bank fails, customers of other banks might begin to worry about the solvency of their own bank and create a run on that bank, so the failure of one bank may be the start of a series of runs on other banks. Sometimes contagion occurs for rational reasons, for example if other banks have made similar mistakes to the one that failed or have lent money to the one that failed it makes sense for customers to be nervous. In any case, many banking panics spread very quickly across most of the banking sector, changing a relatively localized problem for one banking institution into a national or even global macroeconomic crisis. This is what happened in 2008, though the run was more of wholesale funds than of retail funds.

KEY POINT

Banking panics are often 'contagious', spreading from one bank to another very rapidly.

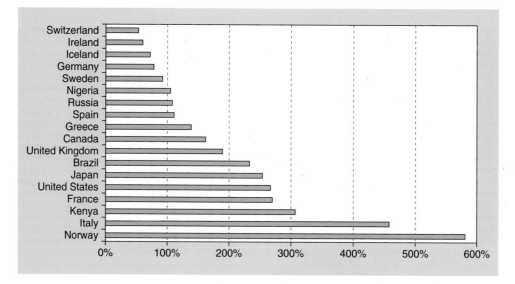

FIGURE 17.9 ● **Deposit insurance around the world. Deposits insured, % of GDP.** Deposit insurance is widespread, but the size of deposits insured varies considerably. *Source:* Demirgüç-Kunt, Karacaovali and Laeven, *Deposit Insurance around the World*, World Bank (2005).

DEPOSIT INSURANCE AND GOVERNMENT GUARANTEES

Bank runs show that the maturity mismatch between banks' assets and liabilities (which is fundamental to how banks operate) can cause severe problems. One response to these problems has been to create a system of deposit insurance. Deposit insurance means that if my bank fails, the government guarantees that I will receive all or most of my funds back. This helps to prevent bank panic: if I know that ultimately the government will pay up for each dollar of my deposit, I have much less incentive to run to the bank because of a rumour that it has got into trouble. Figure 17.9 shows estimates of the level of deposit insurance across a range of countries. Although the amounts insured vary significantly, most developed countries have some level of insurance explicitly to reduce the risk of banking panic, but do not offer to guarantee very large deposits.

In practice, government guarantees usually extend far beyond depositors, as during a banking crisis governments will very often extend loans (perhaps through lender of last resort operations by the central bank) or inject funds into banks in order to try to stem the contagion of the crisis. This type of guarantee is often called an 'implicit' guarantee, as the government does not pre-announce that it will help the banking system in a crisis (in fact, it may vehemently deny that it will do so), but when the crisis occurs, it becomes clear that the economic cost of allowing contagion to spread is far higher than the cost of government intervention, so some form of intervention becomes almost inevitable. This implicit guarantee is most apparent in the case of very large banks, whose failure could have serious macroeconomic consequences. Such banks are often called '**too big to fail**', as most people believe that the government will be forced to guarantee the bank should it get into trouble since its sheer size means that the economic consequences of allowing it to fail would be too extreme to bear.

While the explicit guarantees offered through deposit insurance and the implicit guarantees offered through bank bailouts help mitigate the likelihood and cost of panics by

HSBC Balance Sheet 2009

Assets	$million	Liabilities	$million
Cash and balances at central banks	60 655	Equity	135 661
Loans	1 076 012	Deposits	1 283 906
Financial assets	657 225	Financial liabilities	474 634
Other assets	570 560	Other liabilities	470 251
TOTAL ASSETS	2 364 452	TOTAL LIABILITES	2 364 452

FIGURE 17.10 ● **Summary balance sheet for HSBC, 2009.** *Source:* HSBC and authors' calculations.

depositors and other institutions that lend to banks, they create their own problems, most notably an incentive for banks to take more risks than they otherwise would.

LEVERAGE, MORAL HAZARD AND RISKY BORROWING

Banks are highly leveraged (geared). This means that a relatively small amount of equity capital and a relatively large amount of debt help to finance the loans that banks make. Figure 17.10 shows a summary balance sheet for Hong Kong Shanghai Bank (HSBC) in 2009. Although widely considered a relatively well-capitalized bank, equity makes up only about 6% of its total liabilities and its deposit base is about ten times larger than its equity. Note that since HSBC also has an investment banking operation, many of its assets and liabilities relate to operations in financial markets, rather than just the standard deposit and loans business of a pure commercial bank.

High leverage and highly insured deposits can generate unwelcome incentives for banks. Let us suppose that a bank's depositors are not concerned about insolvency risks, either because of the explicit government guarantee given by deposit insurance or the implicit guarantee of a bailout. In that case, the bank may be able to take in deposits at a relatively low interest rate, even though it may be lending on highly risky projects. But why would a bank take on very risky loans? The answer has to do with the limited liability of shareholders.

Shareholders in banks typically have limited liability, which means that the most they can lose is the money they put in to buy the shares. If the bank becomes insolvent – that is, its assets are worth less than its debt – the shareholders do not have to contribute more money to ensure that the debtors are paid in full. This generates an asymmetry in payoffs. Let us take a simple example. Suppose that a bank has a small amount of equity capital and finances nearly all its loans by deposits. Suppose also that the bank could undertake two types of loans: safe loans that pay 5% interest for certain; and risky loans that might pay back $1.20 for every dollar loaned (a 20% return), but that could go badly wrong, in which case each dollar loaned could only be worth 80 cents (a –20% return). For risky loans, suppose that the bank has an equal chance of good returns (+20%) and of bad returns (–20%). You might think that a sensible bank would prefer to loan at a certain rate of 5%, which is, on average, much better than a 50% chance of earning 20% and a 50% chance of losing 20%. After all, the average rate of return on the risky loan is zero, so even someone who didn't care about risk would prefer 5% with certainty. And if a person is risk averse, surely there is no contest here.

However, we should look at these options from the point of view of the bank's owners. *They aren't the depositors, they are the shareholders.* From their point of view, risky loans could go two ways. Number one, they could make a high profit by getting a 20% rate of return on the funds loaned and paying only a small fraction of that as interest on the deposits that finance the loan. If the interest paid on deposits is 4%, by making risky loans the bank has a 50% chance of making a 16% net return on each dollar loaned. If loans are large relative to equity, then that 16% net return on each loan translates into a huge return on equity. If equity is 6% of all bank assets – like it was for HSBC – then a 16% net return on each dollar of loans creates a return on equity of 267% (i.e. 16%/0.06). Number two, if the risky loan fails and the bank becomes insolvent, its owners get nothing (and the deposit insurance scheme picks up the loss). So equity holders face a 50% chance of losing all their money (a return of –100%) and a 50% chance of earning 267%. This is an average rate of return on equity of 83.5%.

Now suppose that instead the bank makes the riskless loans. These generate 5% for sure, which gives a net profit to shareholders of 1% on every dollar loaned after paying 4% to depositors. That would generate a return to equity of 16.7% (1%/0.06). This is a high number, but only one-fifth of the average return from making the riskier loans. This is because the risk really resides with the government that insures the deposits, which is why the depositors are not unhappy with this gamble.

To take an even more extreme example, imagine that a bank has loans worth $1 000 001 and deposits worth $1 000 000, making its equity worth $1 (i.e. the loans, which are the bank's assets, minus its debt). The owners of the bank are offered a double-or-quits bet on the toss of a coin. Heads and the bank loses all of its assets; tails the bank's assets double in value to $2 000 002. The bank's owners will jump at this bet, since from their point of view heads means losing $1 (with deposit insurance paying the other $1 000 000), while tails means winning $1 000 001 (since the deposits are still only worth $1 000 000).

KEY POINT

Since shareholders do not have to bear the losses of failed banks, they have an incentive to encourage risk taking,

The limited liability of shareholders creates an incentive to take risk. While this is true of all firms that are financed mainly by debt, it is a particular problem for banks, since in their case their creditors (mainly depositors) may not care about this risk taking since they are often guaranteed by the government. For other highly indebted firms, creditors (who, ironically enough, are usually banks) carefully monitor their behaviour in order to control risk taking, and will often impose conditions on their loans that restrict the ability of the firm to take risks.

CAPITAL ADEQUACY AND BANKING REGULATION

As is often the case with government intervention, a policy designed to deal with one problem, in this case deposit insurance and other guarantees to stop banking panics, ends up creating another problem, in this case incentives to take risks to which depositors are indifferent. The government response to the problem of risk taking is then to regulate bank behaviour in order to reduce risk taking. These regulations usually take two forms. First,

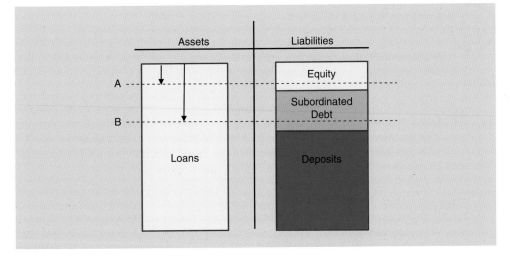

FIGURE 17.11 ● **Stylized commercial bank balance sheet.** Even if the value of this bank's assets falls to point B, depositors will not lose out as equity and subordinated debt must absorb the losses first.

banks are subject to regular inspections by regulators, who analyse their business plans and loans policy in order to root out any excessively risky behaviour. Second, banks are subject to **capital adequacy** requirements, which limit their ability to use leverage by establishing a minimum amount of equity and other liabilities that banks have to hold.

Figure 17.11 shows a stylized bank balance sheet where the bank's assets are loans and its liabilities are a mix of deposits by customers, other debt such as interbank borrowing and equity. Imagine that the some of the bank's loans go bad (i.e. the borrower fails to make any repayments), which reduces the value of the bank's assets to point A. Initially, the fall in value in the bank all falls on the equity holders in the form of a lower share price (lower future dividends); all the creditors to the bank continue to be paid and the bank remains solvent. Now imagine that even more loans go bad so that the value of the bank's assets falls to B. At this point, the value of the bank's equity is wiped out and so, as we discussed above, the bank's losses begin to fall on its creditors, who can force the bank into bankruptcy should their interest payments not be made. However, even if the bank is forced into bankruptcy, that need not mean that depositors have to lose money. In fact, that would not happen if there were other suppliers of debt to the bank whose claims were ranked below those of depositors. Such claims would be subordinated to claims of depositors; they are subordinated debt. So in bankruptcy, all the cash that is realized by selling off the bank's remaining assets goes first to depositors and then to other (subordinated) claimants. So at point B the bank's remaining assets are still valuable enough to pay off depositors, leaving other creditors to bear the losses. It is clear from this example that the larger the share of equity and subordinated debt the bank is required to issue, the larger the losses the bank can make before depositors lose money.

KEY POINT

Capital adequacy rules force banks to use a buffer of equity and subordinated debt funding so that depositors are supposedly protected should the bank's assets go bad.

(17.3) Banking Crises

We have seen that banks are vulnerable to panics, and that these panics can be contagious in the sense that the failure of one bank makes further failures much more likely. History is littered with systemic banking crises where many banks fail all at once, the whole financial system comes under severe stress and the economy as a whole suffers. Even the significant measures to regulate banks that were put in place in many countries after the Great Depression seem to have done little to reduce the rate of crisis. Laeven and Valencia[4] estimate that there were 124 systemic banking crises over the period 1970 to 2007, even before the global crisis that reached its most acute point in 2008 took place.

Figure 17.12 shows estimates of the share of the world economy entering a banking crisis since 1820. Although the banking crisis of the Great Depression still ranks as the most significant in terms of economic damage done, the recent crisis has seen a growing share of the world economy afflicted. In fact, it is notable that the contagion associated with bank panics spreads across national borders, so that crises, when they do occur, tend to hit many countries simultaneously.

REAL ESTATE AND BANKING CRISES

One common feature in many banking crises is the role of real estate. Real estate (both residential and commercial) is fundamental to banking for two main reasons. First, as Figure 17.13 shows, lending for real estate purchase or investment is enormous and so is the most important form of lending for many banks. Second, real estate is the most commonly used form of collateral for bank loans. Buildings are valuable and can't disappear overnight if the borrower gets into trouble, so banks will very often lend on the basis that they have a claim on real estate should the borrower fail.

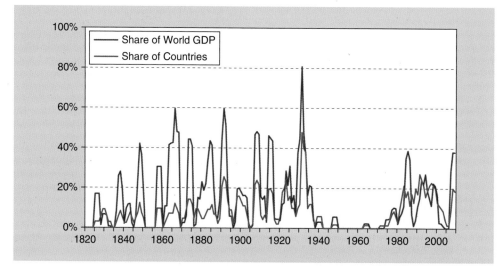

FIGURE 17.12 ● **Banking crises since 1820.** Share of countries entering a banking crisis, three-year moving sum. *Source:* Reinhart, Carmen M. and Rogoff, Kenneth S., *This Time It's Different: Eight Centuries of Financial Folly* (Princeton: Princeton University Press, September 2009).

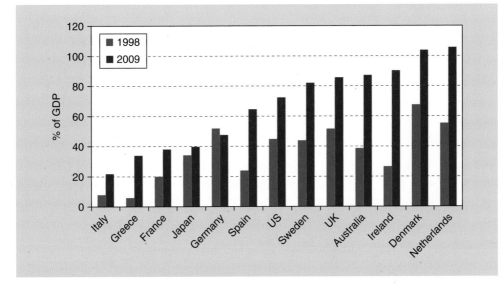

FIGURE 17.13 ● **Residential mortgage lending.** Although it varies across countries, lending for residential property is a large and growing part of developed economies. *Source:* IMF.

As well as being important to banking, real estate prices have another feature that makes them important propagators of banking crises: they are subject to long booms and subsequent busts. In principle, property prices should be determined by the present discounted sum of the future rents that the property could generate, in much the same way that the value of equities is the present discounted value of future dividends (see Chapter 16). Therefore, one might expect the ratio of rents to house prices to be relatively stable over time. Figure 17.14 shows an estimate of this ratio for the United Kingdom since 1970. There are

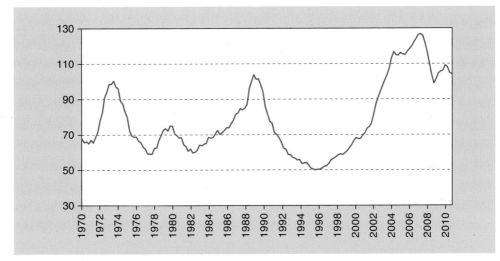

FIGURE 17.14 ● **Property price–rent ratio for the UK (2003=100).** The ratio of property prices to rents has gone through a number of boom–bust cycles in the UK. *Source:* Authors' calculations.

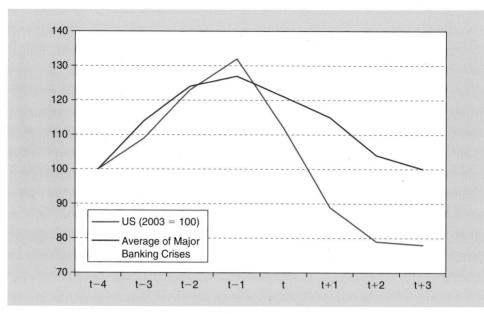

FIGURE 17.15 ● **Real property prices around banking crises.** A house price boom and bust cycle is a common feature of banking crises, both the recent financial crisis and other major post-war banking crises (average of Spain 1977, Norway 1987, Finland 1991, Sweden 1991 and Japan 1992). *Source:* Reinhart, Carmen M. and Rogoff, Kenneth S., *This Time It's Different: Eight Centuries of Financial Folly* (Princeton: Princeton University Press, September 2009).

at least three clear cycles over this period when property prices rose steadily relative to rents before falling back. Moreover, the downturns of two of these cycles were associated with significant banking problems (the secondary banking crisis of 1973–75 and the 2007 crisis).

Figure 17.15 shows the behaviour of property prices around the major post-war banking crises and compares them with US property prices in the recent financial crisis. Here date t indicates the first onset of the crisis. In both cases we see a similar pattern, with real property prices rising dramatically just before the crisis, before falling back when the crisis takes hold. In fact, falling property prices seems to one of the first indicators that a crisis is about to take place. This suggests that a boom–bust cycle in property prices is a common feature of banking crises.

THE ROLE OF THE INTERBANK MARKET

In our discussion of bank panics so far we have focused on bank runs started when depositors withdraw their funds. However, in many cases it is not depositors who start a bank run but banks themselves (and other financial institutions). For example, in the recent financial crisis, the most important driver of banking problems was the failure of the interbank market, where banks and other large financial institutions borrow and lend. Figure 17.16 shows how in 2007 and 2008 the cost of borrowing on the interbank market rose well above the level predicted by looking purely at expected future interest rates. This was particularly

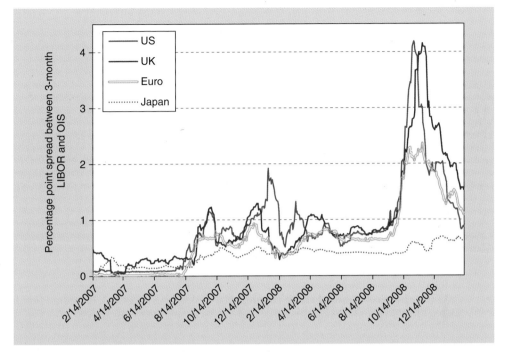

FIGURE 17.16 ● **The breakdown of the interbank market in 2007–08.** Average recorded interest rates for three-month loans between banks rose significantly above normal levels during the financial crisis (measured relative to expected overnight rates from OIS). *Source:* Reuters.

·acute after the failure of Lehman Brothers in September 2008. In fact, after the Lehman failure some institutions found that interbank borrowing was not possible at any interest rate. Effectively, banks became nervous of lending to one another and those with excess funds withdrew that funding from other banks. This withdrawal of interbank lending is an example of wholesale funding (as opposed to retail deposits) drying up. Such problems became severe for banks that did not have a large number of depositors. In particular, pure investment banks (like Lehman Brothers, Goldman Sachs and Morgan Stanley) that have no depositors found it increasingly difficult to finance their operations. Also some commercial banks, such as Northern Rock in the United Kingdom, that were significant borrowers on the wholesale markets (because the total value of their loans was far greater than their deposits) failed due to the unwillingness of other banks to lend to them. In the case of Northern Rock, television coverage that focused on queues of depositors wanting to withdraw their deposits gave a false impression that it was this retail deposit run that caused the problem. In fact, the bank had already failed at that point due to a run on the interbank market. This withdrawal of funds from the interbank market had the standard features of a self-fulfilling bank panic, since it was the withdrawal of funds in itself that caused many banks to fail (or come close to failing) rather than any realized losses. However, it was uncertainty about whether losses would be realized that made those runs happen.

From one perspective, bank runs in the interbank market make sense, since the absence of deposit insurance for interbank transactions makes them more vulnerable to bank failure. However, an important ingredient for a panic is lack of information: depositors may withdraw funds on the basis of unsubstantiated rumours because they have no better information on which to base their decisions. In the case of the interbank market, one might expect that other banks would be better informed about the true state of their competitors. But in a crisis, no one feels very well informed.

(17.4) Credit Crunches

Why is it that problems in the banking sector have such serious macroeconomic repercussions, while downturns in other sectors of the economy, such as agriculture or manufacturing, tend not to spark off recessions? One important reason is that bank credit is important to all other sectors of the economy and if that credit dries up, then the economy as a whole suffers. A situation where firms cannot access credit due to problems in the financial sector is often called a **credit crunch** and means that even if the central bank tries to loosen monetary policy in order to stimulate demand, that policy loosening does not get translated into easier credit conditions, since lenders are restricting the supply of credit. How such credit crunches come about is the subject of much current research, but most models highlight two key channels.

First, there is the **broad credit channel** where, during a recession, firms find that lack of internal funds (profits) mean that they need to borrow money externally. However, at the

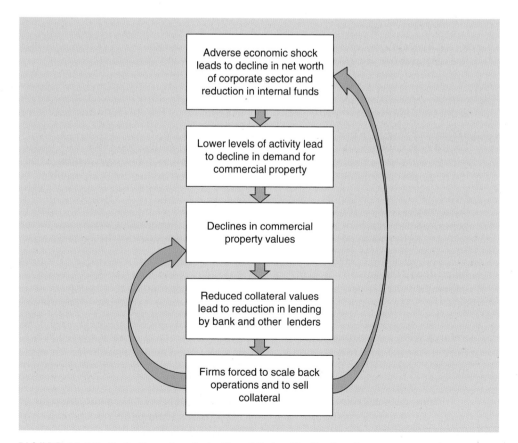

FIGURE 17.17 ● Credit crunch mechanism through the broad lending channel.

same time the downturn means that the value of their fixed assets (commercial property in particular) is falling too. This is important, because these assets are usually used as collateral for loans (because banks are willing to lend if they have a claim on a fixed asset should the borrower fail). With collateral values falling, firms do not have enough fixed assets to cover the borrowings they would like to make. As a result, they are either forced to resort to expensive unsecured loans (i.e. loans that do not require collateral) or are unable to borrow at all, a situation called credit rationing, where firms cannot borrow at any interest rate. Additionally, a credit-rationed firm may well be forced to sell assets, resulting in a further decline in asset values. Figure 17.17 illustrates how a credit crunch can develop through this broad credit channel.

This first channel is called the broad credit channel since it is not restricted to bank lending. Though it will mainly operate through banks, it could also operate for borrowing through financial markets like the bond market. The second credit crunch channel is called the **bank lending channel**, since it focuses purely on banks. In this case the focus falls on small and medium-sized firms, whose only feasible source of borrowing is the banking sector (larger firms can bypass banks by borrowing on financial markets). Through this channel a credit crunch occurs because the banks themselves are in trouble: either bad lending in the past means that they are very unwilling to make risky loans today (since more bad loans could bankrupt them), or regulators are concerned about the financial position of banks and so either explicitly or implicitly encourage them not to make new risky loans. Once again, this channel mainly operates by rationing credit rather than by making loans very expensive.

Some evidence for the existence of this credit-rationing mechanism is shown in Figure 17.18. It shows that there have been two recent periods when small businesses in the

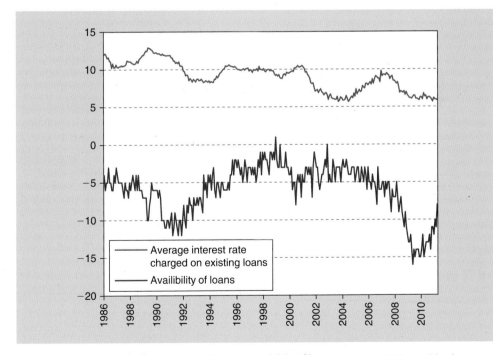

FIGURE 17.18 ● **Small business cost of loans and availability of loans.** Surveys of US small businesses indicate that during a credit crunch they report a significant reduction in the availability of loans rather than a rise in the cost of borrowing. *Source:* NFIB Research Foundation.

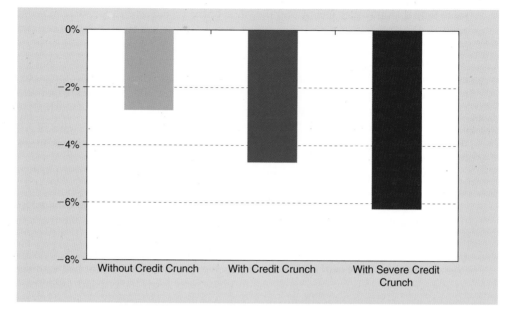

FIGURE 17.19 ● **Output loss in recessions with and without a credit crunch.** Historical evidence shows that recessions associated with credit crunches are more severe (and longer) than normal recessions. *Source:* Claessens, Kose and Terrones, What Happens during Recessions, Crunches and Busts?, IMF Working Paper 08/274.

United States have reported a significant reduction in the availability of loans: 1990–92 and, more dramatically, 2008–10. What is noteworthy is that when the same businesses are asked what interest rate they were charged on loans that they did have, they reported relatively low rates in both of these periods. Their concern was not the cost of credit, but simply its availability.

These credit crunch mechanisms are important, since evidence suggests that recessions associated with credit crunches are far worse than those without. Figure 17.19 compares the average output loss for recessions without a credit crunch with those with a credit crunch and a severe credit crunch (the worst 50% of credit crunches) for 122 recessions between 1960 and 2007 (i.e. not including the recent financial crisis). This evidence suggests that a credit crunch episode results in a far more severe (and longer-lasting) recession than normal. The events following the more recent financial crisis add greatly to the evidence that recessions following banking problems are unusually severe.

SUMMARY

Section 17.1 showed how banks provide an number of important services, ranging from payments services, monitoring of loans (especially to SMEs) and maturity transformation, so that depositors can get instant access to their money while borrowers can get long-term loans. In Section 17.2 we saw that the way banks operate puts them at risk of bank runs and how deposit insurance and banking regulation have been introduced to reduce this risk. Section 17.3 showed that despite this type of regulation, banking crises are relatively frequent and are often associated with down-turns in house prices. Finally, in Section 17.4 we saw how credit crunches can occur and explained why banks have such an important impact on the economy.

CONCEPTUAL QUESTIONS

1. (Section 17.2) 'Governments that support failing banks are encouraging inappropriate behaviour from both savers and banks – bank bailouts represent a huge waste of resources.'

   'Banks are so important that governments simply cannot let them fail – that is what the banking panics and bank failures in the US in the 1930s show.'

   Which position is more defensible? Does it matter which country we are focusing on?

2. (Section 17.1) Consider the links you have with banks. Could you imagine all the services that banks provide to you being provided by non-banks?

3. (Section 17.2) It has been proposed that banks should not be allowed to operate as both commercial and investment banks. What are the advantages and disadvantages of such a proposal? Would it reduce the risk of bank runs?

4. (Section 17.3) Should central banks raise interest rates when property prices are rising rapidly even if general inflation is low? Should other measures be introduced to limit property price fluctuations?

5. (Section 17.3) 'Banking crises are as common now as they were before banking regulation was introduced after the Great Depression, so bank regulation is simply costly and ineffective.' Do you agree?

ANALYTICAL QUESTIONS

1. (Section 17.1) To loan money successfully requires monitoring those to whom money has been loaned. Assume that the annual monitoring cost are $300 a year for each loan regardless of size. Suppose that the typical saver has $30 000 to lend and would not want to lend to fewer than 10 different borrowers so as to diversify risk. Compare a situation in which each saver directly lends money to 10 borrowers and a situation in which each saver joins 1000 others to form a bank that lends to 10 (very large) borrowers. What is the saving in monitoring costs?

2. (Section 17.1) A bank has deposits that are instantly redeemable at no penalty. It makes loans that are repaid gradually over a period of several years. It cannot call the loans at short notice. It also holds some of its assets in the form of cash balances, which it can use immediately to pay out to those who want to withdraw funds. Assume that loans earn a rate of return of 9% a year and that cash balances pay nothing. Explain exactly how the bank should think about the optimal split in its assets between loans and cash balances. Assume that the penalty for running out of cash (not being able to pay depositors) is very large. How does your analysis depend on the availability and cost of loans in an interbank market in which a bank can borrow money in the short term from other banks?

3. (Section 17.2) A bank is near insolvency – its assets are worth $1000 million, only a fraction more than its debt liabilities of $999.5 million. As a result, the true value of its equity is small. The bank is able to take $100 million more deposits from the public in return for a promise to pay 6% return. The bank considers two possible uses to which the new deposits can be put. The safe

option is to lend at a rate of 8%. There is a 95% chance that such a loan will be repaid in full. There is a 5% chance that for each dollar loaned the bank will simply get its money back (but receive no interest). The alternative loan is very risky. There is a 60% chance that the bank can make the risky loan at an interest rate of 40% and be paid back in full (receiving $1.40 for each $1). There is a 40% chance that it will be repaid nothing. Which loan has the higher expected return? Which loan would the shareholders, who have limited liability, prefer the bank to make?

4. (Section 17.2) Explain why a bank run is a Nash Equilibrium and why not running to the bank is also a Nash Equilibrium. Because one of these equlibria is less desirable than the other, it would be useful to devise arrangements that made bank runs unlikely. Describe some possible arrangements that would achieve this.

CHAPTER 18

Sovereign Debt and Default

Overview

We consider the implications of governments running fiscal deficits; that is, not covering their expenditure out of tax revenue. We discuss how deficits and the stock of debt have evolved over time and the implications of the recent financial crisis for sovereign debt. We analyse the long-run implications of current deficits and show how the relative magnitudes of rates of return and growth of GDP are critical to the sustainability of the fiscal position. We also look at how and when sovereign defaults occur and the role of financial markets in those defaults.

Sovereign Debt and Deficits

We saw in Chapter 14 the benefits of government borrowing, both as a means of smoothing tax and spending and as a way to finance investment. One key implication of tax smoothing is that governments should spread the cost of unexpected, one-off events across time by accumulating debt and then paying off that debt with slightly increased tax rates (and/or lower spending), keeping taxes at this higher level for a long time. Figure 18.1 illustrates (for the case of the United Kingdom) the most significant that events that tend to cause a significant increase in government debt are wars. UK government debt peaked at around 260%, 180% and 240% of GDP around the Napoleonic war and the First and Second World Wars respectively, but was subsequently brought back under control.

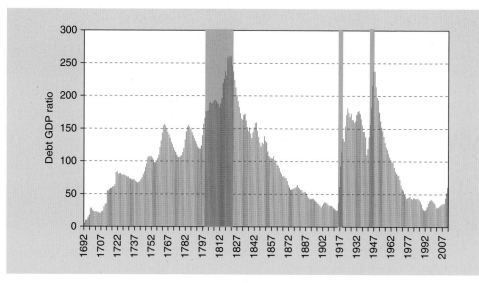

FIGURE 18.1 ● UK net public debt since 1692 (% of GDP). UK government debt has risen most dramatically around major wars. Shaded areas show Napoleonic Wars, First World War and Second World War respectively. *Source:* www.ukpublicspending.co.uk.

More recently, a number of governments have had to deal with a different type of one-off event: the financial crisis of 2008–09. Figure 18.2 shows that the average level of gross government debt of advanced economies rose substantially over this period. By contrast, developing and emerging nations that were generally less affected by the crisis continued to see a steady decline in their debt-to-GDP ratios, largely as a result of rapid GDP growth and the benefits of higher commodity prices for commodity-exporting countries.

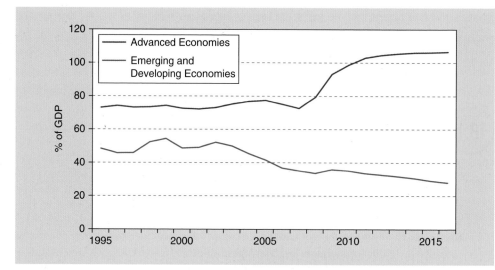

FIGURE 18.2 ● Average gross government debt of developed and developing countries (% GDP). The 2008–09 financial crisis caused a dramatic increase in the debt of developed nations, but had little impact on developing-country debt. *Source:* IMF World Economic Outlook database (April 2011).

TABLE 18.1 ● **General Government Gross Financial Liabilities as a Percentage of GDP.**

The financial crisis has resulted in a significant increase in government debt for a number of countries.

	2007	2008	2009	2010	2011	Debt Increase 2007–11
France	70	76	87	92	97	27
Greece	105	106	120	129	137	32
Iceland	53	102	120	125	117	64
Ireland	29	50	73	105	113	84
Japan	167	174	193	198	204	37
Portugal	69	74	86	93	99	30
Spain	42	47	62	72	78	36
United Kingdom	47	57	72	81	88	41
United States	62	71	84	93	99	37

Source: OECD *Economic Outlook* No. 88, OECD Economic Outlook: Statistics and Projections (database).

Table 18.1 looks in more detail at the debt and deficits of some of the countries worst affected by the financial crisis. Although for some countries, like Ireland, the most important factor behind the increase in government borrowing has been the direct costs of bailing out the banking system, in most cases it has been the indirect effect of the crisis on tax revenue and transfer payments that has been the major driver, along with the cost of fiscal stimulus measures aimed at stabilizing the economy.

In the rest of this chapter we look at the background to large increases in government debt such as the one that occurred in many countries after 2007. We analyse the conditions under which debt is sustainable and when and why default occurs.

(18.2) Deficits and the Business Cycle

As we saw in Chapter 15, there is a natural tendency for government borrowing to increase in recession and fall in booms. This occurs because government revenue tends to fall in recessions (due to falling tax revenue) while spending rises (on transfers such as unemployment benefit). We also saw that it makes little sense for the government to attempt to offset this cycle by trying to increase taxes or cut spending in recessions and vice versa in booms. Such deficits are generally temporary and allowing borrowing automatically to increase in a recession and fall in booms will tend to stabilize the economy by dampening the business cycle. This is why the mechanisms that cause this cycle in government borrowing are called automatic stabilizers. Given this cycle in government borrowing, it is important to try to find a measure of the underlying fiscal position after allowing for the business cycle. Such a measure is called the **structural** or **cyclically adjusted** deficit.

In order to estimate the structural budget balance, we start with an estimate of potential output using one of the methods discussed in Chapter 11. This gives a measure of where output would be if the output gap was zero and so removes the impact of the business cycle. We can then estimate what tax revenue and government spending would have been if actual output was equal to potential output. These estimates are called the structural government revenue and structural government spending respectively and are calculated as follows:

$$\text{Structural Revenues} = \text{Actual Revenues} \times \left(\frac{\text{Potential Output}}{\text{Actual Output}}\right)^{\alpha}$$

and

$$\text{Structural Spending} = \text{Actual Spending} \times \left(\frac{\text{Potential Output}}{\text{Actual Output}}\right)^{\beta}$$

where α is the elasticity of government revenue with respect to output and β is the elasticity of government spending with respect to output. In practice, α tends to be much larger than β, since most tax revenue is sensitive to economic activity while only a small share of government spending changes with the business cycle. The structural budget balance is then given by:

$$\text{Structural Balance} = \text{Structural Revenues} - \text{Structural Spending}$$

Figure 18.3 compares the actual and structural balance for the United States. We see that the structural deficit was far smaller than the actual budget deficit during the recessions of 1975, 1983 and 2009.

In principle, the structural balance is an important guide to policy, since governments should pay less attention to the cyclical pattern of government borrowing and should instead focus on maintaining the structural balance at sustainable levels. But, in practice, estimates of the structural balance can be problematic, since they are not always reliable. Not only are the output elasticity of revenue and spending not easy to estimate, but calculations of potential output are challenging and vary according to the method used. These problems are particularly acute in deep recessions, since it is likely that a particularly acute recession will actually

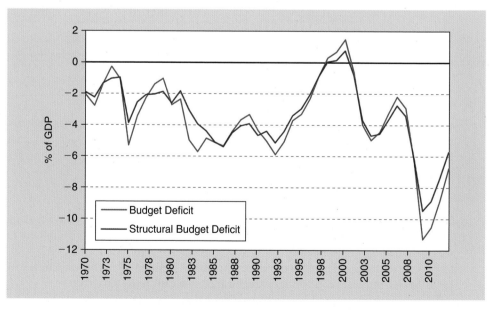

FIGURE 18.3 ● **US actual and structural budget balance (% of GDP).** The structural balance strips out the impact of the business cycle on government borrowing. *Source:* OECD, *Economic Outlook* (2011).

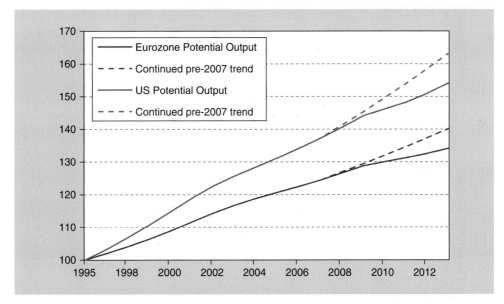

FIGURE 18.4 ● **Estimated path of US and Eurozone potential output pre- and post-financial crisis.** The OECD judges that potential output will be permanently lowered by the crisis as a result of a period of below-trend growth. *Source:* OECD, *Economic Outlook* (2011).

significantly reduce the level of potential output growth. For example, Figure 18.4 shows OECD estimates of potential output for the United States and Eurozone around the financial crisis of 2008–09. The OECD judges that both economies saw some reduction in their potential output growth over this period. This reduction in potential output growth means that, unlike in a normal business cycle where the deficit accumulated during a recession is largely offset by a surplus in the following boom, the structural deficit has increased and so fiscal policy must at some point be actively tightened to bring government borrowing to sustainable levels.

Unfortunately for policymakers, estimates of the structural deficit are highly uncertain. As an illustration, Table 18.2 compares IMF and OECD estimates of the output gap and

TABLE 18.2 ● **Output Gap and Structural Balance Estimates, 2011.**
There are some significant differences between OECD and IMF estimates of both the output gap and the structural balance.

	IMF Output Gap	OECD Output Gap	IMF Structural Balance	OECD Structural Balance
Canada	–1.5%	–3.4%	–3.6%	–2.1%
France	–3.1%	–5.8%	–4.0%	–4.4%
Germany	–0.5%	–1.9%	–2.1%	–2.4%
Italy	–3.0%	–3.9%	–2.8%	–1.5%
Japan	–3.8%	–1.5%	–8.3%	–6.8%
UK	–2.6%	–4.0%	–6.6%	–6.0%
US	–3.7%	–3.0%	–8.1%	–7.4%

Source: OECD *Economic Outlook*, 88, IMF *World Economic Outlook* (April 2011).

the structural deficit for a number of countries in 2011. The estimates often differ markedly. These differences are of significant practical importance, since the size of the structural deficit is widely used by policymakers as a guide to the level of fiscal consolidation (or tightening) required as a result of the crisis.

KEY POINT

Government borrowing varies with the business cycle. Estimates of the structural budget balance are an attempt to control for the effect of the business cycle on borrowing,

---

(18.3) Long-Run Sustainability

Imagine that the structural deficit were correctly estimated. What level of that deficit would be sustainable in the long run? Every period the government runs an overall deficit, its debt increases: when spending plus interest payments on the existing stock of debt exceeds tax revenues, the stock of debt will rise. But it does not follow from this that governments cannot afford to run deficits for long periods. So long as the stock of debt does not keep rising relative to GDP, then a government is likely to be able to keep paying the interest on its debt. At unchanged interest rates, the burden of paying interest would be constant relative to GDP if the debt-to-GDP ratio is steady. This is why stability of the ratio of the stock of government debt to GDP is considered the best way to judge the sustainability of the fiscal position.

Since GDP – in nominal terms – is likely to rise over time, it follows that the nominal stock of debt can rise. For that reason, it can be sustainable for a government consistently to run overall deficits without finding its debt growing out of control. But there will be a limit to the sustainable deficit – the limit being the deficit that is the largest consistent with the debt-to-GDP ratio not rising.

Let us examine the conditions under which a government can consistently run a deficit. Let D denote the stock of government debt and let GDP be denoted Y. The debt/GDP ratio is D/Y. We define the **primary balance** as government revenue minus government spending *excluding* debt interest payments. Table 18.3 shows the size of the primary deficit for a number of countries. If the government runs a primary deficit of zero (a zero deficit excluding interest payments), then debt increases only because of the interest payments on its existing debt. These interest payments are the product of the interest rate (r) and the stock of debt (D). But offsetting this is the fact that the debt-to-GDP ratio falls because of GDP growth (g).

Debt is sustainable if D/Y is not changing. A change in the ratio of debt to GDP can result from any of three factors:

- It rises because of interest on existing debt. This adds r (D/Y) to the debt-to-GDP ratio.
- It falls because of growth of GDP. This reduces the debt-to-GDP ratio by g(D/Y).
- Finally, debt changes by the size of the primary deficit relative to GDP.

Putting these three together we have:

Change in D/Y = $(r - g)$D/Y + Primary Deficit/GDP

TABLE 18.3 ● Government Deficits as % of GDP, 2011.

	Government Fiscal Balances	Government Primary Balances	Government Debt Interest Payments
US	–10.1	–8.2	1.9
Japan	–8.9	–7.3	1.6
Germany	–2.1	0.0	2.1
France	–5.6	–3.1	2.5
Italy	–3.9	0.5	4.4
UK	–8.7	–6.1	2.6
Canada	–4.9	–4.2	0.7
Spain	–6.3	–4.6	1.7
All OECD	–6.7	–4.9	1.8

Note: Column 1 = Column 2 – Column 3
Source: OECD, *Economic Outlook* (2011).

Therefore the debt-to-GDP ratio is constant when

$$(r - g)D/Y = \text{Primary Surplus/GDP}$$

Here we are measuring the interest rate (r) in nominal terms and, for consistency, we also need to measure the growth of nominal GDP (g). If $r > g$, the government has to run a primary surplus in order to control the debt-to-GDP ratio. If $r < g$, then government can always run a deficit (of a certain size) without seeing the debt-to-GDP ratio increase.

Table 18.4 illustrates the dynamics of debt by showing two situations. In both cases g exceeds r. This means that primary deficits can be sustained. Interest rates are 3%, while the growth in nominal GDP – that is, real GDP growth plus inflation, denoted g – adds up to 5%.

TABLE 18.4 ● Sustainable and Unsustainable Deficits.

Because of output growth, a government can always run a deficit but its debt is sustainable (in the sense that D/Y stays at 50%). An economy with a 5% deficit eventually sees D/Y stabilize at 250%.

Unsustainable	GDP	Public Debt	Deficit	Interest	Debt/GDP	Deficit GDP	Interest/GDP
Year 1	$700bn	$350bn	$35bn	$10.5bn	50%	5%	1.5%
Year 2	$735bn	$395.5bn	$36.8bn	$11.9bn	53.8%	5%	1.6%
Year 3	$771.8bn	$444.1bn	$38.6bn	$13.3bn	57.5%	5%	1.7%
Year 4	$810.4bn	$496.0bn	$40.5bn	$14.9bn	61.2%	5%	1.8%
Sustainable							
Year 1	$700bn	$350bn	$7bn	$10.5bn	50%	1%	1.5%
Year 2	$735bn	$367.5bn	$7.35bn	$11.0bn	50%	1%	1.5%
Year 3	$771.8bn	$385.9bn	$7.72bn	$11.6bn	50%	1%	1.5%
Year 4	$810.4bn	$405.2bn	$8.1bn	$12.2bn	50%	1%	1.5%

Note: Assume 5% growth in money GDP – 3% real + 2% inflation; interest rates are 3%.

(We assume 2% inflation, which implies real interest rates of plus 1%.) In the first case, we start with a stock of public debt of $350 billion and a primary deficit of $35 billion. The debt-to-GDP ratio is 50% and the primary deficit-to-GDP ratio is 5%. But we see from the table that this level of deficit implies a rising stock of debt and a rising interest burden. The debt-to-GDP ratio would eventually settle down on this path, but at a much higher level than 50%. Only when the debt-to-GDP ratio is 250% is it sustainable. We know that the sustainable debt-to-GDP ratio is 250% because if we consistently run a primary deficit of 0.05 of GDP and with $r = 0.03$ and $g = 0.05$, the condition for an unchanging debt-to-GDP ratio implies:

$$\frac{(r - g)D}{Y} = \text{Primary Surplus/GDP}$$

which means:

$$(0.03 - 0.05)D/Y = 0.05$$

This implies $D/Y = -0.05/(0.03 - 0.05) = 2.5$, so that the sustainable stock of debt is 250% of GDP.

The lower panel of Table 18.4 shows that if the primary deficit-to-GDP ratio were initially 1%, then although the stock of debt would continue to rise (because the government would consistently be running a deficit), the stock of debt to GDP would remain constant at 50%.

The key issue is whether the real cost of debt exceeds or falls short of the long-run, real sustainable rate of growth of GDP. This is because the key number for sustainable debt dynamics is $(r - g)$. Although both r and g are measured in nominal terms, the difference between them is actually equal to the gap between the real interest rate and the rate of growth of real GDP. This is because:

$$r = \text{Real interest rate} + \text{Inflation}$$

$$g = \text{Growth of real GDP} + \text{Inflation}$$

$$\text{so: } r - g = \text{Real interest rate} - \text{Growth of real GDP}$$

Clearly, whether g exceeds r matters. The sustainable rate of growth of real GDP (g) probably does not exceed 2.5% for mature, developed economies. What about the real rate of return on government debt? One measure is to take nominal yields on government bonds and subtract inflation. But actual inflation over the last 20 to 30 years has probably, on average, exceeded expected inflation in many countries. So the ex post (or realized) average real rate is a poor guide to the real cost of government borrowing in the future. Perhaps a better indication is to look at inflation-proof (index-linked) bond yields. Few governments have issued index-linked bonds, but the biggest market, in UK government index-linked bonds, does provide some data. Since that market was created in the early 1980s, index-linked yields on medium-dated (10-year) government bonds have fluctuated, but the average has been close to 3% – above the likely sustainable long-run rate of growth of developed economies.

Most empirical evidence suggests that rates of return on assets in *general* do, over the long term, exceed GDP growth. That is, r does exceed g. This implies that sustainability of fiscal policies requires that governments do *not* consistently run primary deficits. *Governments with existing debt will need to run primary surpluses at some point to keep the debt-to-GDP ratio from exploding.* Indeed, if the interest rate on debt were to rise with the stock of debt, the need to offset current primary deficits with surpluses in the future becomes even more urgent. Failure to do that quickly could lead to an ever-rising interest rate. Investors can develop a fear that a government may have set off on an unsustainable path that, at some point, could trigger default on debt obligations, because the government cannot raise sufficient revenues even to pay the interest on existing debt. That fear could cause interest rates to rise, as investors need to be compensated for the risk of default on the bonds that they hold. It is easy to see how that fear could become self-fulfilling, a point that we discuss further in Section 18.5.

> **KEY POINT**
>
> In a growing economy, governments can run overall deficits consistently. But unless growth is high relative to the interest rate on debt on average, primary surpluses are needed.

18.4 The Intertemporal Budget Constraint

We have seen that when r exceeds g a government will need, at some point, to run a primary surplus in order to avoid continually rising ratios of debt to GDP. This means that, if the government currently has outstanding debt, the government has to run a fiscal surplus at some point in the future so as to repay the debt.

The links between the stock of debt and future surpluses are easier to understand with a simple example. Imagine a two-period model where the government has to balance its books at the end of two periods. Debt at the end of the first period (denoted period 0) is:

$$D(0) = G(0) - T(0)$$

where $G(0)$ is government spending in the first period and $T(0)$ is tax revenue in the first period.

To pay off the debt in the second period we need:

$$T(1) - G(1) = [G(0) - T(0)] \times (1 + r) = D(0) \times (1 + r)$$

so that debt equals the present discounted value of future primary surpluses:

$$D(0) = [T(1) - G(1)] / (1 + r)$$

This simple result can be generalized into an infinite number of periods. The more general result is that the stock of government debt today must equal the present discounted value of all future primary surpluses. This is the government **intertemporal budget constraint**.

> **KEY POINT**
>
> The government intertemporal budget constraint means that the current stock of debt should equal the present value of future primary surpluses. If that is not true, default will occur at some point.

The intertemporal budget constraint has huge implications. If a country has very good growth prospects, it can expect to be able to repay its debt; if growth is strong, it may do so without needing to raise tax rates. But if growth slows, then a country may need higher tax rates to generate fiscal surpluses. This may be politically difficult.

The intertemporal budget constraint tells us why it is problematic to have similar numerical targets for debt levels across countries. Debt sustainability means that, on the basis of existing government policies, the future will see sufficient fiscal surpluses to pay back current debt. Different countries have different future prospects and so should have different current levels of debt. Countries where future growth will be high can afford to have larger stocks of government debt than those where growth will be lower. Mature, developed countries cannot confidently expect future growth to be higher than the average over the past few decades. The implication is that, for mature economies that are unlikely to experience sustained shocks or changes in growth patterns, future prospects should be stable and so should debt levels. The idea here is that, for the developed economies, large deficits and high debt-to-GDP ratios cannot be sustainable, because a long period of high growth of GDP is unlikely for any country.

However, the intertemporal budget constraint also implies that the reasons deficits are being run are as relevant as the size of the deficits. Deficits used to finance investment (such as health, education and transport infrastructure) may be self-financing through the higher growth and tax revenue that they generate in the future, while those used to finance current spending are less likely to be. The intertemporal budget constraint also makes it clear that running deficits and having the debt-to-GDP ratio rise sharply during a temporary slowdown – even if it is a prolonged one – is not a problem, so long as future surpluses are large enough.

CONTINGENT LIABILITIES

The intertemporal budget constraint also highlights the importance of contingent future liabilities. These are government liabilities that will only become certain on the occurrence of some future event, but are nonetheless very likely to have an impact on future spending and revenue. The most important contingent liabilities that most developed countries face is future state pension payments and the associated health costs of an ageing population. These have the potential to generate large and sustained future deficits and so should be factored into tax and spending decisions today.

State-run pensions in most developed countries are run on a PAYGO (pay as you go) basis, whereby pensions to the current generation of retirees are paid for by contributions from the current generation of workers. This means that as the share of the population in retirement rises, so does the burden of pension payments for the current working population. One indication of the scale of the problem with such systems is shown in Table 18.5. This gives estimates of the required increase in age-related public expenditure between 2010 and 2025 given unchanged policies. What the table reveals is that at current tax rates, if state pensions remain at the levels of generosity seen in recent years, and if there is no significant increase in retirement ages, then deficits are likely to be generated by age-related government expenditures in most developed countries. Such a rise in the scale of deficits would have ultimately to be offset by surpluses at a later date or by simultaneous surpluses on the non-pension part of the government accounts. More likely is that future governments will have to head off the problem by a combination of further increases in the age at which state pensions are paid, some cut-back in the generosity of pensions and public health provision, and further increases in contribution rates.

KEY POINT

The intertemporal budget constraint has different implications for different economies, depending on the purposes for which they run deficits, their contingent liabilities and their future prospects for growth.

TABLE 18.5 ● **Future Spending Commitments Associated with Ageing Population.**

Projected increase in ageing-related government spending from 2010 to 2025, percentage points of GDP.

	Health care	Long-term care	Pensions	Total
Australia	1.3	0.4	0.8	2.5
Canada	1.4	0.5	0.6	2.5
France	1.1	0.3	0.4	1.8
Germany	1.1	0.6	0.8	2.5
Greece	1.2	1.0	3.2	5.4
Ireland	1.2	1.1	1.5	3.9
Italy	1.2	1.0	0.3	2.5
Japan	1.5	0.9	0.2	2.5
Netherlands	1.3	0.5	1.9	3.7
Portugal	1.2	0.5	0.7	2.4
Spain	1.2	0.8	1.2	3.2
Sweden	1.1	0.2	–0.2	1.1
United Kingdom	1.1	0.5	0.5	2.0
United States	1.2	0.3	0.7	2.1

Source: OECD *Economic Outlook* (2010).

(18.5) Sovereign Default

While fiscal consolidation is one route to managing unsustainable government deficits and debt, the alternative is some type of default where the government is no longer willing to service its debt and so fails to honour promised interest payments. As Figure 18.5 shows, such defaults are not at all uncommon and tend to occur in clusters when many countries default simultaneously. The most significant of these clusters of defaults since 1820 (as a share of world GDP) occurred in the Great Depression, though the debt crisis of the 1980s stands out as the most recent example. Since the 1980s the number of defaults has remained at a remarkably low level, though the financial crisis of the late 2000s has brought a number of countries to the brink of default.

Defaults not only tend to occur in clusters over time; certain countries have a history of serial default. Table 18.6 highlights countries that have defaulted at least five times since 1800 (or independence if that occurred after 1800). There is a clear regional pattern of serial default in this data, with many Latin American countries having a history of repeated default, but no Asian countries appearing in the table (the highest number of defaults by an Asian country is Indonesia, with four since it became independent in 1949). Of course, there were a number of defaults before 1800,[1] though these have not been systematically recorded. Spain and France have seven and eight defaults between them prior to 1800 (in the sixteenth to eighteenth centuries), while the UK has defaulted at least twice[2] – once in 1340 and again in 1472.

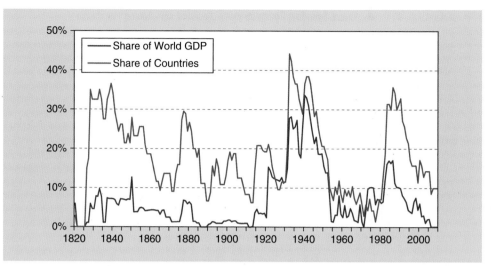

FIGURE 18.5 ● **Share of countries in default since 1800.** *Source:* Reinhart, Carmen M. and Rogoff, Kenneth S., *This Time It's Different: Eight Centuries of Financial Folly* (Princeton: Princeton University Press, September 2009).

THE CHOICE TO DEFAULT

An important feature of sovereign default is that, unlike corporations, sovereigns can default whenever they want to. While a corporation is legally required to honour its debts if it possibly can, sovereign governments are able to write their own laws (and can ignore international law), and so can choose not to pay their creditors whenever they wish. In particular, if those creditors are not citizens of the country, there need be no obvious impact on the government's popular support either. The ease with which a sovereign can default raises two important questions: why do we not see more defaults and why does any overseas entity lend to a sovereign in the first place?

While there are a number of reasons why default might be unattractive to a government, it is not clear if any are likely enough or costly enough to explain why defaults are not more common.

SEIZURE OF PHYSICAL ASSETS   In a corporate default, creditors' ultimate threat is to seize the physical assets of the defaulting firm. In a sovereign default, seizing physical assets (i.e. invasion) is a little more problematic. There are a number of cases in history where foreign creditors have imposed a settlement on a defaulting government by force of arms or other intervention. However, such interventions are now extremely rare and so most sovereigns that default do not fear invasion as a result.[3]

LACK OF ACCESS TO CAPITAL MARKETS AND REPUTATIONAL COSTS   Defaulting borrowers are unlikely to be able to borrow again from international capital markets for some time. However, it is unclear how costly this is to a government that has effectively wiped out its debt (and may have kept some foreign assets), particularly as its creditors may not punish

TABLE 18.6 ● **Serial Defaulters since 1800.**

Countries that have defaulted and/or restructured their debt at least five times since independence or 1800, whichever is the later.

	Year of Independence	Number of Defaults/ Restructurings	% of Years in Default/ Restructurings
Africa			
Nigeria	1960	5	21%
Europe			
Greece	1829	5	51%
Portugal	Pre-1800	6	11%
Russia	Pre-1800	5	39%
Spain	Pre-1800	8	24%
Turkey	Pre-1800	6	16%
Latin America			
Argentina	1816	7	33%
Bolivia	1825	5	22%
Brazil	1822	9	25%
Chile	1818	9	28%
Columbia	1819	7	36%
Costa Rica	1821	9	38%
Dominican Republic	1945	7	29%
Ecuador	1830	9	58%
El Salvador	1821	5	26%
Guatemala	1821	7	34%
Mexico	1821	8	45%
Nicaragua	1821	6	45%
Paraguay	1811	6	23%
Peru	1821	8	40%
Uruguay	1811	8	13%
Venezuela	1830	10	38%

Source: Reinhart, Carmen M. and Rogoff, Kenneth S., *This Time It's Different: Eight Centuries of Financial Folly* (Princeton: Princeton University Press, September 2009).

a defaulter for very long; a recent defaulter may well be a better lending prospect than a highly indebted borrower. On the other hand, there is evidence that the serial defaulters shown in Table 18.6 do pay more to borrow than others (though their overall cost of finance including the benefit of default is lower than that for non-defaulters).

TABLE 18.7 ● Some Recent Debt Restructurings.

Countries rarely default on their debt completely, but instead negotiate a reduction in the timing and amount of debt payments, called a 'haircut'.

Country	Date of Exchange	Amount of Debt ($ million)	Estimated Reduction in Debt Value
Pakistan (external bonds)	1999	610	15%
Ecuador	2000	6700	38%
Russia	2000	31 943	51%
Uruguay	2003	3127	10%
Serbia & Montenegro	2004	2700	73%
Argentina	2005	43 736	77%
Belize	2006	516	24%

Source: Cruces and Trebesch, Sovereign Defaults: The Price of Haircuts, mimeo.

IMPACT ON PRIVATE-SECTOR BORROWING   In a sovereign default it is quite likely that corporations in that country will be unable to borrow overseas, even in the form of trade credit. Such a constraint may have significant economic costs.

IMPACT ON DOMESTIC CREDITORS   In modern financial markets it is often very difficult to identify who is the ultimate holder of a financial asset. So when a government defaults, hoping to impose all the cost on foreign creditors, it may inadvertently default on obligations to domestic creditors, who may be in a position to punish the government directly.

In most cases borrowers agree to a debt restructuring, which is an agreed rescheduling of interest payments between debtors and creditors. Most sovereign-to-sovereign debt restructurings are agreed through a semi-formal institution called the Paris Club, where debtors and creditors negotiate over the terms of a restructuring (there is also the London Club for private-sector creditors), which will usually results in the debtor delaying interest payments and/or making smaller interest payments. Table 18.7 shows estimates of the reduction in the value of external debt agreed in some recent debt restructurings. The terms of the restructuring are often surprisingly generous to creditors; there is some evidence that generous restructurings result in a quicker return to international capital markets.

> ### KEY POINT
>
> Sovereign default, unlike corporate default, is a matter of choice, not necessity, though there are a number of reasons why countries may choose not to default.

INFLATION AS DEFAULT

Rather than default outright, a number of governments have chosen to resort to money printing as a way of dealing with high debt. As we saw in Chapter 12, increasing the monetary base can temporarily help government finances, since the central bank can use the increase in its liabilities to lend money to the government directly. The consequence of this

TABLE 18.8 ● Structure of Debt: Emerging and Advanced Economies, 2005–09.

Original sin means that emerging economies are required to undertake a significant proportion of their borrowing in foreign currency or in short-term instruments.

	Share of Debt in Foreign Currency	Average Maturity of Local Currency Debt
Advanced Economies	1%	7.1 years
Emerging Economies	42%	4.9 years

Source: Cottarelli, Forni, Gottschalk and Mauro, IMF SPN/10 (2010).

money printing is higher inflation and sometimes ultimately hyperinflation. Nevertheless, inflation may also help the government deal with its high debt. Imagine that the debt is a fixed amount of local currency. An increase in inflation can rapidly reduce the debt-to-GDP ratio, since inflation increases the value of nominal GDP (in effect, inflation means that the nominal value of tax payments rises, so paying off the debt becomes easier).

However, in practice a government's debt is rarely fixed in local currency terms. Creditors who fear that inflation may be used to reduce the value of their claims are likely to require either that the government only issue debt denominated in foreign currency, which the issuer cannot erode through domestic inflation, or that the government only issue very short-term debt, which will mature before inflation has eroded its value. And such short-term debt has to be reissued at a much higher interest rate when inflation takes hold. The requirement imposed by creditors that government issue debt in foreign currency is sometimes called an implication of **original sin**, since even if the government has not resorted to high inflation as a way of reducing the real value of its debt in the past, the fear that it might means that creditors will refuse to purchase local currency or long-term debt from it. Table 18.8 shows how original sin means that developing countries are often required to issue much of their debt in foreign currency and that their local currency debt is usually of relatively short maturity. This high proportion of foreign currency and short-term debt means that the incentives to use inflation to erode the real value of debt are quite limited in most developing countries, particularly since inflation imposes significant costs on the local population.

> ### KEY POINT
>
> Inflation can be used to erode the real value of government debt, but borrowers may insist on forms of debt that are less influenced by inflation if they suspect a country of using these means.

18.6 Credit Risk and Credit Agencies

Fear of default is a persistent problem in sovereign debt markets and as a result holders of sovereign debt will usually require a higher interest rate from countries at risk of default, to compensate for the possibility that the promised interest payments do not arrive. This risk of default is called credit risk and higher credit risk means that the interest rate rises above the default-free rate. Figure 18.6 shows how after the financial crisis, the cost of borrowing for a number of Eurozone economies varied significantly, despite the fact that they are all borrowing in the same currency – the euro. This variation in borrowing costs is explained by the risk of default. So, for example, in mid-2011, Greek 10-year government

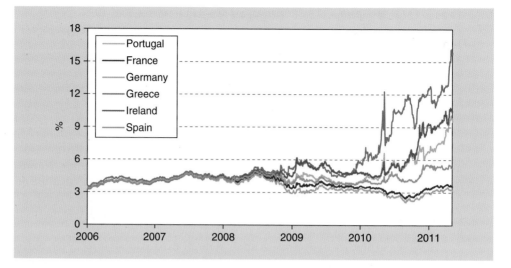

FIGURE 18.6 ● Yields on 10-year Eurozone government debt. A dramatic increase in the probability of default in some Eurozone countries has caused their cost of borrowing to increase significantly above that of 'safe' nations. *Source:* Reuters EcoWin.

debt paid a yield of nearly 16%, while the equivalent debt in Germany paid just over 3%. The difference between these two rates is called a **credit spread** and reflects the different expected probability of default of the two countries.

As well as looking at market prices, investors often use credit ratings as a way of judging the risk of default. These ratings are produced by credit rating agencies such as S&P, Moody's and Fitch, who undertake a detailed assessment of the macroeconomic and political background of the issuer. The credit rating takes the form of letters, ranging from AAA for the highest-quality borrowers who are very unlikely to default to D for a borrower currently in default. The BBB– rating is also important, since ratings below this level are classified as speculative-grade or 'junk' debt. Figure 18.7 shows the recent evolution of S&P credit ratings for some major developed economies, including when ratings have been put on positive or negative watch (which means that the rating is being considered for upgrade or downgrade). Credit rating agencies have been subject to much criticism recently, partly because they are seen as slow to react to borrower problems and only adjust after problems are widely known, and partly because they are seen as subject to conflicts of interest, since the debt issuer pays for the rating. There is some evidence that financial markets react to ratings changes, which suggests that they do contain useful information rather than just reflecting known information or projecting a biased view.

CREDIT RISK AND SELF-FULFILLING DEBT CRISES

Figure 18.8 shows the average behaviour of the interest rate demanded by holders of sovereign debt in the period running up to a government default. It demonstrates how borrowing costs rise dramatically in the year before default. One interpretation of this chart is that markets are relatively good at predicting default and so become increasingly unwilling to hold the debt of a suspect borrower. An alternative interpretation is that it is the

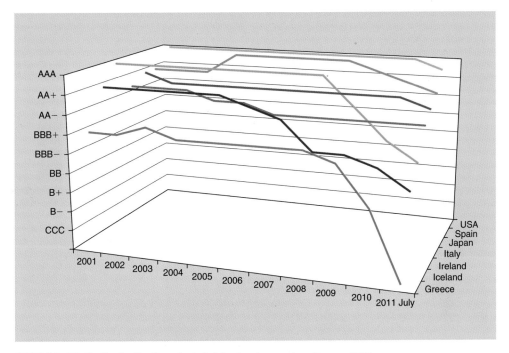

FIGURE 18.7 ● **Credit ratings of selected developed economies.** *Source:* S&P.

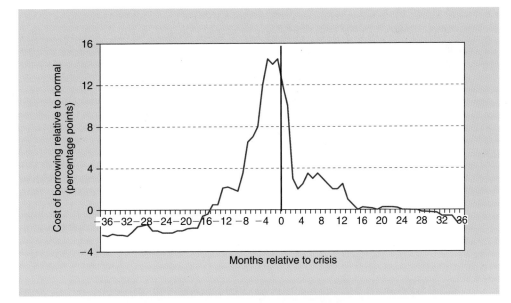

FIGURE 18.8 ● **Government borrowing costs around a default.** The interest rate demanded by lenders rises dramatically relative to 'normal' levels in the year before a default. *Source:* Panizza, Strurzenegger and Zettelmeyer, 'The economics and law of sovereign debt and default', *Journal of Economic Literature* (2009).

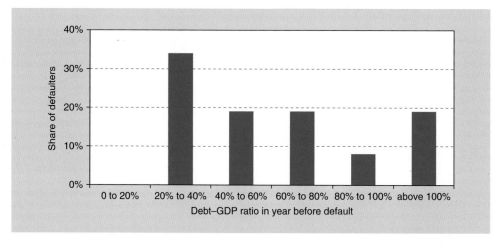

FIGURE 18.9 ● **Debt-to-GDP ratio in year before default.** Debt intolerance means that developing countries are often forced into default at very low debt-to-GDP ratios. *Source:* IMF, *World Economic Outlook* (September 2003).

unwillingness to lend that actually causes the crisis. Very few governments can afford to pay off all their debt in one go, and so rely on financial markets to roll over existing debt (i.e. make new loans when existing ones mature). If potential lenders fear that other lenders will not participate in new lending, they themselves will not lend (or only lend at prohibitively high interest rates). As a result, a **sudden stop** in capital flows may occur, so that the government may be unable to borrow even though it is solvent, in the sense that it could afford to pay reasonable interest payments. These sudden stops are very similar to the banking panic mechanism that we looked at in Chapter 17 and can force a sovereign borrower into default even when its underlying financial position is sustainable.

The risk of sudden stops may explain why debt crises in developing countries often occur at surprisingly low levels of borrowing. This feature of developing country borrowing is termed **debt intolerance** and is illustrated in Figure 18.9, which shows that most developing countries default at a debt-to-GDP ratio of less than 60%, a level of debt that most developed nations would consider as low. The risk of sudden stops is also an important argument in favour of an international lender of last resort like the International Monetary Fund (IMF). By being able to lend, at reasonable interest rates, to countries that cannot access funds elsewhere, the IMF can mitigate the problem of sudden stops. In fact, the mere existence of an organization like the IMF may stop a self-fulfilling panic occurring, since lenders know that the IMF may step in if a fundamentally unjustified withdrawal of lending were to happen and so are less likely to withdraw funding themselves. We look at the IMF in more detail in Chapter 21.

KEY POINT

A sudden stop in financing may force a country into default even if it is able to service its existing debt.

18.7 Debt Forgiveness

While sovereign defaults have been surprisingly uncommon over the last 20 years or so, debt forgiveness has become increasingly popular. Debt forgiveness occurs when creditors agree to write off a significant portion of a country's debt even if default is not threatened. The most important programme of debt forgiveness currently in operation is the Highly Indebted Poor Country (HIPC) initiative operated by the IMF and World Bank. As its name implies, it focuses on the very poorest nations that are also heavily indebted and, at the time of writing, 32 countries have had a significant proportion of their debt service written off through this process.

Although the main justification for debt relief is to benefit the borrower, there is an argument that it may also benefit the lender. The key point is that an excessively high debt burden can so adversely affect an economy that it reduces the capacity of the economy to pay interest on its debt. In particular, by diverting government resources away from health, education and investment spending, high levels of debt can reduce growth and, as we saw in Section 18.3, economic growth is an important element of managing high levels of debt. Some evidence for this effect is shown in Figure 18.10, which compares average growth at different levels of debt. It shows that there seems to be a significant reduction in the growth of countries with debt above 90% of GDP, though below that there appears to be little relationship between debt and growth.

The negative impact of very high debt on economic growth can mean that lenders may receive a larger payout by forgiving some debt than by requiring full payment, leading to low growth and eventual default. This possibility is sometimes called the **debt-relief Laffer**

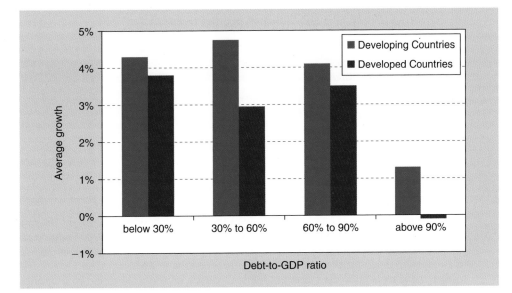

FIGURE 18.10 ● **Growth and debt.** Countries with debt above 90% of GDP seem to grow significantly more slowly than countries with a lower level of debt. *Source:* Reinhart, Carmen M. and Rogoff, Kenneth S., *This Time It's Different: Eight Centuries of Financial Folly* (Princeton: Princeton University Press, September 2009).

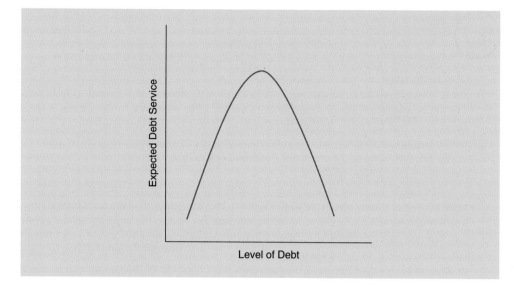

FIGURE 18.11 ● **The debt-relief Laffer curve.** Beyond some point the rise in a country's debt is so large that it reduces growth and reduces its capacity to service that debt.

curve and is illustrated in Figure 18.11. Similar to the other Laffer curves we have looked at in this book, this curve suggests that there is a point where outstanding debt is so large that the probability of repayment is smaller than a lower level of debt that leaves some resources free for growth-enhancing government spending. As a result, a lower level of debt may actually result in a larger repayment.

Nevertheless, many commentators criticize debt forgiveness, as it gives an incentive for poor countries to become highly indebted in order to qualify for HIPC.

> **KEY POINT**
>
> High debt can reduce growth and thus reduce a county's capacity to pay its creditors. As a result, debt forgiveness may actually be in the interest of creditors.

SUMMARY

Government borrowing is an important way to spread the cost of one-off events, like wars and economic crises, over a long period. In Section 18.1 we saw how the 2008–09 financial crisis has resulted in a significant increase in indebtedness for a number of developed economies. Section 18.2 looked in more detail at the relationship between the business cycle and government borrowing and showed how the structural budget balance is used to abstract from business cycle effects. The crucial determinants of the ability to run persistent deficits are the relative magnitudes of the interest rate and the growth rate of the economy. Evidence described in Section 18.3 suggests that most countries cannot persistently run primary deficits, because the interest rate on debt is likely to be above the sustainable rate of growth.

Section 18.4 showed that the intertemporal budget constraint implies that if a country is not to default on its public-sector debt, the current stock of debt should be matched by the present value of future surpluses. Section 18.5 then looked at sovereign default and showed how these tend to occur in clusters and that some countries have a history of serial default. We also saw how a sovereign can choose to default but may incur some costs if it does so. Section 18.6 discussed credit risk and that lenders may make borrowing so expensive for a country that it may be forced to default even if it doesn't want to. We also saw how lenders may require countries to borrow in foreign currency in order to protect themselves again inflation. Section 18.7 described debt forgiveness and how the debt-relief Laffer curve suggests that debt forgiveness may even be in the lender's interest.

CONCEPTUAL QUESTIONS

1. (Section 18.1) Should developed countries have increased their borrowing to mitigate the effect of the 2008–09 financial crisis, given that this borrowing has increased the burden of debt for future generations who were not responsible for the crisis?

2. (Section 18.2) Should the structural deficit be used to guide fiscal policy, given the problems associated with its estimation?

3. (Section 18.3) Because future generations are likely to enjoy higher real incomes than the current generation, shouldn't we aim to run up the stock of debt so that those most able to pay face the higher taxes?

4. (Section 18.4) Does it make sense for there to be any limits on the ability of a democratically elected government to run fiscal deficits? Does the fact that future generations cannot vote have any bearing on this issue?

5. (Section 18.5) Why is sovereign default not more common given the limited costs imposed on defaulters?

6. (Section 18.6) Highly indebted countries are often 'bailed out' by their neighbours, who lend them money at far lower interest rates than they would pay in financial markets. Do such bailouts make sense?

7. (Section 18.7) Should debt forgiveness be extended to countries not yet eligible for HIPC such as less indebted or richer countries?

ANALYTICAL QUESTIONS

1. (Section 18.2) A country has an output gap of –5%, government revenues of 15% of GDP and government spending of 20% of GDP. If the output elasticity of government revenue is 0.5 and the output elasticity of spending is –0.1, what are the actual and structural government deficits as a percentage of GDP?

2. (Section 18.3) A government is running a balanced budget. An election is approaching and the government decides on a one-time, temporary massive tax cut that will cut tax revenue by $50 billion in one year; after the year is over, tax rates and tax revenue return to normal. The government decides to issue perpetual bonds of $50 billion to cover the cost of the tax cut. The interest rate on these bonds is constant at 6%. The tax to pay the interest in the future will be levied on the private sector. Suppose that one half of the population plans ahead and wants to leave enough

in bequests to the next generation so that they are not harmed by future higher taxes. The other half of the population spends all they can now.

(a) What is the impact of the tax cut on domestic saving?

(b) What happens to consumption?

(c) Who buys the $50 billion of debt?

3. (Section 18.4) Suppose that the real interest rate in an economy is 6%. Real GDP grows by 2.75% a year. The new chief economic adviser to the government argues that a tax increase of $20 billion will generate huge benefits, because the real interest rate is much larger than the growth of GDP, so that tax rates will be lower on future generations for ever. What is wrong with this argument?

4. (Section 18.4) Consider the initial situation shown for the two economies in Table 18.4. Using a spreadsheet, calculate the evolution of the stock of debt, debt interest payments and the overall deficit if interest rates are 4% rather than 3%. How much lower would the initial stock of debt need to be for the second country to generate a constant ratio of debt to GDP with a 4% interest rate?

PART FIVE

Exchange Rates and Global Capital Markets

CHAPTER 19

Exchange Rate Determination: The Real Exchange Rate

Key Concepts

Balance of Payments

Balassa-Samuelson Effect

Bilateral and Effective
    Exchange Rates

Capital Account

Current Account

International Investment
    Position (IIP)

Law of One Price

Nominal and Real Exchange Rates

Purchasing Power Parity (PPP)

Overview

The nominal exchange rate is the rate at which the currencies of two countries can be exchanged, whereas the real exchange rate is the ratio of what a specified amount of money will buy in one country compared with what it can buy in another. This chapter focuses on explaining changes in the real exchange rate. We first consider the law of one price, which says that, in the absence of trade restrictions and transportation costs, the same commodity should have the same price wherever it is sold. We use the law of one price to derive purchasing power parity (PPP), which says that identical bundles of goods should cost the same in different countries. This implies that the real exchange rate should be constant and equal to one and that changes in the nominal exchange rate are driven by inflation differences. Reviewing the empirical evidence suggests that only in the very long run does PPP hold and that the real exchange rate is more volatile than inflation alone would suggest. To explain this volatility, we focus on the current and capital accounts of a country. The current account reflects trade in the goods and services of a country, and the capital account reflects the trade in assets. Finally, we review the factors that influence the capital and current accounts and how those factors can explain some, but not all, of the volatility in the real exchange rate.

(19.1) Types of Exchange Rate

Exchange rates can be confusing. Pick up any financial paper and you will see various exchange rates quoted. There are many countries, many different exchange rates and also many terms: bilateral and effective exchange rates, and real and nominal rates. In this section, we clarify these terms.

BILATERAL AND EFFECTIVE EXCHANGE RATES

A **bilateral exchange rate** is the rate at which you can swap the money of one country for that of another. For instance, if €1 can be swapped for $1 US, then the exchange rate is 1:1. If the euro *appreciates*, then it rises in value: it becomes more expensive to buy euros if you are holding dollars. If it now takes $1.10 to buy €1, then the euro has appreciated by 10%, whereas if it costs $0.90, the euro has *devalued or depreciated* by 10%. The exchange rates of major currencies (US dollar, euro and pound sterling) are generally quoted in terms of units of foreign currency required to purchase $1, €1 or £1. For example, if 100 yen are required to buy one dollar, the dollar/yen exchange rate is 100.[1]

Bilateral exchange rates only measure the behaviour of one currency against another. But what if the euro rises against the US dollar and the pound but depreciates against the Canadian dollar and the Japanese yen? Has the euro appreciated or depreciated? To answer this question, we need a measure of how the currency has done on average against *all* countries, rather than just one. The **effective exchange rate** measures this average performance. When calculating the effective exchange rate, it is necessary to recognize that certain currencies are more important than others. For instance, in assessing the average performance of the euro, it is more important to know how the euro has done against the US dollar than against the Thai baht, because Europe trades far more with the United States than with Thailand. We can measure a currency's performance by calculating the effective exchange rate on a *trade-weighted basis*. If a country's trade (the sum of imports and exports) with the United States is ten times more than that with Thailand, the dollar will get a weight 10 times higher. As a result, if the euro appreciates against the dollar by 1% but depreciates against the Thai baht by 1%, while remaining unchanged against all other currencies, the effective exchange rate will rise. Figure 19.1 shows the trade weights used in calculating the effective euro exchange rate.

The effective exchange rate is calculated as a weighted geometric average of bilateral exchange rates. So, for example, if the United States had only two trading partners, the Eurozone and China, with 75% and 25% of US trade respectively, then the US effective exchange rate would be

$$EER = \text{Dollar Euro rate}^{0.75} \times \text{Dollar Yuan Rate}^{0.25}$$

The effective exchange rate is expressed in an index form, so that in one particular year (usually the year to which the trade weights refer) it has a value of 100. Therefore, if the effective exchange rate appreciates on average by 10% from that date, the index will be 110, whereas if it depreciates by 10%, it will be 90.

> **KEY POINT**
>
> Bilateral exchange rates record the behaviour of one currency against another. Effective exchange rates record the average behaviour of a currency against a basket of other currencies, where each currency is weighted by its importance in trade.

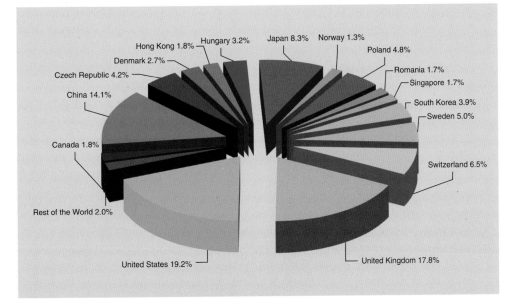

FIGURE 19.1 ● **Trade weights for euro effective exchange rate, 2011.** *Source:* European Central Bank, http://www.ecb.int/stats/exchange/effective/html/index.en.html.

REAL VERSUS NOMINAL EXCHANGE RATES

Throughout this book we have distinguished between *real* and *nominal* variables: real variables reflect quantities or volume measures, while nominal variables reflect money values. The **nominal exchange rate** is the rate at which you can swap two different currencies – this is the exchange rate we have just been discussing. If, at an airport, you wish to swap Australian for Canadian dollars, you can do so at the nominal exchange rate. In contrast, the **real exchange rate** tells you how expensive commodities are in different countries and reflects the competitiveness of a country's exports.

Suppose, for example, a cup of coffee costs ¥200 in Japan and $1 in the United States, and the nominal exchange rate is ¥100 to $1. You can swap $1 for ¥100, but in Tokyo ¥100 only buys half a cup of coffee. The real exchange rate (for coffee) is therefore 0.5 – you can only purchase half as much with your money in Japan as you can in the United States. A New Yorker returning from a vacation who says that Tokyo was expensive is essentially saying that the yen–US dollar real exchange rate is low: goods in the United States are cheap by comparison.

However, the real exchange rate is not just about *one* commodity: it reflects all the goods you purchase in a foreign country. In other words, it is about the overall price level in a country and not only the cost of a cup of coffee. It can be expressed as:

Real exchange rate = Nominal exchange rate
    × Domestic price level/Overseas price level

Consider a case in which what costs $1 in the United States costs 3 pesos in Argentina and where the nominal exchange rate is 3 (3 pesos buys $1). In this case we have:

$$\text{Real exchange rate} = 3 \times \frac{\$1}{3 \text{ pesos}} = 1$$

The real exchange rate is 1 – you can buy exactly the same amount for your money in either country. If, instead, everything that costs $1 in the United States costs 5 pesos in Argentina, then we have:

$$\text{Real exchange rate} = 3 \times \frac{\$1}{5 \text{ pesos}} = 0.6$$

so that in Argentina you can buy only 60% of what the same money (in dollars) buys you in the United States.

Historical data show that fluctuations in the real exchange rate track movements in the nominal exchange rate quite closely. Explaining this similarity in behaviour is a substantial challenge for economists. One argument says that real and nominal exchange rates behave similarly because the real exchange rate is just the nominal exchange rate multiplied by the ratio of domestic to overseas prices. Every minute of the day, the nominal exchange rate changes, often substantially. However, prices in a country change only slowly; as we showed in Chapter 15, prices are sticky. If prices hardly change, then movements in the nominal exchange rate will lead to fluctuations in the real exchange rate. An alternative view suggests that the key factors that determine the real exchange rate are volatile, causing volatility in the real exchange rate that leads to a volatile nominal exchange rate. We will evaluate the strength of these arguments over the next two chapters.

KEY POINT

The nominal exchange rate is the rate at which one currency can be swapped for another. The real exchange rate is a measure of competitiveness and records how much the same amount of money can buy in different countries. When the real exchange rate equals 1, goods cost the same in each country.

(19.2) Law of One Price

In this section, we begin to build a model of real exchange rates by introducing the **law of one price**. This states that identical commodities should sell at the same price wherever they are sold – the same model of television set, for example, should cost the same whether it is sold in Madrid or Barcelona. The basis of the law of one price is *arbitrage*. If the television is cheaper in Barcelona, a firm can buy televisions in Barcelona, sell them in Madrid and pocket the difference. This would increase the demand for television sets in Barcelona and their supply in Madrid. It would thus push up the price of televisions in Barcelona and lower them in Madrid, reducing the price discrepancy between the two cities. According to the law of one price, arbitrage will continue until the price of the television is exactly the same in each city – one price prevails.

The law of one price can also be applied across different economies. Once prices are expressed in a common currency, identical commodities should sell in different economies at the same price. Imagine that the television set retails in Barcelona for €150 and let the US dollar be worth 1 euro. Arbitrage should ensure that in America the television set costs $150 (150/1 = 150). In other words, the law of one price says:

Dollar price of television in US = Dollar/euro exchange rate
                                     × Euro price of television in Barcelona

Does the law of one price hold? The answer is basically no: except for a few commodities, little evidence supports the law of one price. There are several real-life factors that prevent this ideal:

- Transportation costs
- The border effect
- Pricing to market

TRANSPORTATION COSTS

The law of one price says that identical commodities should sell for identical prices. But if transport costs matter, then location is an important feature of a commodity. If transport costs are high and the distance between markets is great, the same commodity will sell for different prices in different locations. We can measure transport costs by comparing the prices of goods when they leave a country as exports to their cost when they arrive at their destination as imports. Exports fob (free on board) refers to the value of commodities when they are loaded on board a ship or plane. Imports cif (cost, insurance and freight) refers to the value of imports when they arrive, including the cost of insurance and freight. Figure 19.2 shows estimates of transport costs using this difference between fob and cif. Costs vary from around 2% for tobacco and transport equipment to around 9% for oil and stone. Figure 19.2 focuses on a few aggregate industries covering all global trade. Figure 19.3 shows the distribution of transport costs for over 25 000 manufacturing industries to a single country, the United States.

For most industries, transport costs are under 10%. However, for a minority of industries, transport costs are over 25% of value. Figure 19.3 is also based on goods that are actually traded; there are many other goods with transport costs so high they are effectively

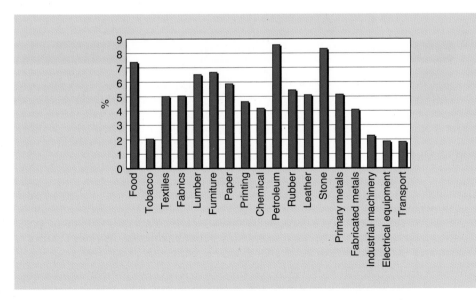

FIGURE 19.2 ● **Estimated transport costs for global trade.** The transport costs of tradeable commodities are significant. *Source:* Ravn and Mazzenga, Frictions in International Trade and Relative Price Movements, London Business School Working Paper (1999).

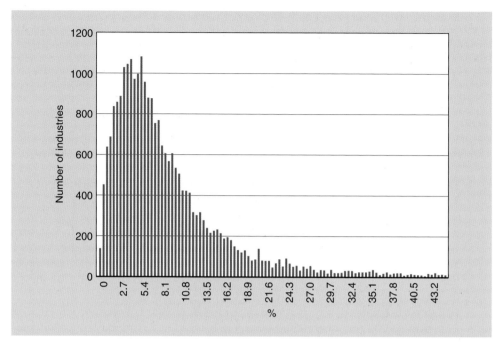

FIGURE 19.3 ● **Estimated transport costs for US manufacturing imports.** Some industries have very large transport costs, which partly explains why the law of one price does not hold. *Source:* Ravn and Mazzenga, Frictions in International Trade and Relative Price Movements, London Business School Working Paper (1999).

non-tradeable. With transport costs of this magnitude, identical commodities will sell for very different prices in different locations.

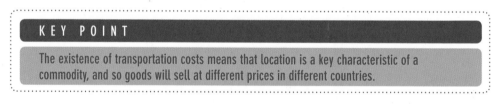

KEY POINT

The existence of transportation costs means that location is a key characteristic of a commodity, and so goods will sell at different prices in different countries.

THE BORDER EFFECT

Transportation costs matter both between and within countries. San Francisco is a long way from Boston, so we can expect that the prices of televisions will be different in these cities just as they are between New York and Barcelona. However, close examination reveals that differences in prices for the same commodity between cities in the *same* country are tiny compared to the differences in price for the same commodity in *different* countries. The difference in prices for the same commodity increases not just with distance and transport costs but also when the commodity crosses a national border. This suggests that border effects are another reason why the law of one price fails to hold.

To see how important this border effect is, consider Figure 19.4, which shows the volatility, or dispersion, of prices across cities in the United States and Canada between 1978 and 1994. The higher the measure, the greater the discrepancy between prices in different cities. If

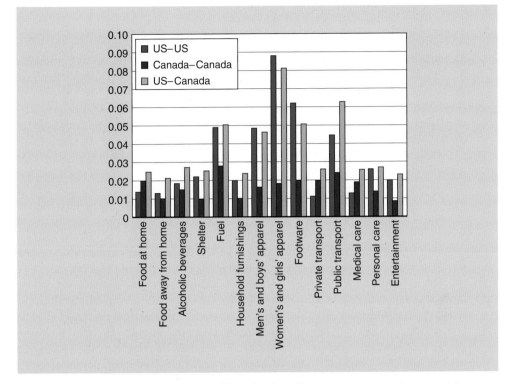

FIGURE 19.4 ● **Price differences between US and Canadian cities.** Price differences between cities cannot be explained just by transport costs: differences in prices between US and Canadian cities are greater than differences within countries, regardless of distance apart. *Source:* Engel and Rogers, 'How wide is the border?', *American Economic Review* (1996), 86: 1112–25. Reprinted with permission from American Economic Association.

prices were exactly the same in each city, volatility would be zero. Except for three categories, the discrepancies in prices between Canadian and US cities are larger than those between US cities or between Canadian cities. The data in Figure 19.4 show that crossing a national border substantially increases price differences – it is equivalent to adding an additional 1800 miles of transport costs over and above the actual distance between a US and a Canadian city.

Why does the border matter so much? One reason is tariffs (as defined in Chapter 8, tariffs are taxes on imports). Tariffs prevent arbitrage and are one reason why the law of one price fails to hold. There are other reasons too: technical requirements (US and Spanish television sets work on different electrical voltages, cars in the United Kingdom need to be right-hand drive but are left-hand drive in the United States and continental Europe) or attempts by firms to obtain regional monopoly power (if a European buys a camera in the United States, for example, its warranty is only valid in the United States). These factors reduce the role of arbitrage in establishing the law of one price.

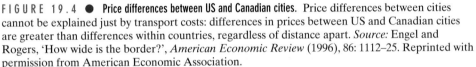

KEY POINT

The border effect shows that transportation costs alone cannot explain why prices differ so much across regions. Goods sold in different countries or denominated in different currencies show large variations in prices unrelated to distance.

PRICING TO MARKET

Consider again the television set that costs €150 in Spain. When the exchange rate is €1 to $1, the law of one price says that the television should retail for $150 in the United States. If, instead, the exchange rate is €1.5 to $1, the US price should be $100. But what happens when the currency changes, but the US price is sticky and remains at $150? At the new exchange rate of €1.5 to $1, the cost of the television in the United States translates to €225 – much more expensive than the price in Spain. The law of one price fails to hold, and the volatility in the exchange rate directly affects the volatility of relative prices across countries.

Table 19.1, which focuses on 65 European cities between 1981 and 1997, shows evidence for this relative price volatility. The first two rows indicate that relative prices between *different* countries (*international*) are far more volatile (by around 20 to 50 times) than relative prices *within* a country (*intranational*). The last row of the table shows why: the volatility in relative prices, or real exchange rates, between countries is almost exactly the same as the volatility in nominal exchange rates. Therefore, because prices tend to be sticky in each country but nominal exchange rates tend to be volatile, as we discussed earlier in the chapter, the real and nominal exchange rates tend to move together in the short run.

One reason why the relative price of a television set varies between countries is that firms may be *pricing to market*. Consider the case of a US television manufacturer who sells to Spain. When the exchange rate is €1 equals $1, its television set retails at $150 in the United States and €150 in Spain. When the exchange rate goes to €1.5 to $1, the firm should charge €225 in Spain to preserve the same equivalent dollar price. But this is a huge increase in price, which will undermine the competitiveness of US products. Therefore, the US producer may keep the Spanish retail price at €150 and sell the product for the equivalent of $100 in Spain but $150 in the United States. The US producer is pricing to market – the price in the Spanish market is set taking into account Spanish circumstances rather than the domestic costs of production and the domestic selling price of the US producer.

As this example makes clear, if firms price to market, then fluctuations in exchange rates bring about large swings in profit margins. This is why exchange rate fluctuations matter to exporters: a low exchange rate and a pricing-to-market strategy mean high profit margins, but when the exchange rate is high, the firm may even lose money if it keeps its foreign currency-denominated export prices fixed.

Pricing to market also opens up another issue: exchange rate pass-through. When the exchange rate depreciates (the euro depreciates in our example when it goes from €1 equals $1 to €1.5 equals $1), imports become more expensive when converted into

TABLE 19.1 ● Relative Price Volatility between and across European Cities.

	Variance of Change in Relative Prices		
	1 Month	1 Year	4 Years
Intranational	0.17	0.96	2.83
International	2.76	52.3	159.8
	Variance of Change in Exchange Rates		
International	2.62	53.1	159

Source: Engel and Rogers, 'Deviations from purchasing power parity: Causes and welfare costs'. Reprinted from *Journal of International Economics* (2001) 51(1), with permission from Elsevier Science.

domestic prices. The $150 television rises in retail value from €150 to €225 in Spain if the law of one price holds. Therefore, a depreciating exchange rate may lead to higher import prices and put upward pressure on wages and inflation. But if pricing to market occurs, then exchange rate changes need not lead to inflation – if the US producer prices to the Spanish market, it charges €150 no matter what happens to the exchange rate. The exchange rate change is not 'passed through' to the Spanish consumers.

The precise amount of pass-through varies for different countries and different industries. If no European-based television producers rival the US firm, it is not constrained by competition. It will pass through a larger portion of exchange rate changes, and euro prices will rise as the euro depreciates. Studies suggest that pass-through is never complete. For instance, one study finds that only around 50% of exchange rate volatility is passed through in changed prices of imports in the United States. For Germany, the estimate is 60% pass-through; for Japan, 70%. For Canada and Belgium, smaller economies and smaller markets, the pass-through is about 90%. For open economies, the degree to which pass-through operates is a critical issue in deciding how to set interest rates to control inflation.

KEY POINT

Firms set prices based on local conditions and prices set by rivals. These prices tend to be sticky, but nominal exchange rates are very volatile. As a result, nominal exchange rate changes feed into real exchange rate changes and the law of one price fails to hold.

(19.3) Purchasing Power Parity

The law of one price is a key part of our first theory of real exchange rate determination: **purchasing power parity (PPP)**. The law of one price refers to particular commodities. PPP applies the law of one price to *all* commodities, whether they are tradeables or not. The PPP exchange rate is the exchange rate such that the same basket of goods costs the same in each country once allowance is made for different currencies. Imagine going shopping in Germany and buying commodities that cost €100. If in Japan, the same purchases cost ¥5000, then according to PPP, the yen–euro exchange rate should be 5000/100 = 50. At this exchange rate, the yen price of your shopping trip equals the euro cost of the same items in Germany. Therefore PPP says:

PPP nominal exchange rate (yen/euro) = Japanese price/German price

If the German price increases to €110 and the Japanese to ¥6000, then PPP implies that the exchange rate should adjust to 54.54 (= 6000/110).

It is worth going back to our definition of the real exchange rate to grasp the implications of PPP. We have:

Real yen/euro exchange rate = Nominal yen/euro exchange rate
× (German Prices/Japanese Prices)

But according to PPP, the nominal yen–euro exchange rate equals Japanese prices divided by German prices. Putting this into our definition of the real exchange rate results in the value 1 – things cost the same in each country.

PPP real nominal yen/euro exchange rate = (Japanese prices/German prices)
× (German prices/Japanese prices) = 1

Therefore, PPP implies that all countries are equally competitive, that commodity baskets cost the same the world over, and that the real exchange rate is forever equal to 1.

Furthermore, the PPP definition of the nominal exchange rate implies that:

Change in nominal yen/euro exchange rate = Japanese inflation – German inflation

In other words, PPP implies that currencies depreciate if they have higher inflation than other countries and appreciate if they have lower inflation. We showed above that when the shopping cost €100 in Germany and ¥5000 in Japan, PPP implies an exchange rate of 50. If German inflation is 10%, so that costs increase to €110, but Japanese inflation is 20%, so the price rises to ¥6000, PPP implies an exchange rate of 54.54.[2] This is an appreciation in the euro of around 10% – or the difference between German and Japanese inflation.

How well does PPP agree with historical evidence? We have already shown evidence that suggests that PPP will perform poorly: we saw that the real exchange rate is volatile and so is not constant at a value of 1, and we have also seen that the law of one price (the basis for PPP) holds for few commodities. However, PPP does have some successes: in particular, PPP appears to be a useful model for explaining long-run data.

We can see the relative successes and failures of PPP in Figure 19.5, which compares for a broad range of countries the behaviour of bilateral exchange rates and inflation differentials over various time horizons. If PPP holds, the relationship should be one for one – for every 1% higher inflation a country has compared to the United States, its exchange rate should devalue by 1% against the dollar. In Figure 19.5a, which shows inflation and exchange rate depreciations over 2010, we see no evidence in favour of PPP. Over this period, exchange rate fluctuations appear to have nothing to do with inflation differences. Figure 19.5b, which looks at the period 2006–10, shows a stronger relationship between countries with high inflation and depreciating currencies, but the relationship is still not reliable. Only in Figure 19.5c, which shows changes in the exchange rate from 1991 to 2010, are the implications of PPP strongly observed: inflation differentials and exchange rate changes are closely connected.

These results suggest that we should not discard PPP completely – over decades, depreciations of nominal currencies are related to inflation differentials. However, PPP does not offer a reliable guide to the short-run volatility of real and nominal exchange rates.

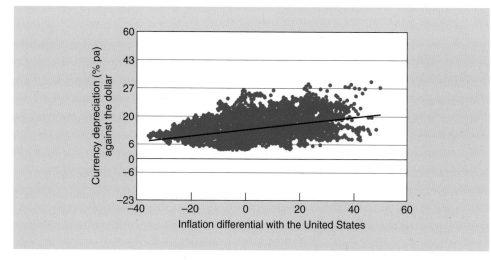

FIGURE 19.5a   ● Annual change in exchange rates and inflation, 2010. *Source:* OECD.

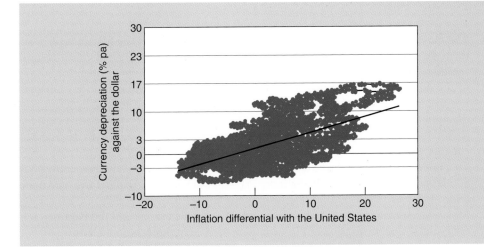

FIGURE 19.5b ● Five-year change in exchange rates and inflation, 2006–2010. *Source:* OECD.

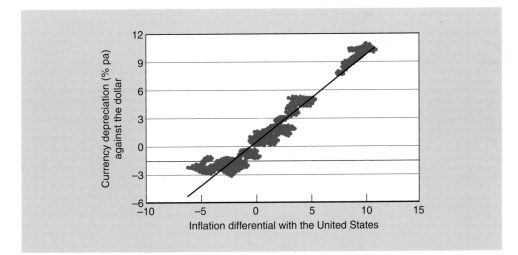

FIGURE 19.5c ● 20-year change in exchange rates and inflation, 1991–2010. In the long run, the implication of PPP that inflation differentials equal currency depreciation is a good approximation, but in the short run the success of the model is very weak. *Source:* OECD.

KEY POINT

PPP assumes that the cost of living is the same across all countries, so that the nominal exchange rate should equal the ratio of prices and the real exchange rate should be 1. As a consequence, high-inflation countries should have depreciating currencies. As a long-run theory, PPP performs well, but it has limited validity in the short run as the real exchange rate shows too much short-run volatility.

THE BIG MAC INDEX

The Economist magazine popularizes a version of PPP with its Big Mac index ('in an effort to make exchange rate theory more digestible'). PPP posits that identical commodities should sell for the same price wherever they are sold. *The Economist* therefore uses a ratio of the domestic price of Big Macs in different countries to estimate PPP exchange rates. For instance, if a Big Mac costs $3.73 in the United States and R18.42 in South Africa, so the implied Big Mac exchange rate is R18.42:$3.73 or R4.94:$1. If the actual exchange rate is R7:$1, then the South African currency is undervalued – South African Big Macs are cheaper than American ones.

Table 19.2 shows actual exchange rates, IMF PPP (based on a representative basket of goods) and the Big Mac PPP exchange rates in 2011 and the implied over- or undervaluation. If we use the Big Mac rates as a guide to PPP, the currencies in China, Egypt and Malaysia appear substantially undervalued. The Swedish krona and the Brazilian real were overvalued, and restoration of PPP would involve their depreciation. Unfortunately, a trading strategy based on the Big Mac index is unlikely to make you rich. As we have stressed, PPP is a long-run influence on exchange rates, and PPP rates exert only a weak short-run

TABLE 19.2 ● PPP Measures and Actual Exchange Rates against the US Dollar, 2011.

	Big Mac price in local currency	PPP Exchange Rates against Dollar		Actual Exchange Rate mid-2011	Under/overvaluation of Actual Exchange Rate against	
		Implied Big Mac PPP	IMF PPP		Big Mac PPP	IMF PPP
Australia	A$ 4.35	0.85*	1.16*	1.06*	25%	−9%
Brazil	R$ 8.71	2.33	1.68	1.64	42%	2%
Canada	C$ 4.17	1.12	1.22	0.97	15%	26%
China	¥ 13.2	3.54	3.89	6.51	−46%	−40%
Egypt	E£ 13.0	3.48	2.59	5.94	−41%	−56%
Eurozone	€3.38	1.10*	1.18*	1.42*	29%	20%
Japan	¥ 320	85.7	108.4	80.8	6%	34%
Malaysia	RM 7.05	1.89	1.82	3.00	−37%	−39%
Pakistan	Rs 210	56.3	35.3	85.5	−34%	−59%
Poland	Zł 8.30	2.22	1.98	2.76	−20%	−28%
Russia	P. 71	19.0	21.3	28.0	−32%	−24%
S. Africa	R 18.42	4.94	5.41	7.00	−29%	−23%
Sweden	kr 6.50	13.0	9.53	6.34	105%	50%
Turkey	Tl 5.95	1.59	1.225	1.59	0%	−23%
UK	£ 2.29	1.63*	1.49*	1.62*	−1%	9%
USA	$ 3.73	–	–			

Source: The Economist (April 2011), IMF, *World Economic Outlook*.

* currencies expressed as number of dollars per local unit.

influence on exchange rates. In the short term, an undervalued currency can become even more undervalued according to PPP measures, and it may take decades to return to its PPP level. While the currency becomes more undervalued, the Big Mac-inspired trade will be losing money.

The Big Mac index has other problems over and above failures of PPP. First, the Big Mac has more to do with the law of one price than with PPP – it refers to one commodity rather than a basket of goods. Second, the Big Mac may be identical across countries, but it is not tradeable: a freshly cooked Big Mac in London is a different commodity from a reheated one imported from China. Third, Big Macs are not identical: a Big Mac consumed in Tokyo reflects the cost of rent for a retail outlet in Tokyo plus various local labour and indirect taxes. This makes it a different commodity from a Big Mac sold in Manila. For these reasons, the Russian price of a Big Mac may always be lower than that of one in Copenhagen without affecting the rouble–krona exchange rate.

WHY DO RICH COUNTRIES HAVE HIGHER PRICES?

One systematic deviation from PPP is that prices tend to be higher in industrial economies than in emerging nations, as Figure 19.6 shows. This is known as the **Balassa-Samuelson effect**.

To explain this, assume that productivity growth in the service sector (which is substantially non-tradeable) is lower than in the tradeable sector. In other words, it is harder to boost the productivity of hairdressers than manufacturing firms. With rising productivity in the tradeable sector, wages will be increasing in these industries. If the non-tradeable sector is to continue to hire workers, then wages in the non-tradeable sector will also have to rise. However, the non-tradeable sector does not benefit to the same extent from productivity improvements, so the only way to finance higher wages is to charge a higher price for services, which can be done because there is no threat of foreign competition. The result is higher prices, originating from the non-tradeable sector, in countries with high levels of productivity in the tradeable sector.

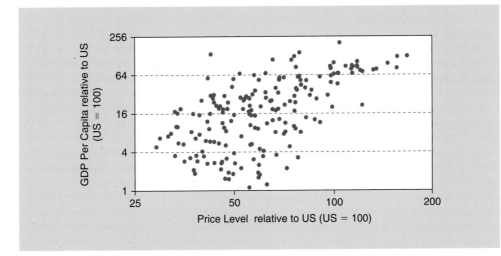

F I G U R E   1 9 . 6   ●   **Wealthy countries have high prices.** *Source:* Heston, Summers and Aten, Penn World Table Version 6.1, Center for International Comparisons at the University of Pennsylvania (CICUP).

According to the Balassa-Samuelson theory, countries with higher productivity growth in their tradeable sectors will have to have higher non-tradeable wage increases and thus higher non-tradeable inflation; this is exactly what Figure 19.6 shows. As a result, fast-growing economies tend to have higher inflation than slower-growing ones.

> **KEY POINT**
>
> Non-tradeable commodities are a key reason why the law of one price does not hold. Countries with high productivity in their tradeable sector tend to have high prices for non-tradeables, so that rich countries are more expensive than poor ones.

19.4 The Balance of Payments

The previous sections have shown that real exchange rates are too volatile for PPP to explain, so we need to develop alternative models. To do this we have to introduce some important concepts. In particular, we have to discuss a country's balance of payments, which is made up of its capital account and current account. The **balance of payments** is a statistical record, covering a particular time, of a country's economic transactions with the rest of the world. The **current account** records the net transactions in goods and services, while the **capital account** records transactions in assets between countries. The relationship between these concepts is:

Balance of payments = Current account surplus + Capital account surplus = 0

In other words, if the current account is in surplus (deficit), the capital account should be in deficit (surplus) by an equivalent amount.

> **KEY POINT**
>
> The current and capital accounts should sum to zero (the balance of payments has to balance).

THE CURRENT ACCOUNT

The current account measures the net flow of goods and services between a country and the rest of the world. It consists of four main categories: goods, services, income and transfers.

Current account = Balance of trade (exports of goods − imports of goods)
                  + Balance on services (exports of services − imports of services)
                  + Investment income and dividends
                  + Net transfers

- *Goods.* Countries both export and import goods (automobiles, wheat, oil and so forth). For instance, in 2009 (see Table 19.3) the United States exported to the rest of the world $1073 billion worth of goods and imported $1577 billion. Therefore its net exports of goods were –$504 billion, what economists term a *balance of trade* deficit.

TABLE 19.3 ● Capital and Current Account Flows, 2009 ($ bn).

China ran a current account surplus in 2009, and the United States and Eurozone ran deficits. All three countries saw an increase in their foreign currency reserves.

	US	China	Eurozone
Balance on Goods	−504	250	32
Balance on Services	129	−29	43
Balance on Goods & Services	**−375**	**220**	**75**
Net Investment Income	121	43	−12
Net Transfers	−125	34	−140
Current Account	**−378**	**297**	**−77**
Capital Account	0	4	12
Net Direct Investment	−134	34	−112
Net Portfolio Investment	−27	39	259
Net Other Investment	429	70	−44
Financial Account	268	143	104
Net Errors and Omissions	163	−43	−33
Overall Balance	**52**	**401**	**6**
Reserve Assets	−52	−401	−6

Source: IMF, *Balance of Payments Statistics* (2010).

- *Services.* Services account for a broad collection of activities, such as transport services, telecommunications, legal and financial services. In 2009, US exports of services were $498 billion against imports of $369 billion, providing a surplus on services of $129 billion and a balance on goods *and* services of –$375 billion (–$504 billion + $129 billion).
- *Income and dividends.* China, as a result of previous investment, owns assets overseas but also foreign companies and investors own assets in China. For instance, the Chinese Central Bank holds US government bonds, and multinational firms run profitable businesses in China. The Chinese Central Bank earns interest on those bonds. Similarly, multinationals in China send profits and dividends back to their overseas investors. The current account records these income flows. In 2009, China received $108 billion in income on its current account and paid out $65 billion, for a balance of $44 billion. For the United States, investment income received was $588 billion but investment income paid out was $467 billion.
- The fact that the United States is a net recipient of investment income despite being a net debtor to the rest of the world (see Figure 19.7) is a little surprising and has caused some to argue that the US balance of payments is misreported (the idea being that the United States is in fact a net creditor and unrecorded assets or 'dark matter' are generating the extra income). The alternative explanation is that US investments (predominately FDI) generate higher returns than its liabilities. In other words, US firms have enjoyed higher returns on their overseas FDI than other countries have earned on their FDI in the United States.

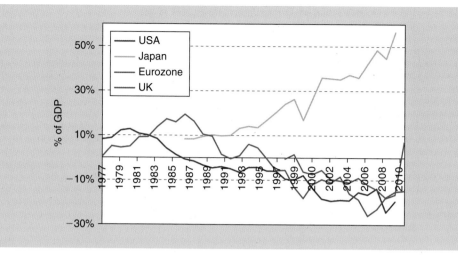

FIGURE 19.7 ● **Net foreign assets (% GDP).** Japan is an important global creditor, the US is a debtor. *Source:* Various.

- *Transfers.* Transfer payments occur when no asset or good is provided in return for money paid. For instance, if the United States donates resources to Sub-Saharan Africa for overseas development assistance (ODA), this is a transfer payment because either goods or money flows in one direction only. Similarly, the remittances that US-based Mexicans send back to Mexico would enter as a transfer debit on the current account. In 2009, the United States paid out $125 billion in net transfers.

If we add transfers to the balance on goods, services and income, we have the total current account for the United States in 2009 – a $378 billion deficit.

THE CAPITAL ACCOUNT

The current account records transactions in goods and services between a country and the rest of the world. The capital account records transactions in assets, both financial and non-financial. Strictly speaking,[3] we should refer to the *capital and financial account*. However, this distinction is rare, and we normally refer to the whole of the capital and financial account as just the *capital account*. We shall follow this practice throughout this chapter, except in the next few paragraphs, where we distinguish between the capital and financial accounts.

Capital and financial account = Capital account + Financial account
+ Errors and omissions

- *Capital account.* The capital account refers to capital transfers (such as debt forgiveness) as well as the acquisition or disposal of non-produced, non-financial assets (like copyright ownership and patents). If the US government were to cancel $2 billion of debt that was owed to the United States by Iraq, this would show up as –$2 billion in the capital account. If a Japanese investor were to buy the copyright for Kanye West's songs, this would show up as a surplus on the US capital account.

- *Errors and omissions.* The balance of payments has to balance so that the current and capital account surpluses add to zero. Logging all the financial transactions between a country and the rest of the world is a Herculean task. First, some transactions, such as money laundering, are illegal and will not be registered, so these transactions will be excluded from the balance of payments. Second, even legitimate transactions will not always come to the attention of statisticians. For these reasons, the capital and financial account will not always exactly offset the current account, and the size of the discrepancy is a measure of the magnitude of the errors and omissions made in the calculations. For the United States in 2009, these errors and omissions amounted to the very substantial sum of $163 billion.
- *Financial account.* The financial account refers to the acquisition and disposal of financial assets and is by far the largest component of the capital and financial account. The financial account is made up of four different categories:

$$\text{Financial account} = \text{Net direct investment} + \text{Net portfolio flows}$$
$$+ \text{Net other investment} + \text{Change in reserve assets}$$

- *Direct investment.* Direct investment occurs when an individual or firm in one country acquires a lasting interest in an enterprise resident in another economy. Direct investment implies a long-term relationship between the investor and the recipient firm, where the investor has significant influence over the enterprise.[4] For instance, if Coca-Cola opens a bottling factory in the Philippines, it would count as US foreign direct investment abroad. If Toshiba opens a production factory in California, it would count as Japanese foreign direct investment abroad. As well as including such 'greenfield' investment, FDI also includes mergers and acquisitions. We need to be careful about what signs we use when we measure the financial account. When Coca-Cola opens its Philippine bottling plant, it is in effect purchasing or 'importing' an overseas asset. Therefore US investment overseas counts as a negative for the US financial account. Table 19.3 shows that, in 2009, the United States had a deficit of $134 billion on direct investment (consisting of $269 billion of foreign investment by US firms compared to investment in the United States by foreign firms of $135 billion).
- *Portfolio investment.* The portfolio assets section of the financial account refers to trade in various assets, but mainly equities (stocks) and bonds. In 2009 for the United States, this part of the financial account saw a deficit of $27 billion – the United States bought this many more equities and bonds than it sold from overseas. In contrast, the Eurozone was a net seller of $259 billion of overseas equities and bonds.
- *Other investment.* Another part of the financial account is investment in other assets. As its name suggests, it reflects a range of different transactions (such as trade credit), but its most important category is bank deposits and bank loans – a category that is sometimes called 'hot money', since it is the most volatile form of investment. When a US investor places funds on deposit in a London account, the funds will appear in the 'other investment' category (with a negative sign for the United States: the United States is acquiring an asset in the United Kingdom). When a Korean firm borrows from a New York-based bank, the loan will also show up in this category (as a positive term: the Korean economy has increased its liabilities to the rest of the world). In 2009, the United States had a surplus (i.e. was borrowing money) of $429 billion on this other investment category (including financial derivatives). In 2008 the same category recorded a deficit of $200 billion.

- *Reserve assets.* The final part of the financial account is the reserve asset category. This reflects mainly the government's financial interactions with the rest of the world and in particular with other governments. Consider the case of China in 2009 (see Table 19.3), which had a current account surplus of $297 billion. Counting trade in goods and services, and allowing for income and transfers, the Chinese economy sold $297 billion more commodities abroad than it purchased from foreign countries. The logic of the balance of payments requires a matching deficit in the capital and financial account of $297 billion. A capital and financial account deficit means that investors were pulling money out of China and accumulating assets overseas. For China in 2009, however, the capital and financial account (including errors and omissions) was a surplus of $104 billion – adding to the inflow of foreign currency coming into China. China had an *overall balance* (current account + capital and financial account + errors and omissions) of $401 billion. This means that overall there was a net inflow of foreign currency into China of $401 billion from net exports, foreign investments in China and so on. However, as its name implies, the balance of payments must ultimately be in balance and in China's case balance is maintained by a large net investment in foreign exchange reserves by the Chinese Central Bank. In 2009, Chinese foreign exchange reserves rose by $401 billion, largely through the purchase of US government bonds.

19.5   Which Countries Are Rich and Which Are Poor?

The capital account records disposals and acquisitions of assets within a particular period. If a country is running a capital account deficit (buying overseas assets) or current account surplus, then its *stock* of overseas assets is rising. The net **international investment position** (IIP) measures this stock of external wealth. If this is a positive number, then a country has more foreign assets than it does liabilities; if it is negative, then the country owes the rest of the world money. Furthermore, if this stock of wealth is invested in assets that increase in value, then the wealth is increasing, *even if there are no further capital account deficits or overseas investments*, because of capital gains.

Figure 19.7 shows the net IIP (expressed as a percentage of GDP) for the United States, Japan, the Eurozone and the United Kingdom. The slow deterioration of the US position from a positive stock of around 10% of GDP to a net debt of 19% reflects the years of persistent current account deficits. By contrast, the Japanese graph shows a continuing increase in overseas assets, from under 10% of GDP in the mid-1980s to over 50% by 2010, due to the continued Japanese current account surpluses.

Table 19.4 shows the net foreign asset position of a range of countries in 2007. Does it matter if a country is a net creditor or debtor? As so often in economics, the answer is that it depends on the circumstances. Sustained periods of negative net foreign assets may be optimal when there are exceptional domestic investment opportunities. For instance, if a country is starting from a low level of capital, then our analysis in Chapters 4–6 suggests that investors could earn a high return from investing in that country. As a result, the country will borrow from overseas (run a capital account surplus) and, as long as the money is invested appropriately, the country's economy will grow fast, which will allow the loans to be repaid. However, if a country is running a current account deficit because of high consumption (rather than high investment), then selling off its foreign assets/borrowing from overseas is a cause for more concern, because eventually foreign assets cannot fall further and consumption will have to be curtailed.

TABLE 19.4 ● **Net Foreign Asset Position (% GDP), 2007.**

Creditors (100% of GDP+)		Creditors	Debtors	Debtors (100% of GDP+)
Kuwait (+311%)	Norway (+59%)	Canada (−2%)	Jamaica (−100%)	
Hong Kong (+234%)	Japan (+50%)	Russia (−11%)	Portugal (−101%)	
UAE (+208%)	Iran (+37%)	US (−17%)	Greece (−104%)	
Singapore (+170%)	Venezuela (+32%)	UK (−20%)	Iceland (−113%)	
Switzerland (+141%)	Germany (+26%)	Italy (−21%)	Lebanon (−130%)	
Taiwan (+137%)	China (+22%)	India (−25%)	Rep. of Congo (−139%)	
Saudi Arabia (+101%)	Nigeria (+15%)	Brazil (−41%)	Seychelles (−232%)	
Botswana (+100%)	France (+12%)	Australia (−65%)	Liberia (−767%)	

Source: Updated and extended version of the External Wealth of Nations Mark II database developed by Lane and Milesi-Ferretti (2007).

If a country does have a positive net foreign asset position, then this enables it to sustain indefinitely a current account deficit of a certain size. The reason is that a country can always maintain a current account deficit if it also has a capital account surplus. A capital account surplus means that a country is selling its assets to overseas investors. If the Netherlands has a stock of overseas assets, then these will be increasing every year either through interest and dividends or because of capital gains. If the Netherlands every year sells foreign assets equal to these gains, it will maintain a constant level of foreign assets (it only sells the gains it realizes from the assets, not the capital itself) and create a continual capital account surplus (it is selling Dutch assets). It can thus maintain a continuous current account deficit.

KEY POINT

If a country runs a capital account deficit (surplus), then it is acquiring foreign assets (liabilities). The level of these foreign assets is measured by a country's net IIP.

19.6 Current and Capital Accounts and the Real Exchange Rate

We focused above on the accounting definitions behind the balance of payments. Before we can use these concepts to explain real exchange rate movements, we need also to consider the balance of payments using the national accounts framework of Chapter 2. This will help provide a deeper insight into both why and how the current account has to be matched by an equal and offsetting capital account position.

The previous section stated that a country running a capital account deficit is acquiring foreign assets. In order for this to happen, the country must be doing more savings than investment. That is,

Capital account deficit = Savings − Investment

Consider the case where net savings is positive – savings within a country exceed investment. The banking system can therefore finance all the domestic investment needs of a country and still have surplus deposit funds left over. But banks want to make a profit and will not simply sit on these surplus funds. Instead, they will lend them overseas and earn profit on them. If the surplus savings are invested in overseas equity markets, then the portfolio asset part of the capital account will show a deficit. If, instead, the bank lends the money to an overseas firm, then the other investment category of the capital account will show a deficit. In all these cases, the level of net savings is equal to the capital account deficit. We now proceed to show why it is that net savings (or equivalently the capital account deficit) has to equal the current account surplus.

In Chapter 2, we showed how GDP is a measure of income: the total of wages and salaries and capital income. We also showed how GNI was equal to GDP plus the net income earned on foreign assets, i.e. $GNI = GDP + NIFA$. The income that the economy earns is used by the personal sector in one of three ways: it is spent as consumption (C); it is used to pay taxes (T); or it is saved in the financial system (PS). Therefore,

$$GDP + NIFA = C + T + PS$$

so that savings equals

$$PS = GDP + NIFA - C - T$$

Chapter 2 also showed how GDP was used in one of four ways: as consumption (C); investment in physical machinery or buildings (I); government expenditure on goods and services (G); or net exports (X – M). Therefore,

$$GDP = C + I + G + (X - M)$$

Using this in our expression for savings gives

$$PS = I + G - T + X - M + NIFA$$

or

$$PS + (T - G) - I = X - M + NIFA$$

PS is the savings of the personal sector, while T – G is the savings of the public/government sector (the fiscal surplus). Therefore $S = PS + T - G$ is savings for the whole economy. Thus the national accounts implies

$$S - I = X - M + NIFA$$

As we have just shown, S – I is the capital account deficit. Furthermore, X – M is the balance of trade on goods and services, and NIFA is net income and dividends on overseas assets. Therefore, X – M + NIFA is the current account surplus. Once again, we have derived the result that the capital account plus the current account have to sum to zero. However, we can now convert that into a more meaningful economic statement: net savings in an economy has to equal net exports. Using this net savings–net export approach enables us to explain why the real exchange rate fluctuates.

Consider the case of an economy that starts to run a large fiscal deficit: T – G declines. If net savings by the personal sector (PS) do not increase, the larger fiscal deficit means a lower level of net national savings (S – I). This, in turn, means that the capital account deficit will reduce in size and may even become a surplus, as the government's borrowing needs leave less funds available for overseas investment. The rise in the capital account (i.e. a move into surplus) means a growing current account deficit, so that a fiscal deficit will worsen

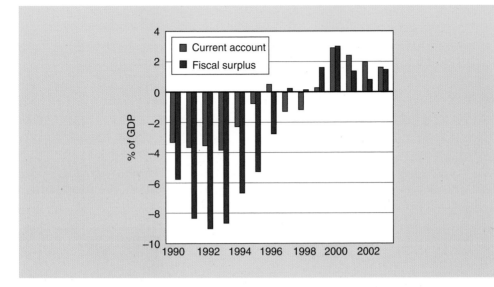

FIGURE 19.8 ● **Canadian fiscal and current account surplus.** The current account is strongly affected by fluctuations in the fiscal surplus. *Source:* IMF, *International Financial Statistics* (September 2003).

the current account (X – M + NIFA). By contrast, an improvement in government finances will be associated with an increase in the current account. This positive relationship between the fiscal and current account surpluses is shown for Canada during the period 1990 to 2003 in Figure 19.8. The positive association between the fiscal position and the current account gives rise to the phrase 'twin deficits': when a country runs a fiscal deficit it often also has a current account deficit.

> **KEY POINT**
>
> The balance of payments implies that net savings (the capital account deficit) must equal net exports (current account surplus), or S – I = X – M.

THE ROLE OF THE REAL EXCHANGE RATE

PPP was rejected by the data because the real exchange rate was too volatile. We will now use this balance of payments framework to show that changes in the real exchange rate are needed to achieve a balance between net savings and net exports. In other words, shifts in net exports or net savings may explain real exchange rate volatility.

As outlined at the beginning of this chapter, the real exchange rate reflects a country's competitiveness: the higher its real exchange rate, the more expensive its commodities are to overseas residents. With a high real exchange rate, a country's exports will be low and imports high because foreign goods are cheap. Therefore, the higher the real exchange rate, the lower the level of net exports and the higher the current account deficit. Figure 19.9 shows this negative relationship between the real exchange rate and net exports.

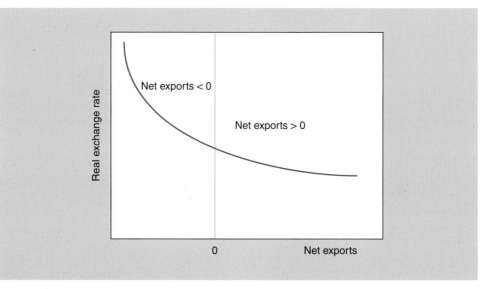

FIGURE 19.9 ● **Real exchange rate and net exports.** Net exports improve when the real exchange rate falls.

Figure 19.9 suggests that when countries experience a real depreciation, their current account should ultimately improve. However, two points need to be stressed:

- It is the *real* exchange rate that matters. If the nominal exchange rate falls but is offset by higher domestic inflation so that the real exchange rate is unaltered, then there is no effect on net exports.
- The beneficial effect of the depreciation may not be immediately felt. In fact, in the short term, the current account may worsen due to the *J-curve* shown in Figure 19.10.

To understand the second point, consider the case when the real exchange rate depreciates so much that the cost of imports rises in domestic currency terms. Eventually this higher import cost will lead to lower demand, and net exports will improve. However, in the short run, firms and individuals may be contracted to purchase, at specified *foreign currency* prices, goods from overseas. While these contracts are in force, the costs of imports will rise without any offsetting benefits from reduced demand. Of course, as contracts come up for renewal, the extra cost means that many will be cancelled and net exports will improve. It may take six months or more before the improvement manifests itself. Economists call this delayed beneficial effect on the current account the J-curve effect, for reasons that should be obvious from Figure 19.10.

Having described how the real exchange rate affects net exports, we need to make an assumption about how exchange rates affect net savings to complete our model. In the rest of this section we assume that net savings do not depend on the exchange rate – whether the currency is high or low, savings and investment decisions are unaffected. This assumption means that net savings is given by a vertical line, as in Figure 19.11.

We can now use this framework to consider the case of a country embarking on an investment boom that leads to a fall in net savings (S–I decreases). This causes the net savings line to shift left in Figure 19.11. Lower net savings means a larger capital account surplus, as the investment boom needs to be financed by overseas funds (assuming that domestic savings does not change). A larger capital account surplus requires an increased

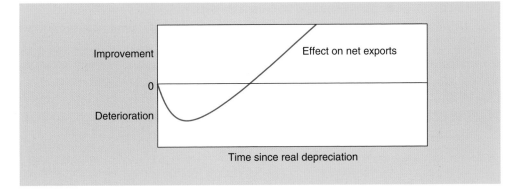

FIGURE 19.10 ● J curve. The current account initially worsens before improving after real depreciation.

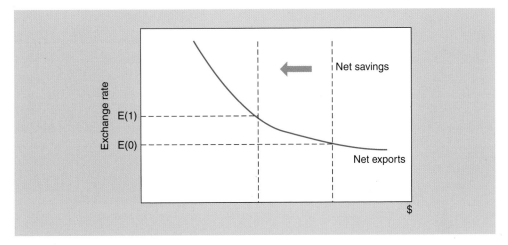

FIGURE 19.11 ● Real exchange rate appreciation from investment boom. An increase in investment reduces net savings and leads to real exchange rate appreciation.

current account deficit; for this to happen, the exchange rate has to appreciate in real terms, from E(0) to E(1). With a higher real exchange rate, exports become uncompetitive and fall, while imports increase. Therefore, the appreciation of the real exchange rate brings net exports and net savings back into line again.

This analysis explains why the US dollar saw a real appreciation in the 1990s (see Table 19.5). US firms increased investment substantially to benefit from the new economy and developments in ICT, and this was financed by significant foreign investment. This produced a large capital account surplus (see Table 19.3) and a large current account deficit. The larger current account deficit was produced as the capital account inflows led to an appreciation of the dollar real exchange rate. Between 1995 and 2001 the dollar appreciated by 34%.

We have shown how shifts in net savings affect the real exchange rate, but shifts in the net exports schedule have similar affects. Anything that shifts the net export schedule will also change the real exchange rate. Consider what happens when Mediterranean goods

TABLE 19.5 ● **US Investment and the Dollar in the 1990s.**

The US investment boom in 1990s led to a fall in net savings and a larger current account deficit through an appreciating real exchange rate.

	Investment (% GDP)	Current Account (% GDP)	Real Effective Exchange Rate
1990	14.6	−1.4	104.8
1991	13.4	0.1	103.7
1992	13.5	−0.8	101.3
1993	14.1	−1.2	104.8
1994	14.7	−1.7	103.5
1995	15.0	−1.4	100.0
1996	15.5	−1.5	104.3
1997	16.0	−1.5	111.9
1998	16.7	−2.3	119.9
1999	17.0	−3.1	119.1
2000	17.2	−4.2	124.9
2001	16.3	−3.9	134.2
2002	15.2	−4.6	133.6

Source: IMF, *International Financial Statistics* (September 2003).

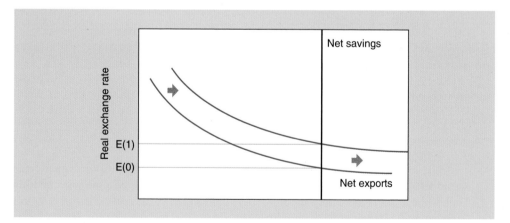

FIGURE 19.12 ● **Shift in export demand and real appreciation.** An increase in demand for a country's net exports leads to appreciation.

suddenly become fashionable. At any particular real exchange rate, exports from Italy will be higher than before – the net export schedule shifts to the right, as in Figure 19.12. However, net savings have not altered and at the existing exchange rate, net exports will be greater than net savings. This cannot happen – the current and capital accounts must sum to zero – so the real exchange rate will have to increase to choke off the demand for Italian goods. Figure 19.12 shows this case, where the increased demand for Italian goods leads to an appreciation of the exchange rate from E(0) to E(1).

Note that we can use the same diagram to examine import controls. If a government introduces import controls, then for a given real exchange rate, the level of imports is reduced, but exports are unchanged, so that net exports increase. As a result, the real exchange rate has to rise to reduce exports in line with the reduction in imports.

This simple model suggests that there are good reasons (shifting net export and net savings curves) for expecting fluctuations in the real exchange rate. However, the key question here is one we posed earlier about PPP: How well does it agree with the data? Examination of the nominal and real exchange rate (see Figure 19.13) shows them both to be volatile and their general fluctuations show a similar pattern. These facts have two potential explanations:

- First, as we suggested in this section, the real exchange rate changes and the factors that lead it to change are volatile. According to this account, volatile economic fundamentals driving net savings or net exports will lead to a volatile real exchange rate, which, in turn, produces a volatile nominal exchange rate.
- The alternative explanation is the idea mentioned earlier in the chapter that, because prices in a country are relatively sticky, changes in the nominal exchange rate feed through into changes in the real exchange rate. According to that analysis, we need to focus on the nominal exchange rate, and in particular monetary models, to understand the volatility of the real exchange rate. In the next chapter we turn to consider some of these alternatives.

Which of these two explanations is correct? While opinions differ, the general consensus is that real exchange rates are far too volatile, especially in the short run, to be explained by changes in the macroeconomic fundamentals that underpin the net exports and net savings curve. As our analysis of the United States in the 1990s shows, we can use changes in macroeconomic fundamentals to explain some of the medium-run fluctuations in the

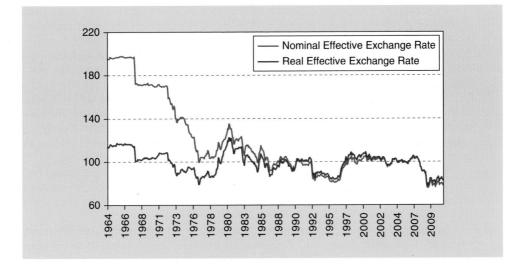

FIGURE 19.13 ● **Nominal and real sterling effective exchange rate.** The short-run volatility of nominal exchange rates is shared by the real exchange rate. *Source:* BIS.

real exchange rate. However, as we see in Figure 19.13, the real exchange rate is too volatile in the short run to be explained by variations in fiscal policy, savings, investment and so forth. For that reason, in Chapter 20 we will move on to discuss changes in the nominal exchange rate. What we have provided in this chapter, though, is a long-run model with which to consider fluctuations in the nominal exchange rate (PPP) and a medium-run model (where real exchange rates shift to ensure that net savings equals net investment). Our focus in the next chapter will be on short-run fluctuations in the nominal exchange rate.

KEY POINT

Fluctuations in net savings and net exports can be used to partially explain why the real exchange rate is so variable compared to the predictions of PPP. However, these fluctuations in economic fundamentals are not large enough or frequent enough to explain more than 3–10-year swings in the real exchange rate.

SUMMARY

In Section 19.1, we defined various concepts of exchange rates. The bilateral exchange rate is the rate at which two particular currencies are exchanged, and the effective exchange rate reflects the behaviour of a currency against a trade-weighted average of all currencies. The nominal exchange rate reflects the rate at which you can swap different currencies, whereas the real exchange rate represents the relative cheapness of one country compared to another.

In Section 19.2, we discussed the law of one price: the idea that the same commodity should sell for the same price in all countries due to arbitrage. We showed that there are substantial deviations from the law of one price due, in part, to tariffs and transportation costs, but also due to border effects and pricing to market on the part of firms.

In Section 19.3 we applied the law of one price to all commodities by using purchasing power parity. PPP implies that the real exchange rate should equal one, as all countries should have the same prices, and that the nominal exchange rate should equal the ratio of prices between countries. As a result, countries with high inflation should have depreciating currencies. In the very long run (over 10 years), PPP describes the data well, but in the short run it performs poorly.

In Section 19.4, we introduced the balance of payments: a statistical record of a country's dealings with the rest of the world. The balance of payments equals the sum of the current and the capital account. The current account details trade in goods and services between countries, while the capital account shows trade in assets. The balance of payments has to balance, so that a current account surplus must be matched by a capital account deficit and vice versa.

Section 19.5 showed how, over time, the capital account of a country determined its net foreign assets or international investment position. Countries that run large capital account deficits are purchasing foreign assets and so will have a positive IIP, while capital account surplus countries will owe money.

In Section 19.6, we discussed how well the balance of payments framework works to explain variations in the real exchange rate. An increase in the real exchange rate reduces net exports and performs a key role in ensuring that the capital account deficit (which equals net savings) equals the current account surplus (net exports). This approach can help explain 3–10-year general shifts in exchange rates, but it cannot plausibly explain the magnitude of short-run fluctuations in the real exchange rate. Instead, the consensus view is that short-run fluctuations in the real exchange rate reflect variations in the nominal exchange rate.

CONCEPTUAL QUESTIONS

1. (Section 19.1) The nominal exchange rate between Eurasian and Oceanian dollars is 3:1. The average shopping trip costs E$400 in Eurasia and O$75 in Oceania. Which country is cheapest? What is the real exchange rate?

2. (Section 19.2) What does the increasing impact of the Internet imply for the law of one price?

3. (Section 19.3) You have been hired as a statistician by an international economic institution and asked to construct estimates of PPP exchange rates. What data do you need and what problems would you expect?

4. (Section 19.3) A multinational company has asked you for a 30-year forecast of various African exchange rates against the US dollar. The firm will give you any macroeconomic forecasts you need. What data would you ask for?

5. (Section 19.4) A German investor places some funds with an emerging-market stock market fund and intends to leave it there for five years and have all dividends paid into a Munich bank account. How will this affect the German current and capital account in each of the next five years?

6. (Section 19.4) Assuming in Table 19.3 that 'Net Other Investment' covers volatile short-term financing that is easily reversed and that central banks cannot continuously use reserves to fund their balance of payments, assess the vulnerability of each country's capital account position.

7. (Section 19.5) Figure 19.7 shows that the UK is a net debtor to other countries, yet it is a net receiver of investment income. What might explain this?

8. (Section 19.6) The Hong Kong dollar depreciates by 5% against the US dollar, but Hong Kong inflation also rises by 5%. What will happen to the Hong Kong current account? How would your answer differ if the authorities managed to prevent inflation from increasing?

9. (Section 19.6) In 2011, several European nations were running large fiscal deficits. What would our net savings = net exports analysis predict should happen to the euro?

ANALYTICAL QUESTIONS

1. (Section 19.1) The United States of Albion does 30% of its total trade with the Republic of Oz, 25% with the Federation of Tropical States and 45% with the Banana Republic. Over the last three years the exchange rates against the United States of Albion dollar (number of local units per dollar) have been

	Republic of Oz	Federation of Tropical States	Banana Republic
Year 0	1	2	3
Year 1	1	1	4
Year 2	2	1	5

Calculate the effective exchange rate for the United States of Albion dollar for years 0 to 2, such that a higher number means a stronger dollar and setting year 0 to 100.

2. (Section 19.3) Calculate the purchasing power parity exchange rate between the following countries (where all goods are purchased in equal amounts).

Commodity	United States of Albion	Republic of Oz
Gasoline	120	180
Meat	80	140
Books	20	33
Fruit juice	40	40
Coffee	15	10
Clothes	70	160

3. (Section 19.5) The New Economic Republic has a net foreign asset position of $0 in 2003, but runs capital account deficits of 3% in 2004, 2005 and 2006. The capital account deficit is used to purchase overseas equity.

(a) Assuming no GDP growth, no capital gains and no change in the exchange rate, what is the IIP in 2004, 2005 and 2006?

(b) Assume no GDP growth or changes in the exchange rate but that the equities purchased experience capital gains of 10% per annum. Recalculate your answer to (a).

(c) In addition to the assumptions in (b), assume that the New Economic Republic currency depreciates by 10% per annum. How does this change your answer to (b)?

4. (Section 19.6)

(a) Use the model of real exchange rate determination in Section 19.6 to analyse the impact on the dollar of a fall in US investment.

(b) Use the same model, but where the net savings line depends positively (e.g. is upward sloping) on the real exchange rate, to analyse the impact of import controls.

5. (Section 19.3 and 19.6) What slope does the net export schedule in Question 4(a) have to be in order to account for purchasing power parity? What is the economic justification of assuming this slope?

CHAPTER 20

Exchange Rate Determination: Nominal Exchange Rates and Asset Markets

Key Concepts

Carry Trade

Covered Interest Parity (CIP)

Global Capital Markets

Home Bias

Order Flow

Risk Premium

Spot and Forward Exchange Rates

Uncovered Interest Parity (UIP)

Overview

This chapter focuses on explaining the volatility in nominal exchange rates. It does so by examining asset markets and capital flows and the relationship between nominal exchange rates and interest rates. We outline the theory of uncovered interest parity (UIP), which implies that when interest rates increase, currencies should appreciate immediately, but thereafter experience a depreciation. UIP also implies that exchange rates are affected by the whole expected path of future interest rates, which helps to explain why exchange rates are so volatile. While UIP captures well the response of exchange rates to interest rate changes, it is in conflict with the data in many other dimensions. The focus of UIP is to use macroeconomics to explain exchange rates, but in the short run this is unsuccessful, as exchange rates seem to be driven by other factors. To understand the short-run behaviour of exchange rates, economists are placing increasing focus on the microstructure of markets and transaction order flows. We conclude the chapter by focusing on the magnitude of capital account flows from both contemporary and historical perspectives. We assess their economic function and consider the issue of whether there really is a single global capital market.

20.1 The Importance of Asset Markets

In this chapter we explain how international asset markets, or investment opportunities, influence the nominal exchange rate. Just as we did with the law of one price and purchasing power parity (PPP) in Chapter 19, we consider what arbitrage implies for exchange rate fluctuations. Whereas with PPP we focused on arbitrage in goods and services, we now

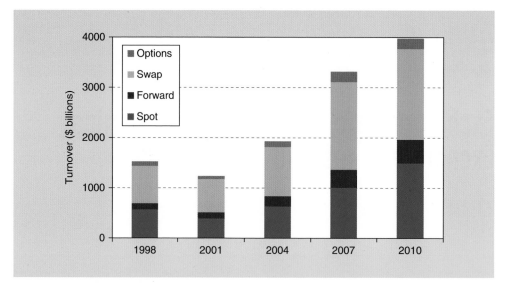

FIGURE 20.1 ● **Average daily turnover ($ bn) in foreign exchange markets.** Foreign exchange market turnover has increased substantially over time. *Source:* Bank for International Settlements, *Triennial Central Bank Survey: Foreign exchange and derivatives market activity in 2010.*

focus on arbitrage between investment opportunities in different economies. We focus particularly on differences in interest rates between countries.

The importance of asset markets in explaining exchange rates is evident when the size of daily market transactions is considered. Figure 20.1 shows daily turnover in foreign exchange markets between 1998 and 2010. Both **spot** transactions (for immediate delivery of one currency in exchange for another) and **forward** transactions (where exchange rates are fixed today but delivery is in the future) have increased substantially over time, although with the introduction of the euro in 1999 there was a temporary fall in turnover. By 2010, the combined level of *daily* turnover was approximately $4 trillion. Less than 5% of these exchange rate transactions are related to trade in goods and services, the focus of Chapter 19. The majority of these transactions are for investment in asset markets, hence our focus on investment returns and interest rates.

Not surprisingly, the world's three largest economic areas (the United States, the Eurozone and Japan) have the three most heavily traded currencies.[1] The most traded combination is US dollar/euro, which had a daily trading volume of $1.1 trillion, followed by US dollar/yen ($568 billion). Table 20.1 shows where these currency trades occur. Even though the British pound accounts for only around 13% of total trade in foreign exchange, geographically London accounts for 37% of all turnover.

KEY POINT

The daily turnover on foreign exchange markets is enormous and far exceeds the level required for trade in goods and services. The motivation for this high level of turnover originates in asset markets and investment flows.

TABLE 20.1 ● **Geographical Distribution of Foreign Exchange Market Activity.**
London is the main foreign exchange market.

UK	36.7
US	17.9
Japan	6.2
Singapore	5.3
Switzerland	5.2
Hong Kong	4.7
France	3.0
Germany	2.1

Source: Bank for International Settlements, *Triennial Central Bank Survey: Foreign Exchange and Derivatives Market Activity in 2010.*

(20.2) Covered Interest Parity

The aim of this chapter is to explain how variations in interest rates and asset returns lead to fluctuations in exchange rates. We start our analysis with **covered interest parity** or CIP. Consider a Japanese investor deciding whether to invest in a yen or a dollar bank account. The yen account pays interest of 1%, the dollar account 4% and the current spot rate is ¥100:$1. For the Japanese investor, the return on the yen account is straightforward – it is simply the Japanese interest rate. However, the return on the dollar account consists of two factors: the dollar interest rate (4%) plus any appreciation of the dollar against the yen. What the investor does depends on what she expects the yen–dollar exchange rate to be.

The Japanese investor has to compare two different investments (as outlined in Figure 20.2). The first is investing ¥100 000 for one year in a yen account and earning interest i^J,

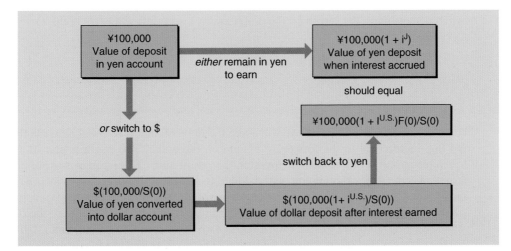

FIGURE 20.2 ● **Covered interest parity.** Covered interest parity implies that the difference between forward and spot exchange rates compensates for any interest rate differential.

which in our example is 1%, or 0.01. The alternative is to invest in a dollar bank account. Assume that the current exchange rate is $S(0)$. (The notation $S(0)$ reminds us that we are talking about today's *spot* rate. In our example, $S(0)$ is ¥100:$1.) The Japanese investor with ¥100 000 would deposit $(100\,000/S(0))$ in the dollar account. This pays interest at the rate i^{US} (4% or 0.04), so that at the end of the year, the account is worth $(100\,000(1 + i^{US})/S(0))$.

However, this is a dollar amount, and to compare it with the yen investment we need to convert it back into yen. With CIP we do this by using the forward rate. The forward rate is the rate at which you can purchase currency at specific *future* dates at an exchange rate that is fixed *today*. Our Japanese investor wishes to know the future yen value of $(100\,000(1 + i^{US})/S(0))$. If she signs a one-year forward contract today at a rate of $F(0)$, then in one year's time, the investor is guaranteed in yen terms ¥100 000$(1 + i^{US})$ $F(0)/S(0)$. It is important to stress that there is no uncertainty here, because all transactions are made today. Therefore, whether the investor chooses a yen or a dollar account, she faces no exchange rate risk if she uses forward contracts. The exchange rate risk is *covered* by the forward contract.

Over the year, the ¥100 000 converted into dollars increases by a factor of $(1 + i^{US})$ $F(0)/S(0)$. If $F(0) > S(0)$, then the dollar is said to have a forward premium – the forward rate includes a dollar appreciation (i.e. at the forward date more yen are paid out for dollars than at the current spot rate). If $F(0) < S(0)$, then there is a forward discount as the dollar depreciates. We can therefore write $F(0)/S(0)$ as $1 + fp$, where fp denotes the forward premium. If the forward rate is 5% above the spot rate, then $fp = 0.05$. Using this notation, the return on the US dollar investment for the Japanese investor is $(1 + i^{US})(1 + fp)$ and the return on her yen investment is $(1 + i^J)$.

If $(1 + i^{US})F(0)/S(0)$ exceeds $(1 + i^J)$, the dollar investment is more profitable than the yen investment and investors will rearrange their portfolio by switching into dollars. In order to do so, the investor will sell yen in the spot market (to open a dollar account) and will buy yen in the forward market (to convert the dollar account back into yen). As the investor sells yen today, it will drive up the spot value of the dollar and so increase $S(0)$. As the investor buys yen forward, it will tend to push up the future price of yen and lower $F(0)$. As this happens, the advantage of investing in the dollar account diminishes as $F(0)/S(0)$ (the forward premium) falls. The investor will switch her funds into dollars as long as the return on the dollar investment exceeds the yen return. But eventually, by switching her funds, the return on the dollar and yen accounts will become the same. That is eventually

$$(1 + i^{US})\,(1 + fp) = (1 + i^J)$$

which is approximately the same as

$$i^{US} + fp = i^J$$

Therefore in equilibrium, arbitrage will make the interest rate differential between the yen and the dollar equal to the forward premium on the dollar. This result is known as covered interest parity. For a Japanese investor, the return on a US account consists of interest earned plus the forward premium on the dollar. In our example, US interest rates were 4% and Japanese rates were 1%. In this situation, covered interest rate parity implies that there is a forward dollar discount of 3% – the forward rate should be 3% lower than the current yen–dollar rate. In order for the return on the two investments to be the same, it must be that the currency that offers a higher interest rate has to be priced at a forward depreciation. CIP therefore pins down a precise relationship between interest rate differentials and the spot and forward exchange rates.

> **KEY POINT**
>
> Arbitrage by investors will lead to the forward premium between two currencies being equal to the interest rate differential. High interest rate currencies are priced at a forward discount.

Does CIP hold? The answer is a resounding 'yes'. If it did not hold, investors could make infinite amounts of money at no risk by switching funds between currencies. There is, however, one caveat. CIP only holds exactly if there is absolutely no risk to either the yen or dollar side of the transactions. Imagine a Japanese investor considering a yen deposit account in Tokyo or a dollar account based in Moscow with a Russian bank. Because the accounts are based in different countries and with different banks, their risk characteristics may not be identical. One country might impose capital controls, or one of the banks might be almost insolvent, in which case the investor will lose his money. In this case, the investor may place funds in the account that offers a lower return because it is less risky. This became a major issue in the financial crisis of 2008–09, as we saw in Chapter 17. If, instead, we concentrate attention on deposits in the same country with the same bank, these risk differences do not exist and CIP holds exactly.

20.3 Uncovered Interest Parity

A key feature of CIP is the use of a forward contract so that the investor faces no uncertainty when comparing the return on yen and dollar accounts. By contrast, with **uncovered interest parity (UIP)**, the investor does not buy forward, but waits before converting dollars into yen at the future spot rate. The risk is therefore uncovered. The result is that instead of comparing ¥100 000$(1 + i^J)$ with ¥100 000$(1 + i^{US})$ $F(0)/S(0)$, the investor compares it with ¥100 000$(1 + i^{US})S^e(1)/S(0)$, where $S^e(1)$ is what the investor *expects* the spot exchange rate to be one period in the future. Of course, the investor could be wrong – $S^e(1)$ may not equal $S(1)$; the outcome may be different from the investor's forecast. But this is the risk the investor takes, because he does not cover his position by a forward transaction.

Under UIP, investors rearrange their portfolio in a similar way to CIP until the return on the yen account is equal to the expected return on the dollar account. In the case of UIP, we have:

Expected appreciation of dollar $[S^e(1) - S(0)]/S(0)$
   = Japanese interest rate − US interest rate

In other words, if US interest rates are higher than Japanese interest rates, investors must be expecting a depreciation (or negative appreciation) of the dollar. If Japanese interest rates are 0% and US interest rates are 2%, then the market must be expecting a 2% depreciation in the dollar. Imagine instead that at these interest rates the market expects the dollar to remain unchanged. Investors will shift funds into US dollar accounts in order to earn 2% compared to 0%. Investors buying dollars will lead to an increase in the dollar, so that (assuming an unchanged forecast) the dollar is now overvalued and expected to depreciate. If the dollar is expected to depreciate by only 1%, it is still worth while shifting funds into dollars that earn 1% (2% interest less 1% depreciation), compared to 0% on yen. Investors will therefore continue to buy dollars until the dollar has risen so far that they expect it to fall by 2%. At this point, the interest rate differential is completely offset by the expected depreciation on dollars. UIP therefore offers a theory to explain expected changes in exchange rates: it is all about interest rate differentials.

THE RISKS OF INVESTING IN HIGH-YIELDING COUNTRIES

UIP helps explain why investors do not place all their funds in countries offering high interest rates or borrow from countries with low interest rates. Although the investors benefit from low interest rates, this benefit is offset by adverse shifts in the exchange rate according to UIP. One recent example of the dangers of such a strategy comes from Iceland, where Icelanders tried to avoid paying the high local interest rates on their mortgages by borrowing funds in foreign currencies like the Japanese yen and Swiss franc, currencies of countries where interest rates were low. Just before the Icelandic currency crisis it is estimated that roughly one-fifth of all Icelandic mortgages were in low-interest-rate foreign currencies. Figure 20.3 shows what happened to the Icelandic krona value of a typical mortgage denominated in yen. Before the crisis the low Japanese interest rate meant that the krona repayments on a yen loan were low and made these types of mortgages seem like a good idea, but over the course of 2007–08 the massive devaluation of the Icelandic krona during their banking crisis saw the krona repayments value of these loans more than double.

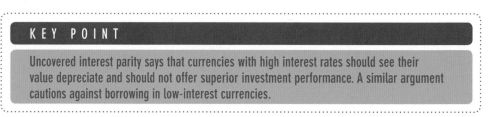

KEY POINT

Uncovered interest parity says that currencies with high interest rates should see their value depreciate and should not offer superior investment performance. A similar argument cautions against borrowing in low-interest currencies.

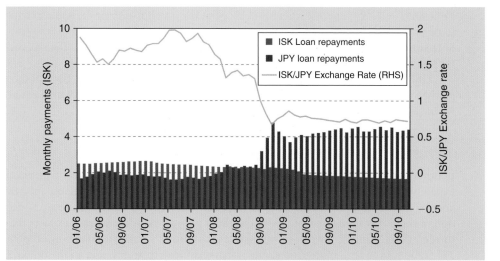

FIGURE 20.3 ● Repayments on a five-year loan denominated in Icelandic krona (ISK) and Japanese yen (JPY). Low Japanese interest rates compared with those in Iceland made borrowing money in yen attractive to Icelandic citizens. However, the currency crisis of 2007–08 meant that repayments on such loans soon outstripped the repayments required on a loan denominated in krona and paying Icelandic interest rates. *Source:* Authors' calculations.

(20.4) Pinning Down the Exchange Rate with UIP

UIP tells us how exchange rate *changes* are related to interest rate differentials. In this section, we use UIP to develop a model of what determines the current *level* of the exchange rate instead. A key feature of this model is to work out today's exchange rate *taking as fixed expectations of where the exchange rate will be tomorrow*. In other words, we reverse the flow of time and take a forward-looking approach. Rather than try to work out expectations of where the exchange rate will be tomorrow by reference to the current exchange and interest rates, we do the opposite: *we calculate the current exchange rate by reference to interest rates and where we expect the exchange rate to be in the future.*

In Figure 20.4 we consider again the case of a US and Japanese investment and use UIP to derive the yen–dollar exchange rate. For the Japanese investor, the yen-denominated return on the Japanese investment is i^J and does not depend on $S(0)$, the current spot rate. For example, if $i^J = 2\%$, then the return on the yen account is 2%, whatever happens to the dollar. The return on the yen account is therefore given by the vertical line in Figure 20.4.

The return on the dollar account for the Japanese investor is $i^{US} + [S^e(1) - S(0)]/S(0)$. The higher are US interest rates and $S^e(1)$, the expectations of the future spot rate, the greater the return on the dollar account. For a given $S^e(1)$, the US return is *decreasing* in $S(0)$. The reason is simple: by keeping fixed the forecast of the future exchange rate but increasing the current strength of the dollar, there is less dollar appreciation and, as a result, a lower return on dollars for the Japanese investor. Therefore, the US dollar return is shown in Figure 20.4 as a downward-sloping line: for given expectations of the future spot rate, the higher the current spot rate the lower the return on dollar investments.

UIP says that in equilibrium, the return on the yen account equals the expected return on the dollar account. This occurs at the point where the two lines in Figure 20.4 intersect, and this determines the current exchange rate, shown as $S^*(0)$.

We now use this analysis to model exchange rate fluctuations in response to:

- changes in Japanese interest rates
- changes in US interest rates
- revisions to expectations of the future value of the dollar

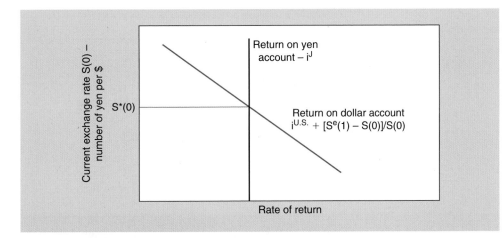

FIGURE 20.4 ● Determining the nominal exchange rate. Domestic and overseas interest rates and expectation of future exchange rates determine the current exchange rate.

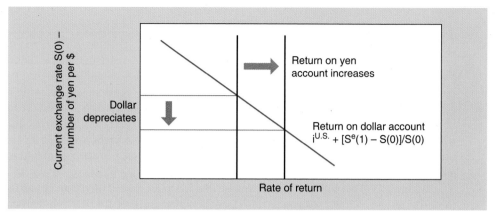

FIGURE 20.5 ● **Increase in Japanese interest rates leads to dollar depreciation.** Higher domestic interest rates means currency appreciates.

IMPACT OF HIGHER JAPANESE INTEREST RATES ON THE DOLLAR

As shown in Figure 20.5, an increase in Japanese interest rates leads to a rightward shift in the yen return curve and a decline in $S^*(0)$, so that a dollar buys fewer yen. Therefore, *an increase in Japanese interest rates leads to a depreciation of the dollar and an appreciation of the yen.*

IMPACT OF HIGHER US INTEREST RATES ON THE DOLLAR

Figure 20.6 shows the impact of an increase in US interest rates on the dollar. For a given current exchange rate, an increase in US rates leads to an increase in the return on dollar investments, so the dollar return line in Figure 20.6 shifts right. As a result, the yen–dollar

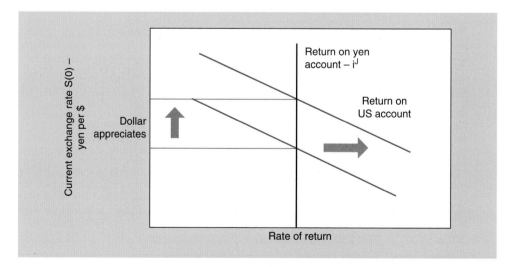

FIGURE 20.6 ● **Increase in US interest rates leads to dollar appreciation.**

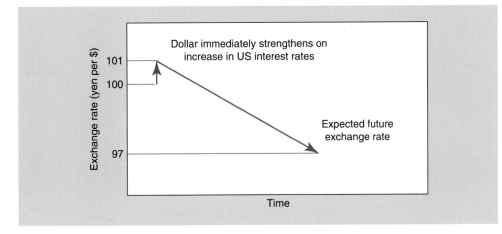

F I G U R E   2 0 . 7   ●   **Appreciation of dollar after increase in US interest rates.** Exchange rate jumps in response to higher interest rates.

rate increases: the dollar strengthens and can be used to buy more yen per dollar. Therefore, a rise in US rates leads to a dollar appreciation/yen depreciation.

Consider the case where US interest rates are 4%, Japanese rates 1% and investors expect the yen–dollar rate to be 97 in a year's time. Because US interest rates are 3% higher, UIP implies an expected dollar devaluation of 3%, which gives a current exchange rate of 100 (3% higher than the expected future value of 97). If US interest rates increase to 5%, UIP now implies an expected 4% devaluation of the dollar, so the current exchange rate should be approximately 101, as shown in Figure 20.7. In response to the 1% increase in US interest rates, the dollar *strengthens* from 100 to 101.

UIP says that countries with high interest rates should see their currencies depreciate, but we have just used UIP to show that an increase in US rates leads to an *appreciation* of the dollar. There is, however, no inconsistency between these two conclusions. The key is that Figure 20.7 shows that in response to higher interest rates the currency should appreciate *immediately*. By contrast, the UIP equation says that *looking forward*, countries with high interest rates should see gradually depreciating currencies. If the dollar did not rise today then, for a given forecast of the future exchange rate, superior returns would be available on the dollar. Therefore, in using UIP it is important to separate out the immediate response of exchange rates from the future effect.

IMPACT OF CHANGED EXPECTATIONS OF THE DOLLAR

We have so far concentrated on how interest rates influence the current exchange rate. However, expectations of future exchange rates are also important, because they influence the expected return on the overseas investment.

Figure 20.8 shows the case where the market revises upwards its expectation of future dollar strength – this increases the expected return from the dollar investment and shifts the return schedule on the US investment for the Japanese investor to the right. The result is an

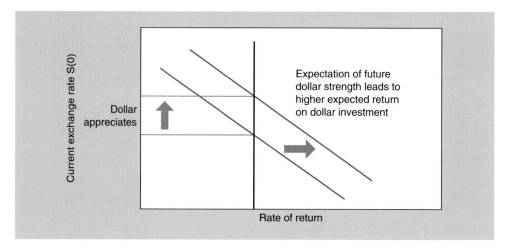

FIGURE 20.8 ● **Expectations of future dollar strength lead to dollar appreciation.** Expectations of future high currency lead to an appreciation today.

increase in the current value of dollars – *market expectations of future dollar strength lead to an immediate appreciation of the dollar.* This makes sense: if investors think the dollar will be strong in the future, they will wish to buy dollars now to benefit from this, which will lead to an appreciation today.

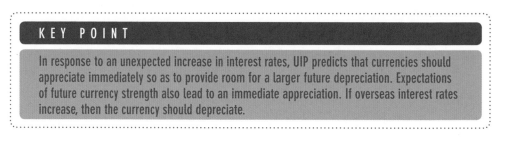

KEY POINT

In response to an unexpected increase in interest rates, UIP predicts that currencies should appreciate immediately so as to provide room for a larger future depreciation. Expectations of future currency strength also lead to an immediate appreciation. If overseas interest rates increase, then the currency should depreciate.

20.5 The Role of Expectations

UIP tries to explain exchange rate volatility through interest rate differentials. However, expectations of the future are critical to UIP. We now show how changing expectations can lead to considerable volatility in exchange rates. In other words, the current exchange rate displays considerable volatility in response to *unanticipated* events. We first discuss changes in expectations concerning interest rates, and then consider changes in expectations about future exchange rates.

INTEREST RATE EXPECTATIONS

Consider the case where the market thinks that the yen–dollar exchange rate will be 100 next period, $S^e(1) = 100$. US interest rates are 4% and Japanese rates 1%. However, the market is expecting that today's meeting of the Federal Reserve Board will raise US rates to 6%.

On the basis of this expectation, the current exchange rate is 105 – at 6% interest rates, UIP predicts a 5% decline of the dollar (the interest differential between US and Japan) to a level of 100 in a year's time. However, the Federal Reserve surprises the market and only increases interest rates from 4% to 5%. With a 5% US interest rate, UIP predicts only a 4% devaluation, so that the dollar falls from 105 to 104, giving it scope to depreciate by 4% to 100. *Note that even though US interest rates have increased, the currency has immediately depreciated.* However, this does not contradict our previous analysis: the key point is that US interest rates in this example are lower than what the market expected, which is why the dollar falls.

> ### KEY POINT
>
> UIP says that predictable changes in the exchange rate are due to interest rate differentials, but that changes in expectations will lead to substantial unpredictable fluctuations in exchange rates.

EXPECTATIONS OF FUTURE EXCHANGE RATES

Crucial to our modelling of the exchange rate was an expectation for future exchange rates, $S^e(1)$. Without knowing how to model $S^e(1)$, however, we have not really arrived at a model that explains the current exchange rate. We need to be able to pin down $S^e(1)$ to fully understand the current exchange rate. However, modelling $S^e(1)$ is easy – we can just use UIP again!

We have shown how to determine the current exchange rate, $S(0)$, based on current interest rates and a forecast of the future exchange rate, $S^e(1)$. However, this analysis should hold for all periods, not just today. In other words, we could use the same analysis to deduce the expected exchange rate tomorrow, $S^e(1)$, given expectations of interest rates tomorrow and the exchange rate two periods from now, $S^e(2)$.

What determines $S^e(2)$? Again, we can use UIP and derive $S^e(2)$ as depending on interest rates two periods from now, as well as on expectations of the exchange rate in three periods' time, $S^e(3)$. We can keep performing this trick until we have expressed the current exchange rate in terms of the expectation of some long-run equilibrium exchange rate ($S^e(LR)$) that will occur at some distant future point and *the whole intervening course of domestic and foreign interest rates*, as shown in Figure 20.9.

How can we pin down this long-run equilibrium exchange rate? In Chapter 19 we showed that, over several decades, purchasing power parity seemed a reasonable guide to how nominal exchange rates behaved. This suggests that we can use PPP to pin down $S^e(LR)$. For instance, if over the next 20 years US inflation is expected to be 40% higher than Japanese inflation, then PPP would suggest that over the next 20 years the dollar will depreciate against the yen by 40% – this pins down $S^e(LR)$. However, the dollar will not experience a straight-line depreciation over this 20-year period; differences between US and Japanese interest rates will add additional exchange rate dynamics.

This dependence on the whole future path of interest rates can potentially account for substantial volatility in exchange rates. Consider the case where the market expects only a temporary increase in US interest rates over the next year. This does not affect $S^e(LR)$ (a temporary increase in interest rates is unlikely to affect long-run US inflation) or even $S^e(1)$ (unless it influences interest rates more than one period from now). Therefore, the

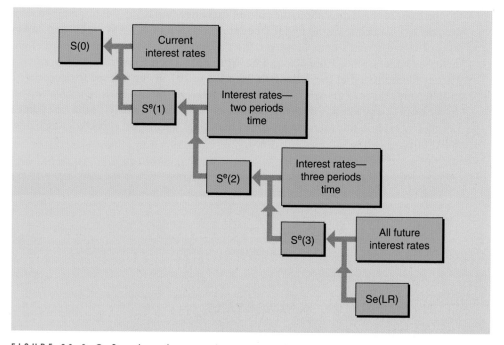

FIGURE 20.9 ● **Dependence of current exchange rate on all future interest rates.** Because the exchange rate depends on interest rates and exchange rate forecasts, the current exchange rate depends on all future interest rates.

effect on the current exchange rate is relatively small – the dollar appreciates by the amount of the interest rate increase.

However, compare this with the case where the United States increases interest rates and the market expects them to stay permanently higher. In this case, the dollar will appreciate substantially. First, the permanently higher interest rates should lower long-run US inflation. As a result, $S^e(LR)$ will increase, because PPP implies that the dollar depreciates less in response to the lower long-run US inflation. Second, the whole future path of US interest rates is now expected to be higher, so that, according to UIP, the dollar now has to *depreciate* by more over the coming years. This faster depreciation is not just in the next year but in every subsequent year. To provide room for this depreciation, the dollar has to appreciate immediately and substantially relative to $S^e(LR)$, which has itself increased anyway. As a result, a permanent change in monetary policy will exert a substantial impact on the current exchange rate and create volatility in the current exchange rates. Therefore, UIP implies that rational, forward-looking investors should generate a highly volatile exchange rate if changes in monetary policy are highly persistent.

> ### KEY POINT
>
> UIP explains exchange rate volatility by suggesting that changing expectations about current and future interest rates and inflation are likely to lead to substantial unpredictable changes in exchange rates.

20.6 Does UIP Hold?

We have spent a lot of time outlining UIP, but we have not yet assessed the empirical validity of the model. Economists have devoted a great deal of effort to testing this model. The standard approach they take is to run the following regression:

% Depreciation of currency = Constant + β × [(Domestic interest rate − Overseas rate)]

If UIP is correct, the interest rate differential should have a coefficient of one ($\beta = 1$), so that the interest rate differential is, on average, equal to the future change in the exchange rate. However, one survey of 75 published estimates of this regression found that the average value was –0.88.[2] In other words, contrary to the implications of UIP, the currency of countries with high interest rates tends to *appreciate*. This violation of UIP means that investors can earn higher investment returns if they invest in high-yielding currencies. It implies that in response to higher interest rates, the exchange rate appreciates immediately (as predicted by UIP) but continues to be strong going forward (in conflict with UIP).

> **KEY POINT**
>
> UIP is correct in predicting how exchange rates respond immediately to interest rates and monetary policy, but it is wrong in forecasting the exchange rate forward. Instead, high-interest-rate currencies tend to appreciate.

THE CARRY TRADE

The result that high-interest-rate currencies tend to appreciate has not been lost on financial market participants like hedge funds, since it suggests that it may be possible to earn superior returns by investing in them. Support for this is shown in Figure 20.10, which compares cumulative returns to a US-based investor with $1 in 1969 from three alternative investment strategies:

1. *US investment:* simply deposit $1 at US interest rates and reinvest interest income.
2. *Lowest-interest-rate currency:* place funds in whichever country has the lowest prevailing interest rate out of the six most heavily traded currencies (US dollar, Japanese yen, euro, UK pound, Australian dollar or Swiss franc). As well as earning interest, a non-dollar investment is exposed to currency fluctuations.
3. *Highest-interest-rate currency:* place funds in whichever country has the highest prevailing interest rate out of the six most heavily traded currencies (US dollar, Japanese yen, euro, UK pound, Australian dollar or Swiss franc). As well as earning interest, a non-dollar investment is exposed to currency fluctuations.

If UIP holds, the three strategies should deliver roughly the same returns (since low-interest-rate currencies should tend to appreciate against high-interest-rate currencies). In practice, the failure of UIP means that, on average, investing in high-interest-rate currencies gives higher returns than normal, while investing in low-interest-rate currencies delivers low returns on average.

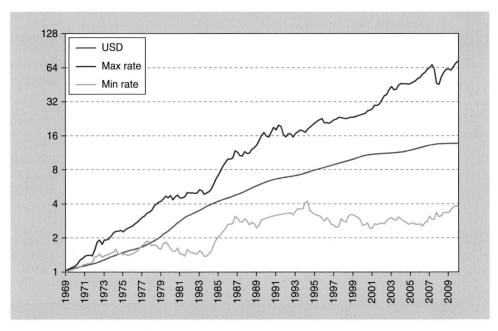

FIGURE 20.10 ● **Investment return on alternative currency strategies.** In contradiction to UIP, high-interest-rate currencies frequently earn a higher return. *Source:* Authors' calculations using IMF data.

In financial markets, the most popular way to exploit this failure of UIP is called the **carry trade** (carry is a market term for net interest earned on a trade). In the standard carry trade an investor will borrow funds in a low-interest-rate currency and deposit them in a high-interest-rate one.

Note, however, that both the high- and low-interest-rate currency strategies expose the investor to currency fluctuations, so the returns are volatile and risky. As our example of the Icelandic krona earlier in this chapter suggests, this risk is substantial. Investors will need to assess whether or not the extra returns shown in Figure 20.10 compensate for this higher risk.

(20.7) Introducing Risk-Averse Investors

In an effort to make UIP fit the data better, this section modifies one of its assumptions: that investors ignore risk. When we moved from CIP to UIP, we stressed that the investor no longer covered the future exchange rate risk by buying forward. As a result, the exchange rate uncertainty makes the US investment more risky for a Japanese investor than the yen investment. If Japanese investors are *risk neutral*, the extra risk/variability involved in the dollar investment does not influence their decisions. The investor only compares the expected return on the yen investment to the expected return on the dollar investment and does not worry about the uncertainty of the latter.

But if Japanese investors are *risk averse*, then when given the choice between two assets with the same expected return, but where one is more risky, they will choose the less risky one. This means that to be indifferent between the yen and dollar investments, the Japanese investor will require a higher return on the US asset. This additional return required to compensate for higher risk is the **risk premium**. In this case we have to modify UIP so that

US return = US interest rate + Expected dollar appreciation
= Japanese interest rate + Risk premium

Imagine that Japanese investors require a risk premium of 2% on US investments. Then if the Japanese interest rate is 1% and the US interest rate is 4%, this equation tells us that the market is expecting a 1% fall in the dollar.

So far we have only been considering the case of Japanese investors, but US investors will also require a risk premium if they are to invest in yen accounts. Obviously, both US and Japanese investors cannot simultaneously achieve a positive risk premium, so the sign and size of the risk premium will depend on the relative risk aversion of each group of investors and the perceived risk in each country.

Figure 20.11 shows the implications of introducing a risk premium into our UIP analysis. Consider the case where the risk premiums that Japanese investors demand from overseas investments decline – in this case the United States becomes like a 'safe haven'. For a given current exchange rate and unchanged US interest rates, this is equivalent to boosting the risk-adjusted return from investing in dollar accounts, so the overseas return schedule shifts to the right. This immediately strengthens the dollar. Therefore the perception that a currency is now less risky, or has become a 'safe haven', will lead the currency to appreciate even if interest rates have not altered. Similarly, an increase in perceived risk will lead to a depreciation of a currency.

A risk premium adds an additional source of exchange rate volatility and can *potentially* explain why the currencies of countries with high interest rates tend to appreciate over time. If, when US interest rates increase, the required risk premium for holding dollar assets increases by *more*, then our risk-adjusted UIP implies that the dollar should appreciate over the coming period. Consider the case where US interest rates are 4%, Japanese interest rates are 1% and the required risk premium on dollar assets is 2%. Our risk-adjusted UIP implies that the market is expecting a 1% depreciation of the dollar. However, if US rates rise to 5% and, at the same time, the required risk premium *increases* to 5%, then our risk-adjusted UIP implies a dollar *appreciation* of 1%.

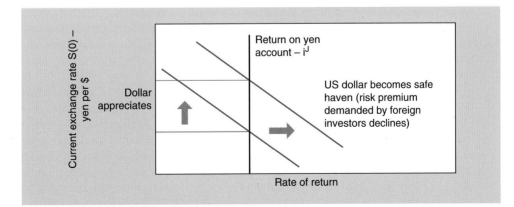

FIGURE 20.11 ● **Risk premiums and exchange rate fluctuations.** Introducing risk premiums produces a more volatile exchange rate.

Do the data support this potential explanation of exchange rate volatility? The answer is no. Empirical studies based on interest rate data and market expectations of future exchange rates reveal that although a risk premium exists, and it varies over time, it is not large enough to account for the magnitude of exchange rate volatility. Even though there is some evidence for 'carry crashes' where carry trades make significant losses over a short period (as they did in 2008), the risk premium generated by such potential crashes does not seem large enough to explain the high average returns earned from such trades.

> **KEY POINT**
>
> Introducing risk premiums into UIP can help explain more of the volatility in exchange rates, but ultimately UIP fails to account successfully for short-run fluctuations in exchange rates. While it correctly predicts how exchange rates react to interest rate changes, there seem to be many other factors that drive exchange rates that are not reflected in UIP.

20.8   What Are Exchange Rate Markets Really Like?

So far, our analysis of exchange rates has repeatedly shown how theories of exchange rate behaviour like PPP and UIP have only a very limited role in explaining exchange rates in practice. As one recent study concludes, 'the exchange rates of low-inflation countries are almost unrelated to macroeconomic phenomena'.[3] Indeed, a seminal study in 1983 (the results of which have remained essentially unchallenged) concluded that a wide variety of economic models of the exchange rate were unable to outperform the simple forecasting rule that the future exchange rate over the next year would remain unchanged.[4] In other words, macroeconomic data are not useful in forecasting short-run changes in the exchange rate. Despite an exhaustive hunt, researchers have struggled to overcome this result. PPP and inflation differences help to predict very long-run changes in exchange rates; the net savings/net exports approach helps explain medium-run changes in the real exchange rate and, using UIP, interest rates have some role to play in explaining how exchange rates respond to monetary policy. However, the majority of the substantial short-run fluctuations in exchange rates seem to be unrelated directly to macroeconomics.

As a result, exchange rate economists are pursuing new avenues. One of the most promising is to concentrate on the operation of foreign exchange markets themselves. To understand the way FX (foreign exchange) markets work, we focus on a survey of the London market.[5]

The first revealing feature is how quickly the market responds to economic information (see Table 20.2). Two-thirds of respondents suggest that the market assimilates new information about interest rates within 10 seconds, and the overwhelming view is that markets have incorporated all macroeconomic developments within one minute. Looking at scheduled macroeconomic releases, we can also tell which economic variables FX dealers think most influence exchange rates (though interest rate changes that most market participants think are very important are not included). Figure 20.12 shows that the most significant data release is that of the figures on the US labour market (called non-farm payrolls or simply payrolls) on the first Friday of the month. Also important are unemployment and inflation, which are key determinants of monetary policy.

TABLE 20.2 ● **Responsiveness of Exchange Rates to Macro Information.**

Number of respondents answering the question: 'How fast do you believe the market can assimilate the new information when the following economic announcements from the major developed countries differ from their market expectations?'

	<10 seconds	<1 minute	<10 minutes	<30 minutes	>30 minutes
Unemployment rate	51	44	10	1	1
Trade deficit	45	46	13	1	2
Inflation	49	40	14	2	2
GDP	29	50	23	1	3
Interest rates	65	30	9	0	3
Money supply	22	61	20	2	2

Note: Exchange rates respond swiftly to macroeconomic data.

Source: Cheung, Chinn and Marsh, How Do UK-Based Foreign Exchange Dealers Think Their Market Operates?, NBER Working Paper 7524 (2000).

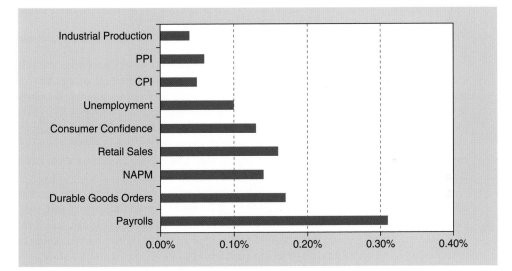

FIGURE 20.12 ● **Impact of economic data on exchange rates.** Average impact of various US macroeconomic data releases on the US dollar.

The survey offers little support for PPP. When asked the following:

In your opinion, the purchasing power parity condition

(a)   can be used to compute the fair spot exchange rate

(b)   proposes national price levels, once converted to the same currency via the appropriate exchange rate, should be the same

(c)   is only an academic jargon and has no practical relevance to the FX market

(d)   other

(c) was chosen by 60% of respondents. Furthermore, 70% of respondents said that they would take no trading action if PPP calculations indicated that the dollar was overvalued;

TABLE 20.3 ● **What Drives Exchange Rates?**

Number of respondents answering the question: 'Select the single most important factor that determines exchange rate movements in each of the three horizons listed.'

	Short Run Intraday	Medium Run (up to 6 Months)	Long Run (over 6 Months)
Bandwagon Effects	51	13	1
Overreaction to News	57	1	0
Speculative Forces	44	42	3
Economic Fundamentals	1	43	80
Technical Trading	18	36	11
Other	3	2	2

Note: In the short run, macroeconomics has little influence on market participants.

Source: Cheung, Chinn and Marsh, How Do UK-Based Foreign Exchange Dealers Think Their Market Operates?, NBER Working Paper 7524 (2000).

only 29% would sell the dollar. This all confirms what we saw in Chapter 19: PPP is a poor guide to short-run exchange rate developments.

The most informative part of the survey asks dealers what factors they think drive exchange rates at different horizons (see Table 20.3). Hardly anyone gives much of a role to macroeconomic fundamentals in the short run. Instead, the momentum of the market and the beliefs of dealers dominate (bandwagon effects, speculative forces and overreaction to news). Over the medium run (up to six months), economic fundamentals play a bigger role, and bandwagon effects and overreaction cease to matter. But even at this horizon, speculative forces are just as important as macroeconomics. Only in the long run (over six months) do the macroeconomic fundamentals exert the main influence.

The idea that non-economic factors may influence exchange rates in the short run has encouraged researchers to look at how the FX markets operate as a way to try to explain exchange rate volatility. Economists call this the **microstructure** approach and it involves analysing the actual trading behaviour of market participants, rather than assuming that the market simply reacts to fundamental information like interest rates and inflation.

(20.9) Global Capital Markets

This chapter has so far focused on how the substantial flow of capital between countries influences exchange rates in response to differences in interest rates and asset returns. In this remaining section we focus on the economic rationale behind these capital flows.

HISTORICAL PRECEDENT

The huge capital flows that we observe today tend to be seen as unprecedented. In terms of their absolute size in billions of dollars, this is true, but not when they are measured as a proportion of the economy. Around the end of the nineteenth century, capital flows between

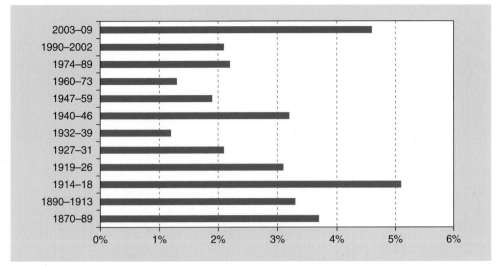

FIGURE 20.13 ● Average absolute capital account surpluses (% GDP) for 12 OECD economies, 1870–2009. Peak years for global capital flows were around the turn of the nineteenth century. *Source:* Obstfeld, 'The global capital market: Benefactor or menace?', *Journal of Economic Perspectives* (1998), 12(4): 9–30, and World Development Indicators (2011).

economies were enormous. Many economies that are now rich and part of the OECD were then emerging markets and were the recipients of huge capital inflows. This is shown in Figure 20.13, which plots the average capital account position (as a percentage of GDP) for 12 countries between 1870 and 2009.[6] To focus on the magnitude of the flows between countries, we show only the *absolute* value of the capital account – whether a country has a capital account surplus of 5% of GDP or a deficit of 5% of GDP, it appears as 5% in Figure 20.13.

Even after the surge in capital flows to developing economies in the 1990s, by 2002–09 overseas capital was only just beginning to finance as much investment as 100 years ago – a situation that has since been reversed again by the financial crisis that began in 2007.

SAVINGS AND INVESTMENT CORRELATION

With investment in most countries between 15% and 45% of GDP and current account positions of an average of 5% GDP, it is apparent that most investment is financed by domestic savings rather than through the capital account. This raises questions over the role of **global capital markets**. Capital markets use funds from savers and lend them to individuals/firms/countries that can invest them profitably. Therefore, countries that invest do not have to be the same as those who save. Indeed, if capital markets work well, we should not expect to find any cross-country correlation between savings and investment. However, Figure 20.14 shows that, among OECD countries, savings are strongly correlated with investment.

Figure 20.15 shows the same calculation of the correlation between savings and investment, but for Japanese prefectures. Regions in Japan show very little correlation between savings and investment. This suggests that, within a country, the domestic banking system allocates funds from savers to investors on a much larger scale than occurs between countries. Even though flows between countries are large and growing, they do not lead to the kind of separation between savings and investment that we observe *within* a country.

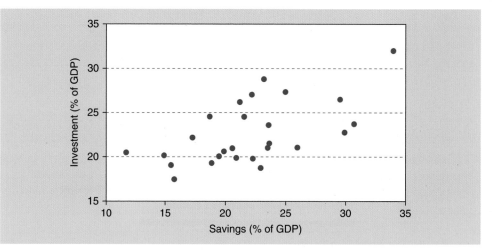

FIGURE 20.14 ● **OECD cross-country savings–investment correlations, 1980–2011.** High-saving economies also have high investment. *Source:* Authors' calculations from OECD, *Economic Outlook* (June 2011), OECD database.

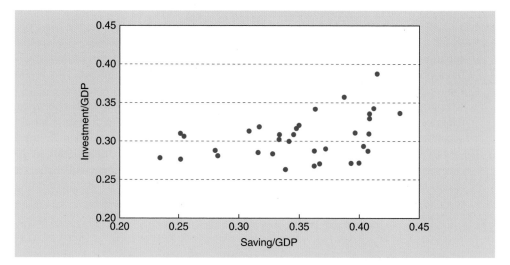

FIGURE 20.15 ● **Savings and investment correlation in Japanese prefectures, 1985–90.** No correlation across Japanese regions between savings and investment means that the market works well. *Source:* Hess and Van Wincoop, *Intranational Macroeconomics* (Cambridge: Cambridge University Press, 2000), Chapter 1, 'Intranational versus international saving–investment correlations'.

A CONSUMPTION PUZZLE

As well as help finance investment, financial markets also finance people through bad times. Consider a construction worker whose income is seasonal: low in the first and fourth quarters of the year, but high in the second and third quarters. To maintain consumption, the worker should borrow from the bank during the low-income quarters (see Chapter 10 for a full analysis). For this example to work, the bank must have funds to lend, and it will if there exists a retail worker who works hard during the Christmas quarter and in the New Year sales period, but not for the rest of the time. Therefore, in the first and fourth quarters, the retail worker, through the bank where she saves, lends the construction worker money. In the second and third quarters, the construction worker repays the retail worker and helps maintain her consumption during her low-income periods. As a result, when financial markets help smooth out income fluctuations, individual consumption should show no correlation with individual income on a quarterly basis.

The above system works only for idiosyncratic income fluctuations; that is, changes that not everyone experiences. Consider, however, the case where the economy moves into recession and the income of both the retail *and* the construction worker falls. Both of them wish to keep consumption high in the recession, so both want to borrow. But because the income of both has fallen, the banking system cannot borrow money from one and lend to the other. As a result, the consumption of both workers will fall. The financial system can help smooth consumption against idiosyncratic shocks to income, but not in response to aggregate income shocks that affect everyone. So, with an efficient financial system, every person's consumption should rise or fall depending on what is happening to aggregate income, but individual consumption should not show any response to purely idiosyncratic fluctuations in income.

Applying this logic to countries suggests that national and world consumption should be strongly correlated and that this should be higher than the correlation between national consumption and national GDP. If, for instance, German GDP is weak today while French GDP is high, then France can temporarily lend money to Germany (Germany has a capital account surplus), which is then reversed when German GDP is stronger than French GDP in the future.

The evidence, however, suggests that global capital markets achieve only limited consumption smoothing with respect to country-specific output fluctuations. Figure 20.16 shows that there isn't a single country for which the correlation between national and OECD consumption is greater than the correlation between national consumption and GDP.

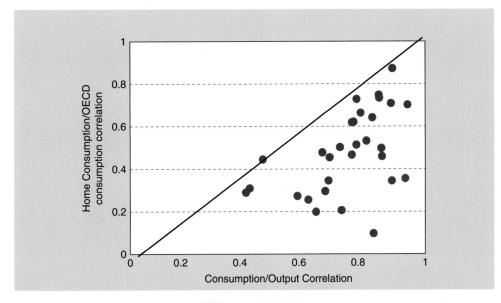

FIGURE 20.16 ● **Risk sharing among OECD nations, 1960–2011.** For OECD countries, output is more closely correlated than consumption over the business cycle. *Source:* Authors' calculations using OECD data.

> ## KEY POINT
>
> Global capital markets have shown substantial increases over the last 20 years due to declining costs and capital account liberalization. However, a large proportion of investment is still financed domestically. Furthermore, national consumption is closely tied to fluctuations in GDP, suggesting limited consumption smoothing across countries.

20.10   A Home Bias Puzzle

We have shown that even though capital markets are large and growing rapidly, evidence suggests that they are not as good as domestic institutions at performing the functions we expect capital markets to do, namely financing investment and smoothing consumption. In this section we show the reason for this: investor portfolios are heavily biased towards their home economy; they show a **home bias**. In other words, holdings of overseas assets are small, so domestic savings has to finance much domestic investment. Savings and investment track each other closely over the business cycle; and each country's consumption relies heavily on its own output because portfolios are not sufficiently diversified.

Table 20.4 shows the percentage of the local stock market held by domestic investors for a number of countries and compares it to a predicted holding if there were no home

TABLE 20.4 ● Home Bias in Equity, 2005.

Theory predicts that domestic investors should have no more reason to invest in their local stock market as in overseas markets, so the share of domestic holding of a stock market should be the same as the market's share in the world stock market. In practice, domestic investors have a strong bias towards their local market.

Country	Predicted Share of Domestic Equity in Domestic Portfolios	Actual Share of Domestic Equity in Domestic Portfolios
Australia	1.9%	83.6%
Brazil	1.1%	99.3%
Canada	3.5%	76.6%
France	4.2%	68.8%
Germany	2.9%	57.5%
India	2.5%	100.0%
Italy	1.9%	57.1%
Japan	13.2%	91.9%
Russia	1.3%	99.9%
South Africa	1.3%	89.0%
Spain	2.3%	86.3%
UK	7.3%	65.0%
US	40.5%	82.2%

Source: Sercu and Vanpee, Home Bias in International Equity Portfolios: A Review, Leuven Working Paper AFI 0710.

bias. Comparing the actual holdings of domestic shares with the predicted holding shows a significant home bias. Why are investment portfolios so internationally undiversified? Each of the following factors helps explain the lack of portfolio diversification we observe:

- Capital market restrictions
- Measurement issues
- Asymmetric information

CAPITAL MARKET RESTRICTIONS

Many OECD economies did not substantially remove capital controls until the 1980s, and only in the 1990s did several emerging markets follow this policy. Restrictions on capital account flows dramatically reduce holdings of overseas equity and can help account for the home bias in portfolios. However, capital controls cannot fully account for the magnitude of the home bias. For instance, there are few capital controls between France and Germany, but equity cross-holdings between these nations are still low.

MEASUREMENT PROBLEMS

Table 20.4 might overstate the lack of international diversification in portfolios. Consider a Finnish investor holding a large portfolio of Finnish equities. This may appear to be an instance of home bias, but closer inspection reveals that Nokia, the telecommunications company, accounts for more than 80% of the Finnish equity market. Nokia is an international firm and earns its profits around the world. Therefore, by buying shares in Nokia on the Finnish exchange, the investor is diversifying her portfolio away from the Finnish economy. Such international diversification through holding domestic equity somewhat (but not completely) alleviates the home bias problem.

ASYMMETRIC INFORMATION

If you are a United States-based investor, you can easily gain information about US firms and economic developments: trading screens, newspapers, television advertisements and even conversations with taxi drivers are all potential sources of information. Getting this information is much more costly for non-United States-based investors. Therefore, US equity will be cheaper for US investors, and they will have a much greater US portfolio holding than non-US investors. Although it might seem surprising that institutional investors like large pension funds and mutual funds should be influenced by these information asymmetries, empirical evidence suggests that they prefer to invest in familiar domestic stocks. In fact, evidence from the United States suggests that mutual fund managers even prefer to invest in nearby companies rather than further afield within the United States.

KEY POINT

Investment portfolios show limited international diversification and a bias towards domestic securities, a home bias. International diversification has been increasing with declines in capital controls and may not be as limited as the data suggest. Asymmetric information seems to be one factor in explaining this home bias. If the home bias falls over time, we can expect global capital flows to increase yet further.

SUMMARY

In Section 20.1, we outlined the enormous size of the foreign exchange markets, which have daily turnover approximately the same as the annual GDP of Italy. Capital, rather than current, account transactions motivate these flows.

In Section 20.2, we introduced covered interest parity (CIP), which states that because of arbitrage the interest rate differential between two countries is equal to the difference between the forward and spot rate. The evidence supports CIP because it involves riskless transactions.

With uncovered interest parity (UIP), the investor does not use a forward contract to buy the currency. Instead, as we described in Section 20.3, the investor estimates the future spot rate and then holds the currency in the hope of trading at that rate in the future. UIP implies that the interest rate differential between two countries equals the percentage difference between the expected spot rate in the future and the current spot rate.

In Section 20.4, we explained why UIP implies that a currency appreciates when its interest rate rises and depreciates when other interest rates increase. In Section 20.5, we saw that expectations play a crucial role in UIP and that the current exchange rate depends on the whole expected future path of interest rates in the two economies.

In Section 20.6, we examined the empirical evidence on the success of UIP. While UIP has some empirical successes, it predicts a negative relationship between interest rate differentials and future exchange rate changes, whereas in practice the relationship is positive.

Allowing for risk aversion among investors helps the empirical performance of UIP, but we concluded in Section 20.7 that macroeconomic data seem to have no role to play in forecasting short-run changes in exchange rates.

To explain both the short-run volatility of exchange rates and the high levels of exchange rate trades, economists have begun to analyse the microstructure of foreign exchange markets. We saw in Section 20.8 that the evidence supports the theory that order flows drive exchange rates in the short run and that market transactions reveal information. This can lead to band-wagon effects and market momentum that may be very different from the forces that macroeconomic fundamentals generate.

In Sections 20.9 and 20.10, we examined global capital flows in more detail. Global capital flows have risen substantially over the last decade, but most investment continues to be financed domestically. Investment portfolios show a lack of international diversification, which means that national consumption is closely tied to GDP and national savings correlate strongly with national investment.

CONCEPTUAL QUESTIONS

1. (Section 20.1) What has happened to the yen–dollar or yen–euro rate over the last month? What factors help explain it?

2. (Section 20.2) UK interest rates are 4%, US interest rates are 3%, and the current exchange rate is \$1.60:£1. What should be the six-month forward rate? The one year ahead forward rate?

3. (Section 20.3) If the chair of the US Federal Reserve Board warns of an overheating economy, what will happen to the dollar? Why?

4. (Section 20.3) Imagine that US interest rates are 5% and Japanese interest rates are 0.5% and you are buying a house in New York. Should you take out a yen-denominated mortgage?

5. (Section 20.4) In response to a 1% increase in inflation, the central bank raises nominal interest rates by 1%. Use UIP *and* PPP to work out what should happen to the current spot rate. How would your answer differ if the central bank raised rates by 2%? Why?

6. (Section 20.5) Imagine that you are a central banker who feels that an exchange rate appreciation would reduce inflationary pressures, but you wish to avoid raising interest rates today. What can you say in public to make the currency rise? What difficulties might this strategy cause?

7. (Section 20.5) Is exchange rate volatility an obvious sign of a poorly operating market?

8. (Section 20.6) Considering Figure 20.10, in what period would holding dollar, rather than yen, assets have performed best?

9. (Section 20.7) Examine the newspapers of recent days. What economic or non-economic factors have they used to predict likely exchange rate changes?

10. (Section 20.8) You are aware of all public macroeconomic information, but note that many dealers are buying the dollar even though you think the dollar is overvalued. How would you respond? Why do you think order flows appear to predict future exchange rates?

11. (Section 20.9) What differences are there between national and global financial markets that can account for Figures 20.15 and 20.16?

12. (Section 20.10) How hard is it for you to find information about companies listed on foreign equity markets? Does this explain the home bias puzzle?

ANALYTICAL QUESTIONS

1. (Section 20.1) The spot €/£ rate is 1.5 and the one year forward €/£ exchange rate is 1.6 per £. What is the forward premium for pound sterling? If covered interest parity holds, what is the euro–sterling interest rate differential?

2. (Section 20.3) What is the dollar rate of return on a $10 000 investment in Tokyo if the Japanese interest rate is 1% and the yen–dollar exchange rate moves from 100 to 110?

3. (Section 20.3) Interest rates between the United States of Albion and the Republic of Oz are currently the same. However, you now think that there is a 50% chance that the Oz dollar will depreciate by 30% over the next week. What has to happen to interest rates in Oz to keep a fixed exchange rate with the United States of Albion?

4. (Section 20.4) This morning the exchange rate between the United States of Albion dollar and the Republic of Oz dollar was 1.50:1 and interest rates in both countries were 6%.
   (a) If the market thinks that later today the Republic of Oz will raise interest rates to 8%, what will happen to the exchange rate?
   (b) If instead interest rates in Oz are increased to only 7%, what will happen to the exchange rate?
   (c) What is the relationship between exchange rates and interest rates in your example? Does this contradict UIP?

5. (Section 20.4) The exchange rate between the United States of Albion and the Republic of Oz is now 1:1, with inflation in both countries expected to be 2% and interest rates 4%.
   (a) What does PPP imply about the exchange rate in 20 years' time?
   (b) If inflation in the United States of Albion increases to 3%, how does your answer change?
   (c) What happens to the current exchange rate if United States of Albion interest rates rise to 5% along with inflation increasing to 3%?

6. (Section 20.9) Total national income in three countries over a recent, and typical, 10-year period are shown below

Year	1	2	3	4	5	6	7	8	9	10
Country A	10	8	7	9	10	14	12	16	18	8
Country B	11	12	11	13	15	8	7	16	18	10
Country C	10	12	13	11	11	7	9	5	4	10

(a) Is there scope for risk sharing between countries? Describe exactly how this might work.

(b) With which country should Country A look to share risk?

CHAPTER 21

Currency Crises and Exchange Rate Systems

Overview

In this chapter we analyse the international financial system; in other words, the manner in which exchange rates fluctuate between countries and how capital account flows are regulated. We begin by examining currency crises: dramatic falls in the value of a currency. We outline a variety of models to explain such crises and consider their applicability. We examine the potential role of foreign exchange intervention by governments and the actions of the IMF in preventing such crises. A controversial factor in explaining currency crises is the role of capital account liberalization, and we review the evidence for and against capital controls. We finally consider the various choices that governments can make over their exchange rate regime: from dollarization and single currencies to purely flexible exchange rates. We analyse the pros and cons of these alternative regimes and recent trends in their popularity.

21.1 Currency Crises

The most dramatic form of exchange rate volatility is a currency crisis; that is, when an exchange rate depreciates substantially in a short period. Such events push macroeconomics to the top of news summaries and onto the front pages of newspapers. They can have huge political and commercial implications. In this section we will examine the frequency of currency crashes and outline theories to explain them.

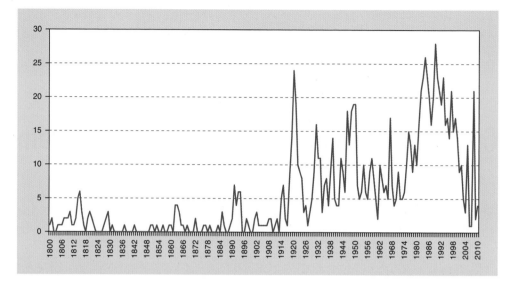

FIGURE 21.1 ● **Currency crises, 1800–2010.** Currency crises (here defined as a depreciation of more than 15% in a year) are a frequent occurrence. *Source:* Reinhart, Carmen M. and Rogoff, Kenneth S., *This Time It's Different: Eight Centuries of Financial Folly* (Princeton: Princeton University Press, September 2009).

A **currency crisis** must have two features: the exchange rate depreciation must be large relative to recent experience, and the nominal exchange rate depreciation must also affect the real exchange rate. In other words, the depreciation must not just reflect inflation and the operation of PPP. Even when we restrict our attention in this way, we still find that currency crashes are frequent. Figure 21.1 shows that between 1800 and 2011 nearly 1200 currency crashes occurred.

Currency crises cause substantial economic upheaval and, usually, sharp falls in output. Table 21.1 shows GDP growth in a number of countries that have experienced currency

TABLE 21.1 ● **GDP Growth during Currency Crises.**
Currency crises lead to dramatic declines in GDP.

	GDP Growth		
	Year Before Crisis	Year of Crisis	Year After
Argentina (2001)	−0.8	−4.4	−10.9
Iceland (2008)	6.0	1.0	−6.5
Indonesia (1997)	8	4.5	−13.1
South Korea (1997)	6.8	5	−6.7
Philippines (1997)	5.8	5.2	−0.6
Russia (1998)	1.4	−5.3	6.3
Thailand (1997)	5.9	−1.4	−10.5
Turkey (2001)	7.4	−7.5	7.8

Source: World Bank, World Development Indicators.

crises. In each case, the currency crisis produced large declines in GDP and a sharp recession, either in the year of the crisis or immediately afterwards.

> **KEY POINT**
>
> Currency crises are large depreciations in exchange rates not driven by inflation differentials. Currency crises are a frequent occurrence, an average of 5.5 happening each year, and are often associated with substantial falls in GDP.

21.2 First-Generation Models

Because currency crises tend to have enormous political, economic and social implications, it is important to identify what causes them. In so-called first-generation models of currency crises, the answer is straightforward: the government is to blame for pursuing inconsistent domestic and external policies. When the crisis occurs, speculators and global capital markets are the main actors, and politicians blame them. But speculators are merely the messengers – and their message is that governments have to change their policy.

Consider the most straightforward first-generation model, where a government announces a fixed exchange rate target but also pursues an expansionary fiscal policy.[1] To finance the fiscal deficit, the government uses the inflation tax (see Chapter 12) and prints money. However, such an expansionary monetary policy leads to low interest rates and capital outflows as investors seek higher returns overseas. In order to invest money overseas, investors sell the domestic currency, leading to downward pressure on the exchange rate. In an effort to stop the exchange rate falling, the government will intervene and *buy* domestic currency and *sell* reserves of foreign currency. This process is called foreign exchange intervention. In this scenario, the country is experiencing a large and continual fiscal deficit, high money supply growth, rapid inflation and a fixed nominal exchange rate, but an appreciating real exchange rate (because inflation is high). Furthermore, government foreign exchange reserves are falling. This situation will continue as long as the government maintains its policy of fixing the exchange rate *and* simultaneously running a large fiscal deficit. If it dropped its commitment to a fixed exchange rate, it would no longer have to sell foreign exchange reserves to support the currency, and the exchange rate could depreciate. Alternatively, if it reduced its fiscal deficit, it would not need to increase the money supply, interest rates could be higher, less capital would flow out and the exchange rate would not be under pressure. However, if the government does not change its policies, foreign exchange reserves will continue to fall, as shown in Figure 21.2.

These circumstances cannot continue indefinitely: eventually the central bank will run out of foreign exchange reserves and the currency will depreciate sharply. However, the currency crash will occur *before* the central bank runs out of reserves. In particular, at a critical level of reserves (R_C in Figure 21.2), a speculative attack will occur and the currency will drop. Why does this happen? Investors will not want to wait until the foreign exchange reserves of the central bank are zero. At this point everyone knows the currency will depreciate sharply, and anyone holding it will lose money. Therefore, the investor will want to sell the domestic currency *before* reserves run out. When the central bank has high levels of foreign currency reserves, it can withstand the pressure of a speculative attack – investors selling the domestic currency. But when reserves reach the critical level, they are too low to

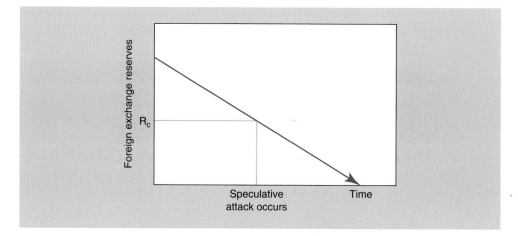

FIGURE 21.2 ● **First-generation models of currency crises.** Fiscal deficits cause foreign exchange reserves to fall and attack comes in advance of reserve depletion.

offset the sell orders for the domestic currency. Investors know that in a few months reserves will be exhausted, and the currency will crash. At this point they sell the domestic currency in large amounts, and the government either wastes what little reserves it has left or immediately devalues the currency.

When all this occurs, the government will blame investors. They will argue that the government was committed to defending the exchange rate and that it still had several months of foreign exchange reserves left. But according to first-generation models, this is beside the point. Domestic and external policy are so inconsistent that a sharp depreciation of the currency is inevitable. By simultaneously pursuing two inconsistent aims, the government has caused the currency crisis. These first-generation models cannot account for all currency crashes. But, they do explain the volatile exchanges of Latin America in the 1970s, when governments tried to target the exchange rate to stabilize high inflation rates while still running large fiscal deficits.

KEY POINT

First-generation models explain currency crises as the inevitable consequence of governments running inconsistent monetary and fiscal policy. In order to control inflation, governments fix their exchange rate but find themselves having to print money in order to finance their fiscal deficit. When reserves reach a critical level, speculators will sell the currency and, in the absence of sufficient reserves or a change of fiscal policy, the government will have to devalue.

21.3 Second-Generation Models and the ERM Crisis

First-generation models imply that currency crises are inevitable as governments are running inconsistent monetary and fiscal policy. Crises are therefore the responsibility of governments and not speculators. We now turn our attention to a more complicated model that has at its heart shifts in investor confidence. If investors remain confident then there is no crisis, while if they begin to withdraw support a crisis occurs. These are called second-generation models and were originally developed to explain the European Exchange Rate Mechanism (ERM) crisis of 1992. The ERM was a system of fixed exchange rates among European countries. In practice, the key country in the ERM was Germany, with countries effectively linking their currency to the Deutschmark. For a country to fix its exchange rate against another country, PPP implies that both countries must have the same inflation rate. UIP implies that they should also share the same interest rates. Therefore, ERM membership meant that countries had to adopt the same monetary policy as Germany. Given Germany's post-war record in achieving low and stable inflation, this was seen as one of the advantages of the ERM for participating countries.

KEY POINT

In a fixed exchange rate system, uncovered interest parity implies that a country has to adopt the same monetary policy as the country against which it fixes its exchange rate.

In 1990 West Germany reunified with East Germany, an event that had significant economic implications for the German economy. Most important for the ERM, West Germany, which had historically run significant current account surpluses and so invested a large proportion of German savings overseas, now diverted those savings into domestic investment in the East. As we saw in Chapter 20, this type of switch from foreign into domestic investment means that the exchange rate will tend to appreciate – precisely what happened to the Deutschmark after reunification. Because of the fixed exchange rate system, this meant that other currencies also had to rise. Elsewhere in Europe economies were struggling with weak GDP growth. In order to maintain a fixed exchange rate against the rising Deutschmark, ERM member countries had to raise interest rates. Internally, however, they wanted to lower interest rates to fight off a recession. There was a conflict between the external and internal goals of monetary policy. This conflict came to a head in Autumn 1992, when almost all ERM currencies came under speculative attack. The three-week crisis saw Italy and the United Kingdom leave the system and substantial devaluations of central rates for other countries, but some countries such as France and Denmark managed to remain in the ERM at their original parities.

What caused the crisis? Table 21.2 suggests that first-generation models cannot account for the currency crash. While countries had different experiences, there were no sharp differences between those that had to leave the ERM, or devalue, and those that remained. Furthermore, although some countries had seen an increase in fiscal deficits, this was due to the fact that 1992 was a recession year for most countries and inflation remained subdued. There were no substantive general signs of large and persistent fiscal deficits (with the exception of Italy).

To account for the ERM crisis, economists developed a new set of currency crisis models (called rather unimaginatively second-generation or SG models). In SG models, a fixed exchange rate can survive indefinitely as long as the currency is not attacked. However, if the currency comes under selling pressure, the fixed exchange rate peg will go. SG models therefore possess *self-fulfilling equilibria*. If investors think that the fixed exchange rate is stable, they will not attack and the fixed exchange rate will survive. However, if they believe that the exchange rate is vulnerable, they sell the currency and the exchange rate target will

TABLE 21.2 ● European Inflation and Fiscal Deficits, 1990–92.

Before the ERM crash of 1992, there were no broad-based signs that European economies were running large fiscal deficits or had high inflation – this is not a first-generation crisis.

	Fiscal Deficit (% GDP)			Inflation (%)		
	1990	1991	1992	1990	1991	1992
UK	1.5	2.8	6.5	8.0	4.7	3.5
Spain	4.3	4.5	4.1	6.5	6.4	6.4
Finland	5.4	1.1	5.5	5.8	5.6	4.1
Ireland	2.3	2.4	2.5	2.1	8.5	5.5
Sweden	24.2	1.1	7.8	9.9	10.3	2.2
Germany	2.1	3.3	2.6	2.7	3.7	4.7
France	1.5	2.0	3.9	2.8	3.2	2.4
Italy	11.2	10.2	9.6	6.3	6.9	5.6

Source: IMF, *International Financial Statistics* (September 2000). Courtesy of IMF.

fail – investor beliefs are self-fulfilling. Such a model can explain the ERM crisis. There is no need to suggest that poor policies were in place before the currency crash. It can also explain why some countries with greater credibility (notably Germany and France) survived the crisis, while other countries (Italy, the United Kingdom) were forced to leave the ERM.

SG models are based on three key assumptions:

- Governments want to maintain the fixed exchange rate because it yields benefits, such as lower and stable inflation.
- Governments also perceive advantages in abandoning the fixed exchange rate. For example, they can loosen monetary policy and stimulate the domestic economy.
- The perceived advantages to dropping the fixed exchange rate increase the more investors think that the exchange rate will depreciate.

In Figure 21.3 we have drawn the benefits from maintaining the fixed exchange rate as being constant regardless of investors' beliefs. However, the benefits from leaving the system increase as investor confidence in the exchange rate target falls. Investors show their beliefs by buying or selling domestic currency. As more investors believe that the exchange rate is going to be devalued, interest rates have to increase to prevent capital outflow. The less confidence investors have in the fixed exchange rate, the greater the required increase in interest rates. The higher are interest rates, the greater the incentive for the government to abandon the pegged exchange rate by devaluing and choosing a looser monetary policy to avoid recession.

Below the point marked C in Figure 21.3, the benefits exceed the costs to the government of staying in the system and it will defend the currency. However, if investor confidence in the fixed exchange rate deteriorates to a position above C, then the system is no longer stable. If investors start to sell the currency, the government will abandon the exchange rate peg because the costs of holding the line exceed the benefits. This model helps to make sense of the lament of ERM-country finance ministers that capital markets forced them to leave the system – without an attack and if investor confidence remains to the left of C, the government is perfectly happy to stay in the system. Only when this confidence deteriorates

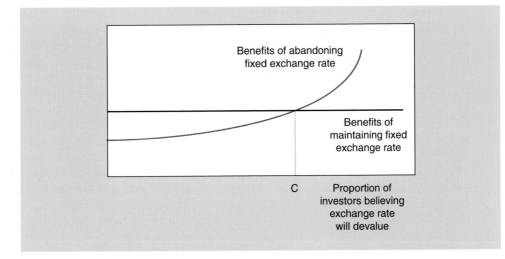

FIGURE 21.3 ● **Second-generation models of currency crises.** With second-generation models, the government no longer defends the exchange rate target when a large number of investors think that a devaluation is imminent.

are governments no longer prepared to pay the price of membership in the fixed exchange rate system.

While SG models allow for self-fulfilling equilibria, fundamentals still play a role. Fundamentals have three relevant ranges. One range occurs where the fundamentals of the economy and policy are so strong that the fixed exchange rate is secure, no matter what investors believe. Another range occurs when a currency crash is inevitable because the fundamentals are so poor. Finally, over an intermediate range, the self-fulfilling equilibria of SG models apply and a currency crisis depends on investor behaviour.

> ### KEY POINT
>
> Second-generation models suggest that currency crises are not inevitable but depend on the beliefs of foreign exchange traders. If a sufficient number of investors believe that a currency is overvalued, then the government will find it too costly to defend the exchange rate and a devaluation will occur. If only a few investors believe that a currency is overvalued, it may be possible for the government to maintain a fixed exchange rate.

21.4 Twin Crises: Banking and Currency

A particularly damaging form of currency crisis is one that also precipitates a banking crisis – a so-called 'twin crisis'. In 1997 the fast-growing economies of Southeast Asia experienced a currency crisis. The problems began in Thailand, but soon spread to Indonesia, Malaysia, South Korea and the Philippines. Taiwan, Singapore and Hong Kong also felt the pressure. During this period, the behaviour of capital markets was so volatile that the Asian currency crises spilled over in a contagious manner to other emerging markets as far away as Russia, South Africa and Brazil. These currency crises blended together aspects of both first- and second-generation models while also containing additional features – in particular the problems of a **sudden stop** in external financing (see Chapter 18) and the way in which domestic financial systems are badly affected by currency crises, which, in turn, contributes to a sharp economic slowdown.

In the early 1990s, many Asian economies *liberalized* their capital accounts to allow for the free flow of capital in and out of the economy. After several decades of fast growth, and with seemingly robust fundamentals, these economies received large amounts of capital inflow from investors seeking high returns. For instance, in 1996 the five largest Association of Southeast Asian Nations (ASEAN) economies had a combined capital account surplus of $55 billion. But by 1998 confidence in these economies was reduced, and they now had a capital account *deficit* of $59 billion. Instead of *receiving* an additional $55 billion a year to fund investment, these economies had to *pay out* $59 billion. External financing (that is, financing of these countries' high investment rates by foreign investors) came to a sudden stop and the shift from a large capital account surplus to a large deficit produced dramatic declines in exchange rates. As these Asian currencies fell, foreign investors became worried about the falling dollar value of their Asian investments and started to withdraw more funds. As a result of this investor flight, the Indonesian rupiah fell by more than 80%, the Thai baht by 50% and the Korean won by 55%.

To prevent these currencies collapsing, Asian central banks sold their foreign exchange reserves (i.e. their holdings of dollars, yen and Deutschmarks) and bought their own currencies (selling well over $50 billion of reserves). They also borrowed extensively from the IMF and other international institutions (over $100 billion of loans were arranged) and aggressively raised interest rates. Eventually the pressure on the currency subsided, but the large increase in interest rates and the dramatic outflow of capital from the banking system left economies in a severe recession (see Figure 21.4).

At first glance, first-generation models seem unlikely to explain the Asian currency crises. In 1996 Indonesia, Malaysia, the Philippines and Thailand recorded fiscal surpluses and, although South Korea had a deficit, it was only 0.1% of GDP. With few obvious fiscal problems and low inflation, the essential mechanism behind first-generation models seems inappropriate in this case. Second-generation models also seem unlikely as an explanation.

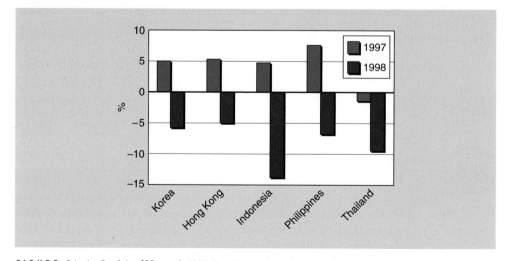

FIGURE 21.4 ● Asian GDP growth, 1997–98. The Asian crisis saw dramatic falls in exchange rates, large increases in interest rates and sharp recessions. *Source:* IMF, *International Financial Statistics*. Courtesy of IMF.

All of these economies were benefiting from fast growth, stable inflation and no unemployment problems. With governments committed to a fixed exchange rate and with no obvious clash between this external target and internal economic aims, the situation in Asia did not mimic that of the ERM and provide the conditions for self-fulfilling crises.

However, closer inspection of these countries suggests that both models may have some explanatory power after all. Although governments were running fiscal surpluses, it can be argued that, due to government guarantees to the financial system, government finances were deteriorating. In other words, first-generation models could explain the currency crisis in Asia.

If the government is expected to bail out the banks, then government liabilities are the level of government debt plus its commitments to the banking sector. Therefore, although the actual fiscal deficit may seem small, the true extent (including off-balance-sheet liabilities) of a government's fiscal liabilities worsens sharply once a banking crisis takes hold. By allowing for this government commitment to the banking sector, we can explain the Asian currency crises (and the more recent Icelandic crisis) through first-generation models.

The role of the banking sector also helps explain the severity of currency crises. As the currency starts to depreciate, banks find themselves lacking funds to repay their foreign currency loans. As a result, they start calling in other loans that they have made to domestic firms. To repay these loans, firms will have to sell off their assets, such as real estate. These sales will lead to a fall in real estate prices in general, which will lead other firms to find that the real estate collateral they have offered to banks when they borrowed has now fallen below the value of their loans. This will further worsen the balance sheets of banks and lead the banks to call in more loans, producing further falls in real estate prices and a general vicious circle. The impact of this banking crisis will be even worse if banks were not very proficient at allocating funds and made large numbers of ill-advised loans, as often occurs in the wake of large capital inflows. This combination of a currency crisis and a banking crisis (a so-called twin crisis) will have a dramatic impact on output, investment and the banking system. One study finds that on average an emerging-market currency crisis tends to lower output by 5.1%, but a twin crisis lowers output by 13.3%.

The fact that the health of the banking sector depends on the exchange rate because of foreign currency debt also opens up the possibility that second-generation models can explain the Asian crisis. If investors believe that the exchange rate is fixed and will not devalue, then governments do not need to set high interest rates to attract funds. But if enough investors believe that the exchange rate will devalue, then the currency will come under pressure. As the exchange rate starts to fall, this will create a deficit in the banks' balance sheets and they will experience a shortage of foreign currency when trying to repay their overseas debts. In order to encourage capital inflows to help finance this foreign currency shortfall, the government will seek to raise interest rates. But higher interest rates make corporate debts harder to service and lower real estate prices, further worsening the value of firms' collaterals and weakening the banking sector. Therefore, the internal target of protecting the domestic banking system conflicts with the external target of achieving a fixed exchange rate. This is the essence of second-generation currency crises.

KEY POINT

Twin crises – a combined banking and currency crisis – are particularly damaging. The Asian currency crises of 1997 have aspects of both first- and second-generation models. In addition, they emphasize the key role of the financial sector and its exposure to exchange rate fluctuations and the danger of abrupt sudden stops in capital inflows.

21.5 Foreign Exchange Rate Intervention

When capital account outflows occur, investors sell the domestic currency and buy foreign currency, which puts downward pressure on the exchange rate. In order to avoid a depreciation, a government can raise interest rates in an effort to persuade investors to keep their money in the country. However, as our discussion of second-generation models suggests, there may be limits to this policy, due to the weakness of the domestic economy or the banking system. Another option is for the government to instruct its central bank to engage in foreign exchange intervention, namely to buy the domestic currency being sold by selling the central bank's foreign currency reserves. The central bank will sell foreign currency if it wants to stop its domestic currency falling, but will buy foreign currency and sell domestic if it wants to stop the exchange rate rising.

FX INTERVENTION AND STERILIZATION

In most countries, the decision whether to undertake FX intervention is made by the Ministry of Finance, but the market operations themselves are undertaken by the Central Bank. To help show how intervention takes place in practice, Figure 21.5 reproduces the simplified central bank balance sheet that we looked at in Chapter 13. When intervention takes place, the central bank either sells foreign exchange and in return acquires monetary base (if the intervention is aimed at strengthening the currency), or purchases foreign exchange and sells monetary base. In either case, the intervention is associated with a change in the money supply and so can result in a change in interest rates. But in most cases foreign exchange intervention is intended to be a substitute for changes in interest rates and so the change in monetary base is an undesired consequence of foreign currency purchases/sales. In order to stop this money supply effect, the Central Bank can undertake a **sterilization operation**. Thus two days after foreign exchange intervention (foreign exchange transactions take two days to go to settlement), the central bank either sells financial assets in exchange for monetary base if the intervention had been currency supporting and so reduced the monetary base, or vice versa for a currency-weakening intervention. Intervention followed by a sterilization operation is called sterilized intervention and is by far the most common form of intervention. However, unsterilized intervention has occurred more often recently – particularly by the Swiss Central Bank – since it is a natural tool to use in a situation of quantitative easing (see Chapter 13).

Assets	Liabilities
Foreign Exchange Reserves	Monetary Base
Other Domestic Assets	Other Debt and Equity

FIGURE 21.5 ● **Central bank balance sheet.** Changes in central bank holdings of foreign exchange reserves (FX intervention) is either matched by changes in the monetary base (unsterilized) or changes in domestic assets (sterilized).

FOREIGN EXCHANGE RESERVES

An important counterpart to intervention is foreign exchange reserves. These are holdings of overseas assets that the central bank can sell in exchange for local currency when conducting currency-supporting FX intervention. In principle, central banks do not need reserves in order to conduct such intervention, since they should be able to borrow foreign currency when required. Indeed, there are a number of countries, such as the United Kingdom after the ERM crisis, that have run a negative net foreign exchange reserves position for a number of years (central bank foreign currency debt larger than foreign currency assets). In developing countries, however the fear of a sudden stop where foreign currency borrowing will not be possible means that holding a stock of foreign assets may be valuable insurance.

Figure 21.6 shows recent trends in the holdings of foreign exchange reserves by developed and developing countries. It shows average **import cover**, a standard measure of reserves adequacy based on how many months of imports reserves could purchase. Given that a standard rule of thumb suggests that three months' import cover is sufficient, the rise in developing country reserves since the Asian crisis looks excessive. However, some argue that financial liberalization and the growing importance of private financial markets to developing countries mean that import cover is no longer a valid metric and that measures of reserves relative to either short-term debt or M2 are more appropriate. On these measures, developing countries' reserves still seem quite large at around four times larger than short-term debt (the **Guidotti-Greenspan rule** suggests that reserves should be equal to short-term debt of one-year maturity or less) and over 30% of M2 (when 20% is generally seen as adequate), but not as extreme as import cover would suggest.

Given the size of global reserves holdings, the currency composition of those reserves has important implications for financial markets. Figure 21.7 shows estimates of the currency composition of reserves (excluding gold) and highlights the continued importance of the US dollar as a global reserve currency, with over 60% of reserves held in US assets

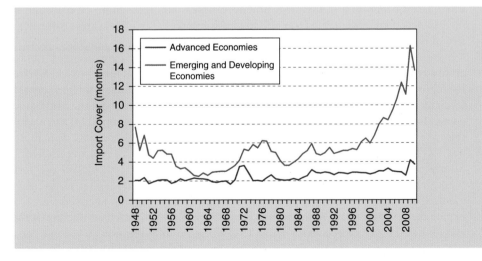

FIGURE 21.6 ● **The growth of foreign exchange reserves.** Using the conventional metric of import cover (how many months of imports could be purchased with reserves), developing country reserves have grown significantly since the Asian Crisis of 1997. *Source:* IMF *International Financial Statistics.*

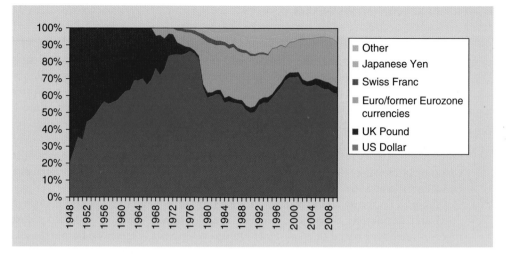

FIGURE 21.7 ● **Estimated currency composition of foreign exchange reserves.** The dollar remains the most important reserve currency. *Source:* IMF *International Financial Statistics,* annual reports and COFER database.

(mainly US government debt). But the post-Second World War decline in the importance of sterling as a reserve currency shows that the currency composition of reserves can change quite quickly.

(21.6) Sovereign Wealth Funds

Foreign exchange reserves are not the only vehicle through which governments acquire overseas assets. Over the last 20 years or so there has been a significant increase in assets held by sovereign wealth funds (SWFs). These funds are state-run entities that undertake a significant proportion of their investments overseas and focus more on risky and illiquid investments than those held in foreign exchange reserves. Table 21.3 shows estimates of the size of some of the major SWFs currently in operation.

Broadly speaking, SWFs are of two types. First there are 'excess reserves' funds (such as those of Singapore and China), where governments decide that foreign exchange reserves have grown to such a significant level that the standard investment principles operated by foreign exchange reserves managers, which emphasize safe investments and investments in assets that can be sold at short notice, are no longer appropriate for all of the reserves. In this case a significant proportion of reserves are shifted to a SWF that invests in more risky and less liquid assets such as equities and property that should, in principle, deliver higher returns than the assets held in conventional reserves. The second type of SWF are 'resource' funds (such as those of Abu Dhabi and Norway). These are funds created to invest government tax revenues (or profits from a state-owned resource company) derived from resource exploitation. These funds serve two purposes. First, they are designed to convert the benefits of a relatively short-lived windfall like oil into a long-run flow of income for future generations. So when the resource runs outs, the government can use the returns from the SWF to avoid raising taxes or cutting spending. Second, they are designed to mitigate one of the symptoms of the 'Dutch disease' that we discussed in Chapter 6, namely excess currency appreciation. A country that is exploiting a natural resource like oil will sell that resource

TABLE 21.3 ● Some Major Sovereign Wealth Funds.

The total value of assets held by all SWFs is estimated to be over $4 trillion.

Country	Fund name	Founding Date	Est. Value ($ bn)
Abu Dhabi – UAE	ADIA	1976	$600
China	CIC	2007	$322
Kuwait	KIA	1953	$295
Norway	GPF-Global	1990	$507
Singapore	GIC	1981	$185
Russia	National Wealth Fund	2008	$87

Source: www.sovereignwealthfundsnews.com (2011).

overseas and then convert the revenue back into domestic currency. This conversion represents an increase in demand for domestic currency and so tends to cause the real exchange rate to appreciate. Real exchange rate appreciation then makes all non-resource industries less competitive in international markets and so tends to cause the non-resource economy to stagnate. Since an SWF holds overseas assets, the resource income that flows into the SWF is not converted back into domestic currency and so does not cause real exchange rate appreciation. This helps the non-resource economy to remain competitive.

21.7 The Role of the IMF

If a central bank begins to run out of foreign exchange reserves, and is unable or unwilling to borrow foreign exchange from financial markets, it may apply to the IMF for a loan. For instance, in 1997 the IMF lent or coordinated loans of $17.2 billion to Thailand, $58.2 billion to Indonesia and $42.3 billion to South Korea. In 1998 it loaned Brazil $41.5 billion and Russia $22 billion. The idea behind these IMF loans is to provide foreign currency reserves to help stop a falling exchange rate. If foreign investors believe that the IMF loan is enough to stabilize the exchange rate, then private-sector capital may return once the fear of further devaluation is removed.

The IMF does not automatically lend foreign currency to countries on request. If the IMF loan is to be used to buy a depreciating domestic currency, then the borrower country will be unable to repay the original loan if the currency continues to fall in value. Therefore, critical to the IMF making a loan is the belief that the underlying cause of the currency crisis is removed. From a first-generation model perspective, this will involve commitments by the country to improve its fiscal position by cutting expenditure and increasing revenue. From a second-generation model perspective, the very provision of the loan by the IMF may be enough to resolve the currency crisis, especially if steps are also taken to improve the health of the financial system.

IMF lending to a country in a currency crisis is extremely controversial. Three key questions are:

- Does IMF intervention work?
- Is IMF intervention good for the economy?
- Does IMF lending make emerging markets more volatile?

DOES IT WORK?

The main aim of IMF intervention is to restore balance of payments equilibrium by reducing capital account outflows and so stabilize the exchange rate. The success of this policy will depend on many factors. One is improved policy. Are the policies that the IMF suggests being successfully and enthusiastically implemented? Is there credibility that these policies will be maintained in the future? For instance, in 1997, when the IMF lent substantial funds to Korea, capital outflows continued because there was widespread doubt about the government's initial willingness to implement the desired IMF reforms.

Another key factor for the success of IMF lending is the size of the loan. Due to capital account liberalization (which is described further in the next section of this chapter), the amount of private-sector capital flows has increased enormously. Therefore, for IMF loans to work, they have to involve ever larger amounts of money to counteract the large-scale private-sector outflows. These loans are now so large that some commentators doubt whether the IMF can respond to future currency crises unless it can boost its own capital reserves.

IS IMF INTERVENTION GOOD FOR THE ECONOMY?

At the heart of most IMF advice is the need to remove the imbalances in the economy that have led to a dependence on capital inflows. This normally leads to policy recommendations to reduce demand and eliminate the need to borrow, and is accompanied by an improvement in fiscal balances and an increase in interest rates. Some observers suggest, however, that the policies recommended by the IMF actually worsen the economic situation and create a severe recession. These critics suggest that countries should pursue alternatives to IMF loans. The two obvious alternatives are to introduce capital account controls and stop investors withdrawing funds from the economy (as Malaysia did in 1997) or simply to default (as Russia did in 1998 and Argentina in 2001), as well as at the same time implementing more growth-orientated policies.

The difficulty in assessing whether IMF intervention helps the economy is in knowing what would have happened had the IMF not intervened. Figure 21.8 compares the performance of a range of emerging-market economies. Both those who borrowed from the IMF between 1973 and 1999 and those who did not are included. All the figures are centred around the time of the crisis for each country. The impact of IMF conditions on these economies is clear: fiscal policy is much tighter and interest rates much higher. Both sets of economies show recoveries, but those in receipt of IMF loans recover somewhat less vigorously. These data are suggestive, but it is not enough for us to conclude firmly that IMF intervention is unhelpful. Perhaps countries that had to borrow from the IMF faced more severe crises than those who didn't borrow and this explains their worse GDP performance. Without a way to compare what happened with IMF intervention and what would have happened to the same economy with no intervention, this debate is hard to resolve.

DOES IMF LENDING MAKE EMERGING MARKETS MORE VOLATILE?

A common criticism of IMF involvement is the **moral hazard** that it creates. Emerging markets are a riskier investment opportunity than the advanced nations. As such, investors should require a higher return. But if investors know that, in the event of a currency crisis,

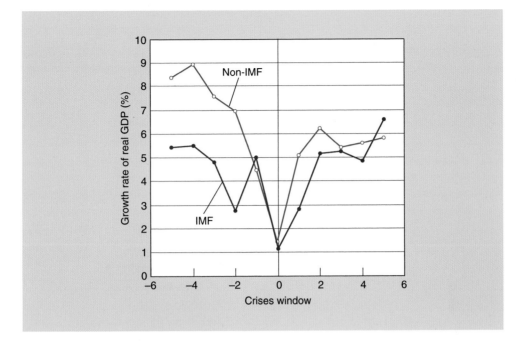

FIGURE 21.8a ● GDP growth compared.

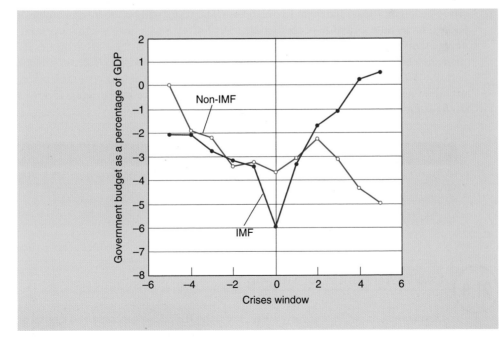

FIGURE 21.8b ● Fiscal deficits compared.

FIGURE 21.8b ● Fiscal deficits compared.

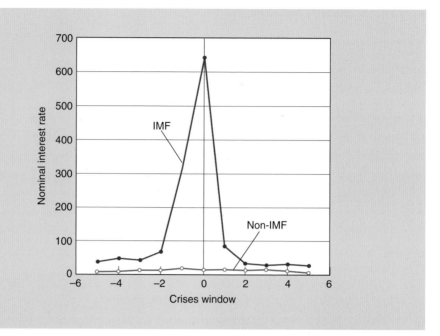

FIGURE 21.8c ● **Interest rates.** IMF intervention leads to tighter fiscal policy, higher interest rates and slightly lower GDP growth. *Source:* Bordo and Schwartz, Measuring Real Economic Effects of Bailouts: Historical Perspectives on How Countries in Financial Distress Have Fared with and without Bailouts, Working Paper 7701, http://www.nber.org/papers/w7701.

the IMF will intervene and use funds to try to stop the currency falling, they face a reduced risk, which may encourage them to overinvest. The result will be too much lending and not enough focus on the quality of that lending. As Jeffrey Sachs once wrote: 'if central banks devote their resources to a defense of the exchange rate and if the IMF dedicates its funds to the defense of the central bank then lending to emerging markets is like shooting fish in a barrel'.[2] Without the prospect of an IMF bail-out, investors would curb their lending, flows would be less volatile and, by implication, there would be fewer currency crises and less need for the IMF to provide huge funds to bail out investors.

> ### KEY POINT
>
> When a country's foreign currency reserves are depleted, it can borrow from the IMF subject to satisfying certain conditions. These conditions are aimed at eliminating the source of a country's borrowing needs.

21.8 Capital Account Liberalization

During the late 1970s and early 1980s, the rich OECD nations removed **capital account controls**, allowing investment funds to flow in and out of their countries with few restrictions. During the 1990s, partly at the prompting of the IMF, this process of **capital account**

liberalization also happened in numerous emerging markets. This policy became increasingly controversial, as many of the countries that removed capital account controls, including Thailand, Korea, Indonesia, Brazil and Argentina, experienced painful economic recessions in the wake of currency crises.

There are several arguments supporting capital account liberalization for emerging markets:

- *Financing investment and stimulating growth.* According to the convergence growth models of Chapter 4, poor countries with low levels of capital should offer a high investment return. Therefore, capital account flows can help finance a high level of investment and rapid economic growth without depending on domestic savings.
- *Risk diversification.* As we saw in Chapter 20, capital account flows also help share consumption risk, so that country-specific fluctuations in output do not need to affect consumption.
- *Improving government policy.* Global capital flows also impose discipline on policymakers. If domestic and foreign investors can withdraw funds from a country that pursues poor policies, the government will be forced to adopt better economic policies (what Thomas Friedman calls the 'golden straitjacket' in his book *The Lexus and the Olive Tree*).
- *Increasing efficiency of financial sector.* Capital account liberalization is also claimed to lead to improvements in financial-sector efficiency through TFP transfer. As foreign banks and financial firms enter along with foreign investment, 'best-practice' techniques and strategies are adopted in the emerging market.

Despite these strong theoretical claims regarding the benefits of capital account liberalization, empirical evidence is much less conclusive. As Barry Eichengreen of the University of California, Berkeley, states: 'Capital account liberalization . . . remains one of the most controversial and least understood policies of our day . . . empirical analysis has failed to yield conclusive results.'[3] This can readily be seen in Figures 21.9 and 21.10, which show

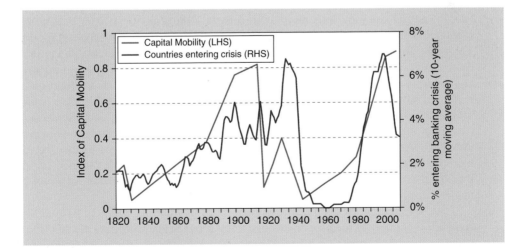

FIGURE 21.9 ● Capital mobility and incidence of banking crises, 1820–2011. Increased capital mobility seems to have been associated with an increased incidence of banking crises. *Source:* Reinhart, Carmen M. and Rogoff, Kenneth S., *This Time It's Different: Eight Centuries of Financial Folly* (Princeton: Princeton University Press, September 2009).

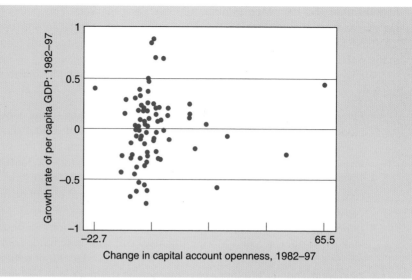

FIGURE 21.10 ● Capital account liberalization and economic growth, 1982–97. There is no simple correlation between capital account liberalization and GDP growth. *Source:* Prasad, Rogoff, Wei and Kose, 'Effects of financial globalization on developing countries: Some empirical evidence', *International Monetary Fund* (March 17, 2003).

that there seems to be a relationship between capital account liberalization and banking crises, but little relationship between liberalization and growth. This suggests, at the very least, that capital account liberalization on its own is not sufficient to generate economic success.

Market imperfections can help explain why capital account liberalization does not boost growth. There may, for instance, be asymmetric information that leads foreign investors to lend too much money and into unprofitable sectors. If the domestic banking system is poorly regulated or lacking experience, then these funds will suffer further misallocation problems. Therefore, capital account liberalization can lead to excessive risk taking and poorly allocated funds and speculative bubbles. Furthermore, the volatility of these capital flows and the resulting economic fluctuations they cause may serve as a further restraint on investment and so slow growth. Many commentators on the 1997 Asian crisis argue that these problems were prevalent. Whether it be the measured tones of US Federal Reserve Board Chairman Alan Greenspan ('In retrospect it is clear that more investment monies flowed into these [Asian] economies than could profitably be employed at reasonable risk') or the more forthright comments of Malaysian Prime Minister Mahatir Mohammed (describing the global capital markets as 'a jungle of ferocious beasts'), the behaviour of global capital markets inspires increasing concern.

The severity and frequency of currency crises in emerging markets have dented the confidence of many of the proponents of capital account liberalization. While there is still belief in the advantages that it brings, there is much greater awareness of the problems that it produces. The growing consensus is that capital account liberalization should be pursued, but not at too rapid a pace. In particular, countries should seek to develop a well-regulated and sound domestic financial system before fully opening up their capital account.

> ### K E Y   P O I N T
>
> Capital account liberalization on its own may not benefit an economy, but needs to be sequenced appropriately with other policies if it is to boost long-term growth. In particular, a well-regulated and experienced domestic banking system would appear to be critical to gain the maximum benefits.

21.9 Exchange Rate Regimes

There are a range of exchange rate regimes available to countries, varying in the flexibility that they allow for the exchange rate. With a **floating exchange rate**, the value of a country's currency can vary freely depending on the forces analysed in Chapters 19 and 20. By contrast, with a **fixed exchange rate**, the government will either change interest rates or sell/buy foreign currency to maintain a fixed value for the currency, as described earlier in this chapter.

Table 21.4 lists the broad categories of exchange rate regimes that countries can adopt. Allowing the most variations in exchange rates are floating systems:

- *Pure float.* The most flexible system is a pure free float. In this case, the exchange rate can rise and fall depending on fluctuations in supply and demand and the government does not need to adjust fiscal or monetary policy or intervene to try to achieve any particular value. The best current example of a pure float is the US dollar.
- *Managed float.* The next most flexible system is a managed float, where although the government does not target a specific exchange rate, it does intervene by buying and selling foreign exchange to try to moderate fluctuations in the exchange rate. This best describes the recent behaviour of the Japanese yen.

TABLE 21.4 ● **Exchange Rate Regimes.**
Countries can choose from a wide range of different exchange rate regimes.

Floating Regimes	Pure float
	Managed float
Intermediate regimes	Target zone
	Basket peg
	Crawling peg
	Adjustable peg
Fixed regimes	Truly fixed exchange rate
	Currency board
	Dollarization
	Single currency

Intermediate between floating and fixed exchange rates are a range of systems that try to fix the exchange rate but allow for changes over time:

- *Target zone.* Target zone systems allow the exchange rate to fluctuate but only within certain prescribed bands, as was the case with the European Exchange Rate Mechanism and currently with the Danish krona against the euro.
- *Basket peg.* More flexibility can also be provided if a country pegs its currency against a basket of currencies (as Botswana and Kuwait do) rather than just one.
- *Crawling peg.* Another option for a country is to adopt a crawling peg (as currently used in Bolivia and Tunisia), where a fixed exchange rate is announced but so too is a profile over time that allows the exchange rate to change in a managed way.
- *Adjustable peg.* The final possible intermediate arrangement is an adjustable peg, where a fixed exchange rate is targeted but the system allows flexibility through periodic revaluations.

Finally there are the more rigid fixed exchange rate systems:

- *Truly fixed.* A truly fixed exchange rate exists when the government commits to a specific exchange rate and there are no tolerance bands or pre-announced option to revalue. An example of such a system was the CFA zone in Sub-Saharan Africa, linked to the French franc.
- *Currency board.* A currency board is a stronger version of a truly fixed exchange rate. Under a **currency board**, the central bank of a country is committed to exchanging its monetary liabilities at a fixed exchange rate. The monetary liabilities of a central bank are essentially the currency that it has issued. Therefore the central bank can only issue as much domestic currency as it has holdings of foreign currency, given the fixed exchange rate. For instance, the Hong Kong Monetary Authority (HKMA) operates a currency board based on an exchange rate of HK\$7.80:US\$1. If the HKMA has US dollar reserves of US\$80 billion, it can issue domestic currency worth $7.80 \times \$80$ billion = HK\$624 billion. The domestic central bank can only expand the money supply by obtaining more foreign exchange. If instead its foreign exchange reserves fall, then so will the domestic money supply.
- *Dollarization.* With a currency board, although a central bank has no choice over how much domestic currency to issue, it still does issue a currency. Under **dollarization**, a country voluntarily eliminates its own currency and adopts a foreign currency, such as the dollar or the euro. In effect, it closes down its central bank.
- *Currency union.* Finally, two or more countries can come together and collectively adopt a **single currency**: for example, they merge their central banks, as the participating countries of the euro have done. The key difference between a currency union and dollarization is that all members of a currency union share seignorage income and have a say in monetary policy decisions.

THE IMPOSSIBLE TRILOGY

To understand the advantages and disadvantages of a fixed exchange rate, we begin with the **impossible trilogy**, which says that a government can choose at most *two* of the following *three* options:

1. Independent monetary policy – the ability to choose its own interest rates to achieve domestic targets.

2. Fixed exchange rate.
3. Capital account liberalization.

In other words, if a country chooses a fixed exchange rate, it must either abandon an independent monetary policy or impose capital controls. Similarly, countries that liberalize their capital account have to forgo either a fixed exchange rate or an independent monetary policy.

To understand the impossible trilogy, consider again the case of uncovered interest parity (see Chapter 20), which is based on an arbitrage relationship in which investors reallocate funds to the country that offers the highest expected return. This reallocation can only happen in the absence of capital controls. According to the impossible trilogy, a government that has liberalized its capital account cannot also operate both a fixed exchange rate and an independent monetary policy. This is because the key result of UIP was that interest rate differentials equal expected exchange rate depreciations. Under a fixed exchange rate, the expected devaluation is zero. Therefore, UIP implies that interest rates should be the same between countries with fixed exchange rates – the countries cannot run independent monetary policies. If the fixed exchange rate regime allows for small fluctuations around a central rate, then interest rates can differ between countries in the expectation of small depreciations. Adding a risk premium to UIP allows for more interest rate differentials. But even if interest rates do not have to be *identical*, there will be strong linkages. Countries that participate in a fixed exchange rate system will tend to raise interest rates together, even if not by exactly the same amount.

With capital controls it is possible to have a fixed exchange rate *and* choose an independent monetary policy. Consider the case of a country with a fixed exchange rate that unilaterally lowers its interest rate. Without capital controls, investors would move funds out of the country to overseas where a higher return can be earned. This would put downward pressure on the currency and threaten the exchange rate target. If capital controls are in place, this outflow can be restricted and so pressures on the exchange rate can be avoided; with capital controls, the government can have an independent monetary policy *and* an exchange rate target. Without capital controls the impossible trilogy tells us that the cost of a fixed exchange rate is the inability to choose a monetary policy to suit the country's specific circumstances.

> **KEY POINT**
>
> Countries face a wide range of options when choosing an exchange rate regime. The impossible trilogy tells us that countries without capital controls effectively face a choice between a fixed exchange rate or an independent monetary policy.

ADVANTAGES OF FIXED EXCHANGE RATES

- *Providing a nominal anchor.* According to the impossible trilogy, a country with no capital account controls and a fixed exchange rate has no choice over its monetary policy. In other words, the exchange rate is a nominal anchor that pins down monetary policy. For countries with a poor or unreliable record in controlling inflation, this is a major advantage – for these nations, giving up an independent monetary policy is an advantage. Figure 21.11 shows which countries are chosen most frequently as an

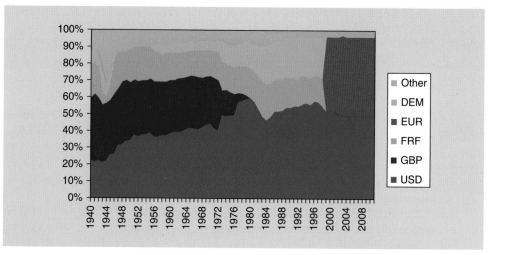

FIGURE 21.11 ● **Anchor currency choices, 1940–2001.** Countries choose the dollar and the euro as obvious pegs due to their low inflation. *Source:* Meissner and Oomes, Why Do Countries Fix the Way They Fix?, IMF Working Paper (2004), and authors' calculations.

anchor currency. Given their good inflation track record, it is not surprising that the dollar and the euro play a major role.

- *Encouraging trade and investment.* It is widely believed that reducing exchange rate volatility boosts trade between countries and encourages FDI and investment, thereby aiding long-run GDP growth.
- *Avoiding speculative bubbles.* Under floating, exchange rates show substantial swings that can lead to long-term and far-reaching misalignments from their fundamentals.
- *Reducing risk premium.* If countries can issue debt in their own currency, then investor fears of devaluation will lead to higher interest rates via a risk premium. A credible fixed exchange rate will remove the risk of devaluation and lower interest costs.

ADVANTAGES OF FLOATING EXCHANGE RATES

- *Independent monetary policy.* By not adopting a fixed exchange rate, the impossible trilogy allows a country to have no capital controls and also to choose interest rates to achieve internal domestic targets rather than influence the exchange rate.
- *Automatic adjustment to trade shocks.* Consider a country that experiences a fall in the price of its major export. With a fixed exchange rate, the only way the country can regain competitiveness is if prices, wages and costs fall. This is a painful and often protracted process, depending on the flexibility of labour markets. With a floating exchange rate, adjustment can occur almost instantaneously through a devaluation.
- *Avoid speculative attacks.* As we have outlined in the first part of this chapter, fixed exchange rates are vulnerable to speculative attack. By not forcing governments to intervene to prop up a currency, floating exchange rates can avoid this problem. However, dollarized countries and currency unions are also free from speculative attack, since speculators cannot sell one member's currency against another's.

EXCHANGE RATE ARRANGEMENTS

The choice of an exchange rate regime will vary from country to country depending on circumstances. Table 21.5 documents exchange rate systems around the world. It shows that a wide range of different regimes are utilized in different countries, suggesting that no one single regime is appropriate for everybody. Furthermore, the choice may change as a country's economy evolves.

Given our discussion of the advantages and disadvantages of fixed and flexible exchange rates, we can say that fixed exchange rates make more sense for a country the more it fulfils the following properties:

- Poor reputation for controlling inflation, so that it benefits from following another country's monetary policy.
- Significant levels of trade with a country whose exchange rate is being targeted, so that there are substantial gains from increasing predictability between the countries' exchange rates.
- Similar macroeconomic shocks to the country whose exchange rate is being targeted, so that little is lost from giving up an independent monetary policy.
- Relatively little involvement in global capital markets, so that the exchange rate is not at risk from sudden stops.
- Flexible labour markets, so that in the face of export price shocks the country can regain competitiveness.
- High levels of foreign exchange reserves, so that in the case of selling pressure, the central bank can intervene to maintain the exchange rate peg.

As Table 21.5 suggests, smaller economies often meet these requirements; in particular, they often are heavily linked through trade with other nations and their business cycle is also driven by developments in the larger nation. This explains why San Marino, Panama,

TABLE 21.5 ● Exchange Rate Regimes, 2008.

Regime	Number of Countries	Examples
No separate legal tender	44	Eurozone, Ecuador, Panama, Eastern Caribbean Currency Union, CFA Franc Zone
Currency board	7	Bosnia, Brunei Darussalam, Bulgaria, Hong Kong, Djibouti
Other conventional fixed pegs	55	Saudi Arabia, Russian Federation, Argentina, Bangladesh, Jordan, UAE
Pegged exchange rates with horizontal bands	5	Denmark, Tonga
Crawling pegs	8	Bolivia, China, Nicaragua, Ethiopia, Iran
Crawling bands	2	Costa Rica, Azerbaijan
Managed float	44	Indonesia, Kenya, Vietnam, India, Nigeria, Egypt
Independently floating	24	Australia, Brazil, Canada, Korea, Norway, Poland, Sweden, UK, US, Japan, Zambia

Source: IMF Annual Report on Exchange Arrangements and Exchange Restrictions (2009) and authors' calculations.

Lesotho and El Salvador have all dollarized and why Belgium, the Netherlands and Luxembourg were all enthusiastic participants in the euro. Larger economies tend to be less exposed to trade and often have more independent business cycles so that flexible exchange rates are more desirable. The obvious reference cases here are the United States, the European Union and Japan. While many of the member states of the EU have joined together in a single currency, the euro has a flexible exchange rate with no specific target against the dollar, yen or any other currency.

THE LAW OF THE EXCLUDED MIDDLE

With increasing numbers of emerging markets adopting capital account liberalization, the logic of the impossible trilogy says that nations either have to adopt an independent monetary policy and float or adopt a fixed exchange rate. Furthermore, the experience of many currency crisis countries and the logic of second-generation models suggests that it is better to have a *very* fixed exchange rate system, such as a currency board or dollarization, rather than a more flexible target zone or fixed exchange rate system. The greater the political and institutional costs of leaving a fixed exchange rate system, the less likely investors are to believe that the currency will devalue and so the peg is more robust, as it is less liable to second-generation crises. This implies that the intermediate regimes described earlier are not a viable long-run choice – countries have to be based at either one of the extremes, a result known as the **Law of the Excluded Middle**. In line with the logic of the Law of the Excluded Middle, a number of countries have recently adopted extreme versions of fixed exchange rates: Ecuador and El Salvador have both dollarized; Estonia, Lithuania, Bulgaria and Bosnia have all adopted currency boards; and in 1999 eleven European countries joined together to launch the euro. Figure 21.12 also shows supportive evidence for the excluded middle:

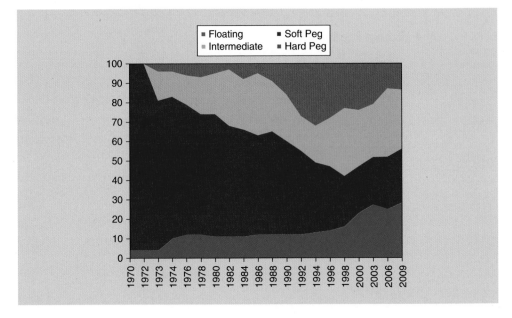

FIGURE 21.12 ● **Law of excluded middle.** Countries seem to be adopting more extreme versions of fixed exchange rates. *Source:* Rogoff, Husain, Mody, Brooks and Oomes, Evolution and Performance of Exchange Rate Regimes, IMF Working Paper 03/243 (December 2003), and authors' calculations.

the proportion of countries with either floating rates or a hard peg have generally risen over time. In the remaining sections of this chapter, we will investigate in more detail two of these more extreme fixed exchange rate systems: currency boards and single currencies.

> ### KEY POINT
>
> The appropriate exchange rate regime will vary depending on a country's circumstances and may even change over time. It will differ from country to country. A number of countries have adopted extreme versions of fixed exchange rates in recent years, leading to discussion of the Law of Excluded Middle — the idea that countries have to choose either flexible exchange rates or extreme versions of fixed exchange rates.

21.10 Currency Boards

At the time of writing, there are seven currency boards in operation: Bosnia and Herzegovina, Brunei Darussalam, Bulgaria, Hong Kong SAR, Djibouti, Estonia and Lithuania. The currency board in Djibouti has been in place for nearly 50 years and in Hong Kong since 1985. More recently, Argentina instigated a currency board in 1991, but was forced to exit in 2001.

As Figure 21.13 shows, currency boards have a good record in improving overall economic performance: inflation, inflation volatility, the fiscal deficit and growth all improve under a currency board compared to alternative regimes. Under a currency board, countries cannot print money not backed by foreign currency reserves, so the central bank can no longer finance the government's fiscal deficit by holding government debt. Therefore,

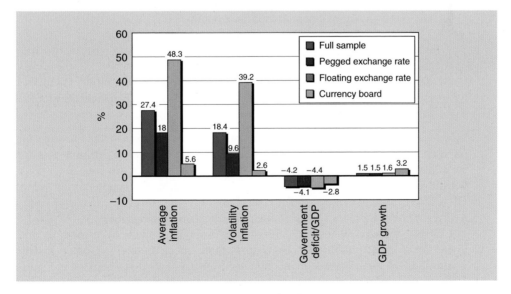

FIGURE 21.13 ● **Economic performance under currency boards.** Currency boards combined with fiscal reform produce substantial improvements in macroeconomic performance. *Source:* Ghosh, Gulde and Wolf, Currency Boards: The Ultimate Fix? IMF Working Paper 98/8 (1998). Courtesy of IMF.

currency boards tend to be adopted as part of an overall package to reduce high inflation. Without broad-based reform, the adoption of a currency board alone will not produce the superior economic performance of Figure 21.13.

> ### KEY POINT
> Currency boards require fiscal reform if they are to be successful at reducing inflation. Argentina's currency board collapsed due to a lack of fiscal reform and wage flexibility and the decision to link to the dollar.

(21.11) Currency Unions

On 1 January 1999, 11 European nations permanently fixed their exchange rate against each other and launched the euro.[4] On 1 January 2002, the countries' legacy currencies, for example the Deutschmark, the franc the lira, were withdrawn and euro notes and coins became legal tender in all countries. The size of these countries and their cooperation in launching a new currency constitute an unprecedented modern money experiment. Does it make sense for these countries to share one currency and one monetary policy?

The theory of **optimal currency areas (OCA)** argues that there are four criteria for adopting a common currency:

- *The degree of trade between countries who adopt a common currency.* If countries trade heavily between each other, then a single currency significantly reduces transaction costs.
- *The extent to which different countries experience similar shocks.* If countries experience the same shocks, then they will wish to set the same interest rates so that they do not lose by having a common monetary policy.
- *The degree of labour market mobility in each region.* If regions face different shocks but implement the same monetary policy, then if labour can move between regions, this will help stabilize the economy.
- *The amount of fiscal transfers between regions.* If regions face different shocks, labour is immobile and both regions face the same interest rates, then fiscal transfers between regions can maintain welfare standards.

Most evidence suggests that as far as the first two criteria are concerned, the Eurozone fulfils the OCA criteria as well as the United States (i.e. a single currency for the Eurozone is as appropriate as a single currency for the United States), but that the latter two criteria are more problematic. Unfortunately, there is no established way of judging the importance of each of these OCA criteria, so although we can judge which countries are more likely to benefit from joining a currency union, we cannot judge whether these benefits outweigh the costs.

Despite these problems in quantifying the costs and benefits of currency unions, some argue that currency unions are likely to become an increasingly common arrangement worldwide. The argument for an increase in currency unions is summarized in Figure 21.14. It shows two important global trends. First, despite some setbacks, there has been an upward trend in world trade since 1945; increasing trade increases the benefits of currency unions. Second, over the last century there has been a steady increase in the number of countries in the world; smaller countries are more likely to fulfil the OCA criteria, as we noted in

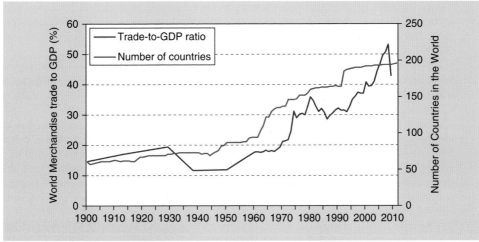

FIGURE 21.14 ● **Trade openness and number of countries.** Increasing trade and a growing number of countries in the world make currency unions more likely. *Source:* Alesina, Barro and Tenreyro, Optimal Currency Areas, NBER Macroeconomics Annual (2002), and authors' calculations.

Section 21.9. Yet the currency union of the Eurozone has faced a number of economic challenges and currently its future is by no means certain. But there are a number of other currency unions that may well come into operation in the next ten years or so, such as that proposed by the Gulf Co-operation Council including such countries as Bahrain, Kuwait, Qatar and Saudi Arabia.

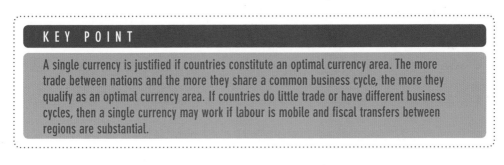

KEY POINT

A single currency is justified if countries constitute an optimal currency area. The more trade between nations and the more they share a common business cycle, the more they qualify as an optimal currency area. If countries do little trade or have different business cycles, then a single currency may work if labour is mobile and fiscal transfers between regions are substantial.

SUMMARY

In Section 21.1, we defined a currency crisis as a large and sharp fall in the real exchange rate. We documented that 7–10 currency crises occur around the world each year.

In Section 21.2, we outlined first-generation models of currency crisis, which explain currency crashes as being the governments' fault when they set inconsistent fiscal and monetary policy. Section 21.3 extended our analysis to include second-generation models, where the currency crises depend on investor optimism/pessimism. In the case where there exists a conflict between the government's internal and external goals, investors may begin to doubt the stability of an exchange rate and it will come under speculative attack.

In Section 21.4, we considered the 1997 Asian crisis and saw that it contained aspects of both first- and second-generation models. In addition, it showed the difficulties that occur when a country borrows heavily in foreign currency but is vulnerable to sudden stops of capital inflows. Section 21.5 outlined how central bank intervention works during a crisis and Section 21.6 looked at the role of sovereign wealth funds. In Section 21.7 we assessed the role and level of success of the IMF in preventing currency crises.

Section 21.8 considered the advantages of capital account liberalization. After much initial hope, most advocates are now more careful in their advice about the pace at which capital controls should be removed. A strong institutional setting and high-quality regulation of the domestic banking system are critical for success.

Section 21.9 listed the various different alternative exchange rate regimes that a country could choose and outlined the impossible trilogy, which states that countries can choose only two of the three options of independent monetary policy, a fixed exchange rate or capital account liberalization. The Law of the Excluded Middle suggests that countries which liberalize their capital account have either to adopt a very rigid exchange rate or move to a floating rate. A number of countries have moved towards strongly fixed exchange rates, offering some support for this 'Law'.

Section 21.10 examined the record of currency boards and. Section 21.11 concludes by focusing on currency unions and the advent of the euro.

CONCEPTUAL QUESTIONS

1. (Section 21.1) Table 21.1 shows that currency crises lead to sharp falls in GDP growth. Why do you think this is?

2. (Section 21.2) Use the insights of the first-generation model to consider the impact of the government refusing to publish its holdings of foreign currency reserves. Would this lower the risk of a currency crisis? How would it affect the timing of a crisis?

3. (Section 21.3) A government has poor opinion poll ratings in a recession, but is attempting to maintain a fixed exchange rate. To defend the currency, it raises interest rates from 5% to 10%. How do you think that the markets will respond?

4. (Sections 21.4 and 21.10) If emerging markets were to abandon their own currency and dollarize, would this help them overcome their debt intolerance?

5. (Section 21.6) How should IMF interventions differ in the cases of first- and second-generation currency crises?

6. (Section 21.7) 'Capital account liberalization is like a medicine that is usually beneficial but often produces horrific side effects. Such a medicine cannot be left unregulated.' Discuss.

7. (Section 21.7) National governments do not try to restrict the flow of finances between regions and sectors within a country. Why should they therefore use capital controls to restrict flows of finance between nations?

8. (Section 21.8) China currently has a fixed exchange rate, capital controls and independent monetary policy. Is this consistent with the impossible trilogy? How do you think that these policies may change as China grows richer?

9. (Section 21.9) In a pure currency board, the central bank can only print domestic currency up to the value of the foreign currency reserves that it owns. What would be the impact if it was allowed to include in its assets not just foreign currency reserves but also the central bank holding of government debt?

10. (Section 21.10) To what extent do you think that the economic success of the United States is due to the fact that it has a single currency? What lessons does this hold for the European Union?

ANALYTICAL QUESTIONS

1. (Section 21.3) Interest rates between the United States of Albion and the Republic of Oz are currently equal. However, you now think there is a 50% chance that the Oz dollar will depreciate by 30% over the next week. What has to happen to interest rates in Oz to keep a fixed exchange rate with Albion?

2. (Section 21.8) There is a fixed exchange rate system between the United States of Albion and the Republic of Oz and interest rates in Albion are always 2% higher than those in Oz due to a constant risk premium. Does UIP hold? What is the relationship between the monetary policy of the two economies?

3. (Section 21.8) The Republic of Argent does 50% of its trade with Eurasia and 50% with Oceania. Over the last three years, the currency has risen from 1 to 1.1 and then to 1.3 against the Oceania dollar. However, against the Eurasian euro it has fallen to 1/1.1 to 1/1.3. What is the effective exchange rate? If the Republic wishes to fix its exchange rate, what exchange rate regime would you recommend?

4. (Section 21.8 and 21.9) A country has GDP of 10 billion pesos and its government has borrowed 1 billion pesos of money domestically and 4 billion in US dollars. The exchange rate is $1 = 1 peso. Interest rates are 10% on peso-denominated debt and 5% on dollar-denominated debt.

   (a) What is the debt-to-GDP ratio?

   (b) How much are interest payments as a percentage of GDP?

   (c) According to UIP, what should happen to the exchange rate?

   (d) If the exchange rate goes to $1 = 4 pesos, how do your answers to (a) and (b) change?

Glossary

Active labour market spending Expenditure by the government aimed at increasing the probability of the unemployed being hired.

Adverse selection A problem of asymmetric information where one side of a transaction will find itself coming into contact with agents that make the transaction unprofitable and is unable to exclude them, e.g. when a bank fears that if it raises interest rates it will attract high-risk borrowers who face a high probability of bankruptcy.

Aggregate demand curve The relationship between the overall price index and the level of total aggregate demand in the economy. Higher prices lead to lower demand.

Aggregate supply curve The relationship between the overall price level and the aggregate level of output/supply that firms wish to produce.

Appreciation An increase in the value of a currency in the market for foreign exchange (opposite of depreciation).

Arbitrage The process of making profit by buying goods where they are sold cheaply and selling them for a higher price. As a result of this process, prices between the two markets converge.

Asymmetric information A situation where economic agents have different information that cannot be revealed to each other.

Asymmetric shocks Shocks that affect different countries/regions/industries differently.

Automatic stabilizer The impact of policies that automatically tend to boost demand in a slump and reduce demand in a boom. For example, taxes on incomes tend to rise in a boom and fall in a slump; government spending on unemployment benefits has a similar impact.

Average propensity to consume (apc) The ratio of consumption to income (C/Y).

Balance of payments A record of a country's international transactions.

Balance sheet A record of the assets and liabilities of a company, an individual or a nation.

Balanced budget A situation where receipts equal expenditures.

Balassa-Samuelson effect The phenomenon where prices (especially of non-tradeables) are higher in richer, more productive countries.

Bank for International Settlements (BIS) An international organization that fosters cooperation among central banks and other agencies in pursuit of monetary and financial stability.

Bank run A situation where depositors withdraw funds from a bank for fear that it may go bankrupt and not honour its liabilities.

Beveridge curve The relationship between unemployment and job vacancies.

Bilateral exchange rates The rate that defines the terms at which two currencies can be exchanged.

Bond A financial instrument that promises to pay flows of money at specific intervals (sometimes called *fixed-income securities*). Bonds are a form of debt issued by corporations and governments.

Borrowing constraint A restriction on the amount an agent can borrow. Individuals unable to borrow against the prospect of high future labour income may be constrained in their current consumption if current income is low.

BRIC economies The large and fast-growing economies of Brazil, Russian, India and China.

Bubble Non-sustainable behaviour of asset prices where values are bid up in a way that is linked to expectations of future capital gains, not based on economic fundamentals.

Budget constraint The requirement that over the relevant horizon, the value of spending must equal the value of receipts.

Budget deficit A situation where receipts are less than expenditure.

Budget surplus A situation where receipts exceed expenditure.

Business cycle Medium-term aggregate fluctuations in output, incomes and employment whereby the economy goes from expansion to recession over a period of normally less than ten years.

Business fixed investment Expenditure on equipment and structures that businesses use in production.

Capacity utilization A measure of the extent to which physical capital and employment are being fully utilized in production.

Capital account A record of a country's assets transactions with the rest of the world. Sales of a country's assets increase the capital account; purchases of overseas assets reduce the capital account.

Capital account liberalization The removal of controls restricting the flow of capital into and out of a country.

Capital accumulation Process whereby the stock of physical capital increases when gross investment exceeds depreciation.

Capital adequacy rules Rules that restrict the amount and type of funding structure that banks can have depending on their assets.

Capital controls Restriction on the free movement of capital in and out of a country.

Capital gain The rise in the price of an asset.

Capital stock The stock of physical equipment and structures used in production.

Carry trade A foreign exchange trade that seeks to exploit the benefits of borrowing in low-interest-rate economies and investing in high-interest-rate ones.

Catch-up (see also Convergence). When rich countries grow more slowly than poor ones.

Central bank The institution that implements monetary policy, such as the Federal Reserve in the United States and the European Central Bank in Europe.

Chain weighting A method of calculating real GDP, which allows for the gradual evolution of prices rather than use of completely constant prices.

Closed economy A country that neither borrows nor invests overseas and does not trade goods and services with other countries.

Cobb-Douglas production function A production function where output is given by $f(K,L) = AK^a L^{1-a}$, where K is capital, L is labour and A and a are parameters. If capital and labour receive their marginal product, a is the share of capital income in total output and $1 - a$ is the share of labour.

Commodity money Money that has an intrinsic value even if it were to become unacceptable as a medium of exchange (e.g. gold, silver).

Comparative advantage A situation where a country has a lower opportunity cost of producing a certain commodity. The industry in which a country has greatest productivity advantage (or smallest disadvantage) compared to other nations.

Competitiveness Productivity in a country compared to other nations (often used with reference to high value-added industries).

Conditional convergence The process whereby countries that share a steady state show convergence to similar levels of GDP per capita.

Constant prices The use of the same prices across several years when calculating real GDP in order to focus on output changes.

Constant returns to scale A situation where the same percentage increase in all factors of production generates an equal percentage change in output.

Consumer price index (CPI) A measure of the general level of prices that consumers have to pay for goods and services, including consumption taxes.

Consumption Goods and services bought and used by consumers.

Consumption function The relationship between consumption and its determinants. The simplest consumption function has spending depending simply on current income.

Contingent liabilities Future liabilities that will only become certain on the occurrence of some future event (e.g. pension payments).

Contractionary policy Government actions that reduce demand in the economy and cause employment to fall, e.g.higher interest rates or taxes (opposite of expansionary policy).

Convergence Process whereby poor countries grow faster than rich ones.

Corruption A form of rent seeking where agents demand extra-market payments for economic services or commodities.

Cost of capital The overall amount of resources that has to be sacrificed to acquire the use of a unit of capital for one period. The cost reflects interest rates, depreciation and any rise or fall in the price of the capital.

Counter-cyclical Tending to move in the opposite direction to aggregate output and employment over the business cycle (opposite of pro-cyclical).

Coupon Regular (normally fixed) payment made to bond holders.

Covered interest parity Prediction that the gap between two countries' interest rates should be the same as that between their current spot exchange rate and the current forward exchange rate.

Credit channel Where monetary policy and the financial system affect GDP not through changes in interest rates and the price of credit, but through the quantity of credit available.

Credit constraint An inability to borrow against future income.

Credit crunch Negative interrelationship between bank lending, property prices and bank assets.

Credit rating An indication of the likelihood of default supplied by a rating agency like S&P or Moody's.

Crowding out The tendency of extra government spending to cause reductions in private spending through inducing increases in interest rates.

Currency Coins and paper money issued by the authorities of a country.

Currency board An arrangement whereby a country can only issue domestic currency if the central bank owns matching quantities of specific foreign currency.

Currency crises Sharp dramatic declines in the value of a currency (say, of more than 25%).

Current account A record of trade between countries in goods and services, including money earned from interest payments and dividends. A country that sells more (less) goods and services overseas than it purchases has a current account surplus (deficit).

Current prices Use of current-year prices when measuring the value of output in each year, which leads to a measure of nominal GDP. Changes in nominal GDP reflect both output and price changes.

Debt intolerance The inability of emerging-market economies to cope successfully with even modest levels of indebtedness to foreign investors.

Debt relief Laffer curve The relationship between the level of debt and the likely repayments on that debt.

Debt sustainability Whether current and future policy by governments, firms or countries can maintain a stable debt-to-income ratio.

Deflation Sustained falls in the general level of prices (opposite of inflation).

Deflator A price index that converts a nominal series to a real one.

Demand deposits Bank deposits that are available on demand and that can be used to settle transactions, e.g. current accounts.

Demographic transition The transition of a country from low life expectancy and high birth rates to high life expectancy and low birth rates.

Dependency ratio Ratio of population of working age to the young and old who are dependent on them.

Deposit insurance Protection of depositors from bank failure.

Depreciation (1) Wear and tear on physical capital that reduces its effective quantity over time.

Depreciation (2) A fall in the value of a currency relative to other (foreign) currencies.

Depression A protracted slump in output; an unusually severe and long-lasting recession.

Devaluation A fall in the value of a currency relative to other foreign currencies.

Diminishing marginal product A situation where increased use of a factor of production leads to ever smaller increases in output.

Discounting Converting future income amounts into their present value, e.g. the amount of money today that, when invested, yields a specified future amount.

Discount rate The interest rate set by the central bank when it provides loans to banks.

Discretionary policy Policy that is not fixed by pre-set rules but that can respond to different events in a flexible way.

Disinflation A reduction in the rate of inflation.

Disposable income Income available after deducting taxes.

Distortions Factors that alter market outcomes away from the optimal invisible hand outcome.

Divergence When poor countries do not catch up with rich ones through faster growth.

Dividend yield Dividend payments on a share expressed as a percentage of the share price.

Dollarization When a country gives up use of its own currency and switches to using foreign currency as legal tender, e.g. the dollar.

Effective exchange rate An index that expresses the average value of an exchange rate against several other currencies.

Efficient market hypothesis Prediction that equity prices reflect all available information about future share price and dividends.

Elasticity The responsiveness of one variable to another measured as the percentage change in one variable caused by a 1% change in another.

Employment protection legislation (EPL) Government regulations aimed at increasing the cost or speed with which firms can reduce employment by downsizing.

Employment rate The proportion of the labour force who are in employment.

Endogenous growth Models that offer an explanation for persistent long-run GDP growth, even in equilibrium.

Endogenous variable A variable whose value is explained by the behaviour of other variables in a model (opposite of an exogenous variable).

Equilibrium A situation of balance between various forces, e.g. supply and demand in a market, such that there are no forces leading to change if the system is left undisturbed.

Equities (also shares or stocks) Paper asset reflecting part ownership of a company and its assets and a claim on the future stream of income that it earns.

Equity premium puzzle The finding that returns on equities have in many countries far exceeded those on other assets, even after allowing for the riskier nature of equity.

Equity risk premium The excess return that equities earn over safe assets that is required for investors to hold this riskier asset.

European Union (EU) An economic union (free trade of goods, services, labour and capital) and (limited) political union between a group of European countries. At the start of 2004, the countries of the European union were: Austria, Belgium, Denmark, Finland, France, Germany, Greece, Ireland, Italy, Luxembourg, the Netherlands, Portugal, Spain, Sweden and the United Kingdom. Ten new countries joined the EU in 2004.

Ex ante real interest rate The nominal interest rate less expected inflation over a specific time horizon. Contrast this with the *ex post* real interest rate.

Exchange rate The rate at which one currency exchanges for another on the foreign exchange market.

Exogenous variable A variable that is not explained by a model but whose value is taken as a given.

Expansionary policy Government policy that raises aggregate demand and increases employment and incomes, e.g. lower interest rates and taxes.

Exports Goods and services sold to other countries.

Ex post real interest rate The interest rate minus actual, as opposed to expected, inflation.

Externality When the behaviour of an agent affects the return of others in a way that is not reflected in market prices.

Factor endowments The level of factors of production, e.g. land, capital, skills and so forth, that a country possesses.

Factor intensity Extent to which a country or industry uses a particular factor of production.

Factor of production A resource used as an input into the productive process, e.g. capital or labour.

Factor price The price of one unit of a factor of production.

Factor price equalization The process whereby returns paid to factors of production for producing output are equalized across countries as a result of trade in goods and services.

Factor share The share of total output paid out as income to a factor of production.

Federal Reserve (the Fed) The central bank of the United States.

Fiat money Money that is not valuable in itself but achieves its value by government legislation/fiat.

Financial intermediation The channelling of funds from savers to ultimate users of funds via financial institutions (e.g. banks, pension funds, mutual funds, unit trusts, insurance companies).

Fiscal deficit Government expenditure less government revenue.

Fiscal policy Government policy relating to levels of spending and taxation.

Fisher effect The one-for-one link between the nominal interest rate and expected inflation.

Fisher equation The relation that makes the nominal interest rate the sum of the real interest rate and expected inflation.

Fixed exchange rate A rate of exchange for currencies that is set by the central bank and that is not allowed to vary in response to fluctuations in supply and demand.

Fixed-income securities Assets that do not have any uncertainty about their future payoffs. Bonds rather than equity are normally considered fixed-income securities.

Flexible prices Prices that move rapidly when supply or demand conditions alter to keep the market in equilibrium.

Floating (flexible) exchange rate A rate of exchange for currencies moving day by day to balance private-sector flows of money across the foreign exchange market.

Flow A variable that is measured per unit of time and that only exists during that time period.

Foreign direct investment (FDI) Purchase of a substantial ownership in, or construction of, a factory/operation in a country by an overseas agent.

Foreign exchange intervention When a central bank intervenes to buy or sell its own currency by using its foreign currency reserves in order to influence the value of the exchange rate.

Foreign exchange (FX) reserves Holdings of foreign currency by a central bank.

Forward rate Price paid today for delivery of a currency at some future point.

Frisch-Slutsky paradigm View of business cycles as being triggered by random shocks that are propagated through mechanisms to influence the economy over time to create business cycles.

Fundamentals The real forces of supply and demand that determine the evolution of output, asset prices and other real economic variables.

G7 Seven largest industrial nations (in order): United States, Japan, Germany, France, United Kingdom, Italy, Canada.

GDP *See* Gross domestic product.

GDP deflator The ratio of nominal (or current-price) GDP to real (or constant-price) GDP. This is a measure of the level of prices for domestically produced output.

General Agreement on Trades and Tariffs (GATT) Precursor to the World Trade Organization, which arranged a sequence of trade negotiations leading to lower tariffs.

Gini coefficient A measure of inequality.

Globalization The unification of national markets for goods, services, capital and labour into a single global market.

GNI *See* Gross national income.

Gold standard A historical exchange rate system where countries defined their currency as worth a specified amount of gold and committed to buying and selling at that rate.

Golden rule Investment criteria that maximizes consumption in the steady state.

Government purchases Goods and services bought by the government. Note that total government expenditure includes *both* government purchases and transfer payments (e.g. social security spending).

Gravity Model Model that relates the level of trade between two countries to their size and proximity.

Gross domestic fixed capital formation (GDFCF) Total amount of output used within a period to augment the capital stock *including* repairs and maintenance.

Gross domestic product (GDP) The total value of output produced in a country without any adjustment for the depreciation of capital. GDP also equals the sum of income earned domestically by both nationals and foreign citizens working in the country.

Gross national income (GNI) The total income of all residents of a nation wherever they produce or earn this income. It includes income from abroad paid to national citizens owning factors used overseas.

Growth accounting Attempt to attribute observed growth in GDP to increases in various factors of production.

Guidotti-Greenspan Rule. Rule that suggests that a country's FX reserves should be equal to its short-term foreign currency liabilities.

Heckscher-Ohlin model Prediction that countries export goods and services that require the intensive use of a factor of production that the country possesses in abundance.

HIPC High Indebted Poor Countries. These may be eligible for debt relief.

Home bias The larger proportion of investor portfolios that are invested in domestic securities relative to what is needed for risk diversification.

Hotelling rule. Rule that suggests that the price of an exhaustible resource should rise in line with interest rates.

Human capital Skills and knowledge possessed by individuals and society.

Human development index A broad measure of welfare constructed by the United Nations based around indicators of health, education and GDP.

Hyperinflation Very high inflation rates (sometimes defined as over 50%) where the increase in inflation is rising over time.

Idiosyncratic risk Uncertainty or income variability that is specific to an individual consumer or firm.

Import cover Number of months of imports that can be purchased with a country's foreign exchange reserves.

Imports Goods and services bought from other countries.

Impossible trilogy The fact that a country can only choose two out of (a) an independent monetary policy, (b) a fixed exchange rate and (c) no capital controls.

Imputed value The value of the services provided by ownership of an asset but not actually received as income in a market exchange, i.e. the imputed rent of a house owner is the rent they would have paid on their accommodation if they did not own it.

Income effect The change in demand or supply for a good when income is different but the price of the good is held constant.

Indifference curves Set of points that show combinations of goods that yield the same level of enjoyment or welfare to the individual.

Infant industry An industry in its early stage of development that is often considered to need protection from more efficient and experienced foreign competitors.

Inflation A sustained increase in the overall level of prices.

Inflation targeting Central bank practice of changing interest rates to achieve a specified inflation target rather than an alternative exchange rate or money supply target.

Inflation tax Revenue raised by a government through printing money (equals inflation multiplied by stock of non-interest-bearing money).

Information and communications technology Computer hardware and software and telephone equipment.

Infrastructure Part of the capital stock that is basic to the operation of an economy, e.g. roads, railways and so forth.

Institutions The formal and informal organizations and practices that define the 'rules of the game' or the ways in which economic agents interact.

Intangible assets Assets that have been accumulated over time but that do not have a physical manifestation, i.e. brand value.

Interest rate The return from lending money or the cost of borrowing money; the price of moving spending from one period to another.

Interbank market Market where banks borrow and lend to one another.

Intermediate target Variable that a government tries to control/influence not because it is of direct policy interest but because it is closely linked with a variable that is.

Intermediation Process whereby financial markets and institutions pass the funds provided by savers to those who wish to invest.

International financial institutions (IFIs) The institutions such as the World Bank, the International Monetary Fund, the Bank for International Settlements, the OECD and the WTO, which attempt to monitor and regulate the global economy.

International investment position (IIP) The accumulated stock of foreign net assets that a country owns.

International Monetary Fund (IMF) The IMF, founded in 1946, is an international organization of 183 member countries, established to promote international monetary cooperation, exchange stability and orderly exchange arrangements; to foster economic growth and high levels of employment; and to provide temporary financial assistance to countries to help ease balance of payments adjustment.

Intertemporal budget constraint The constraint that makes the net present value of all future expenditure equal to the net present value of all future income.

Inventory investment The change in the stocks of finished and intermediate goods held by companies.

Investment Goods purchased by individuals, companies or governments that increase their stock of physical or financial capital.

Invisible hand Adam Smith's result that individuals pursuing their own self-interest will be guided by market prices to an outcome that is efficient for society.

IS curve Relation between interest rates and the level of demand within the economy.

Keynesian cross A component of the IS-LM model that shows the relationship between expenditure/income and planned expenditure.

Keynesian policies Use of fiscal and monetary policy to boost demand in a recession and reduce demand in an expansion.

Labour force Those in the population who either work or are seeking work.

Labour-force participation rate The proportion of the adult population in the labour force.

Labour productivity Output divided by employment (either persons or hours worked).

Labour supply curve Relationship between wages and hours of work supplied.

Laffer curve Relationship between tax rates and tax revenue in which revenue is maximized at tax rates below 100%.

Laissez faire The free operation of markets without government intervention.

Law of the excluded middle The hypothesis that only very flexible or very fixed exchange rate systems are viable and intermediate regimes are untenable.

Law of one price Notion that identical goods will sell for identical prices wherever they are sold.

Leverage Amount of borrowing (normally expressed as a proportion of income or revenue or total assets).

Life-cycle hypothesis A theory of consumption in which individuals plan a path of consumption over their lives that is smooth and that balances the present value of spending against the sum of current wealth and the future values of earnings.

Liquid Easily converted into a form that allows transactions to be completed at a predictable price.

LM curve Key part of the IS-LM model that summarizes the relationship between interest rates, money supply and money demand.

Long-run supply curve The long-run link between output that is produced in an economy and the level of prices. Since sustained variations in capital, labour input and technology are unlikely to be driven by changes in nominal magnitudes, the long-run supply curve is vertical.

M1, M2, M3 Different measures of the aggregate stock of money in the economy. Higher numbers encompass wider definitions of what counts as money and are therefore larger in value.

Marginal product of capital (MPK) The extra output produced when the amount of capital used in production is increased by one unit, holding fixed the labour force and technology.

Marginal product of labour (MPL) The extra output produced when the amount of labour used in production is increased by one unit, holding fixed the capital stock and technology.

Marginal propensity to consume (mpc) The proportion of a rise in income that feeds through into higher consumption.

Market failure Where free operations of markets will not produce an efficient (or optimal) outcome. A failure of the invisible hand argument.

Mean reversion Process whereby a variable eventually returns to its long-run average.

Medium of exchange An item that is accepted as a means of payment for goods and services; one of the roles of money.

Menu costs The resources used in setting and changing prices.

Modigliani-Miller theorem Prediction whereby the financial structure of an institution's liabilities does not influence its value, i.e. the firm's overall value does not depend on whether it is financed by bonds or equity.

Momentum the tendency for asset prices that are rising/falling to carry on rising/falling

Monetarism The theory that inflation results from changes in the money supply and that control of the money supply is a necessary and sufficient means to control inflation.

Monetary policy The central bank's decisions on the terms (usually short-term interest rates) at which it will lend money to and buy securities from the private financial sector.

Monetary transmission mechanism The mechanisms by which changes in monetary policy affect the economy.

Money The stock of assets used for transactions.

Money illusion When individuals confuse nominal and relative prices.

Money multiplier The eventual increase in a measure of the money supply resulting from an increase in central bank (high-powered) money.

Monopoly power The ability of an agent or firm to set market prices above costs.

Moral hazard The tendency of people to shirk or not try hard when their behaviour is not monitored perfectly and where effort is costly.

Multinational enterprises (MNEs) Firms that both produce and sell their output across a range of countries. Also sometimes called transnational corporations (TNCs).

Multiplier Keynesian concept whereby the final impact on demand of an increase in expenditure is greater than the initial impact.

Nash equilibrium A situation where each agent is following an optimal strategy given the actions of other agents.

National income accounting The system used for measuring overall output and expenditure in a country and its constituent parts.

National income accounts identity Output can be used for either consumption, government expenditure, investment or net exports. $Y = C + I + G + X - M$.

National saving A nation's income minus private and public consumption. The sum of government, corporate and household savings.

Natural rate of unemployment The rate of unemployment at which inflation can be steady and to which the economy will move when inflation is neither rising nor falling.

Net exports Exports minus imports.

Net foreign investment The net flow of funds being invested overseas, which equals domestic saving minus domestic investment.

Net investment Total investment expenditure less depreciation of the existing stock of capital.

Neutrality Result that nominal variables (money supply, prices and so forth) cannot influence real variables (output, unemployment and so forth).

Nominal Measured in current prices.

Nominal exchange rate The terms of exchange between a unit of one currency and a unit of another.

Nominal interest rate Interest rate paid/received without making allowance for the fact that the price of goods is changing.

Non-tariff barriers Restrictions on trade other than tariffs, such as quotas, health and safety standards and so forth.

Okun's Law The relationship between output and unemployment.

Open economy An economy in which people can freely engage in international trade in goods, services and capital.

Open-market operations Purchase or sale of assets by the central bank in order to increase or decrease the money supply.

Opportunity cost Activities or revenue forgone through pursuing a course of action.

Optimal currency area Region over which it is optimal to have just one currency.

Organization for Economic Cooperation and Development (OECD) The OECD is a group of 30 member countries (Australia, Austria, Belgium, Canada, Czech Republic, Denmark, Finland, France, Germany, Greece, Hungary, Iceland, Ireland, Italy, Japan, Korea, Luxembourg, Mexico, Netherlands, New Zealand, Norway, Poland, Portugal, Slovak Republic, Spain, Sweden, Switzerland, Turkey, United Kingdom, United States) in an organization that provides governments with a setting in which to discuss and develop economic and social policy.

Organization of Oil Producing and Exporting Countries (OPEC) A group of major oil-producing countries who meet to discuss, and try to control, oil output and prices.

Original sin Refers to notion that all emerging markets are potentially high-risk defaulters even if they have not previously defaulted. As a result, emerging markets have to borrow in foreign currency terms.

Output gap Difference between GDP and its trend level.

Overseas development assistance (ODA) Money given to poorer nations by rich countries to help boost their GDP.

Pareto efficiency Situation where it is impossible to make anyone better off without making someone worse off.

Participation rate Proportion of the population (sometimes non-institutional population) who wish to have a job.

Per capita Amount per person.

Perfect competition Where each agent/firm is small compared to the marketplace and has to accept prices as beyond its control.

Permanent income The level of income that someone can reasonably expect to be sustained into the future without running down their assets.

Permanent-income hypothesis The theory that consumption is proportional to the anticipated value of future average labour income (plus a share of current wealth), as opposed to the idea that current income is the prime determinant of spending.

Phillips curve The relationship between unemployment and inflation, claimed by A.W. Phillips to be negative.

Physical capital Stock of machines and buildings.

Poverty trap Situation where a country cannot grow because it is so poor that it suffers from a low return on investment.

Precautionary saving Saving that reflects the impact of uncertainty about the future and is done as a form of insurance.

Present value The amount today that has the same value as an amount to be paid or received in the future, having adjusted for the interest that could be earned (or must be paid) in the intervening period.

Price index Measure of the price of a basket of goods.

Primary balance Government tax revenue less expenditure *excluding* interest payments.

Private saving Disposable income less private consumption expenditure.

Pro-cyclical Tending to move in a similar direction to aggregate output and employment.

Production function A relationship that describes how increases in factor inputs lead to an increase in output.

Productivity *See* Labour productivity.

Profits A firm's revenue less costs.

Pro-poor growth GDP growth that reduces poverty or, more demandingly, GDP growth that reduces inequality.

Public good A commodity that it is impossible to exclude individuals from consuming, e.g. national defence.

Public saving Government receipts less spending on consumption and transfers. Same as fiscal surplus.

Purchasing power parity (PPP) The theory that exchange rates will move such that the price of goods is the same in all countries, so that a given amount of money buys the same amount in different countries.

q theory of investment The theory that investment depends positively on the ratio of the stock market value of a firm's assets to the cost of buying those assets. In equilibrium, this ratio should equal 1.

Quantitative easing Additional creation of money by the central bank after interest rates are already at or near zero.

Quantity equation $MV = PY$, where M is the money supply, V the velocity of circulation, P prices and Y output.

Quantity theory of money Theory that assumes that the velocity of money is predictable and that money is neutral for output, so that increases in the money supply lead directly to inflation.

Random walk A variable with the property that the optimal forecast of its future value is its current value, because it is impossible to predict whether the variable will rise or fall.

Rate of return Income and capital gains on an asset expressed as a percentage of its price.

Rational expectations A situation where forecast errors are unpredictable and agents' expectations on average equal outturns.

Real Measured in constant prices having allowed for inflation.

Real business cycle theory Theory that variations in total factor productivity cause business-cycle fluctuations.

Real exchange rate The ratio of what a specified amount of money can buy in one country compared to what it can purchase elsewhere.

Real interest rate The cost of borrowing (or the return to saving) in real terms, i.e. after adjusting for inflation.

Real money balances The amount of money measured in terms of the quantity of goods it could buy; the nominal stock of money relative to an index of prices.

Real wages Wages divided by prices. A measure of what workers can purchase with their earnings and so a measure of the standard of living.

Recession A period of falling aggregate output in the economy. Often used to refer to the situation where output declines for two or more consecutive quarters.

Rent seeking Earning income in excess of the value of economic services offered.

Rental price of capital *See* User cost of capital.

Replacement rate Benefits (especially pensions or unemployment benefits) expressed as a percentage of average or previous earnings.

Research and development (R&D) Resources spent on fostering invention or innovation.

Reserve requirement Rules governing minimum levels of reserves to be held with the central bank.

Residential investment Investment in new houses.

Ricardian equivalence The prediction that fiscal deficits or surpluses do not influence GDP.

Risk aversion When consumers prefer risk-free assets even if the return on riskier assets is higher.

Risk premium Additional return required by investors if they are to invest in riskier assets.

Sacrifice ratio The (percentage) fall in output (or rise in unemployment) that is needed to reduce inflation by a full percentage point according to the Phillips curve.

Saving *See* National saving, Private saving and Public saving.

Saving rate Savings expressed as a percentage of income or output.

Seasonal fluctuations Fluctuations in economic variables that repeat themselves but that complete their cycle within a year.

Seignorage Revenue raised by central bank through printing money due to the difference between face value of money and costs of production.

Shock An exogenous and unpredictable change in an economic variable that generates changes in endogenous variables.

Shoe-leather cost The cost of inflation from people holding fewer real money balances and having to incur more costs in financing transactions.

Single currencies When two or more countries agree to abandon their individual currencies and agree to share a new currency.

Small open economy An open economy that is small enough that its actions do not influence interest rates or other prices set in global markets.

Social capital The value of social relations and cooperation that can aid economic development and raise living standards.

Solow growth model Model of growth based around capital accumulation and diminishing marginal product of capital that culminates in a country reaching its steady state.

Solow residual The growth in total factor productivity, i.e.that part of a rise in output not explained by the increase in factor inputs.

Sovereign wealth fund. A government-owned investment fund that invests mainly in foreign assets.

Spillovers Events or actions in one industry or market that affect other industries as well.

Stabilization policy Government policy aimed at keeping output and employment on steady trend paths.

Stagflation A situation of falling output and high inflation.

Steady state A situation in which key variables are not changing. In the Solow growth model, this is where gross investment equals depreciation.

Sterilization The process whereby the central bank intervenes in the bond or money market to prevent its foreign exchange intervention from affecting the domestic money supply.

Sticky prices Prices that are slow to adjust when demand or supply conditions change.

Stock The outstanding amount of a variable at a point in time. Also used to denote a share issued by a firm and traded in the stock market.

Stock market The market in which corporate stocks (or equities) are bought and sold.

Stolper-Samuelson effect Result showing that a factor of production that is in relatively scarce supply sees a fall in its real income as a result of more trade.

Strategic trade policy Use of trade restrictions to achieve long-run advantages for high value-added industries.

Substitution effect The change in demand or supply for a good due to a change in the relative price, holding income constant.

Sudden stop A sudden slowdown in private capital inflows into a country.

Tariff A tax on imported goods.

Tax smoothing Attempts to avoid sharp swings in tax rates while maintaining long-run solvency.

Tax wedge Gap between price paid by consumers and that received by producers because of taxes.

Taylor rule Relationship between interest rates and output gap and inflation.

Technical progress Improvements in knowledge that enable more output to be produced from given inputs.

Terms of trade Price of a country's exports divided by price of its imports.

Time inconsistency Problem where future plans are only optimal when announced but not when they have to be implemented.

Tobin's q The ratio of the market value of a company's existing capital to its replacement cost.

Total factor productivity Efficiency with which factors of production are utilized. Reflects a huge range of influences, both economic and sociocultural.

Trade liberalization Reduction or removal of trade tariffs and other barriers.

Transactions costs Costs incurred in trading assets or goods and services. Includes taxes and brokers' charges as well as transport costs, where relevant.

Transfer payments Payments from the government to people that are not expenditure on goods and services, e.g. unemployment benefits; old-age pensions.

Transitory income A current shock to income that people do not expect to persist into the future.

Trend growth Long-run average growth in GDP per capita.

Uncovered interest parity Prediction that interest rate differentials between countries will be exactly offset by future exchange rate depreciation.

Underground economy Economic activity not reported in official statistics due to tax evasion and illegal status.

Unemployment rate The percentage of those in the labour force who are not working.

Unit of account Units used to measure value of economic activity.

User cost of capital Cost of using a unit of capital during a period of time, including rental and depreciation charges and any capital gains.

Value added The value of a firm's output minus the value of the intermediate goods and raw materials that the firm purchased.

Velocity of circulation The ratio of aggregate nominal spending to the money supply, which reflects the average rate at which money changes hands.

Wage The amount paid for one unit of labour.

Wealth Assets less liabilities.

Wealth effect Influence of changes in value of wealth on consumption and investment decisions.

World Bank The World Bank uses its financial resources and staff to help developing countries achieve long-run sustainable growth and alleviate poverty.

World Trade Organization (WTO) The World Trade Organization deals with the rules of trade between nations. At its heart are the WTO agreements, negotiated and signed by the bulk of the world's trading nations and ratified in their parliaments.

Yield Discount rate that makes the current bond price equal to the net present value of future income stream generated by the bond.

Yield curve Relationship showing how yields on bonds vary with the maturity of bonds.

Notes

CHAPTER 1

1. These figures are quoted in terms of what are called 'constant prices'. We shall go into more detail about this in the next chapter, but essentially it means that everything is measured in terms of what a dollar could buy in the United States in 1990. We should also stress that cross-country comparisons of historical data are not among the most reliable aspects of economic measurement.
2. Lucas, R.E., Jr., 'On the mechanics of economic development', *Journal of Monetary Economics* (1988), 22(1): 3–42.

CHAPTER 2

1. To be precise this should be a geometric average; that is, the square root of the product of the two numbers (this is the GEOMEAN function in EXCEL).
2. Until recently GNI was often referred to as GNP or gross national product. As will become clear, the concept is much more about income than production.
3. Consider the case in which you take your parents out to a restaurant for a meal. GDP includes the entire value added of this transaction. If, by contrast, you buy the ingredients and cook the meal yourself, then GDP includes only the value added of the ingredients. However, the economic activity is still the same: someone is still cooking the meal. GDP includes a chef getting paid for cooking, but not you cooking at home. Of course, if you are a lousy cook then perhaps your value added is zero or negative.

CHAPTER 3

1. Lucas, R.E., Jr., 'On the mechanics of economic development', *Journal of Monetary Economics*

(1988), 22: 3–42. Note that in recent years, India's economy has indeed been growing very fast.
2. This is only a thought experiment – Lucas is not saying that spending this money will produce these results.
3. The following gives a good taste of Malthus's work:

> *The power of population is so superior to the power in the earth to produce subsistence for man, that premature death must in some shape or other visit the human race. The vices of mankind are active and able ministers of depopulation. They are the precursors in the great army of destruction; and often finish the dreadful work themselves. But should they fail in this war of extermination, sickly seasons, epidemics, pestilence, and plague advance in terrific array and sweep off their thousands and ten thousands.*

4. A rising population means that increased employment does not necessarily equate with less unemployment.
5. The following section requires some mathematical knowledge fully to understand the derivations, but the general intuition of the approach should be accessible for the reader who does not have this knowledge.
6. It requires only straightforward differentiation of the production function, since the marginal product of capital equals $\partial y/\partial K$. Write the Cobb-Douglas production function $y = \text{TFP } K^a L^{1-a}$ where y is output, K is capital and L is hours worked. $\partial y/\partial K = a \text{ TFP } (L/K)^{1-a}$ and $\partial y/\partial L = (1-a) \text{ TFP } (K/L)^a$. If capital earns its marginal product, then the total payments to those who supply capital is $K \, \partial y/\partial K = ay$, and if the hourly wage is the marginal product of labour, the total wage bill is $L\partial y/\partial L = (1-a)y$. Thus a is the share of profit (the returns to capital) in total value added (y) while $1-a$ is labour's share.

CHAPTER 5

1. Lucas, R.E., 'Why doesn't capital flow from rich to poor countries?', *American Economic Review* (1990): 92–6.
2. Mohammed, S. and Whalley, J., 'Rent seeking in India: Its costs and policy significance', *Kyklos* (1984): 37: 387–413; and Hamilton, B., Mohammed, S. and Whalley, J., 'Applied general equilibrium analysis and perspectives on growth performance', *Journal of Policy Modeling* (1988): 10(2): 281–97.
3. Hobsbawm, E., *Industry and Empire from 1750 to the Present Day* (Penguin: Harmondsworth, 1969).
4. Balazs, E., *Chinese Civilization and Bureaucracy* (New Haven: Yale University Press, 1964).

CHAPTER 6

1. Mankiw, N.G., Romer, D. and Weil, D.N., 'A contribution to the empirics of economic growth', *Quarterly Journal of Economics* (1992): 107: 407–37.
2. Bloom, D. and Sachs, J.D., Geography, Demography and Economic Growth in Africa, Brookings Papers on Economic Activity (1999).
3. Easterly, W. and Levine, R., 'Africa's growth tragedy', *Quarterly Journal of Economics* (1997), 112: 1203–50.
4. Collier, P. and Hoeffler, A., 'On economic causes of civil war', *Oxford Economic Papers* (1998), 50: 563–73.

CHAPTER 8

1. We discuss a world of two commodities and two economies, but the analysis also holds for any circumstance where the number of countries does not exceed the number of commodities.
2. Terrania will not focus on fish production because, at most, it can produce two bags of fish, which, given international prices, can be swapped for four bags of coconuts, less than it can produce itself.
3. This and many other fascinating trade facts are discussed in detail in Yarbrough, B.V. and Yarbrough, R.Y., *International Economics* (Fort Worth: Dryden Press, 2002).

4. Baldwin, R.E., 'Determinants of the commodity structure of U.S. trade', *American Economic Review* (1971), 61: 126–46.

CHAPTER 9

1. Frankel, J.A. and Romer, D.H., 'Does trade cause growth?', *American Economic Review* (June 1999), 89(3): 379–99.
2. Wacziarg, R. and Welch, K.H., Trade Liberalization and Growth: New Evidence, NBER Working Paper 10152 (2003).

CHAPTER 10

1. Keynes, J.M., *The General Theory of Employment, Interest and Money* (New York: Macmillan, 1936), p. 96.
2. Developed by Milton Friedman, *A Theory of the Consumption Function* (Princeton, NJ: Princeton University Press for National Bureau of Economic Research, 1957).
3. Because of discounting and interest rates, the increased lifetime income is not spread *exactly* equally between periods. The higher the rate at which people mentally discount future satisfaction, the more is spent today because consumers are impatient, and the higher the interest rate, the less is spent today because consumers have more of an incentive to save.
4. The reason why there will be a difference is due to interest rate effects. If interest rates are high, then the consumer will be tempted to save more of any first-period increase in income. Similarly, it is more expensive to borrow against news of higher future income.
5. Carroll, C.D. and Samwick, A.A., 'How important is precautionary saving?', *Review of Economics and Statistics* (1998), 80(3): 410–19.
6. You may have spotted an obvious problem with this argument. Running a company attracts risk lovers and working for the tax authorities attracts the risk averse. James Stewart was the worrying type (which is why he takes the safe job with the IRS), while Sharon Stone doesn't give a damn about tomorrow and loves risk. So maybe Stewart saves more than Stone. This is an example of *sample selection bias*. The point we make in the text, however, relies on holding

attitudes to risk constant. Thus the person in the safe job would save less than the person running the new company. Our James Stewart character will save more if he is starting up a new firm than if he is employed with the IRS.

7. It is important to note that Figure 10.15 is based on data covering different individuals of different ages and not consumption over a single individual's life. Because of productivity growth, income differs across generations.

8. Hall, R.E., The Stock Market and Capital Accumulation, NBER Working Paper 7180 (June 1999). See also the later version of that paper with the same name that appeared in the *American Economic Review* (2001), 91: 1185–202.

9. Internal funds means profit not paid out to shareholders that is available to finance expenditure.

10. Governments in developed countries have often introduced tax breaks to encourage investment expenditure, especially when investment looks low and the economy is in a slump. The effectiveness of tax breaks, which may prove temporary, is questionable given the length of life of much capital equipment. Temporary tax breaks may also affect the *timing* of investment expenditure more than the *amount* of capital accumulation.

11. By Jim Poterba and Lawrence Summers.

12. By the Bank of England.

13. That is, minimum required rates of return on new investment projects.

14. This is effectively a detailed way of modelling the aggregate demand side of the economy, which helps analyse how changes in fiscal or monetary policy can influence the economy. It was developed by John Hicks in the United Kingdom and Alvin Hansen in the United States and was based on their interpretation of Keynes's work.

CHAPTER 11

1. Although it is sometimes said that a recession is when you know someone who has become unemployed and a depression is when you become unemployed!

2. Stock, J.H. and Watson, M.W., Has the Business Cycle Changed and Why?, NBER Working Paper 9127 (September 2002).

3. Wolfers, J., Is Business Cycle Volatility Costly? Evidence from Surveys of Subjective Well-being, NBER Discussion Paper 9619 (April 2003).

4. Ramey, G. and Ramey, V.A., 'Cross-country evidence of the link between volatility and growth', *American Economic Review* (1995), 85: 1138–51.

5. Named after two 1930s economists, Norwegian Ragnar Frisch and Italian Eugene Slutsky.

6. Many have contributed to real business cycle theory, but its origins are in the work of Finn Kydland and Ed Prescott, 'Time to build and aggregate fluctuations', *Econometrica* (1982). Far more sophisticated real business cycle theories have been developed than the one we outline here.

7. Another way of drawing the long-run supply curve is for it to be placed just before the short-run supply curve becomes vertical. In other words, price increases occur when firms try to produce too far above the full capacity level by utilizing machines more than is sustainable or by using too much overtime.

CHAPTER 12

1. The average basket of goods has clearly changed over this time!

2. See Fisher, D.H., *The Great Wave: Price Revolutions and the Rhythm of History* (New York: Oxford University Press, 1996) for an ambitious attempt to summarize 1000 years of inflation and its causes across a range of countries.

3. This is less important for the United States because many commodities are priced in US dollars.

4. See Krugman, P., 'Viagra and the wealth of nations', *New York Times Magazine* (23 August 1998).

5. Shapiro, M.D. and Wilcox, D.W., Mismeasurement in the Consumer Price Index: An Evaluation, NBER Working Paper W5590 (May 1997).

6. Technically this doubling of prices is not inflation – inflation is a *sustained increase* in prices.

7. Fisher, S., 'Towards an understanding of the costs of inflation II', *Carnegie Rochester Conference Series on Public Policy* (1981), 15: 5–41.

8. Barro, R.J., Inflation and Economic Growth, NBER Working Paper 5326 (1995).

9. See Davies, G., *A History of Money: From Ancient Times to the Present Day* (Cardiff: University of Wales Press, 1994) for a broad survey of the history of money.

10. The money multiplier is not a modern invention. Sir William Petty, Professor of Anatomy

at Oxford University, wrote in his 1682 work *Quantulumcunque Concerning Money*, 'We must erect a Bank, which well computed, doth almost double the effectiveness of our coined money.'

11. Strictly speaking, a government finances its activities through taxation or by selling bonds either to the private sector or the central bank, with bonds being purchased by issuing new currency.

12. Loans from the nobility were often politically costly, as was taxation. Plunder from wars and ransoms were other important sources of revenue.

13. Strictly speaking, 'currency' should read non-interest-bearing assets.

14. Germany's fiscal problems were mainly a result of reparation payments to the Allies after its defeat in the First World War. In 1921–22, reparations amounted to 77% of all government expenditure. Refusing to pay reparations was a key part of German fiscal reform.

15. Friedman, M. and Schwarz, A.J., *A Monetary History of the United States 1867–1960* (Princeton, NJ: Princeton University Press for NBER, 1963).

16. Our result will also hold, with only minor modifications, even if there are predictable changes in velocity. Only large unpredictable changes in velocity undermine our results.

CHAPTER 13

1. 'Independent' is a somewhat slippery concept. What we mean here is that the central bank does not merely implement monetary policy decisions that have been made by the government. Full central bank independence means that the bank sets its own targets and chooses monetary policy accordingly. However, in some cases the target is set by government, and the central bank is independent in its choice of monetary policy to meet that target.

2. The intuition is as follows: If one country has a higher inflation rate than another, then its currency will buy fewer items in that country. Therefore people will sell the high inflation currency, leading it to depreciate. If the exchange rate is fixed, it must be because individuals are indifferent as to which currency they hold – they buy both in the same amount. This means that inflation must be equal in the two countries.

3. Short-term securities are certificates that represent ownership of loans to government (treasury

bills) or companies (commercial paper) where the loans are less than six months.

4. Friedman, M. and Schwartz, A., *A Monetary History of the United States 1867–1960* (Princeton, NJ: Princeton University Press, 1963).

5. After the Stanford economist John Taylor. See his 'Discretion versus policy rules in practice', *Carnegie-Rochester Conference Series on Public Policy* (November 1993), 39: 195–214.

CHAPTER 14

1. Of course, these issues also affect the classification of private-sector spending into consumption and investment, but to a lesser extent.

2. See Slemrod, J., 'What do cross-country studies teach about government involvement, prosperity and economic growth?', *Brookings Papers on Economic Activity* (1995), 2: 373–431. See also *The Economic Journal* (1996), 106(439).

CHAPTER 15

1. Alban William Housego 'Bill' Phillips was an inventive man (as well as being a polymath, a crocodile hunter and a school dropout at the age of 15). He built probably the first working model for macroeconomic experiments. The machine was made up of tanks and pipes with different-coloured water to represent levels of consumption and exports; a variety of taps and plugs showed how demand circulated through the economy. For a fascinating account of Phillips and his life, see Leeson, R., 'A.W.M. Phillips MBE (Military Division)', *The Economic Journal* (May 1994), 424: 605–18.

2. Friedman, M., 'The role of monetary policy', *American Economic Review* (1968), 68: 1–17.

3. See, for example, Ball, L., 'What determines the sacrifice ratio?' in G. Mankiw (ed.), *Monetary Policy* (Chicago: University of Chicago Press, 1994), pp. 240–81.

CHAPTER 16

1. The exception is the 20 years starting just before the Wall Street crash of 1929.

2. The expression is an infinite geometric progression that converges if $r > g$.

3. We are using a technical definition of rational expectations: that agents use all the information at their disposal and the appropriate model of the economy and of share prices in forming their guesses of what the future holds. This does not mean that agents do not make mistakes – it just means that they cannot forecast their own mistakes.

4. Mehra, R. and Prescott, E.C., 'The equity premium: A puzzle', *Journal of Monetary Economics* (1985), 15: 145–61.

5. Dimson, E., Marsh, P. and Staunton, M., *Triumph of the Optimists: 101 Years of Global Investment* (Princeton, NJ: Princeton University Press, 2002).

6. As well as depending on risk aversion, the magnitude of the equity premium should also depend on how much risk there is in the world. Focusing on aggregate consumption changes, Mehra and Prescott argue that measured in this way risk is fairly small: consumption changes fluctuate between –2 and 14% per year. Therefore, we can only account for the equity premium if agents are highly risk averse, because measured risk is too small to play a substantial role.

7. For an excellent review of this work, see Shiller, R., *Market Volatility* (Cambridge, MA: MIT Press, 1989).

8. Shiller, R., 'Do stock prices move too much to be justified by subsequent changes in dividends?', *American Economic Review* (1981), 71: 421–36.

9. By the 'fundamental value', we mean the value based on the discounted sum of expected future earnings that the underlying productive asset generates.

10. Garber, P.M., 'Famous first bubbles', *Journal of Economic Perspectives* (1990), 4(2): 35–54.

11. Pastor, L. and Veronesi, P., 'Was there a Nasdaq bubble in the late 1990s?', *Journal of Financial Economics* (2006), 81: 61–100.

12. The cash (or nominal) values are usually known, though the *real* value of those payments is not because inflation is uncertain. Some bonds pay future amounts that are linked to inflation outturns and generate cash flows with known real values.

13. Not all bonds pay amounts fixed in advance. For example, inflation-protected bonds (sometimes called index-linked bonds) pay coupons and have a final redemption payment that depends on what happens to inflation between the time the bond is bought and its maturity. Such bonds have guaranteed real repayments but uncertain nominal repayments. Other bonds have cash flows that vary in line with movements in interest rates (floating-rate bonds).

CHAPTER 17

1. The term commercial bank is also sometimes used to specify a division of a bank that deals primarily with businesses, while retail banks provide financial services to consumers.

2. Cochrane, John H., 'The risk and return of venture capital', *Journal of Financial Economics* (2005), 75: 3–52.

3. The line shown depicts the (weighted) median repricing/maturity gap for the entire US commercial banking sector, in years, based on data from the Call Reports. The repricing/maturity gap is defined as the weighted average reported repricing time or maturity (whichever comes first) of assets less the weighted average reported repricing time or maturity of liabilities. Savings, demand and transaction deposits are included in the calculation of the repricing/maturity gap at their contractual maturity, which, according to the Call Report instructions, is equal to zero. Excluded from the calculation of the repricing/maturity gap are certain assets and liabilities for which repricing time or maturity information is not available. All percentiles are weighted by total bank assets. For further details, see English, W.B., Van den Heuvel, S.J. and Zakrajšek, E., Interest Rate Risk and Bank Equity Valuations, Federal Reserve Board mimeo (2011).

4. Laeven, L. and Valencia, F., Systemic Banking Crises: A New Database, IMF Working Paper 08/224 (2008).

CHAPTER 18

1. The first recorded default occurred in the fourth century BC, when 10 Greek municipalities defaulted on loans from the Delos Temple.

2. Both the confiscation of Catholic lands in 1594 and the 1932 default on inter-Allied debt have been described as a partial default by some commentators.

3. Possibly the most famous recent foreign intervention to resolve a default was the case of Newfoundland in the 1930s, which had its sovereignty removed by the British government and was later made a province of Canada as a result of a default on its debt.

CHAPTER 19

1. There are exceptions to this generalization. As far as the US dollar is concerned, the exceptions to this are sterling, the euro, the Australian dollar and the New Zealand dollar, all of which are quoted the other way (e.g. euro/dollar at 0.9 means that 1 euro is worth 90 US cents).
2. Although Japanese inflation is 10% higher than German inflation, the exchange rate does not depreciate by exactly 10% but by the factor 1.10/1.20 – this is approximately 10%.
3. For those of you who wish to speak strictly on balance of payments accounting issues, there is no better place to learn than the IMF's *Balance of Payments Textbook* (2003). This offers a complete overview of the structure of balance of payments accounting as well as detailed definitions of various terms.
4. The investor does not, however, have to have majority control – a 10% stake or more is normally enough. See IMF *Balance of Payments Textbook*, p. 107.

CHAPTER 20

1. These percentage shares add to 200%, because a dollar–yen trade is recorded as both a dollar share of transactions and a yen share.

2. Froot, K.A., Short Rates and Expected Asset Returns, NBER Working Paper 3247 (1990).
3. Flood, R.P. and Rose, A.K., 'Understanding exchange rate volatility without the contrivance of macroeconomics', *The Economic Journal* (1999), 109: F660–F672.
4. Meese, R.A. and Rogoff, K.S., 'Empirical exchange rate models of the seventies: Do they fit out of sample?', *Journal of International Economics* (1983), 14: 3–24.
5. Cheung, Y.W., Chinn, D. and Marsh, I.W., How Do UK-Based Foreign Exchange Dealers Think Their Market Operates?, NBER Working Paper 7524 (2000).
6. Argentina, Australia, Canada, Denmark, France, Germany, Italy, Japan, Norway, Sweden, United Kingdom and United States.

CHAPTER 21

1. This model is based on Krugman, P., 'A model of balance of payments crises', *Journal of Money, Credit and Banking* (1979), 11: 311–25. Subsequent work has extended the relevance of the model, but the basic insights remain the same.
2. Sachs, J., *The Economist*, September 12, 1998.
3. Eichengreen, B., 'Capital account liberalization: What do cross-country studies tell us?', *World Bank Economic Review* (2001), 15(3): 341–65.
4. The 11 countries were Austria, Belgium, Finland, France, Germany, Ireland, Italy, Luxembourg, Netherlands, Portugal and Spain and they were subsequently joined by Greece, Slovenia, Cyprus, Malta, Slovakia and Estonia.

Index

Note: Page references in *italics* refer to Figures; those in **bold** refer to Tables

A.p.c. (average propensity to consume) 215

Highest Incomes

Country	GNI per Capita (US Dollars)
Monaco	184440
Liechtenstein	128200
Norway	84917
Luxembourg	79577
Switzerland	64030
Denmark	58733
San Marino	50400
Sweden	50337
Netherlands	49043
Finland	47313

Source: World Bank, 2011, World Development Indicators average GNI per capita Atlas method 2008–2010.

Happiest

Country	Satisfaction with Life (survey on scale of 1 to 10)
Costa Rica	8.5
Denmark	8.3
Iceland	8.2
Switzerland	8.0
Finland	7.9
Mexico	7.9
Norway	7.9
Canada	7.8
Panama	7.8
Sweden	7.8

Source: Veenhoven. R. 2011. *Average happiness in 149 nations 2000–2009.* World Database of Happiness. Rank report Average Happiness. Internet: worlddatabaseofhappiness.eur.nl/ hap_nat/findingreports/RankReport_ AverageHappiness.php.

Most Equal

Country	Gini Coefficient (family income)
Sweden	23
Hungary	24.7
Norway	25
Czech Republic	26
Malta	26
Luxembourg	26
Slovakia	26
Austria	26
Kazakhstan	26.7
Finland	26.8

Source: CIA Factbook 2011.

Least Corrupt

Country	Corruption Score
Denmark	9.3
New Zealand	9.3
Singapore	9.3
Finland	9.2
Sweden	9.2
Canada	8.9
Netherlands	8.8
Australia	8.7
Switzerland	8.7
Norway	8.6

Source: Transparency International 2010.

Highest Life Expectancy

Country	Life Expectancy at Birth
Japan	83.2
Hong Kong	82.5
Switzerland	82.2
Iceland	82.1
Australia	81.9
France	81.6
Italy	81.4
Sweden	81.3
Spain	81.3
Israel	81.2

Source: UN Human Development Indicators 2011.

Lowest Government Debt

Country	General Government Gross Debt to GDP ratio
Brunei Darussalam	0
Oman	4.0
Estonia	6.0
Saudi Arabia	7.1
Kuwait	8.1
Equatorial Guinea	8.5
Islamic Republic of Iran	9.2
Chile	10.5
Algeria	10.7
Azerbaijan	10.7

Source: IMF World Economic Outlook (September 2011) 2011 estimates.

Lowest Inflation

Country	CPI inflation
Japan	−0.4
Tuvalu	0.5
Switzerland	0.7
Bahrain	1
Ireland	1.1
Morocco	1.5
Norway	1.7
Slovenia	1.8
Czech Republic	1.8
Brunei Darussalam	1.8

Source: IMF World Economic Outlook (September 2011) 2011 estimates.

Largest Current Account Surplus

Country	Current Account % of GDP
Timor-Leste	196.9
Brunei Darussalam	48.5
Kuwait	33.5
Qatar	32.6
Azerbaijan	22.7
Saudi Arabia	20.6
Trinidad and Tobago	20.3
Singapore	19.8
Gabon	14.8
Oman	14.5

Source: IMF World Economic Outlook (September 2011) 2011 estimates.

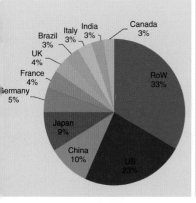

Brazil 3%
Italy 3%
India 3%
Canada 3%
UK 4%
France 4%
Germany 5%
Japan 9%
China 10%
US 23%
RoW 33%

re of World GDP by Country 2010.
rce: World Bank World Development
dicators.

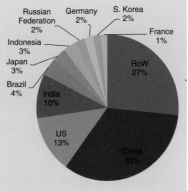

Russian Federation 2%
Germany 2%
S. Korea 2%
France 1%
Indonesia 3%
Japan 3%
Brazil 4%
India 10%
US 13%
China 33%
RoW 27%

Projected Share of World GDP by Country 2050.
Source: Authors' Calculations.

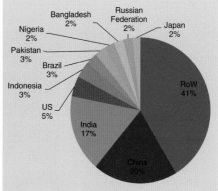

Bangladesh 2%
Russian Federation 2%
Japan 2%
Nigeria 2%
Pakistan 3%
Brazil 3%
Indonesia 3%
US 5%
India 17%
China 20%
RoW 41%

Share of World Population by Country 2010.
Source: World Bank World Development
Indicators.

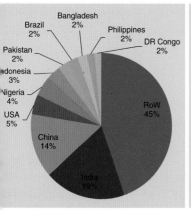

Brazil 2%
Bangladesh 2%
Philippines 2%
DR Congo 2%
Pakistan 2%
Indonesia 3%
Nigeria 4%
USA 5%
China 14%
India 19%
RoW 45%

**jected Shares of World Population by Country
50.** *Source:* UN Population Projection.

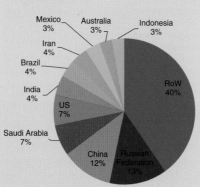

Mexico 3%
Australia 3%
Indonesia 3%
Iran 4%
Brazil 4%
India 4%
US 7%
Saudi Arabia 7%
China 12%
Russian Federation 13%
RoW 40%

Share of Resource Depletion by Country 2010.
Source: World Bank World Development
Indicators.

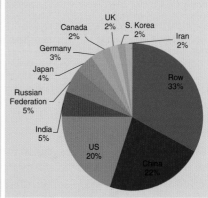

UK 2%
S. Korea 2%
Canada 2%
Iran 2%
Germany 3%
Japan 4%
Russian Federation 5%
India 5%
US 20%
China 22%
Row 33%

Share of CO$_2$ Emissions by Country 2010.
Source: World Bank World Development Indicators.

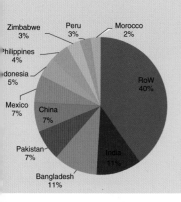

Zimbabwe 3%
Peru 3%
Morocco 2%
Philippines 4%
Indonesia 5%
Mexico 7%
China 7%
Pakistan 7%
Bangladesh 11%
India 11%
RoW 40%

rce of Emigrants by Country 2010.
rce: World Bank World Development
dicators.

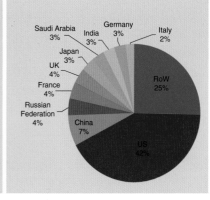

Saudi Arabia 4%
UK 4%
Qatar 3%
Canada 4%
Australia 4%
Russian Federation 4%
Italy 8%
Spain 8%
UAE 11%
US 18%
RoW 32%

Destination of Emigrants by Country 2010.
Source: World Bank World Development Indicators.

Saudi Arabia 3%
India 3%
Germany 3%
Italy 2%
Japan 3%
UK 4%
France 4%
Russian Federation 4%
China 7%
US 42%
RoW 25%

Share of World Military Expenditure by Country 2010.
Source: World Bank World Development Indicators.

Lowest Income

Country	GNI per Capita (US Dollars)
Burundi	153
Democratic Rep. of Congo	170
Liberia	190
Afghanistan	290
Eritrea	293
Malawi	307
Sierra Leone	333
Ethiopia	343
Niger	347
Guinea	377

Source: World Bank World Development Indicators average GNI per capita Atlas method 2008–2010.

Least Happy

Country	Satisfaction with Life (survey on scale of 1 to 10)
Togo	2.6
Tanzania	2.8
Burundi	2.9
Benin	3.0
Zimbabwe	3.0
Congo	3.5
Kenya	3.7
Madagascar	3.7
Mozambique	3.8
Niger	3.8

Source: Veenhoven. R. *Average happiness in 149 nations 2000–2009*. World Database of Happiness. Rank report Average Happiness. Internet: worlddata baseofhappiness.eur.nl/hap_nat/findingreports/RankReport_AverageHappiness.php.

Least Equal

Country	Gini Coefficient (family income)
Namibia	70.7
South Africa	65
Lesotho	63.2
Botswana	63
Sierra Leone	62.9
Central African Republic	61.3
Haiti	59.2
Columbia	58.5
Bolivia	58.2
Honduras	57.7

Source: CIA Factbook.

Most Corrupt

Country	Corruption Score
Somalia	1.1
Myanmar	1.4
Afghanistan	1.4
Iraq	1.5
Uzbekistan	1.6
Turkmenistan	1.6
Sudan	1.6
Chad	1.7
Burundi	1.8
Equatorial Guinea	1.9

Source: Transparency International 2010.

Lowest Life Expectancy

Country	Life Expectancy at Birth
Afghanistan	44.6
Lesotho	45.9
Swaziland	47
Zimbabwe	47
Zambia	47.3
Central African Republic	47.7
Democratic Rep. of Congo	48
Angola	48.1
Sierra Leone	48.2
Nigeria	48.4

Source: UN Human Development Indicators 2011.

Highest Government Debt

Country	General Government Gross Debt to GDP ratio
Japan	233.1
Greece	165.6
St. Kitts and Nevis	148.9
Jamaica	143.3
Eritrea	134.4
Lebanon	126.4
Italy	121.1
Barbados	116.9
Ireland	109.3
Portugal	106.0

Source: IMF World Economic Outlook (September 2011) 2011 estimates.

Highest Inflation

Country	CPI inflation
Belarus	41.0
Venezuela	25.8
Islamic Republic of Iran	22.5
Guinea	20.6
Sudan	20
Kyrgyz Republic	19.1
Republic of Yemen	19.0
Vietnam	18.8
Ethiopia	18.1
Sierra Leone	18.0

Source: IMF World Economic Outlook (September 2011) 2011 estimates.

Largest Current Account Deficit

Country	Current Account of GDP
Sierra Leone	−49.2
São Tomé and Príncipe	−40.5
Liberia	−35.8
Seychelles	−32.2
Kiribati	−31.7
St. Vincent & the Grenadines	−27.4
Niger	−26.7
Lesotho	−26.1
Grenada	−25.4
Kosovo	−25.0

Source: IMF World Economic Outlook (September 2011) 201 estimates.

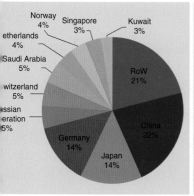

of World Stock Market Capitalization
untry 2010. *Source:* World Bank World
lopment Indicators.

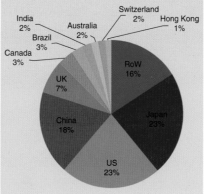

**Share of World Broad Money Supply by Country
2010.** *Source:* World Bank World Development
Indicators.

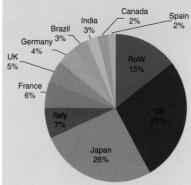

**Share of World Central Government Debt by
Country 2010.** *Source:* World Bank World
Development Indicators.

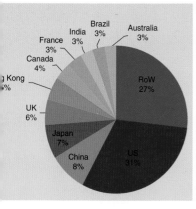

of World Current Account Surplus by
try 2010. *Source:* World Bank World
lopment Indicators.

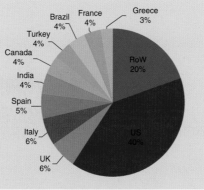

**Share of World Current Account Deficit by Country
2010.** *Source:* World Bank World Development
Indicators.

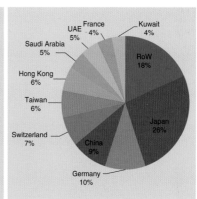

**Share of World Net Financial Creditors by
Country 2007.** *Source:* updated and extended
version of the External Wealth of Nations
Mark II database developed by Lane and
Milesi-Ferretti (2007).

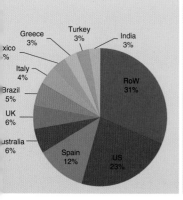

of World Net Financial Debtors by Country

Source: updated and extended version of
xternal Wealth of Nations Mark II database
oped by Lane and Milesi-Ferretti (2007).

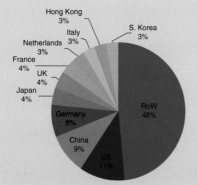

Share of World Trade by Country 2010.
Source: World Bank World Development
Indicators.

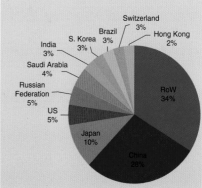

**Share of World Foreign Exchange Reserves by Country
2010.** *Source:* World Bank World Development
Indicators.